LONDON RECORD SOCIETY PUBLICATIONS

VOLUME XLV

LONDON RECORD SOCIETY
2010

LONDON INHABITANTS OUTSIDE THE WALLS, 1695

EDITED BY

PATRICK WALLIS

LONDON RECORD SOCIETY
2010

ISBN: 978-0-900952-45-6

Typeset, printed and bound by
GB Winstonmead, Loughborough, Leics.

CONTENTS

INTRODUCTION

In the summer of 1695 the inhabitants of London were listed as part of the preparations for a new tax on births, marriages and deaths (6 & 7 Wm & Mary, c. 6).[1] The Act imposing the Marriage Duty, as the tax has become known, had been passed in April 1695 to help pursue the war against France 'with vigour', and remained in force until 1706. It instituted a complicated set of duties on vital events together with annual payments by bachelors aged over twenty five and childless widowers. Surcharge levels were determined by status, with a precise set of gradations set out in the statute ranging from dukes to those with an income of under £50 per year.[2] To function, the tax required a full register of the population and a thorough system of registration of births, marriages and deaths. This ambitious fiscal initiative led to one of the first detailed records of the population of the metropolis. The lists of inhabitants produced for the tax offer an unequalled level of information on social, family and household structure. In particular, unlike most comparable contemporary records, they enumerate entire households by name and status, including children, servants and lodgers. Relatively few assessments survive for other parts of the country, making it all the more remarkable that a nearly entire set of records exist for England's largest city for 1695.[3]

An index to the surviving manuscript assessments for the parishes that lay within London's walls was published in 1966 by David Glass as the second

---

1. The digitisation of this index was funded by the British Academy as part of a project on 'Why did apprenticeships fail? Training, mobility and opportunity in seventeenth-century England' (SG-45038).
2. The details of the tax are discussed in *London Inhabitants within the Walls, 1695*, ed. David Glass, (London Record Society, ii. 1966), 'Introduction'; Tom Arkell, 'An examination of the Poll taxes of the later seventeenth century, the Marriage Duty act and Gregory King', in Kevin Schürer and Tom Arkell, *Surveying the People* (Oxford, 1992), pp. 163-171. Some of the possibilities of the source and its accuracy are discussed in: Jeremy Boulton, 'The marriage duty act and parochial registration in London, 1695-1706', in Schürer and Arkell, *Surveying the People*, pp. 222-252; Schürer, 'Variations in household structure in the late seventeenth century: towards a regional analysis', in Schürer and Arkell, *Surveying the People*, 253-278; Vanessa Harding, 'Families and Housing in Seventeenth-Century London', *Parergon*, 24: 2 (2007), 115-138; Mark Merry and Philip Baker, '"For the house her self and one servant": family and household in late seventeenth-century London', *The London Journal*, 34: 3 (2009), 205-232.
3. A list of other surviving assessments is given in Glass, *Londoners*, fn. 18. One of the fullest sets, for Bristol, has since been published in its entirety: E. Ralph and M.E. Williams, *The Inhabitants of Bristol in 1696*, (Bristol Record Society, xxv, 1968).

volume issued by the London Record Society. It has become a widely known and heavily used source, often employed in its own right with no further reference to the original manuscript records. That Glass and his researchers had prepared a typescript index to the assessments for the parishes and precincts outside the walls is less well known.[4] This volume makes this second part of the index to the assessments generally available for the first time.

The thirteen parishes and precincts outside the city walls for which assessments survive contained a substantial portion of the population of the city. The index to the eighty intramural parishes produced by Glass lists around 58,000 individuals, from a likely total of around 70,000 living within the walls, once allowance is made for those parishes for which no assessments survive.[5] By contrast, this volume lists 52,631 individuals. Nonetheless, the assessments indexed here do not offer complete coverage of London beyond the walls. No assessments survive for some large extramural parishes, while only partial assessments exist for several of the parishes included here. Notably, the 162 inhabitants of St Olave Southwark recorded here represent a tiny fragment of the metropolitan population living south of the Thames – indeed, it is only the precinct of London Bridge itself that survives. Over the seventeenth century London had expanded considerably beyond its traditional boundaries. Most estimates suggest that the metropolis, including Westminster and urban parishes in Middlesex and Surrey, contained something over half a million people by the late seventeenth century.[6] The surviving assessments for the Marriage Duty record less than a fifth of this wider metropolitan population.

In some important respects, the parishes and precincts outside the walls differed substantially from those within. Most obviously, they were far larger in size. The average population of parishes within the walls was 728; the largest intramural parish, St Anne Blackfriars, contained 2,833 individuals. Even without compensating for the missing portions of the assessments, the average size of the thirteen parishes indexed here was 4,049 individuals. The largest, St Botolph without Bishopsgate, contained 9,618 people. The parishes outside the walls were also poorer, as Jones and Judges long ago demonstrated by measuring the proportion of the population identified by the assessors as being rich enough to pay a surcharge because of their wealth or status, although parts of the western

---

4. The researcher on the volume on London within the Walls was Terry Gourvish. He subsequently led the work on the second volume, in which he was assisted by Negley Harte and David Ormrod.
5. P. E. Jones and A. V. Judges, 'London population in the later seventeenth century', *Economic History Review*, 6 (1935), 47. Higher estimates of 80,000 and 92,159 are suggested in C. Spence, *London in the 1690s* (London, 2000), p. 65.
6. Vanessa Harding, 'The Population of Early Modern London: a Review of the Published Evidence', *London Journal*, 15 (1990), 111–28; Spence, London, pp. 63-65.

parishes could be as wealthy as the central intramural parishes.[7] One of the most visible effects in the assessments of the extramural parishes' relative poverty was the frequency and number of servants employed by households in these parishes. Only eight percent of those living outside the walls were described as servants, compared to twenty percent in the parishes within the walls.

The size and relative poverty of the extramural parishes also has consequences for the assessments themselves. Sheer numbers of inhabitants meant that it was far harder to list the population of parishes of this size accurately. Assessors could not know the inhabitants of the parish personally, and might not even know the physical layout of its lanes and yards in any great detail. Small and poor households and their lodgers were also more mobile, and thus less likely to be recorded. Those in receipt of alms were exempt from paying the duties imposed by the tax, and it is not clear how comprehensively they were identified in the assessments. Similarly, children appear to have been undercounted.[8] What proportion of the population was omitted from the assessments has long troubled those seeking to use them as the basis for population estimates. Writing at the time, Gregory King added ten percent to his figures for London's population to account for such errors.[9] More recently, Craig Spence assumed a fifteen percent rate of omissions.[10] Whatever the correct figure might be, it seems safe to assume that under-enumeration affected the parishes outside the walls more severely than those within and the index needs to be treated with some caution as a result.

THE ASSESSMENTS

The assessments indexed in this volume are held in the London Metropolitan Archives. At the time of writing, they are catalogued as COL/CHD/LA/04/01/98-110. Each parish is bound as a separate volume, with the exception of the four precincts of St Giles Cripplegate, which are each bound individually. The assessments all follow a similar format, with the names of inhabitants listed to the left of each page followed by a series of columns to the right giving the details of the duties to which they were liable. The households in each list are differentiated, usually by a horizontal line, into a distinct group of names. Within each household, kin and service relationships are normally described. The tax also required that certain kinds of status and wealth be recorded (those found most frequently here are bachelor, widow, gentleman, doctor of law, medicine or divinity,

---

7.   Jones and Judges, 'London population', p. 62; Derek Keene, 'Growth, modernisation and control: the transformation of London's landscape, c. 1500-c. 1760', in *Two Capitals*, ed. P. Clark and R. Gillespie, (Oxford, 2001), pp. 7-37.
8.   Merry and Baker, "For the House", pp. 216, 223.
9.   Jones and Judges, 'London population', p. 55.
10. Spence, *London*, p. 65.

possessing an income of £50 per year). The apparent precision of the listings can be misleading, however. Some of the categories employed, particularly bachelor, could cover a wide range of social positions, from rich young men to single labourers, while servant was used interchangeably with apprentice, and neither might be explicitly defined.[11] Some assessments also give additional information on the location of households, or the occupations of householders, which was not required by the terms of the Act. The list below gives some indication of the size, form, contents and provenance of each volume.

98. St Andrew Holborn: 28cm by 37cm. 88 pages. The listing is divided into streets and courts. Households are clear. No occupations.

99. St Bartholomew the Great: 21cm by 31 cm. 61 pages. The listing is divided into broad areas. Households are clear. No occupations. The volume was signed at the end by the parish assessors on 27 June 1695, and was endorsed as having been viewed and approved by the commissioners for the Act on 28 June 1695.

100. St Bartholomew the Less: 24cm by 39cm. 15 folios, text on one side only. The listing is undivided. Households are clear. No occupations. The parish is not identified in the original MS but was inferred from later returns. Page 1 may be missing. The volume is not dated.

101. St Botolph without Aldersgate (part): 33cm by 40 cm. 110 folios, text on one side only. The heading on page 1 identifies the text as the assessment for the 'freedome part of the parish'. Precincts one to four are identified, but only a few streets or other locations are identified. Households are clear. Occupations are given for a substantial minority of householders. The volume is not dated.

102. St Botolph without Aldgate (part): 25cm by 37cm. 276 pages. The heading on page 1 identifies the text as covering the part of the parish lying within the liberties of the city of London. The parish precincts (Houndsditch, High Street, Barrs, Tower Hill, Covent Garden) are identified, but not the streets within. Households are clear. No occupations. The volume was endorsed on the 12 July 1695.

103. St Botolph Bishopsgate: 24cm by 35 cm. iv + 293 pages, with blank pages at end of volume. Streets, yards and courts are indicated clearly. Households are clear. No occupations. The title on page iv notes that volume is for the year May 1695 to May 1696.

11. Merry and Baker, "For the house", pp. 225-6; Chris Minns and Patrick Wallis, 'Rules and Reality: Quantifying the Practice of Apprenticeship in Early Modern Europe', *LSE Working Papers in Economic History*, 118/09, (2009).

104. St Bride's: 27cm by 41cm. 148 pages. Some locations are indicated, but this is not always clear or consistent. Households are clear. No occupations. The volume was signed by the collector, and the commissioners and assessors on the 29 July 1695.

105. Bridewell Precinct: 31cm by 41cm. 18 pages. The listing is not divided by place. Households are clear. No occupations. The assessment is dated 13 May 1695 on page 1.

106. St Dunstan in the West (part): 26cm by 42cm. 69 pages. The volume covers the part of the parish of St Dunstan in the West that lies in the liberties of the city of London. The listing is divided into streets, courts and alleys. Households are clear. No occupations. The assessment is dated 16 July 1695 on pages 1 and 69.

107A. St Giles Cripplegate, Fore Street Precinct: 32cm by 41cm. 43 folios, text on facing side only. Locations are indicated. Households are clear in most but not all cases. No occupations. The volume is not dated.

107B. St Giles Cripplegate, Grub Street Precinct: 32cm by 40cm. 82 folios, text on facing side only. Locations are indicated. Households are clear. No occupations. The volume is not dated.

107C. St Giles Cripplegate, White Cross Street Precinct: 33cm by 40cm. 42 folios, text on facing side only. Locations are indicated. Households are clear. No occupations. The volume is not dated.

107D. St Giles Cripplegate, Redcross Street Precinct: 33cm by 40cm. 102 folios, text on facing side only. Locations are indicated. Households are clear. No occupations. The volume is not dated.

108. St Olave Southwark, First precinct on London Bridge: 32cm by 40cm. 8 pages. The listing is not divided by place. Households are clear. No occupations. The volume is endorsed at the end by the collector, the assessors and commissioners and dated 28 June 1695.

109. St Sepulchre's, part lying in the ward of Faringdon Without: 38cm by 46cm. 112 folios. The listing is divided into the four precincts (Smithfield, Holborn Cross, Church, Old Bailey), but no other place information is given. Households are clear. No occupations. The assessment is dated 24 July 1695 on page 1.

110. Whitefriars: 30cm by 39cm. 37 pages. The listing is not divided by place. Households are mostly delineated, but with some ambiguities. No occupations. The volume is not dated.

THE INDEX

The index follows the same structure as the volume for parishes within the walls. Names are listed alphabetically by surname. Family members are listed together with the head of the household, and their relationships are indicated in the form in which they are given in the assessments. The location within the manuscripts is given by a two part reference containing a code for the parish before the full stop and the folio after. The parish codes are the same as the catalogue number, and the numbers and locations are also given in full with the map below. Kin ties, particularly between members of nuclear family groups, are thus easily identified. However, non-kin members of households are listed under their own head surname and households cannot therefore be easily reconstructed from the index on its own.[12]

---

12. A full transcript of the Tower Hill Precinct of St Botolph Aldgate was prepared as part of the project 'People in Place: families, households and housing in early modern London' and is currently held by the Centre for Metropolitan History at the Institute of Historical Research. A detailed discussion of household structure in this area is given in: Merry and Baker, "'For the House'", pp. 210-228.

LIST OF ABBREVIATIONS

£50 pa	real estate of £50 or more per annum	**Jac**	Jacob
£600	personal estate of £600 or more	**Jas**	James
		Joa	Johana, Joanna(h)
Alex	Alexander, Allexander	**Jos**	Joseph
alms	almsmen, almswomen	**jr**	junior
And	Andrew	**Jud**	Judith, Judeth
Ant	Anthony, Antony	**Kath**	Katherine
apoth	apothecary	**kin**	kinsman, kinswoman
app	apprentice	**kt**	knight
Art	Arthur, Arther	**Marg**	Margaret(t)
assr	assessor	**Mat**	Mat(t)hew
bach	bachelor	**Mic**	Michael(l)
Barb	Barbara	**Nat**	Nathaniel(l)
Bart	Bartholomew	**Nic**	Nicholas, Nicolas
Benj	Benjamin	**p a**	per annum
Bridg	Bridget(t)	**Phil**	Phil(l)ip
bro	brother	**Rac**	Rachel, Rachael(l)
bt	baronet	**Reb**	Rebecca(h)
Cath	Catherin(e)	**Ric**	Richard
Chas	Charles	**Rob**	Robert
Chris	Christopher	**s**	son
collr	collector	**Sam**	Samuel(l)
commr	commissioner	**Sar**	Sarah, Sara
cwdn	churchwarden	**ser**	servant
d	daughter	**sis**	sister
Dan	Daniel(l)	**Sol**	Solomon
DD	doctor of divinity	**spin**	spinster
Deb	Debora(h)	**sr**	senior
Dot	Dorothy	**Ste**	Stephen
Edm	Edmund, Edmond	**Susa**	Susan(n)a(h)
Edw	Edward	**Thos**	Thomas
Eliz	Elizabeth	**Tim**	Timothy
esq	esquire	**Val**	Valentine
gent	gentleman, gentlewoman	**w**	wife
Geo	George	**Wal**	Walter
Han	Hanna(h)	**wid**	widow
Hen	Henry	**widr**	widower
Humph	Humphr(e)y	**Wm**	William

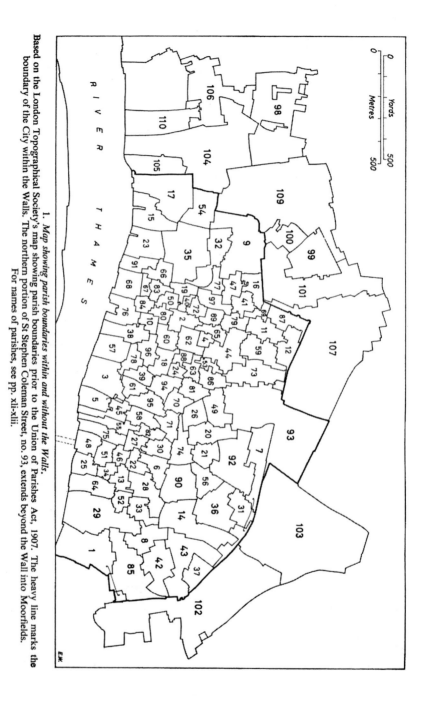

1. *Map showing parish boundaries within and without the Walls.*

Based on the London Topographical Society's map showing parish boundaries prior to the Union of Parishes Act, 1907. The heavy line marks the boundary of the City within the Walls. The northern portion of St Stephen Coleman Street, no. 93, extends beyond the Wall into Moorfields.

For names of parishes, see pp. xli–xlii.

RIVER THAMES

KEY TO MAP OF PARISHES

City within the Walls
1 Allhallows Barking
2 Allhallows, Bread Street
3 Allhallows the Great
4 Allhallows, Honey Lane
5 Allhallows the Less
6 Allhallows, Lombard Street
7 Allhallows, London Wall
8 Allhallows, Staining
9 Christchurch
10 Holy Trinity the Less
11 St Alban, Wood Street
12 St Alphage
13 St Andrew Hubbard
14 St Andrew Undershaft
15 St Andrew by the Wardrobe
16 St Anne, Aldersgate
17 St Anne, Blackfriars
18 St Antholin
19 St Augustine
20 St Bartholomew by the Exchange
21 St Benet Fink
22 St Benet, Gracechurch
23 St Benet, Paul's Wharf
24 St Benet Sherehog
25 St Botolph, Billingsgate
26 St Christopher le Stocks
27 St Clement, Eastcheap
28 St Dionis Backchurch
29 St Dunstan in the East
30 St Edmund, Lombard Street
31 St Ethelburga
32 St Faith under St Paul's
33 St Gabriel, Fenchurch
34 St George, Botolph Lane
35 St Gregory by St Paul's
36 St Helen

37 St James, Duke's Place
38 St James, Garlickhithe
39 St John the Baptist
40 St John the Evangelist
41 St John Zachary
42 St Katherine, Coleman
43 St Katharine Cree
44 St Lawrence Jewry
45 St Lawrence Pountney
46 St Leonard, Eastcheap
47 St Leonard, Foster Lane
48 St Magnus the Martyr
49 St Margaret, Lothbury
50 St Margaret Moses
51 St Margaret, New Fish Street
52 St Margaret Pattens
53 St Martin, Ironmonger Lane
54 St Martin, Ludgate
55 St Martin Orgar
56 St Martin Outwich
57 St Martin, Vintry
58 St Mary, Abchurch
59 St Mary, Aldermanbury
60 St Mary, Aldermary
61 St Mary Bothaw
62 St Mary le Bow
63 St Mary Colechurch
64 St Mary at Hill
65 St Mary Magdalen, Milk Street
66 St Mary Magdalen, Old Fish Street
67 St Mary Mounthaw
68 St Mary Somerset
69 St Mary, Staining
70 St Mary, Woolchurch
71 St Mary Woolnoth
72 St Matthew, Friday Street

73 St Michael, Bassishaw
74 St Michael, Cornhill
75 St Michael, Crooked Lane
76 St Michael, Queenhithe
77 St Michael le Querne
78 St Michael, Paternoster Royal
79 St Michael, Wood Street
80 St Mildred, Bread Street
81 St Mildred, Poultry
82 St Nicholas Acon
83 St Nicholas, Cole Abbey
84 St Nicholas Olave
85 St Olave, Hart Street
86 St Olave, Old Jewry
87 St Olave Silver Street
88 St Pancras, Soper Lane
89 St Peter, Westcheap
90 St Peter Cornhill
91 St Peter, Paul's Wharf
92 St Peter le Poor
93 St Stephen, Coleman Street

94 St Stephen, Walbrook
95 St Swithin
96 St Thomas the Apostle
97 St Vedast

City outside the Walls
98 St Andrew Holborn
99 St Bartholomew the Great
100 St Bartholomew the Less
101 St Botolph without Aldersgate
102 St Botolph without Aldgate
103 St Botolph without Bishopsgate
104 St Bride
105 Bridewell Precinct
106 St Dunstan in the West
107 St Giles Cripplegate
108 St Olave Southwark
109 St Sepulchre's
110 Whitefriars

INDEX OF INHABITANTS OUTSIDE THE WALLS

ABBITT:
Anne, 102.80
Elizabeth, ser, 100.4
Mary, 101.102

ABBOTT:
Abraham; Kath, w; Sam, s, 104.107
Anne, ser, 102.161
Benjamin; Jane, w, 99.24
Edward; Sarah, w; Elizabeth, d, 103.193
Elizabeth, 107C.41
Elizabeth, ser, 107B.73
Ephraim; Sunam, w; Mary, d; Susan, d;
   Thomas, s, 107D.70
James; Dorcas, w, 102.254
Jeremiah; Anne, w, 101.36
John; Sarah, w; John, s; Sarah, d, 107A.5
Judeth; Ellin, d, 109.59
Mary, 104.29
Mary Richard, d of Claver, 107B.52
Michaell, 109.85
Richard; Mary, w; Mary, d, 109.45
Samuel, ser, 109.6
Thomas, 102.233
Thomas; Mary, w; Sarah, d, 104.47
Thomas; Elizabeth, w, 102.13

ABDY:
Margaret, 109.10
William; Johanna, d; James, s; Elizabeth, d;
   Nathaniel, s, 107C.31

ABELL:
John; Hanah, w; Daniell, s; John, s; Richard,
   s, 103.156
John; Rose, w, 104.93
John; Damaris, w; William, s, 104.42

ABERNITHA: Amy; Elizabeth Beale,
   kinswoman of, 98.33

ABERRY: Susan, ser, 107B.79

ABLDIN:
Richard; Mary, w; Margaret, d, 102.172
Thomas; Ann, w, 103.276

ABOURNE: Frances, 107B.69

ABRAHAM:
Jas; Jane, w, 104.81
Margaret; John, s; Anne, d, 98.73
Wm; Bethiah, w; Jas Cundy, s, 104.79

ABRAM:
John, 109.33
John; Mary, w; John, s, 109.112
Nichas; Elizabeth, w; Anne, d, 109.97
Thomas; Mary, w; William, s, 107B.51

ABRAY:
Mary, 110.12
Richard; Margaret, w, 101.76

ABSOLOM: Thomas; Rebecca, w, 107B.43

ABTHORPE: Thomas; Elizabeth, w;
   Alexander, s; John, s, 109.109

ACHES:
Elizabeth, 109.16
Mary, 109.16

ACKERLY: Thomas; Anne, w;

ACOCK: ~, 104.13
Sarah, ser, 107D.1

ACON: Thomas; Mary, w; Mary, d; John, s,
   109.104

ACORMAN: Margaret, 109.82

ACQUITH: Francis, 99.53

ACREMAN: Mary, ser, 104.10

ACRES:
Edward, app, 101.26
John; Anne, w; John, s, 101.98

ACROD: John, £600; Katherine, w; Susan, d;
   Ann, d; John, s, 103.13

ACTON:
John; Jane, w; Jane, d; Sarah, d; Daniel, s,
   107A.5

1

Ralph; Elizabeth, w; Ralph, s; Elizabeth, d,
102.84
Samuell, 102.84
Tho, bach, 104.51
William, £600; Susan, w; Josiah, s; Susan, d;
Mary, d; Rebecca, d; William, s; Sarah, d,
107B.19

ADAM:
Job, app, 104.89
John; Jane, w; William, s; Elizabeth, d, 98.20
Nathaniell, £50 p.a.; Susanna, w, 98.72

ADAMS:
Anne, 107B.49
Anne; Anne, d, 102.190
Anne, ser, 103.120
David, app, 98.20
Edward; Elizabeth, w; George, s, 103.95
Elizabeth; Sarah, d; Martha, d, 102.84
Elizabeth, ser, 103.252, 103.260
Francis, ser, 102.195
Grace, 107D.92
Jane; Ann, d; Joseph, s, 109.35
Jane; Elizabeth, d, 102.235
Joane, 103.23
John; Martha, w; William, s; John, s; Thomas,
s, 104.38
John; Frances, w; John, s; Mary, d; Francis, s;
Sarah, d, 107A.10
John; Anne, w; William, s, 109.101
John, £600; Elizabeth, w; Thomas, s; Mary, d;
Sarah, d; Semuell, s; Joseph, s, 103.13
John, Ironmonger, 103.293
John, ser, 106.2
Jone, 107D.92
Joseph; Mary, w, 103.183
Joseph; Patience, w; Susan, d, 103.279
Katherine, ser, 98.34
Mary; Henry, s, 107A.9
Mary, ser, 106.4
Nathaniel; Elizabeth, w; Henry, s; Sarah, d,
102.250
Richard, 110.4
Richard; Mary, w; Hanna, d; Thomas, s;
Charles, s, 101.47
Richard; Anne, w; Timothy, s, 101.82
Richard; Katherine, w, 102.184
Richard; Elizabeth, w; Daniell, s, aged 30
years, bach, 102.257
Richard; Elizabeth, w; Richard, s, 107B.12
Robert, £600; Jeane, w; Mary, d; William, s;
Samuell, s; Jeane, d, 103.252
Samuell; Sarah, w, 102.18
Sarah, 107B.26
Sarah, 106.8
Sarah, ser, 109.27
Susannah Elizabeth, d of Collins, 107D.19
Thomas; Lucy, w; Sasan, d; Sarah, d, 104.83

Thomas, bach, 103.112
Thomas; Esther, w; Richard Hall, s,
103.124
William, 109.83
William; Ezabella, w, 103.281
William; Mary, w; James, s, 107B.21
William; Sarah, w, 109.5
William; Margaret, w, 109.33
William; Sarah, w; John, s; Phillip, s,
109.58

ADAMSON:
Carles, ser, 108.5
Elizabeth, 103.13, 109.75
John, 98.4
Robert; Joane, w, 102.147
Robert, bach, 98.73
Thomas; Jane, w; Mary, d, 102.99
Thomas; Jane, w; Katherine, d; John, s;
Thomas, s; Anne, d, 102.149
Thomas; Friday, d, 102.274

ADAMSWHITE: Edward; Hannah, w; Eliza, d,
104.14

ADCHURCH: William, 109.69

ADCOCK:
Anne, 102.225
Adward; Jane, w, 110.27
Elizabeth, 109.100
Robert; Mary, w; Mary, d, 107B.2
Robert; Anne, w, 107D.38
Thomas; Chtherine, w, 109.100
William; Martha, w, 101.27

ADDERLY:
Hugh; Mary, w; Hugh, s, 109.2
Thomas; Sarah, w, 103.246

ADDINGTON: Tho, a boy, 104.92

ADDIS: Jas, bach, 104.24

ADDISON:
Daniell, app, 103.283
Francis, 103.163
Francis, wid, 103.16
John, bach, 102.188
Mary, 107B.80
William; Elizabeth, w, 101.76

ADES: Richard, ser, 103.152

ADEY:
Amos; Sarah, w; Christopher, s; Andrew, s;
Joanna, d, 102.247
Rebecca; John, s; Rebecca, d; Benjamin, s,
102.144

3

Edward, bach, 107A.4
Edward, wid no children, 103.79
Elisha; Elizabeth, w; Thomas, s; Susannah, d;
　Hannah, d; Elisha, s, 98.2
Elizabeth; Thomas, s, 98.21
Elizabeth; Mary, d, 102.42
Elizabeth, ser, 103.242,104.7
Ephraim, bach, 106.9
Frances, ser, 101.15
Francis, ser, 106.46
George, 109.74
Henry, 102.114
Hugh; Mary, w; Anne, d; Susanna, d,
　101.24
James; Mary, w, 109.89
Jane, 98.14,98.56
Jeane, 103.77
Joane, 103.25
John, 102.139
John; Elizabeth, w; Alice, d; Elizabeth, d;
　Percye, d; Emma, d, 102.271
John; Jane, w, 104.52
John; Mary, w, 104.81
John; Mary, w; Thomas, s; Deniel, s, 107C.19
John; Mary, w; Samuel, s; Joseph, s; Hannah,
　d; John, s, 107D.96
John; Mary, w, 110.26
John, bach, 99.33,106.9
Joseph; Rebecca, w; William, s; Elizabeth, d,
　101.69
Joseph, £600; Anne, w, 103.181
Josiah, widower; Patience, d; Sarah, d;
　Elizabeth, d, 107D.91
Margarett, 102.16
Martha, 102.19
Mary; John, s?; Thomas, s?, 101.91
Mary, app, 107B.40
Mary, ser, 103.284
Mercy, 101.83
Patrick; kath, w; kath, d, 104.49
Peter, ser, 98.31
Phayllis, ser, 104.88
Rich; Eliz, w; Edw, s; Susanna, d; Marg, d,
　104.46
Robert; Sarah, w, 107D.74
Roger; Benjamin, s, 103.225
Samuell; Agnus, w; Elizabeth, d; Mary, d;
　William, s; Samuell, s, 103.57
Samuel; Mary, w; Samuel, s; Elizabeth, d,
　107B.17
Simon; Ann, w; Sarah, d?; Elizabeth, d?;
　Simon, s?, 99.37
Stephen; Elizabeth, w, 109.20
Susan, 109.89
Thomas, 109.36
Thomas; Mary, w; Augustus, s; William, s;
　Henry, s; Thomas, s, 101.19
Thomas; Hester, w, 101.100
Thomas; Hanah, w, 103.61

Thomas; Mary, w; Thomas, s; William, s;
　Elizabeth, d; Alexander, s, 103.220
Thomas; Jane, w, 109.54
Thomas; Mary, w, 101.40
Thomas; Sarah, w; Henry, s; Anne, d, 110.25
Tymothy, 102.186
William Thomas, 101.91
William; Sarah, w, 102.133
William; Anne, w; Dunstant, s, bach, 103.101
William; Jane, w; William, s; John, s;
　Elizabeth, d, 104.76
William; Anne, w, 107D.64
William; Rachell, w; George, s; John, s,
　109.30
William, £600; Mary, w; Edward, s?; Richard,
　s?; Mary, d?; Elizabeth, d?; Arthur, s?, 99.7
William, bach, gent, 98.17

ALLENBRIDGE: Samuell; Vertue, w, 109.92

ALLENSON: George, £600; Dorothy, w,
　104.63

ALLHALLOWS:
Ann, parish child of All Hallows, Lumber St,
　103.72
Edward, parish child of All Hallows, Lumber
　St, 103.72

ALLIBONE: Job; Katherine, w; Hannah, d;
　Edith, grand-d of, 98.81

ALLIEN: Thomas, widower, 103.275

ALLING:
David, 102.29
Mary, 102.30

ALLINGHAM:
Henry; Ann, w, 109.52
Mary, 109.41
Simon; Alice, w; Simon, s; Anne, d, 107B.78

ALLINGTON:
Thomas, 106.7
William; Mary, w; Sarah, d; Susan, d; Mary,
　d, 100.10

ALLIP: Abigall, ser, 107C.41

ALLISON:
Mary, Mrs, 109.41
William, gent, bach, 106.2
Sarah, 107A.9

ALLITT: William; Susan, w; Mary, d, 102.18

ALLOM:
Anne, 109.13

Anne; Anne, d?; Elizabeth, d?, 102.185
James; Elizabeth, d; James, s, 109.54
James, ser, 106.26
Mathew; Elizabeth, w; Margaret, d;
    Elizabeth, d, 106.26
Sarah, ser, 98.29
Thomas; Sarah, w, 107B.27
William; Jane, w, 106.31

ALLONBY: Rich; Jane, w, 104.83

ALLONSON:
Anne; Katherine, d; Elizabeth, d; Francis, s,
    104.109
Elizabeth, 104.136
George, app, 104.95

ALLOWAY:
Elizabeth, 109.31
John; Anne, w; William, s; Anne, d;
    Elizabeth, d; Susannah, d, 107B.32
Sarah, 107D.86

ALLSOBROOKE: Mary, 109.9

ALLWAY: Thomas, 102.236

ALLY: Morris; Rose, w, 109.31

ALMOND: John; Sarah, w, 104.140

ALPHAGE: Elizabeth, app, 107D.92

ALPORT:
Benjamin; Dorothy, w; Mary, d, 101.18
Johannah, 98.25

ALPRESSE: Thomas, bach,
    104.110

ALPRIS: Anne, 109.75

ALSEBROOKE: Mary, 102.207

ALSOP:
Benjamin, app, 102.114
Dorothy; Rebeccah, d, 98.63
Ellinor, 103.289
Peter; Ann, w, 104.127
Richard, 107A.41
Richard, parish child, 109.14
William, 107B.77
William; Sarah, w; William, s, 102.242

ALSTON:
John, bach, gent, 98.59
Samuel; Judith, w; Ellen, d; John, s; Edward, s,
    107D.20
Samuel, app, 104.39

ALT: Ralph; Marg, w; Simon, s; Eliz, d,
    104.29

ALTHORPE:
John; Mary, w, 104.5
William; Sarah, w, 102.47

ALTON: Ambrose, app, 98.73

ALVIE: Joseph; Elizabeth, w; Elizabeth, d,
    103.275

ALWOOD: John; Christien, w, 102.261

ALWRIGHT: James; Susan, w; John, s,
    107B.22

AMBLER:
Humphry; Anne, w, 109.78
John; Lucey, w, 109.55
Samuel, 105.17

AMBROSE:
Andr; Eliza, w; Tho, s, 104.73
John; Edward, s, 107B.23
Joseph, 98.15
Judith, ser, 101.74
Mary; Mary, d, 104.73
Richard, widower; John, s,
    107C.36
Thomas, 107D.71
William, widower, 107C.3
William, ser, bach, 104.65

AMER?: , 98.25

AMERY: Thomas, 106.3

AMES: Thomas, app, 104.82

AMOSS:
Hesster, 103.9
Jane; William, s; Anne, d, 98.8

AMPES: Elizabeth, 98.65

AMPSON: Edward; Jane, w; Mary, child,
    104.108

AMSDELL:
Joseph, child in house of Andrew Beard,
    102.168
Sarah, child in house of Andrew Beard,
    102.168

AMSDEN:
Pheby, 109.39
Richard; Grace, w; Edward, s; William, s,
    107C.9

6

AMSON:
Anne, ser, 98.43
James; Margarett, w, 109.66

AMY:
John; Eilzabeth, w, 108.5
William;

ANDERSON:
~, 98.46
Daniell, bach, 109.62
Ellizabeth, 102.125
George; Judeth, w, 107D.21
Margery, 101.54
Marian, ser, 106.4
Robert, 106.33
Thomas, 109.4
Vincely, app, 107B.49

ANDERTON:
Ann, wid; James, s, 103.43
Edward, bach, 104.137
James, 104.137
Mary, 107D.68
Nathaniel, app, 107D.13
William, bach, 109.55

ANDESWORTH: Nathan, 105.16

ANDREW: William, assessor;

ANDREWS:
~, wid, 102.61
Abigall, 106.53
Alice, 107A.37
Anne, 107A.27,107C.16
Benjamin, app, 102.107
Elizabeth, 104.32,107D.27
Elizabeth; Elizabeth, d, 109.28
Ellinor, wid; William, s; Mary, d, 103.42
Ellinor, wid; Ann, d, 103.198
Frances, 99.57
Francis, 109.62
Gabriel; Mary, w; Gabriel, s, 109.33
George; Elizabeth, w; Katherine, d, 103.161
Giles, bach, 106.60
Hanah; Hanah, d, 107B.17
Jeane, 103.76
Jeremy; Ann, w; Jeremy, s; Anne, d, 104.132
John; Mary, w, 102.24
John; Elizabeth, w, 104.128
John; Martha, w, 109.21
John, ser, 109.34
Mary, 101.8,107C.16
Mathew, app, 107D.16
Mathew, nurse child, 103.71
Michaell; Margery, w; Rebecca, d, 102.194
Richard, bach, 104.4
Richard, bach, esq, 106.47

Robert; Joyce, w; Elizabeth, d, 107B.13
Robert; Sarah, w; John, s, 109.19
Samuell; Ann, w; Samuell, s; Mary, d;
    Edward, s, 103.250
Sarah, ser, 100.13
Thomas, 110.13
Thomas; Jane, w; Thomas, s?; Samuell, s,
    99.50
Thomas; Elizabeth, w, 107C.16
Thomas; Mary, w, 109.64
Thomas; Sarah, w, 109.74
Wiliiam; Mary, w; William, s; Lyddia, d;
    Elizabeth, d, 103.8
Wiliiam; Hannah, w; William, s, 103.263
Wiliiam, £50 p.a., assessor; Elizabeth, w;
    William, s; John, s; Allen, s; Anne, d;
    Elizabeth, d, 102.4

ANEES: George; Jane, w, 103.214

ANERLY: Thomas, 101.110

ANESWORTH: Mary, ser, 107D.19

ANGE:
Charles; Alice, w; Nathaniell, s; Elizabeth, d,
    106.7
Wiliiam, ser, 103.34

ANGELL:
Ellioner, ser, 106.46
John; Judeth, w, 103.7
Mary, 109.95
Thomas; Ann, w, 103.75
Thomas; ~, w, 103.133

ANGER:
Eleanor, 102.130
Thomas, app, 104.79

ANGLESEY: Mary; Anne, d, 98.27

ANGUISH: Tho; Frances, w; Susan, d,
    104.40

ANGUS: Adam, bach, £50 p.a., 106.66

ANNETT:
Richard, 99.12
Wiliiam; Flora, w; William, s, 99.24

ANNIBALL: Benjamin, 99.40

ANNS: Richard; Frances, w, 102.39

ANNUTT: Joyce, ser, 103.287

ANSCOW: Elizabeth, wid,
    102.25

7

ANSELL:
Edward, bach, 98.38
Elizabeth, 110.8
John, 107D.50
Nicholas, ser, 102.199
Richard; Mary, w; Richard, s; Alexander, s, 98.61
Robt; Susanna, ?w; Eliz, d;

ANSEY: ~; ~, w, 100.7

ANSHAM: Richard, 106.35

ANSLEY: Wiliiam; Elizabeth, w; Solomon, s; William, s; Luke Westwood, s?, 103.117

ANSLOPP: Chas, app, 104.106

ANSTED: Margaret, 109.3

ANSTRY: Katherine, wid; Stonath, d or s, 103.125

ANTES: Frances; Elizabeth, d, 102.254

ANTEY: Samuel; Margaret, w, 107D.86

ANTHONY: Edward, £600; Apphia, w; Apphia, d; Ann, d, 103.276

ANTILL: John; Mary, w; Frances Phillipps, d, 107D.8

ANTONIES: Henry; Civell, w; Henry, s; Sarah, d, 102.197

ANTROBUS:
Daniel; Mary, w; Daniel, s; Richard, s, 109.2
Deborah, 102.242
John, 105.4
Joseph; Barbara, w, 109.34

ANTROM:
David; David, s, 106.32
John; Anne, w, 102.230

ANTWIZELL: Robert; Millicent, w, 99.35

ANWILL?: Anne, ser, 105.15

ANYON: Elizabeth; Nicholas, s, 102.235

APLEING: John, 103.104

APLEYARD: Sarah, ser, 103.13

APPERLEE: John; Jeane, w; Jeane, d; Francis, s, at sea, 103.97

APPLEBY:
John; Kathrine, w; John, s, 109.41
John; Martha, w, 109.91
Simon, ser, 109.6

APPLEGATE: Thomas; Elizabeth, w, 99.20

APPLETON: Wiliiam; Susan, w; Mary, d; William, s; Susan, d; John, s, 105.1

APPRENTICE: Anthony, 98.86

APPS: Henry, 99.54

APSLEY: Henry; Avis, w; John, s; Henry, s, 106.7

APTHORPE:
East; Susana, w, 103.232
James; Catherine, w, 103.181

APULEE: Thomas, 103.19

ARBORY: Anthony; Elizabeth, w; Anthony, s, 110.12

ARCHADINE: Sarah; Wm, s, 104.36

ARCHBOLD: Andrew, app, 107D.11

ARCHDELL: George, ser, 102.166

ARCHE: John; Elizabeth, w, 102.239

ARCHER:
Anne, 98.72, 102.235
Edward, app, 98.65
Edward, bach under age, 103.23
Elizabeth, 109.87
Francis; Zenobriah, w, 107B.41
Jeane, wid, 103.22
Joane, 102.197
John; Alice, w, 107D.83
John, gent; Mary, w, 103.286
Jonathon; Mary, w, 109.35
Jone, 101.38
Martha, 101.42
Mary, 107D.62
Mary, ser, 103.256
Richard; Anee, w, 107D.37
Robert; Joyce, w; Sarah, d; Katherine, d, 102.190
Sam; Mary, w; Sam, s; John, s, 104.145
Sara, 101.5, 109.98
Simon; Susanah, w; Elizabeth, d; Mary, d, 103.278
Thomas; Alice, w, 102.237
Thomas; ~, w, 103.203
Thomas; Elizabeth, w, 107D.67

8

Thomas; Anne, w, 109.34
William, 107B.23, 103.212

ARDISWICK: Isaac, ser, 103.11

ARES:
Frances, 101.36
Mary, 101.59

AREY:
James, bach, 101.109
Thomas, app, 101.107

ARGENT: Robert; Susannah, w, 98.80

ARGILE: Peter; Mary, w; Anne, d; Timothy, s;
John, s, 107A.37

ARINDELL: Sarah, ser, 103.225

ARINGTON: Edward; Emim, w; William, s,
bach; Edward, s, bach; John, bach, under
age; Mary, d; Charles, s, 103.42

ARIS:
Elizabeth, wid; Martha, d; Elizabeth, d; John,
s, 103.165
John; Elizabeth, w, 102.174
Joseph, 107A.42
Nicholas; Hanah, w; Elizabeth, d; Sarah, d;
Honor, d; Joseph, s, 107A.42
Robert; Mary, w; Sarah, d; Mary, d; Robert,
s; Elizabeth, d, 103.44
Samuell, widower; Thomas, s; Abigall, his
mother, 103.21

ARIVALL: Thomas, ser, 103.12

ARKELL:
Martha, ser, 98.61
Peter, 102.103

ARKWRIGHT: Henry, 107D.39

ARLINGTON: Mary, 109.71

ARME: Mary, 103.12

ARMFEILD: Elizabeth, 104.121

ARMIGER: Mary, 107D.13

ARMITAGE:
John; Margaret, w; Thomas, s,
107D.84
Mary, 106.39
Thomas; Mary, w; Mary, d, 103.196
Timothia, 106.39
William, app, 107D.97

ARMITT:
Amy; Alice, d? a child, 102.76
Isabella, ser, 101.109
John, app, 101.83
Thomas, 105.18
Thomas, assessor, 105.15

ARMSHEE: Dorothy, 102.234

ARMSTEED:
John; Isabell, w; Joseph, s; William, s; John, s,
107D.39
Anne, 102.267
Elizabeth, gentlewoman, 102.3
Elizabeth, gentlewoman; Elizabeth, d;
Margarett, d, 98.30
Geo, bach, 104.10
Mary, pensioner, 103.77
Thomas, 107D.85

ARNES: John, ser, 104.5

Arnitt:
Anne, 105.7
Charles, bach, 105.7
Theophilus, 105.7

ARNOLD:
John; Katherine, w, 107C.2
John; Katherine, w, 107D.39
John; Margaret, w, 109.83
Mary, 109.21
Phebe, 109.22
Richard, ser, 109.6
Robert; Margaret, w; Francis, ser;
Margaret, d,
107B.41
Robert, bach, 107D.39
Thomas, 101.100
Thomas; Mary, w, 104.29
Thomas; Sarah, w, 104.100
William, 102.194
Benjamin; Sara, w, 101.14
Bridget, 107B.32
Edward, 109.88
Evan; Dorothy, w; Mary, w, 101.100
Frances?, 104.90
James; Jane, w, 102.142
Jane, 101.70
Jeremy; Elizabeth, w, 109.83

ARON: William; Alice, w; Catherine, d,
109.91

ARONDELL: Nicholas, 102.70

ARRINGTON: Mary, 101.45

ARROW: Mary, 103.94

9

ARROWSMITH:
Africa, ser, 103.94
Anothey, son of a gent, 102.4
Benjamin, 99.46
Hugh; Mary, w, 98.54
John; Dorothy, w, 109.53
Martha, 102.81

ARTERFEILD: Don, bach, 98.36

ARTHER:
Christopher, app, 102.185
Elizabeth, ser, 107B.18
Henry; ~, w, 103.210
Rachell, 109.101

ARTHINGTON: Thomas; George, s;
    Johannah, d; Thomas, s; Anne, d, 98.43

ARWIN: Jane, 109.29

ASBRIDGE: John; Elizabeth, w, 109.34

ASDEN: Francis, ser, 103.235

ASGALL:
Anne, 110.36
Mary, 110.36

ASH:
Elizabeth; Joseph, s, 109.94
John; Mary, w; Hannah, d; Rebecca, d,
    102.48
John; Frances, w; Amey, d; Elizabeth, d,
    110.6
Rachell, ser, 107B.9
William; Susan, w, 103.279

ASHBELL: Prudense, wid, 100.12

ASHBORNEHAM: Elizabeth, 106.60

ASHBOURNE:
Christopher; Elizabeth, w, 99.12
John; Sarah, w, 98.55
John; Mary, w, 101.104
William;

ASHBY:
~, Mrs, 104.138
Ann, 106.62
Elizabeth, 110.10
Jos; Mary, w, 104.87
Nicholas; Elizabeth, w, 98.41
Sarah; Anne, d; Elizabeth, d, 103.221
William, 102.33
William; Ann, w, 103.156

ASHCROFT: John, ser, 104.10

ASHDEN: Margaret, 107B.71

ASHLER: Jane, ser, 104.16

ASHLEY:
Thomas; Martha, w; Lewis, s, 107D.67
Elizabeth, 98.71
James; Grace, w, 107C.26
John, 107D.10
Sarah, w, 107D.10
Hanah, d, 107D.10
Sarah, d, 107D.10
Margeret, ser, 103.14
Randolph; Elizabeth, w, 107C.24
Richard; Katherine, w, 109.93
Susan, ser, 109.77
Thomas; Anne, w, 98.71
Thomas; Jane, w; John Poole, s, 107C.6
Thomas, s of Whitchellow, Charles, 107D.100
William, 101.2

ASHMAN:
Joane, 109.30
William, ser, 103.66

ASHMORE:
Elianor, 109.91
James; Anne, w, 107D.69
John; Mary, w; Mary, d, 107D.10
Mary, 109.4
Mary, wid; Henry, s, 103.134
Richard; Mary, w; Martha, d, 103.93
Thomas; Milecent, w; Thomas, s; Anne, d,
    107C.17
William; Frances, w, 98.88
William; Margaret, w; Mary, d, 107D.58

ASHPOOLE: Ann, wid, 103.186

ASHRIDGE: Elizabeth, ser, 109.103

ASHTON:
Anthony; Ann, w; Luke, s; Anna, d; Mary, d;
    Nathaniel, s, 107D.58
Arthur; Anne, w; Mary, d, 104.66
Elizabeth, 109.103
Henry, ser, 109.8
John; Elizabeth, w; John, s, 98.58
Lucy, 104.96
Margeret; Robert, s; James, s, 103.291
Mary, 103.109, 106.15
Miles, 107B.30
Thomas, 106.55
Thomas; Mary, w, 98.46
William, 107D.65
William; Frances, w; Frances, d; Jane, d;
    Elizabeth, d, 107D.87

ASHURST: Samuell, 101.52

10

ASHWORTH:
Jeane, ser, 103.28
John; Jane, w; Jane, d, 109.40
Thomas; Mary, w; Mary, d; Thomas, nurse
    child of, 107B.31

ASK: Francis, app, 103.103

ASKELL: Thomas, app, 102.173

ASKEN: John; Elizabeth, w; John, s, 103.35

ASKMAN: Anne, 104.51

ASLIN: Ann; Ann, d, 110.21

ASLLEY: John; Elizabeth, w; Elizabeth, d,
    102.10

ASON:
John, 102.225
John; Mary, w, 110.15

ASPIN:
Hanna, 101.53
Richard; Mary, w; Elizabeth, d; Mary, d,
    103.34

ASPINALL: Gilbert; Edward, s, 103.12

ASPINHAM: Mary, ser, 106.48

ASPLIN: Mathew; Elizabeth, w; Thomas, s;
    Agnes, d; Mary, d, 107B.36

ASPLY: Amy, 101.96

ASTELL: Ann, 109.7

ASTREY: James, ser, 106.58

ASTY:
John, 101.21
John; Abigall, d, 101.103

ATCHURCH: Mary, 109.71

ATERELL: Elizabeth, ser, 109.4

ATFEILD: Walter, app, 98.22

ATFEN: ?Edmond; Elizabeth, w, 109.47

ATHE: Ann, ser, 103.224

ATHERLY:
Anthony; Mary, w; Ann, d; John, s; Henry, s;
    George, s, 103.46
Edward; Faith, w; Mary, d, 103.67

Elizabeth, pensioner; Abraham, s, 103.75
Elizabeth, ser, 103.61
Nathaniel; Ann, w, 103.170

ATHEY: Simon; Elizabeth, w, 109.70

ATKINS:
Abraham, bach, 102.63
Alice, 107B.80
Ann, ser, 103.148
Charles, app, 103.8
Deborah, ser, 107A.40
Elizabeth, 102.49
Elizabeth, nurse child, 107C.15
Elizabeth, wid; Mary, d, 103.173
Hanah; Joseph, s; Hanah, d, 107D.33
Isaac, 109.87
James, ser, 106.27
John, 102.46,104.71
John; ~, w; John, s, 100.10
John; Sara, w; Martha, d; Elizabeth, d, 101.94
John; Abigall, w, 102.249
Joseph, 102.93
Judith, 107A.26
Marcy; Joyce, w; Isabella, d, 102.153
Mary, 109.66
Morgan, £600; Sarah, w; Sarah, d; Thomas, s;
    Mary, d; Morgan, s, 102.63
Obediah; Elizabeth, w; Jesse, s, 104.71
Robert; Anne, w, 107C.30
Thomas; Hannah, w; Hannah, d, 109.81
Thomas, app, 102.195
William; Rebecca, w; Thomas, s, 105.15

ATKINSON:
Edmond; Margeret, w; James, s, 103.174
Ellinor, ser, 106.12
Henry; Mary, w; Henry, s, 102.21
Izabellah, ser, 98.39
John; Margarett, w, 99.36
John; Mary, w, 109.46
John, ser, 106.22
John, wid; Honour, d; Anne, d, 103.207
Richard; Barbary, w; Richard, s; Ann, d,
    109.36
Richard, assessor for Holborne crosse,
    109.112
Richard, pensioner; Olive, w; Richard, s;
    James, s, 103.164
Sarah, 102.119

ATLEY:
Susan; Esther, d, 103.146
James, 102.40
John, 109.33

ATTERBURY: Francis; Katherine, w, 105.12

ATTON?: Wm, gent, bach, 104.88

11

ATTY:
Elinor, 109.44
Marmaduke, ser, 98.72

ATWOOD:
Abell; Mary, w; Abell, s; Mary, d, 109.38
Elizabeth, 99.53
Ellen, 107D.57
Hester, ser, 106.40
Isabell; Elizabeth, d; Mary, d, 107B.42
James, app, 107D.10
Mary, gentlewoman; Mary, child d?, 99.53
Mathew, app, 107B.42
Richard, 106.5
Thomas; Anne, w; Elizabeth, d, 100.9
, esq, 109.79

AUBERRY: Isaac; Frances, w; Elizabeth, d;
    Robert, s, 103.62

AUDLEY:
Katherine; Robert, s, 98.73
Millisent, 104.101

AULWINKELL: Gilbert, 102.209

AULY:
Edward; Joanna, w; John, s; Mary, d, 100.6
John; Magdalen, w; John, s, 106.3

AUNGIER:
Thomas, 101.110
Thomas, 102.276

AUREY: Ann, ser, 109.24

AURILL: John; Sarah, w, 109.29

AUSLSTONE: Roger; Catherine, w; Rebecca,
    d, 103.19

AUSSITOR: Katherine, ser;

AUSTIN:
~; John, s; Mary, d, 104.29
Alice, 109.18
Elizabeth, ser, 98.46
Frances, 98.14
Francis, gent; Elizabeth, w, 102.92
Henry, app, 107B.28
Hugh; Elizabeth, w; Elizabeth, d; Anne, d,
    102.116
John, 102.175
John; Mary, w; William, s, 102.113
John; Elizabeth, w, 102.175
John; Elizabeth, w, 104.146
Mary, ser, 102.128, 109.29
Rachell, a nurse child from the Artillery
    Ground, 103.226

Richard; Mary, w; William, s, 103.84
Richard; Anne, w; William, s; Jane, d; James,
    s; Mary, d, 105.6
Richard, £600; Jeane, w; Jeane, d, 103.214
Sarah, ser, 107D.30
Susan; Susan, d; Mary, d; Jane, d, 102.84
Susan, app, 107B.18
Thomas, 101.71
Thomas; Elizabeth, w; Elizabeth, d; William,
    s; Thophilus, s, 98.78
Thomas; Alice, w; Mary, d, 103.168
Thomas; Elizabeth, w, 104.40
Thomas; ~, w, 104.142
Thomas; Margaret, w, 107B.75
Thomas; Jane, w; Thomas, s; Elizabeth, d;
    Samuel, s, 107D.9
William, bach; Anne, sister of, 98.24
Jacob; Martha, w, 103.57
Mary, wid, 103.57
Robert; Susan, w; Elizabeth, d, 103.213

AUTHERSON: Mary; Wm; Eliz, w, 104.20

AUTON: Robert, bach, 102.68

AUTTDAY: Robert; Mary, w; Elizabeth, d,
    103.91

AVELLIN: Augustin, 99.42

AVENOR: Anne, ser, 98.84

AVENS: John, 107D.7

AVENT: Jane, 110.23

AVERET: Anne, ser, 107D.83

AVERLY: Thomas, £600; Martha, w; John, s;
    Martha, d, 101.2

AVERY:
Ann, ser, 106.1
Richard; Susannah, w; Mary, d, 98.58
Richard, wid; Elizabeth, d, 107C.35
Thomas, 109.99
Thomas, app, 102.189

AVIS:
Gilbert, 98.83
Jos, £600; Susan, w, 104.11
Thomas; Winfred, w, 101.62

AVON: Christopher; Penlope, w; Penlope, d;
    Mary, d, 106.53

AWBORNE:
Elizabeth, 101.47
Oliver; Oliver, s, 101.81

AWBREY: Richard; Mary, w; Richard, s; John, s, 101.97

AWOOD: John, 109.72

AX:
Robert, 100.5
Thomas; Mary, w; Mary, d, 100.5

AXDELL: Richard; Elizabeth, w; Ruben Browne, kinsman of, 107D.7

AXHALL: Thomas; Drothy, w, 102.54

AXTELL:
Ann, 109.51
Edward, 102.19
Hannah, 98.88
Robert, 99.31

AXWELL: Mary, 101.46

AYLAND:
Henry; Hanah, w, 103.213
Jonathon; Rebecca, w, 103.117

AYLETT: Ambrose; Mary, w; Ambrose, s; Mary, d, 104.124

AYLIFFE: Bryan; Mary, w; Robert, s; Bengamin, s; Mary, d, 109.79

AYLSWORTH:
Margaret, 99.38
Thomas, bach, ser, 102.146
William, 109.41

AYRES:
Bridgett; Patiense, d, 102.158
Elizabeth, 101.74, 109.29
Elizabeth, ser, 106.2
George; Bridgett, w, 98.47
John; Mary, w; Richard, s; John, s; Elizabeth, d; William, s, 103.111
John; Alice, w; Izabella, d; Elizabeth, d, 103.246
John Horsler, 103.26
John, ser, 103.73
Jonathon, 110.30
Mary; Sarah, d; Thomas Clendon, grand-s of, 107A.2
Richard, app, 107A.43
Richard, ser, 107A.43
Ruth, 107D.17
Thomas; Jane, w, 106.19
Thomas; Susan, w; Anne, d, 107D.85
Thomas, app, 107A.31
Thourborne; Elizabeth, w, 98.48
William; Frances, w; Charles, s; Frances, d; William, s; James, s, 103.37

AYWOOD: Elizabeth, ser, 103.70

AYWORTH: Jas, bach, 104.87

BABB:
Mary, 103.147
Richard; Jane, w, 98.66
Thomas, ser, 106.17

BABBS:
Ezekell; Ellinor, w, 103.266
Francis; Martha, w, 103.20
John; Elizabeth, w, 103.20

BABER:
John, gent, ?b, 104.8
Robert, bach, under age, 103.48

BABHAM: Henry, 109.7

BACKER:
John, 109.19
Matthew, 105.17
Samuel, ser, 109.7

BACKFORD: Anne;

BACKHOUSE:
~, wid, 98.49
Edward, ser, 106.29
Katherine, 104.61

BACKHURST:
Amey, 107B.34
Francis; Barbary, w, 105.4

BACKITT: Anne, 102.28

BACKS: Sarah, ser, 107B.74

BACKSWITH: John; Mary, w; Ann, d; Elizabeth, d, 103.28

BACKWITH:
Elizabeth, child at nurse, 103.36
Mary, child at nurse, 103.36

BACON:
Anne; Elizabeth, d; Thomas, d; William, s; Anne, d, 101.18
Eliza; Mary, d, 104.77
John; Elizabeth, w; Sarah, d, 102.59
Joseph; Jeane, w; Joseph, s; Jeane, 103.128
Richard, gent; Anne, d, 104.95
Sarah, ser, 102.161

BADCOCK:
Alexander; Mary, w, 102.50
James; Elizabeth, w, 107B.29

13

James; James, s; Mary, d; John, s, 107B.29
Jeane, wid, 103.83
Mary, 102.15
Richard, bach, 104.7
William, 103.35

BADGER:
Andrew; Katherine, w; Sarah, d, 98.78
John; Dorothy, w, 102.45
Susan; Mary, d, 107D.73

BADLEY: William, pensioner; Prudence, w;
John, s; Joshua, s; Mary, d, 103.197

BADMORE: Anne, 101.23

BAGG: Stephen, 103.236

BAGGER: Richard, ser, 103.184

BAGGOTT: Edward; Margeret, w; Mary, d;
Martha, d; Thomas, s, 103.48

BAGGS:
Anne; Mary, d, 103.15
Zachary, bach, 104.125

BAGLEY:
~; ~, w, 103.82
Ann, 109.17
Esther, ser, 103.30
James; Mary, w; Mary, d; Dorothy, d;
Elizabeth, d, 109.17
Judeth, nurse child, 103.9
Mathew; Judeth, w; James, s; William, s;
Judeth, d, 103.6
Ruth, ser, 106.28
William; Elizabeth, w, 109.35

BAGNALL:
Anne, pensioner, 109.35
Elizabeth, gentlewoman; Elizabeth, d,
98.31
Elizabeth, ser, 106.12
Sarah, a child, 102.136

BAGNETT: Margarett, ser, 98.69

BAGSHAW:
Edward; Mary, w, 107D.45
Edward, wid, 106.13
John, gent; Elizabeth, w, 106.25
Joseph; ~, w, 100.7
Nicholas, widower; Wm, bach, 104.80

BAGSTER:
Elizabeth, ser, 102.148
John; Lidiah, w; Elizabeth, d; John, s,
102.137

BAILEY, See Bayley

BAKEING: John; Elizabeth, w; Sarah, d,
102.59

BAKEN: Ann;

BAKER:
~, Mrs; ~, wid; ~, wid; Katherine, d, 103.142
Amy, 101.38
Anne; Timothy, s; Ann, d, 103.151
Anne, wid; Sarah, d; Margaret, d; William, s,
103.69
Benjamin; Mary, w; Elizabeth, d; James, s,
106.44
Daniel, 107D.89
Daniel; Mary, w, 109.112
Diana, 104.61
Edward; Anne, w, 103.37
Edward; Elizabeth, w, 103.171
Elizabeth, 102.68
Elizabeth, gentlewoman, 106.41
Elizabeth, ser, 102.73,103.49
Ellinor; Mary, d, 103.15
George, bach, 101.58
Henry, a child, 102.12
James; Margaret, w, 98.56
James, ser, 103.184
Jane, 98.49
John; Mary, w, 98.59
John; Jane, w; Anne, d, 101.16
John; Dorothy, w, 102.12
John; Mary, w; Anne, d; Susanna, d, 104.24
John; Mary, w, 107D.28
John; Sarah, w, 109.7
John; Mary, w; John, s, 109.40
John; Anne, w; Leticia, d; Elizabeth, d; Mary,
d, 109.95
John; Elizabeth, w; John, s; Elizabeth, d;
Ruth, d; Mary, d, 108.2
John, app, 102.71
John, assessor, 108.8
John?, bach, ser, 104.19
Joseph, bach, ser, 107D.27
Joshua, app, 103.179
Martha, wid; Elizabeth, d, 103.56
Mary, 98.87,102.68
Mary; Sarah, d; Elizabeth, d, 102.139
Mary, nurse child, 107B.40
Mary, ser, 102.178,103.197
Moses; Elizabeth, w; Elizabeth, d, 102.185
Rachell, wid, 103.115
Rebecca, 102.261
Richard; Katherine, w, 99.2
Richard, app, 104.31,107B.78
Richard, bach, 98.5
Roger; Hanah, w; John, s; Elishas, s; Hanah,
d, 102.221
Sampson, 109.36

Samuel, 107B.81
Sarah, 109.80
Susan, pensioner, 103.77
Susanna; Heneretta, d, 101.50
Theophilus, 101.50
Thomas; Mary, w, 102.226
Thomas; Elizabeth, w; Martha, d; Charles, s,
    107B.13
Thomas; Elizabeth, w; Mary, d; Sarah, d,
    107B.68
Thomas, app, 107B.22
Thomas Quaker; Mary, w; John, s; Grace, d,
    103.215
William, 102.63
William; Sarah, w; William, s; Richard, s;
    James, s; John, s, 103.29
William; Mary, w; Thomas, s; Anne, d,
    103.205
William; Jane, w, 104.6
William; Katherine, w; William, s, 110.4
William, a bach, 98.2
William, app, 104.99
William, bach, ser, 104.15

BAKERS: Hester, a child, 102.274

BALCH: William, 98.68

BALDER: James; Susanna, w, 99.20

BALDERSON: Richard; Margarey, w, 98.82

BALDIN:
Elizabeth, 99.52
Elizabeth, ser, 102.189
Hanah, 99.52
James, 107D.25

BALDREY:
Edward; Elizabeth, w; Edward, s; Elizabeth,
    d, 103.54
John; Jema, w; Dorothy, d, 101.70
John; Mary, w; John, s; Robeet, s, 102.214

BALDUCK: Nicholas; Joane, w; John, s;
    Samuell, s, 103.170

BALDWIN:
~, 104.47
Anne, 109.77
Elizabeth, 102.126
Elienor, ser, 101.21
George; Marcy, w; Mathew, s; James, s,
    107D.56
George, bach, 98.74
Henry; Anne, d, 104.134
Henry, gent; Anne, w; Samuell, s, 106.22
Humphrey, app, 104.73
James; Katherine, w; Katherine, d?, 99.21

Jane, 109.67
John; Anne, w, 104.99
John; Mary, w; Henry, s, 107D.75
John; Susanna, w, 109.77
John; Elizabeth, w; Robeet, s; Elizabeth, d;
    Lucy, d, 109.100
Margarett, 102.211
Martha, s, 107B.67
Mary, 102.227
Nathan; Elizabeth, w, 107A.12

BALGDEN: Anne; Bridget, d, 101.75

BANSKIN: Edward, 107D.45

BANTHAM: Elizabeth, 106.65

BANTIN?: William, 102.109

BANTON: Elizabeth, ser, 103.285

BANUM: Solomon; Anne, 109.79

BANWICK: Anne, 109.79

BANYAN: Margaret, 102.26

BANYER: Edmond; Abigall, w; Mary, d;

BARBARY:
~, wid; ~, child;

BARBER:
~, wid, 109.23
Anne, 107B.9
Daniell; Martha, w; Elizabeth, d, 109.86
Edward, 103.202
Elizabeth, 109.21
Elizabeth, ser, 103.37, 107D.36
Gregory, bach, 98.73
Henry; Martha, w; John, s; George, grands-s;
    Grace, grand-d, 103.247
James; Elizabeth, w; John, s; Jomes, s,
    107B.53
John; Elizabeth, w, 102.257
John; Mary, w; John, s; Sarah, d, 103.118
Margaret, 109.99
Martha, 102.112
Mary, wid, 103.23
Patrick; Hannah, w; Mary, d; Margarett, d,
    102.159
Sarah, 99.5, 109.30
Thomas; Elizabeth, w; Mary, d; Elizabeth, d;
    Sarah, d; Jane, d; William, s; Thomas, s,
    100.2

BARBEY: Bartron, app, 98.45

BARBOM: Nicholas, app, 101.84

15

BARBOM?:
Elizabeth, 101.77
John; Anne, w; Benjamin, s, 101.86

BARCROFT: William; Jane, w; Henry, s,
107A.11

BARD: Francis; Anne, w; Sarah, d; Elizabeth,
d, 102.207

BARDDON: Henry, widower in prison, 103.90

BARDWELL: John; Grace, w; John, s, 105.6

BARDWIN: Isaac; Martha, w, 107D.1

BARDY:
John; Mary, w; Sara, d, 101.9
Samuell; Elizabeth, w; Elizabeth, d, 103.266

BARE:
Clement, bach, 104.101
Elizabeth, 99.37
Hanah, 99.37
John; Elizabeth, w; Dulcibella, d; Elizabeth,
d, 109.44
Margarett, 99.39
Wm, bach, 104.101

BAREBLOCK: Mary, wid; Elizabeth, d;
Robert, s; William, s, 102.59

BAREBONE: Thomas, a parish child,
102.274

BAREFOOT:
Anne, 102.201
Elizabeth, 102.201
Benjamin; Katharine, w, 102.139

BARFORD: John, 102.16

BARINGTON:
Alice, ser, 102.97
Margery, ser;

BARKER:
~, widower, 98.50
Anne, 106.36
Anne, wid; Elizabeth, d, 103.93
Charles, 102.216
Elianor, 107A.33
Elizabeth; James, s; Judeth, d, 103.77
Ellen, 102.45
Henry, ser, 101.74, 102.104
Jane, 102.170
John, 105.18
John; Sarah, w; Elizabeth, d, 104.103
John, bach, 104.74

BARNY: Anne, ser, 100.11

BARRINGER: Richard, app, 104.14

BARRLE:
Alice, pensioner, 106.8
Mary; Anne, d, 104.37
Robert; Anne, w, 103.265

BARRUM: William, widower, 103.198

BARRWAY: Anne, 105.2

BARRY:
Anne, 98.19
John; Mary, w, 104.115
Mary, 105.5
Mary, ser, 98.33

BARSHAM: Thomas; Katherine, w; Mary, d;
Katherine, d; Thomas, s, 106.27

BARSTON: James, ser, 106.4

BART: John; Elizabeth, w; John, s, 107B.62

BARTHOLEMEW:
Ann; Mary, d, 104.17
Elizabeth, 102.43
George; Sara, w; George, s; Mary, d, 101.6
John, 109.38
John, app, 102.187
Thomas; Rachell, w, 98.17

BARTINTON: Edward; Elizabeth, w;

BARTLETT:
~, wid, 104.55
Alice, 109.81
Anne; Anne, ser, 107A.37
Eliza, 104.78
Elizabeth, 109.2
Elizabeth, wid, 103.99
George, Doctor of Physick; Mary, w, 107D.52
Mary, 109.17
John; Mary, w, 101.109
John; Charity, w, 107D.70
Judeth; Edward, s; Mary, d, 109.18
Richard, 105.18
Robert; Margery, w; Mary, d; Richard, s,
103.93
Samuell, ser, 106.47
Sarah, ser, 103.172, 109.76
William, bach, 109.65

BARTLEY:
Mary, 98.8, 101.57
Mary, ser, 98.38
Susan;

BARTON:
~, in house of Micheal Christmas, 101.16
Alice, 101.19
Chas, ser, bach, 104.25
Daniell; Elizabeth, w; Daniell, s; Elizabeth, d;
    Joseph, s; Richard, s, 109.69
Elizabeth, 101.19
George; Anne, w; Sarah, d, 102.40
George; Patience, w; Abigell, d, 102.253
Hannah, 104.67
Jane; Jane, d, 104.67
John, 102.248, 106.42
John; Dorothy, w; Hannah, d?; Katherine, d?,
    102.46
Mary, 107D.71
Rebaecca, ser, 106.38
Ursula, 101.78
William; Alice, w, 107D.70

BARTRAM:
William, 109.94
Margaret, ser, 106.50
Michael; John, w, 107D.81

BARWELL: William, 102.65

BASEBDINE: Thomas, bach,
    102.193

BASEFEILD: Sarah, ser, 107B.35

BASELY: Alice, ser, 107A.30

BASHAM: William, 99.49

BASKERFEILD: William; Rebecca, w;
    Heaster, d, 109.16

BASKERVILLE: Edward, 101.23

BASNETT: Katherine, wid, 102.43

BASQUET: Nicholas, 102.4

BASS:
Jos; Mary, w, 104.32
Robert; Elizabeth, w; John, s, 106.39
Sarah, ser, 103.289
Susan, wid; Ann, d, 103.41
William, app, 107D.36

BASSAM:
Robert; Rose, w, 107C.12
Robert; Elizabeth, w; Elizabeth, d; Susan, d,
    107D.84

BASSDELL: Jeane, 103.276

BASSELL: Sarah, ser, 103.11

BASSETT:
Edward; Martha, w, 103.45
Edward, parish boy, 103.70
John, 109.6
John, parish boy, 103.135
John, ser, 109.60
Richard; Elizabeth, w; Mary, d; Elizabeth, d,
    109.4
Richard, ser, 106.68
Thomas; Judith, w, 110.26
William; Sarah, mother of, 102.171

BASWICK: Charles, £600; Hanah, w;
    Charles, s; Millecent, d, 102.111

BATALL: Ann, ser, 100.3

BATCH:
Ann, wid, 103.276
Josiah, 99.30

BATCHELER:
Elizabeth, 102.194
Hannah, 102.227
Henry; Elizabeth, w; Temperance, d, 103.242
Joseph; Martha, w, 103.159
Martha; Mary, d, 98.28
Nicholas; Anne, w; Anne, d; Nicholas, s,
    107C.11
Sarah, 107D.5
Thomas; Elizabeth, w; Elizabeth, d; Mary, d,
    109.95

BATCLIFFE: Henry, ser, 109.100

BATEMAN:
Anne, 101.71
Elizabeth, ser, 106.10
Joseph, 107D.37
Margaret, wid, 102.42
Richard; Sarah, w; William, s; Charies, s;
    Frances, d; Sarah, d; Rebecca, d, 107D.93
Stephen, £600; Elizabeth, w; Henry, d; Mary,
    d, 98.57
William; Elizabeth, w, 102.84
William; Margaret, w; Martha, d, 107B.16

BATERNY: Dorothy, ser, 100.2

BATES:
Abraham, 107D.7
Anne, 110.24
Catherine; Elizabeth, d, 109.107
Christopher, ser, 103.202
Elizabeth, 98.55
Elizabeth; Katherine, d, 103.76
Elizabeth, ser, 104.54
Edmond, 106.7
George, ser, 109.12

17

Hanna; Charles, s, 109.65
James, 110.33
Jeremy; Sarah, w; Jeremy, s; Sarah, d, 109.35
John; Jane, w; Thomas, s, 107B.53
John; Anne, w, 107D.76
John, ser, 106.20, 107A.4
Joseph; Anne, w; William, s; Mary, d; Anne,
   d; Joseph, s, 98.57
Mary, 98.60
Mary; Rose, d; Elizabeth, d, 109.33
Nicholas; Grace, w; Anne, d; Sarah, d; Paull,
   s, 103.221
Richard; Mary, w, 98.75
Tho; Dorothy, w, 104.47
William; Mary, w, 103.38

BATESON:
Grace; Martha, d; Elizabeth, d; William, s,
   109.56
Mary, 109.59

BATH:
Abrahm, ser, 103.257
Anne, wid; Henry, s; Edmond, s, 103.16
John, bach, 110.6
Peter, ser, 103.28

BATHURST:
Charles, £600; Grace, w, 103.215
Lancelot, 109.81
Margaret, 103.282

BATON: Thomas, 102.19

BATSON:
Barbery, ser, 100.5
Katherine, 99.31
Mary, 99.31

BATT:
Charles; Elizabeth, w; Rebecca, d, 103.88
John; Margaret, w; Mary, d; Hanah, d,
   103.92
Robert; Margeret, w, 103.107
Samuell, bach, 103.32
Sarah, ser, 103.87

BATTENALL: Tho, ?b, 104.9

BATTENDEN: Elizabeth, 98.49

BATTERELL: Hanah, pensioner; John, s;
   Eccles, s, 103.97

BATTERS: Mary, 104.111

BATTERSBY:
Dianna; Elizabeth, d, 101.6
John, son of a gent, 102.221

Robert; Susannah, w; Winstanley, s;
   Susannah, d, 98.69
William; Sarah, w; Katherine, d, 98.26

BATTERTON:
Elizabeth, 107B.48
John; Anne, w, 107B.48
Tho; Mary, w, 104.125

BATTIMOORE: Eliza, 104.53

BATTIN:
Eliza, 104.95
John; Mary, w; John, s; Tho, s; Eliz, d, 104.53
Mary, ser, 100.1
Tho, 104.95

BATTISON:
George, app, 107B.36
Thomazin; Eliza, d, 104.57

BATTS:
~, wid, 105.7
Sarah, 102.35

BATTY:
Elizabeth, 109.103
Izabell, wid; Margaret, d, 103.25
James; Ann, w, 109.23
John, 109.103
John; Anne, w, 109.103
Stephen; Susan, w; Frances, d; Susan, d;
   William, s, 102.251
Thomas; Mary, w, 109.110
William; Martha, w, 98.68

BAULL: Nathaniell; Margaret, w, 102.214

BAUTIN?: William, 102.109

BAUTON: Hugh, 101.51

BAVE: Grace, 110.6

BAVEGE: Courtney; Mary, w; James, s;
   William, s; John, s; Hannah, d, 109.32

BAVENTON: Margaret, ser; Mary, d, 102.108

BAVIN:
Elizabeth, wid, 103.9
Sarah, 103.276

BAWTREY: Tho, ser, 104.109

BAXINDINE: William, app;

BAXTER:
~, wid, 103.188

18

Alice, 101.3
Ann, 109.95
Christopher, 102.243
Elizabeth, 109.30
Francis, bach, ser?, 104.6
Joseph, bach, under age, 103.64
Oliver; Elizabeth, w, 102.198
Richard; Eleanor, w, 102.122
Samull; Jane, w; Margaret, d; Grace, d,
   106.54
Thomas, junior; Alice, w, 103.64
Thomas, senior; Mary, w, 103.64
William, 109.36
William; Mary, w, 99.30

BAYFEILD: Katherina, ser, 102.117

BAYFORD: Elizabeth, ser;

BAYLEY:
~, 102.102
Ambross; Ann, w, 103.257
Charles, s, 109.95
Edward, 102.87
Edward; Mary, w, 103.126
Elias; Elizabeth, w; Thomas, s, 102.52
Elizabeth; William, s, 109.23
Elizabeth James, d of Fearn, 107D.4
Elizabeth, ser, 104.25, 109.27
Francis, 98.63
George; Elizabeth, w, 107C.25
George, wid no children, 103.1
Henry; Elizabeth, w; James, s; Thomas, s;
   Henry, s, 103.141
James, 107D.25
James; Ellinor, w, 109.17
Jenmiah; Mary, w, 103.132
Joane, ser, 103.292
John; Jane, w; John, s; Joseph, s; Mary, d;
   Rose, d, 104.38
John; Martha, w; John, s, 104.122
John; Jane, w; John, s, 107C.5
John; Jane, w, 109.103
John, app, 102.184, 104.58
John, junior; Anne, w; John, s; Mary, d,
   103.130
John, senior, 103.130
Joseph; Elizabeth, w, 101.98
Joshna; Margaret, w, 107C.16
Lydiah, 102.181
Margaret; Mary, d, 103.244
Mary, 103.257
Mary; ~, d, 103.247
Mary; Martha, d, 109.99
Mattha, 102.193
Rebecca; Rebecca, d; Ann, d, 108.1
Richard; Jane, w, 107A.42
Richard; Susan, w; Susan, d; Christian, d;
   John, s; Richard, s; Thomas, s, 109.105

Richard, app, 107C.23
Robert, 102.24
Robert; Easter, w, 98.25
Samuell, 101.85
Samuell; Anne, w; John, s; Anne, d, 101.100
Samuell; Mary, w; Samuell, s; Elizabeth, d,
   109.16
Sarah, 99.37
Sarah, ser, 100.3, 107A.25
Tho; Marg, w; Eliz, d; Susanna, d, 104.58
William; Mary, w; Katherine, d, 104.60
William; Margery, w; John, s, 109.2
William, app, 98.52

BAYNE: Joseph, ser, 108.4

BAYNEHAM:
Elizabeth, 101.103
Phillip; Mary, w, 101.73

BAYNUM: Pleasant, 103.216

BAYS:
John, £600 or £50 p.a.; Barinton, w, 102.87
Richard; Ann, w, 103.38

BEACH:
Ann, 104.76
Thomas; Margaret, w; Margaret, d, 102.8
William; Elizabeth, w; William, s; John, s;
   Elizabeth, d, 103.274

BEACHUM:
Alice, wid, 103.103
John; Alice, w; Diana, d, 103.184
John; Sarah, w, 109.15
Mathew; Mary, w; Benjamin, s; Susannah, d;
   Henry, s, 103.114
Valentine; Francis, w; William, s; John, s;
   Anne, d, 102.27
William; Jane, w, 102.251

BEACIS:
Elizabeth, wid; Samuell, s; John, s; Joseph, s,
   103.15
Joseph; Elizabeth, w; Joseph, s, 103.71

BEADELL: William, ser, 109.77

BEADLEY: Sarah, 102.62

BEAFOOT: Elizabeth, 99.10

BEAFORD: Jas; Anne, w, 104.66

BEAKKE:
Edmund, 109.26
Elizabeth, 103.209, 109.26
Elizabeth, wid, 103.169

19

Marmaduke; Margaret, w, 98.70
Mary, 102.155

BEALE:
Abraham; Mary, w; Mary, d, 109.46
Agnes, 102.12
Anne, 99.45
Charles, bach, 106.46
Dianah, 109.58
Edward; Ann, w; Easter, d, 109.17
Elizabeth Amy, kinswoman of Abernitha,
  98.33
Francis; Elizabeth, w, 99.46
Henry; Mary, w; William, s; Elizabeth, d,
  109.48
Henry, app, 98.70
John, 109.68
John; Dorothy, w, 103.237
John; Mary, w; Stephen, s; Mary, d, 107B.47
John; Jane, w; Joseph, s; Jemes, s; Jane, d,
  109.88
John; Elizabeth, w; Elizabeth, d, 109.108
Mary, 103.74
Richard; Mary, w, 98.23
Robert; Elizabeth, w, 102.158
Sarah, 104.135
Thomas, 104.128
Thomas, gent; Elizabeth, w; Thomas, s,
  106.19
Thomas, ser, 106.35
Tobias; Judith, sister of, 98.87
Walter, app, 98.74
William; Sarah, w, 110.8
Zachias; Elizabeth, w; Anne, d; Hannah, d,
  110.2

BEAMAN:
Elizabeth, 109.45
Jonathon, app, 103.83

BEAMETH: Garrot, 102.245

BEAMONT:
Carleton; Sara, w; Carleton, s; Anthony, d;
  Lidia, d; Elizabeth, d, 101.49
Edward; Mary, w, 103.181
Jane, 101.3
John; Dorothy, w; Jane, d, 102.17
Nicholas; Lidia, w; Thomas, s, 103.269
Richard, widower, 98.61
Thomas; Elizabeth, w, 104.100
William, 102.56

BEANE:
Elisha; Sarah, w; Johannah, d, 98.2
James, bach, 104.102
John; Joanna, w; Martha, d; Lodwick, s;
  John, s, 104.116
Robert; Elizabeth, w, 107A.5

BEAR:
Mary, 109.105
Michael; Elizabeth, w, 106.3
Thomas; Elizabeth, w; Dorothy, d, 101.61
William; Mary, w; Mary, d, 98.78

BEARD:
Andrew; Elizabeth, w; Joseph Amsdell, s;
  Sarah Amsbell, d; Andrew Beard, s,
  102.168
Anne, wid, 102.232
Jas; Marg, w; John, s, 104.28
Katherine, 102.75
Nathaniell, 99.8
Nicholas, 103.53
Ralph, his wife lives elsewhere, 110.35
Sarah; Sam, s; John, s; Sarah, d; Elizabeth, d,
  104.84
Thomas, 106.38
Thomas, ser, 100.8

BEARDIN: James; Frances, w; James, s,
  107D.42

BEARDSMOSE: John; Susan, w,
  107D.4

BEARLEY: Lewis, dead, 102.275

BEARSLEY:
Mary, 109.10
Sarah; Job, s, 109.10

BEASLEY:
Anne, 109.84
Anne, ser, 109.77
Charity; Charity, d, 104.67
Charles; Alice, w; William, s; John, s;
  Rebecca, d, 109.86
Elizabeth, pensioner, 103.77
Elizabeth, ser, 103.223
Jane, 109.84
John; Sarah, w, 102.65
John; Mary, w; John, s, 107C.9
Nath, 104.67
Richard; Mary, w, 109.84
Thomas; Elizabeth, w; Mary, d, 104.67
William; Elizabeth, w, 98.52

BEASON:
Anne; Anne, d, 107D.32
Rebert; Alice, w; Edward, s; Elizabeth, d;
  Hannah, d; Robert, s, 109.43

BEASSONT: Izabellah, 98.9

BEASTON: Henry; Mary, w, 103.88

BEATHELL: James, 102.122

20

21

BEDWORTH:
Anne; Mary, d, 107B.13
Mary;

BEE: ~, bach, 104.26
John; Sarah, w; Mary, d; John, s; Sarah, d,
107B.8

BEECH:
John; Elizabeth, w; John, s; Mary, d; Ralph,
s; Samuel, s; Elizabeth, d, 107A.6
Mary, ser, 107D.87
Richard, app, 102.8
William; Mary, w; Mary, d, 107D.46

BEECHER:
Anne, 101.11
John, 110.23
Betty; Elizabeth; Elizabeth, ser, 107B.20

BEECHUM, See Beachum

BEEDLE:
James, 110.14
Marcy, 110.14

BEEK(E), See Beak(E)

BEELE, See Beale

BEERES: Robert, 109.75

BEES: John; Elizabeth, w; Mary, d;
Elizabeth, d, 109.65

BEESBY: Nathaniel, 101.14

BEESON: Dorcas; Abigale, d; Robert, s;
Mary, d, 109.8

BEETH: William; Joyce, w; Joseph, s, 103.63

BEETLE: Thomas, 109.62

BEGA: Jane, 102.255

BEGG: Joseph; Anne, w; Joseph, s,
107D.88

BELCHAMBER:
Anne, 109.92
John; Sarah, w, 107D.29

BELCHER:
George, bach, 104.69
George, bach gent, 104.69
Jas, app, 104.2
John, 103.31
Marg, 104.40

Robert, 109.31
Sam, app, 104.111
Thomas; Mary, w, 107A.20
William; Mary, w; Richard Tubb, s; Mary
Tubb, d; Anne Tubb, d; Jane Belcher, d,
107B.4

BELEY: John; Elizabeth, w; John, s, 100.11

BELGRAVE: Anne, 107D.2

BELIS: Elizabeth, ser, 103.233

BELL:
Alexander; Mary, w; John, s; Sarah, d,
107A.16
Anne, 103.237
Anne, ser, 109.37
Benj; Marg, w, 104.20
David; Anne, w, 107D.74
Dorothy, ser, 109.6
Edward; Rebecca, w, 105.7
Edward; Elizabeth, w, 107B.48
Elizabeth, her husband at sea; Richard, s,
103.272
Elizabeth, ser, 98.62
Henry; Mary, w; Mary, d; Thomas, s; Anne,
d, 107B.19
Humphry; Isabell, w; Joseph, s; Humphrey, s;
Anne, d, 107B.6
Issabella, wid, 102.29
Jacob; Mary, w; Rebecca, d; John, s; Joseph,
s; Sarah, d, 102.34
Jane; Mary, d; Susan, d, 107D.40
John; Jeane, w, 103.56
John; Mary, w; Joseph, s, 107D.24
John; Katherine, w, 109.20
John, app, 98.57
Joseph, 110.19
Mary, ser, 103.11,107D.75
Pheneas, ser, 103.277
Richard; Sara, w, 101.50
Richard; Mary, w; Richard, s, 104.32
Richard; Anne, w; Richard, s; Anne, d,
107B.44
Richard, app, 104.2
Samuell, ser, 106.7,107C.30
Tomasine, 103.237
William; Joane, w, 102.23
William, app, 104.13

BELLAMY:
Elizabeth, wid, 103.91
Hannah, ser, 98.63

BENNETT:
John; Mary, w, 103.158
John; Barbara, w, 106.60
John; Anne, w, 107D.47

John; Jane, w; Thomas, s; Henry, s; Job, s,
109.34
John; Jane, w, 109.74
John; Jane, w, 109.98
John, bach, 98.24
Joseph; Anne, w, 98.63
Joseph; Elizabeth, w; Thomas, s; Elizabeth, d;
Sarah, d; Joseph, s; Mary, d, 107D.33
Joseph, ser, 104.90
Joshua; Anne, w, 102.145
Mary; Mary, d, 102.206
Mary parish child, 103.207
Matt; Kath, w; Kath, d; Matt, s; Wm, s; John,
s, 104.11
Moses; Mary, w; Moses, s; Mary, d,
104.47
Nicholas, 109.46
Paul, app, 107D.18
Pradence, ser, 103.116
Richard, 110.36
Robert; Elizabeth, w; William, s; Martha, d,
103.62
Samuel; Mary, w; Samuel, s, 109.11
Sarah, 109.77
Thomas, 106.55
Thomas; Mary, w; Mary, d, 98.71
Thomas; Elizabeth, w; John, s; Rebecca, d;
Hester, d, 104.105
Thomas; Mary, w, 107D.34
Thomas; Mary, w; Thomas, s; Mary, d,
109.23
Thomas, ser, 102.146
William, 102.146, 106.20
William; Elizabeth, w; Elizabeth, d; Susanah,
d; Benjamin, s, 103.34
William; Katherine, w, 106.35

BENNING:
Elizabeth; Timothy, s, bach, 101.66
George, 107B.19
John, app, 107A.37
Thomas; Mary, w; Thomas, s; Elizabeth, d,
107A.38
Thomas; William, s, 107B.19

BENNISON: Francis, 99.20

BENNS: Mary, 109.63

BENNUM: Richard; Catherine, w; Joseph, s;
Richard, s, 103.221

BENNY:
Elizabeth, 102.219
Tho, 104.132

BENSHAW: Elizabeth, 110.18

BENSOE: Anne, ser, 109.101

BENSOME: James; Katherine, w, 101.47

BENSON:
Agnes, 107C.39
Anne, 110.18
Dorothy, 106.18
Edward, 102.214
Ellinor; Francis, ?s; Ellinor, d, 104.111
Hannah, 109.33
Henry; Hannah, w; Tho, s; Eliz, d; Sarah, d,
104.60
Jeffry; Jane, w, 107A.37
John, 107A.33
John, app, 109.27
John, ser, 98.42
Mary, 103.65
Roger; Jane, w, 109.33
Sarah, 107B.71
William; Ellinor, w, 103.41
William; Mary, w; William, s, 109.77
William, wid, 98.33

BENSTEAD:
Ann, pensioner, 103.41
Ann, ser, 103.33

BENT: Hannah, 110.6

BENTHAM:
Joseph; Margeret, w, 103.284
Margery;

BENTLY:
~, 103.163
Benjamin, app, 107A.39
Daniell; Sarah, w, 103.198
Elizabeth, ser, 103.8
Grace, 106.14
Jane, ser, 106.43
Jeremiah; Tabitha, w, 101.43
John, ser, 106.40
Jonathon, 109.30
Martha, ser, 103.286
Mary, 107A.37
Nathaniel; Elizabeth, w; Jeane, d; Jonathan, s;
Dorcass, d; Abigall, d, 103.52
Obadiah; Elizabeth, w, 109.72
Sarah, 110.2
Susana, 106.62
Thomas; Katherine, w; Thomas Keene, s;
John Bently, s, 107A.33
William; Ann, w; Elizabeth, d, 103.15

BENTON:
Penellopa, ser, 98.38
Richard, 99.12
William; Margaret, w, 101.53
William; Mary, w; John, s, 110.5
William; Anna, w; Ruth, d, 104.88

BETON: John, bach, under age, ser, 103.288

BETRIS: Sarah, pensioner, 106.8

BETT: John; Elizabeth, w; John, s, 110.28

BETTERLY: Thomas; Mary, w; John, s;
James, s; Thomas, s; Mary, d; William, s;
Anne, d;

BETTS:
~, 102.99
John, ser, 109.78
Mathew; Elizabeth, w; Richsrd, s, 103.55
Roger; Ann, w, 103.39
Thomas, ser, 106.67

BETTY:
Jenae, ser, 103.37
John, ser, 106.37

BEVERFORD: Susana; John, s; Mary, d,
102.214

BEVERLY:
Charles; Joane, w; ~, child not baptized,
103.65
Elizabeth; Thothy, s, 102.172
Mary, 109.46
Rachell, 104.12
Sarah, 104.12
Thomas, gent; Jane, w; Jane, niece of,
98.40

BEVICE:
Charles, 102.212
Thomas, app, 104.145

BEVIN:
Elizabeth, 101.41
Elizabeth; Elizabeth, d, 101.41
John, 101.7

BEVON:
Edward, ser, 106.37
James, ser, 106.36

BEVRO: Mary, 110.12

BEW: Elizabeth, 102.170

BEWLAND: Susan, 104.69

BEWLEY:
John, 101.44
William; Jane, w; Francis, s; Thomas, s,
103.9

BIADWELL: Joane, ser;

BIBB: ~, wid, 104.75
Thomas; Abigall, w; Thomas, s; Francis, s,
104.75

BIBBY:
Chas; Ellinor, w, 104.126
Henry, pensioner; Mary, d, 103.76
Thomas Jonah, nephew of king, 107C.12
William, ser, 107C.8

BICKESTAFF: Thomas; Ellizabeth, w, 99.37

BICKLEY:
John, 102.152
Robert, 106.36

BICKUM: James; Katherine, w; Benjamin, s;
James, s, 103.137

Bicraft: Christopher; Alice, w, pensioner;
Martha, d, 103.280

BIDDLE:
Elizabeth, ser, 107A.8
James; Mary, w; James, s; Isaac, s; Mary, d,
104C.24
Joseph; Anne, w; ~, Sarah Briteridge, niece
of, 107D.1
Robert; Elizabeth, w, 107A.34
Thomas; Mary, w; John, s; Elizabeth, d,
107B.29

BIFFIN: John, app, 101.30

BIGBANE: Thomas, 107D.85

BIGBY: John; Anne, w, 104.76

BIGDELL: William; Anne, w, 107D.4

BIGELTON: John; Rebecca, w; John, s,
102.119

BIGG:
Martha; Hennry, s, 98.19
Ralph; Elizabeth, w; William, s; Ralph, s;
Elizabeth, d; Joyce, d, 101.106
Ralph, wid; Hennry, s, 103.27
Rebecca, ser, 103.27
William; Elizabeth, w; William, s,
102.164

BIGGER: Robert, 99.40

BIGGERSTAFFE: Ruth; Elizabeth, ser of,
107D.2

BIGGINS: William; Dorothy, w,
106.55

BIGGLESTON: Tho; Eliza, w; Jonathan, s, 104.59

BIGGS:
Ann, wid; Mary, d, 102.41
Edmond, s, 102.41
Edmond, 102.97
Edmund; Anne, w; Edmund, s; Jane, d; Thomas, s; Charles, s, 107B.4
Elizabeth, ser, 107D.40
Jane, 102.27, 102.55
John, 103.19
John; Elizabeth, w, 107A.22
John, app, 109.100
Mary, 102.194
Paul, app, 104.68
Richard, ser, 103.7
Thomas, 102.97
William, 102.184
William, ser, 107A.22

BIGLAND:
Ann, 99.43
George; Anne, w; Henry, s; Dorothy, d, 101.57

BIGNELL:
Abraham; Elizabeth, w; George, s; Sarah, d; Elizabeth, d; Priscilla, d, 107A.24
George; Patience, w; Patience, d, 107B.52
Grace; Thomas, s, 103.19
Richard, app, 109.22
Thomas, app, 102.116
William; Judith, w; James, s; Mary, d, 98.47

BIGSBY: Nicholas, ser, 106.30

BIGTINE: Charles, app, 103.248

BIKER: Pleasant, 102.20

BILBEY:
Francis; Anne, w; William, s; Susannah, d; Rebeccah, d; Anne, d, 98.10
John; Mary, d, 101.91
John; Dorcas, w; Isaac, s; John, s; Daniell, s; Josias, s, 102.256

BILLIN: Christopher; Anne, w; Christopher, s, 101.51

BILLING:
Richard, app, 109.24, 109.42
William; Rebeccah, w, 103.62

BILLINGER: Judith, 107B.39

BILLINGLEY: John, 106.64

BILLINGS: Sarah, wid, 103.57

BILLINGSLEY:
Francis, app, 104.99
Robert; Sarah, w; John, s; Robert, s; Richard, s, 109.69

BILLIOW: Mary, 102.152

BILLS: John; Katherine, w; Katherine, d; Sarah, d, 103.56

BINDDETT: William; Jane, w, 110.27

BINDON:
John; Margaret, w; Nathaniel, s; Mary, d; Elizabeth, d; Margaret, d; Sarah, d, 109.81
John, assessor in Old Baily precinct, 109.112
Samuell, 109.81
Thomas, ser, 106.33

BINDOR: Jane, 110.2

BINGHAM:
Anne, 102.104
Edward; Mary, w; Katherine, d, 102.31
James; Mary, w, 102.104
John; Mary, w; John, s; Sarah, d, 103.105
Rachell, 104.66

BINGLEY:
John; Mary, w; Anne, d, 101.27
John; Mary, w; John, s, 107D.92
John; Sarah, w, 109.82
Joseph; Anne, w; William, s; Jane, d, 109.83
Walter; Jane, w; Sara Clarke, d; Edward Clarke, s, 101.93
Zephaniah; Mary, w, 110.15

BINGLOSS:
Mary, 110.21
William, 110.21

BINLEY: Mathew, ser, 102.144

BINNS: Mary, ser, 98.30

BINSLY: Elizabeth, ser, 98.36

BIR ?:
Nathaniel, child, 102.46
William, 102.29

BIRCH:
Ann, 109.35
John; Anne, w, 104.11
Katherine, 106.48
Mary, ser, 98.69
William, ser, 109.7

BIRCHALL: Samuell, app, 101.59

BIRCHMORE:
Edward; Anne, w; Edward, s, 104.45
John, bach, 109.65
William, bach, 109.65

BIRCOURT: Thomas; Rebecca, w; Sarah, d, 107C.31

BIRD:
Thomas; Mary, w; Mary, d, 107B.67
Thomas; Dorothy, w; Mary, d; Ann, d, 109.26
William, app, 98.59
~, 104.146
Anthony; Elinor, w; Elinor, d; William, s, 99.30
Daniel, app, 107D.3
Edward; Anne, w; Edward, s; John, s; Anne, d; Charles, s, 101.45
Edward, in Aldersgate St. painter, collector, 101.110
Elinor, ser, 103.214
Elizabeth, ser, 101.105
Frances, wid, 103.88
George; Elizabeth, w; Mary, d, 104.148
George; Elizabeth, w; Mary, d, 107C.36
George, app, 107D.21
James, ser, 107C.32
Jeane, ser, 103.17
Jelimiah, bach, 103.31
John; Elizabeth, w, 98.41
John; Ellinor, w; John, s; Ellinor, d; Elizabeth, d, 109.22
John; Mary, w, 109.102
Jonathon, ser, 103.29
Luke, bach, 109.83
Mary, 101.6
Mary, ser, 104.34
Mathew, 109.5
Rebecca, 101.103, 110.9
Rebecca, wid, 102.19
Robert; Dorothy, w, 107C.20
Robert, gent; Elizabeth, w; Elizabeth, d; Sarah, d; William, s; Robert, s; Mary, d, 98.47
Robert, wid; Elizabeth, d; Jane, d; John, s, 98.48
Thomas; Hanna, w; Charles, s, 101.64
Thomas; Sarah, w; George Heel, s, 103.194

BIRDER: Thomas, 109.70

BIRDICUE: Thomas; Mary, w; Thomas, s?; Mary, d?; Elizabeth, d?; Rookes, s?; Anne, d?;

BIRDING:
~, wid, 104.28

BIRDLING: Jane, 109.91

BIRDWHISTLE:
John, app, 101.17
Thomas; Anne, w; Thomas, s; Anne, d, 109.91
William, married since 12th May; Katherine, w, 103.36

BIRGES: Francis, ser, 109.80

BIRKETT:
Edmund; Sarah, w; Edward, s; Margaret, d, 109.44
Geo; Judith, w; William, s; Thomas, s; Chas, s, 104.22
John; Lidia, w; John, s; Thomas, s; William, s, 101.82
Mary, 99.52

BIRKHEAD:
John; Mary, w, 109.94
William; Elizabeth, w; William, s; Elizabeth, d, 109.107

BIRLY: John; Susan, w; Mary, d, 107C.24

BIRREN: Howell; Joannah, w, 102.167

BIRTCH:
Mary, 101.17
George; Isabell, w; George, s; Sara, d, 101.9

BIRTE:
Andrew; Elizabeth, w; Elizabeth, d, 101.17
Nich; Eliza, w; Nich, s; Eliza, d, 104.17

BIRTHES: Thomas; Mary, w; Susan, d, 104.133

BISAKER: Mary, 109.21

BISHANER: Mary, ser, 100.13

BISHOP:
~; Sarah, d; ~, sister, 103.283
Alice, spinster, 103.54
Anne, 98.12
Charles; Elizabeth, w; Francis, s; Sarah, d; Anne, d, 103.136
Daniel; Anne, w, 104.74
Elizabeth, 102.15
Hanah, ser, 106.68
Isabella, 104.39
Jane, ser, 100.5
John, £600; Mary, w; Joseph, s; Elizabath, d, 104.7
John, bach, 103.14
John, wid; John, s, 103.59

Mary, 107D.33
Mary, ser, 102.99,103.271
Richard; Anne, w, 101.51
Robert, 109.48
Robert, hath children elsewhere, 103.123
Sarah, wid, 103.9
Stephen; Anne, w; Mary, d; Stephen, s,
    107B.50
Susan, 102.14
Susannah, ser, 109.57
Thomas; Elizabeth, w, 104.85
Thomas Samuell, child of smith; Martha,
    sister of, 101.77
Walter; Katherine, w, 109.10
William; Sarah, w; William, s, 102.194

BISSE:
John; Elizabeth, w; John, s, 107B.26
Mary, 101.65
Susannah, ser, 98.33
    -
BISSELL:
Andria, 101.6
James; Sarah, w; ~, child, 100.3
John, bach, 99.29
Jonathon; Sarah, w, 103.143
Mary, ser, 101.110
Sarah, 99.29

BISSETT:
John, ser, 109.80
Martha, 102.170

BISSEY: Thomas; Susan, w, 103.24

BISWICK: Kath, ser, 104.27

BITH: Phillis, ser, 100.10

BITOOL: Catherine, 103.234

BITTANY: Thomas; Elinor, w, 98.5

BITTLE: Susan, ser, 109.98

BIVEN:
Job; Elizabeth, w, 110.32
Mary, 110.32

BIX: Thomas, 103.26

BLACK:
Ann, ser, 104.133
Elias, bach, 102.62
Francis Simond, 102.47
Gilbert; Mary, w; Glibert, s, 107B.6
John, 102.218
Mary, ser, 102.153
Mary, wid; Susan, d; Jane, d, 102.224

Richard, ser, 98.45
Shadrick; Mary, w; Shadrick, s; Mary, d,
    102.138

BLACKABY: William; Elizabeth, w, 107B.61

BLACKALL: Richard, ser, 107A.5

BLACKAMOORE: Susan, ser, 103.39

BLACKBRUFFE: Henry; Mary, w, 104.123

BLACKBURN:
Anne, ser, 104.11
Rich; Alice, w, 104.80
Susan, ser, 108.3

BLACKBURY:
Bridget, 102.164
John; Martha, w; James, s; Mary, d, 101.110
Katharine, 102.164

BLACKETT:
Robert, 109.29
Robert, assessor for Holborne crosse, 109.112
Susan, 107B.23

BLACKFORD: Anthony, ser, 103.249

BLACKLEY: Sarah, 106.62

BLACKMAN: Joseph, ser;

BLACKMORE:
~, a woman her husband at sea; Sarah, d,
    103.136
Daniell; Margaret, w, 101.94
Fracis; Anne, w; Francis, s; Anne, d,
    107D.65
Humphry, ser, bach, 103.287
Richard, 109.29
William, 107D.65

BLACKNELL: Thomas, parish child;

BLACKSTONE:
~, wid, 104.44

BLACKWAY:
Francis, ser, 106.2
Mary, 103.269

BLACKWELL:
Mary, ser, 105.3
~, wid, 109.73
Benjamin; Elizabeth, w, 108.6
Charles; Martha, w, 98.35
James, ser, 98.72
Mary, 104.69

28

Nicholas; Magdalen, d; Elizabeth, d; Sarah, d, 107D.41
Philip, 109.41
Sarah, 109.27
Thomas, 108.6

BLADDER: William, ser, 108.1

BLADRICK: Mary, 102.86

BLAGRAVE:
Philip; Jane, w, 109.36
Richard; Hanah, w; Robert, s; Hanah, d; Elizabeth, d; Jane, d, 99.53

BLAGRAVES: Elizabeth, ser, 106.27

BLAGROVE: Alice, 98.60

BLAGUE: Daniell; Ann, w; Mary, d, 100.6

BLAISBY: William; Thomazine, w; William, s; John, s, 109.10

BLAKE:
Alice, ser, 100.6
Ann, wid, 103.33
Edmond; Sarah, w, 102.215
Elizabeth, ser, 103.12
Francis; Ann, w, 109.23
George, 101.2
George; Mary, w; Mary, d, 109.91
James; Jane, w, 109.107
Jane, ser, 101.85
John; Elizabeth, w; John, s, 102.27
John; Mary; Elizabeth, d; William, s, 103.43
John; Ann, w; Elizabeth, d; John, s; William, s; Johana, d; Mary, d, 103.54
John; Stedfast, w; John, s; Alexander, s; Edward, s; Thomas, s, 101.45
John, ser, 103.292
Mary, 102.246
Mary, ser, 101.74
Richard, widower no children, 103.114
William, 99.45, 102.45
William; Hanah, w, 109.92

BLAKEMAN: Sarah, wid; Sarah Bavin, d, 103.276

BLAKESBY:
George, 109.42
Joseph, 109.42

BLAKETT: Elizabeth; Elizabeth, d; John, s, 103.267

BLANCHARD: Ann, 106.26

BLANCHER: Samuell; Anne, w, 107A.21

BLANCHETT: Jane, 102.178

BLAND:
Daniell, gent; Sarah, w, 98.40
Francis; Elizabeth, w; Francis, s; Elizabeth, d; Nathaniel, s; Thomas, s; Anne, d, 107D.93
Francis, gent; Mary, w; Mary, d; Frances, d, 98.71
Henry, 109.28
John, wid; William, s; Mary, d, 100.6
Mary, 109.2, 109.28
Thomas; Katherine, d; Thomas, s, 104.143
Thomas; Mary, w, 109.56
Tobias; Mary, w, 107A.27

BLANDUE: Frances, 110.27

BLANEY: Dorothy, 110.35

BLANK:
Hanah, 102.248
John; Mary, w; Mary, d; Margaret, d, 101.99
William; Sarah, w; Sarah, d; Mary, d; Thomas, s; Anne, d, 107D.45

BLANKINSOPP: Thomas, app, 107D.24

BLANKLEY: John; Alice, w; Samuell, s; John, s, 102.173

BLANSHITT: Mary; Margarett, d, 109.37

BLASHFEILD: Thomas; Elizabeth, d; Thomas, s?, 99.46

BLATCH: John, app, 104.20

BLAUGHTER: Elizabeth, ser, 98.74

BLAWETT:
Jas, app, 104.70
Margaret, 109.59
Mary; Mary, d, 107C.15

BLAXTON: George; Hannah, w, 102.144

BLEAKE: Mary, 109.38

BLECOMB: Anne, ser, 98.67

BLEE: Frances, 98.14

BLEES: William; Ann, w; Mary, d, 103.183

BLENCOW:
John; Sarah, w, 109.71

John; Elizabeth, w; Sarah, d, 109.71
Temperance, 109.71

BLESSE: Jane, ser;

BLESSING:
~, wid, 105.8

BLETHINGTON: Theophilus, gent;
 Elizabeth, w, 98.3

BLETSOE:
Elizabeth, 101.104, 107D.75
William; Dorothy, d; Sarah, d, 109.47

BLEWCOATE: Elizabeth, a parish child,
 109.63

BLEWETT:
Richard; Wilmot, w; Elizabeth, d,
 107A.8
Susan; John, s, 101.88

BLIGHT: Elizabeth, 102.46

BLINCE: James, 99.54

BLINCO:
Elizabeth, ser, 103.138
Richard, bach, 98.4
Samuell; Mary, w; Richard, s, 98.63
Sarah; John, s; Sarah, d, 104.25

BLINKHORNE:
John; Elizabeth, w; John, s; Robert, s; Anne,
 d, 98.74
William, app, 103.214

BLINKINSOP: Anthony, 102.109

BLISSE: Joseph; Elizabeth, w, 107D.6

BLISSETT:
Richard; Anne, w; John, s; Richard, s, 98.37
Tho; Mary, w; Benj, s, 104.76

BLIZARD:
Richard; Dorcas, w; Anne, d; Elizabeth, d,
 102.11
Thomas; Mary, w, 107D.26
William; Susanna, w, 101.23

BLOARE: Martha, ser, 104.112

BLOME: Isaack; Martha, w; Isaack, s,
 102.22

BLOMER: Richard; Sara, w; Richard, s;
 Chareles, s, 101.59

BLOMFEILD:
Hanah, 102.253
Henry, gent; Katherine, w; Anne, d, 98.41

BLOOME:
Ann, 109.107
James, 107B.15

BLOOR: Elizabeth, 106.8

BLOOS: Edmund, app, 109.44

BONNICK: Daniell, ser, 108.3

BONNISH: Peter, ser, bach, 104.12

BONNO:
Edward; Alice, w; Mary, d, 103.86
Robert, ser, 109.6

BONNS: Edward; Elizabeth, w; Edward, s,
 107D.54

BONNY: Elizabeth, 101.11

BONNYFACE: Rich, app, 104.82

BONSOR: Amy, ser, 106.1

BONSY: Ann, 99.51

BONUS: John; Sara, w, 101.58

BONVILL: John; Sarah, w; John, s, 102.30

BOODEN:
Jane, ser, 106.5
Walter; Elizabeth, w; Elizabeth, d; Jane, d;
 Susan, d; Thomas, s; oliver, s, 106.45
William, ser, 106.67

BOODY:
Joane, 105.11
John; Elizabeth, w, 105.11

BOOKER:
Ellen; Elizabeth, d, 102.66
Jas; Elizabeth, w; Elizabeth, d; Mary, d,
 104.40
John; Anne, w, 109.92
Mary, ser, 107D.13
Richard, ser, 107C.41

BOOMER: Mary, Mrs;

BOONE:
~, wid; ~, wid, 105.7
Edward; Mary, w, 109.84
Elizabeth, 98.54

Thomas; Hanah, w; Thomas, s, 107B.44
Thomas; Lucey, w; Mary, d; Sarah, d,
  107B.56
Thomas, app, 98.5
William, 110.19
William, bach, 106.65

BOSWICK: William, 106.63

BOTFORD: John, app, 103.70

BOTLEY: Ann, ser, 103.229

BOTT:
John; Millicent, w, 102.135
Joseph; Sarah, w; Sarah, d; Joseph, s, 103.74
Thomas; Judeth, w; Thomas, s; Ann, d;
  Elizabeth, d, 103.88
Water; Saint, w; Elizabeth, d; William, s,
  109.98

BOTTERELL: Thomas, Doctor of Physick; ~,
  w, 99.58

BOTTLER: Joyce, ser, 102.112

BOTTOM: Phillip, 99.57

BOTTOMLY: Elizabeth, 109.37

BOUCHER:
John; Mary, w, 105.2
Joseph; Mary, w; Joseph, s, 98.77
Martha, 98.77
William, 105.8

BOUGH:
Elizabeth, 106.57
Hannah, 109.19

BOUGHREY: Martha; Martha, d, 98.60

BOULTER, See Bolter

BOULTON, See Bolton

BOUNDS:
Joseph; Catherine, w, 109.90
Mary, 109.15
Sarah, 109.15

BOURNE:
Andrew; Elliz, w; Andr, s; Eliz, d, 104.13
Chris, ser, 104.3
Edward; Barsheba, w; Edward, s; Penelope, d,
  107D.70
Elizabeth, 107D.99
John; Mary, w, 98.80
John; Margarett, w; Mary, d, 102.44

Joshua; Jeane, w, 103.71
Margaret, ser, 107B.65
Mary, 98.34
Samuel; Elizabeth, w; Susannah, d, 107D.4
Thomas; Sarah, w, 107B.12
William, app, 107D.51

BOVEE: Eliza, 104.77

BOW: Jeremiah; Anne, w; John, s; Jeremy, s;
  Elizabeth, d; Thomas, s, 109.95

BOWCHER:
Edward; Denceab, w; Mary, d, 102.56
Mary, wid, 103.44

BOWDEN:
Anne, 98.78
John; Ann, w, 104.139
Joseph, 104.139
Joseph, bach, ser, 104.86
Mary, ser, 104.125
William, 102.274

BOWDIER:
Judith, 98.44
William, gent, widower, 98.44

BOWDLEY: John; Mary, w, 103.277

BOWDRY:
James; Susan, w, 103.244
James, senior; Martha, w; John, s, 103.244
Peter, wid; Mary, d; Rachell, d, 103.155

BOWELL: William; Jane, w; John, s; Sarah,
  d, 99.6

BOWEN:
Alice, a child, 109.60
Ann, 99.13
Margaret, ser, 98.28
Mary, ser, 99.33
Stephen, ser, 106.39
Thomas, 109.77
William, 102.71
William; Elizabeth, w; Griffin, s; Curdelia, d,
  98.45
William; Mary, w, 110.27

BOWER:
Abell; Ann, w; Ann, d; Abell, s, 103.152
Anne; Jeeimiah, s, 107A.11
Joseph, app, 103.150
William; Sarah, w, 103.150
William, 98.44

BOWERS:
Anne, ser, 107C.3

32

Edward, 102.84
Grissell, 104.95
Jonas; Elizabeth, w; Anne, d, 109.64
Richard, app, 103.132
Sarah, ser, 107D.50
William, wid; Saxey, sister of; Elizabeth,
  sister of, 98.16
Elizabeth, 101.66
Thomas; Sarah, w; Samuell, s; John, s,
  103.277
Thomas, ser, 106.15

BOWET: Jone, 107D.72

BOWLDS: Sarah, 109.21

BOWLER:
Edward, app, 98.74
Hester, ser, 98.47
Mary, 101.24
Richard; Elizabeth, w; Richard, s; Thomas, s;
  Rachell, d; Marcey, d, 102.120
Richard, app, 102.122
Samuell, app, 98.86
Stephen, 101.24
William, 102.69

BOWLES:
Abraham; Mary, w, 109.105
Charles; Elizabeth, w, 103.203
Edmund; Rebecca, w; John, s; Mary, d,
  109.110
Eurin, ser, 102.150
Mary, ser, 103.287
Rebecca, 101.96
Richard; Joyce, w; Mary, d, 107A.20
Thomas, 101.31
Urias; Dorothy, w, 107C.23

BOWMAN:
Anne, ser, 107D.63
Chris; Eliza, w, 104.53
Francis, app, 98.5
Simeon de; Jane, w; Mary, d; Wisann, s or d?,
  109.99

BOWNE: Elizabeth, 99.45

BOWRELL: Edward, ser, 100.5

BOWREY: John, 106.41

BOWS: Paul, esq; Bridgett, w, 104.116

BOWTELL: Samuell; Katherine, w;
  Elizabeth, d; William, s, 106.13

BOWYER:
Anne, 107C.11

Dorothy, 98.19
George; Mary, w; Mary, d, 107D.34
John, 109.57
John; Elizabeth, w, 104.81
John; Elizabeth, w; Elizabeth, d,
  104.93

BOWYES: Anne;

BOX:
~, wid; John, s; Dennis, s, 103.105
David, app, 101.79
Elizabeth, ser, 103.72
Mary, ser, 103.14
Thomas; Sarah, w, 104.92

BOXHILL: Samuell; Alice, w, 101.55

BOXLEY:
Ann, 99.42
Katherine, ser, 101.16

BOYCE:
George; Elizabeth, w, 98.49
James; Elizabeth, w, 98.46
John; Rebeccah, w, 98.46
John; Elizabeth, w; Anne, w; William, s,
  109.75
John, bach, 110.8
John, gent, 101.43
Joseph, app, 103.241
Mary, wid, 103.65
Richard, 106.43
Robert; Martha, w; Richard, s; John, s,
  107D.59
Sarah, 103.45
Walter; Honnor, w, 103.34

BOYCOTT: Richard; Mary, w; Katherine, d,
  110.8

BOYD: William; Elizabeth, w; Sarah, d,
  102.213

BOYER: Nicholas, bach, 102.52

BOYES: Anne, ser, 104.28

BOYLE:
David; Anne, w; Samuell, s; Margarett, sister,
  102.164
John, ser, bach;

BOYNTON:
~, Mrs; Mary, d; Fran, d; Eliz, d,
  104.88

BOYTER: John; Elizabeth, w; Ralph, s;
  Mary, d, 102.171

BRABAN:
Dorothy, 103.21
John; Mary, d; William, s, 98.1

BRABANT:
Elizabeth, spinster, 103.56
Stephen, 104.35

BRABINS: Abraham, ser, 103.218

BRABONE: George; Sabina, w; Patronella,
d; Susan, d, 105.7

BRACE: John, ser, 104.1

BRACEY:
Daniell, bach, aged 30 yrs, 102.247
Mary, 102.250
Peter; Tamar, w, 104.84
Phillp; Mary, w; Phillip, s; Sarah, d; Mary, d,
103.193

BRACKENBURY: Edmond; Susanna, w;
Edmund, s, 101.37

BRACKLETT: George; Sage, w, 102.110

BRACKLEY:
Joseph; Sarah, w, 106.64
Sam, ser, bach, 104.4

BRACKWELL: Ann, 99.43

BRADBERRY: Thomas, 109.70

BRADBOURNE: Edward; Rebecca, w,
110.10

BRADDILL: Thomas, bach, 107D.23

BRADDOCK: Sarah, 109.17

BRADFORD:
Frances, wid, 103.65
James; Ann, w; Jeane, d; James, s; Mary, d,
103.20
John; Dorothy, w, 109.99
Mary, ser, 103.250
Richard; Mary, w, 102.93
Richard, bach, 103.50
Thomas; Elizabeth, w, 109.99
William; Anne, w; Rebecca, d, 109.80

BRADING: Robert; Elizabeth, w; Mary, d,
107A.15

BRADLEY:
Alexander; Mary, w; Mary, d, 102.62
Benjamine, 103.28

Ellizabeth; Nathaniell, s, 98.8
Francis, 102.69
George, app, 102.179
Hanah, wid, 103.131
James, ser, 102.15
John; Anne, w, 104.129
Joseph; Anne, w; Thomas, s; Joseph, s;
Benjamin, s, 107D.50
Margeret; Mary, d, 103.94
Nathaniell; Margaret, w; John, s, 103.35
Nathaniell; Arthur, s; Margery, d, 103.35
Oliver, app, 109.103
Ralph; Mary, w; Ann, d, 103.207
Richard; Dorothy, w, 104.116
Richard, app, 101.79
Sarah; Sarah, d; Mary, d; Nathaniell, s,
109.78
Sasan, ser, 104.25
William, 101.49
William; Martha, w, 109.103

BRADSHAW:
Anthony, ser, 106.38
Christopher, 109.41
Croomer; Elizabeth, w; Croomer, s; Rebecca,
d, 103.52
Elizabeth, 103.24
Elizabeth, ser, 104.34
Henry, ser, b, 104.6
Mary, 109.104
Mary; Richard, s; Albion, d; Sarah, d; Mary,
d; John, s, 109.35
Mary, pensioner; Martha, d; Sarah, d; Mary,
d, 103.211
Nicholas; Elisabeth, w; Dorothy, d, 110.6

BRADWELL: Richard; Ann, w; Ann, d;
Daniell, s; Richard, s, 103.102

BRAFEILD:
Robert; Mary, w, 102.13
Thomas; Mary, w; Thomas, s; Mary, d, 109.72

BRAGG: John; Alice, w, 102.220

BRAGRAVE: Sarah, 104.129

BRAINE, See Brayne

BRAISER: John, app, 98.72

BRAKINGTON: William, bach, 98.3

BRAMAN: Thomas, 109.70

BRAMBLE: Elizabeth, 99.36

BRAMER:
Katherine, ser, 109.1

Ralph, ser, 109.1
William, ser, 103.30

BRAMPTON:
Francis; Rebecca, w; Francis, s, 106.62
William, 107D.60
Wm, ser, 104.93

BRAN: Richard; Anne, d, 107D.68

BRANARD: Samuel; Frances, w, 109.88

BRANCH:
George, pensioner; Mary, w; Elizabeth, w, 103.221
Jeane, wid, 103.85
Jerimiah; Katherine, w, 103.49
John; Joane, w, 103.186

BRANCKLIN: Thomas, app;

BRAND:
~; ~, w; ~, child, 104.134
Deniell; Hanah, w; Martha, d, 102.179
Edward; Mary, w; John, s, 109.31
John; Frances, w, 101.88
William, ser, 109.9

BRANDFEILD: John; Jane, w; Jane, d; Anne, d; Thomas, s, 107D.11

BRANDLEY: Elizabeth, 99.29

BRANDON:
Christopher; Sarah, w, 107A.18
Deniell; ~, w, 102.34
Edward; Elizabeth, w; Edward, s, 109.85
Margaret, 109.93
Thomas; Francis, w; Thomas, s, 109.112
Thomas, ser, 106.29

BRANDRIFFE: John; Elizabeth, w; Mary, d, 98.38

BRANDROLLO: Henry, bach, 105.4

BRANDSLY: Edward; Sarah, w; Hanah, d; Phillip, s, 103.20

BRANFEIOD: Edward, 109.103

BRANGMAN: Alice, 104.130

BRANLIN: Jerimiah, ser, 107D.2

BRANSON:
John, 110.24
John; Anne, w; Francis, s; Elizabeth, d; Thomas, s; Ann, d, 109.16

BRANSTON: John; Elizabeth, w, 106.6

BRANT: Richard, 109.77

BRANTHWAITE: Edward, ser, 106.12

BRANWELL: John, ser, 98.48

BRANWOOD: Anne, 102.81

BRATHER: John, ser, 107D.34

BRATHWAITE:
John; Mary, w, 109.5
Thomas; Prudence, w; Prudence, d, 109.95

BRATLEY: Rachael; Eliz, coleby d, 104.66

BRATT: Margaret, 109.34

BRAUGHTON:
Christopher, ser, 106.27
James; Elizabeth, w, 107D.10
Ralph; Elizabeth, w, 107D.84
Sarah, 107A.3

BRAWNE: William; Elizabeth, w, 106.68

BRAXSTON: Sarah, ser, 104.73

BRAXTON: Charles, ser, 106.57

BRAY:
Ann, 109.5
Bartholomew; Mary, w, 103.183
Edward; Mary, w; John, s, 103.131
Elizabeth, nurse child, 107C.15
Henry; Jeane, w, 103.102
Henry; Frances, w; John, s, 103.162
Mary, 101.88
Sara, 101.12
William; Mary, w; Joseph, s; William, s, 103.139
William, app, 107C.8
William, ser, 107C.37

BRAYNE:
Ellis, 107D.71
Joan, 109.73
Joane, wid; Richard, s; William, s, 103.10
Thomas; Elizabeth, w; John, s; William, s, 103.241

BRAYSEY:
John, bach, 102.1
Nathaniell, ser, 102.1

BRAYTHWAITE, See Brathwaite

BRAZILL: Thomas; Dorothy, w, 109.69

BREACEY: George, bach, under age, 103.95

BREAM: Charles; Elizabeth, w; Anne, d, 105.7

BREAMES: James; Margaret, w, 102.225

BREDAH: Francis; Elizabeth, w; Elizabeth, d, 103.21

BREDCUTT: Elizabeth; Thomas, s; Elizabeth, d; Sarah, d, 103.74

BREE:
Anne, 102.11
Esiah; Sarah, w; Mary, d; Elizabeth, d, 102.244

BREECE: Underhill, widower; Richard, s; John, s; Elizabeth, d; Katherine, d; Susan, d, 103.161

BREEMOR: Mary, ser, 98.59

BRENT:
Edward, bach, esq, 106.21
Elizabeth, gentlewoman, 98.39
Francis; Mary, w, 101.51
Jacob, £600; Elizabeth, w; Elizabeth, d; Jacob, s; Richard, s, 102.16

BRENTON: Jeoffory, bach gent, 98.45

BRETON:
Henry, 109.91
Briget, 109.91

BRETT:
Charles; Grace, w, 110.30
George, clerk, 98.28
Susannah; Isaac, s, 107A.36

BREW: ~; Mary, w, 104.122

BREWEN:
Anne, 107D.77
Jonathan, gent; Katherine, w, 106.9
Thomas; Jane, w; Elizabeth, d; Jane, d; Sarah, d; Thomas, s, 109.93

BREWER:
Andr, gent, bach, 104.94
Angell; John, s, 102.233
Dianah, 102.19
Elizabeth; Elizabeth, d, 109.93
Lawrance; Hesster, w; Elizabeth, d, 103.153
Richard, app, 109.25
Samuell; Jeane, w, 103.263

BREWERTON:
Charles, bach, 104.99
John, ser, 109.7

BREWIN: Elizabeth, wid, 103.51

BREWSTER:
Daniel, bach, 105.1
John; Ann, w; Henry, s; Ann, d; Susan, d, 109.42
Samuell, bach, 98.59

BREWTNALL: William, gent; Elizabeth, w, 98.38

BREWTON: Sarah, 98.5

BRICE:
Joseph; Elizabeth, w, 102.112
Mary; Mary, d, 107B.16
Mary, ser, 98.3
Nathaniel; Mary, w, 107A.14
Thomas; Sara, w, 101.1
Thomas, app, 102.117

BRICKLAND: William; Frances, w, 106.60

BRICKNELL:
Elizabeth, 107A.9
James; Jone, w, 107B.35

BRICKWOOD: Margaret, ser, 101.21

BRIDE:
Anne, ser, 106.17
Elizabeth, 102.258

BRIDEN: Mary, ser, 98.73

BRIDGE:
John, 104.20
John, app, 107A.33
Mary, wid, pensioner, 103.16

BRIDGER:
Elizabeth, 110.33
Jane, app, 107B.1
Jonathon, gent; Grace, w; Margarett, d, 106.13

BRIDGES:
Benjamin, bach, 102.11
Clement, 105.5
Dorothy, 98.13
Doughton; Sarah, w; Joseph, s, 103.7
Elizabeth, 102.17
Elizabeth, wid; Elizabeth, d, 103.66
John; Anne, w; Anne, d; Margaret, d, 107A.30

John, 98.39
Katherine, ser, 98.14
Kemp, bach, ser, 104.4
Mary, ser, 106.9
Richard; Mary, w, 100.10
Thomas, app, 98.74

BRIDGMAN:
Thomas; Abigail, w, 109.96
William, widower, 98.58

BRIDGNORTH: Margaret, ser, 109.60

BRIDGWATER: Elizabeth, 107D.101

BRIDMORE: Sarah, 102.65

BRIENTON:
Edward, 109.89
John, 109.82

BRIERLY: Elinor, 109.38

BRIGDELL: Thomas; Ann, w; Elizabeth, d;
Thomas, s; Edward, s,
103.206

BRIGETT: Abigall, 109.71

BRIGG: John, bach, gent, 106.48

BRIGGINS: Pater; Maribella, w; Peter, s?,
99.44

BRIGGS:
Ambrose; Hannah, w; Ambrose, s, 109.31
Anne, 110.26
Christopher, 101.14
Dorothy, ser, 107D.31
Ebin, app, 107C.20
Elizabeth; Mary, w; Thomas, s; Tabitha, d,
109.53
George, 99.19
Jeremiah; Frances, w; Mary, d; Margaret, d,
109.33
John, ser, 109.31
Joseph, 99.41
Mathew; Anne, w; Jessaron, d; Sarah, d;
Elizabeth, d, 103.89
Mathew; Anne, d; Mary, d, 103.89
Michaell; Rachel, w, 103.126
Rebecca, 107D.98
Robert; Mary, w; Thomas, s; Robert, s,
109.24
Susanah, 99.19

BRIGGSTAFFE: Joseph, 107D.53

BRIGHAM: Polliman; Elizabeth, d; Anne, d;

BRIGHT:
~, wid, 105.8
Anne, 104.116
Elizabeth, pensioner, 103.163
Hiam, ser, 103.287
Lettice, 104.116
Martha, 98.75
Thomas; Anne, w; Andrew, s; Anne, d,
102.114

BRIGHTWELL:
John; Mary, w; Joseph, s; William, s, 103.140
William; Mary, w, 102.232

BRIGHURST: Wm; Eliz, sister, 104.3

BRIGMAN: Prisaillia, 103.216

BRIGNALL: Barberah, ser, 107D.21

BRIGSTOCK: Treduskine; Sarah, w, 98.11

BRIMSTEAD: John; Elizabeth, w, 101.6

BRIN: Richard; Elizabeth, w, 110.11

BRIND:
Alice, 101.81
John; Elenor, w; William, s; John, s; Ellen, d,
101.81
John; Mary, w, 104.54
Margaret, 101.81
Thomas, 101.76

BRINDLEY: James; Deborah, w, 106.2

BRINGERS: Mary, wid; Sarah, d, 103.105

BRINGHURST:
Elizabeth, 99.54
Thomas, bach, gent, 106.49

BRINGLY: Thomas, 107C.28

BRINKLEY:
Elizabeth, ser, 103.132
Susan, wid; Martha, d; Loue, d, 103.134

BRINLEY: Anne, ser, 106.69

BRINSMAID: Thomas, 99.19

BRIQUETT: John; Mary, w; John, s, 106.37

BRISCOE:
Anne, 104.45
Edw, bach, 104.65
Francis; Ann, w; Francis, 109.33
John, 110.33

Martha, wid, 103.121
William, ser, 103.114

BRODDELL:
Sarah, 109.105
Sarah, 109.105

BRODDOCK:
Benjamin; Mary, w; Mary, d; Benjamin, s, 107B.68
Benjamin; Mary, w; Mary, d; Benjamin, s, 107B.68

BRODERICK:
George, bach, 106.41
Thomas; Katherine, w, 103.52
George, bach, 106.41
Thomas; Katherine, w, 103.52

BRODGATE:
Anne, 106.47
Anne, 106.47

BROGILL:
Margaret, 102.30
Margaret, 102.30

BROGRAVE:
Francis; Anne, w, 103.137
Mary; Mary, d, 101.59
Francis; Anne, w, 103.137
Mary; Mary, d, 101.59

BROMALL:
Thomas; Elizabeth, w, 109.66
Thomas; Elllizabeth, w, 109.66

BROMAN:
William; Margaret, w, 99.59
William; Margery, w, 99.59

BROMFEILD:
Ann, ser, 106.28
Francis, 109.103
Originall; Ernor, w, 110.5
Ann, ser, 106.28
Francis, 109.103
Originall; Ernor, w, 110.5

BROMHALL:
Thomas; Elizabeth, w; Samuell, s; Richard, s;
James, s; Joseph, s; Hannah, d; Rachell, d,
101.64
Thomas; Elizabeth, w; Samuell, s; Richard, s;
James, s; Joseph, s; Hannah, d; Rachell, d,
101.64

BROMHILL:
Richard; Elizabeth, w; Joseph, s, 101.37
Richard; Elizabeth, w; Joseph, s,
101.37

BROMINGHAM:
Elizabeth; Alexander, s, 109.36
Elizabeth; Alexander, s, 109.36

BROMLEY:
Anne; John Smith, s, 107B.35
Barton, 98.37
Benjamin, app, 102.201
Elizabeth, 103.198, 107D.26
Geo; Susanna, w, 104.86
Mary, 103.198
Thomas; Sarah, w, 107A.16
Thomas; Sarah, w; Thomas, s, 107A.16
William; Mary, w; Rose, d, 101.100
Anne; John Smith, s, 107B.35
Barton, 98.37
Benjamin, app, 102.201
Elizabeth, 103.198
George; Susanna, w, 104.86
Mary, 103.198
Thomas; Sarah, w, 107A.16
Thomas; Sarah, w; Thomas, s, 107A.16
William; Mary, w; Rose, d, 101.100

BROMSDEN:
John; Mary, w; Thomas, s; William, s; John,
s; Daniell, s; Mary, d, 102.223
John; Mary, w; Thomas, s; William, s; John,
s; Deniell, s; Mary, d, 102.223

BROMSELL:
William; Hester, w, 107B.12
William; Hester, w, 107B.12

BROMTON:
Anne, 101.55
Anne, 101.55

BROOKE:
Elizabeth, 106.6
Geo, ser, b, 104.6
John, app, 107D.30
John, wid, 109.25
Robert; Susanah, w; Robert, s,
103.191
Ruth, ser, 107A.39
Samuel; Mary, w; James, s; Samuel, s,
107A.12
Thomas, ser, 109.36
Elizabeth, 106.6
George, ser, b?, 104.6
John, app, 107D.30
John, wid, 109.25
Robert; Susannah, w; Robert, s,
103.191
Ruth, ser, 107A.39
Samuel; Mary, w; James, s; Samuel, s,
107A.12
Thomas, ser, 109.36

BROOKEBANK:
Michell; Margaret, w; Margaret, d; Job, s,
103.146
William; Anne, w, 101.91

BROOKEHEAD: Anne; Rachell, d, 101.406

BROOKER: Mary; Jane, d;

BROOKES:
~, Mr; ~, 109.39
Anne; Anne, grand-d of; William, grand-s of,
107B.81
Anne; Anne, wid; Elizabeth, d, 103.175
Brakia; Sarah, w; Joseph, s, 103.215
Benj, app, 104.143
Charles; Anne, w, 110.22
Edward; Damaresk, w, 99.20
Edward; Anne, w, 102.267
Edward, 107D.42
Elizabeth, ser, 103.256
Ellianor, 101.24
Frances, 98.5
Francis; Sarah, w, 109.39
George, 109.17
George; Grissell, w; Grissell, d, 106.47
George; Mary, w, 107B.23
Hanah, 107C.2
Hanna, ser, 105.13
Henry; Ursula, w; Thomas, s; Jane, d, 106.3
Henry, bach, 109.53
Jeremiah; Hannah, w; Jerimiah, s; Richard, s;
Susanna, d; Avice, d; Murrey, d; Rebecca,
d, 102.228
John; Elizabeth, w, 99.54
John; Ruth, w, 101.31
John; Mary, w, 101.108
John; Isabell, w; Thomas, s; William, s,
106.61
John; Mary, w, 109.66
John, ser, 107C.29
Joseph; Martha, w; Frances, d; Nathaniel, s,
107C.12
Joseph, app, 103.52
Joshua, hath children, 103.215
Joyce, ser, 104.26
Margaret, 107D.90
Margaret, wid; Sarah, d, 103.51
Martha, ser, 107D.16
Mary; George, s, bach, 106.43
Nathaniell; Mary, w; John, s, 110.29
Nevell, bach, 98.52
Phebe, ser, 109.61
Philip, bach, 104.26
Ralph, ser, 109.7
Richard, 109.108
Richard; Mary, w; Mary, d, 104.26
Richard; Thomasin, w; Thomasin, d, 104.86
Richard, ser, 103.3, 103.256

Samuell; Elizabeth, w; Samuell, s, 106.34
Sarah, 104.94
Sarah; Anne, d; Charles, s, 98.37
Sarah, wid, 103.108
Thomas, 99.43
Thomas; Sara, w, 101.49
Thomas; Anne, w; Anne, d, 107D.41
William; Elizabeth, w; Mary, d, 107D.15
William, bach, 104.26
William, gent; Mary, w; Beatry, d; Robert, s,
106.20
William, ser, 107D.29

BROOKHOUSE:
Alice, 107D.6
Daniell; Docilia, w; William, s; Elizabeth, d,
102.129

BROOKLAND: Richard, ser, 103.62

BROOKSBY:
Elizabeth, 109.63
Jane, 98.79
Phillip; Elizabeth, w, 109.63
Phillip, 109.112
Tho; Mary, w; Symon, s; John, s;

BROOME:
~; ~, w, 103.36
George, bach, 98.59
Hugh, 105.18
Hugh; Mary, w; Elizabeth, d, 105.5
Hugh, 105.15
John, dead, 102.81
John, app, 107B.18
Jos; Sarah, w, 104.76
Leonard, bach, 107A.6
Mary, 106.25
Samuell, gent; Rebeccah, w, 98.31

BROOMEMAN: John; Judith, w, 110.6

BROOMER: Barbary, 99.39

BROOMFEILD: John; Eliz, w; John, s, 104.54

BROOMSKILL: John; Mary, d, 105.6

BROSSET: Robert, 107D.13

BROTHERTON:
Edward; Anne, w; Edward, s; Elizabeth, sister
of, 107B.49
John; Margaret, w; Elizabeth, d; Mary, d;
Thomas, s, 107B.67

BROUGHTON:
Samuell; Ann, w; Mary, d; Heneritta, d;
Samuel, s, 109.59

William; Rodah, w; Ann, d; Mary, d; William,
s; Joseph, s; Elizabeth, d;

BROWNE:
~, 102.254
~, children elsewhere, 103.24
Adam; Mary, w; Adam, s; Mary, d; John, s;
Anne, d; Elizabeth, d, 98.64
Alexander; Elizabeth, w, 103.189
Alice, 107B.66,109.102
Alice, ser, 103.229
Ambrose; Mary, w; John, s, 102.269
Andrew, bach, 109.11
Anne; Anne, d, 98.12
Anne, wid; Izerell, s; Benjamin, s, 103.39
Anne, wid; Elizabeth, d, 103.207
Anthony, 101.3
Anthony; Ellen, w, 100.11
Anthony; Lidiah, w; Samuel, s; Mary, d,
107B.44
Benjamin; Mary, w; Benjamin, s, 109.101
Christopher; Ellis, w, 110.24
Dameras; Katherine, d, 107B.47
Dameras, ser, 107B.1
Dorothy, 98.14
Edward; Hanah, w, 106.42
Edward; Katherine, w, 109.15
Edward; Elizabeth, w, 109.111
Edward, bach, 109.62
Edward, ser, 104.116
Elizabeth, 109.22
Elizabeth, nurse child, 103.82
Ellen, 107C.12
Francis; Elizabeth, w; Elizabeth, d, 101.58
Francis; Elizabeth, w; Edmund, s; Elizabeth,
d; Mary, d, 105.15
Francis, collector, 105.15,105.18
Frances, ser, 104.24
George; Jane, w, 102.127
Grace, 98.56
Gundry; Eliza, w, 104.129
Katherine, 98.7
Hanah, pensioner; Mary, d, 103.176
Hannah, ser, 104.57
Henry; Elizabeth, w; Elizabeth, d, 109.21
James, 102.31
James; Mary, w, 101.5
James; Frances, w, 110.8
James; Elizabeth, w; James, s; William, s, 110.29
Jane, ser, 102.200
Jeane, wid, 103.17
Joane, 106.15
John; Mary, w, 98.8
John; Elizabeth, w, 99.40
John; Johanna, w; Katherine, d; Mary, d,
102.136
John; Mary, w; Susannah, d, 103.68
John; Margaret, w; George, s; Anne, d,
103.140

John; Jane, w; Jane, d, 104.89
John; Mary, w, 105.13
John; Elizabeth, w; John, s; Elizabeth, d,
107B.61
John; Mary, w; Sarah, d; Richard, s; John, s;
Samuel, s; Mary, d; William, s, 107C.9
John; Katherine, w, 107D.93
John; Elizabeth, w; Elizabeth, d; Sarah, d;
Thomas, s, 109.55
John; Mary, w, 109.88
John; Elizabeth, w, 109.89
John; Lyddy, w; Martha, d; Mary, d, 110.12
John, assessor, 105.15
John, wid, 103.8
Joseph, ser, 102.199
Josuah; Mary, w; Thomas, s, 109.109
Lidia, 101.63
Lidiah; Elianor, d, 107A.24
Lyon, ser, 102.72
Margaret, 107B.18
Margaret; Alice, d, 101.36
Margaret, ser, 104D.32,101.60
Margaret, wid, 103.92
Marmaduke, bach, 104.11
Mary; Anna Maria, d, 101.41
Mary; Anne, d; Mary, d, 106.9
Mary, d of Browneing, John, 107D.31
Mary Magdalen, ser, 103.183
Mathew; Frances, w; William, s, 109.39
Michael; Mary, w; David, s; Michaell, s; Jane,
d; Mary, d; Anne; Jane Mary, d; Elizabeth,
d, 102.269
Michael; ~, a child (dead), 102.275
Millisent, 109.62
Nathaniel, bach, 109.11
Peter; Jane, w, 104.12
Phillip; Mary, w; Philip, s; Joseph, s, 103.272
Phillis, 107D.51
Prudence, spinster, 103.113
Ralph, bach, 103.208
Ralph Mary, sister of, 103.208
Rebecca, 102.16
Richard; Mary, w; Elizabeth, d; William, s,
98.37
Richard; Susan, w, 102.235
Richard; Elizabeth, w; James, s; Elizabeth, d,
103.110
Richard; Mary, w, 104.3
Richard, app, 98.24
Robert; Sarah, w, 102.17
Robert; Elizabeth, w; Thomas, s, 110.32
Robert, ser, 107C.18
Ruben, kinsman of Axdell, Richard, 107D.7
Samuell; Ellen, w; Samuell, s; Elizabeth, d;
Ellen, d; Robert, s; Debora, d, 102.69
Samuel; Anne, w, 109.56
Sarah; Sarah, d; Rebecca, d, 107B.72
Sarah, d of Browning, John, 107D.31
Sarah, ser, 98.28,103.282

41

Soloman; Hannah, w; Eve, d; Judith, d, 102.140

Susan, 107D.51,109.111

Susannah, 98.10

Thomas, 102.239,110.36

Thomas; Elizabeth, w; Thomas, s, 98.8

Thomas; Feby, d, 101.95

Thomas; Anne, w; James, s; Mary, d; Anne, d; Elizabeth, d; Sarah, d, 101.101

Thomas; Mary, w, 103.22

Thomas; Mary, w; Zachariah, s, 103.83

Thomas; Anne, w, 104.37

Thomas; Susan, w, 106.8

Thomas; Elianor, w, 107B.1

Thomas; Sarah, w; Hanah, d; Martha, d, 107B.12

Thomas; Mary, w, 109.19

Thomas; Anne, w, 109.73

Thomas, Doctor; Henrietta, w, 104.63

Thomas, app, 107B.81

Walter, 109.62

William, 102.173,110.9

William; Katherine, w; Sarah, d; Thomas, s; William, s; Katherine, d; Martha, d, 98.20

William; Mary, w, 98.58

Anne, d, 98.58

William; Sara, w, 101.97

William; Mary, w; Eliza, d; Mary, d, 102.11

William; ~, w, 103.48

William; Hanah, w; Thomas, s; Richard, s; William, s, 103.80

William; Jeane, w, 103.133

William; Mary, w, 104.18

William; Mary, w; Thomas, s, bach, 104.39

William; Joane, w, 105.15

William; Sarah, w; Sarah, d; Mary, d, 107A.24

William; Mary, w; Charles, s; John, s; William, s, 107B.32

William; Sarah, d, 109.41

William; Sarah, w; Elizabeth, d; Joseph, s; Sarah, d; Benjamin, s, 109.111

William; Mary, w, 110.13

William, wid, 104.15, 104.49?

William, alms, 102.190

William, ser, 107C.8, 109.31

BROWNES: Mary, 107B.11

BROWNING:

Ann, 109.33

Elizabeth, ser, 98.30

John; Elizabeth, w; Elizabeth Linly, grand-d; Mary Browne, d; Sarah Browne, d, 107D.31

Rich, 104.2

Samuell, bach, 98.61

BROWNSILL: John, 104.146

BROXTON: Francis, 109.111

BROXUP: Elizabeth, 101.3

BRSDBURY:

~, 105.8

Isaac; Mary, w, 109.93

John, 109.30

Mary, ser, 103.217

Robert; Mary, w, 107D.88

BRUERTON, See Brewerton

BRUERTON, See Brewerton

BRUFFE: William, app, 107C.12

BRUMBLOOM: Elienor;

BRUMELL:

~, 102.167

BRUMHALL: Richard, bach, gent, 106.43

BRUMIDGE: John; Elizabeth, w, 103.226

BRUMSCULL: Mary; Joseph, s, 109.46

BRUNCKARD: Chriastopher, ser, 106.37

BRUNIG: Robert; Margaret, w; Abraham, s; Sarah, d; Jane, d, 102.90

BRUNKETT:

Hannah, 109.93

William, 109.93

BRUNT: Elinor, 99.29

BRUTE: Batrick, 109.112

BRYAN:

Christian, ser, 107B.57

Gervace; Mary, w; Sarah, d, 107D.11

John; Anne, w; Patience, d, 101.9

John; Mary, w, 102.251

Joseph; Anne, w; Joseph, s, 107D.37

Margarett, 99.49

Mary, 109.7

Mary, ser, 104.4

Richard; Elizabeth, w, 103.247

Robert; Jane, w, 109.3

Robert; Elizabeth, w; George, s, 109.62

Samuell, ser, 106.37

William; Mary, w, 107A.7

BRYANT:

Alice, ser, 98.32

Chas; Jane, w, 104.52

BUDESER: Jane, 109.22

BUDGE: Susanna, ser, 101.73

BUDITT: Matthew; Mary, w; Mary, d, 102.188

BUDREE: Agnus, pensioner; Elizabeth, d, 103.148

BUFFETT: William; Mary, w; Elizabeth, d; Mary, d; Susan, d; Sarah, d, 103.222

BUFFORD: Andrew, ser, 103.291

BUFFREE: Susan, 102.231

BUGBY:
John; Jane, w; Ann, d, 109.39
Thomas; Elienor, w; Elizabeth, d, 102.191

BUGDEN:
William; Dorcas, w, 98.54
William, app, 98.54

BUGG: John; Mary, w; John, s; Mary, d, 109.13

BUGGS:
Valentine; Mary, w, 107B.2
William; Ellen, w;

BUKE:
~; William, s, 109.22

BUKEY: Rachell; Richard, s; Sarah, d, 110.18

BULAT: Katherine, 109.39

BULL:
Anne, 101.102
Anne; Aron, s, 102.120
Anne, ser, 98.44
Elizabeth, ser, 106.31, 107D.13
Hannah, ser, 98.39, 106.15
James, app, 107D.29
John; Mary, w, 103.173
Robert; Johannah, w; Mary, d, 107D.61
Seth; Elizabeth, w; John, s; Sarah, d; Elizabeth, d, 102.136
Simon; Mary, w, 107B.48
Stephen; Jane, w, 99.48
Thomas, ser, 103.252
Ursula, 107C.27
William; Mary, w; William, s; Elizabeth, d, 102.122
William; Dorothy, w, 102.145

William, belong to Northern Folgate; Mary, w; William, s; Henry, s, 103.21; Anne, w; James, s; Rebecca, d; William, s, 103.37

BULLARD: Johanah; John, s, 98.79

BULLEN: Henry; Eliza, w, 101.115

BULLER: Thomas; Elizabeth, w; Anne, d, 98.14

BULLEY:
John, 102.74
Martha, 102.250
Mary, wid, 103.244
Tho; Anne, w; Tho, s; Henry, s; Nich, s; Anne, d, 104.30
William, 102.74

BULLIMORE: Ralph; Dorothy, w; Mary, d, 109.70

BULLIN: Dunox; Jane, w;

BULLING:
~, 102.24

BULLIVONT: Robert; Alice, w, 106.56

BULLOCK:
Anne, ser, 104.55
Barberah, 107C.16
Bridgett, 109.70
Elizabeth; Elizabeth, d, 102.112
Henry; Elizabeth, w, 107B.30
Joyce, 101.10
Samuel; Mary, w, 107D.10
Sarah, ser, 107B.7
Susan, ser, 103.218
Thomas; Mary, w; Matthew, s, 107C.29
Thomas; Mary, w; Thomas, s, 109.109

BULLOIGNE: Thomas, 102.156

BULLPEN: Mary, 98.34

BULSTRODE: Whitlocke, gent; Elizabeth, w; Elizabeth, d;

BUNCH:
~; ~, w, 103.185

BUNCHER: Benjamin; Mary, w, 101.102

BUNCKER:
Joseph; Martha, w; Rebecca, d, 102.45
Thomas, bach, under age, 103.116
William; Margaret, w, 103.116

BUNDEY: John; Issabella, w; John, s,
102.193

BUNINGSTONE: Joyce, wid, 102.57

BUNN: Alice, ser, 103.287

BUNNON: Robert; Rebecca, w, 102.56

BUNSTEAD: Anne, 101.94

BUNTING:
Elizabeth, ser, 109.27
John; Mary, w, 110.16

BUNY: George; Jane, w; George, s; Mary, d,
101.40

BURBANCK:
Thomas; Mary, w; James, s, 102.199
Thomas, app, 107D.15

BURBIGE: Elizabeth; Mary, d, 98.52

BURBRIDGE:
Geo; Kath, w, 104.136
Henry; Anne, w, 102.154
Isaack; Rebecah, w; Thomas, s?, 99.48
John, 102.84

BURCH:
Daniell, ser, 100.10
Rebecca, 107B.69
Robert; Mary, w; Rebecca, d, 107B.69
Thomas; Elizabeth, w; Francis, s, 107D.33

BURCHARD: Richard; Elizabeth, w; James,
s; William, s; Stephen, s, 109.41

BURCHER: William; Joane, w; Judith, d,
102.154

BURCHMORE: Ralph; Anne, w; Martha, d;
Henry, s; John, s; Thomas, s, 106.32

BURD:
Arthur, 102.148
Contented, 102.127
Edmond, ser, 102.2
Henry, bach, 102.181
Robert; Rebecca, w; Rebecca, d; Sarah, d, 102.55
Thomas; Frances, w; John, s, 102.192

BURDELL: Jane, 98.37

BURDEN:
Anne, 104.86
Anathaniel; Mary, w; Robert, s; Gray, s;
Hanah, d; Blackborn, s, 102.129

BURDETT:
Ann, 109.52
Francis; Anne, w, 102.209
Francis Francis, s; Mary, d; Anne, d; Jane, d,
102.209
Izabellah, ser, 98.31
Jane; Elizabeth, d; Sarah, d, 109.29
John; Elizabeth, w, 107C.42
Nathaniell, 110.19
Robert; Margarett, w; John, s; Margarett, d,
102.171
Robert; Joane, w, 109.58
Samuell; Susan, w, 103.76
Thomas; Mary, w, 101.58
William; Edith, w, 110.22

BURDWOOD: Hanah, 107B.10

BURDY: Benjamin; Elizabeth, w; Elizabeth,
d; Thomas, s; Valentine, s, 102.160

BURESS: Humphrey; Sarah, w; Kath, d,
104.78

BURFORD:
Ann, 109.41
Samuell, 101.57

BURGE:
Anthony, app, 107D.60
Thomas, bach, 103.121

BURGEN:
Edward, bach, 98.58
Thomas; Mary, w; William, s; Ann, d;

BURGES:
~, Mr, bach, gent, 98.68
Alice; Elizabeth, d, 109.25
Anne, ser, 103.10
Augustine, bach, 104.92
Barbara, 101.50
Elizabeth, ser, 103.286
Ellinor, wid, 103.148
Ellinor, wid, 103.86
Francis; Frances, w; John, s, 107B.20
Hustace; Judith, w, 101.50
John; Margery, w; Hannah, d, 102.229
John; Mary, w; John, s; William, s, 103.198
John; Elizabeth, w, 106.41
John Clarke, 98.44
John, ser, 107A.6
Margarett, 99.24
Mary, ser, 109.100
Richard; Hannah, w, 99.20
Richard; Mary, w; Richard, s; Martha, d,
101.83
Richard; Martha, w, 107B.67
Samuel; Hannah, w, 102.12

Susan, 103.23
Susannah, ser, 107A.28
Thomas; Frances, w; William, s; Mary, d,
103.62
Thomas; Priscilla, w; Hanah, d, 107C.4
Thomas, bach, 109.68
Ustace, 101.5
William; Elizabeth, w, 102.192
William; Mercey, w; Rebecca, d; John, s,
103.248

BURGOTT: James, 105.3

BURKE:
Anne, 106.21
John, a child, 102.6

BURKES: Joseph, 102.81

BURKET:
Jane Henry, d of Broadfeild, 107D.8
Jeane, ser, 103.17
John; Mary, w, 107B.27
Mary Henry, s, 107D.8
Robert; Elizabeth, w; Robert, s; Anne, d,
107D.73

BURKILL:
John; Judith, w; Mary, d, 107B.28
William; Anne, w; Mary, d, 107B.53

BURKLEY: Robert; Elizabeth, w, 106.34

BURLAND: Sara, ser;

BURLEIGH:
~, gent; Elizabeth, w, 104.24
Mervin; Marg, w, 104.108
Tho, app, 104.14

BURLETON: Humphrey; Katherine, w, 106.1

BURLEY: Bridget, pensioner; Mary Willson,
d; George, s; Hanah; William; Susannah,
w, 99.51

BURMAN:
Edward, 102.14
James, gent; Mary, w; James, s; Letitia, d,
98.70

BURNABY: Mary; Elizabeth, d;

BURNALL:
~, wid, 105.2

BURNAM:
Henry, 102.17
John, app, 107D.21

BURNE: John; Hannah, w; Nathaniell, s,
110.26

BURNELEY: Mary, ser, 106.19

BURNETT:
Alexander, 102.211
Catherine, 109.107
John, nurse child, 103.154
Patrick, ser, 101.33
Thomas; Elizabeth, w; Izabellah, d, 98.4

BURNHAM: Elizabeth, ser, 98.65

BURR:
Francis; Elizabeth, w, 103.100
Francis; Anne, w; Richard, s, 109.43
Hester, 102.154

BURRAGE:
Adam; Anne, w, 102.177
Thomas; ~, 102.87

BURRELL:
Ealce, 110.14
Henry; Margaret, w, 101.64
Joseph, app, 107A.28
Sam; Mary, w; Mary, d, 104.38
Thomas; Elizabeth, w; Elizabeth, d; Dorothy,
d, 109.31
William; Sarah, w, 103.13

BURRIDGE:
Elizabeth, 98.3
John, bach, 98.3
Margaret, 102.128

BURRIS: John; Ann, w; John, s; Ann, d,
109.11

BURROW:
Anne, 104.69
Ellinor, ser, 106.3
Joseph, £600; Winifred, w; John, s; Elizabeth,
d, 101.105
Litton, 102.233
William; Elizabeth, w, 103.43

BURROWS:
Anne, 105.15
Anne, ser, 107D.3
Alice, 109.55
George; Elizabeth, w, 102.76
Henry, app, 98.49
Hicks; Anne, w; Margaret, d, 106.5
Joane, wid; Pleasant, d, 103.8
John; Mary, w; Elizabeth, d; John, s, 103.161
Joseph; Elizabeth, w, 109.76
Julian, ser, 109.45

Lidia, ser, 106.64
Robert, ser, 98.4
Samuell, 103.246
Sarah, 107D.71
Tho; Science, w, 104.118

BURRY: John; Amey, w; Thomas, s, 106.58

BURS: Sarah, 102.75

BURSHALL: Elizabeth, ser, 109.27

BURSTON:
Frances, 102.106
Robert; Sarah, w; Sarah, d; Ann, d;
    Catherine, d, 109.79

BURT:
Ellen, 102.212
George, wid; Mary, d; John, s, bach, 103.150
Jeane, spinster; Joane, sister, spinster,
    103.215
Jerimiah; Amey, w; Anne, d, 102.174
Mary; Laurence, s; Sarah, d, 104.130
Thomas; Mary, w; Mary, d, 104.130
William; Mary, w; Mary, d, 109.59
William, bach;

BURTON:
~, wid, 107C.21
Alice, 104.34
Anne, 109.67
Anne, ser, 103.229,109.3
Bridgett; Phillip, s; John, s, 106.19
Dorcas; Elizabeth, d; Dorcas, d; Deborah, d;
    John, s, 98.68
Edward, 103.213
Edward; Anne, w; Elizabeth, d, 103.293
Edward; Margaret, w, 109.17
Eleanor, 109.17
Elizabeth, 99.41,107D.15
Elizabeth, ser, 103.285,108.1
Francis, 109.47
Francis, ser, 103.271
George; Ann, w; George, s; Sarah, d, 103.135
Henry; ~, w; Henry, s; John, s, 103.265
James, 99.30
James; Sarah, w, 102.187
James; Mary, w, 107D.43
Jane, 107B.62
Jerimiah; Margaret, w, 102.258
John, 110.8
John; Hanna, w, 105.4
John; Lettice, w; Lettice, d, 106.11
John, app, 107B.18,107D.19
John, bach, 103.75
Joseph; Heater, w; Elizabeth, d; Joseph, s;
    George, s, 102.95
Judith, 107A.32

Kathrine, ser, 109.37
Margaret, ser, 107A.30
Mary, 98.34,99.43
Moses; Moses, s, bach, 107D.34
Rebecca; Rebecca, d, 106.11
Richard; Emm, w, 103.16
Richard; Anne, w, 107D.3
Richard, app, 103.236
Robe; Sarah, w; Robe, s; Eliza, d; Jane, d;
    Sarah, d; Susannah, d, 104.67
Robert, ser, 109.36
Samuell, 101.103
Sarah, ser, 106.28
Sasan, a girl, 104.40
Ursly, spinster, 103.149
William, 105.18,106.56
William; Mary, w, 101.98
William; Susan, w; Margaret, d; Samuell, s;
    Susan, d; Mary, d, 103.98
William; Mary, w; Henry, s; Mary, s;
    Elizabeth, d, 105.12
William, assessor, 105.15

BUSBY:
James, app, 102.145
Prudence, 107C.19
Thomas, bach, 99.30
William; Permutas, w, 104.112

BUSH:
Elizabeth; James, s; Edward, s,
    107C.28
Elizabeth, ser, 107B.19
Hannah, 98.50
Hannah, ser, 100.13
Joseph, 99.45
Phillippa, 101.62

BUSHELL:
Anne, 109.110
Elizabeth, 109.53
James, app, 107C.22
Jane, 109.104
Margaret, 107A.30
Mary, 99.42,109.110

BUSHER: Robert, ser, 103.19

BUSHFORD: John, 99.13

BUSHNELL:
Elizabeth, ser, 106.29
John; Katherine, w; Elizabeth, d; Mary, d,
    102.269
Jonathon, 109.71

BUSHRETH: Jacob; Elizabeth, w; John, s;
    Hester, d; Elizabeth, d; Mary, d; Susan, d,
    102.219

BUSRION: ~, wid, 104.56

BUSSEY:
Edward; Joane, w; Mary, d, 109.53
Margaret, 101.45
Tho; Mary, w;

BUSSINGTON:
Joseph; Sarah, w; Margaret, d, 107B.11

BUSSVINE: Warrin; Ann, w, 103.262

BUSTIAM: Elizabeth, 104.22

BUTCHER:
Anne, 110.7
Edmond, bach, 103.39
Elizabeth, 101.103
Frances; Frances, d, 110.24
Hanah, 107D.9
James; Tisdall, w; Jane, d; Susan, d, 107B.52
James, parish child, 109.15
John; Ann, w; John, s; Barbara, d, 109.14
Joseph; Mary, w, 101.90
Joseph, ser, 108.6
Mary, ser, 98.8
Robert, 99.11
William; Anne, sister of, 109.75
William, parish child, 109.15

BUTLAND: Richard, bach;

BUTLER:
~, wid; Mary, d; Anna, d; Elizabeth, d, 105.1
Anne, nurse child, 107B.57
Dorothy, app, 98.25
Elinor, 98.25
Elizabeth, 98.56,102.142
Francis, 98.22
Francis, app, 101.56
Francis, gent, wid, 104.74
Gilbert; Elizabeth, w, 109.47
Henry, app, 102.78
Heugh, 103.47
James; Jone, w; John, s; Hanah, d; Sarah, d, 107B.14
James, app, 98.72
Jane, wid, 100.14
John; Elizabeth, w; William, 98.5
John; Mary, w; John, s, 103.19
John; Mary, w, 103.187
John; Frances, w; Alice, d, 104.17
John, wid; Mary, d; Judeth, d; Anne, d, 103.217
Martha, 104.20
Mary, 103.42,109.5
Mary, ser, 98.15
Pearce, bach, gent, 106.46
Ralph, ser, bach, 104.63

Richard; Mary, w, 110.11
Richard, app, 101.108
Robert, 105.18
Robert; Mary, w; Robert, s; Benia, d; Mary, d; Thomas, s; Issabella, d; Joseph, s, 99.35
Robert, app, 102.133,107D.21
Roger; Fortune, w, 104.118
Rupurt, ser, 109.27
Sara, 101.32
Susan, ser, 106.22
Thomas, nurse child, 103.116
William; Jone, w, 98.21
William; Elizabeth, w; Margaret, d; Winifred, s; Lucy, d; John, s, 109.51
William, £600, plumber; Hanna, w; Hanna, d, 101.56
William, app, 101.65
William, assessor, 101.11

BUTSON: Jane, ser, 106.9

BUTT:
Martha, ser, 103.287
Robert, 110.26

BUTTER:
John, 107D.27
Thomas; Rachael, w; John, s; Thomas, s; Jerimiah, s; Ambrose, s; Joseph, s; Anne, d, 107B.95

BUTTERFEILD:
Anne; Anne, d; Margaret, d, 98.62
James; Martha, w; Martha, d; John, s, 109.13
James, app, 107B.21
Robert; Elizabeth, w; Mary Fountaine, kinswoman of, 107D.11
Susan; Elizabeth, d; Anne, d, 102.236

BUTTERLY:
Elizabeth, 101.58
Richard; Elizabeth, w; Richard, s; Cherles, s; Edward, s; Theophilus, s; Elizabeth, d; Mary, d; Jane, d, 104.123

BUTTERNUN: Elizabeth, ser, 109.79

BUTTERWORTH:
John; Margaret, w; John, s; Elizabeth, d, 109.46
Thomas; Elizabeth, w; Thomas, s, 107B.31

BUTTON:
Ann, ser, 103.31
Daniel, 109.80

BUTTS:
Anne, 102.198
Richard; Mary, w, 106.59
Susan, 103.204

CALVERT:
John; Jane, w; Jane, d, 102.232
Mary, ser, 99.2
Thomas; Sara, w, 101.60

CAMBRIDGE:
Elizabeth, 101.44
Elizabeth; Mary, d, 98.53

CAMBRY: Rebecca, ser, 107A.22

CAMDEN:
John; Easter, w; Elizabeth, d, 98.78
John; Eliazabeth, w; Edmund, s, 109.41
Rebecca, 106.9
Thomas; Mary, w; Thomas, s, 101.7

CAMELL:
Jane, 106.7
John; Jane, w, 102.156
William, app, 107A.32
William, wid, 109.24

CAMFEILD: Magdalen, 106.12

CAMMUCK: Edward, bach, 103.50

CAMPIN: Martha, 102.47

CAMPION:
Dorothy, 104.6
Giles, £50 p.a.; Anne, w; Anne, d, 106.30
Henry; Jeane, w; Williams, s, 103.44
John, 109.78
John; Mary, w, 101.106
Richard; Penellopa, w, 98.5

CAMPS: Wm; Deborah, w; Anne, d;
Deborah, d; Sarah, d, 104.19

CANAN: Stephen; Hannah, w; Hannah, d,
102.237

CANBY:
Susannah, 98.40
Theophilus, ser, 98.40

CANDEY:
Nathaniell; Nathaniell, s; Joseph, s; Susan, d,
106.21
William; Mary, w, 104.46

CANDLE: Timothy; Anne, w; Timothy, s;
George, s, 107A.7

CANE:
Elizabeth, 109.104
Francis; Elizabeth, w; Mary, d, 109.66
George; Dorothy, w, 104.49

Henry, 107C.1B
John, bach, 104.101
Sarah, spinster, 103.58

CANFEILD:
Elizabeth, wid, 103.11
Francies, £600; Elizabeth, w, 99.52
Jacob, £600; Ann, w, 99.51
Jeremiah, bach, 99.10

CANHAM: Mary, £600, her husband in the
country; John, s; Anne, d; Katherine, d,
103.17

CANING: Mary, 109.89

CANN:
Mary, ser, 98.29
William; Ann, w, 103.246

CANNELL:
Hanna, 101.90
John, 101.90

CANNER: Edward, at sea; Mary, w; Mary, d;
Elizabeth, d; Sarath, d, 103.50

CANNING: Sara, 101.55

CANNON:
Benjamin; Margaret, w; Mary, d; Margaret, d,
98.21
Charles; Frances, w, 106.7
John; Elizabeth, d; Elizabeth, d, 109.71
Mary, pensioner, 103.212
Robert, 107C.4
Robert; Hanah, w, 107D.37
Thomas; Susannah, w; William; Martha, d,
109.38
Thomas, bach, 98.3
William; Amey, w; Ruth, d, 102.228

CANNY: John, 101.27

CANTER:
Richard; Anne, w; William, s, 101.107
William, 103.201

CANTHORNE: Anne, 98.7

CAPELL:
Eliza, 104.122
Nicholas, 107C.32
William, app, 103.59

CAPEN: Anthony, ser, 109.36

CAPLE:
Elizabeth, 105.5

Grace, ser, 107D.50
Henry; Anne, w; Jane Caple, grand-d,
    109.101
Joseph; Anne, w; Joseph, s; Thomas, s; Peter,
    s; Samuell, d; Mary, d; Anne, d, 103.292
Sarah, 109.105
Thomas; Elizabeth, w, 109.105

CAPON: Simon, bach, 103.221

CAPPS: William, ser, 98.30

CAPSTICK: George; Anne, w; Joseph
    Mason, s, 107B.19

CARALL: Anne, 109.19

CARD: Joseph, 109.106

CARDEN: Robert, 101.52

CARDWELL: Thomas; Abigall, w; William,
    s; Elizabeth, d; Abigall, d, 102.33

CARE:
Grace, ser, 109.51
John, 109.68
Nicholas; Barbary, w, 103.231

CARELESS:
Ann, wid, 103.97
John, wid; Elizabeth, d; John, s, 102.40
Mary, 103.283

CAREW:
John; Juliana, w, 104.41
Thomas; Adrian, w;

CAREY:
~, wid, 104.127
Anne, 109.85
Anne, ser, 106.14
Edward; Jane, w, 109.106
Eliza, 104.135
Elizabeth, wid, 103.30
Francis, 109.30
John; Elizabeth, w; Thomas Monke, s;
    Elizabeth Carey, d; John Carey, s,
    107B.27
Joseph, 103.234
Marg, 104.44
Mary, 103.234
Thomas; Anne, w, 109.105
Wm; Anne, w, 104.114

CARG:
~, 101.60
Anne, 102.211
Margaret, a child, 98.35

CARICK: Robert; Elizbeth, w; John, d; Anne,
    d; Joseph, s; Elizabeth, d; Josuah, s,
    107D.21

CARIN: Grace, 104.51

CARLECRAFT: John; Anne, w; Mary, d;
    Nathaniell, s, 102.179

CARLETON:
Crispass; Winafred, w, 103.38
John; Sarah, w; John, s; Sarah, d, 107C.38
Mary, 103.108

CARLEWIS: James; Mary, w; Mary, d;
    James, s; John, s, 103.59

CARLILE:
Adam; Anne, w, 101.33
Anne, 104.29
Edward; Sarah, w, 107D.73
Elizabeth, 110.28
John; Anne, w; Elizabeth, d, 102.26
John; Susannah, w, 103.65

CARNALL: Jane; Joyce, d, 101.64

CARNE:
Thomas, £50 p.a., commissioner; Mary, w;
    John, s; Mary, d; Ruth, d; William, s;
    Anne, d; Phillip, s; Sarah, d; Ralph, s;
    Susan, d, 102.47
Thomas, app, 98.2
William; Sarah, w; William, s, 109.68
William, gent; Mary, w, 98.33

CARNOLL: Elizabeth, 107D.89

CARPENDER: Stephen; Elizabeth, w; John,
    s; Stephen, s, 100.12

CARPENTER:
Anne, 101.19
Daniel; Jane, w; Mary Newman, d, 107B.74
Daniel, ser, 102.158
Elinor, 110.29
Elizabeth, 109.26
Elizabeth, pensioner, 106.8
Francis; Susan, w, 109.39
Giles; Jeane, w; Lewis, s, 103.196
Henry; Mary, w, 107D.73
Henry, app, 98.81
John; Elizabeth, w; Joseph, s; James, s; John,
    s, 103.71
John, £600; Elizabeth, w, 106.24
John, ser, 100.8, 106.11
James, £600, wid; Elizabeth, sister of, 102.79
James, app, 107C.11
Mary; William, s, 109.36

Richard; Anne, w; Mary, d; Eleanor, d;
Elizabeth, d, 102.112
Robert; Elizabeth, w; Robert, s; Elizabeth, d,
102.28
Sarah, spinster, 103.168
Thomas; Sarah, w; Thomas, s; Mary, d,
109.58
Thomas, £50 p.a., gold beater; Elizabeth, w;
Richard, s; Elizabeth, d, 101.5
Thomas, assessor, 101.111
Thomas, ser, 109.22
William; Katherine, w; John, s; Katherine, d,
103.125
William; Margaret, w, 107B.5
William, £600, commissioner; Katherine, w;
Ralph, s; William, s; Mary, d; Elizabeth, d,
102.78
William, ser, 106.65

CARR:
Frances, ser, 107B.64
John; Anne, w; Francis, s, 107A.42
John, app, 103.195
Kath, 104.104
Marg, 104.88
Mary, 109.55
Mary, ser, 98.36,107B.81
Mary, spinster, 103.47
Ruth; Samuel, s; Sarah, d; Edward, s,
107A.39
Thomas; Susannah, w, 98.82

CARRELL: Joseph; Martha, w, 103.194

CARRIER:
John; Elizabeth, w, 103.25
Thomas, bach, 103.24
William, bach; Elizabeth, sister of, 103.24

CARRINGTON:
Alice, 109.60
John; Jane, w; John, s, 98.84
John, bach, 104.41
Kathrine, 109.45
Ralph; Deborah, w, 106.32

CARROLL: William; Sarah, w; Benjamin, s?;
Sarah, d, 99.5

CARSELLIS: Nicholas, esq; Elizabeth, w,
98.31

CART: Richard; Anne, w; Mabell, d; Mary, d;
Martha, d;

CARTER:
~, wid; ~, wid; Flower, d, 104.99
Anne, ser, 102.159
Anthony, ser, 106.25

Benjamin; Grace, w, 102.5
Charles; Dorcas, w, 109.33
Christian, 107B.20
Edward, gent; Anne, w; Anne, d; Mary, d,
98.29
Edmond, 109.11
Edmond; Mary, w; William, s, 103.268
Elizabeth, 102.213
Elizabeth, nurse child, 103.76
Elizabeth, wid, 103.29
Francis, 109.105
Georg, 102.244
Grace, 109.97
Henry; Elizabeth, w; Thomas, s, 109.102
Hugh; Mary, w; Mary, d, 109.90
Jane, 101.19,109.98
John; Jone, w, 98.80
John; Joyce, w; John, s; Anne, d, 103.32
John; Alice, w, 106.5
John; Peroevall, w, 109.16
John; Flora, w, 110.32
Katherine, ser, 102.132
Laurence; Sarah, w, 109.82
Margaret, 109.75
Martin, bach, £600, 104.5
Mary, 101.24, 109.50
Mary, ser, 104.10
Mathew, 107B.56
Nath; Jane, w, 104.83
Nicholas; Frances, w, 102.103
Paul, 107D.37
Ralph; Elizabeth, w, 106.25
Rebecca, ser, 104.1
Richard, app, 104.72
Richard, pensioner; William, s; Elizabeth, d,
103.75
Robert; Martha, w; Mary, d, 108.3
Royley; Moses, s; Joseph, s; Martha, d; Mary,
d, 107B.8
Samuel, ser, 109.7
Susan, 107B.53
Thomas; Mary, w, 99.38
Thomas; Anne, w, 102.192
Thomas; Mary, w; Anne, d; Elizabeth, d;
Martha, d, 103.157
Thomas; Jeane; w; Christian, d; Elizabeth, d,
103.227
Thomas; Susannah, w; Thomas, s; Susan, d;
Thomas, s, 109.27
Thomas, app, 107D.10
Timohy, app, 109.25
William, 107D.2, 109.15
William; Ellen, w; John, s; William, s,
102.50
William; Elizabeth, w, 103.235
William; Sarah, w; William, s; Samuel, s;
Elianor, d, 107B.17
William, £50 p.a.; Anne, w, 106.36
William, app, 103.201

William, assessor, 106.69
William, bach, 98.65

CARTON: William; Elizabeth, w, 103.61

CARTWRICK: William; Elizabeth, w, 109.99

CARTWRIGHT:
Bridget, 107B.55
Elinor, ser, 98.32
John; Sarah, w; Sarah, d; Peter, s; John, s, 107D.68
John; Mary, w; Willian, s; Jane, d, 109.52
Mary, ser, 107D.29
Robert, 102.30
Thomas; Frances, w; Mary, d, 98.21
Thomas, £600; Mary, w, 107B.73

CARVANO: Jullian, spinster, 103.267

CARVER:
Jos; ~, w, 104.124
Thomas; Elizabeth, w; Sarah, d, 109.12

CARVILL: Edw, app, 104.36

CARWIN: Jane;

CARWITHAM:
~, bach, 104.91

CARWOOD: Mathew, ser, 106.53

CASBECK: Chris, £600; Mary, w; Florence, d; Isabella, d; Mary, d; Eliz, d, 104.125

CASEA: Moses, 102.265

CASELTON: Anne, 109.76

CASEY:
John, 106.47
John; Anne, w; John, s, 107B.24
Martha, 98.6

CASH:
Grace, 109.51
Joseph; Elizabeth, w, 109.10
Sarah, 102.122
Sarah, wid of doctor of physick, 102.136

CASHAW: Joseph; Martha, w; Francis, s; John, s; Abraham, s, 110.17

CASHEIR: John, ser, 109.105

CASKE: William, bach, 103.118

CASON:
Anne, 102.166
Elizabeth, 102.170

CASSELIME: Elizabeth, 99.18

CASSELL:
Elizabeth; Elizabeth, d, 99.15
John; Elizabeth, w; John, s, 103.74

CASSON:
Sarah, wid, 103.30
Thomas; Hannah, w, 109.21

CASTEELE(?): John; Elize, w, 104.58

CASTELL: Joane; John, s, 102.155

CASTLE:
Alice, 109.71
Elizabeth, pensioner; Nathaniel, s; Elizabeth, d, 103.119
Frances, 107B.80
Isaac, 102.88
Izabellah, 98.54
John; Elizabeth, w; John, s, 107D.16
Rich; Ellinor, w, 104.37

CASTLES: George, gent; Sarah, w, 106.4

CASTRO: Lawrance; Margaret, w; John, 107D.19

CASTRY: Francis, 107D.72

CASWELL: William, 98.5

CATER:
Charles, 107C.32
John; Elizabeth, w, 107D.12
Martha, ser, 107D.43
Thomas, app, bach, 98.48
Richard; Mary, w; Anne, d, 103.68
William; Sarah, w; Susanna, d; Anne, d, 102.232

CATERILL:
Elizabeth, 109.32
Jane, 109.32

CATES:
Johannah, ser, 107A.23
John; Mary, w, 107D.81
Ralph; Johannah, w; Ralph, ser; Sarah, d, 107A.36
Willian; Katherine, w; Elizabeth, d, 107D.6

CATESBY: Anne, 98.58

CATLIN:
Daniel; Jeane, w; Esther, d; Daniel, s, 103.74
Edward, 99.4
Elizabeth, 102.64
Henry; Anne, w; Anne, d; Thomas, s, 107C.38
Humfrey, 102.260
James, 99.4
Jeremy, 105.2
John; Anne, w; John, s; Sarah, d; Elizabeth, d,
    102.202
Jonathan, 99.4
Saisley, 104.130
Thomas; Mary, w, 103.69

CATMORE:
Thomas; Mary, w; Henry, s, 107A.33
Thomas, app, 107A.30

CATON:
Elizabeth, 109.44
Mary, 98.18
Thomas; Dorothy, w, 107B.25

CATT: Soloman, 102.233

CATTLE: Thomas, 109.77

CAUSEBROOKE: Thomas; Martha, w,
    102.51

CAVE:
Henry, bach, 104.79
John; Marg, w; John, s; Mary, d, 104.143
William; Mary, w; John, s; Mary, d, 107B.78
William; Elizabeth, w; William, s, 104.53

CAWARDIN?: Thomas; Masey, w, 102.222

CAWCAT: Obediah; Johannah, w; John, s;
    Elizabeth, d; Sarah, d, 107B.9

CAWLES: Francis; Ann, w, 103.276

CAWSETT: Eliza, ser, 104.15

CAWSON: John; Mary, w; Margarett, d?;
    John, s?, 99.49

CAWTHORNE:
Joseph; Elizabeth, w; Mary, d, 107D.53
William; Sarah, w, 109.43

CAXTON: Thomas, 99.38

CEALAR: Bernard; John, s, 98.20

CEARMAN: Mary, 103.73

CEARNACK: William; Elizabeth, w, 102.126

CEARNECK: Sarah, ser, 107B.79

CEARNLEY:
Thomas; Mary, w, 107D.27
Thomas; Sarah, w; Anne, d; Allran, s;

CEARSOCK:
~, esq, bach; Mary, sister, 104.31

CEASSER: Edward, widower, children
    elsewhere, 103.40

CECILL:
James; Anne, w; James, s, 109.70
Mary; Elizabeth, d, 109.33

CESAR: Job; Susanna, w; Elizabeth, d;
    Susan, d, 107A.2

CHADDOCK:
Hannah, 99.37
James; Hanah, w, 99.37

CHADLEY: Anne; Elizabeth, d, 104.32

CHADWICK:
James; Lidia, w, 103.247
John; Susan, w, 103.59
John; Margaret, w; John, s; Thomas, s;
    Elizabeth, d; Anne, d, 107D.57

CHAFFIN:
Hannah, ser, 104.92
John; Anne, w; Anne, d, 102.70

CHAIRE: John; Africa, w, 107C.2

CHALCROFT:
Elizabeth, 106.33
William, bach, 103.189

CHALKLARD: Anne, ser, 102.113

CHALLENDER: John; Mary, w, 98.85

CHALLINGSWORTH: Thomas, 102.94

CHALLINOR: Sarah, wid;

CHAMBERLIN:
~, spinster, 103.9
Anne, 102.95
James; Mary, w; Alice, d; James, s, 107D.96
John; Anne, w; John, s, 100.14
John; Elizabeth, w, 101.35
John; Elizabeth, w; Elizabeth, d, 102.82
John; Mary, w, 104.49
John; Amey, w, 110.20
John, bach, 104.24

George; Margaret, w; William, s, 107B.35
Grace, 103.149
Hanna; Mary, d, 101.12
Henry; Mary, w, 109.55
Henry, app, 102.189, 104.144
Jas, ser, 104.69
Jeffery, 102.53
John; Frances, w, 109.8
John; Margaret, w, 109.15
John; Anne, w; John, s; Joseph, s; Anne, d; Mary, d, 109.72
John; Anne, w, 110.5
John; Elizabeth, w, 110.11
John, junior; Sarah, w; Sarah, d; John, s; Anne, d, 107B.65
John, senior; Anne, w, 107B.65
Kathrine, 109.18
Lidiah, ser, 107D.40
Margaret; Anne, d, 110.3
Mary, 102.95, 103.105
Mary; ~, d, 102.191
Mary; Katherine, d; Murrey, d, 102.236
Mary, parish child, 101.36
Mary, ser, 98.39
Mary, wid, 103.142
Mathew, 107D.98
Matthew; Frances, w, 102.55
Nichas, 109.111
Roger; Elizbeth, w; John, s, 103.12
Samuel; Mary, w; Samuel, s, 107A.7
Sarah, 109.111
Sarah, ser, 106.29
Tho; Sarah, w; Tho, s; Jas, s; John, s; Sarah, d, 104.104
Thomas, ser, 106.23
William, 107C.27
William; Mary, w; William, s; Elizabeth, d, 103.8

CHAPPELHOW: Susannah, 109.8

CHAPPELL:
Charles; Elizabeth, w, 99.47
Joane, 106.7
John; Elizabeth, w; John, s, 98.82
Marg, 104.29
Mary, 98.25
Mary, ser, 98.81
Thomas; Frances, w; Thomas, s, 107A.37

CHARD: Jos; Hester, w; Rich, s; Anne, d, 104.55

CHARE: Sarah, ser, 104.102

CHARGE: John; Jane, w; Mary, d?; ~, d?, 99.16

CHARLES:
John, bach, 98.24
Joseph; Mary, d, 102.225
Joseph, app, 107D.25
Nathaniel, bach, 103.32
Thomas, 101.53
William, bach, 98.24

CHARLEY:
James; Mary, w; Martha, d?, 99.19
Joseph; Anne, w; Joseph, s, 102.31

CHARLOTT: George; Alice, w, 103.78

CHARLSWORTH: Ann, wid, 103.66

CHARLTON:
Anne, 98.74, 102.261
Christian, 109.26
Edward; Jeane, w; William, s; Elizabeth, d, 103.63
Elizabeth; Margaret, d; Francis, s, 109.16
James, 110.10
Jonathan; Mary, w; Elizabeth, d; Mary, d, 102.84
Margarett, 110.24
Richard; Susan, w; William, s, 107C.17

CHARRITY: Hannah, ser, 98.43

CHARTER:
Margaret, 109.25
William; Anne, w; Mary, d; Anne, d; Sarah, d; William, s, 107C.3

CHARTON: Mich; Mary, w; Edw, s; Mary, d, 104.80

CHASE:
John; Mary, w, 103.11
Mary, ser, 104.90

CHATFEILD:
Elizabeth; Mary, d; Ruth, d; Charles, s, 107A.3
John, app, 107A.36

CHATGOOD: Mary, 102.219

CHATWIN: Elizabeth, 109.45

CHAWWER: Henry; Mary, w, 102.85

CHAYNE: Abraham; Eatherine, w, 102.231

CHEAKE: Elizabeth; Mary, d; Anne, d; Allran, s, 107B.7

CHEASLY: William; Elizabeth, w; Mary, d; Elizabeth, d; Katherine, d; James, s, 107A.10

CHEEK: Alice, ser, 100.13

CHEESE:
Jeane, wid; William, s, 103.81
John, bach, 106.59

CHEESKY: William; Elizabeth, w; Anne, d;
Mary, d; Doroty, d, 109.93

CHEESMAN:
~, wid, 104.52
Mary, 106.11

CHEESWRIGHT:
Bridget, pensioner, 103.48
John; Mary, w; Elizabeth, d, 109.1

CHEGOY: Elizabeth, 102.268

CHELLINGSWORTH:
John; Anne, w, 101.73
William, app, 101.73

CHELLINGWORTH: John; Philllpia, w, 98.79

CHELSEY:
George; Sarah, w; Elizabeth Haya, d, 107B.64
Mary, ser, 103.66

CHELSUM: Jethrow, bach, 102.136

CHELTENHAM: William, 99.12

CHELTON:
Henry, 109.14
Robert; Anne, w; John, s, 102.186

CHEN:
George; Anne, w, 99.36
Richard; Lucey, w, 109.41
Robert; Elizabeth, w; Mary, d; Robert, s,
103.78

CHEPSEN: George; Elizabeth, w, 98.36

CHEPSEY: William; Mary, w; William, s;
Mary, d; Anne, d, 98.4

CHERRILL: Bartholomew; Jane, w;
Bartholomew, B, 107D.76

CHERRY: Martha, 104.131

CHERRYHAM: Christian, ser, 106.61

CHESHIRE:
Francis; Mary, w; Jane, d, 109.99
John; Anne, w; Anne, d; John, s; Elizabeth, d,
107B.18

Joseph; Elizabeth, w; John, s, 109.18
Martha, parish child, 106.6

CHESSMOORE: Edmond; Ursula, w;
Francis, kindred; Thomas, kindred, 103.275

CHESSTERFEILD: Thomas; Liddia, w,
103.67

CHESTER:
Granado, widower; Elizabeth, d, 102.67
Margarett, 110.19
Sarah, ser, 107B.3

CHESTERMAN: William; Susan, w, 107C.35

CHETIOM: Mary, wid, £600, 101.56

CHETTLE: John; Mary, w; John, s, 109.36

CHETWIN: John, 109.71

CHHDDINGTON: Benjamin; Sarah, w;
Elizabeth; Cicaly, d, 107B.39

CHIBBUCK: Jos; Elizabeth, w, 104.109

CHICKOE: John, bach, 103.101

CHIDLEY: John; Martha, w; John, s; Mary,
d, 107B.15

CHIFFINS: Jane;

CHILD:
~, wid, 105.10
Amey, 107A.38
Edward, 101.45
Elinor, 109.39
Elizabeth, 98.38, 103.235
Francis; Mary, w; Elizabeth, d, 109.78
Francis, sir, bach, 106.56
Francis, commissioner, 106.69
Hannah, 109.70
Henry, ser, 106.58
Jane, 102.170
John, 102.216
John; Frances, w, 107D.96
John, app, 98.8
John, bach, esq, 106.46
Margaret, ser, 106.43
Mary; Mary, d, 107B.55
Mary, ser, 109.5
Michael; Mary, w, 107B.48
Mosses; Catherine, w, 103.167
Richard, 99.51
Richard; Anne, w, 105.13
Robert, clerk, 98.48
Stephen, ser, 106.56

Thomas, 103.187
Thomas; Mary, w; Thomas, s, 104.2
Willfery; Mary, w, 103.243
William; Elizabeth, w; Elizabeth, d, 102.272

CHILLENDELL: Mary, 109.35

CHILLINGSWORTH: Henry; Eliz, w, 104.19

CHILLINGWORTH:
Elizabeth, ser, 106.5
Hannah, 102.16
Joseph, bach, 102.16

CHILTON: Edward; Hanah, w, 106.54

CHINERY: William; Mary, w; William, s;
Meane, d?; Jeane, d, 103.157

CHINN: Mary, 101.57

CHINREY: Richard, 106.57

CHIP:
Charles; Martha, w; Mary, d, 101.101
John, ser, 103.95
John, wid; Sarah, d; Samuell, s; Charles, s,
102.201
Mary, ser, 102.145

CHIPPS: Thorne, app, 98.74

CHISSELL: Paul, bach, £600, 104.9

CHISSEWELL:
Elizabeth, 103.250
Richard, app, 103.285

CHITTERBUCX: Stephen, ser, 106.37

CHITTEY:
Henry; Sarah, w, 102.132
Thomas, 110.19

CHITTWOOD: Hanah, pensioner; John, s;
Thomas, s, 103.147

CHITWELL:
John, 103.158
Margeret, 103.158

CHITWIN:
Ralph, app, 98.27
Richard; Frances, w; Mary, d; Elizabeth, d,
107A.27

CHIVERS:
John; Elizabeth, w, 102.195
Roger, app, 107C.8

CHOAKLEY: John; Elizabeth, w, 103.55

CHOCKILL: Mary, 100.10

CHORLEY: Henry; Winifred, w; Sam, s,
104.27

CHOTHARN: Anne, 102.120

CHRISLOWE: Thomas; Jane, w, 98.11

CHRISTIAN:
Ben, ser, 104.116
David; Jane, w, 104.103

CHRISTINAS: Ann; Elizabeth, d,
109.64

CHRISTMAS:
Elizabeth, wid; Elizabeth, d; John, s; Alice
Hart, her mother, 103.17
John, 102.72
Michael; Debora, w, 101.16
Thomas, ser, 106.55

CHRISTOPHER:
Anne, 102.105
Anthony; Hannah, w, 102.258
Hannah, 102.105
Marmaduke, 102.105
Thomas, ser, 98.75

CHRISTWAITE: Marvill, 102.242

CHUBBS: Thomas; Elizabeth, w; Elizabeth,
d; Rachell, d, 103.80

CHUCH: Samuell; Jane, w, 101.93

CHUN: William; Elizabeth, w; Hanna, d,
101.41

CHURCH:
Anthony, ?gent, £600, bach, 104.12
Gabrill; Hester, w; Owen, s; Katharine, d,
102.40
Geo; Mary, w, 104.71
John, 109.45
John; Easter, w, 98.33
John, bach, 106.68
Margarett, 110.36
Mary, 102.32
Samuell; Elizabeth, w, 103.257
Susan; Josiah, s; Mary, d; Abraham, s,
102.26

CHURCHELL: Mary, 102.58

CHURCHER: Catherine, 109.83

CHURCHILL:
Henry, 109.41
Joseph; Anne, w; Thomas, s, 102.144

CHURCHMAN:
Aron, w; Lidiah, w; Mary, d, 107D.95
Nathaniel, 109.26

CHURCHWELL: Sarah, 102.12

CHYMIST: Nicholas; Jane, w; Mary, d,
98.5

CIBUS: John, 99.11

CILL: Mary, ser, 106.19

CIMMILL: Elizabeth, 99.13

CITHAM: Elizabeth, wid, 103.65

CLACK:
John, ser, 103.181
Nathaniel; Mabill, w; Mary, d, 103.51

CLACKSTONE: William; Anne, w; Richard
Purcer, grand-s of, 107B.57

CLAN: Mary, 98.83

CLAPHAM:
Duglas, 107D.33
Christopher; Ellinor, w, 104.8
James; Profeisa, w; Anne, d, 103.28
Rebecca; Walter, s, 102.120

CLARANSE: Ann; Isaack, s; Maudlin, d;
Ann, d; Elizabeth, d; Judeth, d;

CLARE:
~, 106.21
Andrew; Hanah, w, 102.267
Ann, a child, 109.14
Benjamin; Anne, w; Anne, d; George, s,
110.16
Francis, gent; Sarah, w; Sarah, d; Susannah,
d, 98.28
Henry, £50 p.a.; Johanna, w, 106.31
Joseph; Jane, w, 107B.68
Joseph; Jane, w; Mary, d, 107D.84
Margery, 107B.37
Robert, app, 101.44, 104.31
William, 107D.93
William, bach, 102.58

CLAREBUT: Elizabeth, 101.22

CLARGIS: Andrew; Faith, w,
104.22

CLARIDGE:
Ann, spinster, 103.85
Elizabeth, spinster, 103.85
Thomas; Elizabeth, w, 104.78
Thomas; Mary, w; Edward, s; Mary, d, 106.14
Thomas, bach, 103.184

CLARISH: Mary, spinster;

CLARKE:
~, bach, 104.16
Alexander, app, 101.85
Alice, 101.87
Anne; Anne, d; Mary, d; William, s, 102.97
Anne, ser, 103.25
Atwood, bach, 102.56
Barbary, wid, 103.55
Benjamin, 110.3
Benjamin; Susannah, w, 98.7
Catherine, 109.82
Charles; Ruth, w; Charles, s; John, s, 103.222
Christopher; Ann, w, 104.117
Christopher; Mary, w, 109.82
Christopher; Jone, w, 110.6
Christopher, ser, 102.115
Delilah; Mary, d, 109.9
Daniel; Eliz, w, 104.20
Edmond; Hannah, w; Edmond, s; John, s,
102.92
Edward, 101.93
Edward, £600; Jane, w, 104.81
Elizabeth; John, s; Elizabeth, d, 98.46
Elizabeth; Andrew, s, 103.168
Elizabeth, pensioner, 103.41
Elizabeth, wid; Richard, s; Elizabeth, d;
Phillip, s, 103.9
Faith, ser, 104.7
Frances, 102.88, 107B.1
Frances, wid, 104.86
Francis, 107D.65, 109.77
Francis; Jane, w; John, s; Elizabeth, d, 98.44
Francis, £600; Anne, w; Anne, d, 106.45
Francis, app, 98.33
Francis Edward, grand-s of Tew, 98.36
George; Anne, w; Mary, d; Anne, d, 100.5
George; Amey, w; George, s, 101.68
George; Elizabeth, w; George, s, 102.272
George; Anne, w; Elizabeth, d; Mary, d,
104.60
George; Mary, w, 106.35
George, app, 103.24
Griffin; Hanah, w; Phillis, d; Samuel, s;
Mary, d, 107B.60
Hanah, pensioner; Hanah, d, 103.144
Henry, 102.163
Henry; Anne, w; Mary, d, 98.71
Henry, bach, 104.15
Henry, gent; Anne, w, 98.27
James, app, 103.249

CLAVELL: Roger, £50 p.a.; Ruth, w, 106.43

CLAVER: Richard; Honor, w; Thomas, s;
Mary Abbot, d, 107B.52

CLAVEY: John; Mary, w, 107D.48

CLAWSON: Thomas; Ann, w; Bridget, d;
Elizabeth, d, 103.72

CLAXTON:
Mathew; Emma, w, 109.4
William, 99.7

CLAY:
Arthur, bach, 104.102
Eliza, 104.102
Elizabeth; Elizabeth, d; Anne, d; Emme, d,
107D.59
Kath, 104.114
Robt, app, ?bach, 104.114
Thomas; Mary, w, 109.9
William; Susana, w; William, s, 102.261

CLAYPOOLE:
Lucy, 101.140
Thomas, 107B.37

CLAYTON:
Anne, 102.72
Edward, 101.57
John; Hanah, w; Febyan, s; John, s, 102.219
John, gent; Lucy, w; Anne, d, 98.39
John, ser, 107B.3, 109.57
Mary, 109.84
Rebecca, wid; Paul, s; Elizabeth, d, 102.50
Robert, ser, 107A.28
Thomas, 102.13
Thomas; Margaret, w, 102.260
Wm; Mary, w; Mary, d; Eliz, d, 104.69

CLEAN: Isaac; Constance, w; Constance, d;
~, child, 100.11

CLEAR:
Jane, 101.14
Joseph; Sarah, w, 107C.13
Mary, pensioner, wid, 103.16

CLEAVE: Martha, ser, 98.39

CLEAVER:
Jane, 98.55
William; Mary, w; William, s; Mary, d;
Elizabeth, d; Sarah, d, 98.49

CLEAVES:
Deborah, 104.109
Mary, 107B.77

CLEDGE: Thomas; Mary, w, 98.9

CLEE: John; Bridgitt, w; Elizabeth, d, 102.42

CLEETER:
Edward, ser, 109.33
George; Sarah, w, 104.123
George; Elizabeth, w, 104.140
Robert; Elizabeth, w, 104.107
William, 104.140

CLEFT:
Elizabeth, ser, 100.12
Francis; ~, w, 100.12
Matthew, ser, 100.12

CLEGG: Isaac; Martha, w, 103.11

CLEGGAT: Mary; William, s; George, s,
101.61

CLEMENT:
Anne, 98.10, 109.13
Elizabeth; Harry, w, 98.10
John; Mary, w, 104.35
Mary, d; Mary, d, 106.63
Phillip, app, 98.16
Samuell, bach; Hester, sister of, 106.15
Thomas; Alice, w; Mary, d;

CLEMENTS:
~, 103.228
Daniell; Johana, d?, 102.130
Edward; Jane, w; Edward, s; Elizabeth, d;
Mary, d, 102.90
Elizabeth, 109.89
George, 107C.30
Joane, 102.130
John; Jeane, w; Anne, d, 103.97
John; Frances, w, 107C.4
John; Frances, w, 109.36
Mary, wid; Jeane, d; Peter, s; Susan, d; Mary,
d; Joseph, s, 103.211
Susan, 103.211

CLEMSON: William; Elianor, w; Elizabeth,
d; John, s; William, s; Thomas, s, 107B.54

CLEN:
John, 102.112
William; Sarah, w, 109.84

CLENCH:
George; Anne, w, 102.122
Thomas; Ruth, w; Elizabeth, d; Hannah, d,
102.131

CLENDON:
Hanah, 107B.17

Henry; Margaret, w; James, s, 107A.3
Thomas;

CLERKE:
~, wid, 105.2
Elizabeth, 106.16
John, 105.16
John; Sarah, w; Samuell, s; Rebecca, d, 106.2
John; Margaret, w; John, s; William, s,
    106.15
Samuel, 105.18
Thomas, ser, 105.16, 106.2

CLETHEROW:
Benjamin; Mary, w; Lucrasha, d; Benjamin,
    s, 103.43
Benjamin; Sarah, w; Benjamin, s, 103.119
Christopher; Ann, w, 103.100
Michael; Ellinor, w, 107D.58

CLEVENGER: John; Mary, w; Jacob, s;
    John, s; Elizabeth, d, 102.122

CLEVERTON: Daniell, app, 98.73

CLEWS: Marg, ser, 104.51

CLEYSON: Francis; Katherine, w; Elizabeth,
    d; Francis, s, 103.40

CLIFFE:
John; Hanah, w, 103.229
Thomas, bach, 109.97

CLIFFORD:
Elizabeth, 102.3
Isaac; Sarah, w, 107B.23
John; Mary, w, 104.48
Kath, 104.71
Mary, 102.59
Temperance, wid, 103.284
William, 107B.24
William; Mary, w; Mary, d, 103.45

CLIFT:
Hanah, ser, 103.237
Mary, ser;

CLIFTON:
~; Anne, w; ~, child, 104.133
Edward; Ellen, w; Mary, d; Sarah, d, 102.25
Elizabeth; Elizabeth, d; Anne, d, 98.62
Henry, 109.44
John, 109.79
Mary, 109.38
Marthew, bach, 106.56
Richard, 106.52
Trehand, 106.52
Wm, bach, 104.42

CLIMPPS: John; Alice, w, 103.4

CLIMSON:
Henry; Grace, w, 109.111
Roger; Elizabeth, w, 103.117
Sarah, ser, 98.71
Thomas; Ann, w; Katherine, d, 103.103

CLINCH:
Anne, 101.93
Elizabeth, pensioner, 103.153
Henry; Elizabeth, w, 106.42

CLINGOE: Elizabeth, ser, 98.29

CLINT: Elizabeth, ser, 98.69

CLIPSON: Elizabeth, 99.52

CLIPTON: John, app, 103.73

CLISALL: Robert, ser, 102.149

CLISBY: Jane Duntham, John, d of, 107B.55

CLISHBY: Anne Duntham, John, grand-d of,
    107B.55

CLITHEROW: Joane, 102.66

CLIVERSTONE: William, 109.15

CLOAKE:
Elizabeth, 101.77
John; Kath, w, 104.23

CLOPTON: Amy, 101.109

CLOTON: Mary, 102.3

CLOUD: Richard, ser, 102.85

CLOUFFE: John; Jeane, w; John, s; Edward,
    s; William, s; Jeane, d, 103.69

CLOUGH:
Izabellah, 98.83
Izabella, wid, 103.66

CLOUNSLEY: Elizabeth, 109.76

CLOUSLY: Martha, 109.94

CLOUTER: Sarah, ser, 109.9

CLOWDS: Joseph; Mary, w; Samuell, s;
    Sarah, d; Elizabeth, d, 102.238

CLOWDSLEY: Paul, bach, £600, 104.4

CLOWES:
James; Jane, w, 98.2
Johana, wid, 103.67
John, a boy, 101.109
Thomas, wid; Thomas, s, 103.266

CLUBB: Edward, 101.28

CLUDSLEY: Elizabeth, 109.111

CLUFFE:
John; Mary, w; Jervas, s; Rebecca, d,
110.24
Robert; Alice, w; Joseph, s; John, s, 110.22

CLUM: John; Elizabeth, w; Elizabeth, d,
102.98

CLUTTERBUCK: John, bach, 98.6

CLYBORNE: Thomas; Mary, w, 106.15

COAKER, See Coker

COALE:
Anne, 102.50
Benjamin, 102.60
Joseph; Elizabeth, w; Benjamin, s; Joseph, s;
Amos, s, 102.20
Margarett, 102.13

COANES: George; Anne, w; Anne, d,
101.60

COAPE, See Cope

COAPSTICK: Robert, ser, 109.27

COARE: Mary, ser, 109.6

COAREY: Fardinando; Jeane, w, 103.55

COAST: Robert, 105.18

COATES:
Alexander, bach, 98.50
Benjamin; Mary, w; Benjamin, s; Joseph, s;
Mary, d, 109.6
Cicely, 110.32
Elizabeth, 102.126
Elizabeth, ser, 106.37
James, 105.17
James; Jone, w, 107C.26
John; Elizabeth, w, 102.129
John, app, 102.195
Lucina, pensioner, wid, 103.15
Nicholas; Frances, w, 103.52
Ralph, app, 107A.40
Richard; Katherine, w, 103.91

COB:
Fredrick, 101.53
George, ser, 106.40
John; Robert, s, 102.257
John; Sarah, w; Sarah, d, 107A.37
Josuah; Elizabeth, w; Elizabeth, d,
107B.15
Robert; Lidia, w, 101.96
Tho, bach, 104.26

COBBETT:
James; Elizabeth, w, 103.290
Sarah, 103.290

COBBIG: Anne; John, s, 102.131

COBBS: Rachell, ser, 103.139

COBDELL: William, app, 103.59

COBDEN:
John, app, 103.283
Rebecca, ser, 103.18

COBHAM:
Fran, 104.87
John; Elizabeth, w; Sarah, d; Mary, d;
Nathaniell, s, 102.53
Priscilla, 104.71
Thomas, app, 98.51

COBLEY: Grace, 104.107

COBNER:
John, 98.77
William, 98.77

COBSON: Robert; Frances, w; Robert, s;
Frances, s, 98.5

COBURNE: Marjery, 109.29

COCK:
Ann, wid, 103.96
Edward; Martha, w, 103.3
Edward John, ser, 109.9
Elizabeth, a parish child, 109.63
Henry; Elizabeth, w, 107B.29
John, bach, 98.65
Mary; Anne, d, 98.10
Mary, ser, 98.3
Robert; Deborah, w; Mary, d; Abigall, d,
103.35
Samuell; Anne, w, 101.92
Susan, wid, 103.94
Thomas; Elizabeth, w, 102.52
Thomas; Elizabeth, w, 102.101

COCKAINE, See Cokayne

63

COCKBILL:
John, app, 98.35
Richard; Rebeccah, w; Richard, s, 98.35

COCKEN: John, clerk, 98.37

COCKER:
Catherine, ser, 103.16
Mary, ser, 103.259

COCKERELL: Susanna, 110.8

COCKERY:
Elizabeth, 110.31
John; Elizabeth, w; John, s; Katherine, d;
    Susan, d; William, s, 103.53
Thomas; Frances, w; William, s, 110.31

COCKETT:
Anne, 98.22, 107A.8
Anne, wid, 103.265
John, 102.91
Leticia, ser, 107D.34
Robert, 109.51
Thomas, 102.91
Thomas; Mary, w, 98.19
Thomas, app, 104.106

COCKHAM: George, wid, 103.145

COCKHILL:
Anne, ser, 102.111
Mary, 107B.23

COCKIN:
Elizabeth, 110.26
Elizabeth, wid; Alice, d; Benjamin, s, 102.64
Hanah, 99.41, 110.26
Jonathan, 99.41
Philipium, 99.41

COCKLE:
John, ser, 103.293
Mary, wid, 102.266
Thomas; Anne, w; John, s, 102.266

COCKLEY: James; Susan, w; Joseph, s,
    102.45

COCKLIN: Daniel, wid, 109.33

COCKNOT: Elizabeth, ser, 100.13

COCKPITT: Henry, app, 98.10

COCKRUM: Margaret, 98.56

COCKS: George, ser, 103.129
Sarah, wid, 103.274

Stephen; Mary, w; Stephen, s, 102.37
Thomas; Anne, w; Anne, d; Thomas, s,
    110.10

COCKSHAW: Isabella, 109.48

COCKSHIT: Robert, 109.31

COCKSHUTT: Katherine, 102.226

COCKSON:
George; Mary, w, 102.179
Stephen; Mary, w; Elizabeth, d, 102.103

COCKWAFT: Caleb; Rebecca, w, 103.118

CODDINGTON: John; Mary, w; William, s,
    107D.63

COE:
Mary; William, s, 103.15
Sarah, 102.32

COEFEILD: James, ser, 109.7

COEING: Robert; Elizabeth, w, 98.7

COETT: Gilbert; Mary, w, 104.40

COFELAND:
Anne, 107A.8
William, 103.275

COFFE: Benjamin; Sarah, w, 98.8

COFFEE:
Mary; Mary, d, 107D.99
Patrick; Katherine, w; Mary, d; Charlott, d;
    Charles, s, 103.25

COFFELL: John; Elizabeth, w, 110.27

COFFLESTONE:
Amos, bach, 104.102
Christopher, 109.110
Mary, 109.78

COFKSTAKE: Mary, ser, 102.1

COGAN: Christian, ser, 106.59

COGDELL:
Elizabeth; William, s, 107A.13
Martha, ser, 103.85

COGDEN: Mary, 104.70

COGGEN:
Anne, 104.29

64

Jos; Eliz, w; Tho, s; Hannah, d, 104.54

Susan, 104.29

COGGER:
John; Eleanor, w, 102.124
William, app, 107D.36

COGGIN:
John; Elizabeth, w; Mary, d; Sarah, d;
Charity, d, 103.30
John, ser, 106.19

COGGS: Edward; Susan, w; Susan Burgis, d;
Mary, d, 103.230

COGSWELL: John; Anne, w; Mary, d, 98.14

COHORNE: George, bach, 103.225

COKAYNE:
James; Elizabetha, w; James, s, 102.9
Peter, app, 107D.87

COKE: Jone; Eliz, w, 104.40

COKER:
Charles; Jane, w, 98.43
Jonathan, a boy, 104.92
Tho; Mary, w, 104.23
Wm, ser, bach?, 104.26

COLBORNE: Anne, 107B.65

COLBRATH: Robert; Joyce, w; Robert, s,
101.13

COLBURCH: George, 102.209

COLCHESTER: Elizabeth, ser, 102.167

COLCOTT:
Elizabeth, 102.102
Thomas, £600; Daniell, s; Thomas, s; Grace,
d, 102.102

COLCUT: Jane, 106.66

COLDROCK: William; Rebecah, w;

COLE:
~, 104.61
~, Mrs, 104.61
Alice, 109.106
Alice, ser, 101.57
Ambrose, clerk, ?bach, 104.75
Anne, 101.4
Anne, ser, 103.92, 104.96
Anne, wid, 103.47
Edward; Elizabetha, w, 98.3

Edward; Elizabetha, w; Henry, s; Sara, d, 101.82
Edward; Jane, w, 109.32
Elizabeth, ser, 104.21
Francis; Mary, w, 109.8
George; Hanah, w; Joseph, s; Sarah, d, 103.57
George; Mary, w; Sarah, d, 109.41
Henry; Elizabetha, w, 109.82
Jas; Kath, w; Rebecca, d, 104.31
Jane; Elizabetha, d, 107D.86
John; Elizabetha, w; Mary, d?; Elizabetha, d?,
99.26
John; Mary, w; Martha, d; Hanna, d;
Elizabetha, d, 101.97
John; Alice, w; John, s; William, s, 103.48
John; Alice, w; John, s; Elizabetha, d;
William, s, 103.72
John; Jeane, w, 103.165
John; Elizabetha, w, 107C.30
John; Elizabetha, w, 109.59
John; Martha, w, 109.82
Jonathon; Joane, w, 103.131
Joseph; Dorothy, w, 104.99
Joseph; Mary, w; Mary, d; Hannah, d;
Margaret, d; Joseph, s; Sarah, d, 109.13
Katherine, 110.15
Margarett, 109.62
Mary, 98.25, 101.74
Mary, dead, 102.275
Mary, wid, 103.10
Nathaniel; Agnus, w; Ellinor, d; Nathaniel, s;
John, s, 103.116
Richard, pensioner; Rebecca, w, 103.253
Richard, ser, 102.107
Robert; Hanah, w, 106.48
Robert, app, 98.82
Samuel; Elizabeth, w; Mary, d, 103.102
Samuel; Mary, w, 107D.89
Susan, ser, 103.123
Thomas, 105.17, 109.82
Thomas; Mary, w; Thomas, s, 102.108
Thomas; Elizabeth, w, 102.196
Thomas; Ellinor, w, 103.47
Thomas; Martha, w; Susan, d, 106.47
Thomas; Sarah, w; Sarah, d, 108.1
Thomas; Margaret, w, 109.21
Thomas; Anne, w; Benjamin, s; John, s,
109.102
Thomas, ser, 106.61
William; Bridget, w, 103.12
William; Ellinor, w; William, s; Richard, s,
103.45
William; Sarah, w, 103.76
William; Sarah, w, 103.156
William; Sarah, w; Mary, d; John, s, 103.156
William; Elizabeth, w; Daniel, s, 104.86

COLEBACKE:
Edward; Margaret, w, 107C.7
William; Mary, w; Thomas, s, 103.52

COLEBECK: Charles, 109.111

COLEBRONE: Sibellah, ser, 98.25

COLEBROOKE: John, £50 p.a.; Mary, w, 102.58

COLEBROUGH: Joseph, ser, 106.14

COLEBY:
Eliz, 104.66
Theodore; Anne, w, 104.25

COLEGRAVE:
John; Sarah, w, 102.184
William; Anne, w; Ann, d; Margaret, d, 104.102
William, app, bach?, 104.108

COLEHAM: Edward; Elizabeth, w, 103.72

COLEMAN:
Alice, wid, 102.10
Anne, 102.232
Avelin, 109.66
Elizabeth, 106.24
Elizabeth, ser, 103.132
Francis, a boy; Sarah, sister, 104.30
Henry; Elizabeth, w; Samuell, s?; Joseph, s?; Elizabeth, d?, 99.48
Jane, 109.105
Jeremiah; Susannah, w; Susannah, d, 98.17
John; Anne, w; Elizabeth, d; Christian, d; Sarah, d, 98.78
Robert; Anne, w; Robert, s; Anne, d; Stephen, s; Elizabeth, d, 102.30
Stephen; Elizabeth, w; Elizabeth, d, 101.21
Thomas, bach, 103.118
Thomas, parish boy, 103.80
William, 110.12

COLES:
Anne, ser, 102.91
Charles; Sarah, w; John, s; William, s; Charles, s, 109.49
Elizabeth, 109.68
John; Mary, w, 103.4
John; Mary, w; Ann, d, 103.142
John, ser, 103.11, 109.61
Jonathan, 102.93
Richard; Mary, w; John, s; Mary, d; Elizabeth, d; Anne, d, 107A.36
Thomas; Elizabeth, 107A.29
Thomas, £50 p.a., assessor; Mary, w, 102.222
Thomas, assessor, 102.276

COLESON, See Coloson

COLLAGE: Sarah, 102.134

COLLEDGE: Richard; Mary, w, 100.6

COLLER: Jeane, ser, 103.235

COLLES: Margaret, 106.35

COLLET:
Christopher; Elizabeth, 107D.36
Elias; Katherine, w; Katherine, d, 102.78
Jeane, ser, 103.286
John; Ellianor, w, 101.55
John; Elizabeth, w; Elizabeth, d; Jamesh, s, 103.55
John; Martha, w; John, s; Elizabeth, d, 107B.72
John; Mary, w; Sarah, d, 109.47
Mary John, d of Williams, 107D.4
Mary, ser, 107B.80
Richard, app, 98.13
Susannah John, d of Williams, 107D.4
Thomas, 103.285
William; William, s, 109.75
William; Rachell, w, 109.91

COLLEY:
Edward; Ursula, w; Elizabeth, d, 102.84
Elizabeth, ser, 106.29
Frances, pensioner, 106.8
James, 102.256
Richard, ser, 106.29
Thomas; Sarah, w; Thomas, s; John, s;

COLLIER:
~, wid; Martha, d; Hannah, d, 109.65
Ann, Shoreditch parish child, 103.36
Ann, wid, 103.194
Doroas, 101.10
Edward; Barbary, w; Mary, d, 103.115
Elizabeth, 98.23
George; Susanna, w; Sarah, d; Mary, d, 102.127
Gilbert; Alice, w, 103.231
Henry, ser, 106.10
Isabell, ser, 101.57
Jeremiah, bach, 106.11
Jervis, ?bach, 104.62
John; Mary, w, 100.4
John, pensioner; Ann, w; James, s, 103.103
John, ser, 103.237, 107A.12
Joseph; Lydia, w; Thomas, s; Susan, d; Elizabeth, d, 108.6
Joseph, £600; Sarah, w; Sarah, d; Joseph, s; Susan, d, 103.237
Mary, ser, 98.25
Mary, wid, 103.13
Nicholas, 101.30
Richard; Margarett, w; Hannah, d, 102.115
Richard, app, 102.19
Thomas, 107C.14

William, 109.99
William, £600, wid; John, s; William, s;
  James, s; Joseph, s; Mary, d; Sarah, d;
  Anne, d; Elizabeth, d, 102.116

COLLINGTON:
Elizabeth, spinster, 103.30
John, a boy, 104.11
Susanna; Anne, d;

COLLINGWOOD:
~, Mrs, 98.59
Daniel; Anne, w; John, s; Daniel, s, 104.58
Rebecca, 98.16
Thomas; Margaret, w, 109.84

COLLINS:
Anne, 101.47, 109.105
Anne; Rosela, d, 98.78
Audery; Sarah, d; Elizabeth, d; Mary, d,
  110.30
Benjamin; Mary, w, 107B.3
Edward, ser, 103.163
Elizabeth; Susannah Adams, d; Elizabeth
  Collins, d, 107D.19
Elizabeth, ser, 98.72
Feby, 102.238
Freeman; Susan, w; John, s; Freeman, s;
  Mary, s; Hannah, d, 109.80
Freeman, assessor in Old Baily precinct,
  109.112
Gabriell; Mary, w; Thomasin, d, 106.55
Hanah, 102.170
Hanah, ser, 103.186
Henry; Sibill, w, 103.7
Henry, ser, 104.61, 106.10
Jane, 101.102
Joane, 106.54
John, 101.47, 109.75
John; Mary, w, 98.38
John; Elizabeth, w; John, s; Mary, d, 103.90
John; Mary, w; William, s; Elizabeth, d,
  109.106
Joseph, 109.111
Joyce, 107D.100
Lewkner, 110.36
Lewkner; Thomasin, w, 110.36
Margaret, ser, 107A.29
Martha, ser, 106.64
Mary, ser, 104.104
Olive, ser, 103.4
Richard; Elizabeth, w, 98.74
Richard; Mary, w; Sarah, d; Elizabeth, d,
  103.170
Robert; Mary, w, 110.22
Samuell; Alice, w, 109.89
Thomas, 101.6
Thomas; Martha, w, 98.7
Thomas; Elizabeth, w, 107D.61

Thomas, bach, under age, 103.53
Ursula; Anne, d, 107D.9
William, 98.20
William; Lucrasha, w; Susan, d, 103.4

COLLIS:
George, 109.105
Lettice, 102.3

COLLISON:
Cisley; Margaret, d; John, s; William, s,
  109.18
Elizabeth, 109.62
James; Mary, w; Mary, d?, 99.50
John; Mary Magdalen, w; Mary, d, 109.89
Mary, 102.182
William; Elienor, w, 102.250

COLLWELL: George, ser, 106.56

COLLYWAY: Mary, 99.33

COLNY: Jane, 102.61

COLRUCK: Elizabeth, 101.82

COLSON:
John, 107C.32
John; Christian, w; John, s; Christian, d;
  Elizabeth, d; Sarah, d, 98.86
Mary; John, s, 98.3
Peter, 109.74
Samuel, wid; Samuell, s; John, s; Owin, s;
  Mary, d, 98.87
Thomas; Alice, w; Elizabeth, d, 103.41

COLSTON: Benjamin, 105.16

COLSWORTH: John, 104.102

COLT:
Elizabeth, 109.66
John; Mary, w, 106.21
Rachell; John, s; Hanah, d, 107B.25

COLTEMOR: Mary, 102.249

COLTHER: John; Elizabeth, w; Benjamin, s;
  John, s; Joseph, s; Sarah, d,
  107B.49

COLTMAN:
Lidia, ser, 106.62
Richard; Elizabeth, w, 103.160
William; Bridget, w; William, s; Henry, s;
  Elizabeth, d; Anne, d, 101.61
William; Anne, w; Anne, d, 104.82

COLTON: Thomas, 102.7

COLTROP:
Mary, 109.4
Thomas; Sarah, w, 103.115

COLVER: Mary, 102.112

COLVERD: Anne, 102.240

COLVERT:
Elizabeth, ser, 98.57
George, 102.250

COLWORTH: George, bach, under age,
103.202

COMBS:
Ann, wid, 100.5
Anthony; Elizabeth, d, 102.121
Caleb, 109.60
Catherine, ser, 100.5
Elifalett; Anne, w; Daniell, s; John, s; Mary,
d; Sarah, d, 102.148
Elizabeth, 101.87
Geo, ?bach, 104.28
John; Mary, w, 101.5
John; Margaret, w, 104.52
John; Sarah, w; Theophilus, s?; Elizabeth, d?;
Richard, s?; Daniell, s?, 110.7
Judith, 98.88
Richard, 101.5
Robert, app, 103.131
Roger, 104.118
Samuell; Dorothy, w; John, s; Margaret, d,
102.93
Sarah, 102.61, 110.6
William; Mary, w; Mary, d; Anne, d; Sara, d,
101.34

COMBY:
Amy, 102.79
Hannah; Hannah, d, 102.101

COMLEY: Richard; Ellinor, w, 103.5

COMMANDER:
Elizabeth, ser, 107D.18
John; Dorcas, w; John, s, 109.54

COMMERFORD: Anne, 98.71

COMMINGS: John; Barberah, w, 107A.18

COMPIER: John, app, 98.27

COMPTON:
Anne, 109.90
Anthony, bach, 109.58
Dinah, 109.58
Elizabeth, ser, 100.11

Gartrite; Rebecca, d; Thomas, s, 107C.11
Hannah, 104.122
Hooper, ser, 100.13
Jonathon, app, 103.84
Joseph; Ann, w; John, s, 109.49
Mary, ser, 109.58
Tho, app, 104.82
William; Fabey, w, 99.31

CONDIT: Richard; Grace, w, 102.249

CONDUIT:
John; Frances, w; James, s; John, s, 103.144
Sarah, ser, 98.66

CONEY:
Ambrose; Mary, w; William, s, 109.99
Daniell, 102.72
Jacob; Frances, w, 107D.54
John, esq; Jane, w; John, s; Mary, d, 104.4
Judey, 102.218
Mary, 104.55
Richard; Anne, w; Mary, d;

CONEYGROVE:
~, 102.235

CONGER: Elizabeth, ser, 98.70

CONGRAVE: William, bach, 106.50

CONIAM: Deborah, 109.94

CONINGSBY:
John; Mary, w, 109.60
Mary, 106.47

CONKLIN: Charles; Elizabeth, w; Dorothy,
d, 107D.32

CONNELL:
Mary, ser, 104.5
Sarah, 102.218

CONNETT: John; Eliz, w; Eliz, d; Mary, d;
John, s, 104.117

CONNEY: Hugh, 106.45

CONNINGHAN: Dorcas, pensioner; Charles,
s; Dorcas, d; Edward, 109.60

CONNINGS: Elizabeth;

CONNOCK:
~, wid; Phillippa, d, 104.60

CONNOWAY: Anne; Hannah, d; Sarah, s,
98.65

Thomas; Margaret, w; Elizabeth, d, 100.5
Thomas; Mary, w; Susan, d; William, s, 101.79
Thomas; Margaret, w, 102.143
Thomas; Susannah, w, 109.26
Thomas, app, 103.196
Thomas, bach, 103.66
William, 109.36
William; Isabell, w, 107B.54
William; Hannah, w; James, s; William, s; John, s; Mary, d, 107C.1
William; Zipra, w, 107C.37
William; Elizabeth, w, 109.18
William; Margaret, w, 109.50
William, esq; Jane, w; Susan, d, 104.75
William, bach, 103.56
William, 101.31
William, ser, bach?, 104.6

COOKES: Edward, 102.195

COOKMAN:
Dan; Ellinor, w; Dan, s, bach; Anne, d; Dorothy, d, 104.90
Samuell; Anne, w; Mathew, s; Anne, d, 110.15

COOKSON: William; Mary, w; Anthony, s; William, s, 102.64

COOLEY:
Abraham; Margarett, w; Margaret, d, 109.35
Charles; Martha, w, 110.12
Dorothy, 102.152
Henry; Elizabeth, w; Henry, s, 102.222
John; Sarah, w, 107D.7
Robert, ser, 107D.90
Thomas; Margarett, w; Abraham, s?, 99.35
William; Mary, w, 107C.40

COOLING:
Noah; Jane, w, 100.9
Joseph, 110.6
William, £600, gent; Margaret, w; Elizabeth, d; Mary, d; Susan, sister of, 104.10

COOMBES, See Combs

COOME: Rcbecca, ser, 106.16

COOMER: Mary, 101.82

COOP: Thomas; Sarah, w;

COOPER:
~, Mr; ~, w; Benjamin, s; ~; ~, w, 104.75
Alice, wid; Rebecca, d, 103.93
Benjamin; Martha, w; Benjamin, s; Joseph, s; John, s, 107A.23

Bridget, ser, 103.225
Caleb, £600; Susanah, w; Joshua, s; Susan, d; Sarah, d; John, s; Caleb, s, 103.245
Charles; Joyce, w; Katherine, d, 102.59
Charles, at sea; Rebecca, w, 103.107
Clement; Martha, d, 98.84
David; Elizabeth, w, 107B.36
Edmund, app, 107D.43
Edward; Jane, w; Edward, s; William, s, 98.6
Edward; Ruth, w; Edward, s; Ruth, d; Mary, d, 107C.6
Francis, 99.33
George; Bridgett, w, 98.72
Grace, 107B.34
Hanah; Richard, s, 103.231
Henry; Alice, w; Henry, s, 104.88
James, 109.82
James; Jone, w; Mary, d, 101.47
Joan, 104.102
John; Anne, w, 98.16
John; Amy, w; Sarah, d, 98.82
John; Sarah, w; Thomas, s; Samuell, s, 102.58
John; Anne, w; Elizabeth, d; Virgin, d, 102.83
John; Anne, w, 102.122
John; Elizabeth, w; Anne, d; Samuell, s; Mary, d, 103.262
John, app, 103.5, 104.77
John, bach, 109.32
John, ser, 98.57
Joseph, wid, 103.187
Katharine, 102.80
Mary; John, s; Jane, d; James, s; William, s, 101.14
Mary, app, 104.94
Mary, ser, 103.79, 106.57
Mary, wid, 103.65, 103.165
Nicholas, 107B.74
Peter; Frances, w; Thomas, s; Ann, d, 109.36
Peter; Elizabeth, w, 99.13
Peter, collector, 109.112
Rebecca; Rebecca, d, 106.15
Richard; Mary, w; Joyce, d; Thomas, s, 103.57
Richard; Hannah, w; Sarah, d; Mary, d, 110.8
Richard, £600, bach, 104.4
Richard John, s of Johson, 109.54
Sarah, ser, 103.287
Thomas; Elizabeth, w; John, s; Elizabeth, d, 102.119
Thomas; Mary, w, 108.4
Thomas; Mary, w; Thomas, s, 110.27
Thomas, senior; Thomas, s, ?bach, 104.99
William, 109.82
William; Mary, w; Peter, s, 107C.29
William; Elizabeth, w, 109.76
William, ser, 102.104, 106.12
William, ser, bach?, 104.15

COORE: Jane, 104.61

COOTE: Agnis, 104.57

COOTES: Frances, 99.37

COPE:
Dorothy, ser, 107D.98
Elizabeth, ser, 107C.12
John; Jane, w, 105.10
John, £600, bach, 106.38
Mary, ser, 104.3
Millington; Alice, w, 101.13
Samuell; ~, w; Ann, d, 100.8
Sarah, 104.86
Stephen, bach, 99.20
William; Sarah, w, 107A.34
William, app, 104.52

COPEE: James; Jane, w; Jamesh, s; Jane, d;
  Martha, d, 102.252

COPINGER: Jarvias; Elizabeth, w; Jarvis, s,
  102.171

COPLANDS: Mary, 102.119

COPLITT: Leonard, 105.5

COPPAGE: Alexander, app, 98.24

COPPING: Mary, 104.47

COPPOCK: Rich; Penelope, w; Rich, s; Jos,
  s; Valentine, s; Robt, s; Susanna, 101.62

COPSON: Christopher; Alice, w, 101.62

CORBETT:
Francis, 106.17
Hanah, 109.17
Richard; Mary, w, 99.3
Samuel; Hanna, w, 105.10
Susan, 109.37
William; Margaret, w, 103.32
William; Elizabeth, w; Peter; Sarah, d, 103.192

CORD:
Elizabeth, ser, 103.89
Henry; Margaret, w; Elizabeth, d; Mary,
  103.75

CORDELL: Richard;

CORDER:
~, 103.163

CORDRY:
Elizabeth, 102.31

Francis, 109.34
Margaret, 107B.56
Samuel; Elizabeth, w; Mary, d, 107C.28
Sarah, ser, 107A.42

CORDWELL: Edward; Mary, w; Edward, s;
  Elizabeth, d, 103.110

CORDWIN: Thomas; Anne, w; Domingo De
  Le Cordy; Pricscilla, w; Rachell, d; Daniel,
  s, 107A.30

COREY: Samuel; Sarah, w; Samuell, s;
  Sarah, d; Anne, d, 102.272

CORFE: Robert; Anne, w; Robert, s,
  102.140

CORK:
Elizabeth, ser, 107C.30
John; Susan, w; John, s; Edward, s; William,
  s; Elizabeth, d, 103.97
Mary, 102.195
Susan, ser, 103.272

CORKER:
Geo; Mary, w, 104.65
John; Anne, w, 105.11
Robert; Robert, s; Mary, d, 101.89

CORKETT: William; Jane, w; Jane, d,
  102.133

CORLEY: Mary, 107D.32

CORMELL: Robert; Sarah, w, 107B.9

CORNBURY: John; Anne, w; James, s;
  Sarah, d; Anne, d; Mary, d, 107A.29

CORNE:
Elizabeth, 107B.63
Francis, ser, 107D.52
John, 107D.5
William; Mary, w; Mary, d; Catherine, d,
  109.95

CORNELIUS:
Henry; Mary, w, 104.123
Martha, 98.22
Robert, 103.129

CORNER:
John; Jeane, w; Elizabeth, d; Jeane, d; Ann, d,
  103.29
George; Mary, w; Elizabeth, d; Martha, d,
  102.31
Hanah, app, 107D.13
William; Elizabeth, w, 107D.79

CORNET:
Ellianor, 101.55
George; Winifred, w; Francis, s, 107A.13

CORNEWELL:
Anne; Anne, d, 101.22
Mary, 107B.61

CORNEY:
John; Abigail, w; John, s, 109.111
Robt, bach, 104.85

CORNIERS: Henrita, 98.60

CORNISH:
Edw, a boy, 104.34
Ellen, 107A.26
George, 103.26
John; Alice, w, 109.13
Joseph, 101.35
Judith, 109.67
Lucretia, ser, 107D.8
Michell; Susan, w; Mary, d, 103.27
Thomas; Jane, w; John, s?; Ann, d?, 99.17

CORNPORT: Robert, £600; Sarah, w;
Robert, s, 102.76

CORNWALL: Tho; Mary, w; Eliz, d; Sarah,
d; Henrietta Maria, d, 104.32

CORPSON: John; Samuell, s; Susanna, d,
106.63

CORTHOFF: Elliza, 104.11

CORTOPP: James; Anne, w; Susannah, d, 98.70

CORY:
Judith, £600; John, s, bach; Eliza, d, 104.1
Sarah, wid; Sarah, d, 102.59

COSEY: John, 109.103

COSHEE: John, 102.116

COSSA: Isaac;

COSSTER:
~, wid, 103.244
John, app, 102.195, 103.202
William, wid, 103.271

COSTIN:
Edward, 109.34
Ellen, 106.8
Hanah, 99.42
Jas; Eliza, w; Jos, s, 104.105
Jane, 99.42

COSYER: Alexander; Alexander, s;
Elizabeth, d; Martha, d, 109.94

COTCHETT: Thomas, ser, 103.240

COTMORE: Edward; Elizabeth, w; Frances,
d, 105.1

COTS:
Anne, ser, 102.86
Elizabeth, 102.222

COTTER:
Edmond, ser, 98.61
John; Sara, w; John, s; Benjamin, s; Jane, d,
105.13
Robert; ~, w; Robert, s, 103.175

COTTERELL:
Isaack; Mary, w, 98.43
Richard; Katharine, w; John, s, 102.12
Sarah, 107C.13
William, ser, 105.15

COTTINGHAM:
Peter, ser, 106.10
Robert; Susannah, w, 109.30

COTTINGTON: Jane, 109.54

COTTON:
Alice, ser, 106.21
Benjamin; Ann, w; Samuell, s, 103.81
James; Mary, w, 109.92
James, £600, bach, 106.58
John, 107B.15, 109.82
John; Marjery, w; Sarah, d, 102.185
John; Ann, w, 103.99
John, app, 98.46
Margarett; Elizabeth, d; Mary, d, 102.233
Mary, ser, 104.27
Richard; Elizabeth, w; Elizabeth, d; Richard,
s; Thomas, s, 109.13
Thomas; Ann, w; Mary, d, 103.137
William, wid hath children in Country parish,
103.109

COTTSFORD:
John; Elizabeth, w, 103.2
William; Elizabeth, w, 103.133

COUDRY: Sarah, wid, 103.135

COULTON: Sarah, 102.7

COUNCELL: Daniell; Mary, w; Sarah, d,
103.181

COURSE: Henry; Alice, w, 110.31

72

COURT:
Dorothy, 109.42
Michaell; Sarah, w; Sarah, d, 106.21
Richard; Mary, w; Richard, s, 109.67
William, £600; Susanah, w; Millicent, d,
102.174

COURTES: Dudley Erasmus, 102.174

COURTHROPE: John, bach, 106.12

COURTMAN: Thomazon, app, 98.44

COURTNEY:
Edward; Frances, w; Frances, d; John, s;
William, s, 107D.34
Robert; Judeth, w; Isaac, s; Henry, s, 103.209

COURTOPP: Anne, 98.3

COUSE: Rebacca, 101.11

COUSENS:
Elianor; Elizabeth, d, 107D.40
John; Mary, w, 107B.62
Joyce, 107C.29
Mary, 107D.28
Oliver; Winifred, w, 107D.35
Samuell; Catherine, w; Nicholas, s; John, s,
103.169
Thomas; Sarah, w, 107B.71

COVANT: Mary, pensioner, 103.137

COVELL:
Christopher, ser, 106.15
John; Hanah, w; Charles, s; Hanah, d,
107D.28

COVENTON: Richard; Sarah, w; William, s,
106.62

COVENTRY: John; Elizabeth, w; Elizabeth,
d, 107A.2

COVER: Thomas; Sarah, w; William, s, 98.6

COVEY: Cordelia, 104.13

COVILL: Elizabeth, 102.264

COWARD:
Hanah, ser, 107C.29
John; Ellianor, w; John, s, 101.84
Margaret, 98.63, 109.75
Martha, ser, 103.10
Mary, 110.34
Richard; Susan, w; Richard, s; Anne, d,
109.81

Robert; Sarah, w, 109.3
Sarah, 101.41

COWART: George, 102.81

COWDELL:
Benjamin, 99.20
Thomas; Friscilla, w; Hanah, d; Mary, d;
Thomas, s; William, s, 107A.18

COWDRELL: Henry, app, 103.153

COWDRY:
Gamaliell, wid, 106.65
John; Elizabeth, w, 99.14
Mary, ser, 103.160
Richard; Constance, w, 101.7

COWELL:
George; Mary, w; Hanah, d; Thomas, s;
Samuell, s, 106.47
Jas, app, 104.147
Margery, 107A.9
Paul; Elizabeth, w; Martha, d?; Mary, d?;
William, s?;

COWER:
~, bach, 98.39

COWLEY:
Alexander, 109.104
Box, wid; Mary, d, 103.133
Elizabeth; Elizabeth, d; Hannah, d; Anne, d;
Martya, d, 109.106
George; Alice, w, 103.229
Mary, 103.234
Sarah, ser, 98.52
William, junior; Martha, w, 103.10
William, senior; Martha, w; Elizabeth, d;
Ann, d; Susannah, d, 103.5

COWOOD: Joane, ser, 103.31

COWSEY: John, app, 107A.42

COWSLADD: Thomas;

COX:
~; Sarah, d, 103.93
Alice, 99.41
Anne, 102.100
Anne, ser, 98.31, 101.32
Benjamin, ser, 106.58
Daniell, Doctor of Physick; Rebecca, w;
Susana, d; Anne, d; Mary, d; Richard, s;
Coldham, s, 101.33
Elianor; Katherine, d; Elizabeth, d, 107B.75
Elizabeth, ser, 98.46, 103.3
Frances, ser, 103.84

Frances, wid; William, s; Elizabeth, d; Jane, d, 104.46
Francis, 109.99
George, app, 107D.101
Hannah, 110.34
Hatton; Mary, w, 104.68
Jane, 104.76
Jonathan; Mary, w; Joseph, s, 103.57
John, 103.201, 110.34
John; Jone, w; John, s; Mary, d; Jane, d, 101.84
John; Elizabeth, w; Mary, d, 102.130
John; Margaret, w; William, s, 102.131
John; Elizabeth, w; John, s, 102.159
John; Mary, w, 103.99
John; Elizabeth, w; Elizabeth, d; Mary, d, 107D.21
John; Mary, w, 109.72
John; Mary, w; Thomas, s; John, s; James, s, 109.99
John; Rebecca, w, 109.110
John, child, 107D.12
Judith, 99.34
Mary, 103.20
Mary; Samuell, s, 102.64
Mary, ser, 102.146
Priscilla, 101.16
Samuel; Rebecca, w, 102.126
Samuel; Anne, d, 104.76
Samuell, child, 107D.12
Sarah, 99.11, 102.258
Thomas; Elizabeth, w; George, s, 102.195
Thomas; Alice, w, 103.117
Thomas; Elizabeth, w; Elizabeth, d; Mary, d; Mosses, s, 103.125
Thomas; Mary, w; John, s, 107C.29
Whiteing; Bridgett, w; Mary, child, 104.107
William, 99.41
William, child, 107D.12

COXED: Henry; Robert, s, 106.11

COXELL: William, app, 101.49

COXHEAD:
Anne, ser, 98.4
Richard; Martha, w, 107A.17
Robert, 102.272

COXSHETT:
Jane, 102.242
Mary, 102.242

COYENS: Nicholas, 102.84

COYTING: Richard; Elizabeth, w; William, s, 105.9

COZBY: John, 103.69

COZEN: Bryann, bach;

COZENS:
~, wid; Francis, s, 103.189
Edward; Margaret, w; Mary, d, 109.80
Elizabeth, 101.38
James; Jane, w, 102.226
John, clerk, 98.31

CRABB:
Ben, ser, bach?, 104.10
Elizabeth, ser; Roger, s?; Elizabeth, d?, 106.34

CRABTREE:
Elianor; Abraham Crabtree, grand-s, 107B.47
Palmer; Mary, w, 110.3
Samuel; Elizabeth, w, 107B.20

CRACE: Wm, bach, 104.30_

CRACROFT: Richard; Faith, w, 101.46

CRADDOCK:
Edward; Phillis, w; Edward, s, 101.242
John; Elizabeth, w; Zachery, s; Elizabeth, d; Joseph, s; Francis, s, 102.72
John; Martha, w; Thomas, s; Elizabeth, d, 109.73
Joseph; Susan, w; Susan, d, 103.166
Richard, 110.12, 110.37
Richard; Esther, w; Susan, his mother, wid, £600; Esther, his d; Sarah, his d, 103.286
Susan, wid, £600, 103.286
Uryas; Sarah, w; Eustace, s, 106.62
William, ser, 108.5

CRADUS: Katherine, ser, 103.70

CRAFORD:
Elizabeth, ser, 103.18
Francis; Elizabeth, w; Benjamin, s; Rebecca, d; Mary, d, 109.90

CRAFT: John; Leticia, w; Elizabeth, d, 109.84

CRAFTON:
Anne; Elizabeth, d, 102.158
Sarah, ser, 102.136

CRAFTS:
Hanah, 102.237
Mary, 102.237
Philadelpha, wid, 103.35
Sarah, 102.237
Sarah; John, s, 103.223

CRAINE: Elizabeth, 98.88

CRIFWELL: John; Elizabeth, w; William, s;
Thomas, s, 107B.51

CRIPPLE:
Mary, 107B.47
William; Dameras, w, 107D.39

CRIPPS:
Christopher, 107B.15
Mary, 107B.53
Nicholas; Barbary, w; Barbary, d, 103.73

CRISLOE: Rebecca; Sara, d, 101.31

CRISLY: William; Sarah, w, 110.34

CRISP:
Ann; Dorothy, d; Ann, d; Hannah, d; Edmund,
s, 109.62
Elizabeth, 107B.69
George, app, 107B.66
Jane, ser, 108.6
Richard, 99.56
Richard; Elizabeth, w, 103.96
Samuel; Mary, w, 107B.57
Tho, ?wid; Mary, d; Sarah, d, 104.27

CRISPEN:
Sarah, ser, 98.77
Jamesh; Mary, w; Rebecca, d; James, s,
103.198
Katherine, 102.175
Paule, 102.175

CRISSEY:
Alice, gentlewoman, 98.45
Eliz, 104.137

CRITCHLOWE:
Elinor, ser, 98.73
George, 98.86
John, 98.86
Richard; Rebeckah, w; Mary, grand-d of,
98.86

CRITON: Anne, ser, 107B.65

CRITTENDEN: Jane, 99.41

CROANE: Thomas, bach, 98.60

CROCKER:
Jeremy; Mary, w, 104.20
John; Mary, w, 109.4

CROCKETT:
Josiah; Margarett, w; Mary, d, 110.23
Lydia, ser, 103.29
Mary, wid; Mary, d, 103.43

CROCKFORD:
John; Elizabeth, w; John, s; Gerrard, s, 98.41
Matt; Hannah, w; Tho, s, 104.56

CROE: Pauel, 101.13

CROFFEILD: William; Annahbellah, w;
Anne, d; Hannah, d, 98.81

CROFTS:
Amey, 107B.5
Edmund, 107D.7
Elizabeth; John, s; Richard, s; David, s;
Edward, s; Elizabeth, d; Mary, d, 107B.9
Elizabeth, ser, 104.144
James, wid, 109.108
Mary, 104.106
Sam, app, 104.47
Richard, 110.20

CROKER:
Anne, 107D.85
Joseph, ser, 107C.39
Thomas; Anne, w; Thomas, s, 107D.32

CROMP:
Richard; Katherine, w, 102.261
Richard, wid, no children, 103.116

CROMPTON:
Edmond, 101.16
Elizabeth, spinster, 103.2
Hester, 110.3
Margaret, 98.80

CROMWELL:
Henry; Anne, w; Henry, s, 107D.31
Thomas; Elizabeth, w, 101.6
William, 101.7

CRONE: Richard; Hannah, w, 106.28

CROOKE:
Anne, 101.11
Bridget, ser, 98.39
Charles, 106.11
David; Mary, w; Benjamin, s, 102.202
George; Mercey, w; Mary, d; Mercey, d;
George, s, 103.22
Henry, bach, 102.162
John; Sarah, w, 103.84
John; Elizabeth, w; John, s; Elizabeth, d,
107B.40
John; Anne, w; John, s; Francis, d; Elizabeth,
d, 107D.25
Mary, 101.11
Mary, wid; ~, child, 100.7
Richard; Mary, w, 103.57
Sampson; Sarah, w, 106.34

CROWLAND: Mary, 107C.35, 107C.36

CROWNE: John; Sarah, w, 102.49

CROWTHER:
Edward; Sarah, w; William, s; Martha, d,
107D.76
Mary, nurse child, 102.162

CROXFORD:
John; Anne, w, 109.92
Richard; Margarett, w; Margarett, d;
Elizabeth, d; Sarah, d; Richard, s, 110.11

CROXON:
John; Elizabeth, w; John, s; Thomas
Massden, s; ~, wid, 104.88
Deborah, 109.109
Joan, 109.98
Thomas; Elizabeth, w; Elizabeth, d, 109.98

CROXWELL: Christopher; Elizabeth, w;
Elizabeth, d, 103.56

CROYLEY:
Mary, 103.20
Thomas; Jeane, w; John, s, 103.250

CRUDG: Alexander, 102.117

CRUMP:
Esther, 104.20
Henry; Elizabeth, w, 102.23
John; Elizabeth, w; Hanah, d, 107B.69
Richard; Elizabeth, w, 109.23
Thomas, ser, 106.45
Walter; Mary, w; George, s, 100.9

CRUMPLE: James, app, 98.35

CSAR: Hanry; Sarah, w, 107D.16

CUDWORTH: Hanah, pensioner; Sarah, d;
John, s, 103.97

CUE: Anne, wid; Anne, d, 102.58

CUERTON: Ralph; Alice, w, 107D.69

CUFF: Jocum, a child, 103.32

CUGGLY: William; Susannah, w; William, s;
Susannah, d, 107A.40

CULL: Mary Susannah, ser to Blundall, 98.8

CULLEY:
Margery, 109.72
William, app, 102.204

CULLIFORD:
John, bach, gent, 106.38
William, esq, 106.38

CULLIN:
John; Ann, w; Thomas, s; John, s; Ruth, d;
Richard, s; Quintine, d, 103.201
John; Joane, w; John, s, 110.18
Mary, 109.88

CULLUM: Elizabeth; Mary, d?; Betty, d?,
102.91

CULPEPPER: Mary, 109.28

CUMBER: John; Elizabeth, w; John, s;
Leonard, s; Sarah, d; Thomas, s; Ann, d,
103.247

CUMBERLAND:
Anne; Wm, s, 104.28
John; Isabell, w, 109.56

CUMBURY: Mary, ser, 104.92

CUMMING:
Joseph; Mary, w; Thomas, s; Joseph, s;
Richard, s, dead, 102.89
Margaret, ser, 103.284
Richard; Margaret, w; Alice, d; Sarah, d;
Samuell, s, 103.106
Richard, ser, 107D.59

CUMPTON: Jane, eid, 102.48

CUNDALL: Richard; Anne, w; Joseph, s,
107C.10

CUNDY: Tho; Mary, w, 104.78

CUNNING: Edward, app, 98.51

CUNNINGHAM:
Eliza, 104.74
Ellias; Mary, w, 102.142
James, 109.36
James, gent; Katherine, w, 104.25
Jeremy, 110.14
Mary, 102.142
Mary, 104.51
Richard, ser, 98.35
Thomas, hostler, 98.73

CUNNINGSBYE:
Charles, bach, 106.47
Christopher, bach, 106.47

CUNNISBY: Humphry; Sarah, w; Mary, d;
Jane, d; Julius, ser, 107B.75

DADD: Mary, ser, 98.8

DADLEY:
Alice, 102.238
Thomas; Grace, w, 102.238

DADNELL: Thomas, bach, under age, 103.55

DAFFIN: Deborah, 104.45

DAFFY: Ellinor; Mary, d; Martha, d, 104.116

DAGE: Hannah, ser, 109.57

DAINTER: Ester, ser, 105.3

DAINTON: Abigall, 101.18

DAINTY: Mary, ser, 98.2

DAKER: Elizabeth, 107D.64

DALBICAN: Edward; Mary, w; Margeret
Wilton, her mother, 103.184

DALBIN:
Alice, ser, 104.95
John, ser;

DALBY:
~, wid; Jane, d, 104.141

DALE:
Elizabeth; John, s; Mary, d; Margarett, d;
Walter, s, 109.24
Henry; Elizabeth, w; Elizabeth, d; Anne, d;
John, s, 109.66
Isaac, 101.75
John; Ann, w, 109.62
Margaret, 101.41
Nathaniel; Anne, w; Ephraim, s, 102.253

DALLIN: John; Susan, w; Elizabeth, d;
Susan, d; Thomas, s, 102.60

DALLISON:
Elizabeth, wid, 103.101
Martin; Esther, w, 103.251
Thomas; Elizabeth, w; Elizabeth Hawkins, d,
103.258

DALLOWBEER: William; Frances, w;
Francis, s, 109.101

DALLUE: Roger; Anne, w; Joseph, s;
Elizabeth, d; Susan, d; Anne, d, 109.89

DALLY:
Aoron, £600; Mary, w; Edward, s, 104.5

Elizabeth, 102.49
Elizabeth, ser, 106.38
Richard; Susan, w; Richard, s, 103.212

DALTON: William, app, 101.45

DALTREY: William; Jane, w, 106.17

DAMES: Anne, 102.134

DAMONE: Mary, wid, 103.198

DAMSELL: Mary, ser, 98.27

DANBY:
Abstripius, Kt, bach, 98.45
Mary, ser, 103.121

DANCE:
Lucy, 98.20
Richard; Ann, w, 109.51
Thomas, 102.79
William; Mary, w, 98.87

DANCER:
Mary, 107D.39
Nath; Bridgett, w; John, s, 104.62
Sarah, 102.257
Thomas; Samuell, s, 102.208

DANCY:
Anne, 106.20
Jas, ser?, bach, 104.90

DANDRIDGE:
John; Anne, w; William, s; Bartholomew, s;
Anne, d, 106.7
John, ser, 106.7
Thomas; Alice, w, 103.34
William; Deborah, w; William, s, 107B.13

DANDY:
Edward; Ellulia, w, 101.53
Edward, wid, 103.71
Thomas; Anne, w; William, s; Mary, d; Rose,
d, 109.88
Willam; Elizabeth, w, 107D.74

DANE: William, 102.247

DANELL: Anne, 101.9

DANFORD: George; Joan, w, 102.127

DANGERFEILD:
Ann, spinster, 103.10, 103.97
Richard; Anne, w; Sara, d, 101.50
Staphen; Elizabeth, w; William, s; Sarah, d;
Elizabeth, d, 102.6

Susanna, 106.67
William; Margery, w; Joan, s; William, s,
  107D.7

DANIELL:
Abraham; Margaret, w, 109.100
Anne, 101.23
Charles; Katherine, w, 107B.32
Elizabeth, nurse child, 107B.40
John; Anne, w, 103.90
John; Joane, mother of; Mary, sister of,
  104.54
John, app, 104.54
John, nurse child, 107B.40
Joseph; Winafred, w, 103.197
Magnus; Mary, w; Thomas, s, 102.172
Peregrine, 101.52
Rebecca, 109.87
Robert; Anne, w; William, s; Robert, s;
  Katherine, d; Mary, d; Jane, d, 110.25
William; Anne, w; Susan, d, 109.65

DANN:
Elizabeth, ser, 107B.81
John, ser, 108.4

DANSFORD: Sarah, 102.261

DANSON: John, £600; Mary, w; John, s,
  101.2

DANZEY: Judith, ser, 101.44

DAPHAGE: Thomas; Mary, w; Mary Staiy, d,
  109.82

DAPHIVER: James, 105.2

DARBES: Elizabeth, 98.9

DARBISON: William, 98.55

DARBY:
Elizabeth; John, s, 103.205
Elizabeth, ser, 107D.38
George; Anne, w; Anne, d, 102.59
John; Alice, w; Mathew, s, 109.52
John; Joane, w; John, s?; Elizabeth, d?, 99.55
Symon; Mary, w; Mathew, s; Symon, s; John,
  s; Samuell, s, 109.27

DARCY: John; Jane, w; Jane, d; James, s;
  Mary, d, 110.20

DARKE: Stephen; Anne, w, 102.198

DARKEY: Richard, ser, 100.6

DARKIN: Robert, dead, 102.275

DARLING:
John; Mary, w; John, s; Charles, s; Francis, s,
  101.71
John, app, 107B.34
Mary, ser, 106.3

DARLOW: William; Mary, w, 109.88

DARMER: John, ser, 103.117

DARMOTT: Peter; Elizabeth, w, 99.51

DARNE: Mary, 102.72

DARSHA: Judeth, spinster, 103.267

DART:
John, 99.41
Robert; Mary, w; Mary, d, 109.41

DARVELL: William, at sea, 103.266

DARVILL: George; Elizabeth, w,
  103.52

DARY: Eliz, 104.123

DASH: Sybell, 104.122

DASHWOOD:
Edward, ser, 109.93
Francis, wid, 103.16
John, 109.63
Richard, 109.11
Samuell, Kt; Ann, w; George, s; Thomas, s;
  Sarah, d; Annabella, d; Jeane, d; Henaritta,
  d; Sophia, d, 103.287
Thomas; Mary, w, 109.8

DASON: John, ser, 109.26

DASSATT: Mary, ser, 109.76

DATE: Katherine, 101.46

DAVELL: John, wid; William, s;

DAVENISH: ~, 98.43
John, ser, 98.30

DAVENOT: Anne, 109.72

DAVENPORT:
Edward; Anna Maria, w; Edward, s; Lidiah, d,
  107D.94
Elizabeth, 107B.23
John; Jane, w; Arthur, s, 109.2
Sarah, 104.112
Sarah, ser, 107D.64

DAVENPORTS: John, app, 101.83

DAVID: William, bach, 102.76

DAVIDGE: Jonathon; Grissell, w, 103.198

DAVIS:
Andrew, 109.6
Anne, 102.264, 109.38
Anne; Thomas, s, 107.22
Arthur, 102.267
Aira; Anne, w; Margaret, d, 107B.6
Bartholomew; Jane, w; Barthew, s; Grisewell, d; Richard, s; Margaret, d, 109.25
Bridget, 101.40
Bridget, ser, 100.2
Catherine, 109.107
Charles, 99.32
David; Elizabeth, w, 103.164
David; Abigale, w; David, s, 109.20
Dorothy, 102.102
Edward; Elizabeth, w; Anne, d?, 99.15
Edward; Margaret, w; Edward, s; Mary, d, 107C.32
Edward; Susann, w, 109.60
Edward, ser, 98.67
Evan; Dorothy, w; Anne, d; Joyce, d, 98.11
Fouch, ser, 109.77
Geo; Phebe, w; Alice, d; Wm, s, 104.41
George; Anne, w, 105.5
Giles; Amey, w; Amey, d; Giles, s; John, s, 107B.76
Grace, 109.17
Hannah, 109.20, 109.102
Hanry; Sarah, w; Thomas, s; Mary, mother; Mary, his sister, 102.151
Henry; Elizabeth, w, 107D.52
Hugh; Elizabeth, w; Elizabeth, d, 98.6
Hugh, app, 107B.12
Heugh, bach, 103.86
Isaak; Ann, w; Ann, d, 104.147
Issabella, wid; Rebecca, d, 102.11
James; Elizabeth, w; Elizabeth, d; Martha, d, 98.12
James, wid, no children, 103.47
Jane, 109.41
Job; ~, w, 104.140
Joan, 99.10
John, 109.17, 110.19
John; Anne, w, 102.98
John; Martha, w; Mary, d; Martha, d, 102.180
John; Frances, w; William, s, 107B.11
John; Margery, w, 107B.34
John; Mary, w; Thomas, s; William, s; Mary, d, 107D.47
John; Anne, w; John, s; Sarah, d; Pheby, d, 107D.51
John; Francis, w, 109.13
John; Elizabeth, w; Elizabeth, d, 109.43

John, bach, 100.4
Joseph; Judith; John, s; Joseph, s, 98.22
Joseph; Ann, w; Katherine, d; Mary, d; Joseph, s, 103.251
Katherine; Anne, d, 107C.8
Lewis; Elizabeth, w, 102.267
Margaret, 106.58, 109.94
Margaret; Margarett, d, 99.39
Martha, 109.65
Mary; William, s; Nathaniell, s, 98.22
Mary, ser, 103.115
Maud, ser, 101.107
Nathaniel; Elizabeth, w; Nathaniel, s; Mary, d; Elizabeth, d, 106.9
Nath, a boy, 104.42
Prew, wid, 102.118
Rachael, 107C.33
Rebecca, child, 102.66
Richard; Dorothy, wid; Anne, d, 98.17
Richard; Sarah, w; Sarah, d, 101.97
Richard; Elizabeth, w; Robert, s, 102.47
Richard; Dorothy, w; Richard, s, 103.87
Richard; Catherine, w, 103.278
Richard; Mary, w; Thomas, s; Mary, d, 109.91
Robert, ser, 102.200
Rose, 102.112
Samuell; Elizabeth, w; Samuell, s, 103.153
Sarah, 107B.76
Sarah, pensioner, 103.144
Sarah, ser, 104.34, 106.10
Sarah, spinster, 103.257
Stephen; Jane, w, 104.140
Stephen; Elizabeth, w; Anthony, s; Stephen, s; Elizabeth, d; Mary, d; Garce, d, 109.63
Susan, 102.64, 104.61
Theophilus, bach, 103.27
Thomas; Susanna, w; Mary, d, 101.50
Thomas; Elizabeth, w; Martha, d; Thomas, s, 102.150
Thomas; Rebecca, w; Katherine, d; Benjamin, s; Thomas, s; Priska, d; Abraham, s, 103.53
Thomas; Elizabeth, w; Martha, d; Mary, d; Robert, s, 103.60
Thomas; Anne, w; John, s, 107A.34
Thomas; Mary, w; John, s; Elizabeth, d, 107A.38
Thomas; Mary, w, 109.3
Thomas, ser, 107A.6, 109.15
William; Jane, w; Mary, d, 102.206
William; Elizabeth, w; Elizabeth, d; William, s; Nicholas, s, 103.90
William; Katherine, d, 104.78
William; Katherine, w, 106.39
William; Ellen, w, 107D.70
William, bach, 104.140
William, nurse child, 107B.68
William, ser, 103.251, 106.21
Winefrid, ser, 103.59

DAVISON:
Daniell, bach, 103.100
John, 110.16
John; Anne, w, 103.281
John, ser, bach?, 104.4

DAVLE: Mainwaring, bach, esq, 106.47

DAWDRY: William; Susan, w; Susan, d;
   William, s, 103.96

DAWES:
Isaac; Isaac, s; James, s; Rebeccah, d, 98.10
John, app, 107B.66
Katherine, ser, 98.29
Mary, ser, 103.214
Perkin, 107D.77
Richard; Jone, w; Richard, s; Mary, d; Anne,
   d; Rebeccah, d; Margaret, d, 98.11
Rich; Ellinor, w, 104.68
Thomas; Mary, w; Mary, d, 102.214
Wm; Joane, w, 104.46

DAWKES: Humphry; Ellinor, w, 109.16

DAWKING:
John, bach, 102.162
Wm; Alice, w; Dorothy, d; Sarah, d; Joshua,
   s, 104.114

DAWLEY: William, ser, 102.147

DAWLING:
Andrew, ser, 108.8
William, £600; Lidia, w, 108.8

DAWLINS: Eleanor;

DAWSON:
~, wid, 102.206
Adam, 101.107
Anne, 104.36
Catherine, 109.68
Edith, 102.13
Elizabeth, 99.7
Elizabeth, ser, 102.150
Hannah, 104.17
Hanah, ser, 107B.72
Henry; Ann, w; Elizabeth, d; Hanry, s,
   103.135
John; Margarett, w, 102.224
John; Mary, w; John, s; Mary, d; Susannah, d,
   104.18
John, at sea; Mary, w; John, s, 103.108
John, bach, 103.25
Joseph; Susannah, w; Susannah, d, 109.1
Joseph, wid, 107A.39
Mathew; Martha, w, 109.75
Moses; Sarah, w; Moses, s, 102.221

Nathaniel, 102.221
Robert; Jane, w, 100.7
Robert, bach, 102.58
Roger, 99.47
Stephen; Mary, w, 104.21
Thomas; Mary, w; Mary, d, 103.200
Thomas; Martha, w, 106.58
Thomas; Elizabeth, w; John, s, 109.101
William, 109.13
William; Mary, w, 103.82
William; Jane, w, 104.128

DAWSTON: Elizabeth;

DAY:
~, wid, 104.128
Alice, 109.45
Alice, pensioner; Elizabeth, d, 103.147
Dorothy, 109.109
Edward, ser, 106.16
Elizabeth; Thomas, s; Frances, d, 98.3
Francis; Jane, w, 110.30
Gyles; Isabella, w; Mary, d; Elizabeth, d;
   James, s, 103.177
Hanah, 107D.71
Isaac; Anne, w; Abraham, s; Jacob, s; Jane, d;
   Anne, d, 109.79
Isabella, ser, 107D.54
Joan, 104.17
John; Anne, w, 101.83
John; Elizabeth, w; John, s; Daniell, s;
   Elizabeth, d, 103.95
John; Frances, w, 104.121
John; Francis, w; Haylston, s, 107D.8
John, app, 107D.24
Leonard; Mary, w, 101.37
Martha, ser, 98.43
Mary, 102.131, 109.46
Mary; Anne, d; Elizabeth, d; Mary, d, 102.32
Michelborne; William, s; Elizabeth, d, 103.31
Rachell, pensioner, 103.166
Richard; Mary, w; Richard, s, 107D.56
Samuell, app, 101.91
Sarah, 98.5
Stephen, app, 107D.48
Tho, app, 104.51
William, 105.18
William; Jane, w, 102.77
William; Mary, w; William, s, 102.79

DE FOUNTAINE: Mary, 109.85

DEA: William; Mary, w; Ann, d; Mary, d;
   John, s, 109.16

DEACON:
Daniel; Margaret, w, 107B.48
Dorothy; Mary, d, 98.28
Easter, ser, 98.65

DEERING:
Anne, ser, 105.12
Joanna, 101.18
Josiah; Frances, w; Jackson, s?; Elizabeth, d?,
99.45
Mary, ser, 106.6
Unton, ?gent; Eliz, w; Susanna, d, 104.11

DEGMAN: William, 110.15

DEHKE: Michaell; Susan, w; Isaac, s; James,
s; John, s; Susan, d, 102.255

DEITER: Samuell; Elizabeth, w; Mary, d;
Samuell, s, 105.12

DELAMAINE: Robert, 105.8

DELAMORE: Christian, ser, 106.67

DELANDER: James, bach, 106.34

DELAVALL: Mary, ser, 106.19

DELL:
John; Anne, w, 107B.24
Jos, gent; Hannah, w; Jos, s, 104.95
Martha, 101.65
Mary, 101.65
Thomas, 101.65
William, £600, wid; William, s; Thomas, s,
101.43
William, assessor, 101.110

DELOAFE:
John; Susan, w; Richard, s; Mary, d; John, s,
103.108
John; Martha, w; Joseph, s, 103.124

DELOW: James; Mary, w, 103.87

DEMAUCK: Rebecca; John, s; Elizabeth, d,
103.170

DEMEANE: Anth; Kath, w;

DEMEER:
~, wid, 103.246

DEMERRY: John, 106.12

DEMISSE: Jane, ser, 107D.32

DEMOCK: Wm, 104.136

DEMOT: Judith; Mary, d; Jerimiah, s,
107D.14

DEMOTE: Mary, 102.253

DENH:
Catherine, ser, 109.78
Elud, 107D.99
Jos; Mary, w; Anna, d, 104.142

DENHAM:
Elizabeth, 98.36
James; Ann, w; Hanah, d, 103.71

DENMORE: Mary; Mary, d, 107B.52

DENNINGOE: Joanna, 101.64

DENNIS:
Anne, 101.88, 103.282
Bridget, 101.48
David; Sarah, w, 109.14
Edward; Joane, w; Anne, niece of, 103.282
Edward, ser, 103.259
Elizabeth, 103.250
Jeane, 103.168
John, nurse child, 107B.60
Katherine, ser, 102.145
Margaret, 103.3
Martha; Martha, d; Sara, d, 101.33
Mary, ser, 98.40
Thomas; Mary, w; Elisha, d, 107D.9

DENNISON:
Eliza, 104.94
William; Ann, w; William, s; Susan, d,
109.107

DENNY: Saints, 109.53

DENSLOE: Elizabeth, 101.26

DENSON: Randulph; Katherine, 102.272

DENT:
Anne, wid, 104.72
Henry; Avis, w; James, s; Mary, d, 98.62
John, 110.4
John; Anne, w; Anne, d; James, s, 110.4
Sarah, 110.4
Thomas, ser, 103.224
William; Sarah, w; William, s; Sarah, d,
106..35

DENTER: Jas, app, 104.39

DENTON:
Elizabeth, 99.59
George, pensioner, wid; George, s; Elizabeth,
d; Mary, d; William, s; Jeane, d,
103.144
Jerimiah; Unis, w; John, s; Thomas, s,
107B.23
Mary, ser, 107D.27

Thomas; Isabella, w; Elizabeth, d; Susanna,
d; Anne, d, 109.64
Thomas Mary, s of Adfin, 103.67

DENVAN: Elizabeth, 102.253

DEPARNE: Noha, ser, 103.129

DEPEER: Isaac; Jeane, w; Abraham, s; Jeane,
d, 103.87

DEPENTERS: Francis, 101.13

DEPOARE: Isaac, pensioner; Elizabeth, w;
Elizabeth, d; Rachell, d; Isaac, s; Mary, d;
James, s, 103.136

DEPON: Mary, ser, 106.15

DEPPER: Susan, app, 107C.13

DEPREE: Wm; Eliz, w, 104.119

DERAM: John; Joane, w; John, s; Martha, s,
102.18

DERAN: Elizabeth, ser, 109.2

DERBY: James; Mary, w, 106.1

DERDS: Mary; Judeth, d, 109.52

DERES: Elizabeth, ser, 101.32

DERMOH: Ann, 104.145

DERRY:
Anne, ser, 100.11
George, app, 101.89
Josiah, nurse child, 107C.15
Sarah, nurse child, 107C.15
Susan, nurse child, 107C.15

DERSON: Barberah, ser, 107D.19

DESAGWILLAW: Sarah, spinster, 103.267

DESBOUROUGH:
Anne, 101.42
Martha, 106.16

DESCAINE: Rebecca, 103.244

DETHICK: Thomas, bach;

DEVAREUX:
~; Elizabeth, w, 101.46

DEVEARGE: William; Anne, w, 98.68

DEVEELL: Mary; Mary, d?, 102.66

DEVELL:
Anne, 98.19
Charles; Mary, w; Sarah, d, 107B.8
Elizabeth, 102.235
Mary, 102.236

DEVERALL: John, ser, 103.10

DEVON:
Michael, app, 107A.31
Rebecca, 102.49

DEVONPORT: James, app, 103.18

DEVORALL: Thomas; Anne, w; Thomas, s;
Elizabeth, d; Mary, d; James, s, 107D.13

DEVOROCKE: William; Anne, w; Ann, d,
102.38

DEW:
John, app, 107D.32
Susanna, 101.48

DEWALL:
Jacob; Elizabeth, w; Mary, d; Joseph, s;
Esther, d; Elizabeth, d, 103.282
Phillip, ser, 106.17

DEWATIME: Judith, 107B.49

DEWBERRY: John; Hanah, w, 107C.12

DEWBREE: Henry, ser, 106.43

DEWEN: Frances; Margaret, w; Elizabeth, d;
Anne, d; Frances, d; Margaret, d,
107D.90

DEWERTINE: Abraham, wid; Abraham, s;
Katharine, d, 102.43

DEWES: Elizabeth, ser, 101.32

DEWETIANE: Simon; Mary, w; Susan,
102.222

DEWEY:
Charles; Mary, w, 98.47
John; Jane, w; Jane, d, 110.7
Mary, 109.43
Robert, 107B.24
Sarah, 107B.24
Thomas, 110.36
Thomas; Susann, w, 110.36

DEWHURST: Samuell, ser, 102.71

DEWICK: Thomas; Elizabeth, d, 106.63

DEWILL: Martha, ser, 107B.24

DEWIT: Anthony; Susanna, w, 101.47

DEWSBERRY: William, ser, 103.171

DIAMENT: Charles; Rebecca, w; John, s;
Charles, s, 102.190

DIAMOND: Elizabeth, 102.218

DIAPER:
Jane, 98.20
Katherine, 104.90
Thomas; Margaret, w; Burgis, s; John, s,
103.100

DIASS: Elizabeth, ser, 103.120

DIBB: Stephen; Elizabeth, w, 103.151

DICK: John, ser, 103.255

DICKASON: John, 109.89

DICKENS:
John; Sarah, w; Sarah, d; Hannah, d,
109.77
Richard; Deborah, w; Richard, s; Deborah, d;
Joseph, s; Anne, d, 109.66
Robert; Anne, w, 100.12
Samuel, ser, 108.2
Susan, 109.30
Susan, ser, 100.11
Thomas, 109.71

DICKENSON:
Alice, spinster, 103.109
Ann, spinster, 103.109
Henry; Ellen, w, 106.32
John Joseph, s of wilson, 107D.4
Joseph; Sarah, w, 103.62
Marg, 104.136
Mary, 109.10
William, 103.62
William, apothecary living in the postern,
collector, 107A.43
William, bach, 107A.25

DICKER: Thomas; Alice, w, 101.3

DICKESE: Anthony; Eliza, w; Eliza, d,
104.71

DICKESON: John, 102.233

DICKS: Robt, 104.132

DICKSON:
Ann, ser, 106.52
Edward; Anne, w, 106.52
Gabriell, 98.36
James; Anne, w, 102.73
Samuell, 99.57
Thomas, 99.57
Thomas, £600, 99.57
William; Margaret, w, 109.90

DIDDY: Winifred, 101.57

DIERLY: Mary, 99.6

DIGBY:
John; Mary, w, 104.96
Thomas, ser, 109.11

DIGG: Christopher, clerk, 98.67

DIGGOR: Ellen, 102.66

DIGGS:
Elizabeth, 98.46
William, app, 98.35

DIKE, See Dyke Dykes

DIKING: William, bach, 109.51

DILKES: Charles, ser, 106.37

DILLINGHAM:
~; Jane, w, 104.143
Thomas; Alice, w; Thomas, s; Elizabeth, d,
110.12

DILLYE:
Hanah, 102.242
Rebecca;

DIMERICK:
~, wid, 103.264

DIMS: Rebecca, 101.107

DIMSDALE: Elizabeth, 101.14

DIMSTALL: Robert, 110.2

DINELY: John, bach, 106.11

DINGLE: William; Isabella, w, 107C.17

DINGLEY: Elizabeth, wid, £50 p.a.;
Elizabeth Thorpe, d; Penticost, d, 101.78

DINING: John; Jane, w; Adam, s,
102.95

DINN: Edward, bach, 110.20

DINSDALE: Nathaniell, 99.41

DIRTY: Jane, 98.12

DISHINGTON: Christian, ser, 106.28

DISNEY: ~; ~, w; ~, s;

DISON:
Mary, 103.97

DISSAMORES: Justine, 102.3

DISSEY: George; Mary, w; John, s?;
　　Margarett, d?, 99.18

DISSMOORE: Richard; Alice, w, 103.47

DISTED: Thomas, bach, 98.66

DISTON:
Rich, a boy, 104.111
Thomas; Mary, w; Thomas, s; Mary, d; Sarah,
　　d; Drucilla, d; Elizabeth, d, 109.72

DITCHAM: John, app, 98.4

DITCHER:
Mary, wid, 103.89
Sarah; Sarah, d, 109.22
Thomas, 103.89

DITCHFEILD:
John; Elizabeth, w; John, s, 109.65
Richard; Elizabeth, w; Elizabeth, d; Martha,
　　d, 98.13

DITINER: Mary, 101.65

DITON:
Mary, ser, 98.3
Stephen; Edith, w; Ideth, d, 103.263

DITTON: Jane, 106.63

DIVINE: Isaacc, bach under age,
　　103.131

DIVIRE: Martin, 101.33

DIX:
Daniell, children, 102.124
Mary, children, 102.124
Elizabeth, ser, 102.73
George, 102.271
Jeremiah, 101.46
John; Mary, w; John, s, 102.220

Mary, 102.271
Mary, ser;

DIXON:
~; ~, wid, 104.106
Abigall, 102.121
Anthony, 104.112
Edward; Sarah, w; Susan, d, 102.254
Gyles, ser, 103.137
Grace, 106.62
Isabell, 101.62
John; Martha, w; John, s; William, s;
　　Elizabeth, d, 102.215
John; Mary, w, 104.30
John; Hester, w; Hester, d; Elizabeth, d;
　　Mary, d, 107B.13
John; Dorothy, w; James, w; Thomas, s,
　　107B.71
John; Elizabeth, w; Susan, d; Elizabeth, d,
　　107C.27
John; Mary, w, 109.63
Martha, ser, 107D.40
Mary; Jeana, d, 103.179
Peter; Ture, w; John, s, 107D.26
Rebecca, ser, 103.277
Richard; Grace, w, 107D.77
Thomas; Mary, w, 107A.34
Thomas; Jane, w; Easter, d; Elizabeth, d,
　　110.32
William; Elizabeth, d, 98.19
William; Mary, w; Grace, d, 107D.71
William, £600; Rebecca, w, 101.1
William, app, 104.49

DOACKLEY: Humphrey, 102.233

DOATER: Henry; Martha, d, 105.3

DOBBELLS: Benjamin, ser, 98.31

DOBBINS: Joseph; Hester, w, 98.30

DOBBS:
John; Mary, w; Elizabeth, d; Mary, d, 98.4
Mary, ser, 107D.52
Wm; Mary, w; Mary, d, 104.46
William, ser, 106.56

DOBINSON: Mich, ?wid; Tho, s; Mich, s;
　　Eliz, d; Sarah, d; Hannah, d, 104.85

DOBLE: Elizabeth, ser, 106.43

DOBSON:
Anne, 102.221
Christopher; Martha, w; Mary, d; Elizabeth,
　　d, 107C.12
Elizabeth, nurse child, 107B.32
John; Hannah, w; Edward, s, 102.26

88

Katherine, ser, 103.106
Mary, 109.66
William, 109.76

DOCKRELL:
Richard, 102.82
Susan, 102.83

DOD:
Alice, 102.55
Ann, 104.134
Benjamin, ser, 107C.33
Chas; Anne, w, 104.41
Dorcas, 102.257
Elizabeth, 102.51, 107A.9
Elizabeth, ser, 106.19
Elizabeth, wid, 103.38
Henry; Martha, w; Henry, s; ~, not baptized,
    103.291
Henry; Hester, w; Hester, d; Rebecca, d, 110.3
John; Hannah, w, 103.161
John, app, 103.214
Peter; Anne, w; Sarah, d, 102.39
Robert; Barbary, w, 103.103
Robert, nurse child, 103.125
Samuell, esq; Izabellah, w; Crooke, s, 98.30
Sarah, ser, 103.158
Thomas; Susanah, w, 99.25

DODDINGTON: Joan, ser, 109.97

DODGE:
Mary, 107B.50
William; Mary, w; Mary, d, 103.151

DODMAN: Mary, 103.251

DODSON:
Elizabeth, 107C.18
John, £50 p.a.; Mary, w, 98.44
John, £600; Sarah, w; Haley, s, 102.98

DODSWORTH:
Christopher; Elizabeth, d; Susan, d; Mary, d,
    105.3
Sara, ser, 105.4
William; Elizabeth, w; Elizabeth, d?; Anne,
    d?; Mary, d?, 99.7

DODWELL: John, bach, 106.2

DOE:
Anne, a child, 102.52
Jane, 98.18
Richard; Margaret, w, 101.49

DOEBEGIN: William, 101.86

DOEDALL: Bathew, 109.49

DOGOOD:
Ralph, 104.135
Ralph, bach, 104.33
Richard, ser, 102.204
William; Elizabeth, w; Mitchell, ser; Sarah, d,
    109.18

DOHERTINE: Elizabeth, app, 101.59

DOIMER: John, ser, 102.178

DOLBEN: Katherine, wid of bishop, 99.44

DOLBY:
Andrew, £600; Dorcas, w; Thomas, s,
    102.132
Judith, 107D.26
Timothy, 102.240

DOLDEN: Anne, 107C.22

DOLE:
Amy, 100.8
William; Ann, w, 103.147

DOLEMAN: Elizabeth, wid; William, s;
    Elizabeth, d, 103.127

DOLFIN:
Elizabeth, pensioner; Joseph, s; Benjamin, s;
    Elizabeth, d, 103.142
Richard, ser, 106.21
William; Katherine, w, 106.55
William, collector, haberdasher, 106.69

DOLIMAN: Henry; Mary, w, 103.154

DOLLING: George, 109.36

DOLLOM: Katherine, 102.223

DOLLY:
Henry; Elnor, w, 110.17
Robert, 110.17
Wm, app, 104.67

DOLSELL: Jas, bach, 104.108

DOLT: William; Susan, w; Elizabeth, d,
    102.265

DOLTON:
Benj, app, 104.80
Thomas, 109.97
William, ser, 106.50

DONCASTLE:
Elizabeth, 99.4
Ottwell; Ann, w; Ottwell, s; Ann, d, 99.4

DONNE:
Richard; Elizabeth, w, 109.50
Roger; Elizabeth, w; Roger, s, 101.57

DONTON:
Eliz, 104.60
John; Elizabeth, w, 107D.19

DOOWORTH: Thomas, 109.103

DOPSON: John; Jane, w; Jane, d, 102.168

DORDRAY: Robt, 104.93

DORF: Thomas, 102.234

DORFELLOW: Elizabeth, wid, ser, 103.288

DORKE: Mary, 106.6

DORKER: Samuel; Sarah, w; Hanah, d,
107D.23

DORMAN: Thomas, ser, 102.189

DORMER:
Gabriell; Bridgett, w, 98.38
John, 109.80
John; Elizabeth, w; Thomas, s; Dorothy, d,
109.81
John, ser, 109.80
Thomas, ser, 107C.37

DORMEY: Mary, wid, 101.21

DORRELL:
Alice, 109.65
Francis, app, 107C.1
John; Elizabeth, w, 103.286
Tho, bach, 104.91

DORRINGTON:
Anne; Robert, s, 101.102
John, app, 109.42
Thomas, app, 101.106
William; Hannah, w, 110.22

DORRISON:
John; Mary, w, 110.9
Luke, 110.9

DORSETT: Kath, 104.59

DORTON: Thomas; Elizabeth, w; Elizabeth,
d, 103.213

DOSISON: John; Anne, w; Anne, d, 102.263

DOSON: William, bach, 109.33

DOSS: Elizabeth, ser, 106.31

DOSSETT: William; Martha, w; Francis, s;
William, s; Rachell, d; John, s, 102.139

DOSTON: Elizabeth, 102.271

DOTCHIN:
Peter, a child, 101.57
William, a child, 101.57

DOUBLE: William, 101.93

DOUBLER: Jacob; Anne, w; Sarah, d; Anne,
d, 98.62

DOUGHTFIER: William, wid; Elizabeth, d;
Mary, d; Henry, s; Hanah, d; Sarah, d;
William, s, 103.116

DOUGHTY:
Eliz, 104.134
Thomas, app, 98.46

DOUGLAS, See Duglas

DOUSE: Clinton, clerk, 98.28

DOVE:
John; Elizabeth, w; Anne, d; Katherine, d;
Richard, s, 102.183
Katherine, 102.167
Nevill; Hester, w; Dorothy, d; Elianor, d;
Hester, d; William, s, 109.66
Robert, £600; Nevell, w; Nevell, d, 102.91
Wm; Mary, w, 104.75
William, bach, 106.68

DOVEE: Jos, senior, £600; ~, junior, £600;
Hannah, w; Hannah, d, 104.31

DOVER:
James, bach, 99.55
Samuel; Jane, w, 109.99
Richard; Deborah, w, 107B.43

DOVEY:
Alice, wid, 103.26
Randolph; Joane, w, 103.185

DOW: Thomasin, 106.45

DOWDELL: Gabriel; Jeane, w; Starling, d;
Judeth, d; Jeane, d; William, s; Gabriell, s;
Susan, d, 103.194

DOWDING: George, app, 107A.36

DOWDY: Elizabeth; Rowland, s, 109.23

DOWERS: John; Jane, w; Edward, s; John, s; Elizabeth, d; Jane, d, 98.26

DOWLE:
Elizabeth, ser, 106.52
Mary, wid, pensioner, 103.16
Thomas, app, 103.79

DOWLER: Mary, ser, 107D.56

DOWLY: Samuel; Hanah, w, 107D.96

DOWMAN: John, 102.210

DOWNE: John; Margaret, w, 107B.48

DOWNEHAM: Elizabeth, ser, 101.70

DOWNER:
Hugh; Frances, w, 99.11
John, bach, 102.38

DOWNES:
~, 98.44
Benjamin, 110.14
Charles, 110.14
Elizabeth, 98.8
Geo; Constantia, w; Marg, d; Hannah, d, 104.102
Jarvis, a child, 107C.3
John; Eliz, w; Arthur, s, 104.95
Margaret, 98.27
Thomas, a child, 107C.3
William, ser, 107A.6

DOWNING:
Elizabeth, 110.3
Richard; Elizabeth, w; Foster, s; Elizabeth, d, 106.23
William; Ann, w; Joseph, s?; Anthony, s?; Robert, s?, 99.54

DOWSE:
John; Anne, w, 107B.26
Mary, 102.185
Sarah, 104.65
Thomas, ser, 107A.4

DOWSON: John; Sarah, w; Penelope, d?, 99.42

DOWZEN: John; Grace, w, 98.87

DRACKLEY: Elizabeth, 110.35

DRAGE:
Joseph; Elizabeth, w, 99.14
Phillip; Anne, w, 101.95
Theophilus, bach, 99.33

DRAKE:
Eliz, ser, 104.109
Joseph, bach, £50 p.a., 106.28
Matt, ser, bach, 104.92
Nathaniel; Ann, w; Thomas, s; Elizabeth, d; Nathaniel, s, 103.84
Rich; Sarah, w; Sarah, d, 104.53
Robt; Ellin, w, 104.88
Roger, commissioner, 103.293
Roger, gent; Mary, w; Margaret, d, 103.289

DRAKELEY: Tho, app, 104.142

DRAKSFEILD: John, 101.54

DRANE:
Elizabeth; Elizabeth, d; Mary, d; John, s; Anne, d, 107B.44
Elizabeth, ser, 100.6
Henry, 106.46
Jas, bach, 104.4
John; Elizabeth, w; Thomas, s; Elizabeth, d, 101.66
John; Dorothy, w, 104.37
John; Anne, w, 107D.44
John, ser, 106.31
Joseph, 103.60
Margaret, 98.86
Martha, 109.63
Mary, 109.70
Mary, ser, 104.21
Rebeccah, 98.49
Richard, app, 107A.27
Robert, pensioner; Jeane, w; Charles, s; John, s; Elizabeth, d; Dorothy, d, 103.49
Sarah, 102.106
Sarah, 106.19
Susannah, 98.79
Thomas, 102.132, 102.206
Thomas; Jane, w, 98.6
Thomas, app, 103.171

DRAPER:
~, gent, bach, 98.75
Abraham; Dorothy, w; Sarah, d, 103.173
Abraham; Sarah, w, 109.23
Alice, 104.131
Charles, app, 107A.22
Ducebellah, 98.65
Jane, 98.51
John, 101.9
John; Ann, w; John, s?; Mary, d?, 99.41
John; Sarah, w; Ruth, d?, 99.55
John; Frances, w; Jeane, d; Elizabeth, d, 103.191
John; Jane, w, 109.110
John, app, 107B.64
John, bach, gent, 106.45
Mary, 99.33, 102.216

Mary, ser, 98.68
Robert, ser, 103.53, 109.60
Thomas; Ellen, w, 108.7
Thomas; Jane, w; Mary, d, 110.30
Thomas, app, 107D.50
Valentine, 99.32
William; Elizabeth, w; Elizabeth, d, 107A.16

DRASLEY: Samuell; Martha, w; Richard, s;
    Samuell, s; Anne, d, 102.79

DRAYCOTT:
Anne; Mary, d, 107B.40
Elizabeth, ser, 107B.47
Lucy, 109.110
Thomas, ser, 109.110

DRAYDEN: William; Elizabeth, w; Alice, d;
    Elizabeth, d; Grace, d, 109.17

DRAYTON: Elizabeth, wid; Elizabeth, d,
    103.205

DREADS: Elizabeth, ser, 98.17

DREATON: John, an infant, 102.210

DREW:
Anne, 102.141
Christopher, 109.94
Christopher; Eliener, w, 102.163
Christopher; Susan, w, 102.169
Elizabeth, 102.141
John; Susan, w; John, ser, 106.23
Mary, 102.68
Sarah, 107C.15
William, wid; Jeane, d, 103.204

DREWELL: Martha, 103.30

DREWIS: Ann, 109.30

DREWIT:
Benjamin, app, 101.103
Henry; Anne, w, 102.153
John; Ephery, w; Henry, s; Michaell, s; Sarah,
    d, 102.153

DREWRY: Charles, 102.13

DRIFFEILD: Elizabeth, 109.59

DRIGUE:
John, assessor, 103.293
John, esq, wid, hath children elsewhere,
    103.163

DRING:
Daniell; Elizabeth, w, 106.68

Dorothy, wid; Jane, d; Dorothy, d,
    106.59
Margaret, 101.16

DRINGDEALE: Esther, ser, 103.206

DRINKELL: Margaret, wid; William, s, bach;
    John, s, bach, 103.70

DRINKWATER:
Anne, ser, 107D.28
Elizabeth, 109.96
Francis; Elizabeth, w; William, s; Richard, s,
    109.96
Hannah, 109.96
James, 109.96
John, app, 107D.28
John, ser, 102.104
Sarah, 104.140
Timothy, 102.15

DRIVER:
John; Elizabeth, w; Sarah, d, 102.143
John; Margaret, w; Thomas, s, 103.196
Margaret; Martha, d, 103.8
Mary, ser, 107D.18

DROSSADEGONE: Sam, 104.28

DROUTE:
Frances, 109.98
Katherine, ser, 103.15

DRUDGE: Edward; Elizabeth, w; Mary, d;
    Elizabeth, d, 102.81

DRUITT:
Mary, ser, 102.80
Rabecca, 104.38

DRURY:
George; Elizabeth, w; Robert, s, 110.1
Margaret, ser, 103.39
Sarah, 101.77
Walter, £600; Bennett, w, 104.87

DRY:
Eliza, ser, 104.60
Henry, £50 p.a.; Elizabeth, w; John, s,
    106.13
Sarah, 107B.78

DRYDEN:
Elizabeth, ser, 100.11
Thomas; Grace, w, 102.144

DUBBIN: Jacob, ser, 107C.37

DUCEY: Elizabeth, wid, 103.23

DUCK:
Andrew; Mary, w; Sarah, d; Martha, d,
102.118
James; Mary, w; Thomas, s, 109.92
John, app, 101.108
Mary, 109.62
William, 109.94

DUCKER:
John; Mary, w; Mary, d; John, s, 103.80
Margaret, 109.92

DUCKETT:
George; Katherine, w, 98.16
Margrett, 99.43

DUCKWORTH: Daniell, 102.18

DUDDS: Joseph, bach, 98.36

DUDGELL: Elizabeth, 109.78

DUDLEY:
Elizabeth, ser, 98.87, 98.88
Jos; Sarah, w, 104.125
Mary, ser, 104.62
Rebeccah, 98.23
Susan, 103.9
William; Margaret, w, 102.177

DUDMAN: Jane, ser, 101.31

DUDNEY:
John; Mary, w; Elizabeth, d, 107B.77
Thomas; Mary, w; Nathaniel Norris, grand-s,
107D.15

DUDSON: Jas; Anne, w; Jas, s, 104.23

DUFFEILD: Richard; Susan, w, 107B.24

DUFFEN: John, ser, 98.71

DUFRAYNE: Elizabeth, pensioner, 103.134

DUGAR: Peter; Mary, w; Peter, s, 110.8

DUGDALE:
Chris, ser, 104.61
John; Elizabeth, w, 109.101
Mary, 109.101

DUGGIN: Susannah, ser, 101.96

DUGLASS:
Elizabeth, 102.69
Elizabeth, ser, 101.81
Hester, 102.66
Israell, bach, 102.69

John, parish boy, 103.71
Margarett, 102.155
Robert; Sarah, w, 102.247
Samuell; Eleanor, w, 102.124
Sarah, ser, 104.67

DUGMORE: Elianor; William, s; Elizabeth,
d, 107D.82

DUHGHILL: Arthur; Sarah, w; Ann, d;
Arthur, s; Elizabeth, d, 109.11

DUHILL: Deborah, 109.11

DUKE:
Elizabeth, ser, 103.158
Frances, 107C.22
John; Mary, w, 102.264
Thomas; Anne, w, 107D.51

DUKES:
Anne, 107D.42, 109.105
William; Elizabeth, w, 103.88
Wm; Alice, w, 104.76

DUKSON: Abigell, 102.165

DULVORCE: Susan, 102.165

DUM: Aron; Mary, w, 102.77

DUMBLETON: Sarah, ser, 103.26

DUNBEAR: Elizabeth; Rachell, d, 101.56

DUNCE: Mary, ser, 107D.10

DUNCH: Edmund, £600; Susan, w; William,
s, 107D.52

DUNCK: Mary, ser, 107D.37

DUNCKLINS:
John, a parish child, 103.220
Richard, a parish child, 103.220

DUNCOMBE:
Alexander; Anne, w, 98.20
Anne, 110.31
Edw, app, 104.59
Hannah, spinster, 103.290
Henry, ser, 106.5

DUNKING: Robert, esq, bach,
106.64

DUNLEY: Richard, bach, 103.100

DUNMORE: Mary, 106.54

DUNN:
Alexander; Anne, w, 102.137
Anne, 107D.60
Benony, 109.63
Elizabeth Decayne, niece of Andrew, 103.14
Henry, app, 98.26
Hester, ser, 106.26
Jas, app, 104.70
John; Mary, w; Sarah, d; Rachell, d, 102.19
John; Sarah, w; Sarah, d, 104.74
John; Mary, w, 107C.41
Mary Grace, d of Nelson; Richard, s?, 98.62
Richard Grace, grand-s of Nelson, 98.62
Sarah, 102.19
Thomas, 102.19
Thomas; Elizabeth, w; Thomas, s, 107D.35
William, 109.44
William; Elizabeth, w; James, s; Elizabeth, d;
    Hanah, d; Ann, d; Sarah, d; William, s,
    103.230

DUNNAGE: James; Hanah, w, 107C.4

DUNNELL:
Jeane, 103.244
John, bach, 98.35

DUNNING: Thomas, 107D.94

DUNSTALL:
Anne, 109.110
Lucy, 98.34
Ralph; Margaret, w, 98.32

DUNSTAN:
Anne, pensioner, 106.8
John, ser, 106.42
Sarah, parish child, 106.6

DUNSTONE:
Elizabeth, 101.54
Thomas, app, 101.65

DUNTHAM: John; Joyce, w; Jane Clisby, d;
    Anne Clishby, grand-d, 107B.55

DUNWORTH: Martha, ser, 106.7

DUPORT: Henry; Martha, w, 107D.39

DUPREE: Charles; Anne, w, 106.7

DURANCE: Elizabeth; Elizabeth, d, 101.37

DURDEN: Ann, 104.32

DURETINE: Margaret, 102.250

DUREY: Judeth, 102.255

DURGEN: Samuell, 109.103

DURHAM:
Ann, ser, 103.5, 106.23
Frances; Richard, s, 106.8
George; Mary, w; John, s, 102.23
James; Elizabeth, w; William, s; James, s,
    109.12
Mary, 107B.11
Nicholas, junior; Ann, w; ~, Twins,
    unbaptized, 103.169
Nicholas, senior; Sarah, w, 103.169

DURLACE: Humfry, esq, 110.8

DUROCELL: Elizabeth, ser,
    103.277

DURRANT:
Alice, ser, 101.18
Anne, 110.23
Grace, ser, 98.43
John, £50 p.a.; Dorothy, w, 106.21
Matthew; Elizabeth, w, 106.15
Prudence, ser, 98.29

DURWYN: Peter; Eliz, w, 104.44

DUSSON: Joseph; Elizabeth, w; Joseph, s;
    William, s, 107B.15

DUSTON: Anne; Anne, d, 109.110

DUTCH:
Cornelius; Ann, d; Cornelius, s; Phillip, s,
    103.81
Edward; Mary, w; Edward, s; Ann, d; Mary,
    d; James, s; Nicholas, s; Arthur, s, 103.11
John; Mary, w; Mary, d; Elizabeth, d; John, s,
    103.82

DUTTON:
Edward, app, 107B.32
Eliza, 104.77
Ellinor, wid, 103.193
Jane, 102.73
John; Margarett, w; Mary, d, 110.24
Margery, 109.2
Mary; Hannah, d; Martha, d, 98.16
Stephen; Mary, w, 104.35

DUVALL: Marg, 104.42

DYARS: Margarett, ser, 100.14

DYASS: Edmond; Alice, w; Alexander, s;
    Elizabeth, d, 103.107

DYATT: Symom, app, 98.85

DYE:
Daniell, 101.102
Francis, ser, 101.102
Jonas; Mary, w; Josuah, s, 107A.25

DYER:
Anne, 105.10
Elizabeth, 110.2
Hannah, 109.43
Joane, wid, 103.274
John, 110.2
John; Elizabeth, w, 110.19
Mary; Elizabeth, d, 109.88
Richard; Mary, w; Richard, s, 102.103
Robert; Elizabeth, w, 98.48
Sara, 101.85
Thomas, 110.2
Walter; Martha, w; Sarah, d; Elizabeth, d,
103.12
Walter, bach; Martha, his mother, 106.60
William, £50 p.a.; Hester, w; Hester, d;
Robert, s; Mary, d, 98.45
William, bach, 103.284

DYKE:
Jane, 99.60
Peter, ser, 109.1
Robert; Dorothy, w; Elizabeth, d,
109.99

DYKES:
Alice, ser, 107D.50
Anne, 104.114
Mary, wid; Mary, d, 103.110
Samuel, 109.6
Ursula, 109.102

DYMER: Wm; Anne, w, 104.30

DYNES:
Anne, £600, 102.201
Hannah, 102.201

DYODATE:
Mary, 102.32
Sarah, 102.32

DYOSS: Richard, pensioner; Katherine, w,
103.123

DYSER: Susan, 102.36

DYSON:
John, app, 107A.38
Philip; Jane, w, 104.141

DYTON: Dotothy, 100.11

EAD: Elizabeth, a child, 102.52

EADEN:
John, 109.63
Nathaniell, app, 98.35
William, bach, 98.27

EADES:
John, 98.11
Michael; Elizabeth, w; Elizabeth, d,
101.67
Windson; Mary, w, 107B.41

EAGLES:
Ann; Mary, d; Sarah, d; Martha, d, 109.37
Henry; Ellinor, w; John, s; ?bach, 104.96
Henry; Mary, w, 107B.40
Mary, 110.3

EAGLESFIELD:
Francis, 109.30
John; Anna, w; John, s; Mary, d, 104.107

EAGLETON:
Henry, bach, 104.12
Thos, bach, 104.12

EAKINS: Giles; Elizabeth, w; Giles, s,
104.44

EALES:
Anne, 110.13
Elizabeth, wid; Thomas, s, 103.21
John; Elizabeth, w, 100.14
John; Elizabeth, w, 110.13
Joseph, 109.9
Thomas, bach, 101.83

EANES:
John, 109.9
Rebecca, 109.9
William, 109.9

EARBY: Anthony, clerk, 106.3

EARE: Winifred, ser, 106.4

EARLE:
Elizabeth; Sarah, d; Susan; Thomas, s,
107B.22
Elizabeth; Margarett, w, 106.20
Henry; Margarett, w; Matthew, s; Margarett,
d; Henry, s; Joseph, s, 99.1
John; Elizabeth, w, 107B.56
Mary, ser, 107D.19
Richard; Anne, w, 107D.89
Thomas, 110.23
Thomas; Sarah, 107B.50
William; Mary, w; Henry, s; Jeane, d,
103.268
William; Mary, w, 104.75

95

EDGOCK: Hannah, 104.90

EDINSOLD: Anne, ser, 102.126

EDIS: Elizabeth, 99.42

EDLIN:
John, bach; Elizabeth, his mother,
 101.44
Samuell, 101.26
Thomas; Israel, w; Anne, d, 107B.35
William; Mary, w; Mary, d; William, s; Sarah,
 d; Richard, s, 107D.98

EDMAYE: Mary, 102.272

EDMERSOME: Ralph, ser, 100.5

EDMONDSON:
Anne, 101.42
Edward; Sarah, w, 102.47

EDMUNDS:
Benjamin, bach, gent, 107B.65
Charles; Anne, w, 107B.37
Debora, wid, 102.51
Esther, pensioner, 103.93
Giles, app, 104.28
Guy; Elizabeth, w; Elizabeth, d; Castle, d,
 101.70
John; Jone, w; John, s; Mathew, s; Ezekiel, s;
 Edward, s, 107C.42
Margarett, 110.27
Mary, 110.10
Robt, 104.131
William, 99.58
William; Mary, w; John, s; Elizabeth, d;
 Mary, d, 109.52
William, £600; Alica, w; Anamariah, d,
 107D.54
William, bach, 99.53

EDOLPH:
Samuell, 110.4
Thomas; Thomasin, w, 110.28

EDON:
~, wid; John, s; Enock, s; Lucretia, d;
 Hannah, d; Hester, d, 109.62
Chas; Mary, w, 104.15
John; Elizabeth, w, 109.16

EDRIDGE:
James, bach, 98.54
Thomas, app, 98.54
William, bach, 98.54

EDRINGHAM: Elizabeth; George, s?,
 102.180

EDWARD:
Daniell, 102.176
James; Ellinor, w;

EDWARDS:
~, Mrs; John, s, 103.207
Alexander, 102.11
Alice, wid, pensioner, 103.16
Anne, 107C.24
Anne; Gyles, s, 98.41
Charles; Elinor, w; Charles, s, 98.38
David; Mary, w, 106.10
Diana, 102.13
Dorcas, 109.70
Easter, 110.24
Edmond; Ann, w; Susan, d, 103.64
Eliza, ser, 104.65
Elizabeth, wid; Rachell, d, 103.102
Edward, 110.21
Edward; Frances, w, 98.38
Edward; Katherine, w, 98.55
Edward; Mary, w; John, s, 102.271
Edward, bach, 104.70
Francis, 109.71
Francis, ser, 106.39
Hanah, 107D.21
Henry; Mary, w; Mary, d, 102.258
Henry, bach, 110.29
James, 105.17
James; Collina, w, 107D.41
Jeane, ser, 103.289
Jeane, wid; Robert, s, 103.238
Jeffry; Sarah, w, 107D.2
John, 99.9, 110.33
John; Elizabeth, w, 102.182
John; Susana, w, 102.272
John; Mary, w, 103.145
John; Sarah, w; Mary, d, 107D.57
John; Mary, w; James, s; Michael, s; Mary, d;
 Elizabeth, d, 109.34
John, app, 107A.36
John, bach, 109.62
John, ser, 109.60
Jonathan, 101.2
Judith, a child, 107C.39
Katherine, ser, 106.56
Lidiah; Sarah, d; Elizabeth, d, 107C.39
Maroy, 102.30
Margaret, ser, 98.68
Michael; Hannah, w, 109.19
Nicholas, 109.5
Phillipp; Philipp, s, 102.225
Reginoll; Jane, w, 106.51
Richard, 103.275
Richard; Margarett, w, 98.31
Richard; Anne, w; Sarah, d; Elizabeth, d, 108.5
Richard, assessor, 108.8
Robert; Elizabeth, w; Hanah, d; Elizabeth, d,
 102.123

Robert; Elizabeth, w, 107C.12
Robert, ser, 103.224
Sarah, 104.12
Susan, ser, 107A.34
Thomas, app, 107D.31
Thomas, ser, 106.63
Walter; Agnes, w, 106.32
William; Anne, w; John, s; Sarah, d; Elizabeth, d, 102.34
William; Judith, w; Anne, d; Richard, s, 104.52
William; Frances, w; Frances, d, 107A.31
William; Margaret, w, 107C.14
William; Susanah, w; Susanah, d; Edward, s, 109.5
William, app, 98.88

EELES:
John; Anne, w; John, s, 102.2
Wm, bach, app, 104.87

EFFINGTON: Francis, ser, 106.50

EGGERTON: John; Frances, w; John, s; Elizabeth, d; Joseph, s; Samuell, s; Thomas, s; Anne, d, 103.85

EGGINGTON:
Edward; Mary, w; Sarah, d; Edward, s, 103.101
William, parish boy, 99.20

EGGLEFEILD: Francis, 101.50

EGIS: William; Margaret, w, 109.32

EGLESTONE:
Edith, 99.2
Elizabeth, pensioner; Samuell, s; Elizabeth, d; Sarah, d, 103.80
Thomas, 102.268
Thomas; Katherine, w, 103.64

EGLETON: Alice, 99.44

EGSHAW: Mary, 99.22

ELAND: Joshua; Elizabeth, w; Elizabeth, d, 102.78

ELBOROUGH: William; Martha, w, 106.61

ELBOW: Lewis;

ELBRIDGE:
~, wid; Mary, d; Eliz, d, 104.87

ELBY: Thomasin, parish child, 106.6

ELCOMB: Alice, 109.53

ELDER: William, 106.26

ELDERTON: Marg;

ELDRIDGE:
~; Esther, w; John, s, 103.25
Bird; Mary, w, 109.100
Bridgett, 109.7
Elizabeth, 107B.37
Elizabeth, ser, 103.33
Mary, 104.3
Sara, 101.80
Tho, app, 104.10
William; Ann, w; William, s, 103.184

ELDRINGTON: William, 102.106

ELFE:
Jane, ser, 98.51
Mary, 98.52

ELFORD: Tho, app, 104.6

ELINER: Luke; Lucy, w, 106.40

ELINOR: John; Hannah, d?, 102.72

ELITT:
Ellinor; William, s, 109.9
Thomas; Ann, w; Thomas, s, 109.8

ELKIN: Robert, 99.15

ELKINTON: Amillyer, 102.154

ELLDERTON:
Ann, wid, 103.20
Ellinor, 103.243

ELLEBORE: Sarah, 109.41

ELLERSHAM: Elizabeth, 101.9

ELLETEES: Jeremiah; Blandina, w; Alice, d; Jane, d, 102.265

ELLETREES: James; Jane, w, 109.104

ELLETSON: John, 102.103

ELLETT: Elizabeth, 109.105

ELLGAR:
Jerimiah; Mary, w, 103.51
William; Mary, w; James, s; Mary, d; Elizabeth, d; Margaret, d, 103.69

ELLICOCK:
Elizabeth, pensioner, 103.220
Sarah, pensioner; Edward, s; Mary, d;
　Elizabeth, d, 103.220

ELLICOR: Bridget, 102.66

ELLILL: Richard; Ellen, w; Elisha, s; Mary,
　d, 98.83

ELLINK: Daniell, 102.226

ELLIOT:
Alice, ser, 106.21
Ann, 99.18
Ann; Francis, s, 109.30
Elizabeth; Anne, d, 98.76
Elizabeth, her husband at sea; John, s;
　Elizabeth, d, 103.134
Elizabeth, ser, 106.34
Giles; Elizabeth, w; Judith, d; Giles, s,
　107B.39
Jane, 99.50
John; Mary, w, 102.206
John, Journeyman, 104.14
Jonathon, £50 p.a.; Mary, w; Mary, d,
　102.109
Jonathon, collector, 102.276
Martha, 109.94
Mary; William, s, 109.32
Millicent, ser, 109.32
Nicholas; Jeane, w; Rachel, d, 103.133
Ralph; Richard, s; Susan, d, 109.87
Richard; Elizabeth, w; Christian, d; Sarah, d;
　Mary, d, 110.13
Sarah, 102.206
Thomas; Hanah, w; Thomas, s, bach under
　age; Mary, d; Peter, s, bach under age,
　103.111

ELLIS:
Abraham; Elizabeth, w; Sarah, d; Elizabeth,
　d, 107D.15
Alice, 107B.16
Alice; Henry, s; Joseph, s, 102.76
Ann, ser, 103.7
Christopher, 107D.51
David; Ellen, w, 104.121
David; Anne, w, 109.94
Dorothy, 101.110
Edmond; Mary, w, 109.47
Edward; Mary, w; John, s?, 99.48
Francis; Anne, d, 102.267
Hannah, 109.47
James; Susannah, w, 98.79
James; Elizabeth, w; Susanna, d; Elizabeth, d,
　104.48
Jane, ser, 99.2
John, 109.65

John; Rebecca, w, 103.291
John; Faith, w, 107C.42
Joyce, 101.110
Luke; Mary, w; Susanna, d; Mary, d; Anne, d,
　101.99
Mary, 103.103, 104.99
Mary; Margaret, d; Mary, d; Penellopa, d;
　Robert, s, 99.58
Richard; Mary, w; Mary, d, 100.15
Richard; ~, w, 104.16
Samuell, 101.3
Sarah, 107D.51
Simon, £600; Mary, w; Simon, s; John, s,
　107A.41
Susan, 100.14
Thomas; Mary, w; John, s; Mary, d;
　Elizabeth, d; Margarett, d, 110.15
Thomas, clerk, 98.61
William; Rose, w; James, s; William, s; John,
　s; Thomas, s; Elizabeth, d; Abigall, d,
　101.105
William; Rebecca, w; Sarah, d, 107C.40
William; Mary, w; Samuell, s, 109.12
William, ser, 100.14

ELLISON:
Ambrose; Elianor, w, 109.109
John, wid; Ruth, d; Kath, d, 104.21

ELLISTON: Susanah, 99.44

ELLISTORE: Joseph; Anne, w; Robert, s;
　Peter, s; Anne, d, 98.33

ELLITT:
Charles; Anne, w; Israell, s, 101.94
Elizabeth, 109.44
Richard; Elizabeth, w; Thomas, s; Elizabeth,
　d, 109.11

ELLORY:
John; Mary, w, 104.142
Robt, app, 104.143

ELLOSON: Joshua, 109.28

ELLSLEY:
Anne, ser, 101.107
Thomas, 105.14
William; Anne, w; Thomas, brother of,
　105.14

ELLSON: Sarah; Ann, d; Mary, d; Martha, d,
　109.18

ELLVIN: Elizabeth, wid, 103.145

ELLWOOD:
Margarett, 99.44

99

Mary, 102.165
Moses, 104.89
Wentworth; Katherine, d; Mary, d, 104.107
William, bach, ser, 104.86
William, pensioner; Ann, w, 103.225

ELMER:
Theoball; Katherine, w; Charles, s; John, s,
102.232
Thomas, ser, 106.3

ELMES:
Frances, 104.59
John, ser, 109.7
Joseph; Jane, w; Joseph, s, 107A.42
Sarah, 109.70
William, app, 107D.36
William, ser, 106.64

ELMOORE:
Henry; Susan, w, 102.57
James; Winafred, w; Mary, d; James, s,
103.119
Mercy, ser, 107D.52
Thomas; Anne, w, 104.29

ELSE: Margarett, 99.55

ELSLEY, See Ellsley

ELSOME:
Katherine, 107D.18
William; Mary, w; William, s; Mary, d,
107D.56

ELTON: Phillip; Elizabeth, w; Sarah, d, 107B.26

ELWICKS: Tho; Eliz, w; Henry, s; Mary, d;
Eliz, d, 104.81

ELWIS: Dionetia, 110.7

ELY:
Alice; Jonathon Haynes, s, 107B.55
Hannah, 104.126
Mary; Barberah, d, 107D.64
Thomas; Elizabeth, w, 105.6

EMANEER: John; Anne, w; Timothy, s,
107B.70

EMBER:
Humphry, ser, 103.2
John, ser, 103.2

EMBRY: Thomas, £50 p.a.; Sara, w, 101.81

EMERSON:
John, 107B.42

Mary; Anne, d; Joseph, s, 102.54
Nicholas, ser, 106.29

EMERTON:
Benjamin; Elizabeth, w; Elizabeth, d;
Thomas, s, 103.67
Grace, 107A.8
John; Elizabeth, w, 107D.94
Jos; Mary, w, 104.141
Mary, 107A.8
Mary, ser, 106.25
Richard; Joanna, w; Richard, s, 109.104
Thomas; Anne, w; John, s; Ann, d; Sarah, d;
Elizabeth, d; Mary, d, 102.116
William, esq; Elizabeth, w; Elizabeth, d;
Sarah, d, 98.29

EMERY:
Mary, wid; Edward, s; Ann, d; Manoss, d,
103.254
Thomas; Anne, w; Elizabeth, d; Anne, d;
Sarah, d; Susan, d; John, s, 107C.9

EMES:
Frances; Eliz, d, 104.56
James; Frances, w; Anne, d; Mary, d, 107C.38
Mary, 107D.64
Thomas, £600; Mary, w; Mary, d; Joseph, s;
Ralph, s; Benjamin, s, 107D.34

EMITT: Sara, 101.105

EMLY: Henry, 102.132

EMMETT:
Anne, 109.97
Eliza, wid, 104.55
John, bach, 109.101
Sam, app, 104.43
Wm, £600; Anna Maria, w; John, s; Anne, d,
104.74

EMMONS: Lucass, bach, 103.31

EMMS:
Alice, 102.30
Anne, ser, 98.66
Elizabeth, ser, 108.3
Folk; Elizabeth, d, 109.79
Ruth, wid; Frances, d; Ruth, d, 102.44
Samuell; Rebacca, w; John, s, 103.26
Thomas, 102.248
Walter, ser, 103.129

EMMUTT: Mary, parish child from Northen
folgate, 103.201

EMORY:
Benjamin; Elianor, w, 109.86

Henry, app, 104.78
Hugh; Elizabeth, w; John, s; Hugh, s, 104.14
William, 109.51

EMOTT: Mary, 102.206

EMPEY: Thomas; Sarah, w, 109.107

EMPSPERT: William, 109.21

EMSON: William, 106.12

ENDE: Patricke, bach, tapster, 109.6

ENDERBY: Anne, ser, 101.23

ENDERLY: Anne, 109.90

ENDERSBY: Ezekell, 102.204

ENFEILD: Richard; Mary, w; Elizabeth, d;
Jane, d; Isabella, d; Richard, s, 107D.64

ENGLAND:
John, app, 98.52, 104.18
Joseph; Dorothy, w; Hannah, d; Elizabeth, d;
Lidia, d, 109.4
Margery, pensioner, 106.8

ENGLE: Anne, 101.63

ENGLEBIRD: Ann, wid, 103.65

ENGLISH:
Anne, ser, 104.26
Chas; Eliz, w, 104.114
Dorothy, 98.14
Margaret, ser, 109.79
Michell; Pheby, w; Mary, d; Michell, s; Jeane,
d, 103.167
Peter, 107D.90
Peter; Rose, w; Peter Vennor, grand-s of, 98.46
Thomas, gent; Joyce, w; John, s; Thomas, s,
98.42
William, app, 107C.42

ENNIS: John; Katherine, w, 106.7

ENOVER: George; Mary, w; William, s,
107D.25

ENSDELL: Margeret, ser, 103.273

ENSER:
David; Mary, w; David, s, 107C.31
William; Mary, w; Mary, d, 102.207

ENSTONE: Thomas; Mary, w; Thomas, s;
Rachell, d, 101.70

ENTRY: Martha, 104.30

ERDESWICK: Thomas, 109.111

ERLINGTON: Francis, 102.79

ESCOURT:
John; Eliz, w, 104.103
Tho, app, 104.1

ESOME: Elianor, ser, 107B.21

ESQUIRE: ~, wid, 103.263

ESSEX:
Anne, ser, 109.78
William, 109.49

ESTWICK, See Eastwick

ESTWOOD, See Eastwood

ESUM: John; Elizabeth, w; Thomas, s,
101.69

ETCHES: Hester, 98.88

ETHELBERT: Wellins, app, 107D.26

ETHERINGTON: George, bach, 106.43

EUBANKE: William, bach, tapster, 98.53

EURATT: Thomas, 109.35

EUSTACE:
John, 109.42
Mary, 104.18

EVANCE: William; Alice, w;

EVANS:
~; Mary, w; ~, 104.79
Anne, 102.180
Anne, ser, 107B.38
Anthony; Hannah, w, 104.56
Benjamin, app, 103.23
Daniell; Hannah, w, 102.55
Dennis; Elizabeth, w; William, s, 103.209
Edward; Elizabeth, w, 107C.28
Elizabeth; Benjamin, s; Richard, s; John, s;
Elizabeth, d; Mary, d, 107C.31
Elizabeth, spinster, 103.33
Elizabeth, ser, 103.18, 106.21
Erasmus, 110.19
Evan, £600; Saint, w; Joseph, s, bach, 108.4
Grace; Mary, d, 107B.74
Henry; Dorothy, w, 103.104
Hester; Hannah, d, 102.231

James; Ellinor, w; Mary, d; Margeret, d,
103.131
Jane, 104.90
Jeane, ser, 103.255
Jervis; Eliz, w, 104.129
John, 101.21, 110.19
John; Anne, w, 102.21
John; Elizabeth, w, 103.152
John; Elizabeth, w, 103.169
John; Rachael, w; William, s, 107C.25
John, app, 104.70, 107A.22
Joseph; Margaret, w; Joseph, s, 101.108
Joseph; Mary, w; Thomas, s, 103.135
Joseph; Margaret, w, 109.13
Katherine; Katherine, d, 107D.91
Katherine, ser, 104.26
Mary, 107C.31
Mary, ser, 98.31, 105.2. 106.30
~, One? bach?, 104.112
Phillip; Mary, w; Jane, d; Mary, d, 102.263
Rebecca, 107B.66
Richard; Jane, w; Dorothy, d, 107B.12
Richard; Alice, w; Elizabeth, d; Mary, d,
107D.67
Richard, ser, 109.24
Robert, 109.6
Robert; Jane, w, 98.59
Robert; Mary, w; Daniell, ser; Anne, d,
102.268
Samuel, ser, 107A.41
Sara, 101.39
Sarah, spinster, 107D.83
Sarah, wid, 103.8
Simon, 109.43
Susanah, 99.12
Thomas, 103.58
Thomas; Rachell, w, 99.47
Thomas; Joanna, w, 104.45
Thomas; Mary, w; Lawrence, ser; Margaret,
d; Elizabeth, d; Thomas, s; John, s,
107D.49
Thomas; Deborah, w; Edward, s; John, s,
109.12
Thomas; Catherine, w, 109.81
Thomas, ser, 103.44
William, 99.30
William; Anne, w; William, s, 105.8
William; Edith, w; Robert, s; Mary, d; Ann, d,
109.53

EVE: Thomas; Margeret, w; Margeret, grand-
d of, 103.239

EVEES: Sarah, ser, 103.206

EVEND: Launcelott, app, 102.107

EVENY: George; Elizabeth, w,
107D.63

EVERARD:
John; Mary, w, 104.42
John, app, 98.13
Marmaduke; Elizabeth, w, 102.16
William; Ann, w; Benjamin, s, 107D.36

EVERETT:
Alice, 109.52
Dorothy, 98.63
Edward; Mary, w; Mary, d, 102.226
Henry, ser, 109.54
John, 101.109
Marke; Elizabeth, w, 102.55
Mary, 102.95, 107A.12
William, 101.109
William, ser, 109.58

EVERINGHAN: Francis, bach, 99.19

EVERIST:
Daniell, parish child, 103.113
Thomas, parish child, 103.113

EVERTON:
Anne, 102.171
Rebecce, 101.52
Anne, 107A.27

EVERY: Jerimiah; Anna, w, 107D.24

EVES:
Elizabeth, 102.209
Hester, 102.209
Mary, 102.209
Robert; Margaret, w, 107B.57
Robert, app, 104.90
Susanna, 104.89
William, a parish child, 103.196

EVETS: Mary; Edward, s, 101.61

EVETT:
Jane, 106.53
John, ser, 106.43

EVILLING: George, esq, wid, 98.67

EWEN:
Elizabeth, 98.17
John, ser, 109.28
William, ser, 109.54

EWENS:
Mary, ser, 100.2
Sara; Elizabeth, d; Sara, d, 101.93

EWER:
Ralph Lord, bach, 98.35
Stephen, bach, 99.55

EWERS:
James, 109.37
Robert, app, 101.86

EWES: Isaacc; Mary, w; Joshua, s; Daniel, s,
103.123

EXETER:
Joseph, a parish child, 101.35
Mary, 103.288

EXON:
Mary, 106.7
Thomas, ser, 106.54

EXTON:
John, £600; Sarah, w; Elizabeth Sicksmith, d
of, 103.217
John, bach, gent, 110.22

EYCOTT:
Mary, 104.84
Rich; ~, w, 104.80

EYLES:
George, 106.66
Henry; Abigall, w; Mary, d; Samuel, s;
Henry, s, 109.60
William, 102.82
William; Elizabeth, w; Elizabeth, d; William,
s, 102.194

EYLOE: William; Alice, w; Elizabeth, d;
Mary, d; Christopher, s, 107D.68

EYRES:
Alice; George, s; Eliz, d, 104.13
Anne, 104.39
Peter, £50 p.a.; Mary, w; Elizabeth, d; Mary,
d, 106.34
Rich, bach, 104.25

EYTON: Peter, 110.10

FACER: Thomas, 102.272

FACKERY: Fallenby, app, 101.17

FAGE:
Edward; Elizabeth, w, 103.91
Robert, pensioner; Hosanah, w, 103.75

FAGG: Richard; Anne, w, 102.120

FAIRBANCK: Elizabeth, 101.47

FAIRBEARD: John, 107D.24

FAIRBONE: Elizabeth, 104.103

FAIRCLOTH:
Litton; Mary, w; William, s; Elizabeth, d;
Jone Clave, mother of Mary, 104.54
Litton; Mary, w; John, s; William, s;
Elizabeth, d, 104.73
Timothy; Jeane, w, 103.187
William, ser, 106.2

FAIREBANCKS: Richard, 107A.36

FAIREBROTHER: Humphrey, pensioner;
Ann, w, 103.164

FAIRECHILD:
Catherine, wid, 103.274
Jonathan; Elizabeth, w; Elizabeth, d; Mary, d;
John, s, 103.78
Thomas; Ann, w; Ann, d; Sarah, d; John, s;
Thomas, s, 103.65

FAIREFAK:
John, 98.58
Margaret, wid; Ann, d, 103.40

FAIREWEATHER: William; Elizabeth, w,
110.28

FAIRIS: Thomas; Mary, w;

FAIRLEY: ~; ~, w, 104.83
Frances, ser, 104.82

FAIRY: Tho, 104.65

FALCON: Anne, 102.246

FALCONBRIGE: Thomas, gent; Anne, w;
Anne, d, 98.57

FALICK: James; Mary, w; Elizabeth, s;
Elizabeth, d, 110.25

FALKLAND: Henry, ser, 107D.87

FALL: Thomas; Elizabeth, w; Hanah, d,
102.152

FANCOATE: Thomas, 101.2

FANDREY: Robert, ser, 109.56

FANFER: Susan, 102.211

FANN:
Freeman; Hannah, w; Mary, d, 109.9
Robert, pensioner; Ann, w; Robert, s,
103.76

FANSHAW: John, bach, esq, 98.67

FANSTER: Dorothy, ser, 106.26

FARDELL:
Elizabeth; Thomas, s, 101.105
Robert, pensioner; Mary, w; Robert, s; John, s; Samuell Peryn, s; Sarah, d; Ann, d, 103.227

FARE: Lidia, 101.32

FARINE: Catherine, 109.87

FARIS: George; Elizabeth, w, 109.23

FARLEE:
Sarah, 104.72
Thomas, app, 107D.38

FARLING: Thomas; Susannah, w; Edward, s; Judith, d; William, s; Anne, d, 98.76

FARLOW:
Richard; Elizabeth, w, 109.81
Sam; Clare, w, 104.129

FARMBOROUGH:
Thomas, £600; Maribella, w, 99.54
Thomas, bach, 99.54

FARMER:
Anne, 110.25
Disnisins, a nurse child, 107D.66
Francis, 109.46
Henry, ser, 106.10
Johanna, 106.9
John, 102.51
John; Dennis, w; John, s; Elizabeth, d, 98.2
John; Mary, w; Henry, s; Mary, d, 101.24
John; Jane, w; John, s, 107D.29
John, nurse child, 107D.66
Kath; Anne, d, 104.32
Martha, 109.67
Martha; William, s, 109.5
Richard; Mary, w; Richard, s, 98.75
Robert, 110.12
Sarah, 107D.68
Stephen; Kath, w; Elizabeth, d; Mery, d, 104.92
Thomas, 99.35
Thomas; Anne, w, 103.264
Thomas, bach, 106.53
Thomas, ser;

FARMORE:
~, wid, 105.3

FARNALLS: Thomas; Susanna, w; Samuell, s; Jane, d, 102.64

FARNBURROW: Jonas, nurse child, 107B.32

FARNELL: Thomas; Elizabeth, w, 98.12

FARR:
Edward; Judith, w; Judith, d, 107D.82
Jane, 107B.38
Joshua; Beateristor, w; Mary, d; Samuel, s; Elizabeth, d, 107D.74
Mary, ser, 109.80
Robert; Mary, w; Charles, s; John, s; Dennis, s, 98.37

FARRINGDELL: William; Alice, w; John, s; Mary, d, 109.64

FARRINGDON: Joseph; Susan, w, 107D.96

FARRINGTON:
George, ser, 103.63
Jo, 110.2
Richard, app, 107B.10
Sarah, 109.37

FARRON:
Ann, wid, 103.176
Elizabeth, ser, 107A.31
Nathaniel; Mary, w; Mary, d;

FARROW:
~, Mrs, 98.53
Dorothy, ser, 98.44
Marg; Marg, d;

FARRYER:
~, wid, no children, 103.28

FARWELL:
John, gent, attorney?; Mary, w; John, s, 106.2
John, ser, 106.19

FASWELL: William; Mary, w; Mary, d, 109.88

FATYERS: Mary, ser, 109.80

FAUKERHAM: William, app, 103.185

FAULKNER:
Anne; Mary, d, 104.86
Edward, ser, 108.8
Ellen, 107C.31
Elianor, 107B.33
John, 101.32
John; Ruth, w, 109.93
Jone, 107C.31
Joseph; Joane, w; Mary, d; Joseph, s; Samuell, s, 103.241
Kenelan, ser, 106.30

Nathaniel; Dorothy, w; Elizabeth, d, 107B.33
Obadiah; Joane, w; John, s; Elizabeth, d;
    Thomas, s; Mary, d, 103.12
Susanna, 101.40
Thomas, ser, 106.68

FAWCETT:
Dorothy, pensioner; Mary, d; Elizabeth, d;
    Dorothy, d; Margaret, d, 103.167
Elizabeth, pensioner, 106.8
Nicholas, 99.44

FAWDREY: Jervis, app, 104.2

FAWKES: Alice, wid; Mary, d, 103.80

FAWLISS: Conyers; Elizabeth, w; Elizabeth,
    d; Mary, d, 106.68

FAWSON:
Elizabeth, pensioner, 103.97
John, 99.9
Steven, £600; Joane, w; Steven, s?, 99.30

FAY: Henry; Ann, w, 109.96

FAZAKERLY: Edward, ser, 106.59

FEACH:
Anne, 101.76
Hester, 101.76

FEALE: William, 102.227

FEARCE: John; ~, w, 102.77

FEARE: John; Mary, w; Rebecca, d,
    101.68

FEARNE:
Godfry; Elizabeth, w; Elizabeth, d; Marry, d;
    Hester, d, 102.64
James; Elizabeth, w; Elizabeth Bayley, d,
    107D.4
John, £50 p.a.; Elianor, w, 107C.22

FEASAND: John; Rejoyce, w; John, s;
    Ambrose, s, 110.36

FEATHERGELL: John, ser, 103.89

FEATHERSTONE:
Elizabeth, 98.18
Francis, ser, 104.65
John; Elizabeth, w; John, s, 107A.24
Samuel, 99.11

FEATLEY: Daniell; Elizabeth, w; Elizabeth,
    d; Robert, s, 101.49

FEE: ~, wid, 98.68

FEESE: Susan, 102.263

FEILD:
Ann, 103.77
Daniell; Jane, w, 103.233
Easter, app, 98.15
Edward; Sarah, w; Ann, d; Mary, d, 109.50
Elizabeth, 107A.33
Francis, 103.177, 105.1
Grace; Mary, d, 107A.6
Hanah, her husband at sea, 103.262
James, 102.14
James; ~, w; Elizabeth, d, 105.2
James, £600; Mary, w; James, s; Elizabeth
    Phillipps, grand-d of, 107D.35
John, 104.127, 107A.31
John; Rebeccah, w; John, s; Elizabeth, d, 98.8
John, clerk, 98.42
John, wid, no children, 103.205
Joseph, 109.32
Katherine, 106.48
Lawrence; Sarah, d; Susannah, d; Peter, s;
    Williams; Hanah, d, 107B.75
Mary, 108.3
Mary, pensioner; John, s, 103.209
Mary, ser, 100.7
Nicholas, bach under age, 103.197
Nicholas, ser, 109.34
Richard, Doctor of Physick, 110.20
Robert; Martha, w, 102.59
Robert, app, 107A.29
Samuel; Elizabeth, w; Samuel, s; Elizabeth, d,
    107B.71
Sara, 101.10
Sara; Penton, s, 101.93
Symon, 101.9
Thomas; Margaret, w; Thomas, w,
    109.47
William; Sarah, w; James, s, 103.141

FEILDER:
Lucratia, wid, 103.132
Richard; Elizaneth, w, 107D.24
William; Elizabeth, w; Alice, d; Williams, s;
    Elizabeth, d?; Thomas, s?, 103.40
William, ser, 98.30

FEILDING:
Edward; Elizabeth, w; Abigall, d; Elizabeth,
    d, 107A.32
Isaak; Joan, w, 104.124
Paull; Ellinor, w; Richard, s; Elizabeth, d,
    103.181
Samuell; Ann, w; Thomas, s, 101.109
William, 110.1

FEILDS: Mary, a child (dead), 102.274

FEIRMIN: Mary, pensioner; Henry, s; Williams, s, 103.204

FELL:
Alice, 98.6
James, 102.83
John; Mary, w; Elizabeth, d, 102.200
Katherine, 106.6
Roger; Alice, w, 98.85
Thomas, app, 101.42
William, a blind boy, pensioner, 103.16

FELLOW: Mary, wid, 103.180

FELLOWS:
Edward; Sarah, w; Mary, d; Sarah, d, 103.128
Joseph; Ann, w; Elizabeth, d; Ann, d; Thomas, s; Nathaniel, s, 109.40
Richard, wid no children, 103.191
Susan, 102.40

FELLS: Thomas; William, s; Mary, d; Thomas, s, 102.89

FELLSTEAD:
Adum, wid, no children, 103.131
George; Sarah, w; Sarah, d; Elizabeth, d; Esther, d, 103.126
Thomas, £600, gent; Mary, w, 104.5

FELSHEED: Jane, wid, 102.236

FELTHAM: Sarah;

FELTON:
~, 104.138
George; Elizabeth, w; Elizabeth, d; John, s; Sarah, d, 103.240
John, nurse child, 103.94
Mary, 103.233
Sarah, 107D.11

FEND: Thomas; Dorothy, w; Thomas, s, 109.33

FENIX: Mabell, 102.219

FENN:
John, app, 103.18
Sampson, ser, 102.166
Sarah, 109.63
Thomas; Ann, w, 103.35

FENNELL:
Hannah, 104.73
William, ser, 107B.7

FENNER:
Frances; Elizabeth, d; Susannah, d; Frances, d, 101.73

Tho, wid; Katharine, sister, 104.14

FENNICK: Robt, B, 104.8

FENTON: Marke; Mary, w; Sarah, d, 98.32

FERBY: Lucey, 105.9

FEREA: Francis; Mary, w; Ester, d?; Anne, d?; Maria, d?, 99.43

FERNE: Samuell; Martha, w, 109.75

FERRERS:
Edmond, ser, 106.47
John; Dulasbella, w, 109.76

FERRES:
Mary, ser, 106.27
Thomas; Ann, w, 106.27

FERRIBY: John, 109.61

FERRILL:
John; Marg, w; Marg, d, 104.45
Thomas, 110.34

FERRIS:
Francis; Mary, w, 104.23
William; Jane, w; Martha, d; William, s, 107D.24

FERVEY: Daniell; Susan, w, 102.230

FESSANT: John, ser, 109.80

FESSON: Elizaneth, 109.78

FETTIPLACE: Jane, 104.95

FEWELL: Phillip; Ann, w, 103.219

FEWTERRALL: Edward; Jone, w; Edward, s; Beatrice, d; Izabellah, d; Richard, s; Jone, d, 98.77

FEWTRELL:
Benjamin; Elizabeth, w; John, s; Elizabeth, d; Hester, d, 109.94
George, £50 p.a.; Katherine, w; George, s; Susanna, d, 101.22
George, assessor, 101.110

FEZEY: Benjamin; Hanah, w; Hanah, d; John, s; Mary, d, 103.111

FIANCE: Jacob; Hester, w; Elizabeth, d, 110.35

Sarah; Debora, d?, 102.51
Susanna, ser, 109.59
Thomas; Elizabeth, w; Elizabeth, d; Mary, d;
   Hester, d, 101.55
Thomas, bach, 103.13
William, 109.47
William; Anne, w, 104.115
William; Elizabeth, w; John, s, 104.147
Winifred, ser, 98.57

FITCH: Penelope, 110.23

FITCHER: Edward; Abigall, w, 103.186

FITCHETT: Richard; Elizabeth, w; Latia, d?;
   John, s?, 99.26

FITCHWALTERS: Henry; Grace, w;
   Elizabeth, d; Grace, d, 98.45

FITTS: Hannah; Ruth, d; Dorothy, d; Hannah,
   d, 109.76

FITZER:
Susanna, 106.16
Thomas, bach, 106.65
Ursley, ser, 106.51

FITZGERALD: Oliver; Mary, w; James, ser,
   110.26

FITZHUGH: Leonard; Anne, w; Mary, d;
   Jane, d; Jane, sister, 104.14

FITZWILLLAMS: William; Annah, his lady;
   Annah, d, 98.47

FIZER:
Jesse, ser, 106.51
Thomas, wid, £50 p.a., 106.51

FLACK:
Ann, 109.63
John, app, 107A.39
William; Jane, w, 98.83

FLAGETT:
John, 102.94
Mary, 102.191

FLAMSTEAD:
John; Hester, w, 104.81
John; Margaret, w, 104.127

FLANNURE: Margaret, 98.49

FLATHERS: Wm; Eliz, w; Faith, d, 104.81

FLAVELL: Phenias; Charrity, w, 98.65

FLAWNE: Robert, 99.5

FLAXMAN: John, 106.38

FLAXMERE: Judith, 106.6

FLEEDE: John, 99.22

FLEETWOOD:
~, ?bach, 104.93
Sarah, 109.21
William, 109.14
William; Anne, w, 101.8

FLEMING:
Elizabeth, 110.11
Frances, ser, 103.28
John; Johana, w, 110.21
John, £600; Anne, w, 107A.4
Martha; Henry, s, 110.11
Sarah, 107A.8
Thomas; Susan, w; Elizabeth, d; Thomas, s,
   103.134
William, bach, 109.6

FLENDALL: John, £6000; Hanah, w; John,
   s;

FLETCHER:
~; ~; ~, w; ~, wid, 104.83
Anne, 102.92
Anne, ser, 104.106
Barnard, ser, 106.68
Elizabeth, 109.72
Elizabeth, wid; Mary, d; Elizabeth, d, 102.43
Henry, 109.39
Henry; Sarah, w, 102.62
James; Elizabeth, w; Issacc, s; Jacob, s;
   Joseph, 103.235
Jeane, wid; Henry, s, 103.273
John, 99.32
John; Elizabeth, w, 101.68
John; Mary, w; Anne, d, 104.79
John; Elizabeth, w, 109.14
John, app, 102.204
John, bach, 103.231
John, parish child, 109.14
John, ser, 103.286, 107A.5
Katherine; Anne, d, 107B.4
Mary, ser, 102.132, 104.75
Mellerent, 109.89
Nathaniell; Elizabeth, w; Mary, d, 109.19
Paul; Isabella, w; Paul, s; William, s, 107B.31
Penellopa, 98.47
Richard; Mary, w; Hanah, d; Mary, d,
   103.237
Samuell; Mary, w; Samuell, s, 103.180
Sara, 101.70
Sarah, spinster, 103.54

Thomas; Lydia, w; Sarah Hill, niece of, 103.59
Thomas; Elizabeth, w; Nicholas, s, 103.128
Thomas; Susannah, w; Mary, d; Elizabeth, d, 109.24
Thomas; Margarett, w; Margarett, d, 110.5
Thomas, assessor, 110.37
William; Sarah, w, 109.25
William; William, s, 109.27
William, ser, 98.53, 102.141

FLEW: Thomas; Frances, w, 109.8

FLEWELLIN: Jane, 109.24

FLEWEN: Richard; Sarah, w, 107C.36

FLINDERS:
Richard, app, 103.208
William; Mary, w; Mary Wooland, d, 103.211

FLINT:
Elizabeth, 109.30
Joyce, 107A.23
Thomas, 109.58

FLOAREY: Elizabeth, ser, 103.36

FLOINE: Gideon; Mary, w; Gideon, s; Abraham, s; George, s, 103.154

FLOOD:
Martha, ser, 98.11,107C.35
Mary, 107B.58

FLORREY:
Alice, 98.14
William; Margaret, w; Martha, d, 109.112

FLOWER:
Geo, app, 104.52
John; Anne, d; John, s; Thomas, s, 107D.16
John, ser, 107B.30
Katherine, 98.65
Martha, 101.71
Mary, 102.69
Mosely, app, 107A.28

FLOWERS: Elizabeth, 109.76

FLOYD:
Jane, 109.50
John; Mary, w; Sarah, d; William, s, 102.149
John; Elizabeth, w; Elizabeth, d; William, s, 109.4
John; Mary, w, 109.26
Richard; Margaret, w; Richard, s, 98.9
William; Clare, w, 109.8

FLUCH: Henry, 102.94

FLUEN: Margaret, app, 98.34

FLYE: Martha; Martha, d; Mary, d; Elizabeth, d; Timothy, s, 102.74

FOARD: Henry, 102.2

FOARDMAN: Luke, 102.1

FODEN:
Edward, ser, 106.54
John; Rachell, w; Thomas, s; John, s; Rachell, d, 98.36

FOLDEN: Robert; Elizabeth, w; John Wainewright, s; George folden, s, 107C.4

FOLDER: Hanah, 103.269

FOLGATE: Edward; Sarah, w, 107C.18

FOLLOW: Mary, 101.48

FONNE: Edw, app, 104.54

FOORD: John, app, 102.79

FOORT: Thomas; Mary, w, 98..11

FOOT:
Daniell, bach, Doctor, 109.71
Edw; Mary, w, 104.70
Isaac; Frances, w, 103.46
John; Anne, w; Sarah, d; Magdalen, d; Jacob, s, 107B.16
Richard; Mary, w; John Cox, s; Elizabeth Cox, d; Charles Though, s; Elizabeth Though, d, 103.201
Thomas, ser, 103.224

FOOTMAN: Mary, 107B.28

FOOTY: Margery, 107B.12

FORACE: Abrahah; Anne, w; Ruth, d; Martha, d; Katherine, d, 102.218

FORBIS: Marg, ser;

FORD:
~, wid, 104.99
Abigall, ser, 106.46
Edmond, ser, 103.19
Edward; Isabella, w, 104.51
Edward, app, 107C.15
Elizabeth, ser, 103.271
Henry; Mary, w; Henry, s, 103.49

Henry; Elizabeth, w; Anne, d, 107D.67
Humphry; Elizabeth, w; Mary, d; Elizabeth, d, 107B.54
Isaac; Mary, w, 107D.50
James, 101.10
John, 102.256, 106.25
Joseph; Alice, w; Elizabeth, d; Rebecca, d; Anne, d, 107B.60
Katherine, ser, 107D.53
Margaret, 109.73
Paul, 104.127
Rich, bach, 104.85
Robert; Charity, w; Mary, d?, 99.21
Samuell; Mary, w; Joseph, s?; Mary, d?; Edith, d?; Anne, d?, 99.9
Sarah, ser, 102.87
Thomas, 107B.41, 109.2
Thomas; Katherine, w; William, s; Thomas, s; Richard, s, 103.10
Thomas; Mary, w; Sarah floming, d, 107A.8
Thomas; Anne, w, 107B.15
Thomas; Judith, app, 107D.59
William; Katherine, w; William, s, 107C.33
William; Jane, w; William, s; Thomas, s; John, s, 107B.70
William, £600; William, s?, 99.6

FORDAINE: Richard, 98.14

FORDHAM: Sarah, 107B.42

FORDIAM: Edw; Charity, w; Edw, s; Mary, d; Charity, d, 104.146

FOREHALL: William; Martha, w, 99.56

FOREMAN:
~, 104.48
Barte, a child, 102.156
Bartholomew, 102.156
John; Elizabeth, w; Frances, d, 102.138
Mary, 109.30

FORESIGHTER: Jas, bach, 104.117

FORINGHAM: Thomas, 109.38

FORREST:
~, 103.44
Anne, 102.166
Benjamin, 102.180
Dan; Sarah, w; Eliz, d, 104.42
Jane, 102.98
Jone; Elizabeth, w; John, s; George, s; Tabitha, d; Elizabeth, d, 104.33
John; Elizabeth, w; Elizabeth, d; Judith, d; Lidiah, d, 107B.17
John, app, 107D.52
John, ser, 106.3

Joseph, 101.97
Katherine, 102.92
Sarah, ser, 109.1
Thomas, 102.109
Thomas, app, 107D.97

FORRESTER: Eliza, 104.43

FORSTER:
Amy, 109.82
Anne, 104.129
Anne, ser, 109.3
Elizabeth, 98.22
Elizabeth; Elizabeth, d, 98.80
Elizabeth, ser, 104.57
James; Anne, w; John, s, 109.86
John; Lydia, w, 98.54
John, clerk, 98.44
Kath; Frances, sister, 104.69
Mary, 109.105 -
Richard; Elinor, w; Elinor, d, 109.3
Thomas; Anne, w; Dorothy, d, 98.77
Thomas; Mary, w; Thomas, s, 102.121
Thomas; Elianor, w; Thomas, s; Joseph, s; Zachary, s; Alice, d; Elizabeth, d, 109.80

FORTE:
Anne, 101.11, 102.35
France, ser, 98.42
Jane, 110.23

FORTESCUE: John; Susannah, w; Elizabeth, d; Jane, d, 98.15

FORTH: William; Elizabeth, w, 101.46

FORTIFAX: Sarah; John, s?; Thomas, s?, 102.21

FORTRES: Judeth, 109.38

FORTUNE:
Andrew; Jane, w, 102.146
Anne, ser, 107D.29
Mary, 107D.25

FORTY: Charles; Elizabeth, w; Edward, s, 103.25

FOSSELL: John, ser, 109.5

FOSSETT:
Alice, ser, 103.237
Barberah; Anne, d; Edward, s, 107C.27
Francis, app, 104.1
George; Susan, w, 102.169
Isaiah, 109.31
Jacob; Mary, w, 104.75

William; Mary, w; Mary Grooms, grand-d,
99.2

FOWLES:
Anne, 98.76
Elizabeth, ser, 103.82
James; Mary, w; Mary, d, 103.18
John; Margaret, w, 102.80
Mary, ser, 109.7

FOX:
Alice, ser, 109.8
Anne, ser, 98.19
Daniell; Elizabeth, w; Daniell, s; Sarah, d,
103.30
Elizabeth; Mary, d, 98.50
Elizabeth, ser, 102.153
George; Ursula Gold, kinswoman of,
107D.37
George; Martha, w, 109.46
Henry, wid, no children, 103.38
John; Anne, w; John, s; Elizabeth, d, 104.48
John; Anne, w, 104.65
John; Mary, w; John, s, 107D.94
John, ser, 103.286
Levy, 104.144
Lydia, ser, 98.35
Mary, ser, 104.5
Robert; Edith, w; Elizabeth, d; George, s,
98.73
Sarah, ser, 98.43, 103.38
Thomas; Mary, w, 104.38
Thomas; Barbara, w; Margarett, d; James, s;
John, s; William, s; Francis, s; Charles, s,
109.29
Thomas, £600, apothecary; Hanna, w,
101.79

FOXALL:
John, 101.32
Zachary, gent, bach, 101.32

FOXCROFT:
Mary, 109.71
William;

FOXLEY:
~, wid; Joshua, s, 103.147
Elizabeth, 102.87
John, 103.216
Sarah, 102.234

FOXON:
Edward; Ann, wid, 103.101
George; Elizabeth, w, 103.226

FOXWELL:
Blanch, 103.134
Sarah, wid, 103.17

FOY:
Israell; Margarett, w, 109.89
Mary, 107B.12

FRAME:
Ann, spinster, 103.24
Elizabeth, ser, 107B.80
Isabella, ser, 104.1
John, 99.47
Lucey, 99.47
Robert, £600; Anne, w, 101.95

FRAMES: Martha, 101.95

FRAMEWELL:
Sam, app, 104.24
William, app, 101.48

FRAMPTON:
John; Mary, w; John, s, 108.2
Katherine, ser;

FRANCIS:
~, bach, 104.78
Brewington; Mary, w; Mary, d, 103.105
Charles; Mary, w, 102.227
George; Anne, w; Anne, d, 107B.35
George; Margaret, w, 107C.19
Henry; Joane, w, 109.35
James, app, 98.74
John; Jane, w; Esen, s, 102.111
John; Lydia, w, 103.158
Martha, 98.17
Mary, 107A.16
William; Mary, w; Thomas, s; William, s,
102.39

FRANCKHAM:
Samuell, ser, 98.51
Samuell, wid, 98.51

FRANKE: Edward, app, 103.1

FRANKLAND: Catherine, 109.104

FRANKLIN:
Abraham; Jeane, w; Sarah, d, 103.99
Edward; Elizabeth, w; Edward, s, 103.191
Elinor, 98.54
Elizabeth; Mary, d?, 102.47
Frances, wid; Sarah, grand-d, 103.146
Jane, ser, 107D.2
Jeane, pensioner, 103.93
John, 107A.21, 109.22
John, ser, 106.2
Katherine, ser, 106.20
Margeret, 103.276
Peter, app, 98.76
Richard; Mary, w, 99.14

Richard; Elizabeth, w; Elizabeth, d, 102.177
Richard; Anne, w; Elizabeth, d, 104.68
Richard, ser, 104.31
Samuell; Judeth, w; Elizabeth, d, 103.4
Sarah, 102.166
Thomas; Hester, w; William, s; Thomas, s, 107B.12
Thomas; Diana, w; William, s, 109.87
William; Mary, w, 98.6
William; Mary, w, 101.9
William; Jane, w; Mary, d, 107B.36

FRANKS:
Anne; Thomas, s, 107A.36
Edward, 101.10
James; Elizabeth, w; James, s, 106.57
John; Hanah, w; John, s; Francis, s, 102.196
John; Mary, w; Mary, d, 102.229
John; Anne, w; Katherine, d, 104.68
John, bach, 107C.29
Joseph, 102.198
Richard; Elizabeth, w, 107D.41
Robert; Elizabeth, w; James, s; Elizabeth, d; Robert, s; Christopher, s, 103.179
Thomas; Alice, w, 103.88
Thomas, app, 102.187
William; Ruth, w; Francis, s, 101.38

FRANKWELL: Francis; Francis, s?; Hester, d, 104.100

FRANSUM: Edward, 109.43

FRASILLYON: John, 110.20

FRASLER: Sarah, 110.24

FREDERICK:
Augustine; Elizabeth, w, 109.35
Thomas, app, 98.8

FREE: Joseph; Alice, w; Bishop, s, 109.72

FREEBODY:
Anne; Rebeccah, d, 102.77
Margeret, 103.225
Martha, 109.30
Thomas, bach, gent, 101.52

FREEBORNE: Joseph; Elizabeth, w, 102.193

FREEMAN:
Andrew; Sara, w; Sara, d; Charity, d, 101.85
Ann, pensioner; Catherine, d, 103.210
Anne, ser, 98.29
Anthony; Elizabeth, w; Mary, d, 107D.6
Aron; Elizabeth, w, 103.60
Arthur, 102.58
Charles; Judeth, w; Charles, ser, 106.20

Chidley, bach, 98.83
Christopher; Mary, w, 98.19
Dorothy, ser, 103.285
Elizabeth, 102.37
Elizabeth; Mary, d, 103.138
Elizabeth, Mrs, £600 or £50 p.a., 109.43
Elizabeth, ser, 98.25
Grace, 101.71
James, app, 103.7
John; Elizabeth, w; John, s; Elizabeth, d, 101.17
John; Sarah, w, 103.92
John; Alice, w; Susanna, d, 104.7
John; Jane, w, 107C.22
John, commissioner, 103.293
John, junior; Mary, w, 103.224
John, ser, 106.2
Jonah; Elizabeth, w, 109.65
Joseph, ser, 106.44
Margaret, 109.31
Mary, wid, 103.49
Owin; Hannah, w, 98.25
Rebecca, 106.36
Richard; Anne, w, 101.25
Richard, ser, 103.32,109.6
Robert, wid; Susan, d; Judeth, d, 103.210
Rose, 102.93
Ruth, ser, 109.12
Samuell, 102.43
Susan, ser, 102.151
Thomas, 102.93, 107D.13
Thomas; Charrity, w, 98.3
Thomas; Jane, w; Phillip, ser, 98.78
Thomas; Judith, w; Thomas, s; Susan, d; Priscilla, d, 104.58
Thomas, app, 98.65,103.60
Thomas, bach, 104.6
Thomas, pensioner; Margeret, w; John, s, 103.77
William; Elizabeth, w; Frances, d, 100.9
William; Martha, w, 101.19
William, £50 p.a.; Elizabeth, d; William, s, 106.57
William, wid, no children, 103.42

FREERE: John; Mary, w, 104.79

FREERSON: William; Sarah, w; Robert, s; Sarah, d; Jeane, d, 103.155

FREGLETON: Robert; Anne, w, 102.69

FREME:
Jane, 99.49
Mary, 99.49

FREMHOUSE: Fall Hannah, 102.119

FREMMINGHAM: Joseph; Mary, w, 98.9

FREMSHORNE: Elizabeth, 102.218

FRENCH:
Anne, 109.109
Charles; Alice, w; Elizabeth, d, 102.90
Daniell; Elizabeth, w; Sarah, d; Elizabeth, d,
   102.50
Elizabeth, 109.93
James, ser, 98.29
John; Grace, w; Susanna, d, 104.32
Margrret, 98.26
Mary, 107C.17, 107D.80
Mary; Jane, d; Frances, d, 102.162
Nicholas; Sarah, w; Mary, d; John, s, 102.99
Samuell, £50 p.a.; Mary, w; Hanah, d, 106.43
Samuell, wid, 109.102
Thomas; Joane, w; Elizabeth, d, 103.35
Thomas, bach, 103.163
William, 102.258
William, app, 98.69

FRENCHAM:
Elizabeth, 99.19
James, app, 104.35
Rebecah, 99.19
Rose, 99.19

FRENCHFEILD: William, ser, 107C.15

FRESHWATER: William, app, 98.36

FRETCHWELL: Hester, 98.33

FRETHY:
Joseph; Jone, w; Anne, d; Mary, d; Joseph, s;
   William, s; Elizabeth, d, 107D.6
William, 105.18

FRETWELL: Thomas; Elianor, w,
   107D.78

FREYER: Tobias; Lucy, w; Mary, d,
   107A.27

FREYSER: Thomas, 110.8

FRICHLEY: Elizabeth, 109.85

FRIEND: Mary, 99.37

FRIMLIN: John; Ester, w; John, s, 105.4

FRIP: Robert, ser, bach, 99.2

FRISWELL:
Francis; Margaret, w, 109.59
Issabella, ser, 102.82

FRITER: Judith, 102.204

FRITH:
Joan, 102.248
Johana, wid, 103.59
John, ser, 103.18
William, 109.87

FRODSER: Thomas, 107D.65

FROGG: Elizabeth, ser, 107D.52

FROGMARTON: James; Marcey, w; Anne, d;
   John, s; James, s, 102.91

FROHOCK: John; Anne, w, 107B.51

FROMANTIEL: Mary, wid; Mary, d, 100.9

FROOME:
Jane, 110.15
Lawrence, 110.15   -

FROST:
Alice; Richard, s; Sarah, d, 102.240
Elizabeth, ser, 103.232
George, ser, 103.257
Grace, 99.5
John, app, 103.7, 107B.2
Mary, 99.5
Richard, 98.32
Richard, pensioner; Ann, w, 103.204
Sarah, 109.74
William; Sarah, w; Elizabeth, d, 109.42
William, app, 109.42

FROUD:
Mary, ser, 98.71
Prudence; Anne, d, 109.64

FRUBISHER: Francis; Marg, w; Francis, s;
   Robt, s; Theophila, d, 104.1

FRYE:
Benj, ser, bach?, 104.12
Hannah, 109.34
Jane; Elizabeth, d, 98.8
John, bach, 103.203
Margaret, 107D.58
Richard, 102.49
Thomas; Katherine, w; John, s; Mary, d;
   Alice, d, 107D.8
Thomas; Mary, w; Patience, d, 109.106
William; Elizabeth, w, 103.251

FRYER:
Anne, ser, 106.41
Joanna, 99.43
John, bach, 103.100
Richard; Frances, w; Thomas, s, 100.10
Sarah, ser, 98.38

114

Thomas; Frances, w; Thomas, s; Samuel, s;
Barbara, d; Francis, s, 109.5
William, wid, hath children not at home,
103.49

FRYERS: Isabella, ser, 104.6

FUDGE:
Ann, pensioner, 103.69
Francis; Jane, w; Thomas, s; Sarah, 102.261
Isabella, ser, 104.55

FULCHER: Edward; Elizabeth, w; Elizabeth,
d, 103.48

FULLER:
Ann, 102.218
Daniell, app, 101.21
Elizabeth, 98.1
Emanuell, under 25 yrs, 102.13
Henry, 101.14
Jane William, d of Medcalfe, 107B.5
John; Martha, w; Martha, d, 98.59
John; Margaret, w; John, s, 102.239
John; Elienor, w; Bartholomew, s, 102.264
John; Mary, w, 103.153
John; Mary, w; William, s; Samuell, s;
Thomas, s, 103.175
John; Elizabeth, w, 109.100
Mary, 106.17
Peter; Elizabeth, w; Charles, s, 102.258
Richard; Frances, w; Frances, w, 107D.53
Richard, wid; Richard, s; William, s,
104.77
Samuell, bach, gent, 106.49
Sarah, 102.14
Sarah; Mary, d, 102.259
Symon, gent; Susan, w; John, s, 106.29
Thomas; Ann, w; Margeret, sister, 103.146
Thomasin; Thomasin, d, 107C.13
Wm; Mary, w, 104.35

FULLERTON:
Joseph, 110.15
Mary, 99.51

FULLHAM: Richard; Temperance, w;
Elizabeth, d; Judeth, d; Richard, s; Joyce,
d, 103.26

FULLUM: Elizabeth, 102.17

FUNGE:
Thomas; Francis, w; Mary, d, 107C.31
Wm, 104.136

FURBOROW: Mary, ser, 106.6

FURBY: Ann, ser, 103.163

FURDEN: Frances; Katherine, d, 106.15

FURMEE: James; Katherine, w; Elizabeth, d;
Sarah, d; Judeth, d, 103.36

FURNACE:
Anne; John, s; George, s; Elizabeth, d; Anne,
d; Mary, d, 107A.15
John; Amy, w; John, s; Wm, s, 104.49

FURNELL: James, 102.30

FURNES: William; Anne, w; Thomas, s,
109.84

FURSEE: Margeret, wid; John, s; Susan, d,
103.273

FURSS:
John; Elizabeth, w; John, s; Elizabeth, d;
Mary, d; Susanna, d, 102.111
John, ser, 106.52

FURTHER: John, 102.33

FUSLAND: Andrew, wid, 102.203

FUSMAN: John; Rebacca, w, 106.28

FUSSELL: Sarah, ser, 103.41

FYANDER:
Dorothy, 109.45
Henry; Mary, w; James, s, 109.102
Martha, 109.45

FYGE: Thomas, £600; Mary, w; Margeret, d;
Hanah, d; Mary, d; Martha, d, 103.219

FYTON: James, commissioner, 108.8

GABBOT: Elizabeth, 106.9

GABRIELL: Elizabeth, 98.55

GADBERRY: Job, 107B.2

GADFEILD: John; Marriam, w; John, s;
Sarah, d, 104.62

GAFFIN: William; Sarah, w; Mary, d,
109.106

GAGE:
Elizabeth, ser, 109.82
Katherine, 106.12

GAINE: John; Sarah, w; Joseph, s,
107B.68

GAINSFORD: Paul, ser,
106.29

GAIRE: Eliz;

GALE:
~, Mrs, 104.94
Alice, 101.65
Charles; Mary, w; Mary, d, 102.107
Elizabeth, wid; Sarah Gardiner, d in law,
103.13
Francis; Martha, w, 103.13
Katherine, 106.4
John, wid, 109.97
Mary, a nurse child, 107D.81
Mary, ser, 104.140
William, £50 p.a.; Martha, w; Elizabeth, d,
106.54

GALES: Joseph, 109.88

GALIER: Robert, app, 107B.79

GALLANT: John, bach, 98.88

GALLARD: Mary, 102.263

GALLION:
John; Frances, w, 104.53
Mary, app, 104.25

GALLOWAY:
James; Elizabeth, w, 107B.18
John; Lucretia, w; Frances, her sister,
104.74

GALLWAY: Richard, ser, 109.9

GAMAGE:
Thomas; Sarah, w, 107C.23
Thomas, app, 107A.36

GAMBALL:
Daniell; Elizabeth, w, 98.19
Eliza; Mary, d, 104.99
John; Alice, w, 103.24
Nicholas; Elizabeth, w; Dorothy, d,
107D.91
William; Elizabeth, w, 107D.75

GAMBLE:
Cordelia, 101.13
John; Mary, w; Elizabeth, d; Mary, d; John, s;
Joseph, s, 101.92
Samuell; Elizabeth, w; John, s; Samuell, s,
101.38

GAME: John; Susan, w; William, s; Joseph,
s; Katherine, d, 102.186

GAMIDGE:
Abraham, £50 p.a.; Rebecca, w; Abraham, s,
103.54
Thomas, app, 103.54

GAMON:
John, app, 107C.36
Michaell; Rachell, w, 106.37
Robert, 109.65

GAMULL: Thomas, 106.43

GANDER: John, bach, 109.103

GANDLITT: Jonathan, 105.18

GANDY:
Elizabeth, 102.66
John; Florenda, w, 107B.58
Thomas; Hannah, w; Hannah, d, 109.77

GANEY: Daniell; Joanna, w, 103.241

GANICK: John; ~, w, 103.35

GANNOCKE: Mary, 110.2

GANT: Jasper; Jane, w; John, s, 107D.11

GANTHORN: John, bach, £600, 102.3

GAPIN:
Stephen, 109.108
Thomas; Sarah, w; Thomas, s, 109.108

GARBUTT: Rich; Marg, w; Mary, d;

GARDNER:
~; Mary, d, 98.56
Ambrose; Alice, w; Obadiah, s, 106.33
Anne, 99.21, 106.45
Anthony; Ellin, w; Anne, d; Mary, d; Kath, d;
Ellin, d; Alice, d, 104.35
Arthur, bach; Elizabeth, sister, 103.192
Benjamin; Catherine, w, 103.186
Charles; Bennet, w; Anne, d; Elizabeth, d,
107A.22
Charles, app, 107C.41
Christian, ser, 107A.3
Edward, ser, 106.26
Elizabeth, ser, 103.95, 106.45
Frances, ser, 104.60
Frances, 101.13
George; Frances, w; Anne, d, 107B.28
Hannah, 102.65
Henry, £600; Anne, w, 104.63
John; Sara, w, 101.65
John; Elizabeth, w, 103.83
John; Jane, w, 104.113

John, bach, 98.38, 109.103
Katherine, ser, 107B.74
Margaret, ser, 98.43
Margaret, wid, 103.40
Mary; Jane, d?, 102.68
Mary; John, s, 104.48
Mary; Frances, d, 107B.68
Mary, ser, 98.73
Nathaniel, app, 107A.34
Sarah; Elizabeth, d; Mary, d, 103.13
Sarah, pensioner, wid, 103.16
Thomas; Margaret, w; Anne, d; Mary, d;
    Thomas, s, 109.106
Thomas, bach, ser, 104.40
Thomas, ser, 103.31
William, 109.98
William; Joan, w; Josias, s; Sarah, d; Mary, d,
    102.128
William; Elizabeth, w, 109.44
William; Anne, w, 110.25
William, bach, 106.45
William, ser, 103.245
Zachariah, bach, 103.31

GAREY: Judeth, ser, 103.5

GARFEILD: Mary; Arrabella, d,
    109.80

GARIOTSON: Richard; Catherine, w;
    Christian, s; Catherine, d, 103.210

GARISH: John; Ann, w, 103.34

GARLAND:
Henry; Soience, w, 104.126
Humphry; Mary, w, 98.13
Lydia, ser, 104.57
Mary; Elizabeth, d, 106.62
William; Elizabeth, w; John, s; Margaret, d,
    102.15
William, bach, 102.75

GARLICK: Chas, app, 104.91

GARLINGTON: Lancellott; Elizabeth, w;
    Mary, d, 98.8

GARMANT: Edward, app,
    102.115

GARMENT: Jane, 102.217

GARNETT:
Eliza, 104.30
Newark, ser, 103.16
Thomas; Barbara, w, 110.15

GARNONS: Elizabeth;

GARRETT:
~; ~, w, 103.75
Ann, 102.225, 107B.33
Anne; Anne, d, 109.13
Charles; Alice, w; Catherine, d; Sarah, d,
    109.108
Elizabeth, wid; ~, d or s, 100.10
Francis, 109.48
George; Frances, w, 101.76
George; Sarah, w; William, s, 102.223
George, bach, 102.148
Hugh; Elizabeth, w; Edward, s; Hugh, s;
    Mary, d; Katherine, d; Jane, d, 102.88
Jane; Bennett, s, 102.186
Jeremiah; Mary, w; William, s; Mary, d,
    102.207
John, 104.62, 109.77
John; Martha, w; John, s, 102.37
John, wid; Thomas, s, 103.26
Jonathan; Mary, w; Mary, d; John, s;
    Jonathan, s, 103.73
Mary, 107D.81, 109.17
Mary; Jane, d, 101.42
Ferkin; Mary, w; Mary, d; Austin, s; Perkin, s;
    Anne, d; William, s; Thomas, s; Elizabeth,
    d; Richard, s, 107B.41
Ralph; Mary, w; Tymothy, s; Mary, d, 102.197
Rebecca; Mary, d; Elizabeth, d, 109.27
Susan, 104.62
Thomas, 101.76
Thomas; Elizabeth, w; Grace, d, 98.75
Thomas; Martha, w; Anne, d, 103.5
Thomas, app, 107B.36
Thomas, ser, 102.148
Timothy; Sarah, w; Sarah, d, 107B.7
William, 99.55
William; Elizabeth, w, 103.67

GARROWAY:
Christopher, app, 104.96
Edmund, 99.34
Thomas, gent; Frances, w; Thomas, s, 104.94

GARTH:
Elizabeth, 107B.67
Jane, 107D.13
Roger, bach, 98.74

GARTHWAITE: Ann, 104.138

GARTHWAY: Ruth, ser, 100.3

GASCOYNE:
Elizabeth, ser, 99.27
Elizabeth, ser, 107A.38, 107D.63
Esther, 103.196
Izabella, ser, 103.287
Robert; Susan, w; Robert, s; Susan, d;
    Thomas, s; Anne, d; William, s, 107D.92

Thomas; Jane, w; Jane, d?; Thomas, s?;
  Susanah, d?; Elizabeth, d?, 99.29
Thomas; Judith, w; Hanna, d; Mary, d; Judith,
  d, 101.52
Thomas; Rose, w, 103.200
Thomas, app, 107D.91
Thomas, assessor, 99.61
William, 110.23

GASEY: John, 102.258

GASKIN:
Katherine, 109.32
Susan, ser, 103.267
William; Ann, w, 103.145

GASLEY: Grace, ser, 103.11

GASSAY: John; Katherine, w; Thomas, s;
  Anne, d, 98.60

GASSERIDGE: Thomas; Mary, w,
  107D.68

GASWAITE: Katherine, 107A.10

GATEHOUSE: John; Mary, w, 98.1

GATELY: Chris, 104.16

GATES:
Elizabeth, ser, 107D.63
Elizabeth, wid, 103.28
Heugh, wid; Gabriell, s; Ellinor, d, 103.216
John; Judeth, w, 109.27
Joslin, 109.69
Rich; Mary, w, 104.29

GATMAN: David, 109.64

GATTON:
John, £50 p.a.; Sarah, w, 106.41
William; Jane, w, 107B.26

GAUTHON: Nathaniel; Ann, w, 103.134

GAVELL: Elizabeth, ser, 98.65

GAWDREN: Mary; Richard, s; Elizabeth, d;
  Jane, d; Martha, d, 109.71

GAWSON: Ann, wid, 103.229

GAWTHORNE: Samuell, 99.34

GAY: Richard, app, 107B.19

GAYNE: Peter, assessor for Holborne Cross
  precinct, 109.112

GAYNES: William, 101.28

GAYNSFORD: Katharine, 102.125

GAYOTT: Peter; Mary, w, 99.49

GAYWOOD: Joseph, app, 107D.28

GAZEY: Paul; Elizabeth, w; Peter, s; Sarah,
  d, 109.111

GEARE:
Henry; Mary, w; Henry, s, 109.65
Mary; Mary, d; John, s; Humberstone, s;
  Elizabeth, d, 98.54
Rebecca, ser, 109.56
Thomas, 109.65
Thomas; Rose, w, 109.53
Wm; Eliz, w; Chas, s; Rachell, d, 104.145

GEARING:
William; Mary, w, 107B.38
William, app, 101.79

GEARY:
Peter, gent; Elizabeth, w; Charles, s,
  104.65
Samuell, 109.29
Thomas; Elizabeth, w, 106.21
Winifred, 109.52

GEATLY: Peter, 110.10

GEDNEY: John, assessor, 99.61

GEE:
Eliz, ser, 104.30
Mary, ser, 106.63
Samuel; Jane, w; Elizabeth, d, 107B.13

GEEKEE: Alex, ?gent; Jane, w; Alex, s,
  104.135

GEESS: Samuell, ser, 103.163

GEFFERYS: Mary, her husband at sea;
  Elizabeth, d, 103.69

GEGG: John; Mary, w, 104.70

GENT:
Edward; Elizabeth, w, 107A.36
George; Olive, w, 110.22
George, child, 102.134
Richard, 102.134
Samuell; Patience, w; Elizabeth, d; Hannah,
  d, 100.5

GENTLE: Frances, ser, 103.262

118

GEORGE: Isaac; Margaret, w; John, s; Hanah, d; Elizabeth, d, 102.178

James, 101.87

John; Rebecah, w; Rebecah, d?; Elizabeth, d?, 99.11

Peter; Debora, w; Debora, d; Elizabeth, d, 102.221

Richard; Elizabeth, w; Sarah, d, 109.25

Richard; Mary, w; Charles, w; Richard, s; Mary, d; Elizabeth, d; Martha, d, 109.81

Tho, 104.120

Timothy, ser, 106.60

GERISH: Mary, ser, 108.2

GERMAN:
Chas; Mary, w; Anthony, s, 104.117
Mary, ser, 104.96

GERNON: Anne, nurse child, 107B.61

GERRALD: Fitz, bach, gent, 106.46

GERRARD:
Gibbert; Mary, w, 110.7
John, 106.36
Justinian, ser, 98.32

GERVIS: Paul, 109.2

GERY:
James; Elizabeth, w, 106.23
Thomas, gent; Mary, w, 106.23

GESS: Ager; Mary, w; James, s, 102.269

GIBBARD: Hannah, 109.19

GIBBIN:
Benj, ser, bach?, 104.106
Mary, 99.54

GIBBINS:
~; ~, w, 104.30
Anne, 101.79
Gabriell, app, 103.84
Richard; Margaret, w, 101.96
William; Elizabeth, w, 102.65

GIBBON: Robert; Jane, w; Martha, d; Mary, d; Rebeccah, d; Katherine, d, 98.65

GIBBONS:
Ann, 99.54, 104.90
Jane, ser, 98.30
John, app, 107D.26
Mary, 99.54
Mary, ser, 106.14

GIBBS:
Alice, 102.160
Elizabeth, 98.11
Elizabeth, ser, 107D.23
George, app, 103.102
Henry; Sara, w, 101.56
John, 101.56
John; Hanah, w; John, ser; Ralph, s; William, s; Elizabeth, d, 103.91
John, app, 98.2
Joshua, 109.73
Katherine, 98.34
Mary, 101.56
Mary; Rebeccah, d, 102.98
Mary; Elizabeth, d, 107C.19
Peter, wid; William, s, 103.96
Rebecca, 106.32
Richard, ser, 106.32
Sarah, ser, 107D.37
Thomas; Hanah, w, 109.41
Thomas; Sarah, w; Samuell, s; Elizabeth, d, 109.73
William, 105.16
Wm; Ann, w; Alice, d; Joyce, d;

GIBSON:
~, bach, 104.122
Anne; Jane, d, 98.56
Benjamin, 102.239
Edward, 110.5
Edward; Katherine, w, 103.95
Elisha; Martha, w; Hanah, d, 102.239
Elizabeth, 109.38
Francis; Magdalen, w; Frances, d; Anne, d; Magdalen, d, 107B.76
Giles; Elizabeth, w; Jeromiah, s; John, s, 102.263
Heugh, bach, 103.24
Izabella, pensioner, 103.96
Joane, 102.134
John; Katherine, w, 101.3
John; Elizabeth, w, 107C.37
John, ser, 107A.39
Jonathan, bach, 100.11
Margaret, 107D.65
Margaret; Jane, d; William, s, 109.98
Margaret, ser, 103.63
Margery; Sarah, d, 107C.37
Mary, wid, 109.77
Nehemiah; Mary, w, 103.67
Penellopi, pensioner; Martha, d, 103.93
Richard, ser, bach, 103.61
Thomas; Anne, w; Mary, d; John, s, 102.194
Thomas; Christian, w; Elizabeth, d; Dorothy, d, 106.11
Thomas; Elizabeth, w, 107A.4
Thomas; Margery, w; Thomas, s; Christopher, s, 107B.53
William, 102.258, 110.29

William; Mary, w; Susan, d, 103.70
William; Sarah, w; Benjamin, s, 107B.22
William, bach, 98.74

GIDDARD: Benjamin; Rebecah, w, 99.35

GIDDIN: Cornelius; Mary, w, 99.13

GIDDINGS:
Alexander; Jane, w; Margarett, d?, 99.24
James; Ann, w; Ann, d; ~, not baptized, 103.101
Martha, 109.42

GIDENS: Elener, 102.153

GIDNEY: John; Sarah, w, 99.33

GIFFORD:
Elizabeth; Easter, d; Mary Horton, grand-d of, 98.47
George; Anne, w, 107B.66
James; Mary, w; James, s, 103.39
Michell; Mary, w, 103.36
Robert; Elizabeth, w, 101.12
Robert; Elizabeth, w; Mary, d; Susan, d; Elizabeth, d, 103.19
Stephen; Charitye, w; Thomas, s; Joseph, s; Anne, d, 102.178

GIGG:
Joanna, 104.40
Phillip; Anne, w; Anne, d, 98.83

GIGGINGTON: Geo, app, 104.52

GILBARD: Elizabeth, 102.263

GILBERT:
Adrian; Katherine, w, 99.23
Anne, 99.59, 101.180
Anne; Thomas, s, 98.43
Anne; Anne, d, 101.71
Elizabeth, ser, 106.7
Ewnice, 102.164
Ezckell; Esther, w; John, s; Ezckell, s; Mary, d; Thomas, s, 103.37
Francis, app, 98.68
Hanah, ser, 107D.24
Henry; Frances, w; Henry, s; John, s; Edw, s; Wm, s; Eliz, d, 104.110
Henry, ser, 106.53
Isabell, 109.16
Jerimiah, bach, 103.20
John, 107B.48
John; Grace, w; John, s, 104.135
John; Jane, w; Elizabeth, d; Ann, d, 109.32
Joseph, 102.117
Margery, 109.84

Mathew; Mary, w, 101.26
Richard; Mary, w; Richard, s, 103.176
Richard; Sarah, w; Jeane, d, 103.176
Robert; Mary, w; Ann, d, 109.37
Stephen, 101.17
Stephen; Mary, w; Anne, d?; Elizabeth, d?, 99.40
Thomas; Unity, w, 109.16
William, app, 98.35

GILBORNE: George, gent; Elizabeth, w; Elizabeth, d; Edward, s; Percivall, s; Sarah, d; Katherine, d, 98.66

GILDER: Blandilla, 109.51

GILDERSLEEVE: Robert; Mary, w; Robert, s, 102.236

GILDERSLEY: Robert; Joseph, s, dead, 102.274

GILES:
Anne, ser, 107B.76
Anne, wid; John, £600, bach, s; Charles, bach under age, s, 103.290
Cornelius; Elizabeth, w; Jeremiah, s; Emanuell, s; Elizabeth, d; Hannah, d, 102.125
Daniell, bach, 102.226
Edward; Judeth, w; Edward, s, 103.41
Hanah, 99.52
Johannah, gentlewoman, 98.33
Margaret, wid, 100.9
Mary, 104.102
Nathaniel; Mary, w, 101.17
Nicholas, £600; Alice, w; William, s; John, s, 107D.29
Thomas; Mary, w, 102.140
Thomas; Frances, w, 107D.38
Thomas, ser, 100.4, 109.50
William; Elizabeth, w; William, s; Elizabeth, d, 101.5
William; Hanah, w, 106.51

GILFORD: Hanah, 103.283

GILGRIFT: Elizabeth; Thomas, s, 109.95

GILHAM: James; Bithack, w; James, s;

GILL:
~, wid; Sarah, d, 102.143
Anne; Rebecca Staines, d, 107D.46
Anne, pensioner, 106.8
Edmond; Margaret, w, 109.21
Edward; Hanah, w, 103.219
Elisha; Margaret, w; William, s; Elisha, s; Mary, d; Margaret, d; Elizabeth, d, 101.7

Geo; Eliz, w, 104.126
John; Sarah, w; Daniell, s; Sarah, d; Anne, d,
    109.75
John, app, 107B.36
Joseph, ser, 107D.53
Katherine, 107B.66
Katherine, pensioner, 103.77
Richard; Elizabeth, w; Mary, d; Susanna, d,
    101.14
Susan, ser, 106.27
Thomas; Margaret, w; Henry, s; Thomas, s;
    Mary, d, 109.106

GILLAM:
Samuel; Elizabeth, w; Samuel, s, 107D.75
Samuel, wid; Arabella, d; Barberah, d,
    107D.75

GILLES: Lambeth; Amy, w; Lambeth, s;
    John, s; Richard, s; Jerrey, s; Mary, d,
    102.212

GILLIBRAN:
Mary; Henry, s, 107D.16
Obedience, 107D.87

GILLIMAN: Anne, 107B.69

GILLING: Joseph, ser, 109.1

GILLINGHAM:
Joseph, 110.19
Margery, 107B.41
Mary, 107A.39

GILLIS: Jane, 104.102

GILLPHY: ~, Dr., 104.9

GILLSTRUPP: Charles; Katherine, w,
    103.114

GILMAN:
John, bach, 100.4
Sarah, ser, 107B.80

GILMEY: Charles, app, 107D.50

GILMORE: Elizabeth, 107A.23

GILPIN: Mary, pensioner, 103.26

GILSTHROPE: Charles, ser, 98.31

GILSTON: John, 103.81

GIMBERT:
Charles, 99.6
Elizabeth, 99.6

Godfrey, 99.6
Richard, 99.6

GIMEY: Peter; Anne, w, 102.229

GIMGE: Elizabeth, 102.75

GINAWAY: John, 102.177

GINGE: Mary, 109.3

GINN: Uriah; Anne, w; Charles, s,
    107B.54

GIRDLER:
Alice, 109.55
Anthony, ser, 109.43
Christopher, child, 109.28
Christopher, ser, 109.28
Joseph, Serjeant-at-Law; Dorothy, w;
    Joseph, s; Edward, s; Thomas, s,
    106.23
Mary, child;

GIRLE:
~, 101.27

GIROME: Margaret, 106.41

GIRTON: Mary, 109.17

GISBEY: Charles, 102.164

GISBURN: Robt; Priscilla, w; Anthony, s;

GISSETT:
~, wid, 103.25

GITHIN: Roger; Mary, w, 103.160

GITHINS:
Daniel, 105.17
Elizabeth, 109.95
Priscilla, ser, 107D.66

GITTINS: Wm; Kath, w; Edw, s; Anne, d,
    104.109

GIVER: Joshua, dead, 102.275

GIXSON: Mathew, 109.34

GLADMAN:
Anne, 109.64
Benjamin; Mary, w; John, s; William, s,
    103.288
Mary, wid, 103.288
Michael, ser, 109.79
Richard, 109.22

GLADSTONE:
James; Hannah, w; John, s; William, s;
Elizabeth, d; Francis, s, 109.91
Thomas, 109.94

GLADWIN:
Edward, bach, 98.67
Elizabeth, ser, 98.68

GLANISTER: John; Anne, w; John, s; Mary,
d, 103.111

GLANVILL: William, esq, wid, 106.29

GLASS: Jeane, wid; Elizabeth, d,
103.69

GLASSINGTON:
Gratrix; Samuell, s; Katherine, d, 98.16
Mary, 102.209
Samuell, a boy, 104.72

GLAVE: Jone, 104.73

GLENISTER: John, £600; Jane, w; John, s,
101.4

GLENN: Thomas; Susanna, w, 101.81

GLOFER:
Alice, 102.116
Elizabeth, 102.269
John, 102.223
Mary, 102.243

GLORYBUSS: Augustin; Katherine, w;
Cornellius, s, 103.103

GLOSSE: Robert; Judith, w; William, s,
107A.16

GLOVER:
Alice; Mary, d, 107D.35
Daniell, 109.79
Elizabeth, 104.26
Elizabeth, wid, 103.135
Henry; Mary, w, 103.99
Henry; Mary, 104.95
John, 102.50
John; Susan, w; Margeret, d; Sasan, d;
Elizabeth, d, 103.268
John; Eliza, w; John, s; Samuell, s; Sarah, d,
104.101
John; Mary, w, 105.4
John, a boy, 104.27
John, collector, 105.15, 105.18
John, ser, 106.26
Jos; Eliz, w; Tho, s; Sarah, d, 104.41
Mathew, 107D.92

Rich; Susan, w; John, s; Susanna, d; Eliz,
Spooner, niece, 104.26-27
Ruth, 109.84
Sara; Charles, s; Richard, s; Elizabeth, d,
101.77
Solomon; Ann, w, 104.82
Thomas; Ann, w; Ann, d, 103.272
Thomas; Mary, w, 104.136
Thomas, boy, 104.27
Walter, app, 103.64
William, pensioner; Sarah, w; William, s,
103.76

GLYNN: Edward, app, 104.73

GOADBY: Benjamin; Margaret, w; Rebecca,
d, 107B.21

GOARE: Elizabeth, spinster, 103.32

GOBBETT: Elizabeth, 109.72

GOBERT: Elizabeth, ser, 106.6

GODBEARD: Phillip, ser, 109.76

GODBURY: Anne, 109.85

GODBY: Edward; Mercy, w, 101.81

GODCHILD: Susan, spinster, 103.97

GODDARD:
Adrian, 109.84
Anne, ser, 98.32
Daniell, 102.245
Elizabeth, 109.60, 103.6
Elizabeth, ser, 104.21
Ellianor; Elizabeth, d; Violetta, grand-d,
101.76
Francis, 101.104
Francis; Anne, w, 104.100
Henry, app, 107A.36
John; Anne, w, 104.8
Joseph; Elizabeth, w, 98.3
Lawrance; Susan, w, 102.132
Martha, 109.103
Matthew, ser, bach?, 104.4
Rebecca, ser, 104.16
Robert; Mary, w; James, s; Elizabeth, d, 101.12
Sarah, ser, 106.23
Susan, 109.84
Tho; Eliza, w; Mary, d; Tho, s, 104.72
William; Alice, w; Sarah, d, 98.46

GODDEN: John, app, 107B.63

GODDERTON: Edward; Elizabeth, w,
107C.17

GOLDSBOROUGH:
~, Mrs; Anne, d, 104.74

GOLDSMITH:
Eliza, 104.82
Isabella, 104.23
John; Anne, w, 101.22
Mathew; Ann, w; John, s, 103.37

GOLDSTON: Mary, wid, 103.79

GOLE: Patrick; Mary, w, 110.18

GOLING: William, 109.89

GOLLEDGE: Haphziboth, 99.52

GOLLY: William, bach, 98.74

GOLSTON: Henry, 107C.11

GOODACRE: Lawrance, pensioner;
Elizabeth, w, 103.223

GOODALE:
James; Frances, w; Elizabeth, d, 102.63
Thomas; Mary, w; Isabella, d, 109.16

GOODALL:
Charles, 109.84
John, ser, 108.8
Joseph; Francis, w; Judith, d; Frances, d;
Phillip, s, 107A.29
Martha, 104.83
Richard, commissioner, 102.276
Robert; Elizabeth, w; William, s; Dorothy, d,
107C.35
William, 99.42

GOODBEY: James, 102.173

GOODBODY: John, 101.10

GOODBURNE: Allen, 102.4

GOODCHILD: Elizabeth; Mary, d; William,
s, 109.23

GOODE:
Francis; Mary, w; Francis, s; David, s;
Daniell, s, 102.253
Greace, 103.24
Henry; Martha, w, 109.16
Jane, 110.8
Mary, wid of gent, 102.78
Richard, 102.272
Robt, app, 104.56
William, 101.99
William, his wife from him, 103.56

GOODEAR:
Benjamin; Izabella, w; Dorothy, d; Sarah, d;
Martha, d, 103.40
John; Mary, w, 103.82
Thomas; Greace, w; Thomas, s, 103.50

GOODEN:
Ann, 109.60
Mary, 109.60
Richard; Elizabeth, w, 109.60

GOODENER: William; Anne, w, 102.105

GOODEY: Hanah, 99.53

GOODFELLOW: William; Francis, w,
107D.78

GOODGAME:
Georga; Elizabeth, w; Mary, d; Elizabeth, d,
103.156
Richard; Ann, w; Mary, d, 103.156

GOODGE, See Goudge

GOODIN: Samuell, 102.259

GOODING: Brick, 109.92

GOODINGTON: Anne, ser, 106.19

GOODLAD:
Jane, 102.217, 109.14
Thomas, 99.46
William, 107D.27

GOODLAND: Elizabeth, 98.58

GOODLITH: Elizabeth, wid, 103.33

GOODMAN:
Anne, 101.22
Anne, ser, 98.54
Arobella, 98.12
Benjamin; Jeane, w, 103.56
Christopher; Elizabeth, w; Elizabeth, d, 98.40
Dorothy, wid, 100.3
Francis; Alice, w; John, s; Anne, d, 104.24
John; Elizabeth, w; John, s?; Mary, d?, 99.13
John; ~, w, 100.8
Mary, 101.87, 104.120
Mary, ser, 107B.15
Rich; Anne, w, 104.141
Samuel, 105.16
Thomas, 101.87

GOODRAY: Tho, ser, bach?, 104.26

GOODRED: William; Anne, w, 98.56

GOODS:
Martha, 104.72
Wm, bach, 104.79

GOODSON:
Anne, 101.67
Edward; Lydia, w; Edward, s, 98.19
Elizabeth, 101.90

GOODWIFE: Mary, 101.99

GOODWIN:
Anne, wid, 102.67
Charles; Elizabeth, w, 107D.77
Elizabeth, 109.13
Ellen, 107B.8
James, £600, 102.200
John; Dorothy, w; Mary, d; Martha, d,
    103.255
John; Penelope, w, 106.35
John, app, 101.44
Mary, 103.33
Thomas; Elizabeth, w; Elizabeth, d, 101.32
Thomas; Elizabeth, w; Elizabeth, d, 107A.21
Thomas; Elizabeth, w; Sarah, d, 107C.28
Timothy, bach, 106.48
Winifred; Abraham, s, bach, 104.147

GOODWORTH: Elizabeth, 103.33

GOODYEARE:
Elizabeth, 109.101
James, £600; Sara, w; John Everet, s, 101.109
Jos; Christian, w, 104.85
Tho; Susanna, w, 104.46

GOOSE: Benjamin, 102.58

GOOSTREE: Richard; Elizabeth, w; Richard,
    s; John, s; Rachell, d, 109.62

GOOZEY:
Elizabeth, ser, 103.160
John; Elizabeth, w; Ellinor, d; Mary, d,
    103.94
Richard; Anne, w, 110.22

GORDEN: Thomas, app, 107A.22

GORE: Richard, 106.66

GOREN: William; Elizabeth, w,
    107A.22

GORGE: Thomas, 109.93

GORING:
Anne, 99.48
Elizabeth, 99.48

GORSON: Mathias; Barberah, w, 107D.80

GORTON: John, app, 104.147

GORVE:
Anne, 109.67
Christopher; Rebecca, w; Christopher, s;
    Elizabeth, d; Martha, d, 101.6
Edward, 101.45
Elizabeth; Mary, d, 109.99
Gabrill; Alice, w; Richard, s, 109.14

GORY: William, 110.3

GOSCOLLER: John; Margery, w; William, s,
    107A.32

GOSDEN: John, ser, 102.93

GOSFREIGHT: Daniell; Anne, w; Daniell, s;
    Charles, s; Katherine, d, 110.36

GOSLING:
Anne, 102.33
Edward, 107B.50
Henry; Ann, w, 104.87
John; Dorothy, w, 107B.67
Mandlin; Anne, d, 102.253
Mary, 101.94
Phillip; Mary, w; Mary, d; Elizabeth, d;
    Thomas, s; Phillipe, s; John, s, 102.151
Robert; Mary, w, 110.32
Robert, assessor, 110.37

GOSNELL:
John; Elizabeth, w, 109.86
Richard, 109.81

GOSSE:
Elianor, 109.83
Elizabeth, ser, 106.25
Lucas, bach, ser, 98.29
Richard; Anne, w, 107A.32
Wm, 104.141
William, ser, 98.38

GOSSON: William, ser, 106.32

GOSTELLER: Jane, ser, 109.9

GOSTING: John, 99.44

GOSTLOW: John, bach, 103.2

GOSTON: George; Elizabeth, w; Anne, d, 102.167

GOSWELL: John; Katherine, w; Katherine,
    d; Dorothy, d; Cornelia, d; Goaver, d or s?,
    98.50

GOTT: Charles, app;

GOUDGE:
~, wid; Margarett, d, 109.63
John; Izabella, wid; John, s; Sarah, d; Hanah, d, 103.220
John; Elizabeth, w, 107B.28
John; Joan, w, 110.29
Mary, wid, 103.281
Matt, ser, bach, 104.11
Richard; Elizabeth, w; William, s, 103.63
Susan, wid, 103.24
Thomas, 109.76
Thomas, app, 102.189

GOUGH:
Anne; Mary, d, 102.120
Benjamin; Tabitha, w, 109.108
Edward, 106.67
Elizabeth, ser, 109.10
John; Susanna, w; Benj, s; Anne, w, 104.21
John; Mary, w, 104.123
John; Jane, w, 106.64
Margaret, ser, 106.46
Mary, 109.38
Robert, 101.21
Unity, 106.18
William, ser, 109.12

GOULD:
Elizabeth, ser, 103.171
Margeret; William, s, 103.76

GOULDING:
Ann, 109.24
Mary, 99.31
Richard, 102.236
Thomas; Anne, 99.16

GOULTER: William; Sarah, w, 102.75

GOULTON: Benjamin; Bridget, w, 102.66

GOVANT: Jane, 102.218

GOVER:
Elizabeth, wid; Mary, d; Joanna, d, 102.231
James; Dorothy, w, 106.2
William; Mary, w, 102.254

GOVERNOR: Jane, 102.217

GOVEY: Francis; Maud, w, 102.219

GOVIN: Maud; Francis, s, 102.219

GOWEN: Richard; Dorothy, w, 107D.56

GOWER:
Marke; Margaret, w; Mary, d, 102.176
Robert, £50 p.a.; Lidia, w, died; Susan, d; Lidia, d, 106.44
Samuel, app, 107D.91

GRABEE: Thomas; Elizabeth, w; Thomas, s, 109.86

GRABY: Susannah, 109.52

GRACE:
Benjamin, nurse child, 107C.15
John; Margaret, w; John, s, 102.189
Richard; Elizabeth, w, 103.260
Robert, ser, 103.103
Samuel; Jone, w, 107C.22
Thomas; Mary, w; Thomas, s; Sarah, d; Elizabeth, d, 102.273
Thomas; Mary, w; Richard, s; Elizabeth, d, 103.32
William, app, 102.187

GRADDY: Nathaniel, ser, 103.214

GRAFTON: Richard; ~, w, 100.8

GRAINFORD: Dorothy, ser, 109.6

GRAINGE: Frances; Frances, d, 106.15

GRAINGER, See Granger

GRALEY: Phillip; Anne, w, 104.114

GRANBUR: Susan; Anne, w, 109.79

GRANFEILD: Elizabeth, 101.43

GRANGER:
Ann, wid, 103.66
Deborah, 107C.2
Edward, 105.17
Elizabeth, of st Alban Wood St., 103.201
Frances, 106.34
Friancis; Eliz, w, 104.20
Henry, ser, 106.52
John; Susanna, w; Geo, s, 104.73-74

GRANT:
Chris; Mary, w; Anne, d; Mary, d; Hester, d, 104.113
Edward, wid; Susan, d; Sarah, d, 103.148
Elizabeth, 110.22
Elizabeth, ser, 98.71
Jacob, 108.6
Jeane, spinster, 103.37
John; Elizabeth, w; John, s; Thomas, s; Judeth, d, 101.40

John; Mary, w; Martha, d; Elizabeth, d;
  Katherine, d, 107B.81
John; Jane, w; John, s; Jane, d; Isabella, d,
  106.10
Mary, 107B.8
Sarah, ser, 106.11
William; Mary, w; John, s, 109.9

GRASON: Jervis, ser, bach?, 104.12

GRASSCOMBE: Samuell; Elizabeth, w;
  James, s, 98.79

GRASWELL: Richard; Mary, w; Nathaniell,
  s; Ann, d, 103.60

GRATEFEILD: Andrew; Hannah, w; John, s,
  109.22

GRATEWICK: James, app, 98.65

GRATRIX: Benjamin; Mary, w; Mary, d;
  John, s; Ann, d; William, s, 103.66

GRAVENER:
Hester, 106.26
John, 99.45

GRAVES:
Catherine, 109.112
Ellinor, 98.55
Guede, grand-s of Guede, Egbert, 107D.92
Joane, pensioner, wid, 103.28
John, 104.136, 10511
John; Thamer, w; Alice, d; Ann, d, 109.16
Jonathon, app, 107D.54
Lancelot; Elizabeth, w, 110.24
Margaret, 109.48
Martha, 104.13
Mary, 99.55. 103.243, 110.22
Mary, spinster, 103.68
Peter, a child, 102.137
Samuell, ser, 106.23
Sarah, ser, 98.26, 103.213
Susan, 102.211
Thomas; Frances, w; Thomas, s; Mary, d;
  Margaret, d; Frances, d, 102.210
Thomas; Sarah, w; Sarah, d; John, s; Mary, d,
  110.9
William; Elizabeth, w, 103.245
William; Elizabeth, w, 109.21
William, bach; Mary, spinster, sister of,
  103.68

GRAVY: Priscilla, ser, 104.9

GRAY:
Anne; Anne, d; Sarah, d, 102.145
Daniel, ser, 109.2

Elizabeth, 103.152
Elizabeth, nurse child, 107C.15
Ellinor, wid, 103.243
Francis; Anne, w; William, s; Francis, s;
  Elizabeth, d; Jane, d, 102.36
Francis; Judeth, w; Francis, s, 103.272
Jane, 102.187
John, 102.58
John; Sarah, w, 107A.20
John, app, 107A.30
John, bach, 109.60
John, wid, no children, 103.203
Joseph, ser, 109.43
Josiah, a child, 102.181
Juda, 102.7
Mary, 107B.31
Mary, ser, 109.76
Nathaniel; Mary, w, 103.155
Nicholas; Elizabeth, w, 102.76
Peter; Ann, w; John, s; Thomas, s, 103.27
Ralph, ser, 102.136
Robert; Margaret, w; Margaret, d; Katherine,
  d; James, s, 103.102
Robert; Mary, w; Samuel, s, 107D.71
Ruth, 98.46
Samuel; Susan, w; Samuel, s, 107D.50
Sarah, 102.144
Sarah; Marke, s, 98.9
Susan, 100.9
Thomas; Elizabeth, w; Anne, d; Francis, s;
  Samuell, s; John, s, 102.179
Thomas; Anne, w, 106.42
Thomas, ser, 102.199
William; Sarah, w; William, s; Mary, d,
  107D.78
William, ser, 106.13

GRAYDON:
John; Elizabeth, w, 98.70
Marg, 104.92

GRAYHAM:
Bassill; Elizabeth, w, 107D.58
Mary, 106.3
Richard; Alice, w; George, s; William, s,
  98.32
Richard, gent; Anne, w; Elizabeth, d; Anne, d;
  Mary, d; Richard, s, 106.49

GREATHEAD: Mary, 110.23

GREAVES: Sarah, 102.112

GREEN:
~, rd; ~, w; William, s; James, s; Richard, s,
  105.7
Alice, 98.58
Anne, pensioner, 103.272
Anthony; Mary, w, 98.75

GREENFEILD: Mary, 109.82

GREENHAM: James, 110.10

GREENHILL:
Elizabeth, wid, 103.43
James; Mary, w, 107D.67
Samuell; Mary, w; Elizabeth, d, 103.98
Thomas; Elizabeth, w; Thomas, s; Stephen, s;
    Elizabeth, d; William, s; Martha, d,
    103.274
William, 109.92

GREENING:
Robert; Elizabeth, w; Elizabeth, d; Robert, s,
    103.163
Thomas; Elizabeth, w; Richard, s; Mary, d,
    103.238

GREENLY:
Elizabeth, 106.11
John; Elizabeth, w, 103.284
Richard; Mary, w; Thomas, s, 106.10

GREENNOW: Margaret, 109.97

GREENOE: Edward; Elizabeth, w; John
    Raven, s, 103.278

GREENOLD: Thomas, app, 101.107

GREENSELL: Elizabeth, wid, 103.55

GREENTREE: Mary, 109.26

GREENWAY:
Elizabeth, 109.43
Randall, gent; Anne, w; Robert, s; John, s;
    Martha, d, 98.28
Robert, gent; Judith, w, 98.28
Sarah, ser, 106.28

GREENWOOD:
Ambrose; Martha, w; Martha, d, 104.66
John, 105.16
Jonathon; Mary, w; James, s; John, s;
    Jonathan, s; Martha, d, 103.59
Mary, 102.97, 107B.38
Mary; Ann, d, 106.64
Mary, ser, 109.54
Miles, 101.31
Richard, bach, under age, 103.206
Robert; Elizabeth, w, 102.199
Tho, bach, 104.57
William; Elizabeth, w; William, s; Elizabeth,
    d, 103.206

GREFERE: John; Anne, w; Robert, s;
    Thomas, s; Frances, d; Mary, d, 110.35

GREGG:
Arthur, ser, bach, 104.5
Benj, gent, bach, 104.77
David, 110.11
Edward; Elizabeth, w, 99.57
Francis, gent; Mary, w; Jane, d; John, s, 98.64
Humphry; Margarett, w, 110.22
Jos, ?gent, 104.77
Mary, gentlewoman, 98.80
Sarah, 110.1
Thomas, gent; Hannah, w; Thomas, s; Ralph,
    s; Hannah, d; William, s; John, s, 98.30

GREGGS: Frances, ser, 98.56

GREGOR: Honor, 106.36

GREGORY:
Anthony; ~, 3 daughters, 104.134
Anthony; Rachell, w; Anne, d, 107A.26
Barbarah, ser, 98.50
Bruch, 109.85
Chas; Eliz, w; Chas, s; Jane, d; Mary, d,
    104.4
Daniell; Martha, w, 106.14
Elianor, 109.36
Hanah, 101.65, 107D.30
Henry; Sarah, w; Henry, s; Sarah, d, 107B.22
Jerimiah; Margaret, w, 107D.30
John; Anne, w; Aaron, s; Sarah, d, 102.101
Lawrence, ser, 98.65
Margaret, 101.56
Mary, 107D.30, 109.89
Moses, app, 107A.42
Pheby; Anne, sister of, 98.76
Samuel, ser, 109.12
Sarah, 107D.30
Susannah, 98.75
Wm; Margery, w, 104.77

GRENER: Thomas, 109.67

GRESON: Daniell, £600; Anne, w, 102.5

GRESOON: Anne, 102.8

GRESSAM:
Abbot, 107D.71
Mary, 109.51

GRETTON:
Charles, £600; Ann, d, 106.19
Joshua; Anne, w; Joshua, s, 102.135

GRETUM: Elizabeth, ser, 103.59

GREVILL:
Benjamin, bach, 109.61
Dorothy, 109.61

Elizabeth, 109.61
John, app, 104.24
Phillip Benja, collector, 109.112

GREW:
Mary, ser, 106.22, 107C.41
Nehemiah, wid; Nehemiah, s, ?bach;
    Obediah, s, ?bach, 104.25
Samuell; Joanna, w, 103.242

GREY:
Christian, 99.31
Dorothy, £600, 104.60
Elicia, 101.49
Geo, app, 104.21
Jas; Alice, w; Fran, a child, 104.15
Nicholas; Elizabeth, w; Anne, d, 110.36
Tho, 104.23
Wm, £600; Mary, w; Wm, s; Eliz, d, 104.82

GRICE:
Joseph; Anne, w; Elizabeth, d; William, s;
    Grace, d, 107B.49
Mary, ser, 98.80
Richard, bach, 98.75
William, ser, 100.9

GRIFFETTS: Elizabeth;

GRIFFIN:
~; ~, w, 104.17
Alice, 109.66
Anne, 107B.38
Daniell; Sarah, w; Elizabeth, d; Sarah, d,
    102.156
Edward, 102.53
Edward; Mary, w, 107B.43
Elizabeth, app, 107B.32
Erasmus, 109.100
Frances; John, s; Kath, d, 104.44
George; Elizabeth, w; Thomas, s; Benjamin,
    s; Matthew, s, 100.13
Jane, 102.27
Jane, wid; Mary, d; Henry, s, 102.27
Joane, wid, pensioner, 103.189
John; Ursulla, w, 103.74
John; Elianor, w; John, s; Richard, s, 109.102
John Edward, s of Lucar, 109.96
Jone, 107B.46
Joseph, app, 98.59
Malachy; Sasannah, w; Richard, s; Sasannah,
    d, 109.11
Mary, 107D.88
Mary, ser, 101.55
Matthew; Martha, w, 98.26
Richard; Elizabeth, w; Henry, s; Ann, d,
    109.45
Samuell, app, 103.143
Sarah, wid, 100.12

Thomas, 109.56
Thomas; Mary, w; Elizabeth, d, 102.182
Thomas; Katherine, w; Thomas, s, 107B.59
William, app, 107D.30

GRIFFIS:
Jane, ser, 102.118
Robert; Elizabeth, w; Jane, d, 109.105
Samuell; Mary, w; Samuell, s; Thomas, s,
    105.5
Thomas, Kt, bach, 106.46
William; Elizabeth, w; Elizabeth, d, 105.2

GRIFFITH:
Bridget, 98.25
Dorothy; Eliz, d; Jane, d, 104.125
Edward; Anne, w; Elizabeth, d; Edward, s;
    Mary, d, 107A.1
Elizabeth, 104.137, 107D.1
Elizabeth, ser, 98.3, 103.213
Isabell, 101.8
Jane, 107B.56
John; Amy, w; Amy, d; Sarah, d; John, s;
    Elizabeth, d, 98.3
John; Mary, w, 109.87
Mary, 104.144
Roger, wid, 104.21
Sarah, 102.198, 109.44
Steven, 101.42
Timothy, bach, 98.50
William, 104.39
William, app, 98.40
William, ser, 106.25

GRIFFITHS:
David; Mary, w; David, s; Alexander, s,
    103.283
Edward; Susan, w, 103.223

GRIFFORD: Mary, nurse child, 103.82

GRIGBY: John; Frances, w; ~, child, 103.278

GRIGG:
John; Anne, w; Anne, d; John, s; Margaret, d,
    107C.11
John, app, 101.92
Rachell, ser, 106.51

GRIGGS: Peter; Mary, w, 104.112

GRIGMAN: Thomas; Mary, w; Stephen, s,
    103.32

GRIGORY:
George; Martha, w; Richard, s; Thomas, s;
    George, s, 101.43
Hiram; Sarah, w; Sarah, d; Janah, d,
    103.87

Michell; Elizabeth, w; Michell, s; Mary, d,
103.163
Peter; Jane, w; Jane, d, 101.44
Sarah, ser, 103.19
Sarah, wid; James, s, 103.147

GRIGSON:
Elinor, 99.50
Mary, ser, 109.3

GRIMDON: Mary;

GRIMES:
~, wid; Elizabeth, d, 109.45
Edward; Hester, w; Samuel, s, 107B.68
Elizabeth; Samuel, grand-s of,
107D.45
Elizabeth, ser, 98.42
George; George, s, 102.192
George; Mary, w, 107D.86
Marg, 104.139
Peter; Susan, w; George, s; Hanah, d; Peter,
d; Samuel, s; Elizabeth, d; Margaret, d;
Susan, d, 107D.31
Robert; Alice, w; Edward, s, 102.158
Robert; Jane, w; Hanah, d, 107D.22
Robert; Mary, w, 110.6
Samuel, 107D.31
Wm, gent; Dorothy, w; Wm, s; Chas, s; John,
s; Eliz, d, 104.80-81

GRIMETT: William; Sarah, w; Sarah, d,
109.1

GRIMSTED:
Eliza; Tho, s, 104.147
John, 102.173
Rachell, 102.173

GRIMSTONE:
John, app, 107D.47
Katherine, 101.6
Margeret, 106.10

GRINDALL:
Elizabeth, 106.56
William; Hester, w; Anne, d; Katherine, d,
102.82

GRINDER: Jeane, 103.90

GRINDFEILD: Thomas; Hanna, w; Mary, d;
Martha, d, 101.42

GRINGE: Elizabeth, 102.75

GRINLY: Jane, 107B.25

GRINNEN: Freeman, 109.104

GRINNING: Mary, 109.96

GRINSEY: Mary, ser, 104.93

GRISDALE: Joseph, ser, 106.68

GRISKOME: Dorothy; Hester, d, 102.137

GRISLEY:
Samuell; Mary, w; Samuell, s; Mary, d,
103.127
Thomas; Elizabeth, w; Abraham, s; Thomas,
s, 103.128

GRISON: George, 109.47

GRISSELL:
Eliazer; Elizabeth, w; Fracis, s; Daniell, s;
Elizabeth, d, 103.88
Mary, 101.38

GRISSEN: Elizabeth; Anne, d, 107B.20

GRISSOLD:
John, pensioner, 103.62
Susan, ser, 103.31

GRISSWELL: William; Sarah, w; Thomas, s,
103.91

GRIZAM: John, dead; Sarah, w; Mary, d;
Sarah, d, 102.37

GROCEMEN: Christopher; Sara, w, 101.109

GROOME:
Edward; Katherine, w; Edmond, s; Katherine,
d, 98.25
Margaret; Mary, d, 102.183
Thomas; Mary, d; Sarah, d, 109.8

GROOMS: Mary, 99.2

GROSVENOR:
Edward; Hope, w; Hope, d; Elizabeth, d;
John, s, 107B.2
Mary; Mary, d, 98.19
Samuell, bach, 98.19

GROVE:
George, wid, 106.62
John, 101.45, 109.73
John; Katherine, w, 101.45
John, ser, 104.116
Katherine, 101.45
Mary, ser, 104.16
Philip; Eliza, w, 104.55
Sarah, 107B.17
Thomas; Elizabeth, w, 103.82

William, 102.93
William, £50 p.a.; Anne, w; Elizabeth, d,
106.44
William, collector, 106.69

GROVER:
Elizabeth, 101.26
Mary, 109.14
Thomas; Elizabeth, w; Anne, d, 101.70

GROVES:
Alice, 107B.78
Catherine, 109.69
Edward; Mary, w, 98.56
Edward; Anne, w; Elizabeth, d; John, s;
Edward, s; Mary, d, 107B.63
Elizabeth, 107C.7
Elizabeth Judith, d of Blowing, 107D.40
George; Dorothy, w; Samuell, s, 103.49
James; Dorothy, w; Dorothy, d; ~, child not
baptized, 103.23
John; Mary, w; John, s; Thomas, s, 102.12
John; Ann, w, 103.99
Martha; Martha, d, 109.95
Nicholas; Elizabeth, w, 107C.18
Paul; Merrian, w; Merrian, d, 107C.13
Rachell; James, s, 107B.33
William, 107C.7
William; Elizabeth, w; John Apleing, s;
Elizabeth, d; William, s; Katherine, d;
Mary, d, 103.104

GROWCOCK:
Dorothy, wid; Mary, d; William, s, 103.5
Edward; Mary, w, 103.45
Rachell, 99.28

GROWETH: Margaret; Grace, d, 101.71

GRUBB:
Elizabeth; Elizabeth, d, 109.104
Giles, nurse child, 107C.15
Joseph; Grace, w; Mary, d; Joseph, s; Sary, d;
Elizabeth, d, 103.34

GRUNDY:
Elizabeth, 109.70
Hanah; James, s, 107B.74
Richard; Susan, w; Mary, d; Susan, d,
109.76
Scissily, 98.80

GRUNSELL: Ann, wid; Ann, d, 103.100

GUBBIDGE: Thomas; Mary, w, 107B.67

GUBBS: Margery; Ursula, d, 104.70

GUDGE: Edward, ser, 109.57

GUDGEON:
John; Mary, w, 103.70
John; Anne, w, 109.74

GUEDE:
Egbert; Anna, w; Gude Graves, grand-s of,
107D.92
Frances, ser;

GUES: ~; Mary, w, 102.101
William; Sarah, w; Thomas, s; Mary, d,
102.196

GUGERFEILD: Elizabeth; Elizabeth, d,
102.90

GUIDER: Richard; Phillis, w; James, s,
109.74

GUILL: Robert; Mary, w, 109.82

GUILLAM: Nathaniell; Mary, w; Elizabeth,
d?; Mary, d?; Anne, d?; John, d?, 102.93

GUILT: John, 101.8

GUISLAND:
Bartholomew, bach, 102.62
Cornelius; Elizabeth, w, 102.62

GULL: John, 106.36

GULLET:
Mary, 103.139
William; Mary, w; William, s; Elizabeth, d;
Ann, d; Sarah, d; Diana, d, 103.197

GULLIFORD:
Henry; Bridget, w, 102.55
Richard; Mary, w, 107B.32

GUMBLY: Hester, 98.84

GUMM:
John, ser, 107C.7
Mary, ser, 102.171

GUMMS: Aron; Sarah, w, 107B.37

GUNIS: Edward, 109.31

GUNNE:
Eliz, ser, 104.82
Frances, 107C.2
John; Anne, w; William, s, 98.75
John, app, 98.19
Mary, 109.78
Moses; Margaret, w; Margaret, d; Moses, s;
Susanna, d, 109.69

Sarah; Thomas, s, 109.48
Tho; Ann, w, 104.127

GUNNER: Amey, wid, 103.29

GUNSON: Humphry, £600; Sarah, w;
William, s; Hanah, d; John, s, 107D.80

GUNSTAN: Mary, ser, 109.76

GUNSTONE:
Anne, 101.30
Hanah, ser, 106.68
Phillip, app, 98.72

GUNTER:
Rebecca, 107A.41
Nicholas, 107B.22

GUNTHORFE: Elizabeth, 109.39

GUPWELL: George, £600; Martha, w;
Dorothy, d; George, s, 102.81

GURDEN: Judeth, 110.24

GURISTONE: Elizabeth, 109.38

GURLING: Robert, 105.17

GURNETT:
Agnus, 103.79
Phillip; Rebecca, w, 103.81
Phillip, at sea; Mary, w, 103.112

GURNEY:
Elizabeth, 109.11
John; Sarah, w; John, s; Bridgett, d, 104.69
John; Mary, w; Abraham, s; John, s; Robert,
s; Anne, d, 107B.81
John, at sea; Mary, w; John, s, 103.46
Richard, bach, 109.11
Thomas; Anne, w; Anne, d, 110.8

GURRATT: Evan; Anne, w, 98.77

GUTRAGE: James; Elizabeth, w, 109.94

GUTTER: Richard; Frances, w; Frances, d;
Elizabeth, d, 100.7

GUTTERIDGE:
Dennis; Hanah, w; Mary, d; Hanah, d,
107B.39
Elizabeth, 101.94, 107D.80
George; Anne, w; Sarah, d; George, s,
109.110
Luke; Elizabeth, w; Elizabeth, d; Luke, s;
Mary, d, 107B.60

Mary, ser, 98.36
Thomas; Margeret, w; Ann, d; Sarah, d;
Thomas, s, 103.159
William; Rachael, w; William, s,
107D.52

GUY:
David, 104.103
Edward, ser, 106.9
Henry, 109.81
James; Margery, w, 109.103

GUYDEE: Philip; Lowis, w; Anne, d;
Stephen, s, 104.110

GWILLIAM: John; Anne, w, 98.53

GWILLIAMS: Mary, 98.70

GWILLIM: Jane, ser, 106.13

GWILT: Howell, app, 98.14

GWINN:
Charles; Mary, w; Mary, d; Elizabeth, d;
Martha, d, 103.231
Charles, collector, farryer, 103.293
Edward; Mary, w, 99.30
Elizabeth, app, 109.25
Jane, 106.57
Richard, 105.15
Richard, £50 p.a.; Grace, w, 106.52

GWYDETT:
Mary, 98.10
Robert; Anne, w; Robert, s; Richard, s;
James, s, 98.42

GYDOTT: Symon, bach, 103.15

GYE:
Dorothy, wid; Mary Pillkin, grand-d,
103.267
Mary, ser; Elizabeth Greene, niece, wid,
103.8
Sarah, spinster, 103.22
William; Catherine, w, 103.167

GYPPES: Elizabeth, pensioner; John, s;
Hanah, d, 103.90

HABBERLEY: Francis; Joane, w; Francis, d;
Phelix, s, 102.183

HABER:
John, 102.214
Ann, w, 102.214

HABERT: Damiseen, 105.9

HACKER:
Eliz; Eliza Robinson, d, 104.96
Henry; Sarah, w; Henry, s; Sarah, d, 107B.60
Susanne, 104.96

HACKETT:
George, 105.16
Samuell, ser, 106.22
Sarah, ser, 98.86
William, 102.45

HACKLEY:
Joseph; Mary, w, 109.99
Joshua, 109.99

HACKNEY:
Eliza, 104.18
Samuell, 102.4

HACKWOOD: Thomas, 109.15

HADDELSHETH: John; Ruth, w; Elizabeth,
    w; Hester, d; Ruth, d, 102.48

HADDEN:
Anne, 107C.12
John; Sarah, w; John, s; Sarah, d, 107D.84

HADDOCK:
Anne, 104.76
Gatty, 109.13
James, ser, 107D.54
Luke; Sarah, w; Luke, s; Sarah, d; Thomas, s;
    Jane, d; Christopher, s, 109.48
Richard; Martha, w; Penellopa, d, 98.9
Roger; Elizabeth, w, 102.119

HADDON:
Adrian, wid, 103.85
John; Sarah, w; Margeret, d; John, s, 103.19
William; Winifrett, w, 99.45

HADDRICK:
Christopher; Martha, w, 101.6
Thomas, 101.6

HADDY: Joane, ser;

HADERELL:
~; Elizabeth, w, 106.7

HADLEY:
Daniel, ser, 106.3
Elizabeth, ser, 98.67
John, 104.72
Joseph; Mary, w, 107D.9
Margery, 104.137
Rebecca, spinster, 103.26
Thomas, ser, 106.23

HADNOCKE: Elizabeth, 106.29

HADNUNCK: Christopher, ser, 98.69

HADRINGTON: Anne, 101.90

HAFFERS: John; Mary, w, 102.113

HAGER:
John; Mary, w; James, s; John, s; Edward, s,
    103.208
Sarah, 102.165
Thomas; Hanah, w; Hanah, d, 103.94

HAGGAS: Robert; Elizabeth, w, 102.182

HAGGERSON: John; Elizabeth, w, 103.190

HAGGETT:
Jeane, ser, 103.56
John; Katherine, w; Elizabeth, d, 102.22
Sarah; Elizabeth, d, 109.106

HAGGIS: Elizabeth, ser, 109.61

HAGGORNE: Ann, wid; Elizabeth, d,
    103.118

HAGGS: Ellinor, 99.25

HAGGUS: John; Elinor, w; John, s; Mary, d,
    102.233

HAGUE: Anne, ser, 107B.5

HAILE:
Elizabeth, pensioner; Esther Mitre, d, 103.222
John, 105.16
Martha, 107D.8
Mary; Elizabeth, d, 102.53
Mary, ser, 103.5

HAILES:
Hanah, 103.61
John; Mary, w; Elizabeth, d; Sarah, d,
    107C.24
Josias, £600; Rebecca, w, 103.3
Nathaniel, ser, 103.3

HAINES, See Haynes

HAINSWORTH: Sam, app, 104.80

HALBURNE: James;

HALE:
~, wid, 109.72
Francis; Alice, w; Francis, s; George, s; Anne,
    d, 101.6

Harcot, 103.234
John; Sarah, w; John, s, 98.56
John, bach, 107B.2
Margarett, 110.21
Martha, ser, 98.32
William; Mary, w, 109.74

HALES:
Eliza, ser, 104.25
Henry; Mary, w, 98.32
Margaret, 109.12
Mary, ser, 98.36
Samuel, app, 107C.10
Thomas, 102.183

HALEY:
Elizabeth; Elizabeth, d; Mary, d, 107D.98
John; Lettice, w; John, s; Alice, d, 102.82
Katherine, 109.24
Mary, 101.94
Ruth, 107D.3
Samuell; Rebecca, w, 102.273
Thomas; Frances, w, 107D.89
William, 101.31, 105.16
William; Elizabeth, w; Richard, s, 98.16
William; Mary, w; Mary, d; Thomas, s,
    103.22

HALFEHIDE: Thomas; Anne, w, 106.40

HALFORD:
Andrew; Sarah, w, 109.75
Andrew, ser, 102.88
Henry; Jone, w; Elizabeth, d; Bell, d, 98.49
Henry, esq; Katherine, w; Katherine, d; Mary,
    d, 98.67
Samuel; Judeth, w, 109.39

HALINS: William; Mary, w;

HALL:
~; ~, w, 104.128
Andrew; Anne, w, 104.55
Ann, pensioner; George, s; Ann, d; Mary, d;
    Emm, d, 103.203
Bartholomew; Elizabeth, w, 110.7
Benjamin; Mary, w; James, s, 107A.3
Benjamin; Elizabeth, w; Elizabeth, d, 109.12
Christopher; Mary, w; Susan, d, 103.205
Edmund; Sarah, w; Anne, d, 107D.62
Edward, 103.48
Edward; Anne, w, 104.44
Edward; Anne, w; Anne, d, 107D.78
Elizabeth; Sarah, d, 102.110
Elizabeth; Richard, s, 102.208
Ellen, 107B.77
Ellis; Rebecca, w; Elizabeth, d; John, s;
    Sarah, d, 107C.15
Francis; Hester, w, 107D.78

George, 99.32
George; Mary, w; George, s; Elizabeth, d,
    101.72
George; Elizabeth, w; George, s, 102.39
George, 103.5
George; Amey, w, 103.129
Hanah, spinster, 103.141
Hanah, ser, 103.6
Henry, ser, 109.28
Humphrey, 99.52
Isaac, wid, 98.53
Jane, 109.70
Joane, 109.51
John; Mary, w; Mary, d, 98.81
John; Anne, w; Samuell, s; Daniell, s; Mary,
    d, 102.247
John; Catherine, w; John, s; Esther, d;
    Charles, s, 103.177
John; Elizabeth, w; Susan, d; Elizabeth, d,
    107B.17
John; Elizabeth, w; Susan, d; Elizabeth, d,
    107B.18
John; Elizabeth, w; John, s; Elizabeth, d,
    107C.8
John; Susanna, w; John, s; Robert, s;
    Susannah, d, 107D.3
John; Elizabeth, w; John, s; Luke, s, 109.44
John; Mary, w, 109.104
John, bach, 103.39, 103.110
John, ser, bach, 98.30
John, ser, 109.19
Joseph, 107D.31
Judith, 101.66
Judith, ser, 107B.77
Lawrence, wife, 98.67
Lidia, 109.3
Margarett, 102.177
Margaret, spinster, 103.10
Mark, 102.83
Martha, 107A.31
Mary; Elizabeth, d, 107B.30
Phillip; Eliza, w; Tho, s, 104.103
Rebecca, 101.89
Richard, 99.32, 107B.35
Richard; Anne, w, 101.66
Richard; Mary, w; Mary, d; Diana, d, 103.46
Richard; Jeane, w; Rebecca, d, 103.110
Richard, pensioner, 103.124
Richard, ser, 104.46
Robert, 102.59
Robert; Dorcas, w; Robert, s; Joseph, s,
    102.59
Robert, bach, 109.51
Samuell, 110.16
Samuell, app, 107B.3
Samuell, bach, 109.56
Stephen, 102.59
Susan; Susan, d, 107A.11
Susannah, 98.63

Thomas, 109.18, 110.22
Thomas; Anne, w; Thomas, s, 101.1
Thomas; Frances, w; Elizabeth, d; Hanah, d,
102.129
Thomas; Elizabeth, w; Bartholomew, s, 104.9
Thomas; Mary, w; Thomas, s; John, s; Mary,
d; Elizabeth, d, 109.28
Thomas; Alice, w, 109.49
Thomas, s, 109.49
Thomas; Sarah, d, 110.5
Thomas, gent, junior; Hester, w, 106.31
Thomas, ser, 106.25
Thomasin, 106.21
Tymothy, a child, 102.147
William; Alice, w, 103.68
William; Elizabeth, w; Michel, s; Mary, d, 103.94
William; Mary, w, 104.13
William; Eliza, w; Benjamin, s, 104.117
William; Ann, w; William, s, 109.28
William; Elizabeth, w, 110.21
William, £600, wid, hath children, 103.218
William, a boy, 104.72
William, esq, 104.102
William, gent; Dianah, w, 98.42
William, ser, 107D.80

HALLETT: Stephen, ser, 106.58

HALLIFAX:
Richard; Elizabeth, w, 107B.39
Sarah, 104.86

HALLS: Mary, 99.6

HALLSHAW: Joseph, bach, 103.292

HALLUM:
Edmond, bach, 102.187
Elizabeth, 109.104
Mary, 109.104

HALSEY:
Robert; Elizabeth, w, 106.7
Susan, 101.77

HALSLY: Elizabeth, ser, 107D.48

HALSTED: Robt, £600; Frances, w; John, s,
?bach; Geo, s, ?bach; Francis, s; Anne, d,
104.101

HALTON: William; Deborah, w; William, s;
John, s, 107B.49

HALTT: Thomas, 102.211

HAMAN: Phillip, app, 103.262

HAMBEROUGH: Thomas, app, 98.24

HAMBLETON:
Anne, ser, 107B.6
George, 106.35
Jane, 110.32
John; ~, w; Sarah, d, 103.160
Mary; Mary, d, 109.96
Matthew, bach, 98.60
Susan, wid, pensioner, 103.136

HAMBLETT: John, 109.89

HAMCOATE: Margaret, 98.63

HAMDEN:
John, wid; John, s; Sarah, d; Hanah, d;
Daniel, s; Rebecca, d, 103.178
William, 102.16

HAMERSLEY: Thomas, £50 p.a.; Charles, s,
106.59

HAMILTON: John; Mary, w, 104.115

HAMITT: Susanna; Thomas, s; Henry, s;
Samuell, s, 108.7

HAMLETT:
Patience, ser, 106.31
Thomas; Mary, w, 106.31

HAMLEY: Mary;

HAMLIN:
~, 102.22
Elizabeth, a child, 102.22
Rebecca, ser, 103.166

HAMM: Thomas; Jane, w; Thomas, s; John,
s; Daniell, s, 102.28

HAMMELL: Leonard; Sarah, w, 107C.17

HAMMERSTER: John; Anne, w;

HAMMOND:
~; Mary, w; Mary, d, 102.262
Abraham; Mary, w, 103.205
Alice, 109.20
Ann, 109.51
Charles; Mary, w, 110.33
Edward, 109.48
Edward, £600; Elinor, w; Martha, d; Edward,
s, 98.32
Elizabeth, 109.92
George, £600; Judith, w; George, grand-s,
107A.28
Hanah, ser, 107D.1
John, gent; Katherine, w; Katherine, d;
Hannah, d, 98.34

136

John, gent; Sara, w, 105.9
Lidia, 101.17
Margaret, 107A.23
Mary, 102.83, 109.21
Mary; William, s, 107C.11
Peter, app, 101.49
Robert; Jane, w; William, s; Mary, d; Robert,
 s, 107A.20
Samuell; Mary, w; Sarah, d, 102.213
Thomas, 102.14
Thomas; Jane, w; Joseph, s, 104.99
William, 102.19

HAMNET: John; Mary, w; John, s; Mary, d;
 William, s; Elizabeth, d; Anne, d, 107D.2

HAMPSHEIRE: Abraham, bach, 98.59

HAMPTON:
Deborah, 99.44
Edward, 109.78
Elizabeth, 109.78
Joan, 109.78
John; Eliz, w, 104.84
Susan, 109.78
William; Anne, w; Anne, d, 107D.57

HANAH: Sarah, ser, 103.42

HANAM:
Bennedict, ser, 109.4
Jonathon, app, 107D.41

HANCOCK: Anthony; Sarah, w, 102.52
Bartholomew; Alice, w, 101.104
Charles; Elizabeth, w; Charles, s; William, s,
 107B.69
Christopher; Mary, w, 102.100
Cornellius; Ellinor, w, 103.181
Daniel; Elizabeth, w, 98.19
Edward; Ellen, w; Lidia, d, 107A.16
Elizabeth; Elizabeth, d, 101.36
James; Elizabeth, w; Matthew, s, 100.13
James; Sarah, w; Martha, d, 109.62
James, ser, 103.286
John, 104.112
John; Elizabeth, w; Anthony, s; John, s;
 Sarah, d, 102.124
John; Dorothy, w; Thomas, s, 103.48
John; Mary, w, 103.107
John; Elizabeth, w, 103.165
John; Elizabeth, w; Mary, d, 107B.59
John, app, 107D.88
Katherine, wid, 100.13
Rebecca, 98.1
Rich; Jane, w, 104.16
Robert; Alice, w; Alice, d; Thomas, s; Mary,
 d; Elizabeth, d, 103.2
Samuell, app, 101.102

Samuell, ser, 103.170
Sarah, ser, 103.283

HAND:
John, 110.20
John, ser, 107D.34
Richard; Elizabeth, w; Mary, d, 103.75

HANDERSON:
Elizabeth; Elizabeth, d; Mary, d, 98.11
Robert, bach, 98.64

HANDFORD: Hanah, wid, 103.121

HANDMER: John; Hannah, w, 109.54

HANDS: Richard, bach, 102.188

HANDSCOMBE:
Ann, spinster, 103.31
Mathew; Ann, w, 103.31

HANDWORTH: Sarah, 109.88

HANGER: John, ser, 100.4

HANGFORD: Hugh, 103.121

HANKINSON:
Mary, 104.58
Samuel; Elizabeth, w; Elizabeth, d, 109.38

HANKS:
Job, bach, 104.84
Joseph, 99.11
Mary, 102.258
Mary; William, s; Elizabeth, d, 102.247

HANLEY: Frances, ser, 104.81

HANNELL: John, nurse child, 103.119

HANNIS: Ann, ser, 100.4

HANNUM:
Elutham, 106.12
John; Alice, w, 99.46
John; Martha, w; John, s; Martha, d, 109.78

HANSHER:
Jane, 109.94
Richard, 109.94

HANSON:
Alice, 104.86
Ann, ser, 103.55
Edward, 101.45
Hugh, 109.73
Jacob, ser, 100.9

James; Dorothy, w, 98.55
Mary, 105.3
Mary, wid; Thomas, s; Mary, d; Mary Fellow,
  wid, mother of Mary, 103.180
Samuell, app, 98.70
Thomas;

HANTHORNE:
~, 103.69

HARBAGE: Mary, 98.15

HARBE: Mary, ser, 105.2

HARBER: Richard, 109.67

HARBERT:
Anne, 107A.29
Anne; Mary, d; Joshua, s, 98.12
Christopher; Anne, w, 98.55
John, 101.91
John; Elizabeth, w, 102.46
Rebecca; Mary, d, 107D.20
Thomas, 109.100
Thomas; Elizabeth, w, 107A.34
Thomas, app, 98.20
William, 106.71
William; Elizabeth, w, 98.55

HARBIN:
John, 104.66
Susan, 102.65

HARBOTTLE:
Hunton; Bridget, w; Richard, s; Ralph, s, 107B.5
Ralph; Sarah, w; James, s, 98.71

HARBURD: Job; Elizabeth, w; Elizabeth, d;
  Hannah, d; Anne, d; John, s, 102.5

HARCOM:
Thomas, app, 101.20
William, 99.56

HARCOURT: Wm; Eliza, w; Wm, s; John, s,
  104.35

HARCY: Thomas, 102.29

HARDACK:
Francis, 99.15
John, 99.15

HARDCASTELL: Samuell; Katherine, w,
  102.208

HARDEN:
Alice, app, 109.96
Elizabeth, 102.35

HARDESSEY:
Francis, bach, ser, 104.34
Robert, bach, 104.15

HARDGRAVE: John; Martha, w; Sarah, d;
  Mary, d, 102.143

HARDING:
Amy, 106.40
Anne, 98.57
Anne, ser, 98.39
Edward; Anna, w, 100.14
Elizabeth, 107D.23
Elizabeth, ser, 98.87, 104.3
Frances, 103.24
Henry; Anne, w; Richard, s, 107B.3
James; Anne, w; Elizabeth, d; Anne, d;
  Martha, d, 107D.42
Jeremy, app, 104.68
John, 102.98
John; Hannah, w; John, s; Sarah, d, 104.22
John; Elizabeth, w; John, s; Elizabeth, d;
  Rebecca, d; Caleb, s, 107D.64
John; Rachell, w; Elizabeth, d; Martha, d,
  109.89
John; Elizabeth, w, 109.111
John, bach, 104.51
John, bach under age, 103.186
Katherine, 107B.70
Margaret, ser, 103.1
Mary, 109.111
Mary, ser, 100.10, 109.86
Mary, wid, 103.150
Matthew; Jane, w, 106.16
Nathaniel; Elizabeth, w, 104.126
Nathaniel; Elizabeth, w; Elizabeth, d, 107C.31
Peter; Susan, w, 106.2
Rebecca; Mary, sister, 104.56
Richard; Mary, w, 98.88
Richard, bach, 103.19
Sarah, ser, 106.11, 107B.75
Thomas; Martha, w, 103.213
Thomas, app, 98.66

HARDIS:
Henry, 109.108
Mary, d of Hatt Ann, 109.108

HARDISH: Mary James, 109.108

HARDLY: Mary, 103.61

HARDUS: Benjamin; Mary, w, 110.28

HARDWICK:
Ann, pensioner; Sarah, d; Elizabeth, d,
  103.220
Elizabeth, 101.52
Thomas; Mary, w; John, s, 101.37

139

Margaret, 107D.95
Martha, 103.137
Mary, 101.25, 106.10
Moses, ser, 102.145
Susanna, 102.229
Thomas; Mary, w; Elizabeth, d; Thomas, s,
109.69
Thomas, app, 98.8

HARRABIN:
Elizabeth, ser, 103.70
William, 104.9

HARRAP:
Jerimiah; Alice, w; William, s; Anne, d,
102.166
Thomas; Elizabeth, w; Anne, d, 107B.70

HARRARD:
Anne, 109.84
Daniell, 109.107
George; Mary, w; George, s; Mary, d,
109.102
John, 109.9, 109.84
Ralph; Elizabeth, w, 109.84

HARRELL: Richard; Anne, w; Mary, d,
109.81

HARRIE: Elizabeth, 106.12

HARRINGTON:
Anne; Rebeccah, d, 98.82
Anthony, 98.87
James; ~, w, 103.237
Mary, ser, 103.286
Robert, bach, gent, 98.62

HARRIOD: Jeane, pensioner, 103.146

HARRIOT: Thomas, bach;

HARRIS:
~, 102.98
~; ~, wid; Elizabeth, d, 109.73
Abraham, 104.79
Adam; Anne, w; Edward, s, 107D.72
Alice; Alice, d, 101.3
Alice, ser, 104.111
Amey, 109.81
Anne; Thomas, s, 103.77
Anne; Anne, d, 107D.43
Anne, child in house of John Townsend,
102.176
Anne, wid; John, s, 102.270
Anthony; Elizabeth, w, 107D.89
Bartholomew; Anne, w, 102.9
Benjamin, app, 107A.42
Charles; Sara, w, 101.107

~, child unchristened, 101.107
Daniell; Margaret, w, 102.116
Daniell; Rachell, w, 103.74
Dorothy, ser, 104.78
Edward; Rachell, w, 102.194
Edward; Sarah, w, 103.8
Edward, nurse child, 107C.27
Edward, ser, 103.33
Elizabeth, pensioner; Mary, d, 103.52
Elizabeth, ser, 104.108
Elizabeth, wid, 103.36
Ellinor, ser, 103.289, 104.99
Frances, ser, 98.50
Francis, 109.47
Francis; Katherine, w; Henry, s; Stephen, s?;
Hanah, d?; Mary, d?, 102.135
George; Mary, w; George, s; Christian, d,
107D.46
George, app, 101.78
George, junior; Mary, w; Elizabeth, d;
Susannah, d, 104.55
George, senior; Rebecca, w; Rebecca, cousin
of, 104.55
Henry; Elizabeth, d?, 102.138
Henry; Susan, w; Henry, s, 109.95
Isaac; Elizabeth, w; Elizabeth, d; Anne, d,
109.96
Jacob; Jane, w; Jacob, s; Anne, d; Elizabeth,
d, 107D.77
James; Deborah, w, 107D.68
Jane, 107C.23
Jane, ser, 98.58
John; Mary, w; John, s?; James, s?, 99.27
John; Sarah, w, 101.11
John; Martha, w, 102.60
John; Elizabeth, w; Elizabeth, d; Benjamin, s;
Rebecca, d, 103.223
John; Ellin, w; John, s; Elizabeth, d, 104.43
John; Mary, w; John, s, 104.103
John; Dorothy, w; Mary, d, 109.4
John; Joyce, w; Mary, d; Sarah, d; John, s,
109.4
John; Rebecca, w; Thomas, s, 109.45
John; Hester, w; Anne, d; Elizabeth, d;
Hester, d; Susan, d, 109.79
John; Elizabeth, w, 109.89
John, £600 or £50 p.a.; Dorothy, w; Charles,
s; William, s; Machell, d, 109.44
John, £600, wheel wright; Mary, w, 101.92
John, app, 103.70, 109.111
John, assessor in Old Baily precinct, 109.12
John, bach, 98.46
John, ser, 103.61, 109.33
Joseph; Sarah, w; Sarah, d; Susanah, d,
103.199
Joseph, bach, 103.122
Judith, bach, 103.122
Katherine, 104.21, 106.58
Katherine, ser, 107D.59

Lambert; Gertrude, w, 107B.21
Martha, 101.11
Martin; Margaret, w; Anne, d, 107D.91
Mathew; Mary, w, 106.13
Michaell, 101.91
Nichas; Ann, w; John, s; Ann, d; Alexander,
 s, 109.49
Rebecca, 102.138
Rebecca; John, s; William, s; Richard, s,
 107A.17
Renatus; Joanna, w; Abigale, d; Elizabeth, w;
 James, s?; Elizabeth, d?; Blance, d?, 99.56
Richard; Elizabeth, w, 109.15
Richard; Amey, w; Joseph, s; Susan, d, 109.87
Richard, 107D.44
Rudkin; Mary, w; Mary, d; John, s, 103.35
Robert, 107D.84
Robert; Elizabeth, w; Hanah, d; William, s;
 Mary, d; Sarah, d; Robert, s, 103.74
Robert; Lydia, w, 104.34
Samuell; Dedfeild, w; Alice, s, 102.101
Samuell; Anne, w; William, s, 109.102
Samuell, esq; Margaret, w, 104.93
Samuell, nurse child, 107C.27
Samuell, wid, 102.44
Sarah, 98.82, 109.19
Soloman, 109.38
Stephen, wid, 106.58
Temperance, 109.21
Thomas, 110.18
Thomas; Martha, w; Richard, s; Anne, d;
 Edward, s, 102.144
Thomas; Elizabeth, w; William, s, 104.82
Thomas; Mary, w; John, s, 107D.35
Thomas; Sarah, w; Sarah, d, 109.3
Thomas; Sarah, w; William, s; Thomas, s,
 109.65
Thomas; Amey, w, 110.16
Thomas, app, 109.95
Thomas, ser, 100.2, 106.38
Ursley, 102.126
William; Elliner, w; John, s; Elizabeth, d;
 James, s; Ellinor, d, 103.47
William; Sarah, w; Mary, d, 103.70
William; Mary, w, 104.84
William; Elizabeth, w, 107B.33
William; Priscilla, w; Joseph, s; Priscilla, d;
 Benjamin, s, 107B.65
William; Elizabeth, w; Elizabeth, d; Sarah, d,
 107C.25
William; Elizabeth, w, 107D.82
William, £600, wid; John, s, bach?, 104.16
William, app, 98.36,104.15
William, Journeyman, 104.10
William, wid, 109.102

HARRISON:
Andrew; George, s; Mary, d, 102.111
Anne, 106.57

Anne, pensioner, 103.164
Anne, ser, 101.78
Arthur; Elizabeth, w; Arthur, s; Mitchell, s,
 103.79
Benjamin; Sarah, w; Elizabeth, his mother;
 Susan, d, 105.14
Bray, ser, 107C.21
Christopher, 102.236
Daniell, 99.8
Dor, ser, 104.19
Edward; Eborah, w; Mary, d; George, s,
 98.66
Edward; Frances, w; Mary, d?; Ann, d?; John,
 s?, 99.10
Edward; Mary, w; Robert, s; Sarah, d,
 102.127
Edward; Mary, w, 104.114
Elianor; Thomas, s; Samuel, s; Elizabeth, d,
 107A.24
Elizabeth, ser, 104.19
Francis, wid, 103.58
George, 106.33
Henry; Mary, w; Thomas, s, 103.164
Henry, app, 102.117
James, 102.176
James, pensioner; Jeane, w; Jeane, d;
 Samuell, s, 103.149
Jeffery; Elizabeth, d, 102.262
John, 109.57
John; Margaret, w, 102.204
John; Elizabeth, w; Elizabeth, d, 109.81
John; Mary, w; William, s; Phillip, s, 109.101
John, app, 98.79
John, pensioner, 103.137
Margaret, 109.99
Margery, 106.31
Martha, 106.57
Mary, 101.49
Mary, ser, 109.6
Peter; Eliz, w; Peter, s, 104.79
Phyllis, ser, 104.79
Ralph, 101.3
Rebecca, spinster, 103.7
Rebecca, ser, 103.202
Richard, app, 98.33
Robert, 107B.27
Robert; Susannah, w, 98.40
Robert; Sarah, w, 107C.11
Robert; Jane, w, 109.67
Sara, 101.2
Susan, ser, 109.79
Thomas, 99.47
Thomas; Mary, w; Mary, d; Elizabeth, d; ~,
 child not baptized, 103.23
Thomas, bach, 109.57
Thomas, wid; Elizabeth, Whiteing grand-d,
 103.68
Timothy; Mary, w; William, s, 102.175
William; Ellen, w, 101.49

141

William; Mary, w; Mary, d, 102.195
William, app, 107B.23

HATLITT: Mary, 105.5

HATORN: Abigail, wid, 100.8

HATRILL: Francis; Jone, w, 107D.10

HATT:
Ann; Mary Hardis, d, 109.108
Elizabeth, 106.24
John; Elizabeth, w, 106.37
Katherine, 101.106
Mary, ser, 104.147

HATTEN:
Elizabeth, 102.20
Elizabeth, ser, 106.51
James; Ann, w; Abigail, d?, 99.34
John, 103.266
John; Mary, w, 100.12
John; Elizabeth, d, 102.270
John; Sarah, w; Elizabeth, d; James, s,
    103.269
Mary; Francis, s; Samuel, s, 107C.15
Pricilla, ser, 106.51
Richard; Elizabeth, w, 109.38
Robert; Anne, w; Sara, d, 101.22
Robert; Mary, w; Francis, s; Amos, s,
    107D.12
Roger, £600; Mary, w; Peter, s; Anne, d,
    102.118
Sarah, 102.268
Sarah, pensioner; Anne, d; Mary, d;
    Elizabeth, d; Robert, s, 103.279
William; Mary, w; Fillagathus, s, 101.94
William, ser, 103.257

HATTERFEILD: Christian; Elizabeth, w;
    John, s; Christian, s, 101.62

HATTOM: Mary, 102.222

HATTON:
Charles; Elizabeth, w; Elizabeth, d; Jane, d;
    Richard, s; James, s; Charles, s, 109.37
Edward; Sarah, w, 106.4

HAUGE: William, app, 103.42

HAUGHTON:
Elizabeth; Anne, d, 98.69
John; Anne, w; Samuel, s, 107D.59
Joseph; Suasannah, w, 99.37

HAVEACARE:
Ann, ser, 109.4
Richard; Sarah, w; Thomas, s, 107D.39

HAVEN: William; Anne, w, 109.103

HAVENS: John; ~, w, 103.239

HAVERD: William; Grace, w; Anne, d,
    107B.12

HAVERFEILD: John, a nurse child, 107D.81

HAVERS: Timothy; Mary, w; George, s,
    102.254

HAWES:
Isaac, 103.26
John, bach, 110.9
Sarah, ser, 100.11
Thomas; Dorothy, w; John, s, 98.79

HAWETT:
Anne; Frances, d, 98.83
Anne; William, s, 98.83
David; Hannah, w, 98.85

HAWFORD:
Francis, £600; Mary, w, 104.3
Richard, ser, 104.3

HAWGOOD: William; Jane, w; Elizabeth, d,
    101.91

HAWISH:
Anthony, ser, 107D.18
James, 101.49

HAWKER:
Elizabeth, 109.56
Richard; Mary, w; Martha, d; William, s,
    109.39

HAWKES:
John, 110.22,110.28
John; Elizabeth, w, 110.26
Jonathan; Martha, w; Martha, d, 104.68
Mary, 110.28
Robert, 107C.1
Samuell, £600; Sarah, w; Sarah, d; Ruth, d,
    103.249
Susanna, 101.59
Thomas; Anne, w, 98.19

HAWKING:
Sarah, 106.19
Thomas, app, 101.80

HAWKINS:
Anne, ser, 102.160
Benjamin; Mary, w; Mary, d; George, s;
    Benjamin, s; Joseph, s, 98.83
Catherine, 109.85

Charles; Elizabeth, w; Charles, s, 107B.24
Christopher; Mary, w; Mary, d, 101.99
Daniell; Elizabeth, w; Daniell, s; Edward, s;
    Elizabeth, d; Jane, d, 109.64
Daniell, ser, 103.73
Edward; Elizabeth, w; Edward, s, 101.10
Edward; Mary, w; Hanah, d, 103.111
Elizabeth, 103.258
George; Elizabeth, w, 109.60
Ja, 104.137
John, 102.175
John; Sarah, w, 102.136
John; Mary, w; John, s; Hanah, d, 102.204
John, £50 p.a., assessor; John, s; Sarah, d,
    102.166
John, app, 98.87
Joseph; Elizabeth, w, 101.10
Karherine, ser, 102.145
Marke; Ann, w, 102.150
Mary, 101.51
Mary, ser, 101.22
Mathew; Dorothy, w; Peter, s, 110.10
Richard; Elizabeth, w, 110.34
Robert; Bridget, w; James, s, 107A.7
Robert; Isabell, w, 107B.11
Sarah, 110.16
Sarah; Mary, d; Sarah, d, 107B.60
Sarah, ser, 98.67
Susan, her husband at sea, 103.165
Susanna, 106.63
Thomas, 104.140
Thomas; Mary, w; Mary, d; Jane, d, 102.130
Thomas; Elizabeth, w, 107D.41
Thomas; Mary, w, 109.52
Thomas, app, 98.69
William; Anne, w, 110.7

HAWKINSON:
John; Mary, w; John, s, 109.1
Wm; Hester, w, 104.75

HAWLEY:
John; Mary, w; John, s, 109.1
Wm; Hester, w, 104.75
Bodnam, 104.89
Elizabeth, 98.56
Joseph; Rebecca, w; Rebecca, d, 103.22
Robert, ser, 106.7
Simon; ~, w, 104.130

HAWLING:
Eliza, ser, 104.65
Wm; Bridgett, w, 104.91

HAWS(S):
Ann, wid, 103.255
Edward; Bridget, w; Elizabeth, d, 103.36
George; Mary, w; Samuel, s, 107D.43
James; Sarah, w, 103.100

Mary, ser, 103.217
Thomas, wid; Thomas, s; Mary, d,
    107D.40

HAWSON: Mary, 102.123

HAWTHORNE:
Alice, 102.66
Hannah, 102.143

HAWTON:
George; Mary, w; Garbrill, d; Susanna, d,
    102.6
Stephen, 105.4

HAWTWELL: Anne, ser, 106.15

HAXBEE: Francis, 109.73

HAY: George, bach, 99.52

HAYDEN:
Anne; Deborah, d, 102.98
Charles, 109.57
Elizabeth, ser, 102.168
John; Dinah, w, 102.98
Martha, 107B.71
Robert, bach, 109.59

HAYES:
Adam; Sarah, w, 102.155
Andrew, pensioner; ~, w, 103.175
Anne, ser, 100.14
Bridget, spinster, 103.69
Daniell; Mary, w, 109.84
Edmund; Anne, w; Anne, d; Sarah, d, 106.2
Edward, 102.236
Elizabeth, 109.75
Elizabeth George, d of Chelsey, 107B.64
Elizabeth, ser, 104.108
Frances, 107B.34
Francis, ser, 109.16
Henry, bach, gent, 106.45
Hester, 109.84
James, 109.79
James, app, 101.86
John; Elizabeth, w, 105.6
Mary, 109.84
Rebeccah, 98.27
Richard; Elizabeth, w; Elizabeth, d; Richard,
    s; Anne, d, 107A.13
William, 109.84
William; Temperance, w; Robert, s;
    Elizabeth, d; Anne, d; Judith, d;
    Temperance, d, 101.108
William; Elizabeth, w, 104.59

HAYFEILD:
Nathaniell; Mary, w, 102.33

William; Sarah, w; Elizabeth, d; Hanah, d;
Sarah, d, 102.137

HAYMAN:
Elizabeth, 107C.7
Susan, 102.183

HAYNE:
Elizabeth, 103.24
Stephen; Hannah, w; Stephen, s; Anne, d;
Murrey, d, 102.234

HAYNES:
Alexander; Mary, w; John, s; Alexander;
William, s, 109.68
Charles; Mary, w; Charles, s, 103.43
Charles, bach under age, 103.122
Clement; Anne, w; Mary, d, 102.104
Dorothy, 105.2
Easter, 98.81
Elizabeth, 99.24, 104.69
Elizabeth; Charles, s; Thomas, s, 107B.69
Elizabeth, ser, 101.28
Enoch; Elizabeth, w, 109.30
Frances, spinster, 103.122
George; Sarah, w; Sarah, d; George, s, 98.82
Hanah; Richard, s; John, s, 102.203
Harbert, 102.55
Henry; Anne, w, 107B.58
James, app, 102.176
Jane, ser, 106.34
John; Dorothy, w; John, s; Elizabeth, d,
101.96
John; Mary, w, 102.142
John; Elizabeth, w, 107D.72
John; Catherine, w; William, s, 109.99
John; Elizabeth, w, 110.9
Jonathon Alice, s of Ely, 107B.55
Jos; Adelina, w; Eliza, d, 104.124
Mary, 102.205, 110.12
Mary, ser, 102.189
Nicholas, wid, 102.153
Rebecah, 99.24
Richard; Jane, w; Joseph, s, 101.73
Richard; Mercy, w; William, s; Anna, d,
107B.56
Robt; Frances, w; John, s, 104.57
Thomas; Emm, w; Thomas, s; William, s,
102.7
Thomas; Mary, w, 103.292
Thomas; Elizabeth, w; Thomas, s; Richard, s;
William, s; Elizabeth, d; Henry, s,
107B.22
Thomas; Mary, w, 107D.11
William; Anne, w, 101.7
William; Frances, w, 103.247
William; Jane, w; Richard, brother of bach?,
104.106
William; Anne, w; Mary, d, 107B.32

William; Elizabeth, w, 109.30
William, ser, 106.29

HAYSMAN: Lucye, 102.7

HAYWOOD:
Richard; Elizabeth, w; Richard, s; Robert, s,
102.55
Thomas, 102.149

HAZARD:
Mary, 107B.16, 109.70
Symon; Elizabeth, w; Mary, d; Simon, s;
Elizabeth, d, 109.19

HAZEY: Henry, parish child to st. Antholins,
103.201

HAZLE:
Andrew; Mary, w, 103.233
John; Anne, 101.16
Mary, 101.24
Matt, 104.105

HAZLEWOOD:
Anne, ser, 98.67
John, 109.61
John; Rebeckah, w, 100.9
Robert, ser, 102.189

HEABERNE: John, wid,
103.142

HEAD:
Edward, 99.49
Elizabeth, ser, 107B.2
Hanah, 103.257
Jane, 102.131
John; Mary, w; Katherine, d; John, s; Sarah,
d, 103.102
Joseph, app, 103.258
Mary, 99.49
Samuel; Martha, w; Joseph, s, 107B.9
Sarah, ser, 103.23
William; Debora, w; William, s; Mary, d;
Thomas, s, 102.40

HEADLAM: Tobias; Mary, d, 102.262

HEADLAND: Thomas; Sarah, w,
103.25

HEADLEY: Katharine, 102.67

HEADY: Elizabeth, 101.85

HEALE:
Elizabeth, 107D.100
Jane, ser, 104.111

HEALEY:
Anne, 106.33
George, bach, 103.288

HEARD:
Anne, ser, 104.65
Rich; Hester, w, 104.34
Robert, ser, 106.34

HEARN:
Dunstan, 109.28
Edward; Susannah, w, 101.12
Elizabeth, 107C.31
George, 109.50
John, 109.43
John; Mary, w; John, s; Mary, ser of, 98.13
Leonard; Alice, w; Leonard, s; Mary, d; Anne, d; Ellen, d, 101.39
Thomas; Dunstan, w; Thomas, s, 109.34
William; Mary, w; Mary, d, 107D.16

HEARTH:
Jas; Sarah, w, 104.48
Jane, 109.5
Jane, ser, 107D.29
Robert, 100.7

HEARTLY: Anne, ser;

HEATH:
~, wid, 109.87
Abigall, 101.3
Anne, 109.77
Elizabeth, 107C.32
Ex, 98.41
George, 101.65
George; Mary, w, 104.9
Jane, 106.15
Joannah, 109.59
John, 101.3
Lawrence, wid, hath children in other places, 103.44
Mary; Thomas, s; John, s, 98.38
Mary, ser, 106.14
Richard; Mary, w, 101.98
Robert; Grace, w, 99.24
Soloman; Mary, w; Elizabeth, d, 101.16
Susan, a parish child, 103.227
Thomas; Elienor, w, 102.243
Thomas, £600; Eliza, w, 104.106
William, 101.48
William; Katherine, w; Sarah, d, 103.74

HEATHCOCK: William; Katherine, w, 101.35

HEATHER:
John, 110.1
John; Jane, w; William, s, 109.50

John, ser, 109.26
Mary, ser, 104.61
Nicholas, 106.33
Sara, 101.16

HEATHERTONE: Margaret, ser, 98.68

HEATLEY:
Francis; Rachell, w; Elizabeth, d; Ann, d, 109.57
George, 103.196
Richard; Anne, w; Anne, d; Mary, d, 102.141
Thomas, ser, 103.166

HEAVER: ~, Mrs, 104.96

HEAYS, See Hays

HEBB:
Barberah, ser, 107A.29
Ellen, ser, 98.45

HEBBS: John; Easter, w, 109.20

HEBELWATE: Robert, bach, 109.10

HEBORNE:
Walter; Mary, w; Mary, d; Sarah, d; Walter, s, 110.10
Walter, collector, 110.37

HECKWITCH: Peter, clerk, 106.3

HEDDISON: Susan, 101.11

HEDGABOUT: Honnora, wid, 103.132

HEDGBUT: John, 106.39

HEDGE: Alice, 102.271

HEDGER:
Ann, nurse, 108.2
John; Catherine, w; John, s; Mary, d; James, s;

HEDGES:
~, wid, 103.270
John; Anne, w; Elizabeth, d, 107C.42
Thomas; Ellen, w, 107D.94
Thomas, bach, 109.110

HEDGSTALL: Mary, ser, 102.185

HEEL: George, 103.194

HEENE: John, app, 101.78

HEFENETALL: William, wid, 109.54

147

HEIFER:
John, bach, 103.127
Mary, spinster, 103.41

HEILD: Ruth, ser, 107A.27

HEILDER:
Charles; Mary, w; Charles, s; Elizabeth, d,
    100.6
Martha, 101.26
Thomas; Susanna, w, 101.26

HELLENS:
Benjamin, St.Helena parish child, 103.36
John, parish child of St. Hellena, 103.222

HELLER: Mary, ser, 109.6

HELLIDGE: Samuell, 101.8

HELLIORD: Elizabeth, 99.25

HELLIS: Heugh, ser, 103.172

HELLMAN:
Margeret, ser, 103.66
Susan, ser, 103.25

HELLOBY: John; Mary, w; Hanah, d, 107D.12

HELMSLEY: Katherine, 105.5

HELY: Mary, ser, 106.7

HEMES: Dorothy, 104.74

HEMMEN:
Hannah, 109.98
Nathaniel, wid, 109.98

HEMMING:
Elizabeth, 107B.20
Hugh, 107B.20
James; Elizabeth, w; Elizabeth, d; Sarah, d;
    Richard, s, 103.124
Richard; Ann, w, 103.187
Robert, 106.69

HEMMINGS:
Edward; Martha, w, 110.33
Henry, ser, 102.190
John, 107D.96
John; Elizabeth, w; John, s; Edward, s;
    Francis, s; Isabell, d; Elizabeth, d, 105.14
Robt; Grace, w, 104.61

HEMMINGWAY: Abraham, bach, 98.75

HENAGOS: Thomas; Sarah, w, 103.8

HENDERSON: Ann, spinster, 103.183

HENDLEY:
Francis; Mary, w, 109.7
John, gent; Mary, w; Mary, d; Robert, s,
    98.61

HENDRICK: Hannah, wid, 102.6

HENDRIX: John; Sarah, w, 103.56

HENDS: Alice, ser, 98.30

HENE: Nicholas; Anne, w, 102.142

HENELY: Jane, ser, 107D.26

HENFREY:
John; Sarah, w; Elizabeth, d, 109.107
Richard; Rose, w; Mary, d; Elizabeth, d,
    106.17

HENGIS: William; Anne, w, 107C.40

HENING: Thomas, bach under age, 103.292

HENLACE: Daniel, ser, 109.12

HENLY:
Elizabeth; Mary, d, 107A.1
Henry; Elizabeth, w, 107D.32
Henry, wid, no children, 103.292
James; Jane, w, 109.83
John; Mary, w; John, s; Mary, d, 110.36
John; Elizabeth, w, 102.119
Litleton; Jeane, w, 103.229
Mary, ser, 107D.82
Thomas, 106.17
Wm; Sarah, w; Marg, d, 104.62

HENN: Christopher; Barthabela, w; Jane, d;
    Christopher, s, 106.17

HENNE: Sarah, 102.35

HENNEST: James, 106.50

HENNY: Philip, app, 104.52

HENSHAW: Jas, 104.36

HENSON:
~, clerk, ser, 106.44
John; Ann, w; Mary, d; Jeane, d; Ann, d, 103.89
Richard; Sarah, w; Mary, d, 103.66

HENTHORNE: Richard, 106.67

HENWOOD: John; Anne, w; Wm, s, 104.43

148

Mary, 109.57
Sarah; Anne, d, 102.134
Susan, app, 107B.74
Thomas, 109.47
William, ser, 102.198, 109.57

HEWETSON: John, 109.5

HEWETT:
~, wid, 109.74
Alice, 101.65
Charles; Mary, w, 99.9
Christian, 101.67
Daniell; Elizabeth, w, 103.24
Edward; Elizabeth, w; Ann, d, 103.108
Elizabeth, 102.273, 109.85
Elizabeth, ser, 103.61
Henry, son of Ann Jackson, 103.63
James, son of Ann Jackson, 103.63
Jane, ser, 106.2
Joane, 104.86
Joane; Eliz, d, 104.86
John, 101.12
John; Rebecca, w; Anne, d, 102.90
Jone; William, s, 107A.8
Katharine, 110.1
Kathrine; Frances, d, 109.48
Margery, 103.285
Mary, 109.15
Nathaniel, £600; Ann, w; Nathaniel, s;
   Margeret Lingham, her mother, 103.49
Roger, 109.85
Soloman; Anne, w; Anne, d, 107D.53
Soloman; Elizabeth, w; Elizabeth, d; William,
   s, 109.68
William; Jane, w; Robert, s; Elizabeth, d,
   102.227
William; Anne, w, 109.94

HEWINS: John, bach, 107A.21

HEWKINS: Slator; Mary, w, 103.33

HEWLET:
Abraham, ser, 107D.62
Sarah Thomas, d of Nottingham,
   107D.73

HEWSON:
Thomas, 109.57
William; Joane, w; Sarah, d; Richard, s,
   103.78
William, gent, wid, 102.68

HEWSTISS: Jeane, 103.274

HEYARD: John, ser, 106.23

HEYBORNE: William, bach, 98.2

HEYCOOK:
Ann, 103.183
Hanah; William, s; Katherine, d, 107B.63
Richard, wid, hath children, 103.186
William, 107D.20

HEYDEN:
Francis, 109.78
John, ser, 104.69
Nicholas, app, 101.63
Samuel, a nurse child, 107D.84
Sara, 101.3

HEYHURST: Robert; Mary, w, 101.14

HEYMAN: Mary; Mary, d, 106.64

HEYMORE: Godfrey; Anne, w; George, s;
   William, s, 101.37

HEYTON: Thomas, £600, wid, 103.13

HEYWOOD: Valentine; Mary, d, 104.132

HIATT: Elizabeth, wid; Robert, s, 102.25

HIBBARD: Thomas, 102.103

HIBBERT:
John, £600; Ester, w; Sarah, d?; Anne, d?;
   John, s?; Ester, d?, 99.56
William, 99.57

HIBBORNE: Mary; Mary, d, 107D.38

HICHCOCK, See Hitchcock

HICHMAN: Nathan, gent; Elizabeth, w;
   William, s; Sarah, d, 106.10

HICKCOCK: Richard, 99.9

HICKETTS: John; Ellianor, w, 101.28

HICKINBOTHAM: Francis; Rebecca, w,
   102.55

HICKIT: Mary, 101.13

HICKLIN: Thomas, wid, 98.50

HICKMAN:
Abraham, £600; Elizabeth, w; Jacob, s;
   Elizabeth, d, 107D.87
Daniell, £600, bach, 103.223
Dorothy, 98.7
Henry; Elizabeth, w; Henry, s, 107B.21
Henry, senior; Anne, w, 104.69
John; Elizabeth, w; Sarah, d, 103.61

Joseph, £600; Elizabeth, w, 102.189
Martha, ser, 104.52
Mary, 106.36
Rich, ser, 104.61
Thomas; Ann, w; Mary, d, 103.199
William; Elizabeth, w; Elizabeth, d, 107B.81

HILLINGLY: Mary Mary, d of Mapplesden, 107A.37

HILLMAN:
Henry, wid, hath children, 103.177
Sarah, ser, 103.13

HILLS:
John, app, 103.35
Thomas, ser, 103.237

HILLUCK: Anne, ser, 102.85

HILTON:
Alexander, 102.183
Anne, ser, 104.27
Benjamin; Mary, w; Abraham, s; Benjamin, s; William, s, 110.29
David, 102.160
Elizabeth, 109.84
Elizabeth; Jeremiah, s, 102.264
Elizabeth, ser, 98.72
John, 109.84
John; Mary, w, 102.264
Phillip; Anne, w, 109.84
Samuell; Mary, w; Mary, d, 102.160

HILUNE: James, 109.31

HINCHMAN:
Alice, wid; Elizabeth, d, 103.10
Maddam, gentlewoman, 98.33
William; Mary, w; William, s; Anne, d; Sarah, d, 107D.25

HINCKLY: Jane, ser, 107A.24

HINCKS:
Edward; Rebecca, w; John, s, 101.9
Elizabeth, 101.109
Jane, ser, 108.5

HIND:
Alice, wid, 103.9
Charles; Mary, w; Charles, s; Mary, d; James, s, 103.180
Chester, ser, 107C.7
Elizabeth, 107A.24
Francis; Rachell, w, 109.92
John; Mary, w; John, s, 103.158
John; Frances, w; John, s; Elizabeth, d, 107D.2

John, gent; Mary, w; Abigall, d, 98.31
Jos; ~, w; Jos, s; Anne, d; Mary, d; Eliz, d, 104.147
Mary, ser, 98.31
Michael; Jane, w, 107A.36
Samuell; Anne, w; Honour, d, 101.64
Thomas, app, 98.23
Thomas, 104.49
Wm; Ellinor, w; Wm, s; Robt, s, 104.83

HINDANA: John, ser, bach?, 104.5

HINDES: John; Mary, w; Phillip, s; John, s; Katherine, d, 98.15

HINDMARSH: Edward, gent; Grace, w; Grace, d; Elizabeth, d, 98.62

HINDRY: Martha, 107B.78

HINE:
Mary, 101.31
Mary, ser, 106.11

HINLEY: William, 109.14

HINMAN: Ann, 109.14

HINNINGS: Elizabeth, 101.82

HINSON: Thomas; Ellinor, w; Thomas, s, 102.168

HINTON:
Benjamin, 101.31
Hugh, app, 101.100
Katherine, 107D.25
Mary, wid; Ann, d, 103.42
Richard, ser, 109.1
Sarah, wid, 103.45
Thomas; Barbary, w, 109.25
William, app, 104.41
William, esq, 106.27

HIPP: Thomas; Anne, w; Susana, d; Thomas, s; Sarah, d, 102.199

HIPPLEY: Francis, 99.8

HIPSLEY: John, £600; Elizabeth, w, 102.147

HIPWELL: Thomas; Sara, w; Joseph, s; Mary, d, 101.66

HIRDSON: Anthony; Jane, w; Singleton, grand-s, 105.13

HISCOCK:
John; Eliza, w; Mary, d, 104.31
Robt, £600; Kath, w; Mary, d;

HITCH:
~, gent; Elizabeth, w; William, 106.4

HITCHCOCK:
Elizabeth, pensioner, 103.15
Francis, 102.251
John; Anne, w; John, s, 101.96
John; Mary, w; Joseph, s; ~, d, newborn,
   103.242
Robert; Alice, w; Jude, d, 102.38
Roger; Lucy, d, 107C.22
Thomas; Hannah, w; Hannah, d, 109.62
William; Mary, w; Samuel, s, 107C.23
William; Barbary, w; Katherine, d, 103.73

HITCHCOCKS: Susanna, 102.130

HITE: Mary, 109.2

HIX:
Ann, 103.126
Daniel; Sarah, w, 107D.42

HLAM:
Bedingfield, gent, junior; Esther, w,
   103.287
Bedingfield, gent, wid, 103.287
Sarah, ser, 103.110

HNNEY: Mathew; Mary, w, 102.167

HOARE:
Elizabeth, 98.57
Elizabeth, wid, 103.105
Henry; Mary, w, 102.85
Jacob, 102.1
Mary, ser, 104.80
Richard, £600; Susan, w; Mary, d; James, s;
   Benjamin, s, 106.44
Richard, commissioner, 106.69, 110.37
Richard, wid; Margeret, d, 103.162
Thomas, 102.104
Thomas, app, 103.162

HOBBS:
Elizabeth, 109.85
George, app, 98.52
John; Susan, w, 103.203
John; Elizabeth, w, 107D.28
John; Mary, w; Ann, d, 109.90
Jos, app, 104.57
Mark, 105.18
Thomas; Amey, w, 107D.27

HOBDEY: William; Eleanor, w, 102.97

HOBERD: Robert; Elizabeth, w, 109.34

HOBKINS: Katherine, ser, 106.11

HOBLING: Richard, ser, 106.55

HOBORNE: Mary, 102.242

HOBSON:
Anne, 104.76
Barbara; Barbara, d, 101.59
Edward, bach, gent, 106.44
Mary, 99.23
Michaell; Jane, w, 101.67
Sarah, 106.14
Walcott, ?gent, bach, 104.12

HOCKLEY:
John; Bridgett, w; John, s; Henry, s, 109.61
Mary, 101.42

HOCKNELL:
Agnis; Elizabeth, d, 106.24
Geo, £600; Eliz, w; Tho, s; Rich, s; Eliz, d,
   104.131
Richard, pensioner; Judith, w, 106.8
Susannah, ser, 98.38

HODDER:
Dorothy, 98.17
John; Ann, w, 104.128
Marke, bach, 98.17
Susannah, 98.17

HODDLE: Joseph; Mary, w; Joseph, s,
   107C.2

HODGES:
Christopher; Anne, w; Mary, d, 107B.18
Duoebellah, niece of wood Rowland, 98.69
Henry; Margaret, w, 109.91
John, 102.105, 107A.31
John; Rebecca, w; Joseph, s; John, s; Sarah,
   d; Sarah, d, 102.207
John, wid, 109.108
Lawrence, 99.36
Mary, 102.110
Nathaniell, gent, wid; Sarah, d; Mary, d,
   98.39
Phillip, 98.51
Thomas, 109.82
Thomas, app, 104.14

HODGESKINS:
Elizabeth, wid, 103.71
Ellinor, wid; John, s; Thomas, s, 103.238
John; Issabela, w; John, s, 102.262
Martha, ser, 103.61
Mary, ser, 107B.5
Nathaniel; Elizabeth, w; Hanah, d, 103.79
Nathaniel; Elizabeth, w, 103.263
Roger; Elizabeth, w; Mary, d; Margaret, d,
   102.60

HODGESON: William; Mary, w, 103.28

HODGIS: Austing; Anne, w, 102.28

HODGKIN:
Anne, 110.32
Anne, ser, 101.74
Thomas, £600, printer; Amy, w, 101.9
William; Elizabeth, w; Elizabeth, d, 109.21

HODGKINS:
Dorothy, ser, 106.60
Elizabeth, ser, 106.25
Thomas, app, 98.52

HODSDEN: Charles; Dorothy, w, 101.49

HODSKIN: Katherine, 107B.47

HODSTON: Tho, ser, 104.92

HOEMAN: Anne, ser, 98.86

HOFFE: Joseph, 102.154

HOGER: Mary;

HOGG:
~, wid, 109.72
Henry, app, 107B.67
Jane, 109.60
Wm; Anne, w; Sarah, d, 104.74

HOGSDEN: Anne, ser, 107D.44

HOGUTH: Richard; Anne, w; Richard, s?, 99.54

HOKEWELL: Jane, 109.31

HOKINS: Bridget, 106.23

HOLAMAN: John, bach, 102.162

HOLBERT: Martha, 103.36

HOLBIDGE: Richard, 103.258

HOLBORNE: John; Rebecca, w, 107B.54

HOLBROOKE: Mary; Mary, d, 98.23

HOLCROFT: Samuel; Hanah, w; Hanah, d;
    Elizabeth, d, 107B.65

HOLDAWAY: Sarah, ser, 103.264

HOLDBIG: Robert, wid, 102.143

HOLDELPH: John; Elizabeth, w, 107C.3

HOLDEN:
Elizabeth, ser, 98.39
Frances, ser, 103.3
George; Sarah, w; John, s; George, s;
    Richard, s; William, s; Sarah, d, 110.25
Jane, 110.22
Margaret; Jane, d, 109.54
Phillip, ser, 98.65
Walter; Margaret, w; Robert, s; John, s,
    107B.64

HOLDER:
John, 102.230
Joseph; Anne, w, 110.21
Thomas, ser, 103.206
William, wid, 98.88

HOLDGATE: Robert, bach, 98.35

HOLDING:
Edward, ser, 102.199
Kath, 104.120, 106.14

HOLDROFF: Jane; Jane, d,
    107D.30

HOLDSHIF:
Charles; Hannah, w, 109.102
Thomas; Ann, w; Richard; ~, child not
    baptized, 103.143

HOLDSWORTH:
Andrew; Elizabeth, w; James, s; William, s;
    Martha, d, 103.22
Rachell, 106.65

HOLE:
Lucy, 106.63
Mary, 107A.33
Nathaniell, bach, 106.63

HOLFORD:
Elizabeth, 101.13
Elizabeth, wid; Mary, d; Robert, s,
    103.54
John; Mary, w, 103.182
John, app, 103.18
Mary, 109.19
Samuell; Hanna, w, 101.47
Samuell; Martha, w; Martha, d, 104.13

HOLFORT: Elizabeth, 99.24

HOLGATE:
John, clerk? bach, 104.131
Mary, her husband at sea, 103.36

HOLGIN: Nich; Margery, w; Mary, d,
    104.102

HOLINES:
Edward; Philis, w; William, s; John, s; Mary, d; Elizabeth, d, 102.208
Luke, bach, 102.208
Samuell; Susanna, w; Samuell, s; Susanna, d; William, s, 101.25

HOLL:
George; Susan, w; Ann, d, 103.149
Henry, pensioner; Iserell, w; Grace Chapman, grand-d;

HOLLAND:
~, wid, 101.97
Chas; Eliz, w; Chas, s, 104.112
Daniell; Mary, w, 102.192
Edward; Anne, w, 98.87
Elizabeth, 107D.73
Elizabeth, ser, 107B.65
Ellinor, 99.17
Francis, 99.17
Jeane, wid, 103.123
John, 99.17
John; Frances, w, 98.87
John; Mary, w; Thomas, s, 107C.25
John, ser, 106.55
Marg, 104.134
Margaret, ser, 104.109
Mary, ser, 98.64
Nicholas; Mary, w, 107B.4
Restorn Richard, s of Smith, 107B.30
Richard; Rachell, w, 109.3
Richard, ser, 107D.18
Robert; Rebeccah, w, 98.46
Robert; Dorothy, w; Susan, d, 107D.83
Robert; Elizabeth, w, 110.27
Sarah; Hester, d?; Hanah, d?, 102.186
Thankes; Hanah, w; Joshua, s; Richard, s, 102.13
Thomas, 99.17
Thomas; Mary, w; Mary, d; Elizabeth, d; Hanna, d; Susan, d; Thomas, s, 105.10
William; Ann, w; Samuell, s, 103.80

HOLLED: Samuell, 101.53

HOLLIARD:
Ann, 110.2
Jas, bach, 104.26
Mary, 109.74
Tho, app, 104.10

HOLLINGS: Mary, 102.85

HOLLINGSHEAD:
Edward; Mary, w; John, s, 103.93
Edward, app, 103.93
Francis, 109.19
Francis; Elizabeth, w, 103.255

John, ser, 103.69
Ralph, wid, 98.49

HOLLINGSWORTH:
Edmund, 107B.71
Elizabeth, 109.101
Francis; Hester, w; Hester, d; Charles, s, 107D.23
John, 106.65
Richard, Doctor in Divinity, 102.53
William; Rose, w; Robert, s, 109.87

HOLLIS:
Elizabeth, 103.31
Hannah, 109.38
Jeremy; Eliza, w, 104.107
John; Margeret, 102.58
John, bach, esq; James, ser of, 98.67
Margaret; Ann, d, 109.5
Mary, ser, 103.256

HOLLISTER:
Alice, 104.141
John, wid, £600; John, s, 103.33

HOLLMAN:
Ann, spinster, 103.33
Ellinor, spinster, 103.33
Mary, ser, 109.7

HOLLMOORE: Francis, app, 103.285

HOLLOWAY:
Ann, wid, 103.19
Elizabeth, spinster, 103.44
Hanah, wid, 103.127
John, a parish child, 101.35
Katherine, 98.11
Mary, 107B.67
Sarah, ser, 98.42
William, 102.58
William; Anne, w, 98.14

HOLLOWELL: Rich, a boy, 104.11

HOLLY: John; Ellinor, w; Elinor, d; Margaret, d, 98.88

HOLLYCROSS: Rebecca, pensioner, 103.136

HOLLYDAY:
Jeane, app, 103.54
Jeane, pensioner, 103.29
Richard; Eliza, w, 104.147
Zachariah; Jeane, w; Mary, d; Hanah, d; Zachariah, s, 103.23

HOLLYOAKE: Thomas; Elizabeth, w, 103.91

William; Sarah, w; Mary, d; John, s; Ann, d;
   Aron Timmera, son-in-law, 103.39
William; Katherine, w; William, s, 109.9
William, pensioner; Mary, w, 103.207
William, ser, 103.14

HOOKE:
Isaack; Anne, w, 98.85
Jeffery; Jane, w, 102.42
James; Anne, w; Anne, d, 98.65
John; Rebeccah, w, 98.68
John; Mary, w, 106.32
John, app, 103.201
Nathaniel, bach, 103.19
Sara, 101.3

HOOKER:
Amy; Sarah, w, 109.28
Edward, wid, 107A.25

HOOKES:
Sarah, 109.40
Thomas, ser, 106.33

HOOLE: Sarah, ser, 98.42

HOOPER:
Abraham; Mary, w, 103.144
Edward, 109.59
Hannah, 106.14
Henry, bach, 104.109
John; Sarah, w; Elizabeth, d; Sarah, d; Anne,
   d; Mary, d; John, s; Arabella, d, 107B.77
Joyce, 110.26
Mary, 102.28, 102.170
Mary, ser, 106.60
Robert; Mary, w, 103.90
Robert, nurse child, 103.88
Susanna, ser, 104.65
William; Mary, w, 107C.34

HOOPES: Susanah, 99.47

HOOSTID: Joseph, 107C.10

HOOTON:
Elizabeth, 109.77
James, ser, 107B.3

HOPDAY:
Elizabeth, wid, 103.192
Joseph; Jeane, w, 103.13
Sarah, spinster, 103.22
William, ser, 103.8

HOPE:
Avis, pensioner, 103.77
Elizabeth, 101.30
Elizabeth, ser, 107A.5

Elizabeth, wid, 103.132
Fowke; Mary, w, 104.120
George; Elizabeth, w, 103.198
John, 107B.65
Mary, ser, 106.5
Ralph; Eliza, w; Ralph, s, 104.83
Samuell, 102.208
Thomas, £600; Sarah, w, 107B.19

HOPEGOOD: Elizabeth, 109.25

HOPES: Anne;

HOPKINS:
~; ~, child, 104.147
Charles; Frances, w, 109.95
Daniel, app, 107D.21
Easter, 99.38
Elizabeth, 101.33
Francis; Joanna, w, 102.48
Henry; Marg, w; Henry, s; Francis, s, 104.135
John, 101.86
John; Elizabeth, w, 103.114
John; Mary, w; Mary, d, 103.278
John; Katherine, w, 104.96
John, bach, 104.136
Margaret, 98.7
Mary, wid; Mary, d; Margeret, d, 103.67
Nullient, 101.19
Oliver; Mary, w, 107A.13
Richard, 102.92
Robert; Elizabeth, w, 98.24
Robert; Mary, w, 107D.57
Thomas, ser, 103.237
William; Elizabeth, w; John, s; Elizabeth, d;
   Ann, d; Mary, d, 109.43
William, app, 98.84
William, ser, 106.52

HOPKINSON: Sarah, 107A.33

HOPWOOD:
Sarah, 104.90
Thomas; Joane, w; Katherine, d, 103.113
Mary, 99.53

HORE:
Benjamin, 102.115
George, 102.3
George; Judy, w; Henry, s; Mary, d, 102.121
William; Anne, w; William, s, 109.104

HORNBLOW:
Mwrtha, 101.13
Richard; Richard, s, 109.12
William, 109.99

HORNBLOWER: Humphry; Mary, w,
   107D.27

HORNE:
Abigell, 102.143
Benjamin, bach, 102.113
James, gent, wid; John, ser of, 98.81
Jane, ser, 106.4
John; Elizabeth, w; Robert, s, 103.39
John; Anne, w; Anne, d; Mary, d; Michael, s,
    107D.90
John, commissioner, 103.293
John, gent; Anne, w; Mary, d; John, s,
    103.287
Mary, 98.26
Matt; Eliza, w; John, s, 104.57
Robert, app; Rebecca, w, 102.202
Robert, app, 107D.29
Samuel; Mary, w, 107C.17
Samuell; Anne, w; Samuell, s, 109.96
Sarah, ser, 102.111
Susannah, 98.27
Thomas, 101.102
Thomas; Sarah, w; Elizabeth, d; John, s, 98.9
Thomas; Mary, w; George, s, 107D.66
Thomas, bach, ser, 98.29
William; Elizabeth, w; Elizabeth, d; William,
    s; Jonathon, s, 98.60
William; Anne, w; Mary, d, 107C.29

HORNEBY:
Anne, 101.55, 101.109
Arthur, ser, 109.80
Elizabeth, 109.31
John; Elizabeth, w; Frances, d, 107D.51
Margaret, ser, 98.84

HORNECK: Phillip; Anna, w; Anna, d;
    Sarah, d; Mary, d; Antony, s, 103.44

HORNELL: John; Margaret, w,
    107D.39

HORNER: Martha, ser, 104.26

HORNET: ~, 103.127

HORNSMITH: Ann, 99.32

HOROBIN:
John, 109.97
John; Sarah, w, 109.97
Robert, 109.75

HORSEMAN:
Ducebellah, gentlewoman; Mary, d; Edward,
    s, 98.30
Elizabeth, 101.61
Elizabeth, ser, 98.42
Mary, 109.30

HORSEY: Dan, ser, bach?, 104.27

HORSLY:
Jane, 102.92
John; Grace, w; Ann, d; John, s; George, s,
    103.103
John; Elizabeth, w; Elizabeth, d, 110.21

HORSNELL: Sarah, 109.16

HORSPOOLE: Dorothy, 103.243

HORT: Josiah, 107D.36

HORTING: Mary, 102.48

HORTON:
Anne; Anne, d, 107D.3
Anne, wid, 103.90
Elizabeth, pensioner, 103.150
Elizabeth, ser, 106.46
Flower; Ellen, w, 107D.92
Francis, app, 98.3
George, app, 98.72
Henry, bach, 98.48
John, 109.66
John; Mary, w; Elizabeth, d, 101.34
John; Sarah, w, 103.48
John; Elizabeth, w, 107D.26
John, pensioner; Susan, w; Susan, d, 103.76
John, ser, 102.73
Mary Elizabeth, grand-d of Gifford, 98.47
Richard, bach, 98.36
Richard, gent; Mary, w; George, s; Ursula, d;
    Susan, d, 107D.54

HORWOOD: Robt; Anne, w; John, s, 104.74

HOSE:
Henry, 102.114
Hester, 109.42

HOSELEY: Elizabeth, 109.94

HOSIER:
Ann, ser, 104.92
Elias, app, 104.74
William; Mary, w; Ann, d?; Mary, d?;
    Elizabeth, d; Martha, d?; Armonetta, d?;
    Sarah, d?, 99.39
William; Rebeccah, w; Mary, d, 102.114

HOSKIN?: Thomas, Doctor in Divinity;
    Letitia, w, 101.3

HOSKINS:
Ann, 103.179
Bennet, £600 or £50 p.a.; Mary, w; James, s;
    John, s; Sarah, d, 109.7
Elizabeth, ser, 98.38
Jane, 104.113

John, 107C.33
John; Mary, w; Elizabeth, d, 98.21
John; Sarah, w; Sarah Spring, d; Isaac Spring, s, 103.89
Jone, 107A.9
Joyce, 102.191
Katherine, 106.9
Rodger, app, 102.71
Thomas, 104.130
Thomas; Mary, w, 107D.26
Thomas, bach, 98.24
William; Anne, w; Mary, d, 107C.33
Wilmott, ser, 106.24

HOSKISSON: Thomas, bach, 103.100

HOSOENBY?: Charles, 98.15

HOSTOCK: Anne, ser, 101.86

HOTHERGELL:
Charles, 103.280
Nicholas, pensioner; Mary, w; Peter, s; Payne, s?, 103.280
Thomas, 103.280

HOUGH:
Aberthia, 98.13
Thomas, ser, 103.91

HOUGHAM: Charles, 109.79

HOUGHTON: Mary, 109.92

HOULDEN: Elizabeth, 102.73

HOULDER: Richard; Sarah, w; Joseph, s?; Charles, d?; Sarah, d?, 99.14

HOULDERCRAFT: John, 109.29

HOULDIN: Thomas, 102.96

HOULT: Elizabeth, ser, 109.10

HOUNSOME: William; Rosomon, w; Mary, d;

HOURD:
~; Jane, w; Anne, d, 104.132
Gabriell; Eliz, w, 104.42
Jas, bach, 104.87
John, bach, 104.41
Wm; Eliza, w, 104.56

HOUSE:
Henry; Elizabeth, w; Ann, d, 109.20
John, pensioner; Margeret, w, 103.143
Patience, 109.13

Sarah, 109.13
William, ser;

HOUSEMAN:
Elizabeth; Elizabeth, d; Susan, d, 103.174
John; Anne, w; John, s, 98.19
Jone, 98.6
Mary, 99.34, 106.50
Tho, bach, 104.67

HOVEY: Alice, ser, 109.77

HOW(E):
Abraham, app, 102.204
Anne, 98.24
Anne; Samuell, s, 98.79
Benjamin; Mary, w; Mary, d, 102.67
Benony, bach, £600; Abigall, sister, 104.6
Daniel; Rachael, w, 107C.5
Daniel, wid, hath a child, 103.115
Dorothy, ser, 106.41
Edward, app, 103.114
Elizabeth, 109.62
George, bach, 98.3
Hanah, ser, 103.30
Humphrey; Mary, w, 104.139
Jane, ser, 106.29
Jeremy; Ann, w; Jeremy, s; Ebenezer, s; Daniell, s, 109.106
John, 98.12
John; Elizabeth, w, 102.49
John, senior; Elizabeth, w; John, junior; Anne, w; Elizabeth, d, 102.157
Joseph; Mary, w; Ruth, d, 98.28
Margaret, wid, 109.21
Mary, 101.62
Mary, a poor child, 103.271
Phillip, 109.73
Ralph, esq, 104.94
Richard; Hanah, w; Ann, d; Margeret, d; Mary, d, 103.154
Susan, 107B.17
Susanna, 101.90
Thomas, 102.232, 109.82
Thomas; Sarah, w; Cassandra, d, 103.87

HOWARD:
Alice, 109.88
Anne, 98.84, 101.53
Anne, ser, 107D.80
Aphraham; Elizabeth, w; John, s; Elizabeth, d, 103.154
Barbara, 102.145
Catherine; Susan, d, 109.101
Charles; Mary, w; Thomas, s, 103.135
Charles; Joyce, d, 109.94
David, 109.73
Edward; Johannah, w; Henry, s, 98.35
Elianor, 109.103

Elianor, ser, 107D.52
Elijah; Elizabeth, w; Mary, d, 101.89
Ester, 110.21
Francis, 109.83
Francis; Sarah, w, 106.29
Francis; Anne, w, 107C.13
George; Elizabeth, w, 103.136
George, ser, 105.7
Henry, 107B.48
Henry; Anne, w, 102.82
Henry; Elizabeth, w; William, s; Elizabeth, d;
     James, s, 107D.63
Henry; Margarett, w; Thomas, s, 110.29
James; Mary, w; James, s; Elizabeth, d; John,
     s; Anne, d, 107D.32
Jeane, spinster, 103.67
Jeremiah; Judith, w; Elizabeth, d?, 99.56
John; Sarah, w, 102.252
John; Gatery, w, 107C.34
John; Mary, w; Mary, d; Anthony, s;
     Elizabeth, d, 109.14
John, £600 or £50 p.a.; Martha, w; Martha, d;
     John, s; Alice, d; Sarah, d, 109.6
Jone, 98.26
Mary, 103.263
Mary; Elizabeth, mother of; Elizabeth, d;
     William, s; Thomas, s; Elizabeth Peirce,
     grand-d of, 109.101
Mary, pensioner; Richard, s?; Sarah, d?;
     Mary, d?; John, s?; Dorcas, d?, 106.8
Mathew; Anne, w, 107D.70
Nicholas, 102.208
Peter; Martha, w; Mary, d, 103.74
Richard; Mary, w; Elizabeth, d?, 99.5
Richard; Jane, w, 102.93
Richard; Elizabeth, w; Hannah, d, 109.43
Robert, bach, 101.105
Robert, pensioner; Susan, w; Thomas, s;
     Mary, d, 103.164
Roger, app, 104.13
Samuell; Elizabeth, w; Samuell, s, 102.89
Samuell, ser, 103.7
Stephen; Bridget, w; John, s, 101.97
Susan, 102.112
Susan; Stephen, s; Mary, d, 107B.33
Thomas, 105.17, 110.29
Thomas; Mary, w, 101.93
William; Elizabeth, w; Anne, d; Elizabeth, d,
     102.45
William; Jone, w; Anne, d, 107D.60
William, ser, 103.94

HOWELL:
Anthony; Ann, w; Thomas, s, 103.22
Cesar, wid, 109.91
Elianor, 102.175
Grace, ser, 102.94
James, 104.75
Jane, 109.70

Kath, 104.79
Marg, 104.1047
Mary; Ann, d, 103.292
Parnell, wid; Parnell, d; Mary, d; Samuell, s,
     102.166
Samuell, £600; Anne, w, 102.166
Sarah, ser, 107D.23
Thomas; Sarah, w, 106.39
Thomas; Elizabeth, w, 107D.93
Thomas; Jane, w; Thomas, s, 109.102

HOWES:
Anne, wid; Anne, d, 107D.28
Ben, £600; Sarah, w, 104.28
Henry; Mary, w, 107C.7
Richard, ser, 106.18
Timothy; Mildred, w; Mary, d; Dorothy, d,
     107D.30

HOWETT:
Richard, 102.227
Thomas; Martha, w; Martha, d, 101.60
Thomas, app, 104.53

HOWGALL: Charles; Sarah, w, 103.246

HOWGIN: John, at sea; Ann, w; Ann, d,
     103.86

HOWGRAVE:
Bridget, pensioner, 103.226
Thomas; Margeret, w; Henry, s, 103.226

HOWING: Walter; Elizabeth, w, 102.25

HOWLET:
Charles, bach, 106.45
Hanah, pensioner; John Powell, grand-s,
     103.77
Joane, ser, 104.7
Nathaniell; Thomas, s, 110.27

HOWLSWORTH: Jane, 102.4

HOWSON :
Thomas; Mary, w; Elizabeth, d; Dewarant, d;
     Mary, d, 102.212
Thomas; Mary, w; Mary, d; Thomas, s,
     107C.19

HOWTON:
James; Martha, w, 109.13
James, ser, 109.13
Thomas; Elinor, w; Henry, s, 109.11

HOY:
Elizabeth, 109.43
Thomas, Doctor; Elizabeth, w; Richard, s,
     106.21

HOYFEILD?: John; Anne, w; John, s; Mary, d; Elizabeth, d, 101.28

HOYLE: Mary, 109.85

HUBAN: Thomas, bach, 109.109

HUBBARD:
Edward; Elinor, w; William, s, 98.34
Francis; Elizabeth, w; Kenden, s; Francis, s; Ann, d, 100.5
Gabrill; Susan, w, 102.67
Gabrill; Elienor, w, 102.240
Joanna, 102.93
Jonathon; Margaret, w; Sarah, d; Jonathon, s, 107B.49
Katherine, wid, 103.133
Mary, wid; George, s; Weborow, s, 102.67
Phillip, 103.244
Rebeccah, 98.51
Richard; Jane, w, 109.103
Thomas; Anne, w; Thomas, s; Anne, d; Robert, s, 102.75
Thomas; Thomas, s; Hanah, d;

HUBBERT:
~; Ann, w; Sarah, d, 103.108
Alice, spinster, 103.219
James, £600; Frances, w; Margeret, d; Thomas, s; James, s; John, s, 103.253
John, £600, bach, 103.277
Martha, wid, 103.264
Robert; Elizabeth, w; Henry, s, 102.21

HUBERSTONE: Katherine, 103.127

HUBNER: Alice, her husband not with her; Sarah, d; Henry, s, 103.90

HUCK: Lewis, app, 101.75

HUCKNALL: Elizabeth, ser, 109.1

HUCKS:
Elizabeth, 109.60
William, ser, 103.219

HUDDLE:
James; Mary, w, 109.12
John; Mary, w; John, s; Francis, s, 104.29
Randolph; Rebecca, w, 103.28
Thomas, bach, 104.29

HUDDS: Benjamin; Elizabeth, w; Elizabeth, d, 107B.42

HUDER: Anne, 107D.41

HUDGBUTT: Eliza, 104.49

HUDIBALL: William; Sarah, w; Daniell, s; Sarah, d, 102.161

HUDLESTONE: John; Ann, w; John, s; Ann, d;

HUDSON:
~, Mr, 105.8
Ann, nurse child, 103.115
Daniel; Mabell, w; Robert, s; Mabell, d; Joseph, s, 107B.24
Daniel, ser, 107C.39
Edw, 104.40
Edward; Elizabeth, w, 103.240
Elienor, nurse, 102.136
Elizabeth; Sarah, d, 102.160
George; Anne, w, 107D.42
George, bach under age, 103.81
Hanah, wid; Lambeth, s, 103.254
Jane, 98.38, 102.9
Jerimiah, nurse child, 103.115
Joane, wid, 102.67
John, 101.34
John; Katherine, w, 109.40
John, wid; Mary, grand-d, 103.74
Joseph, 105.17
Joseph; Mary, w; Mary, d, 107B.12
Kathrine; Elizabeth, d, 109.17
Margery; Elizabeth, d; Mary, d, 109.111
Mary; John, s, 102.129
Mary, ser, 98.59
Mathias; Elizabeth, w, 109.60
Michael; Mary, w, 104.12
Nicholas; Margery, w; Nicholas, s; Mary, d, 101.5
Rachell, ser, 98.67
Rebecca, 102.212
Richard, 101.86
Richard, ser, 107B.79
Robert, bach, 103.41
Sam; Bridgett, w, 104.141
Thomas, 106.45
Thomas; Ruth, w, 107A.38
Thomas; Jane, w; Edward, s; Thomas, s, 107D.65

HUFFE:
Henry, 107B.56
Ralph; Elizabeth, w, 103.14

HUFFINGTON: Magdalen, wid, 98.53

HUGALL: Easter, 99.10

HUGGIN: William; Elizabeth, w; Peter, s, 102.20

HUGGINS:
Anne, 99.10
John; Dorothy, w, 104.120

Robert, gent, wid, 106.28
Thomazin; John, s, 98.12
William, 102.273
William; Mary, w, 104.44
William; Mary, w; Thomas, s; Mary, d, 106.29
William; Elizabeth, w, 109.20
William; Mary, w, 109.73
William, bach, 106.35

HUNCLOCKE: Alice, wid, 103.26

HUNGERFORD: William, 102.210

HUNLOCK: Ann, wid, £600; Thomas, s;
    Susan, d; John, s, 103.18

HUNSDEN: Thomas, ser, 103.139

HUNSMAN: Isaace, 105.16

HUNT:
Alice, a parish child, 102.120
Alice, wid, 102.44
Charles, 106.15
Darcas, 102.169
Edmond, app, 103.84
Edward; Mary, w; William, s, 109.14
Edward; Margarett, w; Edward, s, 110.4
Elioner, ser, 106.40
Elizabeth; Henry, s; Elizabeth, d, 109.14
Elizabeth, wid, 102.48
Geo, ser, 104.90
Gyles, app, 104.53
Hannah, 109.103
Henry, 98.83
Henry; Katherine, w; Thomas, s; Mary, d,
    102.125
Isaac; Sarah, w; Elizabeth, d, 102.40
Jerimiah, 103.179
John; Ann, w; Arabella, d?, 99.59
John; Anne, w, 102.173
John; Anne, w; Joseph, s; Abraham, s; Anne,
    d, 103.58
John; ~, w, 103.93
John; Mary, w, 103.128
John; Mary, w; Mary, d, 104.14
John; Grace, w; John, s; Joseph, s, 107D.61
John; Sarah, w, 109.103
John, app, 107C.20
John, bach, 100.11, 103.113
John, a boy, 104.32
John, ser, 106.19
John, wid; John, junior; Jane, w; Thomas, s;
    Elizabeth, d, 104.119
Jonathan; Alice, w, 102.176
Joseph, 107A.42
Joseph; Anne, w, 102.145
Joseph; Anne, w, 109.3
Jude, app, 103.292

Katherine, ser, 107D.13
Margaret, 109.67
Martha, 102.255
Mary; Margaret, d, 103.175
Mary, ser, 103.289
Mary, wid; Ann, d, 103.179
Oliver; Olive, w; Elizabeth, d; Oliver, s,
    107D.21
Oliver, ser, 106.2
Richard, 105.18
Richard; Jone, w; John, s; Hannah, d, 98.46
Richard; Sarah, w, 106.15
Richard; Jane, w, 110.11
Robert, 102.120
Roger; Mary, w, 103.107
Ruth, ser, 109.9
Samuel; Elizabeth, w; Alice, d, 105.8
Sarah, 104.96
Sarah, ser, 104.3, 104.5
Simon, bach, 103.292
Susan, wid, 103.54
Thomas, 109.70, 109.103
Thomas; Susan, w, 103.1
Thomas, bach, 99.7
William, 107A.34
William; Mary, w; John, s, 102.34
William; Francis, w; William, s; Frances, d;
    Samuell, s, 103.145
William; Susan, w; William, s; Anne, d,
    103.158
William; Margarett, w; Margarett, d; Anne, d,
    109.9
William, app, 101.79
William, a parish child, 102.120

HUNTER:
Ann, ser, 109.10
David; Anne, w, 104.20
Elizabeth, pensioner; Elizabeth, d; Mary, d;
    Thomas, s, 103.109
James; Sarah, w, 109.102
Margarett, 99.10
Michaell; Hester, w, 102.141
Sarah, wid, 103.226
Thomas; Elizabeth, w; Thomas, s, 101.89

HUNTINGDON:
Robert, bach, 101.50
William; Anne, w; Robert, s; Jane, d; John, s,
    102.24

HUNTINGFORD: Elizabeth, 102.79

HUNTLEY: Henry, 104.78

HUNTMAN:
Joseph, £600; Mary, w; Daniel, s; Elizabeth,
    d, 103.283
Joseph, assessor, 103.293

HUNTON:
Elizabeth, 106.1
Stephen; Lucy, w, 107A.22

HUNTSMAN:
Elizabeth, 103.19
Thomas; Elianor, w, 107A.20

HURD:
Elizabeth, 101.33
Elizabeth, ser, 107B.79

HURDIS: Elizabeth, 109.76

HURLES: Abraham; Eliza, w, 104.92

HURLEY:
George; Sara, w, 101.70
Jonathan, bach, 104.105

HURRINGS: John; Alice, w; Grace, d; Mary,
d; John, s, 103.110

HURSE:
John; ~, w; William, s; John, s, 102.35
Thomas, 99.7

HURST:
Clemence; Elizabeth, d, 101.22
Edward, app, 107D.92
Elizabeth, ser, 102.118
Henry; Mary, w, 101.14
James, 106.69
John; Mary, w, 101.97
Lewis; Mary, w, 109.2
Martha, wid, 103.183
Richard; Anne, w; John, s; Elizabeth, d,
101.47
Sarah, 102.258
Thomas; Mary, w; Mary, d; Elizabeth, d,
103.34

HURSTLOW: Dudlow; Elinor, w,
99.35

HURT:
Eliz, 104.137
John; Merriam, w, 103.78
Sarah, 104.127

HUSAN: Gracee; Mary, w, 109.90

HUSBAND:
Abraham; Mary, w; Francis, s; Mary, d,
102.74
Christopher; Anne, w, 102.178

HUSCROFT:
John; Sara, w, 101.25

Mathew; Elizabeth, w, 107A.12
Mathew; Margery, w; Samuel, s, 107C.4

HUSE: Judith Huffeals, 102.170

HUSH: Thomas, wid; Sarah, d, 103.116

HUSK: Joseph, nurse child, 107A.24

HUSON: Ann, 106.49

HUSSEY:
Alice, ser, 102.160
Christopher; Mary, w; John, s; Anne, d,
101.13
James; Mary, w; Mary, d; Elizabeth, d, 98.34
Joane, 103.177
Jos; Fowke, s, 104.56
Penellops, 98.4
Robert; Katherine, w; James, s, 107D.21
Thomas; Mary, w, 103.177
Thomas, bach, 106.53
, £600; Anne, w, 101.95

HUST: Mary, ser, 103.228

HUSTICE: Oliver, 109.36

HUTCHASON:
Francis, ser, 106.58
Mary, ser, 102.147
Richard, ser, 106.35

HUTCHINS:
Dorothy, 109.89
Francis; Frances, w; Joseph, s; John, s;
Daniell, s; Mary, d, 103.11
John; Mary, w; John Woodley, s; Mary
Woodley, d, 109.4
Judeth, 109.25
Magdalen, ser, 107D.59
Margeret, wid, 103.48
Mary, 99.7
Robt; Mary, w; Robt, s, 104.17
Susana, 102.112
Susana, ser, 102.112
Walter; Anne, w, 98.48

HUTCHINSON:
Anne; Anne, d, 101.44
Edward; Elizabeth, w; Sarah, d; Elizabeth, d,
107B.3
Elizabeth; John, s, 107D.97
Frances; Rebeccah, d; Martha, d, 98.76
James; Sarah, w, 98.77
Jeane, ser, 103.217
John; Marg, w, 104.71
Joseph; Esther, w; Joseph, s; Esther, d;
Elizabeth, d, 103.166

Marmaduke; Isabella, w; Elizabeth, d; John,
   s, 109.65
Mary, 102.10
Ralph, £600; Sarah, w; Joseph, s; Sarah, d,
   102.147
Sarah, 109.90
Thomas; Mary, w, 103.24
Thomas, app, 107B.81
William; Mary, w; William, s; Edward, s;

HUTSON:
~, wid, 109.23
Mary, 109.2
Sarah, 102.16

HUTT: Stanford, 102.2

HUTTON:
Grace, £50 p.a., 102.222
John; Elizabeth, w; James, s; Stanton, s;
   Thomas, s; Margaret, d, 107B.66
Mary, 104.146
Mathew, 106.31
Robert; Elizabeth, w; Thomas, s?, 99.11

HUXFORD: Joseph; Phillis, w; John, s,
   103.46

HUXLEY:
William; Hannah, w; William, junior; Mary,
   98.26
William; Anne, d; Hannah, d, 98.56

HUXSTABLE: Charrity, ser, 98.38

HYATT:
Richard, 102.115
Richard, £600; Elizabeth, w; Alice, d; Mary,
   d; Dorcas, d, 102.115
Tabitha; Jonathon, s; Hester, d;

HYDE:
~, Mrs, 104.95
Anne, 107C.21
Arthur; Elizabeth, w, 98.78
Eliz, ser, 104.67
Francis; Judith, w; Mary, d; Martha, d; Anne,
   d, 104.81
John, app, 107C.13
Lucy, 110.24
Mary, 101.9, 107C.37
Mary, ser, 107D.37
Nathaniel; Elizabeth, w; Howard, s, 107D.33
Robert, gent; Mary, w; Frances, d; Dorothy, d,
   98.43
Theodora, ser, 104.80
William, 110.24

HYDER: An, wid, 103.148

HYERNE: Thomas, app, 107C.32

HYMAN: Elizabeth, 101.57, 102.98

HYON:
John; Mary, w; Sarah, d; William, s; Mary, d,
   102.54
Richard, 102.54
Robert; Frances, w, 101.33

HYRON: Susan, 107C.7

IBBITT:
Henry; Mary, w; Hanna, d; Mary, d, 101.99
William, 101.82

IBBOTT: Edmund; Elizabeth, w, 107A.8

IBBS:
John; Mary, w; John, s, 101.42
William; Mary, d, 101.27

IBITTS: Anne, 101.40

IDIA: Joane, 103.86

IKIN: Randolph, a boy, 104.27

ILES: Phillip, ser, 103.249

ILIVE: Thomas; Jane, w, 107D.18

ILSLEY: John; Mary, w, 107D.33

IMER: Izabella, ser, 103.30

IMPEY: Ann, ser, 103.275

INCE:
Alice, a parish child, 101.35
Robert; Ann, w, 109.34

INDIAN: John, app, 98.76

INGALL: Henry; Jane, w; Frances, d; Anne,
   d, 98.74

INGELDEN: Eleanor; Ann, d, 102.217

INGLEDEW:
William; Elizabeth, w; Elizabeth, d, 107D.57
William, 109.108

INGLESBY: Sarah, ser, 98.45

INGLETON: Maudling; Elizabeth, d, 107A.4

INGRAM:
Benj, 104.144

166

Ellinor; Agrippina, d, 104.83
John, 101.2
John; Elizabeth, w, 110.15
Mary, 102.2
Richard; Susan, w, 109.38
Thomas; Mary, w, 104.143
Thomas; Anne, w; Thomas, w; Ann, d,
   109.33
Wm, bach, 104.69

INNMAN:
John, 109.105
John; Elizabeth, d?; Win, d?; John, s,
   104.35

INNOCENT:
David; Elizabeth, w, 103.182
John; Jane, w; Jane, d, 99.25

INSKIP: Edward, 109.61

INSTONE: Richard; Isabell, w; Mary, d,
   107D.80

INWARD:
John; Susan, w, 102.24
Mary, 107C.35
William; Anne, w, 98.50

INYON: Elizabeth, ser, 103.101

IPSHAW: John; Mary, w, 107C.40

IREDELL: John; Mary, w, 101.36

IRELAND:
Elizabeth, 110.3
Francis; Bridget, w, 101.80
Robert; Anne, w, 110.32
Virtue, 109.71

IRESON:
Edward; Sarah, w; Daniell, s; Thomas, s;
   Edward, d; Sarah, d, 103.17
John; Dorothy, w, 107C.22
Thomas; ~, w, 103.173

IRION: John; Susanna, w;

IRISH:
~; ~, w, 103.248
Hanah, 103.246
Samuell; Barbary, w, 103.246

IRONMONGER:
John, 105.18
Joshua, 101.106
Mary, 102.262
Mathew, 101.106

IRONS:
Anne, ser, 109.76
Benjanin, pensioner; Izabella, w, 103.22
John, 102.247
John; Anne, w; Anne, d, 102.270
Margaret, wid, 103.91
Mary, 109.51
Mary, pensioner, spinster, 103.15
Richard; Jane, w, 109.78

ISAAC:
Mary, 106.34
Mary, pensioner; Abraham, s; Susan, d;
   Rebecca, d; Mary, d, 106.8
Sarah, wid, 102.16

ISAM: Elizabeth;

ISDELL: ~, ser, 98.2
Abraham, ser, 106.46

ISENGALL: Anne, ser, 109.95

ISGRIGG:
Esther, wid; William, s; Ann, d, 103.195
John; Elizabeth, w; Elizabeth, d; Hester, d;
   John, s, 107B.51

ISHAM:
Alexander; Elizabeth, w; Jeane, d; Judeth, d,
   103.188
Edward; Elizabeth, w; John, s, 110.26
Zaccheus, Doctor; Elizabeth, w; Jusstinion, s,
   103.15

ISLAND:
Edward; Dorothy, w, 109.55
Mary, 107B.9
Mary, a nurse child, 107C.15

ISLES:
Edward; Anne, w, 107C.14
Jone, ser, 98.28
Robert, bach, 109.1
William; Sarah, w; Rebecca, d, 109.101

ISOM: Margery, ser, 104.31

ISSOD: Tho, £600; Joyce, w, 104.1

ITHER: William, 103.138

IVER: Mary, 101.4

IVERSON: Alice; Hanah, d, 107B.16

IVES:
Christo; Mary, w; John, s; Elizabeth, d;
   Thomas, s; Mary, d, 107C.26

Mary, 110.21
Martha, 101.7
Wm; Anne, w; Wm, s; Rich, s; Anne, d,
104.19

IVESON: Robert; Jane, w; Mary, d; Robert,
s; John, s, 107A.21

IVORY:
Elizabeth, spinster, 103.101
Jane;

IZARD:
~, wid, 109.31
George, 102.78
John, 102.125, 103.188
Mary, 109.3
Wenman, bach, 101.13

JACK:
Richard; Sarah, w; Susan, kinswoman of,
107B.50
Richard; Sarah, w; Susan, kinswoman of,
107B.50

JACKMAN:
John; Margarett, w; John, s; Phillip, s, 102.15
Phillip; Ann, w, 103.17
Richard, assessor, 103.293
Richard, wid; Mary, d; Richard, s, 103.202
John; Margarett, w; John, s; Phillip, s, 102.15
Phillip; Ann, w, 103.17
Richard, assessor, 103.293
Richard, wid; Mary, d; Richard, s; Sarah;

JACKSON:
~, Mrs, her husband at sea, 103.154
Alice, 101.19
Anne; Anne, d, 104.33
Anne; Mary, d, 106.64
Anne, ser, 103.287
Anne, spinster, 103.41
Anne, wid; Henry Hewett, s; James Hewett, s;
Elizabeth Jackson, d; Sarah Jackson, d,
103.63
Charles, ser, 107D.1
Edward, 110.9
Elizabeth, ser, 98.35, 98.41
Elizabeth, wid, 102.40
Ellen, ser, 107B.10
Ellis, 106.56
George, 109.40
Hanah, 102.241
Humphry; Ann, w, 109.105
Humphry, £600; Mary, w; John, s; Sarah, d,
104.106
James; Mary, w, 109.94
Jane, 101.94
John; Anne, w, 104.32

John; ~, w, 104.129
John; Lucy, w, 104.138
John; Johanna, w, 110.12
John, £50 p.a.; Mary, w, 106.59
John, ser, 106.37
John, wid, no children, 103.185
Jonathon; Anne, w, 109.108
Joseph; Mary, w; Joseph, s; Benjamin, s;
John, s, 103.92
Joseph; Anne, w; Anne, d, 104.103
Joseph; Lucretia, w; Daniell, s; Lucretia, d,
109.70
Margaret, 106.59, 109.84
Mary, 102.32, 109.104
Mary; Isaac, s; Mary, d; Joanna, d, 101.95
Mary, dead, 102.275
Mary, ser, 98.25, 104.2
Mary, wid; Elizabeth, d; Mary, d, 103.179
Mathias, 102.124
Peter; Elizabeth, w; Mary, d, 102.273
Richard; Alice, w, 103.26
Robert; Jane, w; Elizabeth, d, 107C.40
Robert; Mary, w; Elizabeth, d; Johanna, d,
110.27
Samuell, 102.97
Samuell; Sarah, w, 104.142
Samuell, ser, 106.27
Sarah, 102.209
Susanna, 101.64
Thomas, 102.65
Thomas; Mary, w, 99.19
Thomas; Hannah, w; John, s; George, s,
102.38
Thomas; Susan, w; Thomas, s; Mary, d,
102.125
Thomas; Mary, w; Thomas, s, 103.57
Thomas; Elizabeth, w, 107A.18
Thomas; Margaret, w; Mary, d, 109.3
Thomas; Joane, w, 109.15
Thomas, app, 104.78
Thomas, bach, 99.33
Thomas, ser, 103.163
William; Elizabeth, w, 101.12
William; Elizabeth, w, 102.32
William; Elizabeth, w; Hannah, d; Mary, d;
Elizabeth, d; William, s, 102.165
William; Susanna, w; ~, child, 104.84
William; Mary, w, 107C.10
William; Hannah, w, 109.22
William, app, 107C.36
William, ser, 107D.58

JACOB:
Isaack, 98.63
James; Elizabeth, w; Mary, d, 109.106
Joane, wid, 103.151
John, wid, 109.46
Katherine, ser, 106.24
Margaret; Grace Williams, d; Paul, s, 98.63

Mary; Phebe, d, 104.37
Moses; Hester, w; Israell, s; Jacob, s;
   Zachary, s; Ephraim, s, 102.10
Robt, bach, 104.77
Sarah, 98.47
William, bach, 98.79

JACOBS:
Charles, ser, 103.257
Elizabeth; George, s, 101.103
Elizabeth, ser, 99.4
John; Mary, w; Elizabeth, d; Sarah, d, 103.98
John; Anne, w; John, s; Stephen, s; William,
   s, 103.112
Joseph, 103.291
Mary, ser, 109.82

JACOCK: Mary, ser, 109.84

JACOMB: Thomas, 99.45

JAELL: Robt; Martha, w; Martha, child,
   104.139

JAGGERS:
Elizabeth, 107D.64
Samuel; Mary, w; Mary, d; Samuel, s;
   William, s, 107B.8

JAKEMAN:
Easter, 98.16
Christopher, 102.95
John; Priscilla, w; John, s; Susan, d, 107B.37

JAKESON: Robert, bach, ser, 98.73

JAKINS: William, a child, 102.77

JALLOF: Mary;

JAMES:
~; ~, wid, pensioner, 106.8
Alice, 101.41
Anne, ser, 103.183
Anthony, 104.148
Dan; Anne, w; Eliz, d; Anne, d; Amy, d,
   104.43
Edward; Mary, w, pensioners; Margaret, d;
   William, s; Elizabeth, d, 103.36
Elizabeth, ser, 103.68
Ellinor, spinster, 103.257
Ellinor, wid; Thomas, s, 103.63
George; Elizabeth, w, 106.21
Hannah, 109.52
Hannah; Elizabeth, w, 102.231
Harris; Elizabeth, w; Elizabeth, d, 107A.1
Jacob; Elizabeth, w; Susan, d; Sarah, d,
   107D.77
Jeane, ser, 103.114

John, 109.103
John; Margaret, w; Samuell, s, 103.60
John, assessor, 103.293
Joseph, pensioner; Elizabeth, w, 103.225
Joyce, 98.82
Mary, 102.35, 106.31
Mary, ser, 104.65
Mosses, 103.291
Richard; Penellopi, w; Penellopi, d, 103.193
Samuel; Elizabeth, w; Jerimiah, s; Anna, d;
   Elizabeth, d; Andrew, d; Thomas, s; Judith,
   d, 107D.13
Sara, ser, 101.78
Susana, ser, 102.136
Thomas; Judith, w, 109.5
Walter; Margaret, d; Elizabeth, d, 109.26
William; Magdalen, w; William, s; Jacob, s;
   Anne, d; Susanna, d, 101.11
William; Blandina, w; Susan, d; Murrey, d,
   102.237

JANAWAY:
Christopher; Elizabeth, w, 102.243
William; Elizabeth, w; Elizabeth, d, b since
   1st May, 102.197

JANCEY: Sarah; Elizabeth, d, 103.152

JANE:
Anne, app, 98.4
Elizabeth, 107D.56
Joane, ser, 105.12
Martha, 106.38
Mary, ser, 106.28

JANES:
Robert, 103.233
Samuell; Ruth, w; Samuell, s; Thomas, s,
   106.23

JANNETT: Ann, ser, 99.3

JAPAN: William, 109.6

JAQUES:
Henry; Elizabeth, w, 109.88
John; Priscilla, w, 104.121
William; Sarah, w; Sarah, d; Hester, d, 109.69

JAQUISH: Dorothy, ser, 106.59

JARMAN:
Mary, 102.30
Mary, app, 103.161

JARRARD: William, 109.41

JARRETT:
Anne, 102.95

George; Ann, w; George, s; Samuell, s,
103.291
Rebecca, 107D.13
Robert; Blanch, w, 107D.25
Sarah, ser, 103.44
Thomas; Benjamin, s, 103.50

JARSON: John, 109.71

JARVILL:
Hanah, wid; William, s; Jane, d, 102.221
John; Rebecca, w; William, s, 102.221

JARVIS:
Edward; Rachell, w, 103.4
Elizabeth, 109.105
Elizabeth, ser, 107B.72
Francis; Judith, w, 107A.11
George, £600; Rebecca, w; Mary, d; Deborah,
d, 102.2
George, collector, 102.276
Jeane, ser, 103.81
John; Elinor, w, 98.2
John; Martha, w; John Gilston, a child they
keep, 103.81
John, app, 101.107
Paull; Mary, w; Susan, d; Diana, d; Mary, d;
Elizabeth, d; Paull, s, 103.223
Phillip; Katherine, w, 98.22
Ruth, 101.80
Samuell; Jane, w, 101.93
Samuell, pensioner; Elizabeth, w; Nicholas, s;
Samuell, s, 103.181
Thomas, 102.264
Thomas, app, 103.161

JAUNCEE: Mary, wid, pensioner,
103.147

JAVIS: Holdgrave; Elizabeth, w,
102.25

JAY: Mary, 104.62

JAYCOCK:
Ann, 103.155
Hester, 107A.27

JAYLE: Margary, 98.76

JEALE: John; Joyce, w, 104.94

JEAMES: Anthony, bach, 104.136

JEANEWAY: Richard; Floarey, w; Richard, s;
William, s; Floarey, d; Jacob, s; Andrew, s;
Mary, d, 103.182

JEE: John; Sarah, w, 98.79

JEFF:
Benjamin, 109.85
Elizabeth, ser, 107D.49
Richard; Jane, w, 107D.58

JEFFCOCK: John; Susannah, w, 98.36

JEFFCUTT: Job; Mary, w, 102.241

JEFFERIES:
Anne, 102.67
Edward; Uriah, w; Ruth, d, 103.254
Edward; Jane, w; Elizabeth, d; Jane, d;
Rebecca, d; John, s, 107D.101
Elizabeth, 98.14
Elizabeth; Sarah, d, 109.55
Fitch, 98.56
Francis; Ann, w; Martha, d, 103.165
George; Elizabeth, w; Hanah, d; John, s,
107D.67
Henry, 98.19
John, 109.59
John; Mary, w, 104.63
Martha, 109.54
Nethein; Sarah, w, 102.129
Rebecca; John, s, 107A.2
Richard, 102.105
Robt; Ellinor, w, 104.129
Thomas; Mary, w; Elizabeth, d, 98.35

JEFFERS: Elizabeth, 101.55

JEFFERSON:
Hannah, 102.71
Jonathan; Alice, w, 99.24
Thomas; Mary, w, 99.27

JEFFRY:
John; Elizabeth, w; Mary, d,
107B.33
Joseph, wid, 109.56

JEFFS:
Francis; Rebeccah, w; Mary, kinswoman of,
98.6
Mary, 99.5

JELEYMAN: John, 109.31

JELLEY: Edw; Sybill, w; Sybill, d; Eliz, d;
Mary, d; Edw, s, 104.89

JELLICOE: Samuel; Mary, w, 107C.32

JELLOTT: Nicholas Denpar, 103.272

JENECKER:
Israel; Anne, w, 107C.1
William, 107C.32

JERVIS:
Henry; Sarah, w; Abraham, s; Sarah, d,
  104.85
John, ser, 106.16
Martha, ser, 106.24
Mary, 106.69
Rich, app, 104.88

JERVISON: William, bach, 106.46

JESSEY:
John, ser, 106.14
Mary, 105.8, 109.5

JESSPER: Lettice, wid, 103.206

JESSUF: Alice, pensioner; Mary, d, 103.98

JESTER: Mary, 110.20

JETT: Thomas; Margarett, w; Sarah, d,
  109.85

JEW:
Alice; Susan, d, 107B.62
Jacob, alias Jue, 102.200

JEWELL:
Mary, wid, pensioner, 103.113
Thomas, gent, see also Juell, 106.28

JEWSNOPES: William; Frances, w; Frances,
  d; William, s, 98.82

JEWSON: William, app, 107D.101

JILLETT: Mary, 103.238

JINNINGS, See Jennings

JOADS: David; Susanna, w, 102.50

JODDRELL: Wm, ser, ?b, 104.6

JOELL:
Augustine; Ann, w; Ann, d, 103.18
Dan; Mary, w, 104.135
Hannah, ser, 102.147
Joane, 109.30
Robt; Hannah, w; Mary, d; Eliz, d,
  104.18

JOERY: Mary, ser, 103.82

JOHNCOCK: Anne, 101.66

JOHNES:
Jane, ser, 107D.23
John; Frances, w; Mary, d, 103.9

John; Mary, w; Lewis, s; Richard, s; Mary, d;
  Ellinor, d; Martha, d; Katherine, d;
  Thomas, s;

JOHNSON:
~; ~, wid; ~, wid; Ahasuarus, s; Margeret, d;
  ~, wid; Robert, s, bach, 109.73
Alexander; Mary, w, 107D.83
Alexander; Lucey, w; Lucey, d, 109.30
Amey, ser, 106.59
Anthony; Anne, w, 102.148
Aoron; Marg, w; John, s, 104.37
Barnet; Hannah, w; Elizabeth, d, 109.19
Charles, 105.18
Charles; Elizabeth, w, 103.85
Edward, wid, no children, 103.50
Elias; Margaret, w; Robert, s, 109.1
Elizabeth, 107D.19, 109.103
Elizabeth Michael, d of Lampryer, 107C.34
Ellen, 102.56
Ellen, ser, 108.1
Francis; ~, w, 103.54
Francis, app, 107A.40
George, ser, 103.170
Glover; Rebecca, w, 102.153
Heugh; Katherine, w; Ann, d, 103.92
Hope, 110.18
Hugh, 102.109
Isabella; Peter, s; Julian, d, 110.29
James, 102.233, 102.266
James; Anne, w; Elizabeth, d; William, s;
  Barshaba, d, 103.46
Jane, 109.24
Jennoway, 98.58
Joane, 109.48
Johana, ser, 103.19
John; Mary, d, 98.59
John; Elizabeth, w, 101.34
John; Margaret, w; Margaret, d, 101.65
John; Sarah, w; Edward, s, 102.103
John; Rebecca, w, 102.182
John; Rachell, w, 103.142
John; Mary, w, 104.22
John; Elizabeth, w, 107A.22
John; Anne, w; Henry, s; Elizabeth, d,
  107D.10
John; Jane, w; John, s; Richard Copper, s;
  Thomas, s?; Dorothy Philps, d?, 109.54
John; Elizabeth, w; Thomas, s; Elizabeth, d,
  109.100
John, £50 p.a.; Mary, w; Alice, niece of,
  101.3
John John, s of Lampryer, 107C.34
John, app, 101.20, 107D.37
Jone, 98.41
Joseph, 109.88
Joseph; Mary, w; Mary, d, 102.50
Joseph; Mary, w; William, s, 102.92
Joseph; Martha, w, 102.264

Jonathan; Arabella, w, 104.6
Jonathon, gent; Mansfeild, w; Anne, d, 98.45
Katherine, 99.13
Margaret, 102.98, 103.269
Margaret, ser, 103.53
Margery, spinster, 103.86
Marmaduke; Hanah, w; Hanah, d; Elizabeth, d, 103.37
Martha, 98.41, 107D.41
Martha, ser, 106.14
Mary, ser, 107D.11
Mary, wid, 103.79
Mary, wid; Elizabeth, d; Honnora, d; James, s, 103.282
Mary; Edward, s; Elizabeth, d; Mary, d, 107D.53
Michaell; Mary, w, 109.75
Peter, 102.97
Priscilla, 107B.44
Rebecca, Mrs, 109.42
Richard; Elizabeth, w, 106.10
Richard; Mary, w, 109.76
Richard, £600 or £50 p.a.; Katherine, w; Richard, s, 109.7
Richard, app, 104.5
Richard, bach, 98.76
Richard, wid, 103.247
Robert; Amy, w; Mary, d?; Sarah, d?; Elizabeth, d?, 99.15
Robert; Jane, w; Robert, s, 102.154
Robert; Mary, w; Elizabeth, d; Martha, d, 102.220
Robert; Bridget, w, 103.69
Robert; Mary, w; Elizabeth, d, 109.57
Robert, assessor for Holborne Cross precinct, 109.112
Robert, ser, 103.122
Roger; Mary, w, 110.18
Roger, bach, 109.7
Samuell, app, 101.18
Sarah; Jane, d?, 102.22
Sibill, 107A.25
Symon, 109.103
Thomas; Sarah, w, 99.33
Thomas; Sarah, w, 104.30
Thomas; Anne, w, 104.31
Thomas; Mary, w; Jane, d, 106.29
Thomas; Sarah, w; Thomas, s; Benjamin, s; Sarah, d, 107B.21
Thomas; Elizabeth, w; James, s; John, s; Anne, d, 109.18
Thomas; Elizabeth, w, 110.25
Thomas, bach, 98.76
Thomas, child, 109.54
Thomas, ser, 98.31
Thomas, ser, 106.48
William, 102.87, 102.109
William; Elizabeth, w; Elizabeth, d; William, s, 98.16

William; Elizabeth, w, 99.2
William; Mary, w, 103.132
William; Sarah, w, 107B.73
William; Mary, 109.15
William; Elizabeth, w; William, s; Thomas, s, 109.36
William; Dorothy, w, 110.28
William, app, 107B.67
William, bach, 98.38, 103.110

JOLETT: John; Anne, w, 102.192

JOLLAND: Thomas; Sarah, d; Mary, d, 107B.79

JOLLIFFE: Wm; Kath, w, 104.20

JOLLIS: John; Elizabeth, w, 107B.32

JOLLY:
Giles; Sarah, w; Sarah, d, 102.87
Mary, wid, 103.198
Thomas, 106.32

JONAS: Ali;

JONES:
~; ~, w; ~, w; ~, wid; ~, wid; Lidy, d, 109.73
Alice, 110.22
Alice, ser, 105.7
Andrew; Susan, w, 106.39
Anne; Anne, d, 101.38
Anne; William, s; Anne, d, 109.1
Anne; Mary, d; John, s; Rotherick, s, 109.3
Anne, ser, 106.39, 107D.19
Benjamin, 106.22
Benjamin; Mary, w, 102.114
Benjamin, bach, 100.12
Bridgett, pensioner, 103.77
Charles; Mary, w; Robert, s; Charles, s, 107D.51
Charles; Elizabeth, w, 104.113
Charles, bach, 104.39
Daniell, 101.50
David; Mary, w; John, s; Francis, s; Mary, d, 104.118
Devorick; Anne, w, 107B.16
Dorothy, pensioner, 103.253
Dorothy, ser, 100.3
Edward, 109.108
Edward; Anne, w; Alice, d; Susan, d, 102.265
Edward; Anne, w, 109.108
Elizabeth; John, s; David, s; James, s, 101.99
Elizabeth, child, 104.133
Elizabeth; Anne, d, 107A.41
Elizabeth; John, s; Mary, d, 109.53
Elizabeth, nurse child, 107B.68
Elizabeth, wid, 103.263
Ellis; Mary, w; Jane, d; Mary, d, 102.13

Esther, ser, 103.290
Evan; Susan, w, 103.156
Frances; John, s?, 102.42
Francis; Martha, w, 107C.25
Francis, parish child, 101.35
George, 107C.35
George; Jane, w, 107A.21
George; Elizabeth, w; Mary, d, 107B.10
Henry, £50 p.a.; Hanah, w, 106.51
Hugh; Margaret, w, 101.23
Hugh, £600 or £50 p.a.; Mary, w, 109.6
Jacob; Jeane, w; Mary, d; Ann, d, 103.91
James, 101.80
John; Mary, w, 101.100
John; Mary, w; John, s; William, s, 102.10
John; Anne, w; Thomas, s; John, s; Grace, d, 102.265
John; Mary, w; John, s; Ann, d, 103.7
John; Sarah, w, 103.25
John; Mary, w; Joseph, s; Benjamin, s, 103.41
John; Anne, w; Elizabeth, d; Mary, d; Susan, d; Richard, s; Anne, d, 103.49
John; Sarah, w; John, s; Mary, d; Joseph, s, 103.249
John; Katherine, w; Mary, d, 104.32
John; Anne, w; John, s; Mary, d, 104.42
John; Anne, w; James, s, 107A.5
John; Elizabeth, w; Thomas, s, 107C.32
John; Jone, w, 107D.101
John; Lidia, w, 109.63
John; Jane, w, 109.96
John; Armineld, w, 109.103
John, app, 107D.17
John, gent, 99.43
John, ser, 102.113, 109.44
Jonathan; Eliza, w, 104.7
Joseph; Jane, w, 102.187
Joyce, pensioner, 103.22
Katherine, 104.119
Katherine, ser, 100.12
Kendrick; Deborah, w, 102.208
Lawrence, 109.79
Leonard; Debora, w; Daniell, s; James, s, 101.74
Lewis, app, 98.60, 102.184
Margaret, her husband at sea, 103.110
Margaret, ser, 98.29, 98.66
Martha, ser, 109.1
Mary; Elizabeth, d, 104.40
Mary; Caleb, s, 107A.14
Mary, pensioner, 103.36
Mathew; Hannah, w, 106.6
Morgan; Hester, w; Geo, s, 104.66
Nathaniell, 110.6
Nathaniell; Ruth, w; Ruth, d, 103.84
Nathon; Sarah, w; Nathon, s; Samuell, s; John, s, 103.155
Oliver; Mary, w, 109.37

Owen, 104.119
Phillipp; Johanna, w; John, s; Phillipp, s, 107C.38
Rebeccah; Francis, s, 98.61
Rice; Steward, w, 102.104
Rice; Sarah, w, 102.177
Richard, 109.69
Richard; Sarah, w, 98.59
Richard; Anne, w; Charles, s; Ann, d; Richard, s; Elizabeth, d; Sarah, d, 109.12
Richard; Anne, w; Elizabeth, d, 109.20
Richard; Katherine, w, 109.33
Richard; Hannah, w; Richard, s, 109.101
Richard, bach, 103.7
Robert, 110.2
Robert; Elizabeth, w, 101.27
Robert; Ellinor, w, 104.84
Robert; Sarah, w; John, s; William, s, 104.141
Robert; Mary, w; Martha, d, 107D.60
Robert; Isabell, w, 110.2
Robert, collector, victualler in Barbican, 107D.102
Roger; Mary, w; William, s; Mary, d, 109.79
Roger, bach, 106.11
Samuel, 105.10
Sam; Dorothy, w; John, s; Mary, d; Rachell, d; Isabella, d, 104.45
Sam; Eliz, w, 104.47
Sarah, 103.222
Sarah, wid, 104.96
Susan, 107A.1
Thomas, 109.71
Thomas; Elizabeth, w, 101.93
Thomas; Ann, w; Mary, d, 103.113
Thomas; Mary, w; Anne, d, 104.72
Thomas; Dorothy, w, 110.11
Thomas, £600 or £50 p.a.; Sarah, w, 109.6
Thomas, ser, 102.181
Thomz, 102.130
Valentine, 109.51
Valentine; Elizabeth, w; Elizabeth, d, 110.24
Walter; Mary, w, 98.5
Walter, a poor boy, 103.257
William; Elizabeth, w, 99.38
William; Letitia, w; John, s; William, s, 101.46
William; ~, w, 103.20
William; Winefrid, w, 107B.32
William; Alice, w; Robert, s, 107B.58
William; Kathrine, w, 107B.58
William; Mary, w; Jacob Pellon, s, 107C.10
William; Sarah, w; John, s; William, s; Robert, s; Sarah, d, 107D.12
William; Anne, w; William, s; John, s; Benjamin, s, 107D.23
William; Susan, w; John, s, 107D.59

174

William, app, 103.54
William, wid; Elizabeth, d, 103.145
Winter; Elizabeth, w, 101.46

JOPLIN: Elizabeth, ser, 102.73

JORDAN:
Alice, wid, 103.29
Anne, ser, 107D.52
Anne, wid, 103.115
Catherine, wid, 103.246
Daniel, app, 103.228
Elizabeth, 101.39, 104.67
Elizabeth; Alice, d, 109.98
Elizabeth, ser, 104.91
Jane, 109.41
Jeane, pensioner, 103.77
John, 104.146, 109.60
John; Anne, w; John, s; Thomas, s, 98.7
John; Sarah, d; Joseph, s; Jane, d, 107D.10
John; Anne, w, 109.66
John, son of £600 man, 102.1
Martha; Martha, d, 107D.25
Mary, 109.69
Oliver; Eliz, w, 104.103
Richard; Elizabeth, w, 98.26
Richard; Mary, w, 104.72
Robert, 109.19
Robert; Elizabeth, w, 102.38
Sam; Eliz, w, 104.36
Thomas; Jane, w; Thomas, s; Jane, d, 109.68
Thomas, £600; Sarah, w, 102.1
William; William, s, 102.113
William, ser, 106.28

JOSLIN: George, app, 101.108

JOSLING: Phillip; Mary, w; John, s; Phillip,
s; Samuel, s, 107D.95

JOVELIN:
Charles; Anne, w; David, s; Sarah, d;
Elizabeth, d, 102.241
John; Elienor, w, 102.241
Samuell; Sarah, w; Charles, s, 102.237

JOY: Bennet; Elizabeth, w; Martha, d,
109.11

JOYCE:
Benjamin; Mary, w; John, s; Jane, d; Mary, d,
109.48
Christopher; Elizabeth, w; Richard, s; Jane, d,
102.127
Elizabeth; William, s; Mary, d, 107C.25
Elizabeth, ser, 106.37
Hannah, ser, 106.11
Patience, 107B.65
Rebecca, wid; Ann, d, 103.20

JOYNER:
Ann, wid; Elizabeth, d; Rachell, d, 103.122
Edmund; Ellen, w; Elizabeth, d; Thomas
Stevenson, nephew of; Edmond, nephew
of, 107B.72
George; Elizabeth, w; Susan, d, 103.9
Robert, 103.127
Theophilus, 109.11
William, ser, 107A.20

JOYNES: Eliza, wid, 104.56

JUBB: Katherine, ser, 106.63

JUDE:
James, bach, ser, 98.28
Joseph, app, 107D.29

JUDGES: John; Jane, w; John, s; Mary, d;
Jane, d, 102.158

JUDITH: John, a child, 107C.39

JUDKINS: Mathew, 101.4

JUDSON:
John; Anne, w, 107B.38
Katherine, 101.40

JUE: Jacob, alias Jew, 102.200

JUELL: Elizabeth, 102.266

JUENS: John, 99.7

JUITT: Richard, 102.9

JURY:
Katherine, ser, 103.232
Mary, 101.1

JUSTER: William; Sarah, w; Michell, s;
Francis, s; Jeane, d, 103.158

JUSTICE: Elizabeth, d of £600 man,
102.152

JUWIN: Thomas; Sarah, w, 102.127

KAMBRAY: William, bach under age,
103.207

KAND: Margery, 102.75

KANDALL: Robert, 102.90

KAPON: John, ser, 102.153

KARM: Mary, ser, 102.86

175

KASH: William; Judith, w; John, s, 107D.74

KATCHING: Elizabeth, 102.101

KATES: James; Grace, w; Henry, s; Sarah, d, 103.151

KATHERINES: Samuel, under age, 103.100

KATHEW: Tho, esq; Mary, w; Tho, s, 104.65

KATHRINE: Mary; Elizabeth, d, 109.32

KEANE:
Christopher, ser, 109.32
Edmond, 102.14

KECKE:
Anne, 110.23
Anthony; Mary, w; Robert, s; Martha, d, 106.20

KECKWOOD: James, app, 98.51

KEDGIN: John, 105.5

KEEBLE:
John; Elizabeth, w; John, s; Henry, s; Mary, d, 109.47
Mary, 106.40
Samuel, £50 p.a.; Mary, w; William, s; Anne, d; Samuell, s, 106.40
Thomas, 101.103
Ursla, ser, 106.28

KEECH: John; Elizabeth, w; Ruth, d, 107D.44

KEEDE: William; Mary, w; William, s; Mary, d, alias Reed, 102.81

KEELE:
Elizabeth, ser, 102.94
Mary, 102.170

KEELEY:
George; Alice, w; Joseph, s, 102.164
Joseph; Elizabeth, d, 102.155

KEELING:
Frances, ser, 103.230
John, ser, bach, 103.18
Prudencw, wid, 103.17
Richard, app, 98.46
Samuel; Elinor, w; Priscilla, d, 109.18

KEEMER: Tho, ser, 104.83

KEENE:
Charles, app, 98.4
Daniel; Jane, w; Elizabeth, d; Jane, d, 107C.6
Exo; Katherine, w, 102.93
John, 107D.37
Martha, ser, 98.48
Rebecca, ser, 106.5
Samuel; Amy, w; Samuel, s; Elizabeth, d, 109.23
Theodore, 101.21
Thomas Thomas, s, of Bently, 107A.33
William; Anne, w, 109.103

KEEP:
Anne, 99.30
Elizabeth, ser, 107D.92
Ester, 99.30
Francis; Dorcas, w, 102.270
Peter; Ellinor, w, 104.126
Rich, app, 104.19

KEEPER: Anne;

KEESE:
~, wid, 102.10

KEESER:
Hanah, 102.267
William; Ellinor, w; Ellinor, d, 104.100

KEESLEY: Anne, 104.100

KEETS: Thomas; Elizabeth, w, 102.169

KEFT: James, bach, 105.2

KEIGHTLEY: Samuell, ser, 106.27

KEILE: Alice, 99.18

KEITE: John; David, s; David, s, 107B.32

KELCEY:
Katherine, ser, 106.28
Thomas; Dorothy, w, 102.72

KELENWORTH: John, 110.22

KELL:
Anne, ser, 101.78
Katherine, 102.121
Rachell, 109.81
Sarah; Abraham, s, 109.102

KELLETT:
John; Isabella, w; Mary, d, 109.66
Nathaniel; Mary, w; William, s; Mary, d, 109.39
Wm; Jane, d; Wm, s, 104.23

KENNISON: Francis, 102.200

KENNISTONE: Elizabeth;

KENNY:
~; Margaret, w, 106.9

KENNYWELL: John; Elizabeth, w;
Elizabeth, d; Susan, d; Mary, d, 102.30

KENSEY:
Robert, ser, 100.5
William, wid; Knowles, s; Richard, s, 106.4

KENT:
Alice, 98.18
Bridget, 107D.63
Edward; Jane, w; Sarah, d; Mary, d; Richard,
s; Edward, s, 107C.41
Elizabeth, 101.51, 104.42
Elizabeth, ser, 109.80
Francis; Elizabeth, mother of, 107C.40
Hester, 104.24
John, 101.32
John; Jane, w, 102.5
John; Mary, w, 104.44
Joseph, app, 101.106
Joshua, 101.2
Margaret, 106.33
Sarah, app, 98.15
William, £600; Frances, w; Ann, d, 103.218
William, £50 p.a.; Mary, w; Anne, d,
106.67
William, bach, 104.34
William, ser, 106.55

KENTISH: Jeremiah, ser, 109.32

KENTON:
Anne; Judith, d; Martha, d, 101.15
Benjamin; Mary, w, 110.15
Elizabeth, 110.15
John; Elizabeth, w; Sarah, d, 103.7
Joseph; Anne, w; Joseph, s; John, s,
102.194

KERBY:
Edward, app, 101.63
Elizabeth, 101.11
Henry; Susannah, w; Susan, d; Henry, s;
Sarah, d, 102.109
Humphry, 107C.16
James; Elizabeth, w; John, s, 107C.37
James, app, 107D.11
Martha, ser, 107D.90
Richard; Dorothy, w; Rebecah, d?, 99.32
Sarah, wid, 103.238
Susan, 102.168
Walter; Martha, w; Mary, d; John, s, 103.65

KERKHAN:
Henry, app, 102.184
Margaret, 102.16

KERKLIS: Thomas, assessor, 100.15

KERKMAN: Lemmell; Mary, w, 107D.30

KERTON: Samuell, 102.11

KESTIAN:
Thomas, 101.81
William; Anne, w; Jane, d, 101.38

KETCH:
Elizabeth, ser, 109.37
Joseph, 109.101

KETCHER: Robert; Jeane, w; Robert, s;
Jeane, d, 103.156

KETCHMAY: Sarah, ser, 98.54

KETLEBY: Arthur, gent; Elizabeth, w, 98.50

KETTERICH: Tho, £600; Eliz, w; Tho, s,
?bach;

KETTERRIDGE:
~, wid, 105.8

KETTLE: Humphrey; Barbara, w, 110.24

KEW:
John; Martha, w; John, s; Martha, d; Thomas,
s; Richard, s; Dorcass, d, 103.121
William, 109.22

KEWELL: John, ser, 102.198

KEY(K):
Arthur; Elizabeth, w, 107C.39
Charles, ser, 106.68
Elizabeth, 109.36
Jane, 98.33
Martha, 109.42
Richard; Anne, w, 102.217
Rich; Amey; w; Robt, s, 104.59
Richard, ser, 109.90
William, app, 101.58

KEYES:
Henry; Anne, w, 102.156
Joane, wid; Susan, d; Anne, d, 102.28
Johana, 103.71
John; Ann, w; ~, mother; ~, child, 104.139
John; Elizabeth, w; Elizabeth, d, 109.27
John; Hannah, w, 109.81
Joseph, 101.94

Nathaniel, 101.94
Ruanah; John, s; Hanah, d, 102.271

KEYNE: Anne, 109.86

KIBLE:
Francis, 103.280
John; Jeane, w, pensioner, 103.280

KICHBELL: Ann, wid, 103.68

KIDBY: Benjamine; Jane, w, 102.156

KIDDER: Richard; Mary; w; Elizabeth, d;
Sarah, d; Lidiah, d; Susannah, d; Thomas,
s, 107B.34

KIDNEY: George; Mary, w; John, s, 101.59

KIDSTONE: John; Faith; w; John, s, 102.242

KIFFE: John; Ann, w; Ann, d; Sarah, d,
103.267

KIFFEN:
Ann, 109.34
Henry, gent; Rachell, w; William, s; Joseph,
s; Susanah, d; Rachell, d; Henry, s,
103.288
William, £50 p.a.; Sarah, w, 107B.79

KIGHT:
Peter; Susanna, w, 102.227
Rebecca, 102.79

KILBEN: Elizabeth, 102.154

KILBY:
Elizabeth, ser, 102.177
Joseph, £600; Katherine, w, 107D.87
Joyce, ser, 103.13
Rebecca, wid, 103.9
William, bach, 109.109

KILCHIN: Anne, wid; Elick, s?, 102.5

KILDER: Robert, 102.94

KILLET:
Anthony; Elizabeth, w; George, s; Anthony, s;
John, s; Valentine, s, 107D.83
Edward; Mary, w, 107B.75
James; Jane, w, 110.4
Richard; Elizabeth, w; Katherine, d;
Elizabeth, d, 103.106

KILLEY: Thomas; Jeane, w, 103.274

KILLGORE: James, bach under age, 103.73

KILLIGREW: Frances; Edw, s, 104.47

KILLINGBECK: Elizabeth; Elizabeth, d,
107D.31

KILLINGHAM: Elizabeth, ser, 98.38

KILLINGLY: William; Ruth, w, 107B.30

KILLINGSWORTH:
Martha; Martha, d, 107C.7
Mary, 103.266
Thomas; Elizabeth, w; Thoma, s; John, s,
103.167

KILLINGWORTH:
Honor, 110.23
Nicholas; Elizabeth, w; Sarah, d, 102.264

KILLPEN: William; Margaret, w; Charles, s;
Anne, d; Martha, d, 98.22

KILLWORTH: John; Mary, w, 103.79

KILLY:
Elizabeth, 107D.63
Elizabeth; Elizabeth, d; Thoma, s; James, s,
107C.29

KILNER: Judeth, wid; Sarah, d; Elizabeth, d,
103.172

KILPECK: James; Mary, w, 109.88

KILPIN: Richard, 101.75

KIMBALL: Francis; Margaret, w; Francis, s;
Sarah, d, 103.38

KIMBER: Robert, ser, 102.150

KIMBERLY: John, 107D.65

KIMES:
John, 101.103
Thomas; Jane, w; Sarah, d, 102.245

KIMIER: Alice, ser, 101.74

KIMNELL: Elizabeth, 98.52

KIMORTHE: Abraham, 102.92

KIND: Jane, 101.25

KINDER: Joseph; Dorothy, w; John, s;
Mosses, s; Elizabeth, d, 103.137

KINDON: Henry, £600; Sarah, w, 107A.32

179

KINES: Timothy; Mary, w; William, s; Mary, d, 109.73

KINESTON: Mary, ser;

KING:
~; ~, w; Anne, d; ~, Mrs, 104.141
Abraham; Elizabeth, w, 109.59
Anne, 98.56
Anne; Anne, d, 109.103
Anne, pensioner, 103.42
Anne, pensioner, wid; Elizabeth, d; William, s, 103.144
Anthony; Hanah, w, 107D.71
Charles; Mary, w, 100.12
Charles; Barbara, w, 102.224
Chud, ser, 106.43
Dameras, ser, 109.24
Daniel; Elizabeth, w, 107B.15
Dorothy, 109.109
Edward, 107C.33
Edward, wid, with children, 102.158
Elianor, 107C.40
Elizabeht, 104.18, 104.86
Elizabeht; Elizabeth, d, 102.236
Francis; Elizabeth, w; Elizabeth, d; Story, s, 107B.13
Francis; Hannah, w; Frances, d, 109.50
Geo; Joanna, w; James, s, 104.11
George, app, 102.118
Gratwick, 102.216
Hannah, 98.5
Henry; Rebecca, w, 109.16
Henry; Elizabeth, w, 109.109
Henry, bach, 104.11
Isaak; Jane, w; Farringdon, s?; Rich, s; John, s; Isaak, s; Mary, d, 104.105
Iserell; Anne, w; Edward, s?; Anne, d?, 102.216
James; Anne, w; Mary, d; James, s, 105.2
James, ser, 106.23, 106.30
Jeane, 103.139
Job; Mary, w; Thomas, s, 101.19
Jonah; Rebecca, w; Penelope, d; Thomas Bibby, nephew of, 107C.12
Jonathon; Rebecca, w; Joseph, s; Christopher, s, 107D.28
Jone, 110.7
John, 102.150, 110.34
John; Margarett, w, 98.49
John; Grace, w; Grace, d; Martha, d, 101.102
John; Mary, w, 103.22
John; Elizabeth, w; Winefrett, d; Jane, d; John, s, 109.22
John; Dorothy, w; John, s; Susannah, d, 109.53
John; Mary, w; ~, wid, mother of, 109.105
John, app, 102.118, 107D.38
John, gent, 102.93

John, ser, 109.82
John, wid, 103.33
Margaret, 107A.36, 107D.71
Mary; Elizabeth, d, 98.24
Mary Margaret, d of porter, 98.82
Nathaniel; Elizabeth, w; Nathaniel, s; William, s, 107D.4
Peter, 106.28
Peter, app, 103.199
Richarde, 107C.18
Richarde; Elizabeth, w; John, s, 102.39
Richarde; Ellinor, w, 103.51
Richarde; Elizabeth, w, 104.125
Richarde; Mary, w, 107D.12
Richard, ser, 109.35
Robert, 109.59
Robert, app, 98.88
Samuell; Margaret, w; John, s; Elizabeth, d, 101.59
Sarah, 98.5
Sarah, ser, 106.38
Stephen; Eve, w; John, s; Sarah, d, 109.75
Susan, wid, 104.2
Thomas, 101.53, 105.10
Thomas; Mary, w; Thomas, s; Elizabeth, d, 107D.62
Thomas; Ursula, w, 109.22
Thomas, app, 109.109, 109.110
Thomas, bach, 103.228
William; Anne, w; George, s; James, s, 107D.9

KINGDON: Mary, 103.255

KINGHAM:
Daniel; Anne, w; Elizabeth, d, 107B.54
Seamore; Ann, w, 106.35
Thomas, 107C.38

KINGMAN: Wm, app, 104.70

KINGS: Julian, 109.47

KINGSBURY:
William, 105.18
William, assessor, 105.15

KINGSON: Samuell, 109.80

KINGSTONE:
Cornelius; Isabella, w; Mary, d; Cornelius, s; William, s, 107B.3
David; Mary, w; Mary, d; Elizabeth, d; Jeane, d, 103.152
John; Elizabeth, w, 109.2
Rich; Mary, w, 104.142
Tho; Eve, w; Rachell, d, 104.68

KINION: John, ser, 103.116

180

Andrew, app, 102.160
Anne; John, s; Anne, d; Elizabeth, d,
  101.61
Diana, ser, 103.3
Elizabeth, 102.142
Elizabeth, ser, 100.2, 105.1
Elizabeth, wid, 103.211
Elizabeth, wid; John, s, 103.22
Francis, bach, 104.94
Griffith, 101.9
Hanah, ser, 103.55
John, 102.58
John; Elizabeth, d, 102.188
John, bach, 104.94
John, ser, 106.47
Margery, 109.105
Mary, 110.21
Mary, pensioner, 103.247
Mary, ser, 100.9
Mathew; Mary, d, 107B.81
Michel; Alice, w; Henry, s, 109.86
Michael, ser, 109.57
Mordecai; Bridget, w; Mordecai, s; Henry, s,
  109.80
Richard, 102.86
Samuell, wid; Susanah, d, 103.36
Sarah, 98.61
Stephen, app, 107C.50
Thomas; Mabell, w; Sarah, d, 102.50
Thomas; Benjamin, s; Thomas, s, 107B.12
Thomas; Elizabeth, w; Thomas, s,
  107C.23
Thomas, app, 102.88
William, 101.72
William; Mary, w; Mary, d, 104.79
William, app, 102.115
William, ser, 106.24

KNIGHTINGALE: John, 101.27

KNIGHTLEY:
John, bach, 104.24
Robert, 110.7

KNIGHTON:
Edward, app, 107A.38
James, 102.229
John, app;

KNIGHTS: Jeane, spinster, 103.290
Sarah, wid, 103.290

KNIPP: John, 103.44

KNITCHING: Hugh, 99.40

KNIVETON: James; Mary, w, 109.82

KNOCK: Lucey; John Izerd, s, 103.188

KNOCKLES: William; Mary, w; Elizabeth, d,
  103.232

KNOTSFORD: John; Susanna, w;

KNOTT:
~, wid, children elsewhere, 103.105

KNOW: Thomas, ser, 109.16

KNOWLE: Ann, 104.25

KNOWLER:
Jone, 98.63
Mary, 109.22

KNOWLES:
Anne, 104.23, 107C.33
Barbary, 102.100
Elizabeth, ser, 107A.21, 103.287
Hester, ser, 107D.21
James, bach, sub hostler, 98.53
John, 104.34
John; Susan, w, 107D.79
John, ser, 103.10
Mary, wid, 103.2
Richard, app, 107C.36
Roger; Dorothy, w, 110.14
Roger, £600, 104.57
William; Elizabeth, w; Elizabeth, d; John
  Cozby, s, 103.69

KNUCKLES: James; Sarah, w, 110.22

KUNTSFORD: John; Christian, w; Samuell,
  s, 101.47

KYNE: Mary, ser;

KYTE:
~, Mrs, 104.146

LABAN:
Esther, wid, 103.207
James; Ann, w, 100.9
Richard; Mary, w; John, s; James, s; Ellinor,
  d, 109.33
William; Alice, w; Ellinor, d; Rachell, d,
  109.35

LACEY:
Anne; Fredrick, s, 98.18
Benjamin, ser, 106.34
Constant, ser, 109.17
Dorothy, 98.59
Fran, 109.17
John; Jane, w; Joseph, s; John, s, 102.238
John; Mary, w, 110.15
Joseph, 109.6

Margaret, 109.17
Mary, ser, 103.252
Robert, ser, 107A.12

LACK:
Edward, bach, 106.64
Thomas; Elizabeth, w, 107B.14
Thomas; Martha, w; John, s; Anne, d, 109.109

LACKFORD: Barbara, 102.52

LACORN: Elizabeth, child, 102.201

LAD(D):
Elizabeth, 109.73
Thomas; Elizabeth, w, 102.223
Thomas, £50 p.a.; Amy, w, 106.56

LADBEROOK: Samuell, app, 102.117

LADBROKE: John, ser, 103.190

LADDS: Anne, 102.163

LADEMAN: John; Elizabeth, d, 102.110

LADKINS: William, 107D.60

LADSTONE:
Ellinor; Mary, d, 107C.27
James, ser, 103.29
Thomas; Anne, w; John, s, 107C.8

LADYMAN:
Hanna, 101.92
James, 107B.80

LAFEILD: Robert, ser, 106.41

LAGOE: Lettice, 99.48

LAINE: John; Mary, w; Henrietta, d?; Maria,
d?; Sarah, d?, 99.38

LAKE:
Anne, gentlewoman, 98.48
Francis; Elizabeth, w; James, s; Joseph, s,
102.46
James; Johannah, w, 98.34
John, ser, 109.54
Samuell; Sarah, w; Robert, s, 98.3
Thomas, app, 98.20
William, gent; Elizabeth, w; Christopher, s,
98.41

LAKEINGS:
John; Susannah, w; Elizabeth, d; Susannah, d,
98.12
Thomas; Anne, w; Anne, d, 98.37

LAMB:
Anne, 107D.51, 107D.90
Anne, app, 107B.75
Anthony; Violetta, w, 101.51
Apher; ~, w; William, s, 100.8
Edmond, clerk, 98.43
Elizabeth, 102.10, 102.219
Elizabeth, ser, 103.171
Emme, ser, 104.39
George; Elizabeth, w; Sarah, d; Pulielin, s;
Ratford, s, 102.36
George, ser, 103.23
Hannah, 110.2
Jacob, 106.41
Jeane, 103.206
John; Joan, w, 99.10
John; Mary, w, 99.12
John; Martha, w, 103.18
John; Dorothy, w, 107C.5
Mary, 107B.14
Percevall; Martha, w; Richard, s; Thomas, s,
109.22
Percivall, app, 107C.20
Richard; Ursula, w, 109.107
Susan, wid, pensioner; Ellinor Barker, d;
Mary Barker, grand-child, 103.15
William, 110.2
William; Mildred, w; Elizabeth, d, 109.92
William, app, 103.208

LAMBERT:
Andrew; Anne, w; Hanah, d, 107D.30
Elizabeth, 101.65
Fenwick; Susanna, w, 106.17
George; Mary, w, 107D.89
Hugh; Sarah, w, 102.227
John, 107D.16
John; Mary, w, 106.24
John; Christian, w; Hanah, d; Christian, d;
John, s, 107B.7
Katherine; Sarah, d, 107B.64
Multen, clerk, 98.44
Robert; Sarah, w; Phillip, s; Thomas, s;
Robert, s; Emme, d; Grace, d, 107B.74
Thomas Ralph Lord, bach, ser to Ewer, 98.35

LAMBERTON: Anne, 99.16

LAMBETH:
Andrew; Hanah, w, 103.78
Marke, app, 103.84
Mary, ser, 103.17
Sam; Mary, w, 104.119
Sarah, wid, 103.111
William, under age, 103.46

LAMBFEILD: Martha, 107C.22

LAMBKIN: Anne, 98.55

LAMDEN: John, 110.16

LAMING: Edward; Elizabeth, w; James, s?;
Elizabeth, d?; Jane, d?, 99.40

LAMMAS: Tobey; Jane, w, 99.46

LAMOUCHE: Esther, wid; Mosses James, s;
Paul, s; Merrion, d, 103.291

LAMPART: Benjamin; Mary, w; Thomas, s?,
99.51

LAMPREY: Richard; Sarah, w; George, s;
Sarah, d, 102.273

LAMPRYER: Michael; Elizabeth, w;
Elizabeth, d; Anne, d; Mary, d; Elizabeth
Johnson, s; John Johnson, s, 107C.34

LAMSKIN: Thomas, ser, 107A.12

LANCASH: Thomas, 99.32

LANCASHEIRE: Geo; Eliza, w; Marg,
104.36

LANCASTER: Matthew, gent; Hester, w;
John, s, 98.42

LANCETT?: Henry; Hannah, d; Anne, d;
Henry, s, 109.106

LANCHETT: Kaleb; Sarah, w, 102.29

LANDAY:
Christopher, bach, 103.292
Thomas, 101.5

LANDE:
Elizabeth, ser, 106.22
John; Rebecca, w, 103.5
William, ser, 109.28

LANDMAN:
~, wid, 101.72
James; Clare, w, 101.88
Thomas; Mary, w; Thomas, s; Sarah, d; Mary,
d, 107A.25

LANDY: Mary; Frances, d, 109.104

LANE:
Alice, 107B.50
Anne, 106.62
Charles; Elizabeth, w; Anne, d, 107D.38
Edward; Susan, w; Mary, d, 102.130
Elizabeth; Roger, s; William, s; Anne, d,
102.211

Elizabeth; Benjamin, s, 102.249
Elizabeth, ser, 98.64, 109.26
Ex, 98.40
George; Thomazine, w; George, s; Jane, d;
Mary, d, 109.23
Henry; Anne, w; Henry, s; Thomas, s;
Elizabeth, d, 102.211
Isaac, app, 107D.23
Jeremiah, bach, 102.174
John, 106.50
John; Mary, w; Mary, d, 109.34
John, ser, 98.49
Jone, ser, 106.18
Judeth, pensioner, 103.119
Katherine, ser, 106.29
Margaret, ser, 98.53
Mary, 107D.26, 109.35
Mary; Mary, d; Susanah, d, 98.75
Mary; Elizabeth, d; Mary, d, 102.250
Mary, ser,-106.40
Owen, wid, hath children, 103.68
Richard; Mary, w; Jeane, d, 103.206
Robert; Elizabeth, w; Thomas, s; Leticia, d,
107B.52
Robert; Jane, w; Mary, d, 107C.25
Sarah, 107B.64, 109.4
Sarah; Sarah, d, 109.14
Timothy; Hester, w; Timothy, s; Isaac, s, 102.108
Walter, 102.15
William, 98.7

LANGBOURNE: Robert, 106.12

LANGBRIDGE: George; Anne, w; Thomas,
s; Anne, d, 105.14

LANGDON: William, bach, 102.63

LANGE: John, bach, gent, 98.27

LANGFEILD: John; Damares, w, 102.272

LANGFORD:
Anne, 99.17
Anne, Mrs; William, s; George, s, 106.25
Henrietta, 99.46
Joane, spinster, 103.183
Richard; Mary, w; Katherine, d; Mary, d;
Phebe, d, 100.14
Sarah, ser, 107D.31
Thomas, 99.17

LANGHAM:
Mary, ser, 98.35
Robert, 102.213
Ward; Eliz, w, 104.71

LANGHLAND: Thomas; Susannah, w; John,
s, 107D.7

LANGHORNE:
Easter; Letetia, d; Martha, d; Cathrine, d,
109.37
Luke; Susanna, w; Susanna, d; John, s; Mary,
d; Anne, d; William, s; Thomas, s, 109.68
William, £600 or £50 p.a., bach, 109.37
William, bach; Anne, sister of, 104.51

LANGLEY:
Andrew; Sarah, w; Charles, s; Sarah, d,
107A.33
Anne, 102.226, 107A.13
Anthony; Margaret, w; Anne, d; Margaret, d,
98.68
Daniell, 102.23, 106.17
David; Mary, w, 106.14
Edward; Elizabeth, w; Daniell, s; Huldast, d;
Hester, d, 102.255
Elizabeth, 98.2
Hanah, ser, 103.81
John; Elizabeth, w; John, s; Nathaniell, s;
Elizabeth, d; Martha, d, 103.150
John; Elizabeth, w; Augustine, s; Christopher,
s, 104.2
John; Alice, w; John, s; Susanna, d,
104.143
Joseph, 102.196
Leonard; Elizabeth, w; Elizabeth, d; Sarah, d,
102.273
Margaret, 98.4, 98.7
Mary, 98.4
Mary; George, s, ?bach, 104.144
Mary, app, 102.188
Mary, wid, 103.162
Roger, 106.20
Susan; Samuel, s; Anne, d, 107B.36
Susan, ser, 103.286
Thomas; Mary, w, 103.50
Thomas; Mary, w, 109.62
Walter; Ursula, w; Elizabeth, d, 103.185
William; Elizabeth, w, 103.113

LANGTON:
Elizabeth, 102.176
William, ser, 106.9

LANGWITH:
Richard; Deborah, w, 101.27
Sarah; Moses, s, 110.27

LANGWORTH:
Jas; Marg, w; Jas, s, 104.43
Moises; Elizabeth, w, 98.16
William, app, 98.48

LANISON: Kath;

LANKESTER:
~, wid, pensioner, 103.71

LANKFEILD: Joseph; Mary, w; Joseph, s;
Mary, d; Elizabeth, d; John, s,
107C.15

LANKFORD: Joseph, wid, 102.152

LANSDELL: Margaret, ser, 100.14

LANSDEN: John; Dennis, w; John, s; Henry,
s; Ann, d, 106.9

LANT: John; Elianor, w; John, s; Francis, s;

LANTHORPE:
~, 103.244

LAPINGTON: Thomas, ser, 106.18

LAPLEY: Martha, 106.6

LAPPAGE: John; Barbara, w; John, s; Jas, s;
Chas, s; Tho, s; Eliz, d, 104.55

LAPTHORNE:
Jane, 110.11
Roger; Mary, w, 110.11

LAPWORTH: Elizabeth, pensioner; Mary, d;
Elizabeth, d; Pheaby, d; Henry, s; Thomas,
s, 103.210

LARGE: Elizabeth, 102.208

LARKIN: Francis, £50 p.a.; Rebecca, w;
Mary, d; Thomas, s, 106.66

LARNOW: Magdalen, spinster, 103.269

LARONE: James, ser, 100.11

LARRETT?: Henry; Hannah, w; Anne, d;
Henry, s, 109.106

LARRIMOOR: Mary; Mary, ?d, 104.47

LARRISON: Sarah, 109.64

LARTER: Maud, 102.219

LASCOE: Francis, £600; Rebecca, w,
101.34

LASEBROUGH: Alice, ser, 98.64

LASEY: Anne, 102.103

LASH: Daniell; Lucye, w, 102.189

LASHBROOKE: Thomas, ser, 109.81

LASHLEY:
Mary, 109.20
Samuell, a parish child, 103.196
Sarah, 104.88

LASINGBY: Richard, ser, 107B.6

LASSENBY: John; Mary, w; John, s, 103.189

LATEWIN: Alice; Richard, s; Samuell, s,
  98.55

LATHAM:
John, app, 98.57
Mary; Jonathan, s; John, s, 101.102
Sarah, ser, 104.6
Thomas, 109.41
Thomas, ser, 106.37

LATHBURY: John, 102.93

LATIMER: Martha;

LATT:
George; Elizabeth, w, 102.208

LATTIMORE:
Elizabeth, 109.54
Henry, 102.99

LAUNDER:
Henry; Anne, w, 98.50
Hester, 98.50
Joseph; Elizabeth, w, 109.5

LAUNDRY: Robert, 105.11

LAVEE: John; Margaret, w; Mary, d;
  Arrobellah, d; Sharlott, d; Anne, d, 98.43

LAVEINDER: Robert; Alice, w; Martha, d,
  102.226

LAVENDER:
Anne, wid, 103.86
Frances, 98.7
James, ser, 103.30
Robert, at sea; Elizabeth, w, 103.48
William; Mary, w; William, s, 107D.46

LAW:
Benjamin; Mary, w; Isabella, d; Elizabeth, d,
  102.70
Dorothy, 107C.18
Edward; Ann, w; Ann, d, 103.240
Grace, 98.17
John, 102.157, 107D.78
Mary, 101.97, 107D.3
Mary, spinster, 103.125

Sarah, 102.249
Susan, spinster, 103.125

LAWES:
Elizabeth, ser, 98.29
Mary, 109.8
Mary, ser, 104.61
Nathaniel, 109.38

LAWN:
Grace, 102.249
Thomas; Frances, w; Thomas, s; William, s;
  Mary, d; Sarah, d; Elizabeth, d, 102.225

LAWRENCE:
Anne, 102.76, 102.211
Anne; Henry, s, ?bach, 104.57
Benjamin; ~, w, 103.92
Daniell, ser, 103.7
Deborah, 104.44
Edward, 99.5
Edward; Elizabeth, w; Edward, s; John, s;
  Elizabeth, d, 102.106
Frances, pensioner; Isaacc, s; John, s; Henry,
  d; Mary, d; Richard, s, 103.221
Hanna, 101.87, 103.287
Henry; Margaret, w; Mary, d, 102.165
Hester, ser, 107D.2
Jane, 110.14, 110.24
John, 98.34
John; Margaret, w; John, s; Susan, d;
  Margaret, d; Anna Maria, d, 107B.79
John; Elizabeth, w; Elizabeth, d, 107D.69
John, 101.31
John, ser, 104.11
Joseph, wid, £600, 103.228
Joyce; Mary, d, 103.165
Katherine, ser, 106.56
Marke, 107B.73
Martha, 104.94, 110.5
Ralph; Rebecca, w; Elizabeth, d, 109.86
Richard, 110.5
Richard; Issabella, w; Sarah, d, 102.180
Richard; Mary, w; Henry, s; Mary, d;
  Elizabeth, d, 105.11
Richard; Mary, w; Alice, d, 110.5
Richard, ser, 103.187
Robert, 107D.3
Samuell, £50 p.a.; Susan, w; George, s;
  Deborah, d, 106.20
Sarah, 107B.67, 109.75
Sarah; Mary, d; John, s, 103.70
Sarah, ser, 98.39
Thomas; Elizabeth, w; Thomas, s, 107C.18
Thomas; Martha, w; Mary, d; Elizabeth, d;
  Thomas, s, 107D.80
Thomas; Anne, w; William, s, 109.83
Thomas; Mary, w; Elizabeth, d; Mary, d;
  Susan, d; Thomas, s; Henry, s, 109.108

LEATHERHEAD: Susan, ser, 103.32

LEATHUM: George; Ann, w; Ann, d; Mary, d, 103.115

LEATHURUM: Thomas, app, 103.207

LEAVAKER: Joane, wid, 103.267

LEAVER:
Easter, ser, 103.18
Peter, wid; Mary, d, 103.216
Robert; Elizabeth, w; James, s, 103.182
William, £600 or £50 p.a.; Abigall, w; William, s, 109.19

LEAVERMORE: Samuell, wid, 109.65

LEAVES: Eliza, 104.23

LEDBEATER, See Leadbeater

LEDGINGHAM: Robt, bach, 104.69

LEE:
~, Mrs; Sarah, d, 104.94
Abraham; Eliz, w; Rebecca, d; Eliz, d, 104.122
Anthony; Mary, w; Anthony, s; Mary, d, 107D.99
Barnard; Hanah, w, 102.246
Caleb, app, 104.14
Charles, 99.32
Charles; Mary, w; Edward, s; Martha, d, 102.43
Charles; Mary, w; Daniell, s, 106.46
Cornelius, 102.104
Cuthbert; Johannah, w; Sarah, d; Ralph, s; Frances, d; Susan, d; Elizabeth, d, 107D.13
Daniell; Elizabeth, w, 109.106
Daniell, app, 103.106
Edward, 109.5
Edward, bach, 102.185
Elizabeth; Mathew, s, 109.16
Ellinor; Ellinor, d; Eliz, d, 104.140
Frances, 101.5
Frances, wid, 103.214
Francis, bach, 103.56
George; Jane, w; Elizabeth, d, 101.62
Hanah, 107C.10
Hanah, ser, 103.234
Henry, 101.40
Henry; Jone, w, 107D.63
Humphrey; Mercey, w, 103.197
James; Anne, w; Anthony, s; Susan, d, 107D.69
Jane, 109.67
Jane; Samuell, s, 101.103
Jane, ser, 101.59

Jeane, wid, 103.56
Jervas; Joanna, w, 109.108
John; Margaret, w; Jonathon, s; Joseph, s, 102.137
John; Elizabeth, w; John, s, 102.172
John; Dorcass, w; Elizabeth, d; John, s; Joseph, s; James, s; Jonathon, s, 103.258
John; Lidia, w; Margaret, d, 109.90
John, app, 107A.28
Joseph, bach, 103.48
Joshua; Margeret, w, 103.281
Margerey, ser, 102.110
Martha, ser, 101.86
Mary, 104.87
Mary, spinster, 103.56
Michael; Susan, w; John, s, 107D.72
Miles, app, 101.27
Philadelpha, ser, 103.120
Richard; Hannah, w; Susanah, d; Hannah, d, 102.142
Richard, ser, 103.233
Rodah, 109.41
Rost, ser, 106.5
Samuel; Mary, w, 107D.53
Samuell, bach, 103.48
Sarah, 100.11
Sarah, spinster, 103.8
Stephen, 107D.77
Susan, 107A.12
Susannah; Mary, d, 98.24
Thomas, 99.33
Thomas; Elizabeth, w, 102.271
Thomas; Mary, w; Susanna, d, 104.58
Thomas; Katherine, w, 107B.23
Thomas, ser, 106.49, 109.7
William; Sarah, w, 103.29
William; Anne, w, 107A.14
William; Martha, w, 109.90
William; Mary, w;

LEECH:
~, wid, 104.42
Anne, ser, 98.48
Anne, spinster, 103.224
James; Anne, w, 107D.48
John; Thomas, s; Mary, d, 102.242
Mary, 107B.27
Mary; Robert, s; Mary, d; Elizabeth, d, 102.252
Samuell, app, 102.176
Thomas, ser, 103.184

LEECHFEILD: William; Frances, w; John, s, 102.98

LEEDS: Thomas; Ann, w, 110.16

LEEK(E), See Leak(E)

LEELAND: Sarah; Sarah, d, 103.243

LEEPOOL: Anne, 107D.41

LEESON:
Bridget, 101.12
Richard; Elizabeth, w; Elizabeth, d, 107B.36
Soloman, 103.234
William, 101.12

LEGATT:
Clement, 110.14
George, ser, 109.111

LEGAW: Jasper; Emme, w; Alice, d, 107D.78

LEGBURY: Rachel, 107B.39

LEGETT:
Elizabeth, a nurse child, 107D.81
John; Deborah, w; John, s; Mary, d; Alenezer,
    s, 103.193
Mary, 110.14
Susan, wid, 103.53

LEGG:
Anne, 109.100
Elizabeth; Elizabeth, grand-d of, 98.11
Elizabeth, ser, 107B.58
Francis, 102.2
Henry; Mary, w; Hamlitt, s; Elizabeth, d,
    102.228
John; Mary, w; John, s; Anne, d; Rebeccah, d,
    98.55
John; Sarah, w; Sarah, d; William, s, 107D.81
Wm, ser, 104.90

LEGITT: Ambrose; Hannah, w, 102.69

LEGO: Edward;

LEGRAND: ~, M, 102.88
Ann, 102.218

LEGROSSE: Tho; Mary, w, 104.31

LEIDGER:
Henry; Anne, 98.16
Mary, 104.207

LEIGE:
Jonah; Elizabeth, w, 107D.73
Magdalen, spinster, 103.269

LEIGH:
Edward; Rebecca, w, 110.1
Jane; John, s; Elizabeth, d, 98.60
John; Susannah, w; Susannah, d, 98.37
Thomas, gent; Honour, w; Elizabeth, d, 98.39

LEIGHS: William, bach, 98.53

LEIISTER: Margaret, 98.51

LEITHILUIER: Abraham, gent; Protasey, w;
    Mary, d; Jeane, d; John, s; Edward, s;
    Abraham, s; Protasey, d, 103.285

LEMMOX: John; Susan, w; Susan, d;

LEMON:
~, wid, 104.71
Anne, 101.31
Elizabeth, 106.21
John, 101.75
Richard, 102.17
Sarah, 109.13
Susan, 102.260
Tanfeild, esq, bach, 106.58
-
LEMOTT: Glode; Mary, w, 104.110

LEMSTEAD: Mary, 109.49

LEMUDE: Elizabeth, 106.24

LENINDE: Mary, 106.34

LENITT: Edward, ser, 103.34

LENTHALL: Francis, ser, 106.4

LENTON: Richard; Sarah, w; Elizabeth, d;
    Mary, d, 107D.79

LENUDE: Ben; Eliz, w; Paul, s, 104.4

LEONARD:
Anthony; Elizabeth, w; Thomas, s; John, s,
    109.100
Elizabeth, 107A.10
Henry; Jane, w; Hannah, d, 104.68
Margaret; Mary, d, 107B.79
Michael; Anne, w; John, s, 107C.10
William; Mary, w; Anne, d; William, s; John,
    s, 107C.33

LEOPARD: William, app, 98.60

LEPIPRE: Peter, gent; Sarah, w, 102.210

LEPPARD: Hanah, ser, 107A.25

LEPPER:
John; Elizabeth, w, 109.82
Kathrine, 109.5
Mary, 109.71
Robert; Sarah, w; Sarah, d; Constance, d,
    107D.5

Thomsa, bach, £600; Alice, sister, 102.115
William; Elizabeth, w; Mary, d; Job, s;
Joshua, s, 107D.5

LEPSON: Dorothy, wid; Elizabeth, d,
100.9

LESAW: John, ser, 107D.58

LESTER:
Elizabeth, 106.39
Richard, 102.2
Thomas, 106.39

LETHER: John; ~, Benedict (sic) wife; John,
s; Mary, d; Hannah, d, 104.68

LETREE: Martha, spinster, 103.267

LETRUE: Isaac, app, 98.84

LETT: Elizabeth, ser, 103.55

LETTERDON: Susan, 102.253

LETTS:
John, 107A.25
Thomas; Elizabeth, w; Elizabeth, d; Mary, d,
103.13
Wm, bach, 104.34

LETTSWORTH: Robert, bach,
103.50

LEVELEY: Maud, 102.219

LEVENTHORP:
John; Katherine, w, 102.271
Margaret; Elizabeth, d, 102.181

LEVER:
John; Isabell, w, 107A.41
Katherine, 107D.85

LEVERSLEY: Josua; Alice, w; William, s,
102.202

LEVETT:
Deborah; Robert, s? child, 102.76
Hanah; Mary, d, 107D.98
Mary, 103.50

LEVIE: Edward; Ann, w; Edward, s;
Elizabeth, d; Hanah, d, 103.104

LEVIN:
Charels; Elizabeth, w; Mary, d; Elizabeth, d;
Anne, d, 109.66
Sarah, wid; Elizabeth, d, 103.5

LEVINGS: Bryant; Elizabeth, w; Katherine,
d; Lettice, d, 98.81

LEVINGSTON(E):
Alexander; Mary, w; Mary, d, 98.68
John, 99.31
Magdalen, 99.31
Sarah, 99.31

LEVINS:
Henry; Anne, w, 104.86
Roger, £600; Elizabeth, w, 102.112

LEWEN: Mary, ser, 98.29

LEWENDEN: John; Elizabeth, w; William, s;
John, s; Joseph, s, 109.65

LEWER: William; Elizabeth, w; Joseph, s;
John, s, 98.4

LEWES: Perkin, dead, 102.274

LEWIN:
Anne, 101.77
Daniell, app, 101.103
Dorothy, 104.120
John, bach, 99.5
Martha; Margarett, d; Sarah, d, 102.62
Richard; Katherine, w, 103.107
Robert; Elizabeth, w; Gamaliell, d; Ruth, d;

LEWIS: ~; ~, w; ~, her husband at sea; ~,
wid; ~, wid; Hannah, d; Edward, s, 102.37
Allen, ser, 103.14
Ann, 103.51
Ann; Edward, s, 104.49
Anne, ser, 99.2
Charles; Sarah, w, 102.178
Charles; Mary, w; Charles, s; Anna Maria, d,
109.63
Charles, ser, 103.101
David; Mary, w; David, s; James, s;
Heneretta, d; Maria, d, 107C.28
Edward, 98.78
Edward; Elizabeth, w, 107C.22
Elias; Sarah, w; Elizabeth, d, 107B.46
Elizabeth, ser, 105.1
Felix, gent; Elizabeth, w; Fretchwell, d or s?,
98.33
Francis, 109.35
Francis; Mary, w, 102.245
Francis; Dorcass, w; Dorcass, d, 103.102
Francis; Elizabeth, w, 109.35
Francis, app, 107B.39
Hannah, ser, 106.21
Henry; Mary, w; George, s; Henry, s, 109.38
Jacob; Blanch, w, 105.8
Jane, 98.9, 106.61

LILLY:
Ann, wid, 103.160
Daniel, app, 107B.66
John; Jane, w; Elizabeth, d, 98.58
Susan, 103.160
William, 109.32
William; Susan, w, 103.173
William; Elizabeth, w, 103.185

LILLYWHITE: Charles, ser, 103.44

LIMBERRY:
Mary, 107B.58
Thomas; Anne, w; Sarah, d; Mary, d;
    Elizabeth, d, 107B.70

LIMBERY:
Caleb; Elizabeth, w, 101.51
Lucey, wid, 103.158

LIMBROW: William; Sarah, w; William, s;
    James, s; Elizabeth, d; Sarah, d, 102.227

LIMPANY: Susanna, 101.66

LIMPENNY: Sarah, 109.90

LINCH: Anne, ser, 98.44

LINCOLNE: Mary, 98.68

LINDALL, See Lyndell

LINDLEY: John; Mary, w; Anne, d, 110.1

LINDOME: Mary, 107B.23

LINDSEY:
Anne, 98.37
Edward; Ann, w; Ann, d, 109.32
Isabella, 109.85
Jane, ser, 109.56

LINDUF:
Ann, ser, 103.271
Elizabeth, ser, 109.48

LINE, See Lyne

LINEY: Joseph, 105.17

LINFORD, See Lynford

LING: Charles; Martha, w; Charles, s,
    103.163

LINGHAM: Margaret, 103.49

LINGOE: Francis, 109.10

LINKHORNE: Elizabeth, 102.181

LINLEY:
Ann, 109.98
Elizabeth John, grand-d of Browning,
    107D.31

LINN:
Edward, bach under age, 103.53
George; Jane, w; Susannah, d; Elizabeth, d,
    109.49
Rebecca; Elizabeth, d, 102.138

LINNAKER:
Ann, wid, 103.67
Henry; Elizabeth, w; Alice, d, 109.55
Sarah, 109.53
William; Margeret, w; Alice, d; Mary, d,
    103.200

LINNETT:
Giles; Jane, w; Francis, s; Ann, d,
    109.49
Johanna, 109.83
Mary, 104.6

LINSKIN: William, app, 103.22

LINSSEY: Thomas, a parish child,
    103.227

LINTELL:
Martha, 102.112
Mary, ser, 108.1

LINTON:
Elizabeth, 102.56
Hester, 98.55
Thomas; Jane, w; Jane, d, 107D.36

LINWOOD: John, ser, 106.55

LIPPINWELL: Benjamin, 103.259

LIPSCOME: John, ser, 106.19

LIPSCUM: Charles; Elizabeth, w,
    109.109

LIQUORISH: Joseph, ser, 103.5

LISNEY: Ruth, 102.259

LIST:
Elizabeth, ser, 107A.6
Mary, ser, 102.174
William; Martha, w, 103.183

LISTON: Sarah; Ann, d, 102.217

James, bach, 109.80
Joshua, £600; Mary, w; Christopher, s?;
  Joshua, s?, 99.44
Margaret, ser, 106.27
Mathias, £600; Ann, w; Phillip, s; Ann, d,
  108.2
Nathaniel; Anne, w; Anne, d, 107A.42
Walter; Winifred, w, 98.24

LOCKER:
Elizabeth, 107B.16
Sarah, ser, 102.162

LOCKET: Harman; Sarah, w; Sarah, d,
  109.91

LOCKEY:
Edward, 106.37
Mary; Mary, d; Martha, d, 102.96

LOCKIN: Anne; Elizabeth, d, 102.265

LOCKINGTON:
Thomas, £50 p.a.; Elizabeth, w, 101.75
Robert, ser, 107C.39

LOCKLEY: John, app, 98.25

LOCKWOOD: Ferdinando; Frances, d; Mary,
  d; Sarah, d, 109.46

LOCUS: Mary, 106.15

LODER, See Loader

LODGE:
Ann, ser, 103.289
James; Elizabeth, w; James, s, 109.3
Thomas, 110.23
Thomas; Anne, w, 104.77

LODLOW:
Nath, gent; Kath, w; Mary Batters, d,
  104.111
Samuel; Hester, w, 107D.28
Stephen; Judeth, w; Mary, d?; Christopher, s?,
  109.28

LOE:
John, 101.46
John, parish child, 101.35

LOFEILD: s, bach, £600, 104.5

LOFTHOUSE:
Mathew, app, 103.260
Richard, app, 103.19
Seth, £600; Ann, w; Joseph, s; Ann, d,
  103.260

LOFTUS:
Robt; Marg, w, 104.121
Thomas; Mary, w; John, s, 107D.18

LOGGINS:
John, ser, 103.32
Kath, 104.24

LOGUS: Jacob; Mary, w; Mary, d, 104.113

LOKE:
Ciprian, app, 109.42
John; Mary, w, 109.39
William, bach, 104.29

LOKER: John; Mary, w, 107D.32

LOLE: John; Margeret, w; Elizabeth, d;
  Esther, d; Mary, d, 103.167

LOMAS: Rebecca, ser, 106.30

LOMBARD: John; Mary, w; Philip, s; Mary,
  d, 103.273

LOND: Jacob, app, 98.74

LONDON:
Edward; Joane, w; Thomas, s; Elizabeth, d,
  102.190
Ellen, ser, 107B.14
Ellinor, pensioner, 103.98
John; Elizabeth, w, 101.62
John, app;

LONG:
~, wid, 109.73
Anne, 99.12, 102.186
Augustine; Katherine, w, 109.25
Francis, 109.99
Henry, junior; Margery, w; Henry, s; Mabill,
  d, 103.51
Henry, senior; Amey, w; Sarah, d, 103.51
James; Edith, w; Mary, d, 109.48
James, assessor for Holborne Cross precinct,
  109.112
Jane, 102.266
Jane; Elizabeth, d, 107B.73
John, 101.51
John; Sarah, w, 107B.38
John; Rebecca, w; Susan, d; Mary, d, 107B.57
John; Elizabeth, w, 109.50
John, £600, wid, 105.14
John, app, 107D.17
Joseph, 109.59
Margaret, wid; Elizabeth, d; Henry, s;
  Johanna, d, 102.44
Marke; Dorothy, w; Susannah, d; William, s;
  John, s, 109.36

Martha, ser, 107D.41
Mary, 101.36, 110.6
Mary; Rowland, s; Mary, d, 109.111
Mary, pensioner; Mary, d, 103.99
Mary, ser, 101.57
Robert; Elizabeth, w; Robert, s, 109.46
Samuell; Judeth, d, 102.101
Solomon; Dorothy, w, 101.9
Thomas; Elizabeth, w; Thomas, s; Elizabeth,
    d, 107D.40
Valentine; Jeane, w, 103.65
William, 103.105
William; Elizabeth, w; Grigory, s; Elizabeth,
    d, 109.12
William, ser, 106.26, 109.84

LONGBOTTOM:
John, £600; Judith, w; Abraham, s, 107A.31
Robert; Alice, w; ~, child, 99.25
Thomas, 107A.31
Thomas; Judith, w, 103.111

LONGDON: Mary, ser, 103.17

LONGFORD:
Jane, ser, 104.116
Wm, gent; Eliza, w; Wm, s, 104.65

LONGHURST: Jervis, ser, 106.68

LONGLAND: Mary, ser, 106.5

LONGWORTH: Richard; Priscillia, w;
    George, s; Richard, s, 103.63

LONGWORTHY: Anthony; Mary, w;
    Anthony, s; Mary, d, 107D.31

LONLEY: Ann, wid, 103.23

LOOM: Sarah, 104.51

LOPEY: Mary, wid; Sarah, d; Jeane, d;
    Daniell, s; Mary, d; Esther, d,
    103.272

LORD:
Anne; Anne, d, 104.38
Edward, Bishop of Gloucester; Anne, his
    lady; Susannah, d; Mary, d, 107D.2
Elisha, 102.145
Elizabeth, 101.88
Mary, 107C.16
Samuell; Sarah, w; Mary, d; Samuell, s;
    Elizabeth, d, 103.85

LORDAN: Hester, 102.218

LORRIMAN: James, ser, 98.31

LOSEBY: Sarah, ser, 107A.36

LOTON:
Elizabeth, ser, 106.24, 109.2
Robert; Hester, w; Robert, s, 102.113
Thomas; Margaret, w; Mary, d, 106.17
Thomas, app, 107A.8

LOTT: Lance, app, 107D.98

LOTTS: William, ser, 106.15

LOUENEA: Abraham; Ann, w; Susan, d;
    Humphry, s; Jacob, s, 103.41

LOUGH: Thomas, bach, 98.74

LOUTON: Edward, 105.16

LOVE:
Anne; Alice, d, 107B.46
Askin, 106.18
Nathaniell, 106.18
William, £600, bach, 108.4

LOVEALL: Edward, 103.266

LOVEBONE: Henry, ser, 106.5

LOVEDAY:
John, 107C.33
John; Esther, w; Susan, d; Ann, d, 103.254
John; Mary, w; Elizabeth, d; John, s; William,
    s, 109.45
Joseph; Anne, w; Hanna, d; Mary, d, 101.49

LOVEDING: Elizabeth, 98.48

LOVEJOY:
Ann; Mary, d, 102.243
John; Ellinor, w; Ellinor, d, 103.89
Mary; Lucy, d, 101.93
William; Ann, w, 102.257

LOVELACE: Francis; Anne, w, 107B.60

LOVELAND:
Richard, ser, 109.57
Robert; Mary, w; Robert, s; Benjamin, s;
    Jonathon, s, 107D.18

LOVELL:
Dorothy, 102.47
Francis, 102.38
Margaret, 107D.16
Parnell, 107D.71
Robert, 101.9
Susan, wid, 103.7
Thomas, 109.103

Thomas, bach, 106.37
William, 109.104
William; Hester, d, 104.71
William; Alice, w; Elizabeth, d, 109.7
William; Elizabeth, w; Elizabeth, d; Richard,
s, 109.34

LOVELOCK: William, £600; Elizabeth, w,
101.63

LOVERAINE: Thomas; Susan, w; Thomas, s,
103.82

LOVERBONE: Henry; Henry, s; Robert, s, 98.20

LOVERON: David, 106.42

LOVETT:
Anne, 102.238
Henry; Catherine, w; Jonathon, s; Elizabeth,
d, 109.97
John; ~, w; William, s, 102.229
Mary, ser, 104.110
William;

LOW:
~, wid, 109.74
Anne, 102.170
Elizabeth, 102.67
Ellinor, wid; Joseph, s, 103.291
George; Elizabeth, w; Elizabeth, d, 98.85
George, ser, 106.59
Hannah, ser, 102.83
James; Agnes, w; Agnes, d; Sarah, d; Daniel,
s, 107D.72
Joane, 107D.43
John; Ann, w; John, s, 103.71
Mary, 109.70, 102.8
Mathew, 107D.6
Richard, app, 104.59
Richard, bach, 104.96
Samuel; Hannah, w; Samuell, s, 109.17
Thomas, 102.8
Thomas; Mary, w; Samuell, s, 104.104
Thomas; Mary, w; William, s, 106.15
Thomas, app, 109.104
Tobias; Eliz, w, 104.126
William; Joane, w; Elizabeth, d; Katherine, d;
Thomas, s, 102.75

LOWATER: Ester, 98.21

LOWBRIDGE: Margaarett, 106.21

LOWDE: Lawrance, 105.10

LOWEN:
Jane, 98.78
John; Eliz, w; John, s; Eliz, d, 104.143

LOWENS: Anne, 109.85

LOWIS: Mary, 110.18

LOWK: John; Margaret, w; Sarah, d; Mary
Wyatt, d, 107C.14

LOWMAM: Thomas, 105.18

LOWNDES:
Mary, ser, 98.8
Thomas; Dorothy, w, 101.48

LOWNES:
Elizabeth, ser, 102.185
Nathaniell, wid, 98.62

LOWREY:
Ann, ser, 103.57
William; Mary, w; Elizabeth, d, 103.6

LOWSON: Dorothy, ser, 98.30

LOWTH: Thomas; Sarah, w; Judith, d;
Dorcas, d, 107D.81

LOWTHER: Elizabeth, 107A.9

LOYNS: Tho, app, 104.61

LUBBOCK:
Dorothy, 109.98
Jane, 109.98

LUCAR: Edward; Catherine, w; John Griffin,
s; Surman Lucar, s;

LUCAS:
~; Mary, w; Eliz, d, 104.133
Alice, ser, 103.37
Catherine; Rebecca, d, 109.67
Charles, bach, 103.228
Edward; Ann, w, 109.82
John; Francis, w, 103.230
John; Frances, w, 104.96
John, £600; Mary, w, 104.95
John, wid, hath children elsewhere, 103.40
Jonathon; Mary, w, 103.219
Mary, belongs to Fish st, 103.212
Mary, ser, 103.212
Nicholas; Sarah, w; Anne, d; John, s,
102.77
Stephen; Martha, w; Edward, s, 103.42
Susan, 102.259
William; Margaret, w, 98.1
William; Anne, w; Anne, d; Margaret, d,
101.53

LUCK: Hanah, ser, 107B.19

LUCKCRAFT: Thomas; Johana, w; Elizabeth Williams, s, 103.283

LUCKER: Elizabeth, ser, 101.75

LUCKMAN: John; Susanna, w; John, s?, 99.39

LUCY:
George, app, 104.11
Richard, ser, 103.218

LUDBEY:
Esther, wid, 103.79
Samuell; Mary, w; Ann, d, 103.177

LUDGATE:
Henry, ser, bach?, 104.34
Margaret, ser, 98.25
Richard; Elizabeth, w, 109.67
Robert; Grace, w; Marjery, d, 109.40

LUDLOW:
Isaac; Mary, w; Elizabeth, d; Samuel, s, 107D.97
Mary, ser, 98.68

LUDWELL: Susannah, 107C.23

LUFCRAFT: Jeremy, 102.209

LUFF:
Jane, 102.89
Richard; Rebecca, w; Richard, s, 109.52

LUFFKIN: Samuell; Jeane, w, 103.75

LUFFMAN:
Austing; Susannah, w, 98.83
Daniell; Mary, w, 109.105
John, 109.65
Susanna; Susanna, d, 109.65

LUFTON:
Edward; Elizabeth, w, 110.17
Thomas; Hannah, w, 110.17

LUGG:
Isaack; Elizabeth, w; Robert, s; Elizabeth, d; Nicholas, s; Christopher, s, 98.56
Peter, 106.1

LUGGER: Susan, 107D.85

LUKAS: Thomas, bach, 102.52

LUKE:
John; Dorcas, w; Samuel, s; Olive, d; Dorcas, d, 107D.93

Sarah, 104.35
Susan, ser;

LUKIN:
~, Mrs, 104.139

LULL: Mary, ser, 100.3

LUMBARD: John, 109.32

LUMBEY: Sarah, ser, 104.92

LUMBLY:
Elizabeth, 98.58
William, 98.32

LUMOUTHE: Elizabeth, ser, 103.260

LUNN:
Anne, 98.86, 102.49
Elizabeth, 101.81
John; Elizabeth, w, 103.159
John, £600; Ursula, w; Francis, s, 106.55

LUNT: Isabella, app, 107D.11

LUPTON:
Jeremy, 98.21
John; Mary, w; John, s; Mary, d; Thomas, s; Thomas, s; Samuell, s;

LUSHEIRE:
~, Mrs, 98.68

LUSKE: Elizabeth, 101.90

LUSOME: Mary, 109.91

LUTHAIGHT: Ralph, 101.109

LUTHER:
James; Anne, d; Martin, s; Dorothy, d, 107B.51
Stephen, app, 102.183

LUTMAN: John, 102.187

LUTTIN: William, ser, 103.255

LYBORN: Mary, ser, 104.5

LYBOURN:
John; Mary, w; John, s?; Dorcass, d?, 99.13
Richard; Elizabeth, w, 99.21

LYCENSE: Jone, 98.56

LYDBEATER: Peter, bach, 104.108

LYDDALL: Thomas; Bridgett, w, 98.58

LYDDYARD:
Anne; Roger, s, 104.11
Elizabeth, ser, 103.228
Nicholas; Mary, w; Dorcas, d; Esther, d;
  Hanah, d; Phillip, s, 103.53
Tho, 104.107
William; Frances, w, 102.60

LYFORD:
Barnard; Rachell, w, 110.18
Richard; Helder, w; Richard, s; Sara, d,
  101.41

LYLEY: Joseph; Mary, w; Anne, d; John, s,
  102.149

LYM: Mathew; Casia, w; Judith, d, 101.84

LYMWOOD: Dorothy, 101.73

LYNAM: George; Katherine, w, 107B.32

LYNCEY:
Elizabeth, 99.27
George, 99.27

LYNDELL:
Dorothy, ser, 106.21
Francis, 110.2
Katherine; Fretchfeild, d, 110.2
Thoms, 110.2
Thoms, bach, 110.2

LYNDSEY, See Lindsey

LYNE:
Ellinor, ser, 103.55
John, 106.13
Thomas; Sarah, w; Thomas, s; Sarah, d,
  103.45

LYNES:
Elinor, ser, 103.45
Phillip, app, 101.89

LYNFORD:
Henry, 109.86
Henry; Elizabeth, w, 109.86
Thomas; Jane, w, 107D.25

LYNUM: Sarah; Robert, s, 107A.18

LYON:
Elizabeth, wid; James, s, 103.217
Hanah, 107B.77
John; Anna, w, 103.255
John; Jane, w; John, s, 107B.23

John, app, 101.84
Joseph; Johanna, w; Martha, d; Mary, d,
  103.72
Mary, wid; John, s, 103.137

LYSLE: Phillip, 106.68

LYTH: George, 106.45

MABLE: Elizabeth, 109.73

MABLEY: Sarah, 103.3

MABOTT: Dorothy, 102.59

MABREY: Mary, 102.220

MACARTLY: Cicill; Richard, s; William, s,
  109.94

MACE:
Anne, 101.110
Elizabeth, 102.88
Gilbert; Esther, w; Esther, d; Priscillia, d;
  Mary, d, 103.186
John; Alice, w, 103.66
William; Hester, w; William, s; Elizabeth, d;
  John, s, 107A.38

MACEY: Thomas, 103.124

MACHANESSE: Thomas; Barberah, w,
  107D.76

MACHINE: John; Mary, w; John, s; Jeane, d;
  Ann, d, 103.225

MACKDONELL: Elizabeth; John, s; Andrew,
  s, 101.27

MACKEINS: George; Anne, w; Mary, d;
  John, s; George, s, 102.71

MACKENNY: John; Martha, w, 102.159

MACKERRY: Anne, a parish child;

MACKIVERR: ~, 104.33
Jas; Joane, w, 104.36

MACKLEY: William, £600; Judith, w; John,
  s; William, s, 101.2

MACKLIN:
Anne, ser, 106.36
Peter; Anne, w; Anne, d; George, s,
  103.257

MACKMATH: Anne, ser, 101.110

MALE:
Charles; Rebecca, w; Michael, s; James, s; Charles, s, 107A.24
George, app, 107B.63
Richard; Elizabeth, w, 110.18
Susannah, 98.12
William, 105.17

MALES: James; Elizabeth, w; James, s; George, s; Daniel, s; Elizabeth, d, 105.14

MALING: Robert, 109.85

MALLABARR: Walter; Eliza, w;

MALLARD:
~, wid; Anne, d; Sarah, d; Christian, d, 102.37
Jeane, 103.269
Tho; Anne, w; Tho, s, 104.132

MALLARY:
Catherine, wid; Eleizer, s, 103.246
John; Amey, w, 102.37

MALLCOTT: John, ser, 102.100

MALLERES: Thomas, 102.243

MALLETT:
Charles, 102.12
Debarah, 102.106
Eliz, wid, 104.4
Mary, 107C.41
Richard, app, 101.85
Roger; Frances, w; Richard, s; Frances, d; Anne, d; Grace, d; Margarett, d, 101.21
Simon; Deborah, w; Deborah, d; Elizabeth, d, 109.2

MALLEY:
James, 110.3
Robert; Mary, w, 110.17

MALLYAN: William; Elizabeth, w; William, s; Elizabeth, d; Richard, s, 103.116

MALPUS: Elizabeth, spinster, 103.2

MALTMAN: Rebecca, 102.97

MALYN: Tho, ser; Tho, s, ?bach; Eliza Lawson, d, 104.101

MAMMELL: Joseph, app, 98.49

MAN:
Anne, 99.21
Anne, ser, 102.152
Daniell, gent; Daniell, s, 109.76

Elizabeth, 106.11
Elizabeth; Elizabeth, d, 107D.36
Elizabeth, gentlewoman; Mary, d, 98.64
John, 109.63
John, gent; Mary, w, 109.76
Jonathan, 101.69
Joseph; Ann, w, 99.23
Mary, ser, 107A.23
Mathew, 106.31
Sarah, wid, 102.68
Silvanus, 101.6
Theophilus, app, 98.46
William; Jane, w; John, s; Jane, d, 107D.82
William, esq, 109.76
William, ser, 106.19

MANATON: Robert, £600; Anne, w, 106.55

MAND: George Chamberlaine; Sarah, w; Rebeccah, d, 98.53

MANDER: John; Mary, w, 102.132

MANDEVILE: Gigon; Isabellah, w; Giggon, s; William, s; Elizabeth, d; Barbarah, d, 98.65

MANERLEY: John; Elizabeth, w; William, s; Martha, d, 102.139

MANFEILD: Anne, 104.9

MANFORTH: Edmond; Mary, w, 98.69

MANGER: William, app, 107D.54

MANIFOLD: William; Elizabeth, d, 107D.72

MANLEY:
John; Mary, w; Jonathon, s; Rebecca, d, 109.101
Matt; Ellin, w, 104.48
Sarah, ser, 107C.14

MANLOVE: Martha, 101.23

MANNING:
Anne, 102.88
Edward, 109.44
Elinor, 98.24
Frances, ser, 98.88
Henry; Isabell, w; Ann, d, 109.57
Henry; Mary, w; Penelope, d; Elizabeth, d, 103.130
Huntington; Anne, w, 98.47
John; Jane, w, 109.77
Robt, a boy, 104.92
Tho; Sarah, w, 104.143

Thomas; Alice, w; Thomas, s; Elizabeth, d,
    106.14
William, 110.23, 110.26

MANNINGHAM: Thomas, Dr.; Elizabeth, w;
    Mary, d; Richard, s; Dorothy, d, 98.25

MANNOOTH: Anne; Elizabeth, d; Anne, d,
    98.80

MANSELL:
Elizabeth, 99.38
Robert, £600 or £50 p.a., bach, 109.46
Thomas; Elizabeth, w, 101.52

MANSER: Jane; Jane, d, 102.147

MANSFEILD:
John, bach, 102.184
Lois, ser, 102.73

MANSLEY: William, 109.85

MANSON: Elizabeth, ser, 107D.2

MANSTING: Ducebellah; John, s; Elizabeth,
    d; Thomas, s; Mary, d, 96.65

MANTELL: Thomazin, 102.208

MANTON: Elizabeth, 98.26

MANWARING:
George; ~, w, 106.16
Sarah, 106.4

MAPLES:
Anne, ser, 98.75
Richard; Elizabeth, w, 107C.11

MAPPLESDEN:
Charles, ser, 108.8
Mary; Mary Hillingly, d; John Mapplesden, s;
    Thomas Mapplesden, s, 107A.37

MAPSON: Jane, 98.30

MARBURY: Charles, bach, ser, 106.48

MARCH:
Jane, ser, 102.152
William; Jane, w; Joseph, s; John, s, 109.14

MARCHALL: Martha, 102.166

MARCHANT:
Mary; Mary, d; James, s; John, s; Sarah, d,
    103.205
Robert, 103.240

Thomas, 98.20
Thomas; Sarah, w, 103.175

MARCROFT: Jonathon; Elizabeth, w,
    107B.72

MARCUM:
John; Mary, w, 99.13
Jonathon; Mary, w; Martha, d, 103.63
Matthew, 102.4

MARCY:
Anne, ser, 98.66
Jane, 102.27
Johannah, ser, 98.16
Katherine, 102.147
Maud, 102.219
Susan; Elias, s, 102.159

MARDEN:
Anne, ser, 105.4
Miles, 105.4

MARE:
Elizabeth, 110.32
John, app, 109.23
Sarah, 99.23

MAREWOOD: John; Sarah, w; Sarah, d,
    107A.7

MARFEILD: John; Mary, w, 105.14

MARGARETS: Thomas, bach, gent, 98.36

MARGERUM:
Benjamin; Mary, w, 103.93
James; Mary, w, 102.193
Mary, wid; Sarah, d; Mary, d, 103.93

MARGIN: Thomas; Arrabella, w; William, s,
    109.34

MARHAM: George; Elizabeth, w,
    109.10

MARIA: Anna, 110.2

MARKE: Thomas, bach under age,
    103.81

MARKEABEE: Elizabeth;

MARKES:
~, bach, 103.194
George, 98.69
George; Rachell, w, 103.210
Robert; Anne, w; Frances, d, 107D.73
William; Elizabeth, w, 107B.68

MARKEWELL: Thomas; Elizabeth, w; John, s, 103.154

MARKHAM:
Alice; James Markham, grand-s of, 107B.55
Anne, 101.24
Avis, 109.44
John; Rose, w, 98.42
John; Sarah, w; Lawrance, s; Sarah, d; Elizabeth, d; Theodor, s, 102.62
John, app, 98.65
Joseph, app, 107C.19
Matt; Eliz, w; Benj, s; Matt, s; John, s; Mary, d; Esther, d, 104.53
Robert; Ellioner, w; George, s, 106.48
Sara, 101.72
Thomas; Elizabeth, w; Nicholas, s?; Elizabeth, d?, 99.19

MARKLAND: Jane, ser, 109.9

MARKLEW: William; Anne, w; William, s; Elizabeth, d, 102.261

MARKLEY: Mary, app;

MARKOW:
~, wid; John, s; Mary, d, 104.41

MARLEY:
Anne; Elizabeth, d; Mary, d, 107B.3
John, 106.12

MARLIN:
Alice, 102.34
Stephen; Elizabeth, w; Elizabeth, d; Sarah, d, 107D.83

MARLOW(E):
Edward; Anne, w; Edward, s; Thomas, s; William, s, 102.197
John; Sarah, w; Sarah, d; Mary, d; Elizabeth, d; John, s, 103.22
John, £600; Anne, w; John, s; Sarah, d, 102.118
Mary; Mary, d, 109.24
Richard, a boy, 98.3
Sarah, ser, 107B.29
Thomas, ser, 106.42

MARMION: James, £50 p.a.; Elioner, w; Richard, s, 106.40

MARNELL: Richard; Ann, w; Elizabeth, d, 103.207

MARQUICK: Anne, 101.5

MARR(E):
Anne, ser, 104.66
Francis, 103.233
Hannah, ser, 106.3
Leonard, clerk, 98.64

MARRABELL: Humphrey; Anne, w, 104.142

MARRANT: Thomas; Jone, w, 107D.39

MARRION: Joseph, wid, 102.156

MARRIOTT:
Esther, wid, 103.268
Foelix; Eliz, w; Sam, s, 104.46
Frances; Robert, s, 109.62
Isaac; Anne, w, 109.97
Jacob; Elizabeth, d; Anne, d; Mary, d; Jacob, s, 98.36
John; Elizabeth, w, 103.223
John, a boy, 103.223
Mary, ser, 98.33, 107D.15
Nich; Eliz, w, 104.78
Rebeccah, 98.36
Richard, 107D.17
Robert, ser, 103.92
Samuell; Ann, w; Robert, s; Samuell, s; George, s; Thompson, s; Bryan, s; Ann, d, 103.284
Stephen; Olive, sister of, 107B.40
Thomas, gent; Rebecca, w; Elizabeth, d; Richard, s; Thomas, s; Samuell, s, 106.3
William, wid; Deborah, d; Marmaduke, s, 103.202
Zachariah(?); Martha, w; Eliz, d; Eliz, Dunton niece, 104.60

MARSH:
Abigall; John, s, 107D.71
Alphonso, ser, 106.2
Anne, 98.58
Elizabeth; Diana, d, 107.34
Hanah, 99.51
Hannah; Wm, s; Rich, s; Dorothy, d, 104.113
Henry, 101.51
Henry; Anne, w, 107C.36
Henry, app, 104.3
Jane, 101.50
John; Jane, w, 107D.71
John, bach, ser, 98.88
Joseph; Elizabeth, w; Hannah, d?, 99.22
Mary, 109.74
Richard; Amy, w; William, s; Katherine, d; Henry, s, 106.13
Robert; Elizabeth, w; Mary, d; Susan, d, 103.281
Robert; Mary, w; Jane, d; Mary, d; Anne, d; Judith, d, 107D.62

Susannah, ser, 98.27
Thomas, ser;

MARSHALL:
~, Mrs, gentlewoman; ~, wid, 103.109
Bridget; Anne, d, 107B.6
Edward, 109.37
Elizabeth, 109.109
Elizabeth, ser, 98.30
Francis, 109.3
Francis; Elizabeth, w; Francis, s; John, s;
    William, s, 107A.25
Francis, ser, 103.152
Fredrick, 98.5
John, 109.41
John; Sarah, w, 107B.69
John; Anne, w, 107B.78
John, app, 101.59
John, ser, 102.85
Katherine, 102.216
Marg, 104.129
Martha; ~, child N.B., 102.146
Mary; Mary, d, 101.65
Mathew; Mary, w; Henry, s; Elizabeth, d,
    109.54
Robert; Margaret, w, 102.185
Robert; Susana, w; Elizabeth, d,
    106.51
Robert; Susan, d, 107C.41
Sam, wid, 104.41
Sarah, 107B.2
Sarah; Mary, d; Elizabeth, d, 107B.7
Sarah, ser, 106.50
Thomas, a child, 98.10
William; Joane, w, 106.13
William; Mary, d; John, s; Elias, s; Anne, d,
    109.109

MARSOW: John; ~, w, 104.66

MARSTER: Martin, 102.250

MARSTON(E):
Dorothy, 109.61
Thomas, ser, 106.12
Zachary; Joan, w; William, s; Zachary, s;
    John, s; Edmund, s; Catherine, d; Grace, d,
    109.93

MARTHER: Sarah;

MARTIN:
~, bach, 104.107
Alice, ser, 102.159
Andrew, ser, 106.16
Anne, 101.67
Anne, parish child, 103.97
Anthony; Sarah, w; Thomas, s; Francis, s,
    103.83

Christopher; Margaret, w; Elizabeth, d;
    Christopher, s; William, s, 107D.74
Cordelia, 101.32
Cutles, app, 102.201
Daniel; Katherine, w; Hester, d, 109.3
Dorothy, spinster, 103.45
Edward; Grace, w; Thomas, s, 103.17
Elizabeth, 109.102
Elizabeth, ser, 98.4
Faith; William, grand-s, £50 p.a., 107A.41
Feby, 107D.72
Francis; Sarah, w; Katharine, d?, 99.29
Francis; Johanna, w; Frances, d; Elizabeth, d,
    109.88
George, bach, 99.3
Hester, 110.10
James; Anne, w, 109.103
Jane, ser, 106.38
John, 102.46
John; Jane, w, 98.20
John; Mary, w, 101.75
John; Margaret, w, 104.1
John; Sarah, w, 107B.47
John; Anne, w; John, s, 109.111
Judith, 105.3
Margaret, 102.112
Martha, ser, 101.33
Mary, 102.138, 109.57
Mary; Mary, d, 103.3
Mary, ser, 104.53
Mary, spinster, 103.45
Mathew; Elizabeth, w; Elizabeth, d, 109.26
Nicholas; Lidia, w; Allen, s; Nicholas, s,
    103.233
Nicholas, app, 107B.67
Peter; Anne, w; Jacob, s, 107A.32
Phillip, bach, 98.38
Richard; Mary, w; John, s, 110.26
Robert, ser, 98.47
Rose, pensioner, 103.44
Samuell, app, 101.44
Sarah, wid, 103.20
Sawdry, bach, 104.57
Seth, ser, 109.7
Susannah, ser, 98.79
Thomas; Anne, w; William, s, 104.27
Thomas; Martha, w; Martha, d, 107B.57
Thomas; Katherine, w; Thomas, s, 107B.73
William; Sarah, w; Sarah, d, 102.26
William; Mary, w, 109.48
William, app, 101.102
William, gent; Elizabeth, w, 98.61
William, ser, 100.4

MARTINGOLE: John; Martha, w, 102.35

MARTON: Sarah, 102.41

MARWOOD: Mary;

MAULDEN:
Elizabeth, 101.11
John; Anne, w; Martha, d, 101.72

MAUND: Elizabeth, 99.52

MAVERLY: Abigall, wid, 103.125

MAW:
Harman, 109.86
John; Mary, w, 104.130
Susan, 107B.43

MAWD, See Maud

MAWDETT: Mrs.Mary, 104.102

MAWHOOD: Samuell; Jane, d, 109.70

MAWKS: Mary, 107D.92

MAWLEY:
Geo; Kath, w; Geo, s; Rich Henry, s; Kath, d;
   Adolina, d, 104.82
William; Martha, w, 102.174

MAWNEY: Elizabeth, 107B.64

MAWSON:
Benjamin; Jane, w; Henry, s, 101.19
John, esq, wid, 106.45
Strainge; Elizabeth, w, 103.254

MAXFEILD: William; Elizabeth, w; Mary, d,
   102.125

MAXON: Robert; Winifred, w, 107B.68

MAXWELL: John; Hannah, w; Elizabeth, d;
   John, s, 98.40

MAY:
Anne; George, s; William, s; Sarah, d,
   107A.27
Bridget, 107D.85
Charles, £50 p.a.; Jane, w; Mary, d, 102.15
Dorothy, 103.257
Francis, 107D.85
Hanah, 103.251
Jane, 107D.93
Joanna, 107A.18
John, 109.88
John; Margery, w, 102.131
John; Ellen, w; Joseph, s, 106.16
John; Mary, w, 107D.66
John; Mary, w; Anne, d; Mary, d, 107D.86
Marcey, 102.102
Margaret, ser, 106.63
Martha, 109.22

Mary, 109.83
Mary, ser, 106.23,107B.19
Nathaniel, bach, 109.45
Samuell, bach, 103.94
Susan, 103.148
Susan, spinster, pensioner, 103.16
Thomas; Anne, w, 109.38
Thomas, bach, 107D.15
William; Katherine, w, 101.76
William; Alice, w; Jeane, d; William, s,
   103.191
William, app, 107B.64

MAYBANCKE: Richard; Jane, w; Margaret,
   d, 107B.34

MAYBURT: John; Mary, w, 109.58

MAYCALT: Anne; John, s, 102.250

MAYCOCK:
John; Anne, w; John, s, 98.12
Thomas; Ursula, w, 98.33

MAYFEILD:
Elizabeth, ser, 103.228
Mary, wid; Ann, d, 103.211

MAYHEW, See Mahew

MAYLE:
Isabell, ser, 106.14
Paul, 102.238
Philipp; Constance, w; Margarett, d, 102.125

MAYLORD: John, app, 107D.38

MAYNARD:
Elizabeth, 107B.62,107D.48
James; Hanna, w; Rebeccah, d; James, s,
   101.60
Jeane, wid, 103.253
Thomas; Dorcas, w, 109.53

MAYNE:
Charles, bach, under age, 103.100
Elizabeth, 106.14
John; Elizabeth, w; Elizabeth, d; Phillis, d;
   Jane, d, 107A.5
John, £600, wid; John, s, 103.228
John, assessor, 103.293
John, ser, 103.228
Thomas; Mary, w, 109.82
William, 101.106

MAYO:
Elizabeth, ser, 107A.28
John, 109.76
Nicholas; Jeane, w; Joseph, s, 103.25

MAYON: John, 106.65

MAYOR:
John; Mary, w; John, s; Joseph, s, 103.42
Margaret, ser, 107B.30
Thomas, bach, 104.9

MAYWAY: John; Jone, w, 107C.17

MEACHEM: Elizabeth, 109.103

MEACHIN: Edward, £600, wid; Godfry, s,
102.15

MEACOCK:
Rober, bach, 107A.38
William, 101.69

MEACOME:
Joseph, 101.78
Sara; William, s; Samuell, s; Anne, d; Sara, d,
101.94

MEACON: Anne, wid;

MEACUM:
~, bach;

MEADCALFE, See Medcalfe

MEADE:
~, 102.83
Ann, ser, 103.139
Jane, 110.29
John, 102.271,109.79
John; Elizabeth, w; Katherine, d; Thomas, s;
John, s; Elizabeth, d; William, s,
102.135
John; Mary, w; Richard, s, 102.154
Joseph; Elizabeth, w; Joseph, s; Thomas, s,
103.55
Joseph, bach, 103.184
Margeret, pensioner; John, s; William, s;
Robert, s; Charity, d, 103.148
Sarah, 109.69,110.29
Thomas, 105.10,105.17
Thomas; Elizabeth, w; Mary, d, 102.91
Thomas; Elizabeth, w; Thomas, s; Elizabeth,
d; Mary, d, 102.106
Thomas; Mary, w; William, s; Thomas, s;
Sarah, d, 103.242
William; ~, w; William, s, 103.63

MEADES: Joseph, 105.17

MEADMAN: Sam; Anne, w,
104.78

MEADOW: William, ser, 103.29

MEADOWS:
Elizabeth, wid, 103.18
Erseby; Mary, w; George, s, 98.36
Gilbert; Elizabeth, w; Mary, d?, 99.23
Isabell, 107B.3
William; John, s, 106.33

MEADUPS: John; Catherine, w; John, s;
Thomas, s, 103.199

MEAGE: Guy, 110.19

MEAKIN: Richard, ser, 102.87

MEAKINE:
John, bach, aged 27, 102.247
William; Frances, w, 101.77
William; Elizabeth, w; Jane, d, 101.82
William; Issabella, w, 102.146

MEALE: Mary, 110.18

MEALES: Elizabeth, wid, 103.10

MEALING:
Ellinor, wid, 103.67
John; Abigall, w, 107D.79
Rebecca, wid; John, s, 103.54
Sarah, ser, 98.85

MEANLY: Elizabeth, ser, 101.103

MEARES:
Anne, 110.24
Anne, ser, 102.100
Charles; Elizabeth, w; John, s, 101.73
Daniell; Rachell, w; Mary, d, 107B.35
Mary, 101.30
Mary; Agnes, d, 107B.25
Sarah, 103.243
Stephen, app, 98.58
William; Judith, w, 102.122
William; Mary, w; William, s,
107D.15

MEATAN: Elizabeth, 102.206

MEATES: Jeane, ser, 103.288

MEATURES: Hugh; Susan, w; Mary, d,
107B.20

MEAUX: Amey, 99.53

MEAZEY: Richard; Bridgett, w; Edward, s;
Richard, s; Elizabeth, d, 109.31

MECANY: John; Alice, w; John, s,
102.243

MECHAM:
Deborah, 109.38
Edward; Katherine, w; Edward, s, 98.16
Thomas; Mary, w, 107D.75
William, 102.104

MEDALFE:
Anne, 105.10
Elienor; Mary, d, 102.252

MEDBURY:
Henry; Mary, w, 107B.40
Nathaniell; Mary, w, 102.41
Thomas, 109.10

MEDCALFE:
George; Jeane, w, 103.56
Joane, wid; Ann, d; Mary, d, 103.288
John; Martha, w; Robert, s?, 99.17
John; Mary, w; Samuell, s, 103.49
William; Anna Maria, w; Richard, s; Jane
   Fuller, d, 107B.5

MEDDUPPS: Anthony, 107C.38

MEDGATE:
Charles; Elizabeth, w, 107A.40
William; Elizabeth, w, 107A.40

MEDHURST: Richard; Bridgit, w; Richard,
   s, 102.187

MEDLEY:
Michael; Sarah, w, 109.44
William; Elizabeth, w; Elizabeth, d; John, s,
   103.196

MEDLIN: Francis; Ann, w, 99.25

MEDLOE:
Frances; Deborah, d; Anne, d; Ralph, s,
   101.35
Elizabeth, ser, 109.91

MEDUS: Sarah, 109.31

MEE: Benjamin, ser, 103.120

MEEKS: Ann, 99.9

MEGGENSON: George; Mary, w, 109.41

MEGGS: Thomas, 102.109

MELL:
Elizabeth; Constance, d, 109.107
James; Anne, w, 106.37

MELLIS: Elizabeth, ser, 103.121

MELLS: Robert, 107B.63

MELLY: Elizabeth, ser, 109.100

MELMOTH: William, £600 or £50 p.a.; Ann,
   w; Mary, d; Elizabeth, d, 109.41

MELMOUTH: William, gent; Sarah, w;
   Anne, d, 98.31

MELTON:
Elizabeth, 102.14
Francis; Mary, w; Mary, d, 107C.24
John; Elizabeth, w, 102.255
John, app, 98.50
Richard; Elizabeth, w; Elizabeth, d; Timothy
   Regar, s, 102.150
Robert; Elizabeth, w; John, s, 103.257

MEMBER: Hezekiah, 109.25

MEMOREY: Richard; Margeret, w; Francis,
   s; Mary, d; John, s, 103.208

MEN: Sarah, 103.51

MENCE:
Jeane, wid; Elizabeth, d, 103.45
Richard; Susan, w; Charles, s; Richard, s;
   Sweething, d; Francis, s; Susanah, d,
   103.261
Robert, 101.21

MENDUM:
Andrew, 109.78
John; Hannah, w, 109.12

MERCER:
Dorcas, mother of Elizabeth Moore, 106.27
Edward, 106.33
Francis; Mary, w, 102.141
Grace, wid, 103.55
Mary, ser, 98.71
Samuell; Mary, w; Jerimiah, s, 103.188
Samuell; Mary, w; Elizabeth, d,
   107D.86
Sarah, wid, 103.41
Thomas; Martha, w; Thomas, s; Elizabeth, d,
   103.140
William; Mary, w, 103.192
William, ser, 106.6

MERCY:
Bartholomew; Mary, w, 107D.38
Jane, 104.117

MEREDIFF: Samuell; Elizabeth, w, 99.17

MERIDEE: Elizabeth, 109.73

METCHELOR: Elizabeth, ser, 109.7

METHRINGHAM: John, 109.42

MEW: Elizabeth, a child, 102.49

MEWS:
Elizabeth, ser, 107D.96
John; Elizabeth, w, 102.238
William; Isabell, w; John, s; Ellen, d;
William, s, 107D.95

MEYTEER: John; Mary, w, 103.240

MIAS: Salathiel, ser, 103.223

MICHAELS: Elizabeth, 107A.13

MICHAM: Richard; Ann, w; Elizabeth, d,
103.140

MICHELL, See Mitchell

MICHELLS: Anne; Anne, d, 102.161

MICKLETHWAITE: Joseph; Frances, w;
Mary, d; Elizabeth, d, 98.41

MICKLETON: Thomas; Elizabeth, w;
Frances, d, 101.38,101.38

MICKLEWRIGHT:
Andrew; Elizabeth, w; Elizabeth, d, 102.57
Robert; Elizabeth, w, 109.39

MICKLEY: Mary, 109.108

MICOM: Elianor, 107A.4

MIDDEN: Mary, 109.17

MIDDLETON:
Anne, 104.114,107A.18
Arthur; Elizabeth, w; John, s; Anne, d,
106.35
David; Elizabeth, w, 104.16
Elizabeth, 102.230.107A.18,107B.11
Ellinor, 104.71
Guift, ser, 101.102
John, 110.17
John; ~, w, 100.3
John; Jane, w, 107C.35
John, gent; Susannah, w, 98.53
Mary, 102.246
Maximilian, ser, 106.3
Ralph; Anne, w; Anne, d, 102.269
Robert, ser, 106.53
Thomas, bach, 98.86
Thomas, ser, 106.31

MIDDLEWRIGHT:
Erasmus; Elizabeth, w; Rebecca, d; Mary, d;
Margaret, d; Erasmus, s, 109.100
Robert, 101.11

MIDLEHURST: Thomas; Anne, w, 101.70

MILBORE: John; Sarah, w; Isabell, d, 109.51

MILBORNE:
Alexander; Elizabeth, w; Charles, s, 109.90
Ann, 98.5
Elizabeth; Elizabeth, d, 102.222
Elizabeth; Judey, d?, 109.90
Elizabeth, wid, 103.145
Jane, ser, 98.66
Mary, wid £600, 103.8
Robert; Mary, w, 110.27
Thomas, wid, 107D.13

MILCORLEE?: ~, 102.235

MILDMAY: Edward; Anne, w; Anne Maria,
d, 104.59

MILES: Anne, ser, 108.1
Charles; Elizabeth, w, 107D.66
Christopher; Susannah, w; Rebecca, d,
107D.88
Elizabeth; Elizabeth, d, 104.135
Elizabeth; Elizabeth Tallent, her ser, 107A.26
Perdinando; Elizabeth, w, 109.28
Hanna, 101.5
Hanna, wid; William, s; Elizabeth, d, 103.243
Isabellah, ser, 98.40
James, 109.33
James; Soience, w; John, s, 104.118
Jane, ser, 107A.27
Joseph; Elizabeth, w, 103.91
Joseph; Elizabeth, w; Alice, d; Joseph, s,
103.124
Joseph; Prisoilla, w; George, s, 104.43
Margeret, pensioner, 103.116
Mary, 101.18,104.87
Mary, wid, 103.54
Richard, app, 109.100
Robert; Sarah, w, 103.56
Robert, ser, 103.23
Sam, app, 104.70
Thomas, 107B.50
William, 102.222
William, app, 98.37
Zachariah; Grace, w, 103.30

MILFORD: Elizabeth, 107B.63

MILKS?: Thomas, 101.82

MILL: Charles, 102.8

MILLARD:
Anne, ser, 101.80
John, app, 98.32
Mary, 102.36
Samuell;

MILLER:
~, wid, 103.236
Anne, 102.28
Anne, ser, 102.18,107B.73
Benjamin; Hanah, w; Barbary, d; Benjamin,
  s, 103.19
Benjamin; Jane, w; Robert, s; Samuel, s,
  107A.17
Benjamin; Anne, w, 107B.70
Edward, ser, 109.12
Elizabeth, pensioner, 103.74
Elizabeth, ser, 103.82
George; Martha, w, 103.102
Henry, bach, gent, 106.56
Isaac, app, 101.101
Jane, ser, 104.107
Jervis; Eliza, w, 104.66
John, 99.36,102.73
John; Elizabeth, w, 101.92
John; Elizabeth, w; Elizabeth, d, 102.122
John; Hannah, w; John, s; Heugh, s, 103.51
John; Mary, w, 103.120
John; Mary, w; Elizabeth, d; Mary, d;
  Elizabeth, mother of, 107B.62
John; Anne, w; Mary, d; Edmund, s, 107D.35
John; Mary, w, 109.66
John; Mary, w, 109.110
John, ser, 102.197
Margaret, 104.48
Martha, 107A.7
Mary, 107A.15
Mary, ser, 107D.41,107D.10
Ralph, app, 104.101
Richard; Prudence, w; Patience, d; Mary, d,
  107D.60
Robert, at sea; Jeane, w, 103.124
Samuell; Elizabeth, w; Charles, s; Samuell, s;
  Elizabeth, d; Joseph, s; Martha, d; Richard,
  s, 103.203
Sarah, 102.20
Susan, pensioner, 103.77
Thomas, a parish child, 103.196
William; Jane, w, 102.229
William, ser, bach?, 104.19

MILLET:
Caleb, 101.11
Caleb; Martha, w, 99.45
Elizabeth, 101.17,101.80
Frances, ser, 98.45
Margaret, 101.17

MILLIAN: Lawrance; Elizabeth, w, 102.132

MILLINER: Thomas, ser, 103.33

MILLINGTON:
Edward; Edward, s; Mary, d, 101.14
Elianor, 109.86
Hester, 101.72
John; Mary, w; Mary, d, 103.130
Lidia, 101.14
Mary, 106.64,107C.30
Sarah, ser, 109.43

MILLION: Henry; Susannah, w; Henry, s,
  98.48

MILLIS: John; Mary, w; Samuell, s; John, s;
  Elizabeth, d, 103.141

MILLMAN: Mary;

MILLS:
~, Mrs; ~, old Mrs, 104.131
Adam; Mary, w; William, s, 107D.14
Alexander; Elizabeth, w; James, s; Elizabeth,
  d; Margaret, d, 98.20
Benjamin, 109.29
Charles, 107B.15
Dorothy, 102.22
Elias, ser, 107A.15
Elizabeth, ser, 102.85
Ellin, 104.42
George; Johannah, w, 98.15
George, a parish child, 101.35
Grace, 104.137
Henry, ser, 102.198
Isaac, 101.60
Jane, 109.109
John, 109.74
John; Elizabeth, w, 106.3
John; Elizabeth, w, 107D.7
John; Elizabeth, w; Margaret, d, 109.88
John; Elizabeth, w; Elizabeth, d, 110.6
John, at sea; Sarah, w, 103.38
John, bach, 104.108
John, wid, 106.37
Joseph, 106.38
Judith, 109.21
Leonard; Elizabeth, w, 107D.67
Margarett, 110.29
Margarett; Anne, d, 98.37
Margery, 102.119
Mary, 110.12,110.15
Mary; Mary, d; Phillip Mills, grand-s of,
  107B.50
Mary, ser, 98.58
Ralph, ser, 106.19
Richard, 109.108
Richard; Susanna, w, 101.55
Richard, at sea; Mary, w; Elizabeth, 103.125
Robert; Ann, w, 109.22

Samuell, 101.77
Stephen; Sarah, w; Phillip, s, 109.27
Susan, 109.108
Thomas, 101.82
Thomas; Easter, w; Easter, d; Susan, d;
  Elizabeth, d; Thomas, s, 98.15
Thomas; Elizabeth, w, 102.198
Walter, bach, 104.131
William; Rebeccah, w; Mary, d, 102.76

MILLWARD: Joseph; Alice, w; Elizabeth, d,
  102.96

MILLWAY:
Ambrose, 109.70
Thomas, 101.21

MILLY: Thomas, 101.36

MILNER:
~, wid, 104.36
Frances, ser, 98.76

MILOR: George; Margaret, w, 109.39

MILTON:
Anne, ser, 104.54
Daniell; Mary, w; Samuell, ser, 109.111

MIMPRESS: Abraham, 109.24

MINARD: Richard, 110.36

MINCE: James; Mary, w; Mary, d, 106.16

MINCHELL: Frances, 101.60

MINCHIN:
Edward; Anne, w; Edward, ser; Mary, d;
  John, s, 102.22
William; Mary, w, 103.250

MINERS: Elizabeth, app, 107D.11

MINETT: Elizabeth, wid; Elizabeth, d,
  103.270

MINGHAM: Anne, 106.7

MINOS: John, ser, 107C.24

MINOTT: John, bach, 103.188

MINSHILL: Andrew; Jane, w; Samuell, s?;
  Mary, d?, 99.38

MINSHULL: Thomas, £600; ~, w, 106.36

MINTIN: Sara, ser, 101.45

MINTY: Richard; Abigail, w, 110.33

MIRAS: George; Ann, w; George, s; Mary, d;
  Ann, d, 103.26

MIRES: Richard, ser, 107A.39

MISSINDEN: Marmaduke; Mary, w, 101.11

MITCHAM: Thomas, app, 109.25

MITCHANNELL: Wm, app;

MITCHELL:
~, Mrs; ~, s, 98.53
Ambrose, bach, 102.63
Anne, 107D.79,109.35
Anne, app, 107D.1
Anne, ser, 100.14,106.59
Edward, 109.70
Elizabrth, 110.28
Elizabrth; Samuel, s, 107C.27
Henry, 110.25
Henry; Mary, w; John, s; Jane, d, 109.22
Henry; Mary, d, 109.66
Hester, 107D.78
Horatio, ser, 109.61
James, 99.17
John; Elizabeth, w; Mary, d, 103.188
John; Jane, w; John, s; Valentine, s, 104.46
John; Sarah, w; Martha, d; Sarah, d, 109.67
John, bach, 103.31
John, ser, 106.16
Joseph; Anna, w; Joseph, s; Rebecca, d,
  107D.59
Martha, 107B.25
Martha; Mary, d; Martha, d; John, s, 109.50
Mary, 104.76,109.52
Mary, ser, 106.60
Ralph; Mary, w, 103.147
Richard; Elizabeth, w, 110.31
Robert, 101.9
Robert; Mary, w; Robert, s, 103.101
Samuell; Elizabeth, d, 102.126
Stephen; Sarah, w; John, s; Sarah, d, 106.56
Susan, 102.214
William, 105.7
William; Mary, w, 102.197
William; Jane, w, 104.35
William; Hannah, w; William, s, 106.18

MITRE: Esther, 103.222

MITTIN: Charles; Rebecca, w, 103.40

MITTINS:
John; Martha, w, 109.88
Martha, 109.88
Martha, a child, 109.88

212

MITTON: Thomas; Anne, d, 107B.57

MOAKES:
Massey, ser, 109.54
Rich, 104.35

MOARTEN: Joseph, 105.18

MOBBS:
John; Rebecca, w; John, s, 101.88
Thomas; Anne, w; Thomas, s, 109.84

MOCHER: Richard; Anne, w, 109.90

MOCKSAM: Susan, ser, 107B.3

MODES: Mary, ser, 109.26

MOFFIT: Bridget, ser, 106.26

MOGG: John; Elizabeth, w; John, w;
    Christopher, s; Medad?, 98.19

MOGGS:
Dan; Jane, w, 104.70
James, 102.84

MOHEN: Bridget, ser, 107A.17

MOKE (E):
Hanah, wid, 103.8
John; Sarah, wid; Elizabeth, d, 109.23
Mary, 101.25
Mary; John, s; Thomas, s; William, s, 101.24
Mary, ser, 98.57
Parthenia, 110.2
Peter; Katherine, w, 103.153
Thomas John, s of Carey, 107B.27
William, ser, 106.57

MOKE(E):
Elianor; John, s; Sarah, d, 107B.44
Francis; Anne, d; Jeane, d, 103.39
Francis; Mary, w; Francis, s; Mary, d, 106.67

MOLDS: John; Elizabeth, w; Marg, d; Jane,
    d, 104.22

MOLE: Jane, ser, 106.3

MOLEY: Samuell; Hannah, w, 102.105

MOLLINS:
Elizabeth, 104.65
Lesr, 98.9
Mary, 98.13

MOLLISON: Gilbert, £600; Margery, w;
    Barbara, his sister, 101.32

MOLLUM: Thomas; Judith, w; Elizabeth, d?,
    99.38

MOLT:
Cicely, ser, 107A.5
John; Margaret, w; Valentine, s; Mary, d;
    John, s, 107C.30

MONCASTER: Margaret, 101.56

MONCKS: William, 106.18

MONDAY:
Adryan; Dorothy, w, 109.31
Thomas; Jane, w; John, s; Mary, d, 98.50
Thomas; Mary, w; Richard, s; Mary, d;
    Elizabeth, d, 103.83

MONDEN: Robert; Jeane, w, 103.55

MONEING: Anne, 102.180

MONEORD: Edward; Jane, w; Joshua, s,
    102.252

MONEY:
John; Mary, w; Alice, d; Mary, d; John, s;
    Joshua, s, 106.42
John; Jane, w, 109.60
Richard; Jane, w; William, s; Thomas, s,
    109.111

MONGER: Jone, 102.214

MONIMENT: Alice, ser, 105.12

MONKSFEILD: Mary, ser, 103.81

MONNUMENT: Soissillah, ser, 98.32

MONTAGUE:
Ann, spinster, 103.47
Elizabeth, ser, 101.96,102.187
Elizabeth, ser, 109.1
Henry; Anne, w, 107D.76
Susan, ser, 103.223
Wm, £600; Elizabeth, w, 104.28

MOODY:
Christopher; Katherine, d; Henry, s, 110.24
Edward; Frecillah, w; George, s; Mary, d,
    102.182
Edward; Sarah, dead, 102.275
George, ser, 106.25
Hanah; Hanah, d; Sarah, d, 107B.57
Jane, 110.4
John; Mary, w; Elizabeth, d, 107B.18
John, wid, hath children elsewhere, 103.91
Mary, 102.271

Mary, wid, 103.55
Robert, 110.4
Thomas, 110.4
William; Margaret, w; Thomas, s; Margaret,
d; William, s, 107B.18

MOONE:
Mary, 98.56
Sara; Elizabeth, d, 101.64

MOONEY: Mathew; Ellinor, w; Mary, d;
John, s;

MOOR (E):
~, bach; ~, wid, 103.65
Alice, 105.5
Alice, wid, 103.42
Andrew; Ann, w, 103.45
Andrew; Martha, w, 105.3
Anne, 104.76,109.87
Arthur, esq, ?bach, 104.63
Benjamin, app, 107D.14
Caleb, 109.40
Daniell, bach, 102.181
David; Mary, w, 106.30
Deborah, 103.182
Edward, 109.95
Edward; Ann, w, 109.47
Edward, app, 104.71
Elianor, 106.78
Elizabeth, 101.198,102.176
Elizabeth, ser, 107C.13
Elizabeth, wid; Ann, d, 103.267
Frances, ser, 104.130
Francis; Elizabeth, w, 106.27
Francis, ser, 109.57
Isaacc; Sarah, w; Isaacc, s; Elizabeth, d,
103.249
Jane; John, s, 104.33
Jeane, ser, 103.253
John, 103.267
John, his wife not with him, 103.102
John; Anne, w; John, s, 103.46
John; Francis, w, 103.114
John; Elizabeth, w; John, s, 104.103

MOORE:
John; Margery, w, 107B.58
John; Mary, w, 107B.77
John, app, 107C.18
John Elizabeth, nephew to More, 101.37
Joshuah, 102.104
Katherine; Elizabeth Clifton, d; Elizabeth, d;
Anne, d, 98.62
Marke; Elizabeth, w; Katherine, d; Ellen, d;
Elizabeth, d; Anna, d, 101.42
Martha, 109.59
Mary, 104.72
Mary; Martha, d, 101.85

Phillipp; Elizabeth, w, 110.27
Rebecca; William, s; Ellinor, d, 103.27
Rich; Anne, w; Eliza, d, 104.102
Robert; Hester, w, 110.21
Samuell; Ann, w, 103.257
Samuell, £600; Arabella Maria, w; Samuell,
s, 101.28
Sarah, 107D.41
Sarah, wid, 103.31
Thomas, 110.16
Thomas; Mary, w; Thomas, s; Mary, d,
103.118
Thomas; Elizabeth, w, 103.182
Thomas; Mary, w, 104.14
Thomas; Jane, w, 104.105
Thomas; Elizabeth, w; Mary, d, 107B.67
Thomas, app, 98.19,103.139
Thomazine; Mary, d; Sarah, d, 109.52
Timothy, ser, 109.9
Uriah, 109.11
William; Mary, w; Martha, d, 103.70
William; Mary, w; Emmanuell, s, 104.21
William, app, 107A.42

MOORECOCK:
Thomas; Anne, w; Anthony, s, 104.41
Thomas, wid; Anthony, s, 98.1

MOOREFEILD: Mary, ser, 107D.48

MOOREHOUSE: Nathaniel; Katherine, w;
Sarah, d; Patience, d; Mary, d, 103.56

MOORETON:
Charles; Elizabeth, w; Elizabeth, d, 98.25
Elizabeth, 98.85
George, 98.85
Johannah; Thomas, s; Johannah, d, 98.66

MOORING: Edward, ser, 103.87

MOORLAND: Ellinor, 109.10

MORANE:
Jane, 102.246
Tamsell, 102.246

MORBEY: Anne;

MORDANT:
~, 102.193
Charles; Frances, w, 106.68
Hanah, 102.193,102.223

MORDEN:
John; Martha, w; Rebecca, d,
102.224
Thomas; Mary, w, their father and mother
lodgers, 103.70

MUCKLEBURY: John; Hanah, w; Richard, s; Ellinor, d, 103.233

MUCKLWRAY: John; Sarah, w; Ann, d; John, s, 103.29

MUDAY: Henry, ser, 102.197

MUDDOX: William; Anne, w; Hanah, d, 103.56

MUGGE: John; Anne, w, 99.28

MUGGLESTON: John; Hanah, w; William, s; John, s, 101.3

MUGLETON: Mary, a parish child, 103.225

MULFORD: John; Elizabeth, w, 109.94

MULLER: Jerimiah, parish child, 103.105

MULLEY: James; Alice, w; Martha, d; James, s; Margeret, d, 103.279

MULLICE: Sarah, 109.72

MULLIER:
Joseph, parish child, 103.105
Samuell, parish child, 103.105

MULLINEUX: Thomas, 107D.13

MULLINOX:
Elizabeth; Mary, d; Elizabeth, d, 103.12
Margeret, wid, 103.21

MULLINS:
Isaac, 101.88
Margaret, 102.85
Mary, 101.88
Thomas; Priscilla, w;

MUMFORD:
~; ~, w, 104.118
Elizabeth, 106.45
Ralph; Mary, w; Wm, s; Mary, d, 104.39
Simon; Alice, w, 107B.14
Thomas, 98.59
Thomas; Sarah, w, 103.68
William, app, 98.3

MUN: Elizabeth, 102.170

MUNCHINGHAM: Judeth, ser, 106.59

MUNDAY:
Elizabeth, 106.38
Henry, ser, 106.22

Jasper, ser, 107D.19
John, 109.93
John, ser, 100.4
Jos, 104.106
Joyce, 104.71
Mary, ser, 100.4
Samuell; Ann, w; Samuell, s, 103.65
William, 102.8
William; Christian, w, 106.39

MUNERY: Ann, wid, 103.269

MUNK: Jane, ser, 109.53

MUNKIN: William; Sarah, w, 109.56

MUNKUS: Issabella, 102.36

MUNN: John; Elizabeth, w, 109.11

MUNNINS: William; Anne, w; Edward, s, 107D.29

MUNNS: Ann, spinster, 103.86

MUNSEY: Owen; Mary, w;

MUNT:
~, 104.139

MURDIN: Elizabeth, 102.9

MURDOCKE:
James; Rebecca, w; John, s, 103.214
John, £600 or £50 p.a.; Susannah, w; John, s; Susannah, d; Barbara, d, 109.47

MURFIN: Daniell; ~, w; Daniell, s; William, s; John, s, 102.85

MURINS: Susan, 102.103

MURPHEW: Richard, 109.18

MURRELL:
~, wid; Susanna, d; Jane, d, 104.68
Easter, 109.51
Richard, bach, 106.1

MURREN: Dorothy;

MURRY:
~, wid, 102.28
Anne, 107A.9
Charles, ser, 106.32
Elizabeth, 107B.36,109.56
Ellen, 107D.85
George, 102.30
John; Sara, w; George, s, 101.55

John, bach, 102.28
Jos, 104.77
Penelope, 106.15
Robert, 106.15
Robert, ser, 98.39

MURSKEW: Elizabeth; Pheaby, d, 103.52

MUSCETT: Elizabeth, 98.27

MUSHEE: Susan, 102.230

MUSSEY: Elizabeth, ser, 98.31

MUSSGRAVE:
Elizabeth, ser, 103.92
John, 103.132

MUSSIT: Amey, 107A.3

MUSSLE: Ann, 106.62

MUSTIN: Elizabeth, 107C.15

MUTCHET: Katherine, ser, 107B.76

MUTTON: John; Sarah, w, 98.56

MYLAND: Edw; Eliz, w, 104.107

MYMON: William; Cicill, w, 110.6

MYNN: Clemence, 107A.9

MYNNS: Nicholas; Mary, w; Anne, d,
107D.96

MYSOM: Sarah; Sarah, d, 107C.28

NAGG: Thomas; Constance, w; Thomas, s;
Susan, d, 110.32

NALL: Mathew; Mary, w; Elizabeth, d,
102.172

NANDICK: Charles; Elizabeth, w, 104.77

NANFAN?: Thomas, 101.63

NANSON: Hanah, 103.284

NANTS: Susanna, 104.104

NAPP: Henry; Alice, w; Robert, s; John, s;
Henry, s, 102.32

NAPPER: Charles, 106.11

NARBUT: Richard; Anne, w, 107B.24

NARD?: Thomas, app, s of £600 man,
102.161

NASEBY: Thomas;

NASH:
~, 103.197
Anne, ser, 100.13
Dorcas; John, s; Elizabeth, d; Rebecca, d,
107B.61
Edw, bach, 104.85
George; Dorothy, w; Francis, s; Mary, d,
107C.4
John, 102.77
John; Elizabeth, w; Elizabeth, d; John, s;
Sara, d; Jane, d, 101.89
John; Mary, w; James, s; Robinson, s;
Elizabeth, d, 103.31
John; Anne, w, 106.34
John, ser, 103.29
Marg, 104.40
Phillip; ~, w, 99.49
Richard; Sarah, w; Sarah, d, 107B.55
Richard, bach?, clerk, 104.95
Samuel; Ruth, w; John, s; Samuel, s; Ruth, d,
107D.75
Sarah, ser, 103.61
Thomas, 102.81
Thomas; Anne, w, 98.72
Thomas; Elizabeth, w; Mary, d; Thomas, s;
Elizabeth, d, 103.126
William, app, 103.125

NASHFORD: Joshua, 101.24

NASHLEY: Richard; Elizabeth, w, 98.34

NASHTON: Sarah, 103.36

NASON: John; Margaret, w, 101.87

NASSBY: Elizabeth, ser, 103.277

NATHRICKE: Hanah, 102.203

NATRIS: Sarah; Sarah, d, 104.2

NATT:
John; Victoria, w; Thomas, s; Mary, d, 98.59
Mary, 98.15

NAYCOCKE: Sarah, 110.11

NAYLOR:
Benjamin; Mary, w, 109.47
Elizabeth, 102.3
Jaine, 102.78
John; Elizabeth, w; John, s; George, s,
107B.59

John; Anne, w, 107C.1
John; Elizabeth, w, 107C.35
John, app, 107D.38
Johnson; Elizabeth, w; Johnson, s, 109.40
Robert; Mary, w; George, s, 101.46
Walter; Elizabeth, w, 98.40
William, 98.21

NEALE:
Daniell, 102.40,104.119
Daniell, £600 or £50 p.a.; Mary, w; Mary, d;
    Joseph, s; Frances, d, 102.188
Edward; Sinchin, w; Edward, s; William, s,
    102.161
Elizabeth, 99.22
Jacob, 109.57
Jeames, app, 103.66
John; Sarah, w, 103.239
Mary, 99.22,99.22
Mary; Elizabeth, d, 109.22
Peter, ser, 109.24
Richard, app, 102.204
Robert, 99.22
Samuell, 100.2
Sarah, 110.2
Simon; Mary, w, 100.7
Susannah, ser, 98.67
Uriah, 99.22
William; Jane, w; Mary, d; Jane, d, 102.204

NEAM: Elizabeth, 102.184

NEATHERALL: Richard; Elizabeth, w;
    Elizabeth, d; Ann, d; Mary, d, 103.65

NEATON:
John, ser, 109.6
Richard, 101.80
Richard; Mary, w, 109.55

NECHER: Elizabeth, 110.36

NEEDHAM:
M, bach, 104.62
Benjamin; Katherine, w; Mary, d; Benjamin,
    s; Joseph, s, 100.6
Charles; Elizabeth, w; Charles, s; Elizabeth,
    d, 110.22
Edward; Abigall, w; Mary, d; Sarah, d;
    Abigall, d, 103.218
Elizabeth; John, s, 102.198
Joseph, £50 p.a.; Mary, w; Anne, d, 106.57
Margarett, 102.6
Samuell; Anne, w; Sarah, d, 102.31
Stephen, 102.31

NEEDLER: John, ser, 109.79

NEEL(E), See Neale

NEENE: Elizabeth, wid, pensioner, 103.16

NEEVES:
Charles, at sea; Mary, w; Mary, d; Elizabeth,
    d, 103.105
Edward; Elinor, w, 99.16
Mercy, ser, 107D.63

NEGE: Lawrance; Margarett, w, 102.159

NEIGHBOUR:
Jane; John, s, 98.12
William, bach, 104.62

NELHAM: Samuell, assessor, 99.61

NELLUM: Samuell; Elizabeth, w, 99.12

NELME: Elizabeth, ser, 103.286

NELMES:
John; Jane, w; Sarah, d; Elizabeth, d;
    William, s, 106.17
Sarah, 99.44

NELSON:
Ann, 100.13
Anthony, ?b, 104.8
Grace; Mary Dunn, d; Richard Dunn, grand-
    s, 98.62
John; Sarah, w, 110.18
John; Anne, w; Martha, d, 102.155
Richard; Anne, w; Isaack, s, 98.40
Robert, ser, 109.93
Sarah; Jane, d, 98.40
William; Alice, w; William, s; Henry, s;
    Elizabeth, d; Mary, d; Richard, s; Thomas,
    s, 107D.36

NELTHROP: James; Ann, w; Ann, d?;
    Samuell, s?; Lucey, d?; Sarah, d?; Charles,
    s?, 99.59

NEND: Robert; Alice, w; John Smith, s;
    James Smith, s; Joseph Smith, s; Robert, s;
    Susanna Nead, d, 107A.33

NEPREW: Isaacc; Alice, w, 103.146

NERRAWAY: Elizabeth, 102.185

NESBITT: John; Elizabeth, w; John, s; Isaac,
    s, 101.107

NESBY: Mary, 101.62

NESFERN: Hanah, 102.61

NEST: Christopher; Hanah, w, 102.207

Henry, app, 98.81
John; Elizabeth, w; Mary, d; Elizabeth, d,
102.11
John; Mary, w; Anne, d; William, s; John, s,
102.106
John; Sarah, w, 103.185
John; Elizabeth, w, 103.196
Jonathan, 102.69
Joseph; Eliazbeth, w; Richard, s, 103.162
Justin, app, 109.104
Mary, 109.20
Mary Daniel, d of Carpenter, 107B.74
Mathew, 102.17
Nath, app, 104.9
Robert; Mary, w; Mary, d, 103.278
Robert; Mary, w; John, s; Robert, s; Sarah, d;
Martha, d, 109.60
Robert, ser, 109.77
Sarah, wid, 102.33
Susanah, wid; Susanah, d, 99.31
Thomas; Audry, w; Joseph, s?; Thomas, s?,
99.31
Thomas, bach, ser, 104.27
Walter; Martha, w; John, s, 102.69
William, 106.60
William; Mary, w; Mary, d; Sarah, d;
William, s, 102.51
William; Mary, w, 109.49
Zacherish, bach, 102.183

NEWPORT:
Elizabeth, 102.77
Peter, app, 101.84
Sarah; Richard, d; Hannah, d, 102.210

NEWSOM: John, aged 23 years, 106.27

NEWSON: Jos, bach, 104.87

NEWSTED: Elinor, 109.59

NEWTH: Adrian, junior; Joyce, w; Mary, d;
Sarah, d; James, s; Adrian, s, 103.106

NEWTON:
Bridgett, ser, 104.6
Edward; Elizabeth, w; John, s; Elizabeth, d;
Katherine, d, 102.140
Elizabeth, ser, 106.13,107D.93
Godfrey; Daniel, s, 107D.64
James, dead?, 110.21
John; Sarah, w; Sarah, d, 102.170
John; Hanah, w; Sarah, d; Rachael, d,
107D.99
John, at sea; Pheaby, w, 103.51
John, bach, 106.66,109.51
Jonathan, 102.148
Mary, 98.52,107D.82
Mary, ser, 103.1

Mary, wid, pensioner, 103.15
Nicholas, 102.178
Rebeckah, ser, 100.8
Samuell, bach, 106.67
Thomas, ser, 106.54
William; Margaret, w; James, s, 101.15
William, at sea; Elizabeth, w, 103.44

NIBB: Anne, 98.19

NIBBS: Joseph; Barbara, w, 109.19

NIBLETT: Mary, 109.105

NICHOLAS:
Charles, 102.221
Elizabeth, 107C.22
Jane, ser, 98.65
John; Abigail, w; Anne, d, 110.25
Robert, 102.105

NICHOLL:
John, commissioner, 99.61
John, esq; Mary, w; Sarah, d; John, s, 104.72
Michael, 109.41
Sarah;

NICHOLLS:
~, bach, under age, 103.54
Ann, pensioner, 103.96
Anthony; Elizabeth, w; Elizabeth, d; Anne, d,
106.9
Christopher; Adery, w; Joannah, d, 102.90
Christopher, ser, 102.181
Elisha; Eliz, w; Wm, s, 104.57
Elizabeth, 101.8,103.177
Frances, 107C.42
James; Margaret, w; Mary, d; Margaret, d;
Esther, d, 103.141
James; Mary, w; Johana, d, 103.171
James; Dorothy, w, 107D.2
Jane; William, s; Cornelius, s, 109.25
Jane, ser, 104.93
Jane, wid; Jane, d, 107A.31
Jeane, spinster, 103.31
Jeane, wid, 103.120
John, 104.108,109.69
John; Elizabeth, w; John, s; William, s,
101.4
John; Hester, w, 101.43
John; Elizabeth, w; Philodelpha, d, 107B.10
John; Margaret, w; William, s; John, s; Sarah,
d, 107B.20
John; Elizabeth, w, 109.98
John, esq; John, s, bach, 98.2
John, ser, 103.252
Joseph, app, 103.104
Martha, ser, 104.5
Mary, 98.43,109.5

222

Mary; Robert, s; Mary, d; Magdalen, d, 103.19
Nathaniell; Alice, w; Sarah, d, 110.1
Ralph, 109.40
Ralph, wid, 109.41
Rebecka, 104.134
Rebecca, wid, 103.138
Richard, ser, 107B.79
Roger; Elizabeth, w; Elizabeth, d; Thomas, s; James, s, 103.47
Samuell, 109.92
Sarah, pensioner, 103.223
Susan, 102.255
Susannah, ser, 98.80
Thomas, 101.6,101.21
Thomas; Elizabeth, w, 103.58
Thomas; Elizabeth, w, 110.4
Thomas, £600, bach, 104.27
Thomas, ser, 103.218
Walter; Jane, w; Walter, s; Jane, d, 104.86
William; Mary, w, 98.11
William; Judith, w; Mary, d; Jane, d, 98.48
William; Elizabeth, w; Grace, d; John, s; Anne, d, 103.75

NICHOLSON:
Anne; Anne, d, 99.24
Arthur; Jane, w, 109.107
Benjamin, 99.51
Edward; Sarah, d; Thomas, s; Edward, s; John, s; George, s; Lidiah, d, 102.109
Issabella, 102.109
Jas, app, 104.109
John, 109.107
John; Anne, w, 106.33
Jos, £600; Eliza, w; Mary, d; Susanna, d, 104.109
Joseph, ser, 99.4
Rachel, 98.80
Robert, bach, 98.60
Sarah, ser, 103.15
Thomas, 109.31

NICHOSON: Anne, ser, 107A.21

NICKINGS: John; Pheaby, w, 103.290

NICKOBES: Isayah; Judith, w; John, s; Sarah, d; Mary, d; Judith, d, 102.244

NICKOLDE: Richard, ser, 106.48

NICKS:
Ann, 103.33
Leonard; Katherine, w; Katherine, d, 102.178
Margaret, ser, 109.25

NICKSON: Sarah, ser, 98.28

NIFFN: Henry; Elizabeth, w; Sarah, d?, 99.25

NIGHTINGALE:
Andrew; Elizabeth, w, 109.51
Anne, 101.90
Elizabeth, wid; Elizabeth, d, 103.57
Jane, 105.9
John, bach, 109.6
Sarah, 107B.2
Stephen; ~, w, 103.24
Thomas; Anne, w, 101.90

NIGHTINGERL: John; Sarah, w, 102.253

NIPP:
Daniel; Elizabeth, w; Elizabeth, d, 105.14
John, 105.2

NIPPING: David, app, 107A.40

NIX:
Issac, 109.25
Mary, 109.25
Rebecca, 109.25

NIXON:
Elizabeth, 102.32
Frances; Henry, s, 104.105
John, 110.11
Jonathan, ser, 106.2
Margaret, 106.16
Margaret, pensioner, 106.8
Martha, 110.11
Mathew, 110.11
Robert, £600; Mary, w, 106.37

NOADS:
John; Hannah, w, 104.47
Joseph; Mary, w, 106.14
Sarah; Hannah, sister of, 98.26
Wm; Mary, w; John, s; Wm, s; Geo, s; Mary, d; Eliza, d, 104.41

NOAH:
Geo; Marg, w; Cornelia, d; Ellinor, w, 103.262
William, ser, 107D.54

NOBB: Francis, 110.27

NOBES: Elizabeth, ser, 109.86

Noble:
~, wid, dead, 102.274
Edmond, gent; Elizabeth, w, 102.94
Elizabeth, spinster, 103.107
Mattew; Susannah, w; Marke, s, 98.74
Nathaniel; Jane, w, 109.42

Richard, app, 103.284
Sarah; Elizabeth, d, 106.41
Susanna, 101.60
Thomas, wid, 102.124
William; Mary, w; George, s; Martha, d; John
Katton, s, 103.266
William; Barberah, w, 107C.26
William, app, 103.43

NOBSON: Daniell, bach, 103.276

NODDING: Wm, bach, 104.6

NOELL: Rebecca, ser, 109.7

NOLLIBOY: Stephen; Eliza, w; Eliza, d;
Sarah, d, 104.11

NOLTON: Jane, 102.211

NOMS: Robert, app, 102.189

NOONE:
Anne, ser, 107D.18
Benjamin, 109.2
Elizabeth, ser, 101.91
Hanah, 99.44
John, 99.44

NOONES: Francis; Elizabeth, w; Elizabeth,
d; Mary, d, 107D.49

NORBERY: William; Margaret, w; William,
s, 103.143

NORBURY:
Mary, 109.102
William; Elinor, w, 98.49

NORCLIFFE: Marmaduke, app, 98.68

NORCOCKE:
James; Frances, w; Mary, d; Richard, s,
106.66
Tho, bach, 104.51

NORCOTT:
John; Elizabeth, w, 102.142
Joseph; Elizabeth, w; Samuell, s; Elizabeth,
d; William, s, 109.47

NORCUTT: John, 107D.71

NORDEN:
Katherrine, wid, 103.284
William; Mary, w; Mary, d; John, s, 107D.49

NORFOLKE: Richard; Marian, w; Margaret,
d; Thomas, s, 106.56

NORGATE:
Elizabeth, 102.217
Priscilla, 102.217
Thomas; Frances, w, 109.53

NORHAM:
Elizabeth, 102.67
Margaret, 102.23

NORLAND: Elizabeth, 107B.9

NORLEY: John; Margaret, w;

NORMAN:
~, 105.12
Elizabeth, 104.89
Elizabeth, nurse child, 103.107
Elizabeth, wid, 100.12
Francis, ser, 98.75
John, 102.270
John; Mary, w, 107A.9
John; Elizabeth, w; Edward, s; Andrew, s,
109.51
John, ser, 103.6
Mary, 98.51,99.51
Richard, 109.76
Richard, £600; Mary, w; Mary, d; Richard, s,
103.280
Richard, assessor, 103.293
Sarah, 104.65.109.99
Thomas; Ann, w; Thomas, s; Mary, d, 109.37
Thomas, app, 103.95
William; Sara, w; Jane, d, 105.16
William; Phedy, w; Sarah, d, 107D.61

NORMANSELL: Elizabeth, £600, 101.32

NORRINGTON: Margaret;

NORRIS:
~, 103.73
Daniell; Sarah, w, 98.69
Dorothy, wid; Mary, d, 100.8
Francis; Eliz, w, 104.87
Henry; Rebecca, w, 103.238
Humphrey, app, 104.31
John; Mary, w; Elizabeth, d; Hanah, d,
103.146
John; Margaret, w, 107D.30
Margaret, 102.189
Nathaniel Thomas, grand-s of Dudney,
107D.15
Robert, 109.43
Samuell; Anne, w; Samuell, s, 109.111
Samuell, bach?, clerk, 104.131
Sara, 101.99.102.25
Thomas; Ellinor, w, 107D.10
Thomas, bach, 104.87
Thomas, wid;

NORTH:
~, bach, 104.63
Anne, ser, 102.136
Elizabeth, 109.59
Elizabeth, app, 98.76
Elizabeth, ser, 98.42,102.78
Francis, 109.71
Francis, ser, 106.2
Henry, £50 p.a.; Elizabeth, w; Charles, s;
    Henry, s; Elizabeth, d; Mary, d, 106.59
Issac, app, 107B.42
Jane, ser, 104.11
John, 102.91,104.127
John; Rebecca, w, 110.5
Martha, 102.187
Mary, 102.142,110.5
Mary, ser, 103.265
Moses, 102.3
Robert, bach, 106.52
Robert, ser, 107A.25
Tho, app, 104.26
Walter, 104.127

NORTHALL:
James; Hanah, w; Mary, d, 106.52
Samuell, 106.52

NORTHEN: John; Elizabeth, w, 106.13

NORTHERNE: Alice, 104.110

NORTHORP: Elizabeth, 109.103

NORTHOVER: George; Elizabeth, w;
    William, s; Thomas, s, 98.62

NORTHWORD: George; Elizabeth, w;
    Elizabeth, d;

NORTON:
~; ~, w, 104.132
Abraham; Anne, w; John, s, 107C.40
Anne, 101.28
Anne, ser, 107B.19
Anne, wid, 103.57
Daniell; Elizabeth, w, 99.44
Edward; Anne, w, 109.103
Eliza, 104.105
Frances, ser, 104.4
Francis; Joane, w; Robert, s; Elizabeth, d;
    Samuell, s; Sarah, d, 109.3
Isabella, ser, 109.11
Jas, ser, 104.136
Jane, ser, 107B.19
John, 105.16,105.17
John; Anne, w, 107B.76
John, app, 103.37
Margeret, ser, 103.181
Margery, ser, 103.181

Mary, 107B.53
Rebecca, ser, bach, 103.86
Richard, ser; Jane, w; Thomas, s; Mary, d;
    Jane, d, 107A.31
Roger; Martha, w; William, s; Elizabeth, d;
    Martha, d, 100.10
Shadrick; Mary, w; Elizabeth, d; Joseph, s;
    Ann, d, 103.37
Thomas, wid, 98.23
William; Elizabeth, w, 106.38
Wm, ser, 104.14

NORWOOD:
Arthur; Elizabeth, w; Eliza, d; Jane, d;
    Edward, s, 107D.53
Elizabeth; William, s, 107A.26
John; Ellinor, w, 107D.16
Margaret, 109.60
Richard; Mary, w; Mary, d, 101.92
Robert, 102.249

NOSE: Ann, 102.218

NOTT: Thomas, 109.97

NOTTINGHAM:
Henry; Rebecca, w; Henry, s; Simon, s,
    103.127
Thomas; Alice, w; Sarah Hewlet, d, 107D.73
William; Sarah, w, 107D.75

NOWDEN: Randolph; Ann, w, 104.122

NOWELL:
John, app, 104.111
Mathew, ser, 106.54
Nathaniell; Mary, w; Nathaniell, s; William,
    s; Mary, d, 100.5

NOWLAND: John, bach, 104.93

NOYES:
John, £600; Eliz, w; Wm, s, 104.92
Symon; Margery, w; Joseph, s, 109.111

NUCE:
Elizabeth, 101.79
Mary, 101.79

NUMES: Margarett; Samuell, s; Mary, d,
    102.228

NUNIS: ~, a jew child, 107B.32

NUNN: Francis; Mary, w, 103.224

NUNNE:
Tho, ser, bach?, 104.102
William, at sea; Elizabeth, w, 103.40

NUNNS: Elizabeth, wid; William, s; Anne, d, 102.24

NURSEY: John; Hester, w; Nicholas, s, 107B.4

NURSLING: Charles, 109.104

NURSS:
Elizabeth, ser, 103.283
John, 103.138,103.283
John; Mary, w, 103.241
Margeret, ser, 103.285
Rich, bach, 104.5
Thomas, 106.3

NUSS: Benjamin; Jane, w; Samuell, s; Jane, d, 102.42

NUTSHELL: John, app, 107D.4

NUTT:
Edward; Elizabeth, w, 103.50
Elizabeth, wid, 100.7
Robert, dead, 109.61
Thomas, £600; Mary, w; Joseph, s, 107D.27
William, bach; Margaret, his sister, 102.176

NUTTALL:
James; Anne, w, 102.146
Jane, 109.13
Susanah, 99.18
William, ser, 100.5

NUTTHALL: John; Elizabeth, w; Joseph, s, 105.3

NUTTING: Joseph, ser, 103.191

NUTTON: Richard, under Tapster, 103.4

OADIUM: Ann, 99.29

OAGLE:
Alice; Mary, d, 98.11
Elinor, 98.36

OAKE:
Benjamin, 107A.41
Elizabeth, ser, 103.44
Judith;

OAKES:
~, wid, 104.92
Anne, 107A.26,109.64
Caleb; Hanah, w, 103.132
John, 105.17
Mary, wid; Mary, d; Martha, d; Sarah, d, 103.141

Thomas; Mary, w; James, s; Thomas, s, 103.96
Anne, 101.96

OAKEY:
Robert; Mary, w, 103.204
Thomas, app, 109.95

OAKLEY:
Daniel; Anne, w, 107B.60
Edward; Anne, w, 101.68
Elizabeth, 102.50
John, 105.18
Katherine, ser, 104.14
Robert; Mary, w, 107D.59
Thomas; Elizabeth, d; Jane, d; Thomas, s; John, s; Barbary, d, 107B.21
William; Mary, w, 109.107

OAKMAN: Nicholas; Anne, w, 107C.6

OARE: Sarah;

OATLY:
~, wid, 103.127

OBEN: Richard; Elizabeth, w; Elizabeth, d, 107D.7

OBITT: Samuell; Elizabeth, w, 98.55

OCKFORD: John, 109.102

ODAM:
John; Hannah, w; Marg, d, 104.104
William; Elizabeth, w, 107B.74

ODDY: Thomas; Elizabeth, w, 106.4

ODEIR: Nicholas; Sarah, w, 103.82

ODELL:
Isabell; George, s; William, s, 107B.1
John; Mary, w; Robert, s; Elizabeth, d; John, s; Benjamin, s, 109.27

ODENT: Peter, 110.23

ODES: Arthur; Eliza, w, 104.91

ODOLPHUS: Jasper, bach, 98.70

ODUM:
Hannah; ~, ser, 103.177
William; Hanah, w; Mary, d, 103.253

ODWAY: Hester, 102.54

ORPIN: John, ser, 106.35

ORR: Susannah, ser, 98.41

ORRELL:
Mary, ser, 106.13
Richard; Susannah, w; Mary, d, 98.80
Sarah, 106.13

ORSON: Frederick; Anne, w; Valentine, s;
    Mary, d, 110.33

ORT: Mary, ser, 107B.78

ORTON:
Edward, 109.111
Edward; Ann, w, 109.86
Isabella, 107B.5
John, ser, 106.52
Peirce; Thomas, s; Elizabeth, d, 109.90
Rebecca, 109.60

ORWELL: George; Mary, w; James, s; Mary,
    d, 103.113

OSBASTON:
Hanah; Jonas, s; Hanah, d; Sarsh, d, 107D.6
John; Eliz, w; Eliz, d; Mary, d, 104.44
Mary; William, s; Mary, d; Jane Godden,
    grand-d, 107B.31
Matt, bach, 104.48

OSBORNE:
Alexander; Elizabeth, w, 109.39
Alexander; Elizabeth, w; Phettyplace, s,
    102.151
Ann; Ann, d, 106.48
Anne, 109.108
Charles, ser, 106.66
Dorothy, 109.104
Edward; Philodelpha, w; Edward, s;
    Philodelpha, d, 107B.30
Elizabeth, 109.72
Elizabeth; Mary, d; John, s; Elizabeth, d,
    109.14
Elizabeth, ser, 102.134
Elizabeth, ser, 109.83
George; Hessebeth, w, 103.32
Hester, ser, 101.28
John, 103.290
John; Elizabeth, w; William, s, 100.11
John; Hanah, w; John, s; Mary, d, 103.26
John; Eliz, w, 104.129
John; Elizabeth, w, 107B.13
John, ser, 109.78
Jone, 101.33
Jos, app, 104.34
Joyce, 99.9
Ludia, ser, 103.283

Margeret, 103.280
Mary, ser, 107B.79
Philadelpha, 109.52
Richard, 107A.26
Richard, 109.93
Richard; Anne, w, 109.93
Richard, £600; Rose, w; Mary, d; Anna
    Maria, d; Rose, d; Anne, d, 104.31
Rich, esq; Eliza, w; Anne, d; Mary, d,
    104.116
Samuel; Mary, w, 107C.20
Sara, ser, 101.20
Stephen, 101.31
Thomas, a parish child, 101.36
William, 110.20

OSEWLL: Joane, 109.39

OSGOOD: John, 103.252

OSMAN: Robert, app, 107A.25

OSMOND:
~, wid, 104.134
Amey; Elizabeth, w, 107C.8
James, bach, 107B.72
John; Anne, w; Sarah, d, 107C.20
Mary, 98.6
Thomas; Anne, w; Barberah Page, d,
    107D.84

OSSTWOOD: Sarah, pensioner; William, ser;
    John, ser, 103.89

OSSWALD: John; Elizabeth, w, 103.194

OSTRUPP: Henry; Elizabeth, w, 98.55

OTEN:
John, app, 104.26
Margaret; Samuel, s; John, s, 107B.5

OTES: Hester; Thomas, s; Mary, d, 107D.68

OTEY: Hugh; Mary, w; Hugh, s; Henry, s,
    107A.36

OTTAMORE: John; Mary, w; Mary, d;
    Martha, d, 109.106

OTTERIDGE: Bridgett, ser, 104.1

OTTEWAY: George William, s of lewis,
    107B.59

OTTWAY: Anne, 109.1

OUARTERMAN:
John; Alice, w, 98.46

PACE:
Elizabeth, ser, 107C.37
Mary, 107A.4
Thomas; Sarah, w; William, s?; Mary, d?,
99.7

PACK:
Christopher, £600; Elizabeth, w; Christopher,
s; Graves, s; Edward, s; Richard, s,
107B.73
James; Jeane, w, 103.172
Job, ser, 101.43
Mary, 109.17
Sarah, ser, 103.172
Thomas; Elizabeth, w; Elizabeth, d; James, s,
102.56

PACKER: Edward; Sarah, w, 109.8

PACKETT:
Francis, 99.28
Nathaniell; Sarah, w; Jacob, s?; Sarah, d?,
99.28

PACKHOOD: Rebecca, 102.146

PACKHURST:
Elizabeth, 107B.25
Mary, 107B.25

PACKINGTON: Jane, 99.14

PACKMAN:
Elizabeth; Mary, d, 98.11
Thomas, 102.148

PACKWOOD: Eliza, ser, 101.1

PAdDESTER: Yeaye; Elizabeth, w, 103.155

PADDISON:
Jeane, wid; Rebecca, d, 103.138
Jerimiah, ser, 103.224
Sarah; Grissell, d, 107D.79
Thomas; Rebecca, w; Mary, d, 103.92

PADGE:
Prisca, 102.262
Thomazin, 102.271

PADGET: Mary, ser, 107D.35

PADLEA: Timothy; Judeth, w; Joseph, s,
103.61

PADLEY: Elizabeth, 110.29

PADON: Robert; Elizabeth, w; James, s;
Robert, s;

PAGE:
~, wid, 104.82
Anne, 102.247,109.94
Anne; Anne, d; John, s; Charles, s; Elizabeth,
d; Sarah, d, 107A.18
Barberah Thomas, d of Osmond,
107D.84
Benjamin, £600; Elizabeth, w; Rose, d;
Benjamin, s, 107B.57
Bridgett, 106.41
Charles; Sarah, w; Sarah, d, 107A.42
Charles, bach, 109.96
Dorothy, pensioner; Elizabeth Hewes, grand-
d, 103.72
Edward; Marg, w, 104.3
Ellinor, ser, 103.7
Frances, 107B.69
George, 106.66
Grace, 100.3
Hanah, ser, 102.117
Henry; Sarah, w, 102.148
James, 109.90
Jone; Richard, s; Samuell, s; Benjamin, s,
98.78
John, 109.60
John; Elizabeth, w, 98.84
John; Elizabeth, w; John, s, 103.10
John; Ann, w; Elizabeth, d; John, s; Ann, d;
Thomas, s, 103.132
John, gent; Dorothy, w, 103.286
Joshua; Deborah, w; Jane, d, 108.8
Judeth, 110.23
Martha, 99.28
Martha; Martha, d, 104.83
Mary, 99.52
Mary; William, s; Thomas, s, 102.115
Mary, ser, 103.31
Mary, wid, 103.143
Samuell, 103.87
Thomas; Dorcass, w; William, s; Mary, d,
103.56
Thomas; Mary, w; Thomas, s; Harcoate, s,
103.216
Tho; Mary, w, 104.141
Timothy; Anne, w; Elizabeth, d; Martha, d;
Timothy, s, 107A.14
William; Margaret, w; Margaret, d; Frances,
d, 106.12
William; Elizabeth, w; Hester, d; Judith, d,
107C.18
William, app, 107D.28
Zaphania, ser, 103.287

PAGGEN: James; Anne, w; John, s; Thomas,
s; Anne, d, 102.156

PAGGETT:
Elizabeth, 103.105
Mary, 110.18

230

Richard; Ann, w, 103.22
William; Martha, w, 103.245

PAIN, See Patne

PAINTER:
Alice, wid, 103.41
Dameris, wid, 102.66
Edmond; Ann, w; Avis Paine, grand-d,
103.183
Jessee; Sarah, w; Sarah, d; Elizabeth, d;
Mary, d; Jessee, s; James, s, 106.35
John, 109.13
John; Eliz, d; Henry, s, 104.125
Margarett, 110.7
Rachell, 98.29
Robert; Ann, w; Simond, s, 109.2
Samuell, 102.232
Sarah, wid, 103.86
Thomas; Jane, w, 109.44
Wm; Anne, w, 104.105

PAIRTRIDGE, See Partricge

PAITE:
Wm; Francis, ?s; Eliz, d; Mary, d, 104.19
Wm; £600, ?bach, 104.108

PALEY:
Henery; Dorothy, w, 106.62
Wm, wid, 104.10

PALFEE: John; Mary, w; Mary, d; Jane, d;
Mary, d, 102.251

PALFRYMAN: Margaret; Sarah, d, 107A.17

PALLARD: Robert; Catherine, w;

PALLETT:
~; Frances, d, 102.177

PALMER:
Andrew, 110.12
Angell, ser, 104.95
Anthony, wid, £600; Elizabeth, his sister,
102.161
Carolina; Mary, d; Wm, s, 104.54
Dennis, 103.163
Edward; Alice, w; Richard, s; John, s; Mary,
d, 107B.39
Edward; Elizabeth, w; William, s; Mary, d;
Elizabeth, d, 107D.85
Elizabeth, 101.39,102.43
Elizabeth; Edward, s, 98.82
Elizabeth; Elizabeth, d; Anne, d; Joseph, s;
Dorothy, d, 107C.34
Elizabeth, ser, 107A.43,107D.24
Francis, 109.58

Francis; Sarah, w; Anne, d; Elizabeth, d;
Jane, d, 102.157
Francis; Sarah, w; Rebecca, d, 107D.62
Francis, ser, 107D.87
George; Jane, w; Mary, d; Thomas, s; Jane, d,
107B.61
Greene; Jane, w; Humphry, s, 107B.43
Hanna, 101.39
Henry; Eliz, w; Eliz, d, 104.54
James, 99.22
John, 102.265
John, 109.90
John; Elizabeth, w, 103.254
John; Sarah, w; Hanah, d; William, s; Sarah,
d, 107C.36
John; Mary, w, 109.85
John, app, 107B.49
Joseph, 101.22
Joshua, Doctor; Ann, w; Joshua, s; Ann, d;
Martha, d, 103.289
Katherine, spinster, pensioner,
103.15
Lawrence; Dorothy, w, 110.2
Margaret, 98.66
Mary, 102.254,109.109
Mary; Sara, d, 101.97
Mary; Grace, d, 107D.26
Peter, 102.254
Rachel, 102.254
Rich; Hannah, w, 104.32
Rose, 99.22
Ruth, 101.39
Samuell; Mary, w; John, s; Henry, s,
103.184
Samuell, ser, 98.29
Susan, 99.35
Thomas, 107B.53
Thomas; Deborah, w, 104.2
Thomas; Margery, w; William, s; Anne, d,
104.34
Thomas, gent; Lucy, w, 106.38
William; Elinor, w; William, s, 101.39
William; Sarah, w; Mary, d, 102.25
William; Susan, w; John, s; Mary, d; Henry,
s; Custing, s; William, s, 102.57
William, app, 107B.5,109.98
William, ser, 106.1

PALPHS:
Elizabeth, ser, Parish child, 103.62
Richard, pensioner; Ruth, d; Jeane, d;
Jonathan, s, 103.68

PAMP:
Anne, 102.215
John; Temprance, w; Elizabeth, d; Mary, d;
Temprance, d, 102.215

PAMPLIN: Priscilla, 101.36

PANCOTT: William; Mary, w; William, s; Mary, d; Thomas, s;

PANETHORN: ~, wid, 102.3
Jane, 102.3

PANIE: Anne, 102.28

PANKE: Susan, wid, pensioner, 103.15

PANKIN: John; Mary, w; Elizabeth, d, 107B.46

PANTENEA: Sarah, ser, 103.29

PANTIN: Elizabeth, wid; Mary, d, 103.96

PANTON:
Ann, wid; Elizabeth, d, 103.66
Anthony; Sarah, w, 107A.27
Caleb; Elizabeth, w; Caleb, s; Joshua, s; Richard, s, 103.78
Rob; Eliza, w, 104.7
Samuel, ser, 109.56
Wm; Ellinor, w, 104.12

PANTRY: John; Elizabeth, w; Bewch, s; John, s, 103.168

PANTWELL: Elianor; Margaret, d, 101.10

PAPE: John; Mary, w; William, s; Rebecca, d, 107D.94

PAPWORTH:
Elizabeth, wid; John, s, bach, 103.252
Mary, 107D.23
Robert, wid, 98.27

PARCEVALL: Thomas, ser, 102.115

PARCHMORE: Mary, 109.99

PARDOE:
Marke; Mary, w, 109.81
Thomas, 109.63

PARDY: Thomas; Elizabeth, w; Thomas, s; Elizabeth, d; Arabella, d, 102.268

PAREMAN: William, 101.41

PARGITOR:
Joseph, app, 107A.14
Mary, ser, 106.36
William, 102.249

PARING: Joseph; Joyce, w, 100.9

PARIS: Richard; Rose, w, 107B.9

PARISH:
Ann, ser, 103.233
Elizabeth, 106.16
John; Mary, w, 107B.1
Margeret, 103.146
Sycilla, pensioner, 103.77

PARK(E):
Anne, 102.92
Bridget, wid, 103.281
Joseph, 99.12
Sarah, 102.92

PARKER:
Alice, 109.44
Anne, 98.75,109.32
Anne, ser, 104.143
Benjamin, 99.49
Dorothy, ser, 103.11
Edward; Anne, w, 107D.74
Edward; Mary, w, 107D.77
Edward, lad, 103.250
Edward, ser, 106.50
Elianor; Richard, s; Sarah, d, 102.74
Elizabeth, 99.49,104.46
Elizabeth; Elizabeth, d, 98.85
Elizabeth, ser, 103.95
Elizabeth, ser, 103.95
Ephraham, 103.250
George; Elizabeth, w; Sarah, d, 103.157
Geo; Penelope, w, 104.129
Grace, ser, 106.16
Hanah, 99.49
Hannah, wid; Elizabeth, d; Mary Hayle, grand-d; Elizabeth Hayle, grand-d; Mary Parker, grand-d; Edward Parker, grand-d, 102.53
Henry; Frances, w; Thomas, s; Timothy, s, 107B.36
Hugh; ~, w, 104.111
Isabell, ser, 107A.34
James, 109.108
John; Dorothy, w; Anne, d?; Dorothy, d?; Mary, d?, 99.18
John; Mary, w; Mary, d, 102.10
John; Elizabeth, w, 102.193
John; Mary, w, 102.214
John; Elizabeth, w; John, s; Christopher, s, 103.27
John; Elizabeth, w, 103.280
John; Elizabeth, w; Elizabeth, d, 109.109
John, £600; Mary, w, 103.73
John, bach, 99.27,103.32
John, ser, 106.35
Johathon, wid; Nicholas, s; Johana Penduck, mother-in-law, 103.271
Joseph; Anne, w; Lephamah, d, 102.107

John, bach, 104.12
Richard; Elizabeth, w, 109.49

PATRICKSON: Agnus, gentlewoman, 98.41

PATRIS: Petre, 102.103

PATSHALL: Jos, £600, ?bach; Jane Read,
  sister, 104.51

PATTEN:
Andrew, 107B.47
Elizabeth, 109.78

PATTIN:
Anne, 101.15
John; Martha, w; Henry, s, 102.193
Thomas, app, 107C.20

PATTISON:
Alexander, wid, 102.36
Anne, 102.211
George, app, 98.34
John, 102.85
John; Martha, w, 102.112
John; Jane, w; John, s; Edward, s, 106.17
Mathew, 101.54
Robert, 102.36
Thomas; Jane, w; Charitye, d; John, s, 102.27

PAUL:
Cornelius; Grace, w, 103.31
Francis; Mary, w; Anne, d; Francis, s,
  107A.25
Joseph; Elizabeth, w; John, s; Mary, d,
  109.84
Mary, wid; Josiah, s; Benjamin, s; Mary, d,
  103.118
Phillip; Sarah, w; Sarah, d, 102.142

PAULET: Joseph; Elizabeth, w;

PAULEY: ~, 103.273
James; Amye, w; James, s; Thomas, s,
  102.22

PAVY: Francis; Elizabeth, w, 107D.59

PAWLET:
David, app, 101.63
Edward, £50 p.a.; Elizabeth, w; Edward, s;
  Robert, his brother, 106.61
Robt; Alice, w, 104.21
Samuel; Elizabeth, w, 109.8

PAWLIN: Mary, 102.63

PAWLING:
Francis; Elizabeth, w; Richard, s, 107D.11

Richard; Mary, w; Mary, d; John, s; Ann, d;
  Martha, d, 106.11
William; Hannah, w; Hanah, d, 102.11

PAWNOM?: Henry, 102.226

PAXFORD: Martha, 102.150

PAXSON: Thomas, 102.31

PAXTON:
John, 110.9
Sherad, 103.165
William; Elizabeth, w; James, s; Cornelius, s;
  Judith, d; Jane, d, 98.13

PAYBODDY:
Ann, wid, 103.99
Eliz; Mary, d; Edmund, s, 104.146

PAYE: Francis, esq; Isabella, w, 106.19

PAYER:
Elizabeth, 107C.13
Richard, assessor, 107A.43

PAYNE:
Alice, gentlewoman, 98.25
Alice, spinster, 103.42
Anne, 101.9,102.213
Anne; Elizabeth, d, 98.24
Anne, ser, 102.145,105.12
Avis, 103.183
Benjamin; Anne, w; Benjamin, s; Elizabeth,
  d, 102.235
Edward; Jane, w; Nathaniel, s; Sarah, d,
  109.40
Elizabeth, 98.5,98.53
Elizabeth, pensioner, 103.23,103.48
Elizabeth, ser, 101.20
Francis, 109.82
Grace, ser, 106.23
Hanah, ser, 107D.18
Henry, ?wid; Tho, s; Mary, d, 104.74
James; Elizabeth, w, 101.61
Jerimiah; Ann, w, 103.44
John, 106.32
John; Mary, w, 104.99
John; Sarah, w, 104.117
John; Elizabeth, w, 104.123
John; Sarah, w; John, s; James, s, 109.55
John; Anne, w; Rebecca, d; Elizabeth, d,
  110.8
John, app, 109.98
Nicholas, 103.280
Robert, ser, 100.13
Samuel; Sarah, w; Samuel, s, 107D.51
Susan, 107B.11
Susan; William Brittaine, s, 107D.17

Susan, wid, 103.266
Thomas, 101.17,106.22
Thomas; Ann, w; James, s; Rowlins, s;
    William, s; Crcs, s?, 100.7
Thomas; Elizabeth, w, 101.33
Thomas; Katherine, d; Mary, d, 107B.59
Thomas, bach, 102.213
William; Elizabeth, w; Elizabeth, d; John
    Siblec, s, 103.58
Wm; Susannah, w, 104.16
William; Anne, w; James, s; Anne, d; Mary,
    d, 107A.34
William; Mary, w; Mary, d; William, s,
    107D.61
William; Elizabeth, w; Jane, d, 109.62

PAYTON: Henry; Mary, w, 103.65

PEACH:
John; Margaret, w; Margaret, d, 102.61
Lawrence, clerk, 106.4

PEACHEY:
Ann, 109.7
Mary, 103.24
Samuell; John, w, 101.35
Thomas, 109.89

Peacock:
Dorothy, 104.40
Elizabeth, 101.22,107D.12
Francis, app, 107D.40
Grace, 104.74
Henry, ser, 106.38
John, 102.74
John, bach, 110.31
Joyce, 102.61
Katherine, ser, 98.67
Martha, 104.29
Mary, 104.29
Robert, 102.29
Sarsh, 104.39
Susanna, 101.31
Thomas, 105.17
Thomas; Elizabeth, w, 102.173
Thomas; Martha, w, 107D.8
William; ~, w; William, s, 103.72

PEAKE:
Anne, 109.82
Elizabeth, 99.54
Elizabeth, app, 107B.31
Elizabeth, ser, 104.4
James; Elizabeth, w; James, s, 109.39
Jane; James, s, 102.98
John; Mary, w, 102.126
Mary, ser, 104.17
Richard; Mary, w; Richard, s, 109.31
Sarah, 103.148

Thomas, 102.68
William; Hanah, w, 103.278

PEAKLIN: John, app, 107A.2

PEALE:
Ann, 109.3
Jeremiah, app, 101.95
John, ser, 106.43
Margaret; Mary Vaughan, d, 107B.38
Morton; Elizabeth, w; Morton, s; Elizabeth,
    d; Mary Peale, sister of, 107B.48
Soloman; Elizabeth, dead, 102.275
William; Elizabeth, w, 107D.23

PEALING: William, nurse child, 107C.15

PEAR:
Elizabeth, 106.38
Thomas; Mary, w; Elizabeth, d, 106.6

PEARCE:
George, bach, gent, 106.44
Mary, 102.121
Peter; Anne, w; John, s; Thomas, s,
    102.123
Prudence, 106.37
William, ser, 106.18

PEARCY: Elizabeth, 106.32

PEAREPOINT:
Francis, 102.2
Jane, 102.2
John, bach, £600, 102.2

PEARMAN:
Mary, wid, 102.40
Thomas, 102.63

PEAROW: Francis; Elizabeth, w; Mary, d,
    103.7

PEARSE: Mary, 110.12

PEARSLEY: Elizabeth, ser,
    106.19

PEARSON:
Richard; Sarah, w, 106.26
William; Anne, w, 102.231

PEART:
Elizabeth, 102.57
John; Dianah, w; Dianah, d; Mary, d; John, s;
    Elizabeth, d, 107B.24
Sarah, 107B.78

PEARTREE: William, app, 109.104

PEASLEY:
John, 109.93
Rebecca, 103.139
Rich; Anne, w, 104.80

PEATE:
Ellen, 101.88
Henry; Sarah, w, 107D.1
Knightly; Mary, w; Charnell, d, 102.128
Mary, 102.174
Mary, ser, 103.53
Wm; Eliz, w, 104.79
William, £600; Elizabeth, w, 102.166

PEATON:
George; Anne, w; Anne, d, 102.161
Humphrey; Katherine, w; William, s,
102.234

PECHEY: Margaret, 102.143

PECKETT: Mary, 110.29

PECKHAM:
Edmund, bach, gent, 99.49
William; Anne, w; Thomas, s, 110.28

PECR:
Ann, 106.61
Edward; Margaret, w; Thomas, s; Edward, s,
98.6
Elizabeth, 103.167
Elizabeth; John, s; Elizabeth, d, 98.69
Francis, app, 107D.12
Hannah, ser, 109.95
John, 110.5,110.6
John; Anne, w, 104.129
Mary, 110.5
Richard; Anne, w; Lydia, d?; Elizabeth, d?,
99.28

PEDDAR:
John; Rachel, w; Thomas, s; Martha, d;
Rachel, d, 105.2
Tho; Alice, w; Lydia, d, 104.37

PEDLER: Richard, 107A.13

PEECHE: Edward, app, 103.260

PEELE:
Charles, ser, 103.26
Elizabeth, pensioner, wid, 103.15
Elizabeth, ser, 102.161
Samuell, ser, 103.261
Sarah, wid; Sarah, d; Mary, d; Thomas, s;
John, s, 102.29

PEELEING: Thomas; Dorothy, w, 98.38

PEEPS:
Elizabeth, 109.42
John; Mary, w; Richard, s; John, s; Thomas,
s; Mary, d, 109.77

PEER: Mary, 103.234

PEERS: Mary, wid, 103.85

PEETE:
Edward; Sarah, w; Susan, d; Dorothy, d,
106.27
John; Hester, w; John, s, 102.163
Mary, 101.101
Rebert, 102.151

PEGEN: Walter, 109.93

PEGG:
Alice, 99.29
John; Susan, w; Susan, d; Mary, d; Judeth, d,
103.64
William, wid;

PEIRCE:
~, bach; ~, Mr, 98.66
Abraham; Ann, w, 103.233
Clifford; Elizabeth, w; Gabrill, s, 109.7
Dulcibella; Jos, s, 104.43
Edward, 101.8
Eliz, 104.28
George, 101.64
George; Hanah, w; John, s; Hanah, d,
107D.36
George Gilbert, esq, bach; bach,
98.33
Isaac; Margaret, w, 107D.49
Jeremy, £600; Sarah, w, 104.10
John, 105.16
John; Mary, w; Anne, d, 107D.37
John, app, 107D.88
John, bach, ser, 104.27
John, gent; Lowis, w, 104.101
Jonathon, 103.275
Margaret, wid, pensioner, 103.16
Richard; Sarah, d, 107C.4
Thomas, 101.75
Thomas; Ann, w; John Foxley, s; Joseph, s;
Elizabeth, d; Thomas, s; Abraham, s; Edia,
d, 103.216
Thomas; Jane, w, 107C.7
Thomas; Arabella, w, 109.84
Thomas, wid, 109.102
William; Jane, w, 109.45
William, app, 103.213
William, ser, 109.11

PEIRCIFALL: Isaac, bach, 28 years,
102.269

237

PEIRCIVALL:
Robert, junior, bach, 103.172
Robert, senior, wid, 103.172

PEIRPOINT: Moses; Mary, w, 106.3

PEIRSEY:
Anne, 102.16
Sarah, 107A.32

PEIRSON:
Allen; Mary, w; Allen, s; John, s, 109.87
Gilbert; Sarah, w; Joshua, s, 103.283
Greace, spinster, pensioner, 103.16
Isaac; Katherine, w; Elizabeth, d; William, s, 98.11
James; Edy, w, 107C.6
John; Elizabeth, w; John, s, 103.236
John; Mary, w, 107B.75
John, app, 107D.91
Joseph; Margaret, w, 107B.25
Joseph, bach, 98.75
Leonard, 109.109
Mary, 103.216
Ralph; Mary, w; Anthony, s; Mary, d, 109.48
Richard, 102.49
Richard, £600; Ruth, w, 106.57
Richard, ser, 109.57
Roger, 109.36
Samuell; Mary, w, 102.16
Stephan, 98.11
Thomas; Susan, w, 107D.91
Thomas; Susan, w; Sarah, d, 109.22
Thomas; Lidy, w; Thomas, s; Henry, s, 109.110
William; Anne, w, 107B.1
William, bach, 103.286
William, parish child, 107D.91

PEISLEY:
Margeret, pensioner; Henry, s; Ellinor, d; Henry, grand-s, 103.227
Mary, ser, 103.1

PELCHEIFE: Nicholas; Mary, w, 106.32

PELFREE: Mathew, app, 102.204

PELL:
John, app, 106.25
Mary; Jane, d; William, s, 109.19
Susan, ser, 104.77
Thomas; Jane, w; Thomas, s; Charles, s, 110.28

PELLEN: Carey, gent; Jane, w; Jane, d, 98.42

PELLON: Jacob William, s of Jones, 107C.10

PELLS: Hannah; Mary, d; Hannah, d, 104.20

PELLSON: Mary, a nurse child, 103.84

PELLUN:
Elizabeth, spinster, 103.52
Mary, wid, 103.2
William; Hester, w; Hester Fellom, mother of, 107B.76

PEMBERTON:
Elizabeth, 109.66
Elizabeth; Alice, d, 107D.9
Francis, Serjeant-at-Law; ~, w; Elizabeth, d; Jane, d, 106.29
John, ser, 106.22
Margarett, ser, 101.48
Richard; Anne, d; Elizabeth, d, 101.34
Roger, ser, 106.33

PEMBLE:
Frances; Frances, d; Elizabeth, d; Frances, grand-d, 101.63
Richard; Mary, w; Mary, d, 109.7
Richard, assessor for Smithfield Precinct, 109.112
Thomas; Elizabeth, w; Elizabeth, d, 100.14

PEMBLETON:
John; Mary, w; Mary, d; Edward, s, 107A.7
Thomas, ser, 107A.7

PEMMELL:
John; Anne, w, 107D.96
Thomas; Anne, w, 106.48

PEN, See Penn

PENDLETON:
Charles; Anne, w; Charles, s; George, s; Mary, d, 106.41
Roger, ser, bach?, 104.27

PENDRID: Wm; Marg, w, 104.40

PENDUCK: Johnan, 103.271

PENHALLOWE: John, gent; Sciesilly, w; Mary, d; Elizabeth, d, 98.28

PENIALL: John; Jane, w; Edward, s; Thomas, s; John, s, 105.2

PENINGTON:
Ann, 106.21
Cisley, 106.21
John; Jeane, w; William, s; Stephen, s; Daniell, s, 103.205
Robert; Hannah, w, 109.37

PETHER: John Cooke, £50 p.a.; Susanna, w, 101.23

PETLEY: John, bach, 104.66

PETRE: Simon, 109.107

PETT:
Ann, ser, 103.164
Edward, app, 103.92
Joseph; Mary, w; Josias, s; Jeane, d, 103.179

PETTFEILD: Elizabeth, ser, 103.179

PETTIFER:
James, bach, 101.78
John; Elizabeth, w, 107D.28
Mary, 107B.54
Richard; Elizabeth, w, 107D.1
Wm; Mary, w, 104.145

PETTIS: Giles, ser, 103.89

PETTIT:
John; Merrian, w, 107D.101
Martha, 101.67
Susan, ser, 103.245
William, 101.59
William; Mary, w, 110.13

PETTS: Mordica, bach, 102.190

PETTY:
Charnell, 109.70
Edward; Elizabeth, w, 103.90
George; Elizabeth, w; George, s; Richard, s, 103.259
Humphrey; Mary, w; Humphrey, s; William, s, 102.80
Jeane, pensioner, 103.279
John; Anne, w; John, s; Elizabeth, d, 100.12
John, nurse child, 103.36
Mary, ser, 102.80
Mathew, parish child, 103.47

PETTYFORE: Samuell, app, 98.14

PEW:
Edward, ser, 106.27
Eliz, ser, 104.6
Humphrey, bach, 98.59
Mary, ser, 103.263
Richard; Grace, w; Margaret, d; Francis, s, 107D.3
Sarah, 107D.62

PEWERCFAT: Hester, 102.254

PEYDEN: Rebecca, ser, 102.111

PEYE:
Humfrey, 102.203
Thomas; Clemett, w, 102.203

PEYNOLLS: William, wid; Aron, s, 102.53

PEYPS: Richard, bach, 106.12

PHARCH:
Cutbeard; Ann, w, 103.66
Robert, at sea; Ann, w; Richard, s; Rebecca, d; Joyce, d, 103.281

PHEEPS: Elizabeth, 102.191

PHELPS:
Dorothy, child, 109.54
Elizabeth; Mary, d, 102.91
Hanah; William, s; Edward, s, 103.142
Hester, ser, 98.40
John; Ellioner, w; John, s; Anne, d, 102.27
John; Mary, w, 102.252
Nicholas; Alice, w; Charles, s; Elienor, d; Anne, d; Mary, d, 102.257
Richard, £50 p.a.; Anne, w; Elizabeth, d, 106.20
Thomas; Anne, w; Katherine, d, 102.110
Thomas; Sarah, w; Thomas, s; Sarah, d; Robert, s, 109.43

PHENIX: Thomas, 109.95

PHENY: Susan, 109.65

PHILIMOTT: John; Mary, w; John, s; James, s, 103.85

PHILLION: Francis, bach;

PHILLIPS:
~; ~, w; ~, sister; ~, bach; ~; ~, d, 104.138
Abell; Alice, w, 101.99
Amy, 101.74
Andrew, gent; Elizabeth, w, 98.29
Anne, ser, 104.75
Anne, wid; William, s; Mary, d, 102.248
Benjamin, 106.64
Benjamin; Elizabeth, w, 98.35
Benjamin; Elinor, w; Elinor, d, 110.17
David, 110.10
Edmond, gent, wid, 98.41
Edward; Alice, w, 107A.14
Edward; Hanah, w, 107B.68
Edward; John, s; Elizabeth, d; Margaret, d; Lucey, d, 109.27
Eliza, 104.54,101.104
Elizabeth James, grand-d of Field, 107D.35
Elizabeth, ser, 107D.60
Elizabeth, wid, pensioner; Flora, d; Bridget, d, 103.60

William; Mary, w; Joseph, s; Mary, d,
102.241

PINCOCK: Daniell;

PINDAR:
~, wid, 102.7
Anne, 101.85
Anne, ser, 103.73
Frances, pensioner; Ellinor, d; William, s;
Ann, d, 103.176
Henry; Elizabeth, w, 109.15
James; Bridget, w, 109.3
Jane Jane, kinswoman of Worth, 107B.77
John, 109.97
John; Anne, w; Mary, d?; Ann, d?, 99.42
Joseph, 109.85
Joseph; Elizabeth, w, 107B.15
Lawrence, £600; Sarah, w; Thomas, s,
107A.28
Thomas; Rebecca, w, 107B.54
William, 102.104
William; Mary, w, 102.217
William, app, 107D.1

PINDFORD: Margaret, 98.27

PINE: Jane, wid, 102.251

PINEGER: Jane, ser, 102.187

PINES: Mary; Anne, d, 98.22

PINFOLD:
Chas; Erances, w; Carlina, d; Garterhood, d?,
104.131
Richard; Elizabeth, w; Cicilia, d; Ann, d;
Mary, d; William, s; Elizabeth, d; Joyce, d;
Edmund, s, 109.3

PINGO:
Elizabeth, 99.42
John; Eliz, w, 104.67

PINHORN:
Elianor, ser, 109.80
Mary, 109.21

PINKAMAN: John; Ann, w; Alice, d;
Elizabeth, d, 109.25

PINKE: Gabriel; Ann, w, 103.165

PINKERD: John; Bridget, w; John, s; Giles,
s; Elizabeth, d, 103.10

PINKETON: Febye; Mary, d, 102.259

PINNELL: Sarah, 98.18

PINNOW: Peter; Hanah, w; Hanah, d,
103.247

PINSHALL: Sarah, ser, 106.46

PINSHON: Jane, 102.225

PINSOLD: John, 102.244

PINSON:
Charles; Elizabeth, w, 102.194
Mary Edward, d of Tench, 109.104
William, 109.104

PIOZETT: Charles; Mary, w; Charles, s;
Marrion, d; Elizabeth, d, 103.269

PIPE: Richard, app, 102.145

PIPES: -
Elizabeth, 102.18
George; Judith, w, 107C.39

PIPINS: John; Alice, w, 109.38

PIPPIN: Joseph, £600; Mary, w; Elizabeth, d;
Mary, d; Marytine, d, 103.259

PIPPING:
John, ser, 106.27
Richard; Rebecca, w; Rebecca, d, 106.63

PISTOR: Thomas; ~, assessor; Katherine, d,
103.31

PITCHES: Richard; Mary, w; Mary, d, 102.94

PITCHLAND: Joyce, ser, 98.67

PITCOCKE:
Greace, wid, 103.27
Samuell; Susanah, w; Thomas, s, 103.278

PITHAM:
Gerrat; Elizabeth, w; Gerrat, s, 99.20
Jane, 104.22

PITHER: John; Ellianor, w; Ellianor, d,
101.56

PITHEY: Stephen; Hanah, w; Thomas, s,
103.33

PITMAN:
Anne, 109.108
Charles, 102.15
Elizabeth, 109.15
John, 109.108
John; Alice, w, 104.122

John; Mary, w, 101.27
Sarah, 109.108
Wm, app, 104.121

PITSTOE: Margarey, ser, 98.57

PITT:
Ann, spinster, 103.286
John; Elizabeth, w, 98.88

PITTFORD: John, 99.33

PITTIS: Elizabeth, wid; Katherine, d;

PITTS:
~, 104.11
Anne, 106.62
Edward; Mary, w, 103.59
James; Judith, w, 107A.28
Jane, ser, 106.60 -
John; Mary, w; John, s; Richard, s; William,
   s; Mary, d; Margarett, d, 109.86
Joyce, 107B.56
Kath, ser, 104.5
Mary, 110.27
Mary, nurse child, 107B.55
Nicholas; Elizabeth, w, 103.235
Thomas, 107B.22
Thomas; Elinor, w; John, s; James, s, 103.30
Thomas; Katherine, w; Jane, d, 107C.5

PITTUM:
Ellinor, wid, 103.209
Jeane, ser, 103.288

PLACE:
John, £600, wid; Edward, s; Elizabeth, d;
   Jane, d, 98.48
Nathaniel; Mary, w; Esther, d, 103.64

PLAISTED:
Frances, 102.170
Thomas; Elizabeth, w, 102.46
Thomas, £50 p.a.; Rebeckah, w; Stonier, s?;
   Thomas, s, 98.79

PLAISTON: Henry, bach, 106.54

PLANK: Elizabeth, 103.233

PLANNER: Rebecca, ser, 107D.30

PLATEFEILD: Thomas, ser,
   106.27

PLATT:
John, 104.116
Luke; Hannah, w, 109.46
Margarett, 110.7

Mary, 98.20
Mary, ser, 106.19

PLATTMAN: Mary, 109.105

PLATTS: Christopher, bach under age,
   103.293

PLAYER:
Charles; Elizabeth, w, 98.20
Isaack; Mary, w; Isaack, s; Abraham, s; Mary,
   d, 98.15

PLAYNOR: Jeremy; Elizabeth, w; Elizabeth,
   d, 110.9

PLAYT: Gratiana, 106.17

PLEAHILL:
Mary, 98.59
William, wid, 98.68

PIEDWELL:
Charles; Mary, w, 106.26
Nicholas; John, w, 103.199

PLEVEY: David; Eleanor, w; William, s,
   102.89

PLIMRTON: Robert; Elizabeth, w; Anthony,
   s; Robert, s; Elizabeth, d; William, s,
   107A.23

PLOMER:
Thomas, bach, 101.83
William; Jane, w; Margarett, d, 102.130

PLOWMAN:
Alice, 110.20
Edward, pensioner, 103.77
Walter; Ann, w; Robert, s, 103.23

PLOWRIGHT: Mary; Elizabeth, d,
   102.130

PLUCKWELL: Anne, ser, 100.5

PLUM: Martha, ser, 106.43

PLUMBB: Jeane, ser, 103.201

PLUMBER:
Elizabeth, 98.34
William; Lidia, w; Sarah, d, 107D.45

PLUMLEY:
Ambrose; Ellinor, w; Matthew, s,
   110.8
Elizabeth, 109.96

Eldridge, bach, 103.61
Elizabeth, 99.39
Ellen, 107B.74
Emory, 98.88
John, app, 107D.33
John Thomas, s of Ashley, 107C.6
Lidiah Richard, d of Waylet, 107B.67
Mary, ser, 103.6,106.40
Mary, wid, 103.251
Randolph; Rose, w; Robert, s, 103.52
Rebecca, 106.29
Richard; Elizabeth, w; Mary, d?; Elizabeth,
  d?; Judith, d?; Anne, d?, 99.12
Richard, app, 98.2
Stephen; Mary, w; Alice, d; Mary, d;
  Elizabeth, d, 102.192
Thomas; Mary, w, 102.248
Thomas; Saphira, w; Godfry, s, 107B.21

POOLEY: Matthias, 104.3

POOLING: Jane, 102.88

POOPE: Christopher, 102.146

POORE:
Margarett, 106.13
Richard; Mary, w, 101.24
Walter, gent, 106.36
William, ser, 107C.35

POPE:
Anne, ser, 104.27
Elizabeth, ser, 104.20
Henry; Barbary, w, 101.85
James, 102.17
John, 109.107
Nicholas; Rebecca, w; Rebecca, d; Thomas, s,
  101.67
Nicholas; Mary, w; John, s, 107D.83
Sarah, 109.110
Thomas, bach, 102.150
William, 102.261
William; Mary, w, 104.128
William; Hannah, w; Thomas, s, 109.49

POPELOW: Margaret, 109.21

PORCER: Margaret, wid, pensioner, 103.108

PORCH:
Rebecca, a parish child, 103.196
William, 101.40

POREE: John, ser, 109.36

PORKS: Hannah, ser, 109.47

PORRINGER: Sarah, ser, 107A.36

PORT:
Katherine, 107A.9
Thomas; Elizabeth, w; Elizabeth, d; John, s;
  Jolly, s, 103.211

PORTER:
Alice, ser, 109.37
Alice, wid; Sarah, d, 103.12
Anne, 101.42
Benjamin; Dorcas, w; John, s, 109.16
Daniell; Elizabeth, w, 103.115
Elizabeth, 109.85
Gilbert; Martha, w; Mary, d; Elizabeth, d;
  Abraham, s, 98.61
Jane, 99.3
John, 109.85
John; Ruth, w; Elizabeth, d?; John, s?, 99.22
John; Highway, w, 102.17
John, ser, 107A.5
Joseph, 105.18
Margaret; Mary King, d, 98.82
Margaret, Mrs, 109.79
Martha, ser, 102.190
Mary, 98.18
Mary, esq, 109.25
Matthew; Jane, d; James, s; Zacar, s, 102.34
Robert, wid, 110.13
Rowland; Sarah, w; Ann, d, 109.27
Thomas, 109.63
Thomas; Mary, w; Martha, d; Mary, d, 103.7
Thomas; Anne, w; William, s, 103.67
Thomas; Mary, w, 109.107
Thomas, wid, 98.7
Timothy; ~, w, 102.60
William; ~, w, 99.19
Wm; Sarah, w, 104.15
William; Elizabeth, w; Francis, s; Sarah, d,
  109.28
William; Elizabeth, w, 109.98

PORTLETON: John; Mary, w; Debera, d;
  Elizabeth, d, 102.34

PORTLOCK: Mary, ser, 103.206

PORTRIDGE:
Samuell, ser, 103.251
William; Ann, w, 103.182

PORTRISS: Richard; Hanah, w, 102.239

PORTSMOUTH: William; Jeane, w;

POSEY: ~, wid, 109.87
Martya, 109.87

POSSELWORTH: ~, wid, 109.92

POST: Thomas, ser, 98.57

POSTON: Roger, £600; Elizabeth, w;
Richard, s; Mary, d, 107A.40

POTHORNE: Thomas; Hannah, w, 109.20

POTLEY:
Mary, wid; William, s, 103.157
Matt; Sarah, w, 104.44

POTTEN: Henry; Elinor, w; John, s?; Henry, s?;

POTTER:
~; Mary, d, 109.70
Amy, 98.48
Anne, 107A.9
Anne, ser, 101.65
Anne, wid, 103.63
Ben; Eliz, w; Eliz, d, 104.91
Dorothy, 107C.13
Elijah, bach, 103.37
Elizabeth, 107C.22
Elizabeth, ser, 103.60
Frances, 98.78
John, 101.80
John; Dulcibella, w, 101.80
John; Mary, w; John, s; Thomas, s, 103.140
Richard, wid, 109.2
Sarah, 107B.46

POTTERTON: Eliza, 102.148

POTTINGDON: Martha, 101.53

POTTINGER:
Andrew; Mary, w; Ester, d?, 99.41
John, ser, 103.228
Thomas; Mary, w; James, s, 102.126

POTTS:
Alice, ser, 98.42
Margaret, 98.14
Martha, ser, 101.95
Richard, bach, 103.214
Sarah, 102.183
Thomas, app, 98.69
Thomas Chamberlin, 109.6
William; Elinor, w; John, s, 98.21

POULTER: William, 109.38

POULTNEY: Augustine, app, 101.75

POUND:
Anne, parish child, 109.14
Mary, 102.218
Mary; Elizabeth, d, 109.56

POUNTNY: Francis; Susan, w; Sarah, d;
Rebeccah, d; William, s, 103.193

POVEY:
John; Mary, w; John, s; Mary, d, 109.22
Rob; Cicilia, w; John, s; Anne, d, 104.43

POWDER: Mary May, 106.66

POWE: Jeremiah, bach, 100.6

POWELL:
Adum; Mary, w; Mary, d; Elizabeth, d,
107C.6
Alice, ser, 103.269
Anne, 107B.44109.57
Anne, ser, 109.77
Barbara, ser, 106.49
Benjamin, ser, 106.27
Christopher, at sea; Elizabeth, d; Mary, d,
103.96
Dorothy, 104.26
Edward; Mary, w, 101.5
Edward; Alice, w, 102.54
Edward; Jone, w, 107D.81
Edward; Priscilla, w; John, s; Mary, d,
109.102
Elianor, 101.6
Elizabeth, 109.89,109.90
Elizabeth, ser, 103.9
Ellen, 98.6
Francis; Katherine, w, 107C.5
George; Abigall, w, 103.263
Henry; Mary, w; Jonatha, s; Elizabeth, d;
Mary, d; Henry, s; Martha, d; Jane, d,
102.165
Hugh; Mary, w, 102.203
Jane, ser, 109.2
John, 102.130,103.77
John; Sara, w, 101.24
John; Martha, w; Thomas, s; Bartholomew, s;
Joseph, s; Susanna, d, 104.13
John; Jane, w, 110.1
John, ser, 98.69,106.31
Jos; Mary, w, 104.15
Margaret; Margaret, d, 101.99
Marg, ser, 104.106,106.30
Mary, 98.8
Mary, wid, pensioner; Elizabeth, d, 103.205
Prudence, 109.18
Richard; Mary, w, 107D.47
Richard; Esther, w; Mary, d; Richard, s,
103.39
Robert; Frances, w; Thomas, s; Frances, d;
Elizabeth, d, 101.17
Robert; Joyce, w, 103.48
Robert, ser, 106.55
Roger, app, 107D.29
Rose, ser, 103.218
Samuell; ~, w, pensioner, 109.5
Samuell, esq, 106.38
Samuell, 109.6

PRONOW: John, 102.236

PROPHET: Katherine, 106.6

PROSSER: Edw, 104.54

PROSSON: Josesh, ser, 106.51

PROUDFOOTE:
Edmond; Elizabeth, w; Elizabeth, d, 109.6
Joseph, ser, 109.1
Patrick, bach, 109.6

PROUT: Amy, 98.82

PROVERBE: Elizabeth, 101.10

PROW: Richard; Jeane, w; John, s, 103.18

PROWDMAN: Edward; Elizabeth, w, 101.4

PRUDY: William; Hester, w, 107C.42

PRUNET: Mary, 107B.21

PRUNEY: James, wid; Anthony Ulline, s, 103.273

PRYOR:
Hannah, 109.67
John, 105.16
John; Mary, w; Frances, d?, 99.58
John; Mary, w; John, s; Thomas, s, 103.38
John; Dorothy, w, 104.68
Jone, 101.38
Samuell; Sarah, w; John, s; Joseph, s,
   102.121
Sarah, ser, 98.81
Thomas; Elizabeth, w; Thomas, s; Elinor, d,
   109.18

PRYOX: Paull, gent; Rose, w;

PUCKLE:
~, bach, 103.17

PUDDEPHAT: Joseph, £600; Anne, w;
   Joseph, s, 101.96

PUFFER: Elizabeth; John, s, 102.85

PUFFERD:
Edward, dead, 102.274
Francis, app, 101.109
Joseph; Eliz, w, 104.8
Hugh; ~, w, 104.78
Jane, 104.78
Maurice; Anne, w; Richard, s; Maurice, s;
   John, s, 98.59
Tho; Eliz, w, 104.42

PULCHRES: Ann, a parish child, 109.63

PULFFRRE: Grace; Kath, d; Mary, d; John,
   s, 104.84

PULFORD:
Edw, 104.138
Geo; Mary, w, 104.138
Thomas, 101.4

PULLEN:
James; Elizabeth, w; Joseph, s; James, s,
   98.38
William; Mary, w; John, s; James, s, 110.31

PULLER:
John, bach, 109.35
Jonathan; Margarett, w, 106.21
Sampson Taylor, £600, 101.60
Samuel, ser, 107D.60

PULLEY: Josiah; Mary, w; Elizabeth, d,
   102.222

PULLIN: Jeremiah; Elizabeth, w; Richard, s;
   Jeremiah, s; Mary, d, 101.58

PULLING: Francis; Sarah, w, 103.129

PUMELL:
Alice, ser, 101.74
Richard, 101.72

PUN:
James, 101.55
Jasper; Dorothy, w; Elizabeth, d,
   102.167

PUNNETT: Susan, ser, 103.42

PUNTER: Daniel; Deborah, w, 107A.8

PUNTON: Rebecca, ser, 102.164

PURCHASE:
James, 102.2
Robert, wid, £600, 102.2
Sam, a boy, 104.27

PURDEW:
John; Joane, w; John, s, 103.202
Patience, a parish child, 101.36
Rice, a parish child, 101.36

PURDY: Mary, ser, 107D.2

PUREFOY: Martha, 104.72

PUREFULL: Ann, wid, 103.51

PURLE: Susan, app, 107D.43

PURLEY: Thomas, junior, 106.38

PURRIOR: Robert; Mary, w; Mary, d, 103.39

PURRS: Timothy; John, w, 109.29

PURRYER: Salsbury, app, 103.25

PURSE: Susana, 101.86

PURSELL:
Lucy; Sarah; Joseph, s?; Mary, d?, 109.105
Michael; Sarah, w, 104.104
Rich, gent; Eliza, w, 104.94
Thomas; Anne, w, 102.143

PURSER:
Edward, ser, 105.1
James, ser, 105.1
John; Judith, w; John, s, 107A.26
John, wid, 103.80
Katherine, wid, pensioner, 103.16
Samuel, 107C.32

PURSLOW: John, bach, junior, 103.25

PURSS: Timothy; Alice, w; Timothy, s; John,
s; Mary, d; Sarah, d, 103.125

PURTON: Christian;

PURVILL:
~, bach, 104.91

PUSEY: Christopher, 110.5

PUTNAM:
Mary, 104.27
Richard; Sarah, w, 107D.28

PUTNAN: Hannah, ser, 106.18

PYBUSH: Thomas; Elizabeth, w, 107D.95

PYE:
Ann, spinster, 103.25
Humphry; Frances, w, 109.103

PYKE: Mary, ser; Richard, ser; Sarah, ser,
104.47

PYLE: John, ser, 109.110

PYMAN: James; Elizabeth, w; Mary, d; John,
s, 101.24

PYNE: Nath; Christian, w, 104.142

PYNNE: Jane, ser, 104.10

PYOTT: Benjamin; Hester, w; Benjamin, s,
109.89

PYPER:
Christopher; Elizabeth, w, 110.37
Mary, 110.7

PYSIN: William, 109.70

PYSING: Richard, dead; Elizabeth, w;
Rebecca, d, 108.1

QUADRAN: Jane, 99.27

QUARIDE?: Abraham, assessor, 103.293

QUARLES:
-Daniel; Rebecca, w; Thomas, s; Rebecca, d;
Daniell, s, 107A.37
Daphia, 107D.97

QUARRYER: John; Anne, w, 107C.16

QUATHEN: Thomas; Mary, w, 107D.3

QUENNELL: Peter; Elizabeth, w; Peter, s,
106.37

QUESTED: Ralph; Elizabeth, w, 102.196

QUILTER:
James, £50 p.a., wid, 107D.20
Joseph, 102.73

QUIMANCE: Lawrance; Katherine, w;
Sarah, d; Mary, d; John, s; Ann, d, 103.56

QUINE: John, 103.272

QUINEy:
Deborah; Elizabeth, d, 102.57
Thomas; Sarah, w; William, s; Elizabeth, d,
102.162

QUINSEY: Anne, ser, 107A.40

QUINTON:
Nathan; Elizabeth, w; John, s; Nathan, s,
107D.101
Richard, app, 107B.64

QUINTREY: Eliza, 104.28

QUISTENBOROW: Praise; Christian, w;
Mary, d; Jonathan, s; Joseph, s, 102.76

RABET: Rebeckah, ser, 100.14

RABLIS: John; Margaret, w, 109.64

RABON: Dobora, 102.132

RABSON: Wm; Sarah, w; Wm, s; Eliz, d,
104.21

RABY:
Mary, 101.58
Thomas; Susan, w, 102.248
William; Sarah, w, 107C.26

RACE:
John, 110.16
John; Elizabeth, w, 110.15

RACHELSON: Phillip, 102.67

RACTLIFFE: Richard, bach, 98.74

RADBURNE: George, ser, 109.94

RADD: Alexander; Elizabeth, w, 102.267

RADDAN:
Ebenezer; Hanah, w; Hanah, d, 102.183
Elizabeth, ser, 107B.75

RADDERFORD: Katherine, dead, 102.275

RADDUMS: Ann, wid, 103.225

RADFORD:
Anne, 107B.21
John; Susan, w, 107C.40
John; Anne, w; Joseph, s; Susannah, d,
107D.100

RADLEY: Anne, 102.170

RADNER: Susan, ser, 102.144

RAGDALE: Andr; Eliz, w, 104.63

RAGG:
Jonathon; Jane, w, 109.87
Martha, 109.87

RAGLAND: Judith, 99.58

RAINE, See Rayne

RAINER, See Rayner

RAINES: Edward; Rebecca, w; Rebecca, d;
Ann, d, 109.9

RAINSBURY: William; Martha, w,
109.98

RAINSDEN: Henry; Martha, w; William, s;
Henry, s; Mary, d, 109.50

RAINSON: Mathew?, bach, 105.10

RAINTON: Elizabeth, ser, 106.13

RALPH:
Abraham; Anne, w; Mary, d, 107B.78
Thomas; Anne, w; Martha, d; Mary, d,
107D.25

RAMKE?: Andrew, 98.17

RAMM: John; Elizabeth, w, 103.79

RAMMAGE: David; Mary, w, 103.32

RAMPRIS: William, 109.2

RAMSDEN:
Jonathon; Jeane, w, 103.206
Johnthon; Marg, w; Eliz, d; Mary, d, 104.145
Jos, 104.99
Richard; Sarah, w, 107B.72
William, bach, 109.10

RAMSEY:
Anne, 102.243
John, 102.243,109.69
John; Alice, w, 102.154
Joseph; Elizabeth, w; Elizabeth, d; John, s;
Mary, d; Rebecca, d, 103.262
Marg; Isaak, s; Eliz, d, 104.23
Mary, 109.49
Mary, wid, 102.243
William; Susannah, w, 98.59

RAMSKER:
Issabella, 102.175
Katherine, 102.175

RANCE: Henry; Margaret, w, 109.36

RAND:
John, ser, 109.90
Rebecca, 101.30
William, 107C.18

RANDALL:
Edward; Martha, w, 102.139
Eliener; Sarah, d; Mary, d, 102.172
Elizabeth, 98.66
Emanuell; Susannah, w, 98.27
Hannah, 109.99
John, 102.105,109.22
John; Elizabeth, w, 102.141
John, 109.36
Katherine, 107D.94

RAWITT: Katherine, 98.7

RAWLEIGH: John; Elizabeth, w, 102.196

RAWLINS:
Anne, 98.48
Anne, ser, 107D.63
Anne, spinster, 103.38
Benjamin, bach, gent, 106.14
Cyprian, wid, 106.67
Frances; ~, 106.14
Jane, 109.48
Joane, 102.195
John; Sarah, w, 109.49
John, app, 104.15
Joshua, 109.110
Marg, 104.61
Martha; William, s, 107D.79
Mary, ser, 101.56,104.92
Rebecah, 99.51
Sampson, 107D.92
Sarah, 110.37
Sarah, wid, 102.232
Susan, wid, 103.204
Thomas; Mary, w, 103.182
Thomas, pensioner; Susan; w; Sarah, d,
    103.146
Thomas, ser, 109.20
Willliam; Martha, w; Thomas, s?, 99.11
William?; Rachell, w, 102.244
William, £600; Mary, w, 99.51
William, 99.61
William, gent; Margaret, w, 98.48

RAWLINSON:
John; Christian, w, 102.89
John; Mary, w; Anne, d; Elizabeth, d;
    Margarett, d, 102.150
Samuell; Sarah, w; John, s; Ann, d, 103.47
Thomas; Mary, w, 109.103
Thomas, £600; Mary, w; Thomas, s; Mary, d,
    107A.30
Thomas, 109.112,110.37
Thomas, sir, kt; Mary, w; Susanna Mariad, d,
    109.80

RAWLMER: Margeret, pensioner, 103.119

RAWORTH: Robert, £600; Rebecca, d,
    104.108

RAWSON:
Anne; William, s, 98.21
Anne; Thomas, s, 102.98
Geo; Mary, w; Chas; s; Roberts, s, 104.112
Izabellah, 98.55
John; Ann, w, 103.186
John; Lowry, w, 104.87
Mary, 107D.2

RAWSTONE: Anne, 102.218

RAXEY: Obediah; Ann, w, 103.139

RAY:
Christopher, app, 107B.21
Edward; Mary, w; Thomas, s, 107D.65
Henry, 109.54
Jas; Anne, w, 104.126
John; Anne, w, 107A.8
John, app, 107C.9
Margaret, ser, 109.30
Mary, ser, 105.7
Peter, app, 104.30
Sarah, ser, 106.33
William, app, 103.1

RAYCUT: Henry; Susan, w; Mary, d, 109.83

RAYMAN: Elizabeth; John, s, 103.280

RAYMENT: Robert, £600; Elizabeth, w;
    Elizabeth, d; Sarah, d; Robert, s, 103.261

RAYMOND:
Elizabeth, 102.230
Jonathan; Anne, w; Mary, d; Mabell, d,
    102.31
Thomas, wid, 102.31

RAYNE:
Lawrence; Christian, w, 106.67
Thomas, £600; Ann, w; Mary, d; Hanah, d;
    Thomas, s, 103.14
Thomas, ser, 106.65
William, 102.243

RAYNER:
Easter; Francis Thomas, s, 109.40
Elizabeth; Mary, d; Elizaberth, d, 98.33
John; Sarah, w; Mathew, s; Elizabeth, d,
    102.238
Stephen; Sarah, w, 103.70
Susannah; David, s, 98.66
Thomas; Mary, w; Mary, d; Robert, s;
    Martha, d, 103.78

RAYNOLDS: Joseph, 109.50

RAYSON: Mary, 107C.9

READ:
Adum; Esther, w, 103.151
Adum; Esther, w, 103.190
Alexander, £600, wid; John, s; Anna, d;
    Francis, s; Marah, d, 103.217
Edmund; Frances, w, 109.36
Edmund, assessor for Smithfield Precinct,
    109.112

Elizabeth; Katherine, d, 104.36
Elizabeth, ser; ~, spinster, 103.285
Francis; Mary, w, 109.75
George; Alice, w, 107C.26
Grace, 102.120
Isabell, 107D.6
James; Anne, w; James, s, 101.62
Jane, 104.51
John; Elizabeth, w; Elizabeth, d; John, s,
    107B.71
John, app, 107D.101
Joshua, ser, 107D.101
Mary, 104.48.107B.38,109.23
Ralph; Grace, w; James, s, 107D.14
Richard; Merriam, w; Richsrd, s; Issabela, d,
    102.266
Thomas; Elizabeth, w, 110.22
Thomasin, ser, 108.4
William; Jeane, w; Ann, d, 103.100
William; Alice, w; Elizabeth, d, 107B.56
William; Martha, w, 107D.66
William; Dorcas, w, 109.29

READER:
John, 102.58
Mary, ser, 103.100

READING:
Ann, 109.60
Elianor; John, s, 107B.56
Elizabeth; Mary, d; Elizabeth, d,
    102.144
Elizabeth, ser, 106.35
Theop; Ellen, w; Theop, s, 101.86
William; Katherine, w; John, s; Katherine, d;
    William, s; Daniell, s, 103.259
William, app, 103.200

REALTON: George; Sarah, w, 98.75

REASON:
Anne, 109.13
Jane, 107B.52
Martha, app, 98.75
William, 102.59

REBBORN: Leonard, 102.120

RECKETT: Robert, 110.19

RECORD: Jas; Mary, w, 104.61

REDAT: Soloman; Jane, w; Mary, d; Jane, d,
    102.260

REDDALL:
James; Elizabeth, w; Alice, d, 110.24
Mary, ser, 102.116
Olive, 107B.69

REDDARFORD: Richard; Margarett, w;
    Sarah, d; Elizabeth, d; Margarett, d,
    102.169

REDDING:
Ann, 109.24
Joseph, ser, 109.77
Mary, ser, 104.12
Rechel; William, ser, 107A.25
Thomas; Joyce, w; Charles, s; William, s;
    Sarah, d, 109.76

REDDROPP: Henry; ~, his brother dead,
    102.275

REDFEILD: Mary, 104.9

REDFORD: Mary, ser, 105.7

REDGES: William, 99.33

REDHEAD:
Anthiny; Jane, w; Elizabeth, d, 109.67
Gabriell; Hanah, w; Catharine, d,
    103.219

REDIN: Joane, 102.268

REDISH:
John, 109.66
John, bach, 103.229
Susan, wid, 103.229

REDLY:
Elizabeth, 106.22
Martha, 106.22

REDMAN:
Elizabeth; Mary, grand-d, 107D.15
Jerimiah; Anne, w, 107A.6
Nathaniel; Jeane, w; George, s; Francis, s;
    Nathaniel, s; Elizabeth, d, 103.55
Richard; Jane, w, 110.36
William; Phillippa, w; Roger, s; Samuel, s;
    John, s, 107D.15

REDNAPP: Francis, 104.114

REDROY: Henry; Elizabeth, w; Hanah, d,
    103.256

REDSHAWE:
John; Mary, w; Beck, d; Mary, d; Elizabeth,
    d; Rachell, d; Ellen, d, 98.72
Susan, 102.227

REDWOOD: Elizabeth, 110.26

REEBORNE: Richard, ser, 103.87

259

Timothy, app, 104.92
Ursula, 107A.27
William, 103.277
William; Margaret, w;

RICHARDSON:
~, 98.1
Anne, 101.43
Anne, pensioner, wid; Jeane, d; Anne, d,
   103.75
Charity, 107C.4
Christopher, app, 107C.42
Edward; Anne, w, 109.98
Elizabeth, wid; Leonard, s, 103.239
Jane, 98.58
John; Sarah, w; John, s?; Mary, d?; Sarah, d?,
   99.11
John; Esther, w, 103.24
John; Martha, w; Susan, d?, 103.230
John; Joyce, w, 107B.11
John; Anne, w, 107C.10
Katherine, 107B.11
Lyonell, gent; Elizabeth, w; Lyonell, s; John,
   s, 98.44
Margaret; Margaret, d, 109.64
Martha, ser, 109.100
Mithias; Martha, w; John, s, 107C.34
Nathaniel; Mary, w; Mary, d, 109.40
Read, ser, 103.230
Richard, at sea; Katherine, w, 103.64
Robert, ser, 98.47
Sarah, wid, 102.117,103.122
Thomas, 109.34
Thomas; Katherine, w, 101.33
Thomas; Elizabeth, w; Thomas, s; John, s;
   Martha, d; Hanna, d, 101.80
Thomas; Anne, w; Sarah, d; Edward, s;
   Elizabeth, d, 102.90
Thomas; Mary, w; Francis, s, 109.6
Thomas, app, 107A.43
Thomas, bach, 104.105,109.98
William, 109.83
William; Martha, w, 106.4
William, app, 104.3

RICHBELL: Richard; Richard, s,
   102.181

RICHESON:
Joshua; Alice, w; Elizabeth, d,
   102.226
Sarah, wid; Sarah, d; Rebecca, d; Alice, d;
   Murrey, d, 102.234

RICHMAN:
Anne; William, s; Nicholas, s, 107A.23
Mary, 109.29
Richard; Joanna, w; Richard, s; Joshua, s;
   Benjamin, s; Joseph, s;

RICHMOND:
~, Mrs, 98.61
Beatrix, wid, 103.197
Jas, a boy, 104.26
John; Susan, w; Susan, d; Mary, d, 103.40
Margaret, 98.19
Peter; Sarah, w, 99.35

RICK: William; Elizabeth, w; Mary, d;
   James, s, 109.80

RICKABY:
Anne, 107C.22
Barthew; Sarah, w; Sarah, d; Ann, d,
   109.7

RICKETTS:
Anne, 109.98
Anne; John, s; Elizabeth, d, 107D.35
Edward; Margaret, w; William, s; Mary, d;
   Hester, d, 107C.3
Elizabeth, 109.98
Francis; Eliza, w; Edw, s, 104.56
Hester, ser, 98.76
Jeane, pensioner, 103.220
John, app, 104.56
Mary, ser, 104.116
Richard, 109.98
Thomas; Mary, w; Martha, d; Sarah, d,
   109.31

RICKLIS: James, ser, 109.54

RICKS:
Charles; Sarah, w; Hester, d; Grace, d,
   102.212
William; Ann, w; Ann, d, 103.200

RICKSTAN: Joseph, £600, 102.94

RICRI|OFT: John, 109.39

RIDDLE: Elizabeth, 99.22

RIDER, See Ryder

RIDGATE: Mary, 104.96

RIDGE: Rob; Eliza, w, 104.16

RIDGES:
Elizabeth, 109.81
John, 110.7

RIDGLEY:
Christopher; Ann, w, 109.5
Elizabeth; Pual, s; Katherine, d, 107D.31
John, app, 107A.41
Joseph, 109.25

Thomas; Rebecca, w; Rebecca, d, 103.6
Thomas; Mary, w; Katherine, d, 107D.13

RIDGWAY:
Edward, app, 107B.3
Mary; Rebecca, d, 107A.20
Edward, app, 107B.3
Mary; Rebecca, d;

RIDLEY:
~; ~, w; ~, child, 104.117
Alice, new borne, 110.19
Anne, 102.94
Anthony, app, 102.132
Eliza, ser, 104.107
Izabellah, ser, 98.28
John, 102.5,110.19
John; Dorothy, w; Peter, s, 107B.28
Joseph; Joane, w; Rachell, d, 103.2
Mary, 101.51,110.19
Mary, ser, 105.15,107A.18
Robert; Mary, w; Mary, d; Thomas, s,
    102.57
Timothy; Deborah, w; Timothy, s; Jane, d,
    102.214

RIGBY:
Anne, 104.62
Rich, £600; Christian, w; Edward, s, 104.6
Thomas; Mary, w; Mary, d, 109.39

RIGG:
George; Hanah, w, 107B.50
Katherine; John, s, 107D.100
Mary, 99.19

RIGGS:
Henry; Sarah, w; Sarah, d, 104.39
Nicholas; Ann, w, 99.16

RIGHT:
Elizabeth, 102.269
Epephraditos; Sarah, w, 102.259
Etheldra, 104.17
Hannah, ser, 104.91
Katherine, 102.127,102.229

RIGHTNNELL: John, bach, under age,
    103.84

RIGMAIDEN:
Ann, pensioner, 103.225
Francis, ser, 106.45
Thomas; Mary, w; Mary, d, 103.119

RIGSON: Richard; Elizabeth, w; Thomas, s,
    102.33

RIGWORTH: John, bach, 98.53

RILE:
Anne, 107C.5
Richard, 107C.5

RIMAGE: William, wid, 109.89

RIMER: Sarah, ser, 103.218

RIMMER: Richard; Mary, w; Elizabeth, d;
    Sarah, d; John, s, 103.105

RING(E):
John, 102.42
Samuell; Elizabeth, w, 103.37
Thomas, 99.33

RIPLEY: John; Mary, w; John, s; James, s,
    98.27

RIPPER: Joshua; Elizabeth, w, 102.63

RIPPIN: Margarett, 110.4

RIRE: William; Elizabeth, w; Elizabeth, d;
    Grizell, d, 102.233

RISE: Mary, 109.39

RISSBY: John; Rebecca, w, 103.145

RISSLY: Elizabeth, pensioner; Ann, d, 103.86

RITCH: Hugh, 101.104

RITCHINSON: John; Sarah, w; William, s?;
    Ann, d?, 99.23

RITT: Elizabeth, 102.51

RITTER: Michael;

RIVERS: ~, esq; Mary, w; Rose, d, 104.90
John, bach, 109.109

RIVETT: William, gent; Hannah, w,
    102.211

ROACH:
Jacob, 110.34
John, 110.34
Richard, 99.9

ROADES:
George, 109.44
John; Ann, w; Elizabeth, d, 103.64
Sarah, 107C.3
Sarah, wid; Thomas, s, 103.199

ROADLY: Thomas, ser, 107C.7

Izabella, wid, 103.45
Jacob; katherine, w; Robert, s; Sarah, d; Mary, d, 102.128
James; Elizabeth, w, 106.67
James; Anne, w, 107C.30
James; Mary, w; Isabell, d, 107D.5
James, assessor, 102.276
James, ser, 106.54
Jane, 109.46
Jeane, wid, 103.164
John; Mary, w, 99.17
John; Elizabeth, w, 103.113
John; Eliza, w, 104.146
John; Mary, w; Edy, d; Mary, d, 107A.6
John; Jane, w; Rebecca, d, 109.37
John, ser, 102.72
Katherine, ser, 100.6
Lancelott, ser, ?b, 104.8
Levinas; Mary, w; Mary, d; Sarah, d; Jeane, d, 103.33
Luke; Grace, w; Luke, s; Mary, d; Diana, d, 103.109
Margaret, 101.70
Margaret, ser, 106.44
Margery, 110.26
Martha, wid, pensioner; John, s, 103.69
Martha, ser, 103.69
Mary, 109.8,109.54
Merrill, bach, 110.1
Moses, 109.65
Nathaniell, 102.87
Priscilla, 104.124
Randolph; Mary, w, 104.49
Richard, 102.48
Rich; Eliz, w; Henry, s, bach, 104.37
Robert; Ann, w; Jeane, d, 103.87
Robt; Eliz, w; Sam, s; Sarah, d, 104.95
Sara, 101.4
Sarah, ser, 106.14
Simon; Winifrid, w, 107D.70
Susanna, 109.21
Tanckard, bach, Dr in Physick, 106.48
Thomas, 109.21
Thomas; Ellen, w; Elizabeth, d; Anna, d; Ann, d; John, s; Mary, d; Sarah, d; Robert, s, 106.16
Thomas; Alice, w, 107D.3
Thomas; Anne, w, 107D.26
Thomas; Mary, w, 107D.97
Thomas; Grace, w; Elizabeth, d; Ann, d, 109.49
William, 99.39,99.52
William; Hannah, w; William, s; Hannah, d, 98.84
William; Hanah, w, 103.181
William; Isabell, w; William, s; Mary, d; John, s; Hanah, d; Rachell, d, 107A.32
William; Gertrude, w; William, s, 107B.50
William; Margaret, w, 109.13

William; Mary, w, 109.79
William; Elizabeth, w; William, s; Elizabeth, d, 109.97
William, ser, 109.28

ROBISON:
George; Anne, w; James, s; John, s, 102.151
James, £600; Anne, w, 102.74
Joseph; Mary, w; Benjamin, s; John, s; Thomas, s; Elizabeth, d, 102.162
Sarah, 102.134

ROBSON: Richard; Sarah, w, 98.86

ROCESTER: Roger, 104.139

ROCHESTER:
James, s of £50 p.a. man, 102.29
Luke, s, £600 or £50 p.a. man; Martha, w; Mathew, s, 102.69

ROCHFORD:
John, 109.67
Mary, a nurse from St. Giles in the field parish, 103.24

ROCK(E):
Eliz, ser, 104.101
Joseph; Sarah, w; Richard, s; Sarah, d, 110.1
Samuell; Judith, w, 107D.90
Sarah, 107C.5
Susan, ser, 102.117
William, 107C.5

ROCKLAEY: Charles, 101.104

ROD: William, wid, 102.52

RODEN: Thomas; Elizabeth, w, 103.208

RODERS: Henry, ser, 106.56

RODWAY: Anne, ser, 106.62

ROE:
Anne, 102.143
Edward; Mary, w; John, s; Sarah, d; Abraham, s; Edward, s, 102.136
Gilbert, ser, 106.44
Hannah, 99.39
Henry, ser, 103.12
John, 99.57
John, £600 or £50 p.a.; Rebecca, w; William, s; Elizabeth Street, d?, 102.7
Robert; Mary, w, 102.77
Stevan, bach, 99.29
Thomas, 101.21,109.112

ROEFEILD: James, app, 98.5

ROGERS:
~; Hester, w, 102.192
Alice, nurse child, 107B.52
Anne; Katherine, d, 107D.81
Anne; Martha, d, 109.14
Anne, her husband at sea; John, s, 103.144
Charles; Mary, w, 101.40
Charles; Alice, w; Elizabeth, d; Alice, d,
    106.5
Charles, wid £50 p.a., 103.290
Daniel; Frances, w, 107C.37
Edmoud, bach, 103.110
Edward; Mary Levitt, wid, d; Alice, d, 103.50
Edward, app, 107D.99
Elizabeth, 101.88,1103
Elizabeth; Elizabeth, d; Martha, d, 107D.100
Henry; Katherine, w; Samuell, s; Anne, d,
    101.7
Henry; Mary, w; John, s, 109.28
Hinton; Catherine, w, 103.32
Hugh, ser, 106.28
Humphery, ser, 106.30
Jacob, 110.13
James, gent; Elizabeth, w; James, s; Daniell,
    s, 106.31
John; ~; Mary, w; John, s; Sarah, d; Mary, d,
    98.78
John; Rachell, w, 105.11
John; John, s, 107B.8
John; Prudence, w, 109.36
John, £600, 106.56
John, nurse child, 103.77
Joseph; Elizabeth, w, 103.157
Martha; Mary, d, 104.55
Mary; Elizabeth, d, 109.34
Mary, her husband doth not live with her, 103.49
Mary, ser, 98.47
Nicholas, 102.7
Owen; Jone, w; Thomas, s; Barbara, d, 101.84
Peregrine; Mary, w, 101.84
Rich; Eliz, w, 104.15
Rich; Susanna, w, 104.89
Richard; Frances, w, 107D.77
Richard; Mary, w; Henry, s, 109.7
Robert, pensioner; Ann, w, 103.68
Theophilus; Anne, w, 109.75
Thomas, 107D.46
Thomas; Martha, w; Martha, d; Mary, d;
    Sarah, d; Thomas, s, 109.19
Thomas, nurse child, 107B.51
William, 107B.58,109.75
William; Katherine, w; Daniell, s, 100.9
William; Alice, w; Thomas, s, 103.46
William; Sarah, w, 107C.33
William; Dorothy, w; Thomas, s; Marke, s,
    109.98
William, £50 p.a.; Mary, w; Elizabeth, d;
    Mary, d, 106.49
William, app, 98.77

ROGERSON: John, bach, gent, 106.49

ROGOT: Hannah, ser, 100.14

ROLES: Daniel, app, 107B.71

ROLFE:
Angell, ser, 104.96
John; Ann, w; John, s; Millford, s; Anne, d;
    Martha, d; Elizabeth, d, 103.14
John, wid, no children, 103.38
Richard; Sarah, w; Mary, d, 101.86
Sarah, ser, 107C.22
Sarah, wid, 103.14
Thomas; Anne, w, 101.6

ROLLE: Samuell, bach, gent, 106.46

ROLLINGS: John, 109.37

ROLSTER: John, 103.245

ROMANIE:
Anne, 110.35
Thomas, bach, gent, 110.35

ROODE:
Elizabeth, 98.52
William; Martha, w; Pheby, d; William, s;
    Hannah, d; James, s, 98.4

ROOKE:
Anne, 110.34
Benjamin; Anne, w, 110.34
Edward, 110.34
Elizabeth, 110.34
Elizabeth, wid, 103.79
John; Elizabeth, w, 103.284
John; Frances, w, 107A.29
Mary, 98.79
Mary; Anne, d, 107B.29
Richard; Elisha Maria, w; Elisha Maria, d,
    106.20
Thomas, 110.34

ROOKES:
Francis, wid, 100.14
Henry, bach, 109.23

ROOKEWOOD: Nicholas; Sarah, w, 106.50

ROOKSBY:
Esther, pensioner, 103.76
Frances, 103.99
Milcah, gentlewoman; Joseph, s, 98.71

ROOME:
John, 105.7
Mary, a child, 109.60

William, £600 or £50 p.a.; Barbara, w; William, s; Elizabeth, d; Hannah, d; Rebecca, d, 109.6

ROOPER: Richard, ser, 103.30

ROOSBY: William; Anne, w, 107B.81

ROOT: Ann, her husband at sea, 103.83

ROOTER: Penelope, 101.16

ROOTS: Briggett, 99.50

ROPER:
Abell, bach, 106.46
Elizabeth, ser, 106.55
Sarah, 106.61
Thomas; Constance, w; Elizabeth, d; John, s, 107D.54

ROSE:
Alexander, wid, 109.56
David, wid, 102.68
Elizabeth, 109.38
George, 109.94
George; Abigal, w; Alice, d; Haanah, d; Anne, d, 107D.19
John, 102.202
John; Ann, w, 103.24
Martha, 106.69
Mary; Joseph, s; Jonathon, s, 109.47
Richard, bach, 109.56
Stephen, 104.141
Stephen, parish child, 103.204
Thomas; Anne, w; Edward, s?; Hanna, d?, 101.70
William; Susana, w, 102.202
Wm, £600; Eliza, w, 104.19
William, wid; Ann, d; Elizabeth, d; William, s, 103.240

ROSEBOTTOM: Daniell, 102.81

ROSEBY: Anne, 102.2

ROSELL: Margarett, 102.104

ROSEMAn: Richard; Anne, w, 102.217

ROSIN: Mary, 109.53

ROSS(E):
Elizabeth, spinster, 103.226
John; Sarah, w; William, s; Jane, d; Sarah, d; William, grand-s of, 107D.78
Joseph, ser, 107B.7
Joshua; Elizabeth, w; John, s; Ellinor, d; Joshua, s, 103.43

Richard; Rachell, w; John, s, 107B.75
Richard, app, 104.67
William, bach, 102.67

ROSSENDALL: Francis, app, 98.78

ROSSER: Sarah, 104.17

ROSSWELL:
Mary, 103.87
Samuell; Sarah, w; Joseph, s, 103.86

ROTHMILL: Robert; Elizabeth, w, 103.271

ROTHWELL:
Alexander; Mary, w; Mary, d, 109.67
Daniell; Elizabeth, w, 99.15
Elizabeth, wid; Martha, d, 107B.80
James, child, 109.22
Sarah; Alice, d, 109.49

ROUCH:
Anne, 104.86
Mary, ser, 104.144
Tho; Agnis, w; Tho, s; Eliz, d, 104.144

ROUGHTON: Mary, wid; William, s; Mary, d, 103.47

ROUNCE: Robert, bach, 103.25

ROUNCEFALL?: William; Ann, w, 109.98

ROUND: Elizabeth, 102.200

ROUNDLEY: Elizabeth, child, 109.3

ROUNDS: Ann, parish child, 109.14

ROUNDTHWAYTE: Wm; Margery, w, 104.52

ROUNDTREE: John, a boy, 104.56

ROUSE:
Francis, app, 104.92
Joane, 104.22
Sarah, ser, 106.55

ROUT: Robert, 106.17

ROUTLAGE: Isabell;

ROW(E):
~, wid; Anne, d, 105.6
Benjamin, app, 101.45
Francis; Joanna, w, 104.43
Francis; Susan, w, 104.44
James; Sarah, w; Elizabeth, d, 106.20

John, ser, 109.29
Mary, 104.104,107B.28
Nich, app, 104.5
Nicholas, gent; Antonia, w, 106.6
Thomas; Mary, w; Thomas, s, 107B.52
Thomas, app, 104.46
Thomas, bach, 102.162
William; Mary, w; Ann, d, 103.210

ROWCH: Richard; Jeane, w, 103.269

ROWDEN: Caleb, bach, 103.42

ROWELL:
Edward; Abigal, w; William, s; Jane, d,
    109.74
George, app, 102.180
Henry; Mary, w, 106.32

ROWLAND:
Anne, 98.63,107C.20
Bartholomew; Mary, w, 107D.76
George, app, 98.71
Grace, ser, 107D.54
Jane, 109.57
Mary, ser, 104.66
Sarah, ser, 103.24
Thomas; Ann, w, 103.139

ROWLES:
Charles; Mary, w; John, s; Rachell, d,
    109.18
Mary, pensioner; Frances, d; Jeane, d,
    103.149
Richard, 109.75

ROWLETT: John;

ROWLEY:
~, wid, 105.7
Edward; Sarah, w, 107A.29
Nathaniel; Elizabeth, w, 103.6
Thomas; Mary, w; Mary, d, 107A.23
Thomas, bach, 101.91
William; Judeth, w; John, s; William, s,
    109.40

ROWLIDGE:
Ann, wid, 103.66
William; Mary, w; Mary, d, 103.66

ROWLINGTON:
John; Barberah, w; Henry, grand-s of,
    107D.47
John; Elizabeth, w; John, s; Samuel, s; Sarah,
    d; Anne, d, 107D.74
William; Mary, w; Barberah, d, 107D.81

ROWLT: Edward, bach, 103.263

ROWORTH: Richard; Mary, w; William, s,
    107A.7

ROWSE, See Rouse

ROWSEY: Elizabeth, 102.33

ROWSHAM: Joseph; Hannah, w, 102.104

ROWSON: Mary, 107C.5

ROXBOGG: James, ser, 106.60

ROXLY: Mary, 107B.68

ROYALL: Thomas; Mary, w; Anne, d, 105.10

ROYCRAFT: Samuell, £600; Sarah, w;
    Frances, d?; Sarah, d?; Anne, d?, 99.54

ROYDEN: Richard, ser, 103.232

ROYLES: John, 107A.31

ROYLEY: William; Berbary, w; Sarah, d,
    106.18

ROYSTON:
Ann, 99.57,102.69
John; Anne, w, 107A.25

ROZIER: Gabrill; Mary, w, 102.32

RUBBISH:
Evan, bach, 109.105
William, bach, 109.105

RUCKE: Elizabeth; Martha, her sister,
    106.65

RUDD:
Joseph, ser, 103.218
Katharine, wid, 102.48
Soloman; Susan, w, 107D.35
Thomas, 109.40

RUDDLE: Mary, ser;

RUDGE: ~; ~, bach, 104.77
Alice, 99.39

RUDSBY: Andr; Alice, w; Andr, s; Sarah, d,
    103.56

RUDSTALL: Ruth, 110.7

RUE:
Sarah, 109.105
Thomas, 109.105

William; Margarett, w, 110.32
Wm, £600; Mary, w; Wm, s, 104.19

RUSSFORTH: Alice, ser, 103.285

RUST:
Elizabeth, ser, 109.80
James; Mary, w, 99.10
John, bach, 99.10

RUSTELL: Sarah, 107B.28

RUTCHDELL: Bridgett, ser, 106.49

RUTH:
Elizabeth, 98.54
Thomas; Mary, w; Elizabeth, d; Anne, d;
    Ellioner, d, 106.61

RUTLAND:
Grace; Rebecca, d; Alice, d, 109.97
Margeret, 103.179

RUTON: Ann, ser, 106.54

RUTT:
George; Esther, w; John, s; George, s; Mary,
    d; Martha, d, 103.270
Mary, ser, 103.240

RUTTER:
Charles; Mary, w; Mary, d; Ann, d, 103.46
Elizabeth, ser, 107D.27
Geo, ser, bach?, 104.5
John, ser, 106.46
Thomas; Anne, w; Thomas, s, 98.60

RUTTY:
Ann, 109.43
John, 109.43

RYAN: Walter; Mary, w; Ellinor, d; Thomas,
    s, 103.39

RYBALL: Susanna, 110.34

RYCROFT:
Arthur, 107D.35
Bridgett, 102.120
Richard, bach, 106.63

RYDER:
Deniell; Elizabeth, w; Sara, d, 101.90
Hugh, 109.77
John, 102.250
Mary, wid; Robert, s; Mary, d, 102.232
Richard, assessor, 100.15
Thomas, app, 109.100
William; Jane, w; Thomas, s, 100.11

RYDEX: Symon, 110.3

RYDLEY, See Ridley

RYDOX: Symon; Elizabeth, w, 110.3

RYHMELL:
Mary, 98.81
Rachell, 98.81,101.87

RYHMER:
Anne, ser, 98.42
James, ser, 106.44
Joyce, 104.71
Matthew; Elizabeth, w; Mary, d, 98.86
Sarah, ser, 98.86
William, gent; Frances, w; Elizabeth, d;
    Mary, d, 98.44
William; Dorothy, w; Ursula, d, 98.87

RYLAND:
Anne, 104.33
Catherine, 109.64
Edward; Alice, w; Elizabeth, d; Letitia, d,
    109.64
Mary, 101.106
Sarah; Thomas, s; Priscilla, d, 109.18
Thomas; Lyddia, w, 103.62

RYLEY:
Daniell; Elizabeth, w, 103.130
Jacob, app, 101.45
Jane; Katherine, d, 98.52
Thomas; Mary, w, 102.259
Thomas; Rebecca, w, 103.192

RYMALL: Thomas, 105.18

RYMES: Edward; Elizabeth, w; Elizabeth, d;
    Edward, s, 102.202

RYMILL:
Charles, nurse child from Moorefields,
    103.82
John; Sarah, w; John, s; Sarah, d, 103.171
Jonathan, ser, 103.31
Mary, nurse child from Moorefields, 103.82

RYNER: Christopher; Anne, w; Elizabeth, d;
    Agnes, d, 107D.40

RYTON:
Francis, bach, 102.4
Tho; Eliz, w; Jane, d, 104.119

RYVES: Brime, ser, 106.13

SABBERTON: Frances; Joseph, s? a child,
    102.181

SABILL: Jeane, 103.181

SABIN:
Joshua, junior; ~, w, 103.245
Joshua, £600; Sarah, w, 103.245
Nathon, wid, pensioner, 103.149
Thomas, bach, 103.46
William; Priscillia, w; Thomas, s; Elizabeth,
  d; Sarah, d; William, s, 103.284

SACHARY:
Elizabeth, 101.62
Winifred, 101.62

SACHELL, See Satchell

SACHEVERELL: Benjamin; Mary, w,
  102.5

SACHWELL: John; Elizabeth, w; Elizabeth,
  d; Anne, d, 102.270

SACKBOLT: Alice, ser, 103.29

SACKINTON: Thomas; Mary, w; Martha, d,
  102.57

SACKSPEE: John, ser, 103.58

SACKSPURR: Jonathan, bach, 103.52

SACKWOOD: Susan, 102.38

SACUS: Ann, 104.72

SADDINGTON:
Elizabeth; Rebecca, d, 109.56
Hannah, ser, 102.147

SADGROVE:
Elizabeth, 109.46
John; Phillis, w; Elizabeth, d, 107B.10

SADLER:
Ann, 99.49
Edward; Elizabeth, w, 99.60
Elizabeth, 107D.10
Elizabeth, ser, 109.8
Giles, ser, 106.21
John, 102.62
John; Hester, w, 104.119
Mary, 109.69
Ralph; Elizabeth, w; Edwin, s, 107D.17
Richard; Elizabeth, w; John, s, 102.171
Samuell; Elizabeth, w; Hanah, d; Elizabeth, d,
  103.44
Thomas; Mary, w; Alice, d, 107D.47

SADWOOD: Thomas; Mary, w, 105.9

SAELL: Katherine; Carloss, s, 98.56

SAGE:
Wm; Phillis, w, 104.41
William, app, 109.100

SAILEMAKER: Isaac; Elizabeth, w;
  Elizabeth, d, 110.23

SAKERY: Hephsheba, 102.79

SALE:
Anne, 101.7
Anthony; Elizabeth, w; Michall, s?, 99.26

SALISBURY:
Ann, 104.45
Chas, bach, 104.69
Elizabeth, ser, 109.98
James, 98.77
Margaret, 98.7
Richard; Mabell, w, 109.27
Robert; Elizabeth, w; William, s, 101.42
Thomas, 110.5

SALKELD: Nicholas; Jane, w, 106.39

SALLAWAY: Samuel, ser, 108.5

SALLERS: Sarah, ser, 107A.14

SALLERY: Sarah, ser, 103.69

SALLIS:
Benjamin; Jone, w, 107D.44
Elizabeth, ser, 103.145
Hester; John, s, 107B.44
Hester; Samuel, s; Elizabeth, d,
  107D.20
Susan; Sarah, d, 107B.55

SALLMAN: Mary, 109.44

SALLOCK: William; Elizabeth, w; Rice, s;
  Mary, d, 103.175

SALLY:
Abigall, 103.16
Benjamin, bach, junior, 103.282
Benjamin, senior; Abigall, w, 103.282
Joseph, bach; Abigall, sister, 103.16

SALMON:
Elianor, ser, 107D.12
Margaret; Mary, d; Jermiah, s, 102.101
Mary, 101.11,107D.35
Robert; Mary, w; Robert, s; Mary, d,
  102.237
William, Doctor; Anne, w;

271

SCAMPTON: Elizabeth, 109.102

SCANELL: Mary, ser, 101.100

SCAPE: John, wid, 109.46

SCARBOUROUGH:
Elizabeth, ser, 98.48
John; Sarah, w; Elizabeth, d, 109.36

SCARE: Elizabeth, 109.70

SCARLET(T):
Elizabeth, ser, 107D.23
John; Martha, w; John, s; Martha, d, 110.32
John, gent; Katherine, w; Elizabeth, d; Mary,
   d; Bridgett, d; John, s, 98.28
Robert; Beatrix, w, 110.36
Thomas, bach, 103.192
Thomas, ser, 99.3
William; Abigall, w; Mary, d; Sarah, d,
   107D.101

SCARSE: Jerimiah; Elizabeth, w; Thomas, s;
   James, s, 107D.75

SCATES: ; Mary, w, 104.26

SCATH: Thomas, 105.9

SCEELY: John; Anne, w; Sarah, d; Joseph, s;
   Mary, d, 102.199

SCHOALER: Thomas, wid, 98.38

SCHOOLER: Anne, ser, 101.101

SCIENCE: John; Susanna, w; Thomas, s,
   101.17

SCLATER:
Elizabeth, ser, 106.48
Joane, pensioner, 106.8

SCOAVELL: John; Jane, w, 98.37

SCOBY: Henry, gent; Anne, w, 106.36

SCOEFEILD:
Thomas, 103.158
Susannah, ser, 98.69

SCOFFEILD: Sarah, ser, 109.2

SCOLDEFEILD: Margeret, wid, 103.96

SCOLDFEILD: Mary; Mary, d, 105.9

SCOOT: Joana, 99.53

SCOOTER?: Dorothy, ser, 109.78

SCORRIER: Matt; Martha, w;

SCOTT:
~, wid, 104.106
Abraham, 99.30
Anne, 106.14
Anne, ser, 107A.21
Anne, wid, 103.98
Daniell, bach, 98.71
Daniell, ser, 109.6
Esther, wid, 103.193
Henry, 102.76
Izabellah, ser, 98.3
James, 107C.42
John; Mary, w; Mary, d, 107B.15
John; Ann, w; Elizabeth, d; George, s, 109.24
John, ser, 109.56
Joseph, 109.24
Joseph, ser, 103.152
Joshua; Elizabeth, w; Caleb, s; Joshua, s,
   109.110
Margarett, 109.81
Mary, 99.21
Mary; Elizabeth, d, 103.94
Michael; Jane, w, 107B.22
Richard; Jeane, w, 103.140
Richard; Rebecca, w, 109.57
Robert, 99.21
Robert, £50 p.a.; Elizabeth, w; Robert, s;
   Elizabeth, d, 101.15
Sam, app, 104.31
Sarah, ser, 102.150,104.30
Susan, 103.266
Susan; Susan, d, 102.184
Thomazine, 109.24
William, 105.16

SCOULDING: Thomas, 102.15

SCRAPER?: Thomas, 103.257

SCRATCHLEY: Roger; Sarah, w; Sarah, d?;
   Mary, d?; John, s?; Richard, s?; Thomas,
   s?; William, s?, 99.38

SCREBY: Martha, ser, 98.32

SCRIPPS: Alice, 107A.17

SCRIPTURE: Giles; Alice, w, 109.20

SCRIVEN: Isaak; Ann, w, 104.132

SCRIVENER:
John, app, 98.33
Sarah, 98.33
Thomas, 109.90

SCRIVENS: Henry; Ellen, w, 98.85

SCROGGS: John; Sarah, w; Sarah, d; Ralph,
s, 103.24

SCROOPE: John, ser, 98.5

SCRUBEE: Margaret, 102.52

SCRUBY: Elizabeth, 109.41

SCUCE: Johannah; Margaret, d, 109.96

SCUCKINGTINE: Unit; Judeth, w; Jonas, s;
James, s; Jane, d, 102.249

SCUDAMORE: Thomas; Ruth, w; Sarah, d;
Henry, s; Quintine, d, 103.201

SCUDER: Sarah, 102.195

SCULTHORP(E):
Edmund; Brisbent, w, 109.57
John; Prudence, w; Sarah, d, 109.57

SCULTROPE: Thomas; Ann, w, 103.152

SCULTROX: William, bach, 103.4

SEA: Elizabeth, wid; Mary, d; Samuell, s,
102.85

SEABOURNE: Anne, ser, 107A.27

SEABROOKE:
Elizabeth, 109.21
John; Mary, w; John, s; Jonas, s, 101.87
John; Mary, w, 107D.37

SEAGER: Judith, 109.95

SEAGOOD: Francis; Elizabeth, w; John, s;
Frances, d, 99.3

SEAGRAVE:
John, ser, 108.2
Martha; Ruth, w; Richard, s; Mary, d,
109.74
Mary, 104.57

SEAKER: Robert; ~, w, 103.30

SEAKINS: Mathew, app, 103.195

SEALE:
Alice; John, s, 103.24
Elizabeth; Ruben, s, 109.1
Henry, app, 101.75
Richard, bach, 103.61

Ruth, a child, 107D.97
Susana; John, s; Ellinor, d, 103.61

SEALEY: Edward, 102.111

SEALON: William, 109.112

SEAMER: Anne, 102.259

SEAMORE, See Seymore

SEARCH: Daniell; Mary, w; Elizabeth, d,
110.1

SEARES:
Mary, wid; Mary, d; William, s; Elizabeth, d,
103.195
Richard, 107B.9
Robert; Amey, w; Robert, s, at sea; Samuell,
s; Ellinor, d, 103.266
Susan, ser, 107D.43

SEARLE:
Edmund, 109.74
Eliz, ser, 104.2
George, gent; Susannah, w; John, s, 98.39
John; Ellen, w; Elizabeth Lloyd, d; Sarah
Lloyd, d; Elizabeth Lloyd, d, 108.7
John; Mary, w; George, s; Mary, d, 110.23
John, assessor, 110.37
Martha, 109.75
Richard, 102.238
Samuell; Margaret, w, 109.75
William; Elizabeth, w, 106.17

SEARLES:
Sarah; Anne, d; Stephen, s; Isaac, s,
100.12
Thomas, ser, 106.33

SEARNE: Anne, 107B.25

SEAROSS: Judey, 102.218

SEARS: Jane, ser, 100.12

SEARSE: Elizabeth, 107D.31

SEATE: Alice, wid; Luke, s; Elizabeth, d,
102.33

SEATON:
John; Anne, w; John, s, 100.7
Nathon, wid, pensioner, 103.118
Samuel; Anne, w; Anne, d, 107A.4
William; Elizabeth, w; Jarvis, s; Jonathan, s;
Samuell, s, 102.188

SEBBRY: Mary, 110.14

SEBROTT: Robert, wid; Robert, s; Susan, d; James, s, 106.26

SECHEVEREL: George, bach, 100.4

SECURR?: Elizabeth, 109.93

SEDDON: Martha, 104.18

SEDGWICK:
Elizabeth, ser, 107D.38
George; Mary, w, 107C.24
Robert; Francis, s, 107C.6
Thomas, £600; Elizabeth, w, 101.53

SEDLING: Richard, 109.89

SEDWELL: John; Mary, w, 109.95

SEELY: Elizabeth; Elizabeth, d; Sarah, d, 102.57

SEERS: Wm, 104.74

SEGLEY: Susanah, 99.7

SEISER: Johanna, 109.83

SELBAVAND: Delvis; Sarah, w, 107A.20

SELBY(E):
Elizabeth, 106.40
George, app, 107D.14
Hanah, ser, 102.118
Isaac; Hannah, w; Isaac, s, 109.57
James; Margaret, w; James, s, 102.123
Jos; Mary, w, 104.59
Margarett, £600; Elizabeth, d, 99.4
Mary, 103.106
Mary, ser, 104.8
Richard; Richard, s?, 102.73
Robert; Mary, w; Jane, d; Mary, d, 109.69
Samuell; Mary, w; Mary, d, 102.23
William, a child, 102.77

SELFE: John; Mary, w; Elizabeth, d, 102.45

SELL: Rachell, ser, 98.46

SELLARS:
Anne, 104.87,104.131
Mary, 99.22

SELLON: Humphry; Jane, w; Jane, d; Mary, d, 104.33

SELSBY: John; Judith, w, 102.39

SELWOOD: Deborah; Elizabeth, d, 102.100

SEMER:
Elizabeth, 107C.29
Mary;

SEMLEY:
~, wid, 109.76

SENDALL: William; Anne, w, 107D.56

SENNY: Richard; Mary, w, 109.98

SERGOOD: John; Mercy, w; Katherine, d, 101.41

SERJEANT:
Anne; Richard, s; William, s; Susan, d, 107C.39
Anne, ser, 106.37
Elizabeth; Mary, d, 98.66
James, bach, 99.59
John, 104.71
John; Elizabeth; Judith, d, 107D.34
Joseph; Sarah, w; Thomas, s, 107D.29
Sherrard; Eliz, w, 104.108

SERMON: Jervis; Mary, w, 104.58

SESSIONS:
Anne; Rich, s; John, s, 104.35
Mary, ser, 103.10
Peasant, app, 107C.10

SEWARD:
Charles, bach, 103.184
Dorothy, 98.71
Elizabeth, 98.71

SEWELL:
Henry; Hannah, w, 106.7
John; Frances, w, 104.115
Sarah, app, 104.94

SEWERIDGE: John, ser, 107A.14

SEWSMITH: Hanah, ser, 107B.2

SEX: Peter; Isabella, w, 103.66

SEXTON:
Clement, 110.2
Crissill, 110.2
Sarah, 102.21
Tho, ser, bach?, 104.106
Timoty; Joane, w, 102.21

SEYBOND: Eliza, ser, 104.26

SEYDON: Mary;

SEYMORE:
~, wid; Margarett, d, 102.8
Anne; Elizabeth, d, 110.2
Edward, 106.63
Elizabeth, 106.42,109.102
James, bach, £600, 106.42
John, ser, bach?, 104.34
Mary, 98.76
Rich, bach, 104.95

SEYNELL: Amey, 103.72

SEYS: Rowland, ser;

SHACELL:
~, wid, 102.60

SHACKBOULT: Thomas; Mary, w; William,
s; Sarah, d, 102.216

SHACKFORD: John, ser, 103.5

SHACKLETON:
Geo, 104.81
Jonathon, 109.63
Margarett, 99.33
Mary, ser; Thomas, 99.33

SHADD: Charles; Mary, w; Richard, s;
Samuell, s; Hannah, d; Charles, s; Mary, d,
102.140

SHADWELL: Francis, 105.18

SHAICROSSE: John; Judith, w; Elizabeth, d,
107D.31

SHAKESFEARE:
Anne, 109.103
Manassah; Anne, w; Mary, d; John, s, 98.34

SHAKILL: Richard, bach, 108.5

SHAKLETH: Robert; Mary, w, 103.113

SHAKMAPLE: Sampson; Anne, w; Stephen,
s; Rachell, d; Elizabeth, d, 102.244

SHAKSHAFT: Mary; Henry, s, 102.143

SHALCROSSE: Henry, esq; Adigall, w;
Elizabeth, d; Katherine, d; Thomas, s,
107D.19

SHALER:
Anthony, bach, 104.137
Elizabeth, 106.38
Sarah, ser, 100.14
William, bach?, gent?, 104.137

SHALL: Walter, 109.43

SHALLEY:
Joseph, app, 98.13
William; Elizabeth, w; Martha, d, 98.13

SHALTRUM: William; Katherine, w;
William, ser; Elizabeth, d; Mary, d,
102.245

SHAMBOW: Jane, 102.239

SHAMBROOKE: Samuel; Mary, w, 107B.25

SHAMPEIRE: Mary, 98.22

SHANE: Jane, 99.43

SHANKES: Samuell; Elizabeth, w, 103.34

SHANN: Martin; Elizabeth, w; Martin, s;
Elizabeth, d; Ann, d, 102.245

SHANTLEY: John; Constant, w, 109.20

SHAPLY: John, 107A.18

SHAPTON: Rebecca, 101.41

SHARANKE: Thomas; Mary, w; Samuell, s,
103.190

SHARD: Edward; Katherine, w, 109.41

SHARFE:
Jane, 109.99
John, 104.81,109.10
John, app, 103.141
John, nurse child, 103.113
Leonell; Mary, w; Jane, d, 107A.26
Mary, 106.31
Richard; Sarah, w, 107C.41
Richard; Christian, w; John, s; Christian, d,
110.25
Robert; Elizabeth, w; Sarah, d; Robert, s,
103.79
Robert; Elizabeth, w; Elizabeth, d, 103.159
Robert, app, 102.108
Sam, ser, bach?, 104.51
Sarah; Sarah, d, 98.79
Stephen; Elizabeth, w, 107D.94
Susan, wid, 103.33
Thomas; Elizabeth, w, 107C.7
Thomas; Menesa, w; Thomas, s,
107D.37
William; Hanah, w, 103.189
William; Elizabeth, w, 109.86

SHARNELL: Mary, wid;

SHARP(E):
Bookbimder, 103.33
Adam; Eliza, w, 104.81
Durham, ser, 107B.9
Edward; Ellinor, w, 103.46
Elizabeth, 99.45
Ellizabeth, ser, 102.111,106.52

SHARPENDER: James, 107D.7

SHARPLES: Thomas, 101.32

SHARPLEY: John, 98.12

SHARRARD: Tabitha, 109.84

SHARRET: John, app, 107A.40

SHARWOOD: Elizabeth;

SHAW:
~, 103.56
Anne, 107B.43
Edmund, ser, 106.68
Elianor, 107B.41
Elizabeth, 109.24
Elizabeth, ser, 103.6
Francis; Mary, w, 103.11
Gervais, ser, 100.4
Gyles, bach, 98.70
Henry, app, 102.191
James; Anne, w; Elizabeth, d, 107B.31
James; Jane, w; Henry, ser; Priscilla, d,
  107B.31
John; Katherine, w; John, ser; Katherine, d,
  98.57
John; Mary, w; Elizabeth, d, 98.73
John; Elizabeth, w, 99.16
John; Margaret, w, 103.165
John; Elizabeth, w; Sarah, d, 107C.34
John, bach, 109.40
John, boy, 104.109
John, ser, 98.31,98.49
Jonathon; Elizabeth, w; Elizabeth, d,
  103.228
Margaret, 107B.31
Mary, 103.165
Mary, ser, 101.74,106.68
Mary, wid; Thomas, ser; John, ser, 103.92
Richard; Anne, w, 102.58
Richard; Jane, d; Elizabeth, d; Richard, ser,
  109.10
Robert; Joane, w, 102.30
Thomas, 110.24
Tho; Eliz, w; Geo, s; Anne, d; Eliz, d; Mary,
  d; Martha, d; Susanna, d,
  104.84-85
Thomas, app, 107B.57
William; Emmory, w, 103.177

SHAWELL:
Abraham; Elizabeth, w; Thomas, s; Abraham,
  s, 98.77
Thomas, gent; Jane, w; Mary, d, 98.31

SHAWLER: Mary, 101.70

SHAXBY: Mary, 109.84

SHAYLES: Anne, app, 104.25

SHEAR(E)S: Thomas; Martha, w; Martha, d,
  110.19

SHEARBORNE: william; Anne, w; William,
  s, 103.10

SHEARCROFT:
Sara, 101.1
Thomas, 101.1

SHEARS: Richard, 102.223

SHEATH: Elizabeth, 98.6

SHEBEGE: William; Elizabeth, w, 102.20

SHECKLS:
Hugh; Elizabeth, w; Stophen, s; Elizabeth, d,
  109.50
John, 109.50

SHEDALL: Mary, 109.2

SHEDRAKE:
Jacob; Elizabeth, w, 101.45
Jacob, bach, 101.45

SHEERS:
Anne; Mary, d, 104.47
Richard, ser, 106.5
Sarah, ser, 98.30
Wm, bach, 104.15,104.47

SHEERWOOD: John, 99.14

SHEFIELD:
Edw, 104.103
Edward, app, 107A.28
James; Anne, w, 107B.28
John; Mary, w; Thomas, s; Mary, d, 103.74
John, gent; Mary, w, 98.62
Mary, wid; Mary, d; Elizabeth, d; Katherine,
  d; Ann, d; Daniell, s, 109.24
Millicent; Eliz, d; Grace, d; John, s,
  104.79
Nicholas, wid; George, s; Elizabeth, d; Anne,
  d, 106.15
Robert; Elizabeth, wid, 98.65

Sarah, 107C.24
Thomas, 109.47

SHEILD:
John; Mary, wid; John, s, 107C.28
Thomas, 106.33

SHEIN: Ann, pensioner; Claudius Savage,
grand-child, 103.77

SHEIRMAN: Thomas, bach, 106.38

SHEIRS: Elizabeth, 99.45

SHELDON:
Daniell, esq, 99.44
Gilbert; Ann, wid, 103.74
Grace, ser, 98.3
Jubeth, 99.44
Mary, 99.44
Thomas, 98.17
William, 99.45
William, app, 98.32

SHELDRICK: Anne, 104.84

SHELL:
Ralph; Eliz, w; John, s, 104.57
Robert; Ellinor, w; Mary, d; John, s, 109.1

SHELLITOE:
Robt, 104.114
Wm; Eliza, w; Eliza, d, 104.83

SHELLY:
Anne; Eave, d, 98.9
John; Mary, w; John, s; Benjamin, s; Charles,
s, 103.14
Mary, 102.91

SHELMERDINE:
Robert; Mary, w, 101.75
Thomas; Agnes, w, 101.13

SHELT: Rodolphus; Elizabeth, w, 109.40

SHELTON:
Anne, ser, 107C.37
Edmund; Elizabeth, w, 107C.37
James; Mary, w; Jane, d, 98.80
Jethor; Joane, w; Margaret, d, 102.259
John, 109.77
John; Mary, w, 107B.42
Margaret, pensioner; Elizabeth, d,
106.8
Margaret, wid, 103.78
Richard, bach, esq, 106.49
Richard, ser, 107C.35
Sara; Mary, d, 101.13

William; Mary, w; William, s; Ann, d,
103.180
William; Elizabeth, w; Isabell, d, 109.17
William, ser, 107C.37

SHEMETT: John; Mary, w, 106.18

SHENTON:
Hannah, 102.20
Sam, bach, 104.110
Wooliston, 102.36

SHEPLEY: Anne; Wm, s;

SHEPPARD:
~, wid; Ralph, s; Ann, d, 109.74
Anne, 101.6,107D.13
Charles, 105.18
Char; Sarah, w, 104.25
Eden, ser, 104.8
Elizabeth, 101.4,101.30
Elizabeth, ser, 98.31
Gilbert; Martha, w; William, s; Elizabeth, d;
Martha, d; Isabella, d, 107C.36
Hannah, 102.138
Henry, 109.8
Henry; Issabell, w, 99.45
Henry, app, 103.218
James; Issabella, w, 102.140
James; Sarah, w, 107D.42
Jane, ser, 106.31
John, 109.76
John; Anne, w; Sarah, d; Mary, d, 102.74
John; Mary, w; Mary, d, 102.195
John; Elizabeth, w, 102.241
John; Jane, d, dead, 102.274
John; Hannah, w; Margaret, d; Hannah, d,
109.107
John, £600, merchant; Susanna, w; William,
ser; Elizabeth, d; Susanna, d; Mary, d;
Thomas, s, 101.56
John, app, 107D.22
John, 101.31
John, ser, 98.58,102.198
Joseph; Mary, w, 98.25
Joseph; Chtherine, w; Margaret, d; Elizabeth,
d, 109.74
Joshua, app, 102.160
Margaret, ser, 98.72
Mary, 107B.59,109.110
Mary; Elizabeth, d; Susannah, d, 109.29
Matthias; Anne, w, 98.58
Michaell; Johana, w; Jane, d, 102.147
Richard, 109.97
Richard; Sarah, w; Lydia, d, 102.114
Richard; Katherine, w; Thomas, s,
102.126
Richard; Anne, w, 104.86
Richard, bach, 109.8

Peter; Jeane, w; John, s; Katherine, d;
Thoricke, s; Jeane, d, 103.45

SHIP: Katherine, 101.63

SHIPLEY:
Edward, 101.41
Eliz, 104.73

SHIPMAN:
Elizabeth, 103.291
Mary, ser, 102.71
Samuell; Joanna, w; Samuell, s, 102.22
Winifred, ser, 106.63

SHIPPEY:
Mary, ser, 105.12
William, 102.91

SHIPSIDE: George; Dorothy, w; George, s;
Whitter, s, 106.40

SHIPTON: Joseph, wid; Esther, d,
103.122

SHIPWAY: John; Mary, w; Robert, s;
William, s; Ellinor, d, 103.107

SHIRE: Owen, app;

SHIRLEY:
~, 101.140
Eliz; Eliz, d; Mary, d; John, s, 104.67
Francis; Eliz, w, 104.58
John, app, 104.1
Sarah, a girl, 104.140

SHIRT:
Jane, ser, 106.61
Lancelott, app, 104.28

SHITTLEWOOD: John, bach, 109.7

SHIVERSTORY: Mary, 102.195

SHOEMAKER:
Abraham; Dianah, w, 103.106
Elizabeth, wid; Elizabeth, d; Aulgrine, d;
William, s, 103.45

SHOERS: Michael, a boy, 104.13

SHOOTER:
John, wid, 99.10
William, ser, 103.70

SHORE: Ann, 109.83

SHORING: Ellinor, 103.147

SHORT:
Edward; Christian, w, 109.94
Elizabeth, 109.94
Isaac, 109.94
John, 102.74
Leonard; Margrett, w, 99.25
Leonard; Mary, w; Thomas, s; John, s,
107D.42
Phillip; Agnes, w; Alice, d, 107D.76
Rebecca; George, s, 107D.44
Robert; Mary, w; Mary, d; Ellen, d, 102.29
Roger, 107C.40
Thomas, 110.26
Thomas, app, 109.30
Wm, app, ?bach, 104.28

SHORTER:
~, 107D.99
Benjamin; Alice, w; Nichas, s; Margarett, d;
William, s, 109.4
George; Elizabeth, w, 107D.66
John; Elizabeth, w, 102.139
John; Elizabeth, w; Katherine, d; Elizabeth, d,
103.22
Mary, ser, 100.13
Rebecca; Susannah, d, 109.50
Richard; Mary, w; Mary, d; Elizabeth, d,
109.55
William; Elienor, w; Richard, s, 102.140

SHORTLANDS: John; Margaret, w; Ann, d;
Elizabeth, d; Vincent, s, 109.52

SHORTRIDGE: John, wid; Elizabeth, d;
Mary, d; Sarah, d, 102.46

SHOTTON: John, ser, 103.288

SHOULDER:
Abraham, bach, 103.288
Isaac, bach, 103.288

SHOURMAN: Peter, bach, 104.9

SHOWELL:
Thomas, 101.60
William; Jane, w; Sarah, d, 109.63

SHOWRING: Wm; Eliz, w, 104.88

SHRAYHEARNE: Rachell; Rachell, d,
101.107

SHRED: Elizabeth, 101.102

SHREEFE: Anne, 102.33

SHRESHBRIDG: Thomas; Mary, w; John, s;
Thomas, s, 102.54

SHREWSBURY: William; Mary, w; Mary, d, 100.6

SHRIFE: Susan, 109.85

SHRIMPTON:
Anne, 107C.40
John; Sarah, w, 103.195
Lucrass, ser, 103.4
Richard, ser, 102.147
William, bach, under age, 103.215

SHROUDBRIG: John; Elizabeth, w, 102.83

SHUFFY: Mary, ser, 107D.54

SHUGAR: Wiilliam, wid, 99.22

SHUGSBEY: Edmond, app, 102.108

SHURKELL: Margarett, 102.182

SHURLEY:
George, app, 98.17
James; Elizabeth, w, 109.92

SHURLOW: Mary, 107C.1

SHURMER: Richard, bach, 98.35

SHURY: Joseph; Elizabeth, dead, 102.275

SHUTE:
Elizabeth, spinster, 103.41
Joyce, spinster, 103.41

SHUTTLEWORTH:
John, ser, 109.15
Mary, 109.60

SIBBERT: Margaret, 98.10

SIBITT: Edward; Anne, w, 107A.25

SIBLEY:
Daniell; Elizabeth, w; Jane, d, 98.28
Elizabeth, 109.25
Henry; Lettice, w; Edmund, s; Rebecca, d, 104.51
John, 103.58
John; Mary, w; Elizabeth, d, 102.103
John, app, 104.29
Joseph, 109.86
Thomas, bach, 98.71
Thomas, ser, 103.172

SICKSMITH: Elizabeth, 103.217

SIDDALL: Sarah, pensioner, 103.279

SIDDERN: Mary, 102.229

SIDDINS: Susanna;

SIDDON:
~, 101.76

SIDELL: George, 102.92

SIDERSON: Samuell, 106.61

SIDLEY:
Edward; Mary, w, 109.63
Elizabeth, 106.69

SIDNAM: Mary, gentlewoman, 102.78

SIEDON: Richard, wid, 106.25

SIER: Elizabeth, ser, 103.224

SIGNELL: Elizabeth, 102.55

SIGNER: Anne, ser, 106.33

SIKES, See Sykes

SILBY: Jonas; Mary, w; Mary, d, 107D.17

SILKE:
Andrew, 102.138
John, 109.68
John; Mary, w, 102.103
John, £600, wid, 102.146
Josiah, 102.138
Robert, £600; Mary, w; Martha, d; Tobias, s, 102.185
Robert, bach, under 25, 102.176
Simon; Susan, w; George, s, 102.171

SILL: Wellosborn, 110.3

SILLS: Eliza, 104.29

SILLY: Anne, ser;

SILVANUS:
~, bach, 104.135

SILVER:
John; Ann, w, 104.138
Richard, 104.138
Thomas, 109.64

SILVERWOOD: William; Blanch, w, 109.15

SILVESTER:
Anne, 102.44

Mathew; Ellinor, w; Mathew, s; William, s;
  Frances, d, 103.136
Morris; Mary, w, 102.87
Peter; Elizabeth, w; Thomas, s, 109.20
Robecca, 110.19
Robert, 103.69
Samuel; Elizabeth, w, 109.32
Sarah; Sarah, d, 106.18
Thomas, 110.18
Thomas, 110.18
Thomas; Alice, w, 102.131
William, 110.18
William; Elizabeth, w, 103.177

SINBALL: John; Mary, w, 110.12

SINDARY: Eliz, 104.18

SINER: Grace, 101.4

SINGE: Hanah, 106.38

SINGER: Mary; Rebecca, sister;

SINGLETON:
~, bach, 104.136
Elizabeth, ser, 102.182
Hester, ser, 107D.30
Jane; Alice, d, 109.63
Mary, ser, 104.116
Thomas, 106.7

SION: Mary, spinster, 103.289

SIPHER: Phillip, 107B.30

SIPTHORPE: Edmond, bach, 103.39

SIROTT: Anne, ser, 98.57

SISE: Elizabeth; Sarah, d, 98.63

SISSELL:
John; Mary, w, 102.138
Thomas; Frances, w, 101.72

SISSNOR: Mary, spinster, 103.275

SISTED: John, ser, 106.36

SITWELL: Ann, ser, 109.9

SIVERS: Penelope, ser, 106.50

SKAMTON: Robert, 102.18

SKEATE:
John, 109.73
John, bach, 102.58

SKEEMAN:
Francis; Margaret, w, 98.75
Judeth, 102.249

SKEERES: Susan, 107B.68

SKEGG: John, app, 103.60

SKELLINGTON: William, 99.27

SKELTON:
Elizabeth, ser, 103.17
Frances, ser, 104.1
Richard; Mary, w; Barbary, d; Thomas, s,
  103.143

SKEVINGTON: Wm; Eliz, w; Wm, s,
  104.28

SKILDEN: Mary, 107C.31

SKILLETT:
John, 103.62
William; Ann, w, 103.145

SKINN: John; Mary, d; James, s, 102.162

SKINNER:
Abell; Jane, w; Abell, s; Martha, d; David, s,
  107D.38
Anne, ser, 98.30
Benjamin; Jeane, w, 103.277
Christopher; Mary, w; Susan, d, 102.218
Edward; Anne, w, 102.133
Elias; Mary, w; Mary, d, 102.107
Eliza, 104.87
Frances, 107C.12
Hannah; Daniell, s; Cesar Augustus Obrian, s,
  109.102
Israell; Margarett, w; Mary, d, 102.83
John; Anne, w, 104.100
John; Elizabeth, w; Mary, d, 107C.29
Joseph; Elizabeth, w; Sarah, d; Elizabeth, d,
  102.223
Joseph; Sarah, w; Mary, d; John, s; Richard,
  s; Edward, s; Elizabeth, d, 103.81
Joseph, bach, under age, 103.81
Luke, bach, 99.49
Lyonell; Martha, w; Martha, d, 102.177
Nathaniel, 105.16
Obadiah, app, 103.21
Richard, ser, 106.58
Thomas, app, 109.108
William; Sarah, w, 102.49

SKIPP:
Francis; Judith, w; Mary, w, 107D.83
Matt; Eliz, w, 104.63
uriah; Sarah, w, 103.11

SLY:
Elizabeth, 109.42
John; Margarett, w, 99.40
Mary, ser, 107D.84
Thomas; Sarah, w; Anne, d; John, s,
102.82

SLYDER: Henry; Prudence, w; Roger, s,
109.10

SLYDUM: Elizabeth, 109.76

SMALBONE:
John; Elizabeth, w, 110.23
Mary, 102.259

SMALBONES:
Joseph; Anne, w; Thomas, s, 109.74
Patience, ser, 103.59

SMALBROOKE:
Henry; Elizabeth, w; Anne, d, 109.93
Thomas, 109.93

SMALDRIDGE: Wm; Mary, w, 104.53

SMALE: Anne, 107B.25

SMALL:
Mary, 102.15
Robt; Mary, w; Hannah, d, 104.35

SMALLBOON: Edward, 102.83

SMALLEY:
Abraham; Alice, w, 102.233
Andrew, 107C.18
Henry; Adris, d, 109.73
James; Susan, w; John, s; Elizabeth, d,
109.40
Mary; John, s, 98.72
Richard; Sarah, w, 109.40
Richard; Elizabeth, w, 110.4
Thomas, 102.63
William; Grace, w; Abraham, s; William, s,
103.178

SMALLPIECE:
Barbara, ser, 106.36
Michell; Ann, w; John, s; Susan, d,
103.260

SMALLWOOD:
Arthur; Hannah, w; Samson, s; John, s,
102.22
Dorothy, 102.77
Isaak; Mary, w, 104.23
Joseph, 109.95
Richard; Susanna, w; William, s, 98.75

SMALMAN: James; Sarah, w; Elizabeth, d;
Mary, d; Martha, d; Anne, d; Sarah, d;
Susannah, d, 98.75

SMALT: Harman; Eliz, w; Peter, s; Harman,
s; Geo, s; Eliz, d, 104.104-105

SMART:
Anne, ser, 107B.6
Elizabeth, 109.85
Francis, app, 107B.57
Henry, 102.2
John; Anne, w, 107C.2
Mary; Elizabeth, d, 107A.11
Michael; Elizabeth, w, 107B.62
Phillis, 107C.16
Richard, 102.148
Samuell, ser, 106.55
Thomas; Sarah, w; Thomas, s; Elizabeth, d;
Margaret, d; John, s; Richard, s, 103.71
William; Elizabeth, w, 98.72

SMEATH: Thomas; Mary, w; Mary, d;
Simon, s; Alice, d; Elizabeth, d;

SMEATON: ~, wid, 104.96
Anne; Jane, d, 98.72

SMEDLEY:
Anne; Anne, d, 98.37
Mary; Martha, d, 103.138

SMITE: Thomas;

SMITH:
~; ~; Elizabeth, w; John, s; Barbara, d; ~; ~,
w; ~; Anne, w; ~, wid; ~, wid; Susannah,
d; Widow Milner, d?, 104.68
Aaron, gent; Prudentia, w; Joshua, s; Aaron,
s, 106.14
Abigail, 110.30
Abraham; Margaret, w, 100.10
Abraham, ser, 103.4
Alice, 107B.33,107C.10
Alice, wid, 103.37
Andrew; Mary, w; Thomas, s; Samuell, s;
Mary, d; Elizabeth, d; Anne, d, 110.28
Anne, 107B.79
Anne; Mary, d, 104.71
Anne; David, s; Geoege, s, 107A.3
Ann; Richard, s, 109.20
Anne Rebecca, d of Walker; Rebecca, sister
of, 107B.27
Anne, spinster, 103.75
Anthony, ser, 106.57
Aquilla; Elizabeth, w, 101.78
Barnaby, 110.5
Bartholomew; Elizabeth, w; John, s, 103.214
Barth; Eliz, w; Jolly, s, 104.36

Benjamin, 99.12
Benjamin; Elizabeth, w; Thomas, s?;
   Rebeckah, d?, 99.19
Benjamin; Hanah, w; Elizabeth, d, 102.178
Benjamin; Elizabeth, w, 107A.3
Benjamin; Elizabeth, w; Benjamin, s;
   Elizabeth, d, 107B.33
Benjamin; Elizabeth, w, 107D.80
Benjamin, £600; Elizabeth, w, 106.19
Benjamin, ser, 106.4
Bentley, 109.86
Bridget, 107C.5
Caleb; Mary, w; Richard, s; Joshua, s, 98.85
Charles; Mary, w; Richard, s, 109.110
Charles, parish child, 109.5
Charles, wid, 102.158
Christopher; Hanah, w; James, s, 103.198
Cressatt, 99.12
Daniell; Ellinor, w; Hanah, d; Daniell, s;
   Ellinor, d, 103.44
Daniel; Elizabeth, w, 107A.15
Daniell, ser, 102.95
Dorothy, 100.11
Dorothy, ser, 102.201
Edward, 100.4
Edward; Elizabeth, w; John, s, 98.81
Edward; Elizabeth, w; Elizabeth, d; Rachell,
   d, 102.194
Edward; Mary, w, 104.12
Edward; Clemence, w, 107B.41
Edward, ser, 99.2
Edward, wid, 100.14
Elizabeth; Joseph, s, 101.94
Elizabeth; Elizabeth, d, 107B.4
Elizabeth, wid, pensioner, 103.15
Elizabeth, wid, 103.32,103.65
Ellinor, 104.95
Ellinor, ser, 103.287
Ellinor, spinster, 103.65
Frances, 109.25
Frances, ser, 99.3
Francis; Mary, w, 98.77
Francis; Mary, w; Susan, d; Elizabeth, d;
   Anne, d; Richard, s, 101.69
Francis, £600; Martha, w; Frances Saunders,
   niece of, 103.1
Francis, assessor, 103.293
Francis, ser, 103.245,109.90
George, 105.16,107B.19
George; Jane, w; George, s; Cyrus Lawe?, s?;
   Elizabeth, d, 98.27
George; Mary, w, 101.59
George; Ruth, w, 102.264
George; Anne, w; George, s; Elizabeth, d,
   107A.24
George, ser, 106.2
Grace, 98.36
Guy; Margaret, w; Mary, d, 102.192
Hannah, 102.134,103.98

Hannah; Elizabeth, d; Anne, d, 101.57
Hannah, pensioner; Elizabeth, d, 103.196
Hannah, ser, 104.82
Henry; Jane, w; Jane, d, 99.46
Henry; Elizabeth, w, 101.23
Henry; Mary, w; Daniell, s, 104.23
Henry; Margaret, w, 107D.4
Henry, app, 103.112
Henry, parish child, 109.63
Hercules, a boy, 104.65
Hugh; Margarett, w, 102.154
Hugh; Anne, w; Hugh, s; John, s, 110.6
Humphry; Elizabeth, w; Elizabeth, d, 103.66
Humphry, ser, 103.287
Hurd; Ann, w; Mary, d; Sarah, d, 106.25
Isaac, commissioner, 109.112
Izabellah, 98.81
James; Violett, w; Barbara, d, 102.157
James; Elizabeth, w; Joseph, s; Martha, d,
   103.33
James; Kathrine, w; Jeane, d; Jerymiah, s;
   Sarah, d; Hanah, d; Mary, d, 103.59
James; Mary, w; Sarah, d; John, s; Mary, d,
   103.135
James; Jane, w; Jane, d, 107C.11
James; Hannah, w; Elizabeth, d; John, s;
   Anne, d; Mary, d, 106.30
James; Elinor, w; James, s, 109.50
James, £600; Mary, w, 103.277
James, app, 104.41
James, bach, 104.41
James, commissioner, 106.69,110.37
James, gent, £600; Elizabeth, w; Athania,
   niece of, 104.4
James Robert, son of Nend, 107A.33
John, brother of, 107A.33
Joseph, brother of, 107A.33
Jane, 102.170,102.253
Jane, ser, 107A.39
Joanah, ser, 102.153
Joane, 102.167
John; Sarah, d; Henry, s; Mary, d, 98.26
John; Anne, w, 98.42
John; Anne, w; John, s, 98.51
John; Anne, w, 98.55
John; Elizabeth, w; John, s?; Elizabeth, d?,
   99.56
John; ~, w; John, s, 100.8
John; Mary, w; Mary, d; Thomas, s, 101.25
John; Mary, w, 101.42
John; Elizabeth, w, 101.84
John; Sarah, w, 102.40
John; Anne, w, 102.171
John; Elizabeth, w; Benjamin, s, 102.224
John; Mary, w, 102.225
John; Anne, w; Elizabeth, d, 102.251
John; Sarah, w, 103.26
John; Elizabeth, w; Mary, d, 103.102
John; Jeane, w, 103.243

Robert; Katherine, w; Katherine, d;
Elizabeth; Benjamin, s, 101.15

SNOWDEN:
John, 109.47
Jos; Mary, w; Tho, s; Chas, s; Jos, s; Mary, d,
104.20
Joshua; Sarah, w; Susanna, d; Mary, d, 109.65
Mary, ser, 98.64

SNOWSMARY: Tho; Martha, w; Olive, d;

SOABER:
~, Mrs, 98.51

SOAMES:
George; Ann, w; Henry, s; Ann, d, 103.67
John, 99.31
Mary, 101.28

SOANE: Elizabeth, ser, 106.31

SOARE: Sara, 101.67

SOARES:
Hester, 110.15
James, wid; Susanah, d; Sarah, d, 103.168

SOEWELL: Rander, 105.4

SOFLA:
Anthony, 102.124
Joseph, 102.124

SOFTLY: Jane, a child, 107D.97

SOLAR: Stephen, wid, 110.22

SOLE: Alice, 109.53

SOLESBY: John, app, 107D.24

SOLOMON: Charles; Elizabeth, w, 109.75

SOLUE?: Mary, ser, 109.105

SOMERFORD: John, 101.36

SOMERS:
Anne, 101.44,102.255
Henry, 106.13
John, ser, 106.13

SOMERSETT:
Mary, ser, 98.37
Richard; Elizabeth, w, 105.5

SOMERTON: Edward; Margarett, w,
110.8

SOMES: Aathur; Anne, w; Arthur, s;

SOMMER: ~, 98.57
William, 98.30

SOMMERBY: Temple, app, 98.24

SOMMERSOME: Eliza; John, ?s; Anne, ?d,
104.70

SOMNER:
Elizabeth; Thomas, s; Elizabeth, d, 98.51
Elizabeth, gentlewoman; Henry, 98.67
Mary, gentlewoman, 98.44

SOOLEY: John; Mary, w; Mary, d, 101.73

SOPER: Thomas, his wife not with him,
103.271

SORRIVEN: John; Elizabeth, w; Sarah, d,
98.23

SORRYLL: John; Hanah, w, 103.112

SORY: Mary, ser, 106.29

SOUCH:
Ann, 110.5
Arthur, bach, 98.39
Joseph; Mary, w, 106.59
Mary, 110.5
William, 110.5

SOUIBB:
Esther, ser, 103.245
William; Mary, w; John, s; James, s; Mary, d,
103.57

SOUTH:
Elizabeth, 107A.17
Hannah, ser, 106.15
John; Mary, w; John, s; William, s; Joseph, s,
107D.62
William;

SOUTHBY:
~, bach, gent, 104.1
Richard; Elizabeth, w; Elizabeth, d, 101.83
Susan, 106.29

SOUTHEAN:
~, wid; Jeane, d, 103.67
John; Mary, w, 102.224
John; Margaret, w; John, s; George, s;
Rigden, s, 103.119

SOUTHEN:
Anne, ser, 102.246

Elizabeth, 107D.89
James; Elizabeth, w, 103.82
John; Margaret, w, 101.46
Richard, £600, bach, 108.3

SOUTHERLAND:
Margaret, 106.64
Tho, £600, bach, 104.107

SOUTHERN:
Rebecca, wid; Josiah, s, 103.32
Robert; Ursula, w, 107D.7
Sarah; Sarah, d, 98.76
Wm; Eliza, w, 104.95

SOUTHEY:
Alexander, 105.16
Henry; Elizabeth, w, 110.4

SOUTHSUN: Katherine, 102.30

SOUTHWELL:
Edward, gent; Frances, w; Edward, s, 98.42
Hannah, wid, 102.44
Humphrey; Eliz, w; Valentine, s; Marg, d;
 Mary, d, 104.120
Susanah, 102.106
William; Mary, w; Daniell, s; Samuell, s,
 106.66

SOUTHWORTH: Francis; Mary, w; Francis,
 s; Elizabeth, d, 105.8

SOWARD:
Hannah, 109.33
John, bach, 109.33
William; Ann, w, 103.206

SOWDEN: Daniel; Catherine, w; Daniel, s;
 John, s; Catherine, d, 109.62

SOWELL:
Ann, ser, 103.287
?John; Alice, w; Alice, d; John, s,
 103.77

SOWERBY:
Hanna, wid, £600; Hanna, d; Samuell, s,
 101.88
William; William, s; Mary, d, 98.10

SOWERSBY: Alice, ser; John, app; Richard,
 bach, 98.78

SOWND: Richard, bach, 102.16

SOWTHING: John; Mary, w, 103.82

SPACKMAN: Elizabeth, 109.32

SPAKEMAN: Thomas, app, 102.183

SPARHANKE:
John, 102.266
William, 102.266

SPARING: Benjamin; Mary, w, 105.10

SPARKEMAN: John; Alice, w; John, s,
 101.11

SPARKES:
Chris, gent; Eliz, w; Tho, s; Chris, s; Arthur,
 s; Eliz, d; Magdalen, d; Mary, d, 104.111
Dorothy, 110.33
Edward; Joane, w, 106.63
Elizabeth, 102.87,109.85
James, app, 98.12
John; Mary, w, 107A.24
Margarett, 110.33
Mary, 109.23
Mary, ser, 98.64
Percevall; Elizabeth, w; Katherine, d, 109.5
Thomas; Ruth, w; Christopher, s; Mary, d;
 Elizabeth, d, 102.235
Thomas; Mary, w, 103.109
Thomas; Elizabeth, w, 103.115
Thomas; Mary, w, 109.90
Thomas; Anne, w, 109.91
Thomas, app, 98.8
Thomas, ser, 103.13,106.23
Wm; Margery, w, 104.48

SPARLING: Anne, 107C.32

SPARROW:
Daniel, bach, 104.59
George, 102.83
Jane, 109.98
John; Hannah, w; John, s; Samuell, s;
 Joshuah, s; Mary, d, 102.106
John; Mary, w; Jerimiah, s; Mary, d, 103.129
Sarah, ser, 98.59

SPATCHURST: Symon; Katherine, w,
 110.19

SPATTON: Elizabeth, ser, 103.67

SPEADMAN: Elizabeth, wid; Robert, s,
 102.19

SPEAKE: Richard; Mary, w, 107A.1

SPEAKMAN:
Richard, app, 109.100
Thomas; Anne, w, 107C.1

SPECKS: Wm, ser, 104.14

STANFORD:
Alice, 99.26
William; Matha, w, 107D.44

STANHOP: Robert; Elizabeth, w, 106.10

STANLEY:
Alice, wid; Alice, d; Sarah, d, 109.75
Anne, 107B.26
Dorothy, ser, 108.7
Edward; Millecent, w; Edward, s,
   102.130
Elinor, 99.25
John, 109.72
John; Sarah, w; Sarah, d, 102.167
John; Lettice, w, 104.37
John; Martha, w, 104.57
Katherine, 107A.4
Marg, 104.20
Richard; Elizabeth, w; Pleasant, d, 102.19
Samuel, 109.61
Samuel, ser, 105.16
William, 101.90
William; Mary, w; Mary, d, 103.252
William; Abigale, w; Kathrine, d, 109.31

STANNAWAY:
Elizabeth, 107B.43
Richard; Mary, w; Richard, s; Margaret, d,
   102.121

STANNING: Thomas, 109.12

STANNION: Anne, ser, 98.39

STANTON:
Anne, 107B.3,109.96
Anne, ser, 105.14
Benjamin, ser, 107D.87
Jane, ser, 106.52
John, 110.28
John; Mary, w, 98.49
John; Sarah, w; Edward, s, 102.160
John, £600, wid, 107B.66
John, app, 102.114
John, bach, 107A.36
Nathaniel, app, 107D.19
Richard, 98.49
Richard; Elizabeth, w, 107D.52
Samuel, 109.50
Samuell; Ann, w; Mary, d; Jarvis, s;
   Catherine, d; Cellum, d, 103.170
Samuell, £600, wid, 98.72
Susannah, 98.64
Thomas, 107B.76
Thomas, bach, 98.53
William; Dorothy, w; Edward, s, 98.24
William; Mary, w, 98.48
Wm; Mary, w, 104.22

William, gent; Margaret, w; Rebeccah, d;
   Elizabeth, d, 98.64
William, ser, 103.5

STANWORTH:
Elizabeth, 109.109
Richard, wid, 109.109

STAPE: John, 102.72

STAPLEFORT: William, bach, under age,
   103.270

STAPLER:
Robert, 105.17
Sarah, ser, 107D.60

STAPLERTON:
Eliz, 104.88
Marg, 104.88

STAPLES:
Anne, 107B.50
Anne; Anne, d, 107B.33
Dorothy, ser, 107D.93
Gartrite; Joseph, s, 107C.14
John; Jane, w; John, s, 107B.81
Mary, 102.236
Nicholas, 102.70
Richard, 102.23
Samuell, bach, 106.49
Thomas, 102.95

STAPLETON: Thomas; Anne, w; William, s;
   Anne, d, 107C.15

STAPLEY:
Elizabeth, 102.96
Thomas; Barbary, w; Richard, s; Mary, d,
   102.96

STAPLOE: John; Katherine, w; John, s,
   101.91

STARBIN: Henry; Elizabeth, w; Repentance,
   d; Thomas, s; Dorothy, d, 101.90

STARBUCK: John; Mary, w, 107C.11

STARKE: Ann, wid, 103.108

STARKEY:
Charles, app, 107A.33
Henry, app, 109.25
William, ser, 109.9

STARLING:
Anne; Elizabeth, d; William, s; Henry, s,
   107D.74

Humpld?, 101.87
John, bach, 102.56
Mary, pensioner; Francis, s; Anthony, s,
103.220
William; Elizabeth, w; William, s, 103.67
William; Elianor, w; Elizabeth, d; Mary, d,
107B.55

STARR:
James; John, s, 104.146
James, ser, 107C.37
William, 106.5

STASELY: Hanna, 101.10

STASMORE: Mary, 109.79

STATE: Richard, ser, 106.25

STATEHAM: Daniel; Katherine, w;
Elizabeth, d, 98.3

STATON: Mary; Wm, s; Mary, d, 104.42

STAVELY:
Anne, 101.55
Arthur, £600; Barbary, w; Martha, d,
103.73
Jane, 101.8
Nicholas; Elizabeth, w, 101.78
Richard, ser, bach, 98.45

STAVERTON: Deodatus, £600, bach,
108.7

STAYNER: Anthony; Margarett, w; Kathrine,
d; Richard, s, 102.157

STEABIN: William; Jeane, w, 103.87

STEACEY:
Joane, wid; Mary, d; William, s, 103.36
Mary, spinster, 103.38

STEAD: Elizabeth; Benjamin, s; Joseph, s;
Ann, d, 106.14

STEALE: Sandere, 99.28

STEARNE: Mary, wid, 103.51

STEARS: Elizabeth, 109.26

STEBBING:
Robert; Sarah, w; Robert, s; Sarah, d; Anne,
d, 106.43
William, 99.28

STEBBINS: Lycias, ser, 104.10

STEDMAN:
Elizabeth, ser, 98.42
Nathaniel, 102.52
Reginold;

STEED(E):
~, wid, 101.48
John, app, 98.72
John, bach, 105.3
Thomas Chamberline, 103.4

STEELE:
Anne, 104.95
Daniell; Elizabeth, w; Daniell, s; Elizabeth, d;
Jeane, d, 103.35
Dosephens, app, 103.70
Elizabeth, 102.110,103.38
James, 102.74
Mary, ser, 104.24
Richard; Susan, w, 107D.52
Robert; Jane, w; Sara, d, 101.8
Thomas, bach, 98.61
Thomas, clerk, 98.29
William, 109.15

STEER:
Jone, 107D.21
Thomas; Margarett, w; Elizabeth, d?, 99.20

STEERS:
John; Eliz, w; Eliz, d, 104.112
Thomas, 99.45

STEFPHALL: Mary, 107B.48

STENNETT:
Anthony, 110.13
Jane; Rowland, s; Robert, s, 109.9
Mary; Mary, d, 109.10

STENT: Jane, 105.7

STEPNY: Frances, ser, 108.2

STERK: Anthony; Dorothy, w, 107D.98

STERNS: John, app, 102.132

STERRY: Joseph;

STEVENS:
~, 102.36
Alexander, 106.45
Alice, 104.65
Anne, 109.24
Anne; John, s; Joseph, s, 107D.35
Anthony; Elizabeth, w; John, s, 102.244
Dorothy; Thomas, s; Christopher, s, 107B.64
Dorothy, ser, 98.67

STIBBS: Marcus; Jeane, w, 103.96

STICHER: Thomas; Mary, d, 102.236

STIDMAN: Thomas, 107D.98

STIFF(E):
Barbara, ser, 101.109
Francis, pensioner, 103.221

STIFFE:
Isaac, app, 101.78
Thomas; Margaret, w, 102.146

STIGMAN: James; Elizabeth, w; Elizabeth,
d; Sarah, d, 107B.47

STILE:
Anne, 101.19
Mary, 109.81
Patranella, 105.9

STILEMAN: Isaac; Elizabeth, w; Elizabeth,
d; Mary, d; Sarah, d, 109.78

STILER: Joyce, 98.21

STILES:
Anne, 107A.11,100.18
Benjamin; Mary, w; Thomas, s; Mary, d, 103.267
Bridget, 107D.75
Dorothy, 102.131
Edward; Mary, w; Ann, d?; Peter, s?, 99.36
Elizabeth, 109.2
Henry; Anne, w, 107C.23
James; Sarah, w; Edward, s; Priscilla, d;
    Elizabeth, d, 102.128
John; Rachell, w; Mary, d; Rebecca, d, 102.27
John; Grace, w, 103.161
John, app, 107A.2
John, ser, 106.22
Nathaniell, 109.74
Robert; Esther, w; Esther, d; Mary, d, 103.88
Sarah, pensioner, 103.77
Susan, 101.23
Thomas; Mary, w, 107C.25
Thomas, ser, 107C.23
William, 102.132
William, app, 98.48
William, ser, 103.225

STILGOE: Zacheriah; Anne, w; Anne, d;
    Zacheriah, s, 107C.13

STILL: Francis, app, 104.101

STILLMAN:
Elizabeth, ser, 107A.2
John, 102.113

STILLYMAN: Jane, ser, 107B.11

STINT:
Anne, ser, 98.67
Francis; Mary, w, 109.51
John, bach, 102.2
Joseph, gent; Elinor, w; Elinor, d, 98.43
Peter, bach, 106.58

STINTON: John; Sarah, w, 107B.14

STINTSON: Anne, ser, 107B.14

STIRKE: Samuell; Ann, w; Samuell, s;
    Joseph, s; Mary, d, 103.27

STIRRUF:
Elizabeth, 102.173
Rachell, 102.173
Thomas, 102.173
Thomas; Jane, w; Thomas, s; Jane, d; Anne,
    d; Mary, d, 101.20

STIRUNT: Henry; Mary, w;

STISTED:
~, 104.10

STNDFAST: Richard, 106.57

STOAKER: Anne, ser, 98.28

STOAREY: Mary, wid, pensioner, 103.16

STOCK:
Elizabeth, pensioner, 103.199
John; Margarett, w; Jacob, s; Jaboss, s; Sarah,
    d; Ruth, d, 102.209
Mary, 101.46
Richard; Elizabeth, w; Jane, d, 102.117
William; Elizabeth, w; Thomas, s,
    103.134

STOCKDEN:
Catherine, 109.102
Joanna, wid; John, s, 102.48
Sarah, 99.45

STOCKEN:
John, living in grubb-street, collector,
    107B.82
Thomas; Anne, w, 107D.17

STOCKEORTH:
Joseph, 99.46
Richard, 99.46
Sarah, 99.46

STOCKER: Obediah, app, 104.3

STOURCH: Matthew; Elizabeth, w;
Katherine, d; Martha, d; Edward, s,
98.87

STOURMAN: Mary; James, s, 98.4

STOURT: Thomas; Elizabeth, w; Elizabeth,
d, 98.57

STOWE: John, 102.30

STOWERS: Robert; Elizabeth, w; William, s,
98.11

STOY: Elizabeth, 107A.9

STOYDEN: William; Margaret, w, 106.24

STRABERRY: John, 109.33

STRADLEY: George, 105.6

STRADWAY: John, 102.51

STRAITE: John; Jane, w;

STRANGE:
~, Mrs; Eliz, d, 104.138
Edward; Elizabeth, w; Edward, s; Elizabeth,
d; Mary, d, 101.79
Elizabeth, 101.81
John; Mary, w, 104.101
John; Margaret, w, 107D.58
Nich, £600; Millicent, w; Millicent, d; Eliz,
d; Mary, d; Nich, s, 104.91
Sam; Susanna, w; Cornelius, s; Mary, d,
104.38
Sarah, 107B.65
William, 99.9

STRANGER:
Charles; Mary, w, 107A.14
Mary, 109.39
Sarah, 109.38
Sarah, wid; Sarah, d; Elizabeth, d,
103.3

STRANGWIDGE: Henry; Mary, wid;
Hannah, d, 109.49

STRATFORD:
Charles; Margaret, w, 109.50
Elizabeth, 99.25
Marg, ser, 104.33
Thomas; Margaret, w, 100.10

STRATTON:
Elizabeth, 99.30
Frances; Henry, ser, 107A.17

Joseph; Margaret, w; Anthony, s; Elizabeth, d;
Margarett, d; Mary, d; Joseph, s; John, s,
109.71
Marke, 101.110
Marke, £600; Anne, d; Hannah, d; Nathaniell,
s; William, s, 101.86
Selin, 109.69

STRAYHEARNE:
Elizabeth, ser, 101.57
Henry; Elizabeth, w; George, s; Henry, s;
Rebecca, d, 101.50

STREAME: Thomas; Mary, w; Elizabeth, d;
Mary, d, 103.24

STREAMES: Henry; Mary, w; Mary, d;
William, s, 109.85

STREETE:
Ann, ser, 103.21
Elizabeth, 99.48,106.64
Elizabeth; Joseph, s; Samuel, s, 107B.38
Elizabeth, child, 102.7
James, 102.14
John, ser, 107A.15
Richard, 106.36
Roger, wid, £600; Roger, s, 103.290
Susan, 109.111
William, £600; Frances, w, 103.21

STREIKLAND: Jane, 98.79

STRETCH: John; Elinor, w; Mary, d, 98.12

STRETTON:
Daniell; Jane, w; William, s; Mary, d, 102.254
Elizabeth, 98.52
John, ser, 100.11
Joseph, app, 101.107
William; Anne, w; Anne, d; Sarah, d, 100.11
William, assessor, 100.15

STRICKLAND:
Charles, 109.95
Elizabeth, ser, 109.80

STRIGLEY: John, bach, 99.19

STRIGWOOD: Thomas; Dorcas, w, 102.131

STRINGER:
Elizabeth, 102.191
John; Margaret, w; John, s; Dorothy, d;
Joseph, s, 102.180
John; Ann, w; Jacob, s, 103.155
Joseph, ser, 106.52
Martha, 107D.3
Mary, ser, 101.75

Samuell, £600; Lucey, w; Samuell, ser; Lucey, d, 103.1
William; Sara, w; Thomas, s; Mary, d, 101.71
William; Elizabeth, w; John, s, 109.41

STRINGFELLOW: John; Elizabeth, w, 101.82

STRONG:
Daniel, 109.48
David, app, 103.158
John, 105.17
Ralph; Elizabeth, w, 107C.3
Richard; Mary, w, 109.105
William, ser, 106.54

STROOD: Thomas; Katherine, w; Mary, d, 102.58

STROTTON: Francis, 102.266

STROUD:
Abraham; Martha, w; Ann, d, 109.34
Edw; Sarah, w, 104.34
Feby, 102.238
Marg, 104.76
Richard, wid, 106.58
Willawbee, bach, under age, 103.186

STROULGER: Jobe; Elizabeth, w; William, s, 102.102

STRUDE: John; Jooane, w; Joseph, s; Elizabeth, d, 102.26

STRUDNER: Richard; Elizabeth, w, 103.94

STRUDWICKE:
George; Martha, w, 109.42
John; Phebe, w, 109.44
William, Mr, £600 or £50 p.a.; Jane; w; Jane, d; Lucy, s?, 109.43
William, commissioner, 109.112,99.60

STRUGLES: Benjamin; Elizabeth, w, 103.41

STRUTT:
Margarett, 109.81
William, ser, 109.7

STRUTTON:
Benjamin; Frances, w, 98.5
Hanah, ser, 103.60
John; Elizabeth, w; Elizabeth, d, 103.247
Sarah, ser, 103.60

STUBB: Anne, ser, 107A.3

STUBBORNE: Anne, ser, 98.71

STUBBS:
Grace, 98.51
John; Elizabeth, w; John, s; Elizabeth, d; William, s, 107C.26
John, ser, 100.10
Joseph; Elizabeth, w, 102.101
Mary, ser, 100.13

STUBERFEILD: Thomas; Ann, w; John, s, 103.266

STUDDS: John; Anne, w, 107B.40

STUDHAM: Ann, 100.9

STUDHOLM: John, app, 102.79

STUDLEY: John, 101.21

STUKNER: Thomas, 109.75

STUNSTONE: Francis, 107B.57

STURGEN: Richard, app, 102.84

STURGER: John; Christian, w, 110.12

STURGES:
Edward; Mary, w; Thomas, s; Edward, s, 102.88
Henry; Sarah, w; Mary, d, 107C.2
Lydiah, ser, 102.147
William; Lettice, w, 102.215

STURMEY:
Edward; Elizabeth, w; Elizabeth, d, 106.63
Thomas, bach, 106.65

STURNEE: Mary, wid, pensioner, 103.15

STURT:
John; Mary, w, 107D.88
Joseph; Elizabeth, w; Joseph, s?; John, s?; Alexander, s?; Mary, d?; Elizabeth, d?; Anne, d?; Richard, s?; Robert, s?, 99.8
Mary, ser, 103.10

STURTON: John, bach; Samuell, his brother, 106.65

STURWOOD: Dorothy, 109.6

STUTTER: John; Mary, w; Wm, s; Mary, d; Jane, d; Eliz, d; Susanna, d, 104.53

STYES: William, 104.60

STYHAM: Wm; Eliz, w, 104.76

SWINNOCK: Michael; Barbary, w, 109.80

SWINSTEED: Richard, £600; Anne, w;
  Thomas, s; Sarah, d, 102.133

SWINTON: William; Anne, w, 107D.8

SWOMTON0: Thomas; Christiana, w, 110.9

SWYNN: Mary, ser, 98.36

SYDDEY: Richard; Dorothy, w, 98.63

SYKERNE: Timothy; Joanna, w; Robert, ser;
  Johanna, d, 102.227

SYKES:
Darcas, 102.2
Geo; Anne, w; Mary, d, 104.144
Grace, 102.241
James, a child, 102.52
John; Katherine, w; John, s; Edward, s,
  107B.20
Thomas; Susanna, w; Susanna, d, 101.65
Wm; Mary, w; Eliz, d; Mary, d, 104.7

SYLE: Margarett, 109.82

SYMCOX: Mary, 101.33,101.82

SYMES, See Simes

SYMON:
Greenestreete, wid; Symon, s, 98.63
John, £600; Katherine, w; Thomas, s; John, s;
  Rebecca, d, 104.34

SYNIER: Cassandra, ser, 104.34

TABOTT: Mary, 109.63

TACKER: Anne, ser, 98.24

TACLOCK: Thomas; Elizabeth, w,
  103.195

TAFT: Sarah, 106.61

TALBOTT:
Ann, ser, 103.283
Anthony; Arabella, w, 105.5
Thomas; Jeane, w; Susan, d, 103.235
William; Mary, w; William, ser; Anne, d;
  Mary, d, 102.197

TALEBY: Anne, 104.80

TALLENT:
Elizabeth, ser, 107A.26

Margaret; Frances, d, 107B.62
Thomas, app, 107D.50

TALLEY: Charles; Rebecca, w, 104.20

TALLFOOT:
James, 102.108
James; Joannah, w, 102.92

TALLIS:
Emma, 99.48
John; Emma, w; Emma, d; Ann, d; Elizabeth,
  d; John, s; Joseph, s, 103.35

TALLOW: Robert; Ruth, w; Elizabeth, d, 109.68

TALVER: John; Isabella, w; Joshua, s; Mary,
  d; Ellen, d, 107A.14

TAME: Mary, 107D.49

TANDY:
Anne; Frances, d; Hester, d, 107D.45
Henry; Sarah, w; Sarah, d, 107D.46
Margaret, 107B.37
Mary, 107B.36
Richard; Mary, w, 107B.33

TANNER:
Edward, ser, 109.6
Eliza, 104.17
Hannah, 109.4
James, 109.81
James; Mary, w, 102.175
Joan, 109.68
John, 110.27
Joseph, 103.215
Mary, 103.272,109.66
Mary, app, 98.15
Samuell; Martha, w, 103.61
Tho; Joane, w; John, s; Marg, d, 104.113
Thomas; Alice, w; Thomas, s, 106.14
William; Rebecca, w, 109.104

TANT:
Elizabeth, 109.109
John; Sarah, w; George, s; Elizabeth, d;
  Mary, d; Ann, d, 109.63
Mary, 109.109

TANTON:
Mary; Anne, grand-d of, 107B.78
Tho; Hannah, w, 104.18

TAPLEY: Elizabeth, 109.2

TAPP:
Mary, ser, 103.3
William, app, 103.54

TAPPERTOE: Edward; Mary, w, 107B.70

TAPPS: Jane, 101.81

TAPSLEY: Anne, 110.21

TARBUAK: Robert; Anne, w, 98.62

TARBUCK: John; Ester, w; Edward, s?,
99.43

TARLES: Lidia, 102.107

TARNER:
Elizabeth, 110.25
John, 110.25

TARRANT:
Hugh; Elizabeth, w; Mary, d, 109.111
Thomas; Elizabeth, d; Mary, d, 98.22
Thomas; Jane, w; Thomas, s; Jane, d,
110.33

TARRATT: Joseph, 109.54

TARRETT: Jane; Benjamin, s; Hannah, d,
109.110

TARREY: Hester, 102.255

TART:
Beatris, 102.170
John; Judith, w, 107B.74
Richard; Sarah, w; John, s, 100.2
Susan; John, s, 102.127
William, 100.8

TARVIN: Mary, ser, 106.28

TASH: John, ser, bach?, 104.27

TASKER:
James; Anne, w; Mary, d, 110.1
James, parish child, 103.280
Jane, 107C.23
John, 107C.18
Rowland; Martha, w; Sarah, d, 102.202
Thomas, 107C.35

TASSELL:
Mary, 103.235
Ursula, 103.235

TATE:
Elizabeth, 109.51
Exan, ser, 98.24
John; Sarah, w; Sarah, d; Mary, d,
107B.59
Robert; Mary, w, 107B.46

TATEHAM: Thomas; Sarah, w; George, s;
Anne, d, 98.10

TATEMAN: Agnilla; Hanah, w; William, s,
107B.6

TATHAM: William; Catherine, w; William, s,
110.10

TATLOCK:
Henry, ser, 104.10
Hester, ser, 101.95

TATMAN: Susan, pensioner, 103.75

TATNELL:
Jessper, app, 103.6
Margaret, 101.32
Mary, wid, 103.9
Thomas; Anne, w; Thomas, s; Elizabeth, d,
109.107

TATNOM:
Ann, 102.234
Henry, 102.234

TATTERSALL: Grace, 101.2

TATUME: Mary, 109.30

TAVERNER:
Elizabeth, ser, 107D.62
Michael; Mary, w; John, s, 109.40
Samuel; Jane, w; Thomas, s?, 99.13
Susan, 107B.38

TAW: Jane, ser, 104.92

TAWMAN: William; Elizabeth, w, 102.236

TAWNEY:
Martha, ser, 107A.4
Ursula, 98.63

TAY: Richard; Mary, w;

TAYLOR:
~, wid; ~, child, 103.249
Abigail, 102.119
Abraham, 102.60
Alderne; Ann, w, 103.22
Alexander; Elizabeth, w; Elizabeth, d;
Thomas, s, 102.82
Amey; Elizabeth, d; Amey, d; Rebecca, d,
107A.34
Anne; Hannah, d; Patience, d, 109.45
Anne, ser, 101.105,106.51
Anne, wid, 103.87
Benjamin; Judith, w, 107D.89

William, 99.23,105.16
William; Mary, w, 102.247
William; Mary, w; William, s, 103.2
William; Hanah, w; Hanah, d; Elizabeth, d;
 William, s; John, s, 103.130
William, £600; Martha, w, 104.29
William, app, 107A.21,107A.38
William, ser, 98.69,100.4

TEA: John; Mary, w, 104.8

TEAGUE:
Eliza, a child, 104.44
Jane; ~, s, 104.66

TEARE: Elizabeth, ser, 103.89

TEAT: Elizabeth, pensioner; Sarah, d, 103.47

TEBBATT: Bennony; Ann, w, 109.50

TEDDAR: Martha, 98.56

TEDDER: Stephen; Ann, w; Jeane, d, 103.99

TEDHAM: Hannah, ser, 98.88

TEDMAN:
John, 107D.58
Sarah; Anne, d; Elizabeth, d, 107B.22

TEERES: Elizabeth, 102.176

TEGGE: Elizabeth, 102.4

TEILURE:
John, gent, wid; Frances, d, 98.30
John, ser, 106.26

TELEWER: William; Elizabeth, w; Dorothy,
 d; Elizabeth, d, 98.39

TEMPEST: James; Elizabeth, w,
 102.200

TEMPLE:
Anne, ser, 101.60
Christmas, 110.15
Elizabeth, 110.23
John; Dorothy, w; James, s, 110.23
Mary, 101.44
Thomas; Mary, w; Mary, d, 109.15

TEMPLEMAN:
Dorothy, 109.69
Thomas, 109.43

TEMPLER:
Ellinor, 103.183

Robert; Elizabeth, w; Elizabeth, d; Rebecca,
 d, 103.81

TENAY: William, 102.246

TENCH:
Edward; Mary, w; Mary Pinson, d, 109.104
Joseph; Ann, w, 104.132

TENDRILL: Chas; Ann, w; Chas, s; Sarah, d,
 104.132

TENNANT:
James; Elizabeth, w, 99.45
John, at sea; Ann, w; Stephen, s; Mary, d;
 Joph, s; Elizabeth, d, 103.68
Thomas, 102.226
William, bach, 98.74

TENNETT: Thomas, app, 103.131

TENNEY: Ezechia; Jane, w; Jacob, s; Susan,
 d; Jane, d; Sarah, d, 102.238

TERBOX: Emma, 101.104

TERRETT:
Deborah; Deberah, d; Mary, d; Elianor, d;
 Hester, d, 107B.42
Rebecca, ser, 106.49

TERRILL:
Ann, pensioner; Benjamin, s; Joseph, s,
 103.64
David; Mary, w, 101.73
Elizabeth, 99.9
Joseph; Mary, w, 103.23
Joseph; Margaret, w; Martha, d, 109.88
Robert; Mary, w; Thomas Collet, s, 103.285
Susannah, ser, 98.66

TERRINGTON: William, ser, 107D.27

TERRITT:
Daniel, app, 103.228
William; Mary, w; Ann, d; Benjamin, s; Ruth,
 d, 103.248

TERRY:
Alice, ser, 98.44
Ann, wid; Robert, s, 103.73
Edward, 109.37
Edward; Elizabeth, w; Ellen, d, 102.49
Edward, bach, 103.288
Elizabeth, 109.5
Henry, ser, 100.4
James; Jeane, w; James, s; Robert, s; Jeane, d,
 103.123
John; Martha, w, 103.146

John; Katherine, w; John, s, 107B.47
Mary, 101.32
Michaell, gent; Elizabeth, w, 98.29
Nath; Cicilia, w; Mary, d; Anne, d; Judith, s,
   104.109
Rebecca, 107A.12
Richard, 102.45
Robert; Rachell, w, 99.27
Robert; Joane, w, 102.50
Roger; Elizabeth, w; Ann, d?, 99.49
Samuell, £600; Mary, w; Samuell, s; John, s;
   Elizabeth, d; Mary, d, 102.113
Sarah, 107B.24
Susan, 107D.30
Thomas, 107B.48
Thomas; Anne, w, 109.71
William, nurse child, 103.259

TERVELL: Martha, 109.86

TESMOND: Michaell, £50 p.a.; Audery, w,
   106.33

TESSTASS: Aron; Mary, w, 103.271

TEST: Sarah, 107B.43

TEW:
Edward; Sarah, w; Sarah, d, 98.18
Edward; Margaret, w; Francis, clerk, grand-
   son of, 98.36
Elizabeth, 101.36
Hanna, 101.22

TEWSLY: Martha, 98.17

TEY:
John; Dorothy, w; Mary, d, 107D.97
Richard; Elizabeth, w; Elizabeth, d,
   102.102
Richard, app, 107D.97
Thomas; Fenix, d, 102.224

THACKAREY: John; Frances, w; Robert, s?;
   Mary, d?;

THACKER:
~; ~, w; ~, s; ~, d, 104.118
Francis, 109.101
James; Margarett, w, 110.10
John; Elizabeth, w; Elizabeth, d, 109.90
Mary, ser, 106.40

THACKHAM:
James; Ursula, w, 101.12
William; Prudence, w; William, s; Martha, d,
   110.35

THACKLADY: Jane, 101.87

THACKSTONE: Mary, ser, 103.166

THAFTER: Elizabeth, ser, 102.146

THAIR(E):
Arthur, pensioner, 103.77
Robert, £600; Sarah, w, 103.120
Thomas; Grace, w, 103.179

THANNEY: George; Mary, w, 109.55

THARIS: Mary, 102.118

THARP(E):
John; Elizabeth, w, 99.19
Joseph, ser, 109.9
Mary, ser, 101.26
Thomas; Elizabeth, w, 99.19

THATCHER:
Anne, ser, 107D.87
Elizabeth, 107B.32
Nicholas; Ann, w, 103.207
Samuel; Elizabeth, w, 107D.86
Samuel, junior; Mary, d; Sarah, d, 107D.86
Sarah, nurse child, 107B.55
Thomas; Margaret, w; Elizabeth, d; Mary, d,
   107D.53
William; Elizabeth, w, 103.23

THATCHEY: Mary, ser, 107D.101

THEAD:
John, £600; Rebecca, w, 103.282
Samuell, bach, 106.2
Thomas, app, 98.3

THELWALL: Anne, 100.12

THETFORD: John, wid, 98.7

THEW: Thomas; Mary, w, 110.21

THEYER: George, ser, 102.87

THICKPENNY: Nathaniel; Anne, w;
   Nathaniel, s, 107B.23

THIMBLEBY:
Ann, wid, 103.53
William, 102.141

THIRLE: John; Hester, w, 110.33

THISDEN: Elizabeth, ser, 103.68

THISLEWIGHT: Robert; Margaret, w, 98.6

THISSLEWAITE: Margaret, wid, 103.113

THISTER: Agitus, ser, 106.2

THOMAS:
Abraham, 104.32
Abraham, ser, 102.197
Anne; Thomas, s, bach; Anne, d, 104.37
Anne, pensioner, wid; Elizabeth, d, 103.191
Anne, ser, 98.77
Charles; Martha, w, 102.140
Charles; Elizabeth, w, 109.106
Daniell; Mary, w; Daniell, ser, 102.152
Daniell, collector, 102.276
David; Elizabeth, w, 103.31
Drucellah, 98.63
Edward, 101.100,105.17
Edward; Elizabeth, w, 102.180
Edward; Jane, w; Katharine, d, 102.182
Edawrd; Elizabeth, w, 106.44
Edward; Elizabeth, w, 107B.4
Elizabeth Richard, d of Siedon; Richard, s,
    106.25
Elizabeth, ser, 98.53
Elizabeth, wid, 102.41
Ellen, ser, 98.13
Ellioner, ser, 106.60
Frances, 107B.23
Frances; John, s; Frances, d, 102.193
George; Mary, w; Mary, d, 103.184
George; Sarah, w, 107B.19
Gowen, 109.95
Grace, wid; Uriah, s; Mary, d, 102.18
Henry, 101.56
Hester, ser, 107A.5
Jane, ser, 104.10
Johanna, 109.103
John; Isbell, w; Mary, d, 102.213
John; Elizabeth, w, 104.22
John; Margery, w; John, s; Martha, d, 109.64
John; Mary, w, 109.105
John; Mary, w; Mary, d, 110.6
John, app, 102.241
John, ser, 103.224
Magdalen, 101.48
Marg, 104.25
Mary, 99.7,109.71
Owena, 107B.73
Peter; Elizabeth, w; Elizabeth, d; Mary, d;
    George, s, 103.187
Phillip, wid, 101.48
Rice, bach, gent, 98.67
Richard; Frances, w, 103.35
Richard; Elizabeth, w; Mary, d; Rebecca, d,
    103.119
Robert; Elizabeth, w, 109.108
Robert, ser, 106.22
Sarah, 102.14,109.69
Susanna, 110.12
Symon; Hannah, w, 109.89
Tho, gent; Mary, w, 104.26

Thompson; Joane, w, 103.65
Timothy, bach, 103.288
William, 110.4
William; Mary, w; Edward, s, 101.85
William; Agnus, w; William, s, 103.8
William; Elizabeth, w, 104.68
William; Phebe, w; Sarah, d; Henry, s,
    104.103
William; Mary, w, 106.6
William, app, 109.25
Winifrett, 109.71
Zachens; Issabell, w; Zachens, s; Mary, d;
    Elizabeth, d; Jane, d; Issabella, d, 102.240

THOMASON: Mary, 98.5

THOMAZIN: Sam, bach;

THOMLIN, See Tomlin

THOMLINSON, See Tomlinson

THOMPKINS, See Tomkins

THOMPSON:
~, wid; ~, d, 104.39
Alice, ser, 106.68
Anne, app, 102.124
Anne, ser, 107D.45
Anne, wid, 103.195
Bryan; Sara, w; Elizabeth, d, 105.8
Charles; Elizabeth, w, 98.85
Charles, wid, 103.81
Christopher, pensioner; Sarah, d,
    103.147
Daniell; Susan, w; William, s; Susan, d,
    103.149
Dorothy, wid, 103.65
Eleanor, 102.92
Elizabeth, ser, 98.10
Enoch; Ann, w; Robert, s, 103.87
George, app, 98.36
George, bach, 103.65
Hanah, ser, 107D.88
Henry; Anne, w, 102.35
Henry; Jeane, w; Rowland, s; Simion, s;
    Deniell, s, 103.160
Isaac; Elianor, w; Thomas, s, 109.73
James, 102.107
James, £600; Mary, w, 104.110
James, pensioner, 103.72
Jane, 98.11
Jeremy, 101.6
John; Elizabeth; w; Jane, d, 98.4
John; Jane, w, 101.72
John; Elizabeth, w, 101.100
John; Mary, w; Anne, d, 102.42
John; Joane, w; Sarah, d; Mary, d; Seth, s;
    Thomas, s, 103.41

John; Elizabeth, w; Elizabeth, d; Susannah, d; Ruth, d, 103.190
John; Anne, w; Mary, d; Anna, d, 103.215
John; Elizabeth, w, 104.94
John; Margaret, w; Margaret, d; Anne, d, 107B.27
John; Elizabeth, w, 107D.6
John; Elizabeth, w; Elizabeth, d, 107D.32
John; Mary, w; John, s; Mary, d, 109.57
John; Rebecca, w, 109.83
John, bach, 99.40
Joseph; Ann, w; Richard, s, at sea, 103.107
Joseph, app, 103.7
Joseph, ser, 107D.79
Leonard, ser, 107C.6
Lidia, 101.18
Lidiah, 107B.31
Lundo, 102.249
Margeret, 103.276
Margeret, ser, 107D.45
Martha, 109.66
Mary, her husband at sea, 103.127
Mary, ser, 104.3,106.51
Michell; Susan, w; Elizabeth, d, 103.161
Peter, bach, 109.57
Philip; Mary, w; Philip, s; Francis, s; Elizabeth, d, 109.19
Ralph, £600; Elizabeth, w; Ralph, s, 107D.36
Ralph, wid; Katherine, d; Susan, d, 107D.82
Richard; Hanah, w, 103.85
Richard; Ann, w; Mary, d; Richard, s, 103.159
Samuell; Elizabeth, w; Elizabeth, d, 102.66
Samuell; Ann, w; Elizabeth, d; Ann, d, 103.33
Sarah, 99.10
Sarah; Richard, s, 109.26
Sarah, ser, 107B.80
Thomas, 107D.57
Thomas; Elinor, w; Elinor, d?, 99.50
Thomas; ~, w, 103.183
Thomas; Elizabeth, w; John, s; Thomas, s; Joseph, s; Daniel, s, 103.189
Thomas, £600 or £50 p.a.; Rachell, w, 109.31
Thomas, bach, 103.89
Walter, 101.9
William; Mary, w, 109.68
William, ser, 109.1

THORLY: Thomas; Mary, w, 100.9

THORNBURY:
Jane, 109.77
Lewes, 109.77
Samuell, bach, 98.3

THORNE:
Elizabeth, 109.21
Elizabeth, wid; Elizabeth, d, 103.29

Hannah; John, s; Mary, d; Anne, d; Frances, d, 98.73
James, 103.98
John, 99.7
John; Susan, w, 103.109
Katharine, 99.39
Mary, 98.56
Richard, ser, 103.271
Sarah, wid, pensioner, 103.15
Thomas, 102.114
Thomas; Margaret, w, 98.73

THORNELL: Mary, 107C.10

THORNTON:
Agnus, 99.19
Alice, 101.69
Anne, 102.219
Edward, 102.233
Francis, 102.233
Henry, app, 107B.28
James; Sarah, d; James, s; Susan, d, 110.12
John; Elizabeth, w; Rosaman, d, 103.75
John; Susan, w; Sarah, d, 109.107
John, £600; Samuel, s; Machelbyes, d, 102.145
Sarah; Sarah, d; Thomas, s; ~; Martha, d; William, s, 109.4
Simon; Elianor, w; John, s, 107A.11
Thomas, bach; Elizabeth, his sister, 106.66
William, 102.76

THOROWGOOD:
Francis, 102.227
John; Rebecca, w, 109.32
John, assessor for Holborne crosse, 109.112
Robert; Elizabeth, w; William, s; Elizabeth, d; Mary, d?, 99.4

THOROWKETTLE:
Sarah, ser, 99.4
William; Sarah, w; Benjamin, s?, 99.27

THORPE:
Dorothy, 107B.16
Easter, 98.2
Edward, 109.64
Elizabeth Elizabeth, d of Dingley, 101.78
Elizabeth, ser, 109.93
Francis, 101.31
George, 103.44,107D.96
John; Frances, w; John, s; Mary, d; Susana, d, 104.24
John, bach, 104.102
John, bach, under age, 103.215
John, ser, 106.31
Olive, 101.45
Mary, 109.64
Robert, ser, 107A.18

Thomas; Elizabeth, w; Francis, s; Benjamin, s; Elizabeth, d; Richard, s, 103.232
Thomas; Margery, w, 107C.40
Thomas, collector, victualler living in white cross St., 107C.42

THORTON: Richard; Mary, w, 103.87

THREDGOLD: Thomas; Ann, w; Susan, d, 103.7

THRESHER: Jane, app, 101.109

THRIFT:
Elizabeth; Richard, s, 102.96
James; Cecilia, w, 102.90
Katherine; Thomas, s; Frances, d; Hannah, d; James, s; Katherine, d, 102.138

THROCKMORTON: Robt; Anne, w, 104.70

THROWGOOD: Edward; Judith, w; Elizabeth, d; Samuell, s; Rebecca, d, 102.163

THRUM: Sara, ser, 101.44

THRUSH: Ann, pensioner, 103.221

THUNDER: Susanna, 110.22

THURBINE: Rachell; Joseph, s; Elizabeth, d; Hanah, d, 107B.6

THURLAND: John; Ann, w, 109.59

THURLANDS: Elizabeth, ser, 101.102

THURLOW: John; Phillis, w; Phillis, d, 106.11

THURSTON:
Ailce, 106.40
Anne, ser, 104.74
Thomas; Anne, w; William, s; Anne, d, 107D.85
Thomas; Mary, w; Mary, d; Thomas, s; Martha, d; Malachy, s, 109.21
William; Joannaa, w, 101.54

THWAIGHT:
Mary, 101.10
Thomas, app, 101.94

TIBB: Percivall; Jane, w; Martha, d?; Sarah, d?, 99.36

TIBBALLS: Ann, spinster, 103.24

TIBBETTS: Matt; Ellinor, w; Eliz, d; Mary, d, 104.146

TIBBITT: Wm; Sarah, ?d, 104.70

TIBBY:
Robert, pensioner; Margaret, w; Francis, s; Thomas, s; Mary, d, 103.77
Samuell, ser, 103.180

TIBLETT: John; Mary, w, 103.2

TICHENER: Sarah, ser, 102.146

TICKLE: William; Elizabeth, w; Hanah, d; William, s, 107A.22

TICKLER: John, app, 107D.26

TICKNER:
Elizabeth, 98.57,102.231
Susan, ser, 107D.52

TIDBURY: John; Margaret, w; Sarah, d, 102.73

TIDLEY: Rebecah, 99.22

TIDMAN: James, 109.92

TIDMARSH: Thomas; Mary, w; Anne, d; Thomas, s; John, s; Richard, s; Mary, d; Elizabeth, d, 101.21

TIDMASH: Richard; Elizabeth, w, 106.61

TIEADER: Avis, wid, pensioner, 103.16

TIFFERTON: Jone, 98.35

TIGMAN: John; Mary, w; Mary Perkins, d, 107B.47

TILBURY: Edward; Sarah, w; Edward, s; Phillip, s, 102.18

TILCOCK:
Elizabeth, 107B.13
Henry, dead; Elizabeth, w, 102.139

TILKS: John, ser, 104.90

TILL: Mary, 101.4,104.106

TILLER:
Francis; Jane, w; Rosamond, d; Francis, ser; Elizabeth, d, 109.26
John, 109.36
John, bach, 109.26

TILLESON?: Stephen; Susan, w, 110.10

TILLET:
John; Mary, w; Arathea, d; Amy, d, 101.68
John, app, 101.107
William, 102.78
William, £600; Mary, w, 99.8

TILLIARD: Thomas, 101.71

TILLIENTINE: Mary, 102.95

TILLIER:
Edward; Elizabeth, w, 107A.12
John; Amy, w; John, ser, 101.74
John; Mercy, w; John, s; Rich, s; Phebe, d, 104.77
William; Jane, w; Mary, ser of, 107D.16

TILLINGHAM: Tabitha, 107C.31

TILLOTSON:
Ann, 109.88
Thomas; Ellen, w; Elizabeth, d; Anne, d; Mary, d; Katherine, d;

TILLY:
~, ?gent, ?bach, 104.12
Elias; Ann, w; Elias, s; Ann, d; Elizabeth, d; Mary, d, 103.143
Francis; Phillis, w, 107C.17
John, ser, 109.99
Mary; Henry, s, 101.60
Sarah, 109.78
Sarah, wid, 102.15
Thomas, ser, 107C.8
William; Jeane, w; John, s, at sea, 103.90
William, £600; Sarah, w; Mary, d; Elizabeth, d; Martha, d, 102.173

TILMAN: Katherine, 107C.15

TILNEY: Jas, 104.21

TILSLEY: Sarah, 102.27

TILSON:
Nathaniell, gent, wid, 106.42
William, clerk, 98.45

TILSTON:
Christopher; Mary, w, 107B.50
Susan, wid; Francis Wheatly, d, 103.133

TIMBERLAKE: Sarah; Tabitha, d, 107D.16

TIMBERLY:
Anne, 107D.60
Thomas; Elizabeth, w, 101.67

Thomas; Elizabeth, w; John, s, 107A.10
William; Anne, w; Elianor, d, 107B.64

TIMBERMAN:
Elizabeth, pensioner, 103.28
Ellinor, wid; Elizabeth, d; Nicholas, s, 103.48

TIMBRELL:
John, app, 107D.13
Joseph, 107B.76

TIMEY: John, app, 103.53

TIMMERS: Aron; Alice, w, 103.39

TIMMONS?: Edward; Elizabeth, w; Elizabeth, d; Susannah, d, 109.52

TIMMS:
Benjamin, app, 101.92
Jacob; Mary, w; John, s, 109.106
John; Eliza, w; Mary, d, 104.30
John, bach, under age, 103.85
Peter, 102.96
Richard, app, 102.194
Sarah, 109.3
Tho, bach, 104.68

TIMOTHY: Judith, ser, 107A.27

TINCKARD:
Elizabeth, 106.11
Jeremiah, 106.11

TINDALL: Mary, 109.18

TINDER: George, 109.81

TINERY?: Thomas, £50 p.a.; Sara, w, 101.81

TINGEY:
Anne, 101.23
Edward; Anne, w, 101.23

TINISTON: Thomas; ~, w; Mary, d; Robert, s, 100.7

TINKLER: Charles; Alice, w, 101.53

TINS: Anne, ser, 107B.81

TINSLEY:
Elizabeth, wid, pensioner; Margaret, d; Elizabeth, d; John, s, 102.54
Jane, 109.54
Sarah, ser, 103.264

TINSON: Charles; Ann, w, 109.29

TINSTON: John, 107D.6

TIPEROR: John, ser, 106.24

TIPHINE:
Magdalen, 103.234
Mary, 103.234
Rachell, 103.234

TIPLER: Robert, app, 102.202

TIPPER: Edw; Eliz, w; Benj, s; Wm, s; Tho,
s, 104.69

TIPPETT:
Abigale, 109.43
Ellianor, 101.19
John, app, 98.84

TIPPING: William, Doctor of Physick;
Elizabeth, w; Ursula, d?, 99.59

TIPPITT:
Margery, wid, pensioner, 103.199
Martha, ser, 103.67

TIRAR: Robert; Elizabeth, w; Thomas, s; Martha,
d; Hanah, d; Diana, d; Jessper, s, 103.45

TIRES: Mary, app, 101.27

TIRINGHAM: Elizabeth; Charles, s; Mary, d;
Anne, d, 98.11

TIRKE: Jeane, pensioner, 103.86

TISBURY: Richard, 102.94

TISDALE:
Benj, £600; Sarah, w; Eliz, d, 104.15
Eliza, 104.31
Eliza; Elizabeth, d, 104.2
Richard; Mary, w, 98.35
Robt, ser, bach?, 104.5
Sarah, 98.72

TISDALL:
Edward; Jane, w, 102.111
Michaell, 106.29

TISDELL:
Roger; ~, w, 103.205
William; Elizabeth, w; William, s, 106.12

TISSLEY: Richard, app, 103.208

TITCHBORNE: Thomas, pensioner;
Elizabeth, w; Elizabeth, d; Elias, s;
Timothy, s; Susan, d; William, s, 103.227

TITCHBURY: Elizabeth, a nurse child,
103.47

TITCOMB:
Elizabeth, 107A.25
Elizabeth; Daniell, s; John, s, 109.23
John; Sarah, w; Sarah, d; Mary, d; Ralph, s;
Catherine, d, 109.110
Thomas; Sarah, w, 109.18

TITNALL: Tho, ser, bach?, 104.109

TITTFORD: Ralph; Esther, w; Charles, s;
Mary, w, 103.171

TITTOLOW:
Sarah, 102.14
Thomas; Hannah, w; Mary, d, 102.14

TITULOR: Elizabeth, ser, 103.62

TIVEY: Sarah, 110.16

TOACH: Isabella, 107A.16

TOAMER: Susan, wid, French, 103.267

TODD:
Anne, app, 107D.11
Anne, ser, 104.65,106.34
Edmond; ~, w, Constance; ~, d Constance;
Susanah, d, 103.43
Elizabeth, 102.273
Henry; Abigall, w, 102.60
John; John, s, 109.96
John; Rachell, w; Anne, d, 102.127
John, ser, 108.5
Josia; Amey, w, 102.134
Mary, 106.20
Mathew; Margeret, w, 103.82
Sarah, ser, 106.45
Wm; Jane, w, 104.48

TODE: Elizabeth, 98.49

TOFFT: Humfrey; Margaret, w,
102.175

TOKE: Robert, app, 109.101

TOKEFEILD:
George; Sarah, w; George, s; Catherine, d;
Damara, d; Sarah, d, 109.85
Joseph, bach, 107D.12

TOLES: Thomas; Anne, w, 109.87

TOLLINGTON: Peter; Esther, w; Esther, d,
103.114

TOPHAM:
John; Anne, w; Mary, d, 102.148
Mary; Rachell, d, 107A.29

TOPLADY:
Alice, 107D.41
Thomas; Anne, w, 107D.77

TOPP:
Edward, a nurse child, 107D.84
Richard, app, 107A.37

TOPPING:
Elizabeth, 99.14
Frances, ser, 104.11
Lucy; John, ser, 104.35

TOREY: Mary, 109.96

TORINGHTON: Jacob; Jeane, w, 103.113

TORLES: John, gent, ?bach, 104.67

TORRINGTON: Anne, 104.90

TOSSELL: Thomas; Mary, w; Mary, d;
Thomas, s; Frances, d, 103.133

TOTHALL: Sarah; Elizabeth, d; Sarah, d,
106.15

TOUGH:
Charles, 103.201
Elizabeth, 103.201

TOVELL: Peter; Martha, w; Samuell, s;

TOVEY:
~, 104.29
Edmund, app, 104.142
Elizabeth, wid, 103.81
Jane, 109.75
Joshua; Anne, w, 98.65
William; Anne, w, 102.65

TOWELL: Eliz, ser, 104.4

TOWER: Elizabeth, 107B.56

TOWERS:
Edward, 102.86
Elizabeth, 101.1
Gabrill, 102.2
John, 102.178
John; Sarah, w, 102.86
John, bach, 102.86
Joseph, app, 103.82
Leonard, 104.137
Margaret; Mary, d, 98.82

Rich; Edey, w, 104.40
William, wid; James, s, 103.243

TOWLE: Elizabeth; Elizabeth, d; Sarah, d;
Thomas, s; William, s; Mary, d; Richard, s,
102.184

TOWNE:
James, 102.79
Kersheba, 102.79

TOWNLEY: Hannah;

TOWNSEND:
~, wid; Martha, d; Hester, d, 104.24
Edmund, bach, 107A.39
Elizabeth, 99.43
Frances, 99.42
George; Elinor, w; Mary, d, 98.14
George, bach, gent, 109.70
Jeane, spinster, 103.50
John, 107A.39
John; Mary, w; John, s; Anne Harris, d,
102.176
John, bach, 109.23
Mary; Henry, s, 102.89
Mary, ser, 101.59
Rachell; Elizabeth, d?; John, s?; Anne, d?;
Francis, s?, 102.51
Robert, bach, 102.12
Robert, ser, 103.271
Sarah, 102.168
Susan, 102.205
Thomas; Hannah, w, 98.24
Thomas; Jeane, w; Thomas, s; Samuell, s;
John, s, 103.50
Thomas; Elizabeth, w; Thomas, s, 103.118
Thomas, app, 102.133
William; Sarah, w; Susana, d; Martha, d;
Drusillah, d, 102.205
Wm; Alice, w, 104.75

TOWNSON:
John, ser, 106.5
Thomas; Elizabeth, w; Edward, ser; James,
ser, 102.35

TOWSE: Tho; Mary, w, 104.36

TOWSON: Stephen, 99.52

TOY: Samuell; Anne, w, 101.28

TRACEY:
Elizabeth, 109.63
Lydia, 98.63
Nathaniel; Anne, w, 107D.90
Robert; Anne, w; Edward, ser, 107C.41
Stephen, 102.203

Tho; Ann, w, 104.115
Thomas, wid, 102.180
William, 109.63
William, bach, esq, 106.9

TRANTER:
Alice, ser, 106.55
Samuel, app, 107D.26
Soloman; Alice, w; Elizabeth, d, 107D.96

TRAPP:
Edward, app, 107A.42
John; Jone, w, 107B.76
Micheal; Dulcabella, w; William, s; Ann, d;
   John, s, 103.159

TRASHEIR: Thomas; Elizabeth, w; Thomas,
   s; Ellinor, d, 109.6

TRATMAN: John; Samuell, s?, 102.93

TRAUNTER: Thomas; Mary, w; Thomas, s;
   William, s; Mary, d; Elizabeth, d;

TRAVELL:
~, wid, 109.63
Alexander, 109.34
Anne, ser, 107D.26
Elizabeth, ser, 109.34
James, 109.29
John; Ann, w, 106.18
Thomas, 109.63
Thomas; Mary, w; Elizabeth, d,
   102.263

TRAVIS: Nathan; Elizabeth, w; Nathan, s,
   108.3

TRAWLLEY: Elizabeth, 102.197

TRAWTER: Alice, ser, 106.55

TRAY: John; Mary, w; John, s; Samuell, s,
   102.222

TRAYFORD: William, 99.45

TREACEY: John; ~, w; Job, s, 103.78

TREBLE: Mary, wid, 103.29

TREDAWAY: Joane; John, s, 109.25

TREDENNUM: Joseph, app, 98.24

TREDWELL:
Casia, ser, 106.27
Wm; Hannah, w; Hannah, d,
   104.103

TREFUZE:
John, 101.5
Joseph; Anne, w, 101.5
William, 101.5

TREHEARNE:
John, 102.106
John; Elizabeth, w, 98.71
Mary, 106.62

TREMHARD: George; Elizabeth, w, 100.12

TRENCHARD: Sarah, ser, 98.30

TRENEALE: Francis, pensioner, 103.62

TRENT:
Jeane, pensioner, 103.163
Mathew; Luce, w; Mathew, s; Mary, d,
   107D.32

TRESHAM:
Thomas, clerk, 98.45
William, 102.30

TRESPASS:
Anne, ser, 107D.41
Margaret; Elizabeth, d;

TRESS:
~, 102.216

TREVAINE: Gerrard; Elizabeth, w; Samuell
   Page, s, 103.87

TREVELL: Robt, app, 104.144

TREVETT:
John; Mary, w; Sarah, d, 98.26
Thomas, ser, 109.8

TREVISE: Peter; Sarah, w; Peter, s, 104.120

TREVOR:
Edward, 109.2
Jane; Francis, s, 102.265
Mary; Joseph, s; William, s, 110.26
William; Mary, w, 102.102

TREWCOCK: Mary, ser, 98.70

TREWLOVE: Margaret, 106.41

TRIBE: William, bach, 106.41

TRIGG:
Anne, 109.85
John, app, 102.117
Mary, 107A.30

315

TUCKER:
Jeremiah; Jane, w, 102.181
John, bach, 106.42
Mary, 102.47,110.33
Susan, wid; Ann, d, 103.39

TUCKEY:
Anne, 107B.55
Bridgett, 110.30
Christopher, bach, esq, 106.47
Edward; Mary, w, 107B.54
Robert, 107B.56
Thomas, 107B.37
Ursula; John, s, bach; Sara, d; Elizabeth, d;
    William, s, 101.63
William; Sarah, w; Martha, d, 107C.24

TUCKNELL: William; Judah, w; William, s;
    Sarah, d; Elizabeth, d; Thomas, s,
    110.3

TUCKNEY:
Margaret; Abraham, s, 98.7
William, ser, 108.5

TUDMAN: Thomas; Mary, w, 101.63

TUDOR: William; Mary, w; William, s;
    Joseph, s, 102.60

TUFF: Hannah, ser;

TUFFIN:
~; ~, w; ~, s, 104.18

TUFFNELL: William; Katherine, w; Daniell,
    s; William, s; Sarah, d; Mary, d,
    102.56

TUFINBORNE: Thomas, 110.3

TULCHER: John; Eliz, w; John, s; Eliz, d,
    104.61-62

TULL:
Hugh; Margaret, w; John, s; Katherine, d,
    102.11
Mary, 107C.35
William; Jeane, w, 103.51

TULLY:
Deborah, 106.43
Susanna, 101.64

TULSE: Mary, 101.69

TUNE:
James; Martha, w, 105.10
Robert, 102.69

TUNKS:
Jane, 107A.23
Mary; Thomas, s; Mary, d, 107C.34

TUNNE: Simon, 104.142

TUNSOON: Thomas, 102.12

TUNSTALL: John, ser, ?b, 104.6

TUNSTEAD: Francis, nurse child, 103.266

TUNYCLIFT: Elizabeth, ser;

TURBILL:
~, gent; Hannah, w; John, s; Hannah, d; Eliz,
    d; Martha, d, 104.130

TURBIT: Isaac; Grace, w; John, s; Frances, d,
    107A.33

TURBUTT: Benj; Phillipa, w; Robt, s, 104.56

TURDALL: John, 102.29

TURENE: William, 109.68

TURFE:
Mary; Frances, d, 102.100
Ralph; Katherine, w, 103.48

TURGIS:
Edward, bach, gent, 106.12
Henry, 109.37

TURLIN: Ellioner, ser, 106.60

TURLINTON: Richard, 99.46

TURNER:
~, bach; ~, esq; ~, wid, 103.185
William, s, 103.185
Aaron, ser, 106.3
Abraham, bach, hostler, 98.53
Adam; Dorothy, w, 109.86
Anthony; Mary, w; Mary, d, 110.32
Arthur, esq; Elizabeth, w, 98.31
Chris; Hannah, w, 104.48
Daniell, bach, 103.1
Edward, 102.223
Edward; Mary, w, 102.112
Edward, bach, 103.273
Edward, bach, gent, 98.31
Elias, £600; Abigall; w; Abigall, d, 103.273
Elizabeth; Elizabeth, d, 109.11
Elizabeth, ser, 103.234,107D.95
Elizabeth, wid, 103.133
Ezekell; Ann, w; Rebecca, d; Elizabeth, d,
    103.38

John, ser, 103.73
Mary, wid, 103.138

VALLENWICK: James, ser, 107A.5

VALLY: Mary; Rebecca, d; Elizabeth, d;
Richard, s; Thomas, s, 107D.23

VAN OVAN: Agnes; Elizabeth, d; Rachell, d,
107B.73

VANBARIN: John; Mary, w, 102.194

VANCOURT: James; Rachell, w; John, s;
James, s, 107A.16

VANDERHELME: Susannah, 109.21

VANDERSTALL: Francis; Sara, w, 101.60

VANDIKE: John; Elizabeth, w; Lettice, d;
Cornelius, s;

VANDROSSE:
~; ~, w, 104.118

VANDUM: Anne, 98.47

VANEE:
Isaacc; Mary, w; Esther, d, 103.254
Mary, ser, 103.81
Susan, spinster; Katherine, spinster, sister;
Rebecca, spinster, sister of, 103.114

VANMILDER?: Daniell, gent; Leonorah, w;
Abraham, s; Leonorah, d; Mary, d;
Hannah, d, 102.105

VANN: John; Elianor, w, 109.83

VANNUM: Ann, 103.120

VANPOKER: Mary, 102.232

VANROY: Tho, wid, 104.8

VANS: Susannnah; George, s, 98.63

VANT:
Susan, 102.243
Walter; Mary, w, 110.36

VARDY: Elizabeth, 109.92

VARGON: Samuell; Elizabeth, w, 103.255

VARIE: Mary, ser, 104.9

VARNHAM: Mary, 109.21

VARRILL: Henry; Anne, w; Henry, s;
Elizabeth, d; James, s, 102.190

VASSIERE: Alice, wid; Martha, d; Mary, d,
103.42

VAUGHAN:
Arden, 98.49
Elizabeth; Elizabeth, d, 109.90
John, ser, 106.55
Henry; Elizabeth, w; Thomas, s, 98.66
Henry; Ruth, w; Elizabeth, d, 102.121
James; Elizabeth, w; Elizabeth, d; Jane, d;
Anne, d; James, s, 107B.11
Jane, ser, 98.68
John; Jonathan, s; Sarah, ?d, 104.72
Katherine, ser, 98.31
Martha; Susan, d; Elizabeth, d; Ann, d,
102.210
Martha, ser, 104.63
Mary, 102.173
Mary; John, s; Samuel, s, 98.26
Mary Margaret, d of Peale, 107B.38
Roger; Anne, w; Thomas, s; Jane, d; Matthew,
s, 98.73
Stephen, a child, 102.195
Thomas, 105.16
Thomas; Elizabeth, w, 102.117
Tho; Mary, w; Tho, s; John, s; Mary, d; Jane,
d; Eliz, d, 104.115
William, 109.46
William; Anne, w; Mary, d; Catherine, d;
Henry, s; Henrietta, d; Elizabeth, d, 109.67

VAUGHTON: John, £600; Elizabeth, w;
Susann, d; Rebecca, d, 101.44

VAUNEY: Anne, 98.6

VAUNT: Elizabeth, wid, 103.187

VEAL(E):
John; Elizabeth, w, 102.21
Joseph, 102.21
Katherine, 101.8
Margarett, 109.101
Susan, 102.97

VEARES:
Elizabeth, 102.126
Elizabeth, ser, 103.63
John; Mary, w; Anne, d; Joseph, s,
107C.17

VEAVES: Mary, a parish child, 102.110

VEBORD: Bethell, 102.74

VEERY: Jas, bach;

VENABLES: ~, wid, £600, 104.7
Anne, 109.73

VENER: Joseph; Isabella, w, 107C.16

VENICUM: Henry; Hester, w, 109.97

VENNOR: Peter Peter, grand-s of English, 98.46

VERDOUTHE: Antanono, bach, 103.289

VERE:
John; Anne, w; Anne, d; Joseph, s, 101.58
Thomas, app, 101.58

VEREY:
Elizabeth, 109.61
Jonathon, bach, 109.61

VERGACE: Alice, 107B.73

VERMIN?: Edward, gent; Elizabeth, w; Henry, s, 102.106

VERNEY:
John; Joel, s, 107B.7
John, bach, 104.17
Mathew, 109.70

VERNON: Miles; Elizabeth, w, 107D.38

VERS: Anne, 109.73

VESITELLA: Isaac; Isaac, s; Hester, d, 102.159

VICCARIDGE:
Charles; Anne, w, 109.71
Thomas, bach;

VICCARS:
~, wid, 104.85
Anne, 107C.24
Eliza, 104.38
Elizabeth, 107B.29
Henry, app, 104.109
James; Dorothy, w, 98.20
Jane, 101.32
John; Dorcas, w, 102.271
Jos; Eliz, w; Wm, s, 104.45
Mary, ser, 104.25
Sarah; Anne, d, 104.43
Wm; Rhody, w, 104.56
William, gent; Leticia, w; Mary, d, 101.59

VICE: Elizabeth, 101.31

VICKERY:
George; Sarah, w, 109.72
Jonathan; Abigall, w; George, s; Dulsabella, d, 102.180

VILLAS: Samuell, 102.270

VILLERS:
Katherine, nurse child, 103.103
Magdalen; Magdalen, d; Cornelius, s, 107B.16

VINCELY: John; Olive, w, 107D.91

VINCENT:
Anne, 98.53
Charles, bach, esq, 106.46
John, ser, 100.13
Michael, app, 107D.33
Robert, £50 p.a.; Sarah, w; Elizabeth, d; Thomas, s; Robert, s, 106.69
Thomas, 107D.76
Wm; Eliz, w, 104.126

VINER: Elizabeth, 107B.78

VINES: Thomas, 101.4

VINNELL: Sarah, 104.38

VINSON: Thomas; Sarah, w; William, s, 107D.20

VIOLETT: Mich; Frances, w, 104.88

VIPER: Eliza, ser, 104.15

VIRGIN: John, 102.96

VIRGO: Anne, ser, 104.4

VISAR?: Mary, 110.21

VISSETELLA: Michaell, 102.155

VITLIN: Wm; ~, w, 104.120

VITTORY: Phillis, ser, 98.69

VOICE:
Jonathon; Anne, w; Johnthon, s; Mary, d, 107D.17
Service; Margeret, w; Margeret, d, 103.284

VOKENS: Robert; Elizabeth, w, 107C.21

VOKINS: John, app, 101.95

VOLLERY: Elizabeth, ser, 107B.54

VOTIER: George; Mary, w; George, s; Peter, s, 110.33

VOUCH: Jane, ser, 98.25

VOVELL: Joseph; Eleanor, w; Elizabeth, d; Sarah, d, 102.124

VOW: Anne, 99.22

VOWELL: Ellinor, wid; Mary, d; John, s, 103.124

VYNER: Dorothy, ser, 107D.59

W:
Elizabeth, d; Sarah, d, 103.173
John; Bridget, w, 103.188
John, 102.159
Mary; Thomas, s, 109.29
Michaell; Elizabeth, w; Elizabeth, d?, 99.48
Richard; Margaret, w, 98.7
Richard; Elizabeth, w; Richard, s; Mary, d, 104.5

WACOR: William; Kathrine, w; Kathrine, d; William, s; Mary, d, 109.25

WADDHAM: Edw; ~, w, 104.124

WADDINGTON: Joshua; Margaret, w;

WADE:
~, Mrs, 101.70
Anne, 106.14
Eliz, 104.2
Gerter, 109.49
George; Jane, w; George, s, 109.45
George, ser, 106.27
Hannah, 99.20
Jane, 107D.60
John, 104.2
John, bach, 103.194
Margaret; John, s; Thomas, s, 109.53
Peter, 109.80
Thomas; Martha, w, 105.4
Wm; Anne, d; Sarah, d; Wm, s, 104.109

WADGWORTH: Joell; Elizabeth, w, 109.15

WADLEY:
Elizabeth, 107D.23
Elizabeth, ser, 104.133
Francis; Jeane, w; Henry, s; Manashah, s?, 103.26
John, ser, 109.10
Joseph; Elizabeth, w; Elizabeth, d, 107D.22

WADSWORTH:
Elizabeth, 102.71
Margaret; Elizabeth, d, 106.35

WAGG: Elizabeth, ser, 101.33

WAGGETT: John; Dorothy, w; George, s; Dorothy, d, 109.94

WAGRAM: Mildred, ser, 107B.79

WAGSTAFFE:
Anne, 102.274
Anne, parish child of Gracions St., 103.113
Robert, ser, 103.122
Thomas, 102.23

WAIGHAM: William; Rachell, w; Elizabeth, d, 109.87

WAINER: Daniell; Anne, w; John, s, 102.264

WAINFORD: Elizabeth, parish child, 101.97

WAINRIGHT:
Hendrick, child, 102.6
Henry; Mary, w; Sarah, d, 102.14
John Robt, s of Folden, 107C.4
Mary, 102.78

WAINSLEY:
Edward, 102.212
Elizabeth; Edward, s; Thomas, s, 98.13

WAITE:
Elizabeth, spinster, 103.41
John, 107B.36
John; Rebecca, w; Mary, d; Jonathon, s; Rebecca, d; John, s, 107B.46
Nicholas; Elinor, w; Alice, d, 109.28
Richard; Elizabeth, w; Sarah, d; Richard, s; Hanah, d; Mary, d; Lydia, d; Joseph, s; Samuell, s, 103.264
Thomas, ser, 109.48

WAITTON: Margaret; John, s, 102.198

WAKE:
Ann; Elizabeth, d, 109.59
Grace, 107C.20

WAKEFEILD:
Anne, 106.18
Elizabeth, 102.162
James; Hannah, w; Elizabeth, d; Charrity, d, 98.16
Jasper, bach, 109.54
John, 109.93

John; Sarah, w; Sarah, d; Ann, d; John, s,
  103.94
Thomas; Elizabeth, w, 102.230
William, 102.82

WAKEHAM: John, app, 104.52

WAKELAND: Elizabeth, ser, 98.43

WAKELING:
Anne, ser, 104.91
Clement, £600; Katherine, w,
  104.26
James, 109.88
William, app, 107B.20

WAKEMAN: Martha, 101.3

WAKER: John, 109.35

WAKNER: Judeth, 103.17

WALCH:
James, 105.16
Sam; Mary, w, 104.104

WALCHET: John; Mary, w; Richard, s; Mary,
  d; John, s, 106.31

WALCOATE: Mary, 109.37

WALCOT:
Eyre; Elinor, w; Rebeccah, d, 98.33
George, gent; Katherine, w, 98.29
John, ser, ?b, 104.6
Thomas, app, 98.20,98.34
William, 106.36

WALDEGRAVE: Sarah, 98.73

WALDELL: Anthony; Sarah, w; Mary, d,
  109.3

WALDEN:
Anne, 102.126,110.19
Edward; Susan, w, 102.261
Mary; Mary, d, 101.94
Thomas; Susana, w; Johana, w; Elizabeth, d,
  103.236

WALDER:
Elisa, 105.17
Robert, ser, 102.178

WALDRAM: Robert, £600; Alice, w; Robert,
  s; Mary, w, 102.117

WALDRON:
Anne, 107D.97

Thomas, 101.81
Thomas; Lidia, w; Mary, d; Sara, d, 101.81

WALE:
Ann; George, s, bach, 103.252
George, bach; Ann, his mother, 103.252
Robert, ser, 103.252
Samuel; Mary, w, 109.15

WALEBANKE: Augustin, 102.67

WALEIS: James; Elizabeth, w; James, s;
  Elizabeth, d; Ann, d, 109.48

WALER: Elizabeth, ser, 102.95

WALES:
Jane; Wm, s, bach, 104.46
Marg, 104.45
Susannah, 104.45
Tho; Anne, w, 104.23

WALFORD:
Richard; Dorothy, w; Benjamin, s; Richard, s;
  Roger, his father, 103.11
Roger, 103.11
Samuell; Mary, w; John, s; Mary, d, 103.290
William; Elizabeth, w; Joseph, s; Elizabeth,
  d; Mary, d; Ellinor, d; Faith, d, 103.91

WALINES: Elizabeth, 109.83

WALKE:
Jane, 102.268
John, ser, 103.29

WALKEDIN: Mary, ser;

WALKER:
~, wid, 98.49
Anne; Martha, d; Anne, d, 109.76
Anne, ser, 106.30
Anne, wid, 103.76
Benjamin; Ann, w, 103.153
Bridget, pensioner, wid, 103.15
Cutbert; Susan, w; Susan, grand-d, 105.12
Edward; Mary, w, 102.216
Edw; Ede, w, 104.112
Edward; Elizabeth, w; John, s; Edward, s;
  Elizabeth, d; Sarah, d, 107A.41
Edward; Anne, w, 109.93
Elizabeth, 98.27,104.87
Ester, 99.47
Francis, ser, 100.11
George, bach; ~, bach, 104.8
Giles; Alice, w; Thomas, s, 109.110
Grissell, 101.85
Isaac, 109.26
Jas; Joane, w; Mary, d, 104.36

WALLSON: John, wid, 99.3

WALLSUM:
Katherine, ser, 103.58
Robert; Mary, w, 103.185

WALLY:
Barbarah, 98.14
George, app, 107B.24
Jonathon; Elizabeth, w; ~, d; Sisley, d, 103.24

WALMSLEY:
John; Mary, w, 104.12
Mary, wid; Mary, d, 103.71
Thomas, 106.61

WALPOOLE:
George; Anne, w; Anne, d; Elizabeth, d;
  George, s, 107B.61
Thomas; Lidiah, w; Thomas, s, 102.136

WALSH: Mary, ser, 100.3

WALSINGHAM: Eliza; Kath, d, 104.38

WALSOME: Mary; William Wisdome, s,
  101.83

WALSOP: Francis, 109.39

WALTER:
Hester, ser, 106.28
Margaret, 101.34
Richard; Mary, w, 110.23

WALTERHOUSE: Sarah; Dimeat, d;
  William, s; John, s, 102.95

WALTERS:
Elizabeth, 102.27
George, ser, 102.178
Mary, 102.15
Mary, ser, 102.152
Robert; Martha, w, 103.172

WALTHEW: Thomas; Elizabeth, w;
  Christopher, s; Elizabeth, d, 109.45

WALTHOE: John, 100.31

WALTON:
Bar, 104.59
Daniel; Anne, w, 107A.11
Elizabeth, 106.20,107B.5
Geo, app, 104.101
John; Ann, w; Samuell, s; Mary, d; Jeane, d;
  John, s; Thomas, s, 103.250
Margaret, 104.74
Margaret, ser, 107D.14

Martha, 109.92
Nathaniel, app, 107A.21
Richard; Elizabeth, w; Mathias, s; Susan, d;
  Robert, s, 107A.39
Susan, 109.92
Thomas; Rebecca, w; William, s; Elizabeth,
  d, 102.206
Thomas; Alice, w, 109.92
Thomas, app, 109.96

WANDELL: Henry, 110.9

WANKELING:
Richard, ser, 103.56
Thomas; Ann, w; Thomas, ser, 103.113

WANLY: Robert, 107D.98

WANNELL: Charles, ser, 106.31

WANSELL:
Clement; Anne, w; Wm, s, 104.71
Thomas; Jane, w; Martin, s; Hanah, d,
  107C.29

WANSFORD: Elizabeth, 101.65

WANT:
Elizabeth, ser, 102.173
Joshua, ser, 103.9

WANTSELL: Richard, wid, hath children
  elsewhere, 103.38

WAPLE:
Edward, bach, arch deacon, 109.65
Thomas, 106.66

WAPSHOTT: Charles; Rebecca, w; Rebecca,
  d, 109.9

WARBERTON: Henry, ser, 106.59

WARD: Anne, ser, 106.5
Avelin, ser, 104.93
Bartholomew; Mary, w; Sarah, d; John, s,
  102.169
Bartholomew, app, 102.194
Caezar, ser, 106.2
Charles; Anne, w; John, s; Robert, s; Anne, d,
  102.273
Edmond; Elizabeth, w; Anne, d, 98.37
Elizabeth; Mary, d, 103.65
Elizabeth; Thomas, s, 103.71
Elizabeth, ser, 100.5,106.24
Ellinor, ser, 103.252
George; Anne, w; Thomas, s; Edward, s,
  101.10
George, app, 107C.38

George, bach, 109.94
Gilbert; Mary, d, 102.258
Henry, 109.86
Henry; Mary, w; John, s?; Elizabeth, d?;
   Mary, d?, 99.18
Henry; Jeane, w; Jane, d; Hanah, d;
   Elizabeth, d, 103.4
Isaac; Margaret, w, 101.105
Isabell; Margaret, d; Elizabeth, d, 109.67
James; James, ser, 109.8
Jane, 107A.29,110.5
Jerimiah Judith, d of Demot, 107D.14
Joane, 102.185
John, 101.77,106.18
John; Anne, w; Mary, d; Anne, d; John, s,
   102.191
John; Mary, w, 103.65
John; Elizabeth, w; Ellinor, d; John, s,
   103.142
John; Martha, w; Elizabeth, d, 107B.1
John; Abigall, w; Barbara, d; Elizabeth, d,
   109.2
John; Elizabeth, w, 109.51
John, £600; Deborah, w; Thomas, s; Anne, d,
   107B.77
John, £50 p.a.; Margaret, w, 101.86
John, app, 103.43,107D.97
John, assessor, 101.11
John, ser, 109.77
Jonathan, 101.9,110.5
John, 98.6
Joseph; Martha, w; Mathew, s, 102.8
Joseph; Sarah, w; Solomon, s; Joseph, s;
   Mary, d, 106.32
Joseph; Faith, w, 110.27
Judith, 102.58
Katherine, wid, 103.74
Mary Judith, d of Demot, 107D.14
Mary, ser, 103.291
Rebecca, 107A.9
Rebeccah, ser, 98.27
Richard; Mary, w; James, s; Anne, d;
   Rebecca, d, 102.201
Richard; Elizabeth, w; Joseph, s; Richard, s;
   Mary, d, 103.33
Richard; Susan, w; William, s, 107B.44
Richard; Elizabeth, w; Henry, s, 109.93
Robert, 101.71
Robert; Elizabeth, w, 109.42
Rose, 109.107
Ruth, wid; John, s, 102.59
Samuel; Mary, w; Mary, d, 107B.6
Samuell, ser, 109.10
Sarah, 102.122,102.231.104.72
Stephen; Arabella, w, 101.99
Stephen; Ellenor, w, 101.104
Susan, 103.232
Thomas, 109.60
Thomas; Alice, w, 102.179

Thomas; Anne, w; Mary, d; Thomas, s;
   Prudence, d, 105.2
Thomas; Sarah, w; Elizabeth, d; Thomas, s;
   Robert, s, 107D.9
Joseph; Sarah, w; Solomon, s; Joseph, s;
   Mary, d, 106.32
Joseph; Faith, w, 110.27
Judith, 102.58
Katherine, wid, 103.74
Mary Judith, d of Demot, 107D.14
Mary, ser, 103.291
Rebecca, 107A.9
Rebeccah, ser, 98.27
Richard; Mary, w; James, s; Anne, d;
   Rebecca, d, 102.201
Richard; Elizabeth, w; Joseph, s; Richard, s;
   Mary, d, 103.33
Richard; Susan, w; William, s, 107B.44
Richard; Elizabeth, w; Henry, s, 109.93
Robert, 101.71
Robert; Elizabeth, w, 109.42
Rose, 109.107
Ruth, wid; John, s, 102.59
Samuel; Mary, w; Mary, d, 107B.6
Samuell, ser, 109.10
Sarah, 102.122,102.231.104.72
Stephen; Arabella, w, 101.99
Stephen; Ellenor, w, 101.104
Susan, 103.232
Thomas, 109.60
Thomas; Alice, w, 102.179
Thomas; Anne, w; Mary, d; Thomas, s;
   Prudence, d, 105.2
Thomas; Sarah, w; Elizabeth, d; Thomas, s;
   Robert, s; Susan, d, 107D.9
Thomas; Mary, w, 107D.65
Thomas, ser, 103.283,109.60
William, 109.91,110.23
William; Jane, w; William, s, 102.110
William; Susan, w; John, s; John Collier, s;
   Thomas, s; Sarah, d, 103.267
William; Elizabeth, w, 103.279

WARDEN:
Martha, spinster, 103.11
Nathaniel; Anne, w; John, s, 109.107

WARDER: Edw; Mary, w; Mary, d;

WARDMANS:
~, 106.15

WARDNER:
Elizabeth, 102.170
Jane, 107B.39

WARE:
Archibald, 110.35
Daniell; Mary, w; George, s, 110.33

327

Edward, ser, 106.19
James, app, 107A.17
John; Eliz, w; Rich, s; Eliz, d, 104.22
John, ser, 105.6
Nicholas, £600; Elizabeth, w; Nicholas, s, 107D.18
Peter, 103.293
Samuell; Easter, w, 109.17
William; Sarah, w; Mary, d, 102.227

WAREMAN: Henry; Anne, w; John, s; Henry, s, 102.203

WARING:
Elizabeth, 107B.3
Joan, ser, 102.107

WARKEMAN: Robert; Elizabeth, w; Sarah, d; Susan, d, 108.3

WARKER: Robert; Bridget, w, 102.56

WARLY:
Abraham; Alice, w; Abraham, s; Mary, d, 103.172
William, bach, under age, 103.229

WARMAN:
Anne, 107D.14
Anne, ser, 103.250
Anthony; Rebecca, w; Edward, s; Thomas, s, 103.106
Elizabeth, 109.4
John; Bridgett, w, 104.122
John; Elizabeth, w; George, s; John, s; Elizabeth, d, 109.63
Richard, 107D.14
Richard, £600; Anne, w, 107D.14

WARMINGTON: Elizabeth, ser, 106.48

WARMSLEY: Elianor, 109.76

WARNBEE: Ann, 109.62

WARNER:
Abraham; Isabella, w, 110.18
Anne, 109.13,109.82
Elizabeth, wid, 103.31
Frances, ser, 103.73
Jane, 109.106
Jane, ser, 109.106
John; Mary, w, 99.43
John; Grace, w; William, s; Mary, d, 102.85
John, 99.61
John; Tomasine, d; Susana, d, 103.178
John, ser, 98.29
Jonathon, 109.23
Joseph; Mary, w; Mary, d, 103.155

Judith, 107A.9
Mary, 109.110
Mary; Sarah, d, 102.86
Phenix, 102.123
Richard; Mary, w; Samuel, s, 109.35
Richard, ser, 106.64
Robert, 110.18
Robert, ser, 106.52
Roger; Elizabeth, w; Thomas, s, 105.9
Sarah, ser, 98.27
Thomas, app, 107D.67
Thomas, ser, 98.44
William; Jane, w, 102.216
Wm; Eliza, w; Robt, s; Wm, s, 104.43

WARNFORD:
Edmund, £600; Jane, w, 104.111
Thomas, bach, £50 p.a., 106.38

WARNHAM: Thomas, assessor, 106.28

WARPOOLE: Richard; Sarah, w; Mary Williams, d; Sarah Warpoole, d, 109.97

WARR:
John; Mary, w, 102.210
Robert, app;

WARREN:
~, 104.18
Alice, a nurse, 102.154
Andrew; Joyce, w, 107B.33
Asia, 103.244
Christopher, 107A.41
Daniell; Frances, w, 99.34
Deborah, wid, 103.37
Elizabeth, £50 p.a., 98.76
Elizabeth, ser, 101.20
Ednund, app, 104.7
Edward; Elisabeth, w; Elisabeth, d, 110.17
Edward, pensioner; Mary, w; Hanah, d; Martha, d; Mercy, d, 103.31
Esther, 103.76
Gilbert; Anne, w, 104.115
Grace, 109.102
Hannah, 102.127
Henry; Jane, w, 102.72
James; Elizabeth, w; James, s; John, s; Anne, d, 101.106
John; Elizabeth, w, 98.34
John; Frances, w, 109.105
John, app, 103.218
Katherine, 106.10
Lionell; Hanah, w; John, s; Lionell, s; James, s, 103.117
Mary, 107D.42,109.89
Rachell, 109.30
Rachell; Sarah, d; Mary, d, 109.4
Rebecca, ser, 104.31

Samuell, app, 109.103
Symon; Mary, w, 110.16
William, 103.222
William; Elizabeth, w, 109.92

WATSON:
John, ser, 106.2
Judith, ser, 98.73
Mary, 107D.93
Mary; William, ser; Mary, d, 101.1
Mary, ser, 104.5,107B.65
Randolph, £600; Margaret, w, 107D.26
Rebecca, 110.3
Robert; Elizabeth, w; Mary, d, 106.16
Samuell; Mary, w, 103.6
Sarah, ser, 102.198
Sarah, wid, 103.269
Tho; Anne, w, 104.100
Thomas; Anne, w, 107B.79
Thomas; Judith, w; Jonathon, ser; Elizabeth,
    d; Judith, d; Thomas, s; Mary, kinswoman
    of, 107D.18
Thomas, app, 107A.37
Thomas, bach, 102.188
Ursula, 110.16
William, app, 103.216

WATT: Thomas, ser, 107C.37

WATTIS: Marg; Mary, d, 104.69

WATTLETON: John, 102.62

WATTON: John; Dorcas, w; Elizabeth, d;

WATTS:
~, 103.64
Bronnker; Ursula, w, 106.38
Edmoud, app, 98.62
Edmoud; Jemima, w, 104.10
Edward; Rebecca, w; Edward, s; Rebecca, d;
    Elizabeth, d, 102.213
Elizabeth, wid; Elizabeth, d, 102.222
Esther, wid; John, s, 103.147
George, gent; Ann, w; Thomas, s, 106.4
James, 109.42,109.67
Jas; Jane, w, 104.70
James; Elizabeth, w; Mary, d, 109.74
Jane, 102.33
Jeane, 103.292
Jeffry; Margarett, w; Margarett, d, 109.29
John, 104.28
John, 109.38
John; Ann, w, 103.284
John; Elizabeth, w, 109.16
John, £600, bach, 101.100
John, app, 104.16
John, bach, 106.4
John, ser, 106.24

Jone, 106.63
Joseph; Jane, w, 106.23
Josiah, 109.48
Mary, 107A.17,110.13
Mary, 104.9
Mary, pensioner, wid, 103.147
Mary, ser, 107A.26
Parnell, pensioner, 103.220
Richard, 102.202
Rich; Mary, w, 104.2
Robert, 99.8
Robert; Elizabeth, w, 107B.40
Sarah, 99.16
Sarah, ser, 102.104,102.165
Sibill, ser, 103.282
Susan, ser, 103.245
Susanah, 99.11
Thomas, 101.83,109.16
Thomas; Joane, w, 103.71
Tho; Anne, w, 104.31
Tho; Anne, w, 104.44
William; Mary, w, 98.25
William; Anne, w, 99.2
William, wid, hath children apprenticed,
    103.132

WATTY: Edw, ?£600; Mary, w, 104.62

WAWPOLE?: Jeane, ser, 103.265

WAY: John; Dorothy, w; Anne, d, 98.80

WAYLE: Samuel; Elizabeth, w; William, ser,
    107D.12

WAYLET: Richard; Katherine, w; Lidiah
    Poole, d; Mary Waylet, d, 107B.67

WAYLIM: Sarah, ser, 106.18

WAYMAN: John, his wife doth not live with
    him, 103.50

WEAD: Alice, 99.11

WEALE: Sibellah, ser, 98.46

WEATHERBUD: Anne, ser, 107D.101

WEATHERED: William; Margaret, w;
    Thomas, s; William, s; Fenata, d, 102.245

WEATHERLY:
George, nurse child, 107B.58
Jane; Jane, d, 107B.20
Jane, nurse child, 107B.58
John; Elizabeth, w; John, s, 107D.33
Terry; Mary, w; Jonathan, s?; Terry, s?;
    Judith, d?; Mary, d?, 99.40

Thomas, 109.8
Thomas, ser, 103.184

WEATHEROW: William, parish child,
103.253

WEATHERSTONE:
James; Deborah, w, 103.112
John, pensioner; Lydia, w; John, s; James, s;
Phillip, s; Samuell, s; Susan, d;

WEAVER:
~; ~; ~, w, 104.18
Anne, 107D.76
Edward, 110.3
Grace; Mary, d; Rose, d; Edward, s, 109.51
James, ser, 107D.34
Margeret, 103.26
Mary, ser, 102.93
Robert, 99.34
Samuell; Mary, w, 102.189
Sam; Mary, w; John, s, 104.46
Thomas;

WEAVERHAM:
~, w, 103.247

WEAVILL:
Elianor, ser, 109.77
Richard; Ann, w; Jeane, d; Elizabeth, d;

WEAVOM:
Jeia, d, 103.17
Thomas, a parish child, 101.36
William;

WEBARD:
Alice, w, 101.26

WEBB:
Mary; ~, 104.68
Anne, 98.59,102.267
Anne, ser, 109.28
Daniel; Mary, w; Elizabeth, d, 107C.37
Daniell; Alice, w, 109.111
Edward; Deborah, w; Edward, s, 103.86
Edward; Ann, w; Richard, s, 109.33
Elizabeth, 102.214,107D.85
Elizabeth, pensioner; Thomas, s, 103.76
Elizabeth, ser, 98.42
Elizabeth, wid, 103.38
Francis; Penelope, w, 107C.2
George, 99.7
George, bach, journeyman, 98.52
Hugh; Eliza, w, 104.40
Jane, 109.72
Joan, 102.272
John; Anne, w, 98.6
John; Martha, w; Ann, d, 103.160

John; Catherine, w; Deborah, d; John, s;
Edmond, s, 103.168
John; Elizabeth, w, 107B.47
John, app, 107D.93
Joseph; Elizabeth, w; Joseph, s; Margeret, d,
103.128
Joseph, ser, 109.18
Marg, 104.52
Margaret, wid, 103.105
Martha, 109.58
Mary, 98.9
Mary, ser, 106.23,106.59
Mary, wid, 102.231
Nath, app, 104.139
Richard, 102.211
Richard, £600; Deborah, w, 98.69
Richard, esq; Anne, w; Katherine, d; Richard,
s; Sarah, d, 98.29
Robert, 105.16
Samuell; Katherine, w, 98.20
Samuell; Elizabeth, w; Samuell, s, 103.95
Sarah, ser, 98.8
Susan; John, s, 107D.79
Thomas; Elizabeth, w; Elizabeth, d; Frances,
d, 98.84
Thomas; Ann, w; Ann, d, 103.107
Tho; Rachell, w; Jos, s, 104.8
Tho; Mary, w; Susan, sister; Tho, s, 104.32
Thomas; Mary, w; Thomas, s; Elizabeth, d,
107B.59
Thomas; Hanna, w; Thomas, s, 110.17
Thomas, app, 107C.8
William; Mary, w; Mary, d; William, s;
Richard, s, 103.91
William; Elizabeth, w; Robert, s; Mary, d,
107B.40
William; Mary, w, 107B.57

WEBBER:
Elizabeth; Elizabeth, d, 98.51
Elizabeth, ser, 98.29

WEBLE: William, a child, 102.157

WEBLEY:
Elizabeth, 107B.66
James, ser, 106.34
John; Anne, w; Elizabeth, d, 104.8
John, bach, 104.8

WEBSTER:
Benj; Anne, w; Edw, s; Eliz, d, 104.102
Elizabeth, 98.85
Elizabeth, wid, 103.32
John; Sarah, w, 103.2
John, bach, 109.51
John, ser, 109.58
Lettice, 107C.21
Mary; Susan, d, 107B.70

Moses; Dorothy, w; William, s; Edward, s,
109.51
Nicholas; Anne, w, 102.154
Richard, 102.273
Richard; Philadelphia, w; Mary, d; Jacob, s,
102.142
Sabina, 105.3
Thomas, 109.92
Thomas; Olive, w, 98.84
Thomas, £600; Martha, d; Jane, d, 102.15
William; Martha, w; John, kinsman of, youth,
98.14
William; Frances, w, 104.53
Zepora, 106.67

WELSHMAN: Thomas, 106.67

WELSMAN: Sarah, 102.174

WENHAM:
Edmond; Lucey, w, 103.203
Frances, ser, 98.46
Mary, 101.30

WENN: Ellinor, 104.129

WENNAM:
Thomas; Ellinor, w; Andrew, s; George, s,
107D.20
Warner; Elizabeth, w, 107D.20

WENT: Alice, 106.64

WENTWORTH:
Maddam, gentlewoman, 98.32
Wm;

WESSTALL: ~, 103.66
Katherine, ser;

WEST:
~, 104.115
Ann, app, 109.1
Anne, ser, 109.90
Charles; Margaret, w; Edward, a parish child,
103.35
Frances, wid; Elizabeth, d, 102.68
Francis; Frances, w, 109.62
James, 105.18
James; Elizabeth, w; John, s, 103.153
John; Margarett, w, 110.6
John, £600; Mary, w; Elizabeth, d; Sara, d,
101.10
John, £600 or £50 p.a.; Mary, w; Mary, d;
Ann, d, 109.42
John, app, 98.86
John, ser, 103.282
Joseph; Beate, w; Rose, d, 102.66
Joseph; Elianor, w, 109.99

Josias; Alice, w, 107A.30
Margaret, ser, 106.57
Mary, 98.86,104.49
Mary, ser, 106.3
Samuel, app, 107A.40
Sarah, 102.10
Stephen, bach, 102.11
Thomas, 101.3
Thomas, bach, 106.13
Tymothy, app, 102.180
William, ser, 109.61

WESTALL:
John; Mary, w; John, s; Thomas, s; Henry, s;
Mary, d; Elizabeth, d; Sarah, d, 109.58
Mary, ser, 103.249

WESTBROOKE:
Ann, wid; Rachell, d; Martha, d, 103.162
Caleb, ser, 106.27
Henry, 109.55
Sarah, 102.260
Susan, 102.260
Thomas, ser, 98.88

WESTBY: George; Elizabeth, w; Thomas, s;
Rebecca, d, 101.80

WESTCOATE: Apolina; Elizabeth, d; Sarah,
d, 98.74

WESTCOME: Robert, ser, 106.41

WESTCOTT:
Mary, 106.5
Mary, ser, 104.12
Sara, 101.83

WESTERBURNE: Marg, 104.143

WESTERMAN: Lancelott, 104.8

WESTFEILD: Susannah, ser;

WESTLEY:
~, wid, 109.24

WESTMACOT(T):
Mary, ser, 108.5
Obadiah; Mary, w; Obadiah, s, 100.4

WESTMORLAND: Tho, bach, 104.10

WESTON:
Anne, 104.36
Edmond; Rebecca, w; Mary, d, 102.176
Ellinor, 107D.42
Francis; Jane, w, 109.104
Henry, ser, 100.4

Jonas; Margarey, w, 98.38
Joseph; Sarah, w; Joseph, ser, 102.229
Margeret, her husband gone from her, 103.69
Marjery, 109.13
Mary, 109.3
Nihimiah; Elizabeth, w; Elizabeth, d; Sarah,
    d; Clemencia, d, 107B.66
Peter; Mary, w; Judith, d, 102.262
Sam; Mary, w, 104.20
Thomas, bach, 106.68
Wm, bach;

WHEELER:
~, wid, 104.88
Abraham, bach, under age, 103.36
Andrew; Mary, w; James, ser; Mary, d,
    102.51
Anne, 101.32
Anne, ser, 98.4,109.2
Charles, 98.32
Christopher, 109.104
Elizabeth, 101.32,109.34
Elizabeth, ser, 107D.54
Francis, 110.13
Frances, ser, 107B.73
George, gent, wid; Elizabeth, d; Martha, d,
    106.24
Hannah, ser, 104.12
John; Elizabeth, w, 103.276
John, app, 98.81
Katherine; Katherine, d, 107A.28
Mary, app, 109.96
Robert, 102.75
Samuell, 102.217
Thomas, 106.58
Thomas, bach, ser, 104.4
William; Elizabeth, w, 109.78
William, app, 109.100

WHEELRIGHT: John, ser, 102.121

WHELPDALE: Thomas; Sarah, w,
    98.54

WHENELL: John, 102.213

WHESTER:
Elleanor, ser, 105.7
William, bach, 105.7

WHETHERBONE: Katherine, 99.30

WHETHERLY, See Weatherly

WHIBLEY: Susan, ser, 103.283

WHICHARD: Francis, ser, 106.27

WHIFFEN: Thomas, app;

WHIGHT:
~, Mrs, 104.135

WHILD: John; Martha, w; Martha, d, 101.44

WHIPP: Robert; Ellianor, w; Robert, s; John,
    s, 101.35

WHIPUM: Thomas, 109.9

WHISKER:
Christopher; Susanna, w; Martha, d, 104.8
Daniel; Ann, w, 109.31

WHISSTONE:
Thomas; Priscilla, w, 103.27
Ann; Mathew, s, 109.37
Thomas, 107C.14

WHITBY:
Elizabeth, 98.22
Jeremish, ser, 102.198
Thomas, app, 109.24

WHITCHELLOW: Charles; Frances, w;
    Thomas Ashley, s, 107D.100

WHITCHELLS: Potter; Hopestill, w; Abiel,
    d; John, s; Sarah, d, 107A.3

WHITCHER:
Edmund; Alice, w, 107D.47
John; Mary, w; Daniel, s; John, s, 107B.37

WHITCHURCH: Ruth; Isaac, s; Jonathon, s,
    109.98

WHITCHURST: Sarah, ser, 106.52

WHITCOME: James; Mary, w;

WHITCROFT:
~; Anne, w, 99.46

WHITCUTT: Jeremy, gent; Elizabeth, w;
    Sarah, d; Mary, ser of;

WHITE:
~, wid; ~, wid; Anne, d; Elizabeth, d, 106.24
Abigail, wid; Abigail, d, 100.2
Anne, her husband from her, 103.44
Anne, wid; Francis, s, 103.230
Arthur; Margarett, w; Mary, d; Arthur, s;
    Margarett, d; Elizabeth, d, 107A.13
Bridget; Elizabeth, d, 109.10
Charles, app, 107B.75
Daniell; Anne, w, 98.49
Edward; Mary, w; Mary, d, 107A.12
Edward, ser, 109.13

Elianor, ser, 109.91
Elizabeth, ser, 98.27,109.79
Francis, 102.214
George, 107C.36
Gilbert; Mary, w; Thomas, s, 107B.4
Grace, 98.30,109.102
Hamnet; Joyce, w; Thomas, s; Hamnett, s, 103.186
Hanah, 107C.21
Henry; Sarah, w, 110.9
Henry, £50 p.a., assessor; Elizabeth, w, 102.152
Henry, assessor, 102.276
Henry, ser, 102.73
Hope, ser, 98.73
Hugh; Sarah, w; Benjamin, s; Elizabeth, d; John, s, 102.23
James; Dorothy, w, 109.29
James; Mary, w; Mary, d; Martha, d, 109.94
James, collector, 109.112
Jane, ser, 109.6
Joanna, 109.38
John, 102.91
John; Katherine, w, 98.13
John; Anne, w, 104.104
John; Susan, w; George, s, 106.13
John; Elizabeth, w; Elizabeth, d; Edward, s; Anne, d; Mary, d, 107B.62
John; Rose, w; John, s, 108.6
John, app, 102.195
John, gent, 106.36
John, pensioner; Frances, w, 103.76
John, ser, 103.1,107C.41
Jonas; Anne, w; John, s; Anne, d; Sarah, d; Mary, d; Elizabeth, d, 102.236
Joseph, app, 103.282
Margaret, ser, 102.115
Martha; Martha, d, 107B.41
Mary, ser, 101.44,109.97
Michael, 107D.95
Nicholas; Mary, w, 98.60
Rebecca; Mary, d, 101.19
Richard, 104.141
Richard; Elizabeth, w, 103.253
Richard; Mary, w; Mary, d, 107B.32
Richard; Mary, w; Richard, s, 109.28
Richard; Rachell, w, 109.103
Richard, app, 103.61
Richard, bach, 103.122
Robert, 99.34
Robert; Mary, w; Thomas, s, 102.17
Robert, ser, 106.24
Rose, ser, 102.204
Samuell; Elizabeth, w; Elizabeth, d; Mary, d, 107B.22
Sarah, 109.54
Thomas, 110.11
Thomas; Elizabeth, w; Anne, d, 99.77
Thomas; Martha, w; ~, child, 100.13

Thomas; Frances, w; Thomas, s; Mary, d, 102.125
Thomas; Alice, w, 107C.41
Thomas; Elizabeth, w; Thomas, s; Alice, d, 107D.58
Thomas, £600; Katherine, w, 102.147
Thomas, collector, 100.15
Thomas, pensioner; Elizabeth, w, 103.158
Tracy; Elizabeth, w; John, s, 102.16
William; Johannah, w; William, s; Margarett, d, 102.114
William; Ellinor, w; Mary, d, 103.238
William; Bridget, w, 107B.28
William; Martha, w; William, s; Elizabeth, d, 109.14
William, app, 98.24,98.35
William, boy, 104.14
William, ser, 100.2

WHITEBREAD: Wm, app, 104.24

WHITECAKE: John; Silence, w; William, s; Priscilla, d, 107A.13

WHITEHALL:
Anne, ser, 104.110
Elizabeth, 102.141,102.176
Jane, 98.54

WHITEHAND: Wm; Mary, w; Sarah, d, 104.13

WHITEHEAD:
Charles; Grace, w; Thomas, s; Elizabeth, d; William, s; Mary, d, 107A.15
Deborah, 104.40
Elizabeth, 107C.39
Gabrill, bach, 106.53
George, £600; Anne, w, 103.6
Jane; Chas, s; Eliz, d; Anne, d, 104.72
Jonathan; Eliza, w; John, a son, 104.75
Joseph, bach, 106.53
Margaret, 107C.39
Mary, 107D.27
Sentley; Audrey, w, 109.56
Sentley, assessor for Holborne Cross precinct, 109.112
Sentley, ser, 109.56
Thomas; Mary, w; James, s; John, s, 103.149
Thomas, £600; Sarah, w; Sarah, d; Jane, d, 99.4
Thomas, assessor, 99.61
Thomas, ser, 106.7
William, £600; Frances, w, 107A.27

WHITEHORSE: William, ser, 98.67

WHITEING:
Anne, 106.19

WHITTLE:
~, wid, 102.65
Alice, ser, 107A.27
Elizabeth; Elizabeth, d, 102.254
Francis, 102.97
John; Sarah, w, 99.41
John; Elizabeth, w, 107D.4
Josesh; Elizabeth, w; Mary, d; Anne, d;
    Thomas, s; Elizabeth, d; Sarah, d, 102.65
Samuell; Mary, w, 102.214
Samuell; Sarah, w; Samuell, s; Martha, d,
    103.139

WHITTOME: Mary, ser, 98.72

WHITTON:
Clay, ser, 109.80
Elisha, assessor, 110.37
Mary, 106.12

WHITTWAY: Caleb; Michall, w; Elizabeth,
    d?, 99.6

WHITWELL:
Katherine; John, s, 98.47
Sarah William, d of Pickering, 107B.37

WHITWICK:
Alexander; Amey, w; Amey, d, 107D.6
John; Rebecca, w, 107C.16

WHOTTOFFE: Richard, 101.6

WHYBART: George, 103.162

WIBSHEARE: Thomas, ser, 102.153

WICKAM: Charles; Anne, w, 107B.20

WICKERSBAM: Benjamin, 102.228

WICKHAM:
Alice, ser, 98.48
Barbara, ser, 101.18
James; Rebecca, w, 101.61

WICKS?:
Charles, 109.70
Elizabeth; Susannah, d, 109.15
John; Mary, w; Mary, d, 103.28
Josesh; Elizabeth, w; Joseph, s; William, s;
    John, s; Elizabeth, d; Sarah, d, 109.82
Lidiah; Mary, d, 107D.11
Magdalen, app, 107B.81
Rachell, 99.4

WICKSON: Mary, 99.9

WICKUM: Susan, 103.148

WICKWORD: William; Susannah, w,
    107B.33

WIDDOWSON:
Jane, ser, 104.51
Jonathan; Sarah, w; Sarah, d, 99.2
William; Sarah, w; Margaett, d?, 99.47

WIDGER: William; Hester, w, 107D.66

WIDMERPOOLE: Nich; Hannah, w; Jos, s;
    Wm, s; John, s; Hannah, d, 104.17

WIDMORE: Richard, 110.14

WIDNELL:
Anne; Anne, d?, 110.16
Francis; Hester, w; Charles, s; Anne, d,
    102.61

WIFE:
Alice, 102.249
William; Elizabeth, w, 107D.81

WIGG:
Eliza, 104.70
Thomas; Joane, w, 102.70

WIGGIN: Fanny, ser, 103.23

WIGGINS:
Alice, ser, 101.75
Edward, 107B.7
Edward; Anne, w; Anne, d; Sarah, d;
    Lawrance, s, 102.75
Henry, ser, 98.84
John; Izabellah, w, 98.84
Mary, a nurse child from St. Martins,
    103.40
Thomas, 109.34
Wm, 104.59

WIGGON: John, app, 109.96

WIGGONS:
John; Ann, w; John, s, 103.149
John; Ann, w, 109.38
Robert; Jane, w, 98.9

WIGHT: William, 102.206

WIGLEY: Edw; Mary, w; Kath, d; John, s;
    Wm, s; Edw, s, 104.21

WIGMORE:
Elizabeth; Sarah, d, 102.110
Robert, ser, 102.198

WIHS: John, wid, 102.48

Edward, £50 p.a.; Ellioner, w, 106.50
Elizabeth; Christopher, s; Hannah, d;
    Elizabeth, ser; Giles; Anne, w; Mary, d;
    Anne, d, 107B.61
James, 109.2
James, gent; Anne, w, 98.66
Jane, 98.49
Jeremiah; Christian, w; Christian, d, 110.1
John, 109.2
John; Sarah, w; John, s; David, s, 107C.39
John, app, 107C.39
John, bach, under age, 103.75
Jos; Hannah, w; Rich. Jesse, s, 104.39
Joshua; Sarah, w, 106.38
Margaret, 105.9
Margaret, ser, 102.92
Mary, 103.25,103.236
Mary; Mary Nevill, d; Anne Nevill, d;
    Frances Wilkinson, d, 107B.14
Mary, ser, 106.4,106.24
Richard; Tomasine, w, 103.8
Rich; Sarah, w; John, s; Rich, s; Jane, d, 104.124
Richard; Margaret, w, 107A.23
Robert, bach, 103.219
Susannah, 98.51
Thomas, 109.6
Tho; Martha, w, 104.23
Thomas, ser, 107D.90
William; Martha, w; Elizabeth, d, 109.26
William, app, 101.89

WILKS:
Anne, ser, 106.7
Edw, bach, 104.80
Elizabeth, 110.1
Hester, 102.46
Mary, 101.78
Thomas; Elizabeth, 110.1

WILLAND: Dorothy, 102.233

WILLAW:
Andrew, esq; Anne, w, 103.288
Andrew, assessor, 103.293

WILLERSTONE: William, ser, 103.178

WILLETT:
Ann, spinster, 103.101
George; Mary, d, 98.64
Jerimiah, bach, about 25, 103.101
Katherine, pensioner; Hanah, d, 103.71
Mary; Mary, d, 98.36
Sarah, d of Thomas Spencer, 106.62

WILLETY:
Hanah; Sarah, d; Mary, d; Rachell, d; Susan,
    d, 102.186
Katherine, 109.30

WILLIAM: John;

WILLIAMS:
~, wid; ~, wid; ~, wid, no children, 103.48
Abigaile, ser, 109.31
Alex, bach, 104.100
Alice, 107D.98
Alice, ser, dead, 108.7
Andrew; Sarah, w; Susan, d, 107C.20
Anne; Robert, s?, 102.96
Anne, ser, 106.43
Barbary, pensioner, 103.278
Benjamin; Sarah, w; George, s, 103.65
Cassandra, ser, 104.13
Christian, 98.70
Christopher, £600, innholder; Ellianor, w;
    Christopher, s, 101.93
Christopher, at sea; Elizabeth, w; Christopher,
    s, 103.226
Deliverance, 104.87
Daniel, £600; Elizabeth, w, 107B.79
David, 102.150,11024
David, wid; William, s; Mary, d; Katherine, d;
    Elizabeth, d, 106.12
Edward, 106.38
Edward, app, 98.11,104.1
Elinor, ser, 98.8
Elizabeth; Thomas, s, 98.88
Elizabeth; Elizabeth, d, 109.53
Elizabeth; Elizabeth, d, 109.68
Elizabeth, pensioner, wid; Thomas, s; Anne,
    d; Isaac, s; Sarah, d; Elizabeth, d; Edward,
    s; Mary, d, 103.226
Elizabeth, ser, 98.35,103.286
Elizabeth, spinster, 103.105
Elizabeth, wid, 102.19
Frances, 107B.69
Francis; Margaret, w, 109.20
Francis, app, 103.201
George; Judeth, w, 102.179
George; Grace, w; George, s; William, s;
    Martha, d, 103.104
Grace, d of Jacob, Margaret, 98.63
Griffith; Ellen, w; John, s; William, s;
    Elizabeth, d, 98.23
Henry; Mary, w; Elizabeth, d; Henaritta
    Maria, d, 103.117
James; Sarah, w; John, s, 98.16
James; Susan, w, 103.50
James; Jane, w, 107D.47
James; Sarah, w, 107D.100
Jane, 102.265
Jeane, wid, 103.67
Jeffry; Martha, w; Elizabeth, d?, 99.14
Joan, 102.220
Joanna, 101.85
Joell, 102.17
John; Mary, w; John Barnwell, s,
    107B.43

John; Mary, w; John, s; Susannah Collet, d;
  Mary Collet, d, 107D.47
John; Elizabeth, w; Sarah, d, 110.26
John, app, 98.19
John, bach, 102.19
John, ser, 106.33,109.8
Joseph; Clement, w, 109.52
Joseph, bach, 99.35
Katherine, pensioner, 103.77
Katherine, ser, 107D.36
Luke; Sarah, w, 102.123
Margaret, ser, 106.18
Mary Richard, d of Warpoole, 109.97
Mary, ser, 109.59
Matt; Thomazin, w; Mary, d of Warpoole,
  104.62
Nicholas, pensioner, 103.76
Peircy, 101.50
Phillip, ser, 103.192
Rachell, 107A.17
Rachell, wid, 103.41
Rebeccah, 102.112,102.162
Rebeccah, ser, 98.31
Richard, 99.14,105.16
Richard; Mary, w, 107C.11
Robert, bach, 98.74
Sarah, ser, 103.40,106.30
Susan, 101.83
Susanna, 109.74
Thomas, 109.99
Thomas; Anne, w, 101.96
Thomas; Anne, d, 102.208
Thomas; Elizabeth, w; Elizabeth Midwinter,
  kinswoman, 107B.51
Thomas; Mary, w; Thomas, s; John, s;
  Benjamin, s, 107D.57
Thomas; Mary, w, 109.97
Thomas, app, 104.93
Walter; Martha, w, 103.103
Walter; Mary, w; John, s; Wm, s; Rich, s,
  104.14
William; Mary, w; Daniell, s, 102.157
William; Judeth, w; Elizabeth, d, 103.189
Wm; Kath, w; John, s, 104.41
Wm; Mary, w; Sarah, ?d, 104.84
William, app, 107D.92

WILLIAMSON:
Anne; Cuthbert, ser, 107C.14
Elianor, 107D.74
George; Elizabeth, w; George, s, 103.57
Hannah, 102.27
Henry; Mary, w; Mary, d, 107D.46
John, 105.17
John; Jane, w, 101.74
Katherine, ser, 106.13
Randall; Hannah, w; Isabell, d?; Anne, d?;
  Martha, d?, 99.15
Thomas; Ann, w, 102.232

Thomas; Mary, w; Disnisins, d; Elizabeth, d,
  107D.66
Thomas, bach, 109.10,109.66

WILLIARD: Susanna, 101.95

WILLINE: Ann, 109.23

WILLING: Edward; Margaret, w; Anne, d;
  Elizabeth, d, 102.235

WILLINGHAM: Elizabeth, ser;

WILLIS:
~, 102.169
Andrew; Elizabeth, w, 102.131
Anne; Mary, d, 102.215
Dorothy, 102.60
Elizabeth, 102.64,107B.48
Ellinor, 99.44
George, ser, 109.27
Henry; Elizabeth, w; Henry, s; Thomas, s,
  106.10
Henry, ser, 106.38
James; Elizabeth, w, 107A.16
Jane, 107C.30
John; Mary, w; John, s; Martha, d, 107D.30
John; Mary, w, 109.6
John, ser, 106.36,109.94
Jonothan; Katherine, w, 103.98
Judith, 107D.38
Mary, ser, 101.21
Nicholas, ser, 106.45
Quinborough, wid, 103.170
Richard, a child (dead), 102.274
Samuell, 101.103
Thomas, bach, 98.49
William; Issabela, w; Elizabeth, d; William, s;
  Anne, d, 102.196

WILLOUGHBY:
Giles; Anne, w; Anne, d, 107D.57
Jane, 110.5
John; Mary, w, 101.98
John; Mary, w; John, s; Benjamin, s; Grace,
  d; Mary, d, 109.85
John; Mary, w, 109.92

WILLS:
Elizabeth; Mary, d, 109.23
Jeane, wid, 103.55
John; Margerett, w; William, s; Thomas, s,
  103.47
Thomas, 98.4
Thomas; Deborah, w; John, s, 107D.44

WILMER:
Edward; Hannah, w, 102.176
Elizabeth, 107B.51

WINSLOWE: Dorothy; Thomas, s, wid, 98.53

WINSON: Elizabeth, 99.11

WINSOR: Thomas; Mary, w, 99.55

WINSPURR: Mary; Margaret, d; John, s, 109.17

WINSTANDLEY: James; Margaret, w, 106.40

WINSTER: Rachell, wid, 103.194

WINSTON:
Edward; Rebecca, w; Edward, s; Rebecca, d, 107A.34
Elizabeth, wid, 103.55
Richard, 102.70

WINTER:
Andrew, 98.11
Anne, 98.52
Daniel, nurse child, 107C.9
Elizabeth; Richard, s; Francis, s, 110.30
John; Elizabeth, d; John, s; William, s; Thomas, s, 101.46
Mary, 107A.37
Ralph; Rose, wid; Mary, d, 107D.7
Rebeccah, ser, 98.50
Robert; Ann, w; Catherine, d, 103.212
Thomas; Jane, w, 101.84
Thomas; Alice, w, 107D.70
William, 99.5
William; Ann, w, 102.234

WINTERBORNE: William; Hannah, w; Hannah, d, 102.209

WINTERBOURNE: Anne, 101.63

WINTERSON: Sarah, 109.67

WINTON: Thomas; Elizabeth, w; Martha, d; Anne, d, 102.15

WISDOME:
Amy, 101.83
Charles; Elizabeth, w, 109.89
George, 109.89
George; Thomazine, w, 109.89
William; Amy, w, 101.83

WISE:
Anne; Elizabeth, d; Mary Anne, d, 98.36
Elizabeth, 101.93
Francis, bach, 102.182
Humphry; Mary, w, 107B.42

John; Mary, w; Susan, d; Sarah, d; Mary, d; Robert, s, 107A.30
John; Mary, w; Ann, d, 109.50
John, app, 102.118
Joseph, 102.2
Margaret; Elizabeth, d, 109.11
Mary, 103.87
Mary, ser, 98.59,107C.40
Robert; Joane, w; Mary, d; Robert, s; William, s; Thomas, s, 103.258
Rob; Anne, w; Peter, s; Chas, s; Jacob, s; Anne, d, 104.37
Samuel, 107C.3
Thomas; Jone, w, 107B.74
Thomas; Ann, w; John, s; Thomas, s; Ann, d, 109.32

WISEMAN:
Cave, 104.1
Charles; Susanna, w, 101.44
Mary, wid; Mary, d; Martha, d, 103.217

WITCHELL: Sarah; Elizabeth, d, 107D.95

WITCHER: Benjamin; Mary, w; Thomas, s, 103.60

WITH:
Richard, 109.38
Richard; Joane, w; John, s, 103.19

WITHAM:
Francis, 101.32
Francis, assessor, 99.61

WITHERED:
Mary, wid, 103.62
William; Elizabeth, w; Mary, d, 103.62

WITHERELL:
Elizabeth, ser, 103.242
John, child, 103.242

WITHERINGTON: Henry; Elizabeth, w, 103.165

WITHERS:
Edward; Martha, w, 107B.15
Elizabeth, 107B.80
Foulke; Hester, w, 101.17
John, bach, 104.8
John, ser, 107D.2
Samuell; Elizabeth, w; Joseph, s; John, s, 109.32
Thomas, 107C.28

WITHINGBROOKE: Dulcebellah, 98.5

WITHNELL: Thurstan, £600, bach; Elizabeth Woodstock, kinswoman, 107B.10

John; Margaret, w; Margaret, d; Elizabeth, d,
107B.64
John; Anne, w; Anne, d, 107D.26
John, app, 104.9
John, gent; Elizabeth, w, 98.42
Joseph, 101.110
Joseph, app, 109.101
Katherine, 99.24
Katherine, ser, 103.56
Margaret, 107B.44
Margaret, 110.24
Margaret, pensioner, 103.77
Marke; Anne, w; John, s; Mary, d, 110.14
Mary, ser, 98.28,103.237
Mathew; Elizabeth, w; Jonathon, s; Martha, d,
103.138
Mathew; Elizabeth, w; Martha, d; Jonathon,
s, 103.231
Nathaniell, clerk, 106.4
Nucholas; ~, w; William, s, 103.175
Phillip, ser, 103.167
Rebecca, 109.107
Richard; Elizabeth, w; Elizabeth, d, 98.52
Richard; Elizabeth, w, 99.31
Richard; Alice, w; Sara, d, 101.104
Richard; Oliva, w; Jeane, 103.126
Richard; Alice, w, 107B.25
Richard, ser, bach?, 104.12
Robert; Elizabeth, w; Elisha, s; Sarah, d;
Elizabeth, d, 107D.34
Robert; Elizabeth, w, 109.24
Robert, ser, 106.53
Ruth, 109.28
Samuell, ser, 103.7
Squire, 110.2
Stephen; Martha, w; Joseph, s, 104.81
Susan, ser, 100.4
Thomas, dead, 102.274
Thomas; Dorcas, w; Thomas, s, 102.179
Thomas; Ann, w, 103.94
William; Dorothy, w; Elizabeth, d?; Rose, d?,
99.25
William; Elizabeth, w; William, s; Thomas, s,
103.140
William; Bridgett, w; Bridgett Page, d,
106.41
William; Mary, w; John, s; Elias, s; Mary, d,
107A.11

WRIGHTS: Katherine, a child (dead),
102.274

WRIGHTSON: William; Ann, w; Mary, d;
Thomas, s; Ann, d, 103.168

WRITE: Jeremy; Elizabeth, w; John, s, 102.9

WYAN: Peter, £600 or £50 p.a., bach,
109.73

WYATT:
Anne; Anne, d, 107B.43
Elizabeth; Alice, sister?; Mary, sister?, 102.4
Elizabeth, ser, 107D.92
Expedient; Expedient, d, 102.45
Henry; Rebecca, w, 103.134
John, 105.16
John; Margaret, w, 102.161
John; Grace, w; Elizabeth, d, 103.148
John; Sarah, w; William, s, 109.77
Joseph; Magnes, w, 109.101
Margarett, 102.69
Mary, 107C.32
Mary John, d of Lowk, 107C.14
Ralph; Margaret, w, 107B.27
Richard; Alice, w; George, s, 107C.40
Sarah, ser, 103.122
Susan, ser, 103.245
Thomas, bach, 98.61
Thomas, bach, 104.55
William, 107D.94
William; Barsheba, w; Anne, d, 107A.17
William; Jane, w, 109.30

WYBEARD: Edward, 102.19

WYBERGH: Redman; Margaret, w; Sarah,
ser of, 98.32

WYBORNE:
Anne, 106.31
Jesper, ser, 109.15
Thomas, ser, 106.51

WYBOURNE: Elizabeth, 107D.13

WYBUT(T):
Eliazer, app, 103.60
Susan, ser;

WYCELEY:
~, Mrs, 104.77

WYCH: Thomas, £600; Mary, w; James, s;
Benjamin, s; Thomas, s, 102.203

WYDBLOOD: John, 98.80

WYE: Gilbert; Elizabeth, w; Charles, s; John,
s, 107B.7

WYER: Samuell, £600 or £50 p.a.; Ruth, w,
102.149

WYKE: Abraham; Eliz, w, 104.44

WYKES:
Anne, 98.56
Henry, gent; Jane, w; Frances, d, 98.31

APPENDIX: NO SURNAME

Abraham, a Black boy, ser, 103.286
Abigall, 103.24
Alice John, app, of Hert, 107B.2
Alice, ser, 104.138,106.50
Andrew, ser, 103.61
Anne, 103.74
Anne, child, 102.56
Anne James, ser, in house of Pullen, 98.38
Anne Joseph, ser, to Stint, 98.43
Anthony Henry, bach, in house of Wykes, 98.31
Avis, ser, 104.60
Barbary, 103.217
Charles, app, 104.79
Charles Thomas, app, to Watkins, 98.12
Christian, a ser, 104.106
Clernencha, 102.154
Cornelius, ser, 104.75
Dorothy, ser, 104.28,104.138
~, bach, 104.76
Edmond, 103.183
Elizabeth, 102.195,106.61
Elizabeth, parish child, 109.14,99.18
Elizabeth; Hanah Edward, sister of?, in house of Wilmer, 102.176
Ellen, a child, 102.56
Elin, ser, 104.19
Ellinor, ser, 104.124,98.70
Ester, ser, 99.12
Frances, ser, 104.132
Grace, a parish child, 98.12
Hanah Samuel, lodger with Drasley; Elizabeth, sister of, 102.79
Hanah, ser, 104.28,106.64
Henrietta Jos, child in house of Bymas; Mary, sister of, 102.124
Hester, ser, 106.37
Hope, a maid, 104.102
Izabella, ser, 103.197,103.287
Jacober; Elizabeth, d; Honour, d, 110.28
James Edward, in house of James; Barbary, w, 103.36
James, boy, 104.24
James, ser, 98.66,98.67
Jane John, lodger with Radinson, 109.37
Jeane, ser, 103.4
Jeane Wm, wid, in house of Shaw, 103.177
John, 103.177

John, boy, 104.93,104.102
John, Dutch shoemaker, bach, 104.30
John, ser, 98.81,103.287
Jone Izabellah, lodger in house of Smith, 98.81
Joseph James, app, to Tusley, 102.99
Joseph William, lodger with Hosier; ~, w, 102.114
Joseph, ser, 106.64
Joyce, ser, 104.21
Judeth, ser, 106.37
Katherine, 103.27
Leond, ser, bach?, 104.76
Lucye, child, 102.13
Lucy, ser, 104.127
Margaret, her husband at sea, 103.69
Margaret Henry, lodger with Hales, 98.32
Marsh; ~, w; ~, d, 105.8
Martha, ser, 104.144
Mary, 99.21,102.53
Mary Daniell, child in house of Greson; Sarah, sister of; Elizabeth, sister of, 102.5
Mary, girl, 104.81
Mary, nurse child, 103.89
Mary, poor girl, 104.61
Michaell, 99.53
Michaell, black boy, 103.217
Nathaniel, app, 104.91
Nolo, a child; ~, nurse child; Henry, a nurse in house of Buckland, 98.27
Penelope, 99.21
Rebecca, 102.53
Rebecca, parish child from St.Grigorys, 103.214
Richard, bach, 98.51
Richard, ser, 98.66
Robert, app, 102.132,102.133
Ruth, lodger in house of Wm Kitchen, 103.148
Samuel, app, 104.79
Sarah, 103.51,103.74
Sarah; Sarah, d, 102.53
Sarah; John, ser; Pryox, servants in house of Paull, 103.289
Stephen Thomas?, app to waraicke, 102.164
Stephen, ser, bach?, 104.26
Steward, 99.41
Susan, ser, 103.8

Thomas; Ann, w; Ann, d, 103.186

Thomas Wm, bach, in house of Warrin, 102.105

Thomas John, child in house of Stevans, 102.27

Thomas Thomas, nurse child at Ashworth, 107B.31

Thomas, parish child, 99.18

Thomas, ser, 106.19

Timothy Edward, app, to Pratt, 98.1

William Nichlas, in house of Coates; Francis, w; Mary, d, 103.52

William, app, 104.145

William Giles?, app, to Joley, 102.87

William, boy, 104.19,104.57

William, gent, 106.55

William Ralph, lodger with Hughes, 98.5

INDEX OF OCCUPATIONS

---

1   Edward Fowler (d. 1714) bishop of Gloucester. The compiler of the index omitted his surname and listed him under 'Lord'.

LONDON RECORD SOCIETY

President: The Rt. Hon. the Lord Mayor of London

Chairman: Professor Caroline M. Barron, MA, PhD, FRHistS
Hon. Secretary: Dr Helen Bradley
Hon. Treasurer: Dr David Lewis
Hon. General Editors: Dr Robin Eagles, Dr Stephen O'Connor,
                         Dr Hannes Kleineke

The London Record Society was founded in December 1964 to publish transcripts, abstracts and lists of the primary sources for the history of London, and generally to stimulate interest in archives relating to London. Membership is open to any individual or institution; the annual subscription is £18 (US $22) for individuals and £23 (US $35) for institutions. Prospective members should apply to the Hon. Secretary, Dr Helen Bradley, London Record Society, PO Box 691, Exeter, EX1 9PH (email londonrecordsoc@btinternet.com)

15. *Joshua Johnson's Letterbook, 1771–4: letters from a merchant in London to his partners in Maryland*, edited by Jacob M. Price (1979)

16. *London and Middlesex Chantry Certificate, 1548*, edited by C. J. Kitching (1980)

17. *London Politics, 1713–1717: Minutes of a Whig Club, 1714–17*, edited by H.Horwitz; *London Pollbooks, 1713*, edited by W.A. Speck and W.A. Gray (1981)

18. *Parish Fraternity Register: Fraternity of the Holy Trinity and SS.Fabian and Sebastian in the parish of St. Botolph without Aldersgate*, edited by Patricia Basing (1982)

19. *Trinity House of Deptford: Transactions, 1609–35*, edited by G.G.Harris (1983)

20. *Chamber Accounts of the sixteenth century*, edited by Betty R. Masters (1984)

21. *The Letters of John Paige, London Merchant, 1648–58*, edited by George F. Steckley (1984)

22. *A Survey of Documentary Sources for Property Holding in London before the Great Fire*, by Derek Keene and Vanessa Harding (1985)

23. *The Commissions for Building Fifty New Churches*, edited by M.H.Port (1986)

24. *Richard Hutton's Complaints Book*, edited by Timothy V. Hitchcock (1987)

25. *Westminster Abbey Charters, 1066–c. 1214*, edited by Emma Mason (1988)

26. *London Viewers and their Certificates, 1508–1558*, edited by Janet S. Loengard (1989)

27. *The Overseas Trade of London: Exchequer Customs Accounts, 1480–1*, edited by H.S.Cobb (1990)

28. *Justice in Eighteenth-century Hackney: the Justicing Notebook of Henry Norris and the Hackney Petty Sessions Book*, edited by Ruth Paley (1991)

29. *Two Tudor Subsidy Assessment Rolls for the City of London: 1541 and 1582*, edited by R.G.Lang (1993)

30. *London Debating Societies, 1776–1799*, compiled and introduced by Donna T. Andrew (1994)

31. *London Bridge: selected accounts and rentals, 1381–1538*, edited by Vanessa Harding and Laura Wright (1995)

32. *London Consistory Court Depositions, 1586–1611: list and indexes*, by Loreen L.Giese (1997)

33. *Chelsea settlement and bastardy examinations, 1733–66*, edited by Tim Hitchcock and John Black (1999)

34. *The church records of St Andrew Hubbard Eastcheap, c. 1450-c. 1570*, edited by Clive Burgess (1999)

35. *Calendar of Exchequer Equity pleadings, 1685–6 and 1784–5*, edited by Henry Horwitz and Jessica Cooke (2000)

36. *The Letters of William Freeman, London Merchant, 1678–1685*, edited by David Hancock (2002)

37. *Unpublished London diaries. A checklist of unpublished diaries by Londoners and visitors, with a select bibliography of published diaries*, compiled by Heather Creaton (2003)

38. *The English Fur Trade in the later Middle Ages*, by Elspeth M.Veale (2003; reprinted from 1966 edition)

39. *The Bede Roll of the Fraternity of St Nicholas*, edited by N.W. and V.A. James (2 vols., 2004)
40. *The estate and household accounts of William Worsley, Dean of St Paul's Cathedral, 1479–1497*, edited by Hannes Kleineke and Stephanie R. Hovland (2004)
41. *A woman in wartime London: the diary of Kathleen Tipper 1941–1945*, edited by Patricia and Robert Malcolmson (2006)
42. *Prisoners' Letters to the Bank of England 1783–1827*, edited by Deirdre Palk (2007)
43. *The Apprenticeship of a Mountaineer: Edward Whymper's London Diary 1855–1859* edited by Ian Smith (2008)
44. *The Pinners' and Wiresellers' Book 1462–1511* edited by Barbara Megson (2009)
45. *London Inhabitants outside the Walls, 1695*, edited by Patrick Wallis

Many volumes are still in print; see http://www.londonrecordsociety.org.uk.